ADVANCES IN CANCER RESEARCH

VOLUME 51

ADVANCES IN CANCER RESEARCH

Edited by

GEORGE KLEIN

Department of Tumor Biology
Karolinska Institutet
Stockholm, Sweden

SIDNEY WEINHOUSE

Fels Research Institute
Health Sciences Center
Temple University
Philadelphia, Pennsylvania

Volume 51

ACADEMIC PRESS, INC.
Harcourt Brace Jovanovich, Publishers
San Diego New York Berkeley Boston
London Sydney Tokyo Toronto

ACADEMIC PRESS, INC.
1250 Sixth Avenue
San Diego, California 92101

United Kingdom Edition published by
ACADEMIC PRESS INC. (LONDON) LTD.
24-28 Oval Road, London NW1 7DX

LIBRARY OF CONGRESS CATALOG CARD NUMBER: 52-13360

ISBN 0-12-006651-3 (alk. paper)

PRINTED IN THE UNITED STATES OF AMERICA
88 89 90 91 9 8 7 6 5 4 3 2 1

CONTENTS

PREFACE ix

The Etiopathogenesis of Prostatic Cancer with Special Reference to Environmental Factors

MAARTEN C. BOSLAND

I. Introduction 1
II. Descriptive Epidemiology 3
III. Animal Models for Prostatic Cancer 28
IV. Environmental Factors: Life-Style 31
V. Non-Life-Style Environmental Factors 68
VI. Endogenous Factors: The Hormonal System 82
VII. Concluding Remarks 87
References 94

Transforming Growth Factor β

ANITA B. ROBERTS AND MICHAEL B. SPORN

I. Introduction 107
II. TGF-α and Its Relationship to EGF 110
III. TGF-β 113
References 138

Oncogene Activation in Chemical Carcinogenesis

ALLAN BALMAIN AND KEN BROWN

I. Introduction 147
II. Activation of Oncogenes during Carcinogenesis *in Vivo* 148
III. The Role of Oncogenes in Carcinogenesis *in Vitro* 169
IV. Conclusions 177
References 177

The Intracisternal A-Particle Gene Family: Structure and Functional Aspects

EDWARD L. KUFF AND KIRA K. LUEDERS

I. Introduction 184
II. Structural and Genomic Organization of *Mus musculus* IAP Sequences 185
III. Relationships between IAPs and Other Retroviruses 191
IV. Chromosomal Distribution of IAP-Related Sequences: Association with Other Repetitive Sequence Elements 201
V. IAP Component Proteins 203
VI. Transmission 212
VII. IAP-Related RNAs 214
VIII. Regulation 219
IX. IAP Gene Expression in Normal Somatic Cells 227
X. IAP Expression in Early Development 230
XI. IAP Expression in Mouse Teratocarcinoma Cells 236
XII. IAP Element Transpositions 243
XIII. IAP Gene Products as Immunoglobulin Regulatory Factors 249
XIV. IAP Gene Expression in Genetically Determined Mouse Diabetes 252
XV. Type-R Particles 253
XVI. Occurrence of IAPs in Other Species 257
XVII. IAP Expression in Relation to Neoplastic Transformation 259
References 267

Immunologic Unresponsiveness to Murine Leukemia Virus Antigens: Mechanisms and Role in Tumor Development

LUIGI CHIECO-BIANCHI, DINO COLLAVO, AND GIOVANNI BIASI

I. Introduction 277
II. Early Work on Immunological Tolerance to Murine Leukemia and Sarcoma Retroviruses 279
III. Immune Reactivity to Viral Antigens in Mice Carrying Endogenous M-MuLV 282
IV. Immune Reactivity to Viral Antigens in Mice Infected with Exogenous M-MuLV 287
V. Lack of Virus-Specific T Lymphocyte Generation in Neonatally M-MuLV-Infected Mice 290
VI. Role of Antigen-Presenting Cells in Immune Reactivity to M-MuLV 293
VII. Role of Immune Reactivity on Lymphoma Development in Mice with Persistent M-MuLV Infection 296
VIII. Discussion 296
References 301

Advances in Human Retroviruses

Angus Dalgleish and Miroslav Malkovsky

I. Introduction 307
II. The Search for Human Retroviral Isolates 309
III. Specific Isolates 311
IV. Significance of SSAV/BaEV Human Isolates 312
V. HTLV-I 313
VI. HTLV-II 315
VII. AIDS and HIV 316
VIII. Simian AIDS (SAIDS) and the New African Isolates 317
IX. Cell Biology and Immunology of Human Retroviral Infections 320
X. HIV 321
XI. Molecular Biology of HTLV-I and HTLV-II 327
XII. Molecular Biology of HIV 329
XIII. Epidemiology of Human Retroviruses 335
XIV. Origin of the AIDS Virus 339
XV. AIDS and Children 340
XVI. From Infection to Disease 341
XVII. AIDS and Cancer 342
XVIII. Approaches to Treatment 344
XIX. Conclusions and Prospects 351
References 352

Homing Receptors and Metastasis

Beverly Taylor Sher, Robert Bargatze, Bernard Holzmann, W. Michael Gallatin, Dana Matthews, Nora Wu, Louis Picker, Eugene C. Butcher, and Irving L. Weissman

I. Introduction 361
II. Metastasis, Adhesion, and the Cell Surface 362
III. Lymphocyte Homing Receptors 367
IV. Lymphocyte Homing Receptors and Metastasis 376
V. Summary and Conclusions 386
References 387

Dehydroepiandrosterone and Structural Analogs: A New Class of Cancer Chemopreventive Agents

Arthur G. Schwartz, Jeannette M. Whitcomb, Jonathan W. Nyce, Marvin L. Lewbart, and Laura L. Pashko

I. Introduction 391
II. DHEA and Breast Cancer 392
III. Glucosce-6-Phosphate Dehydrogenase Inhibition 394
IV. Antiobesity Action of DHEA 396
V. Cancer Prevention 400
VI. Mechanism of Cancer Preventive Effect 404
VII. Glucose-6-Phosphate Dehydrogenase Deficiency and Human Cancer 415
VIII. Other Therapeutic Effects of DHEA 417
References 421

Index 425

PREFACE

With the publication of this volume (51) of *Advances in Cancer Research* my coeditorship comes to a close after twenty-seven years. This serial publication began in 1953 with Alex Haddow and Jessie P. Greenstein as coeditors. On the death of Jessie Greenstein in 1961, I was appointed to replace him, and for the next six volumes, 6 through 11, I worked with Alex Haddow until failing health required him to relinquish this post. Until his death a few years later in 1976, we enjoyed his contact with the *Advances* as a consulting editor.

My coeditorship with George Klein began with his appointment in 1969, and the ensuing eighteen years, covering Volumes 12 through 51, have been most happy ones of close and friendly collaboration. The quickening pace of cancer research has made it desirable to publish two or more volumes per year. Since the initiation of this publication, we have continued the practice of geographic division—the coeditor in the United States taking major responsibility for contributors in the Western Hemisphere and the European coeditor for the rest of the world. With very few exceptions, only contributions solicited by the coeditors have been accepted, and these are determined by mutual discussion and agreement. These practices will no doubt be continued. Starting with Volume 52, my successor will be George Vande Woude (NCI-Frederick Cancer Research Facility, P.0. Box N, Building 469, Frederick, Maryland 21701).

The twenty-seven years of my coeditorship have witnessed exciting advances in our knowledge of the neoplastic process, and it has been a privilege to have shared with Alex Haddow and George Klein the recording of much of these awesome developments. These will be, I am sure, but a prologue to even more magnificent accomplishments in cancer and related biomedical science, which George Klein and George Vande Woude are superbly equipped to document in future volumes. They have my heartfelt good wishes.

I take this opportunity to thank the many people who provided indispensible help. Foremost is my secretary, Dorothy Wyszynski, whose cooperative spirit and efficiency added much pleasure to my continued dealings with contributors and the publisher. I owe special thanks to the staff of Academic Press for their invaluable help, forbearance, and professional skill in preparing manuscripts for publication. Finally, I express my deepest appreciation to George Klein for his collaboration, wise counsel, and major contributions in maintaining the high quality of scholarship of this publication.

SIDNEY WEINHOUSE

THE ETIOPATHOGENESIS OF PROSTATIC CANCER WITH SPECIAL REFERENCE TO ENVIRONMENTAL FACTORS

Maarten C. Bosland

Institute of Environmental Medicine, New York University Medical Center, New York, New York 10016
Department of Biological Toxicology, TNO CIVO-Toxicology and Nutrition Institute, Zeist, The Netherlands

I. Introduction 1
II. Descriptive Epidemiology 3
A. Geographic Variation 3
B. Migrant Studies 6
C. Racial Differences 7
D. Geographic Pathology of Latent Carcinoma of the Prostate 9
E. Special Populations 14
F. Socioeconomic Status 15
G. Urban–Rural Differences 16
H. Time Trends and Cohort and Age Effects 17
I. Correlations with Other Sites and Multiple Primary Tumors 18
J. Relations with Benign Prostatic Hyperplasia and Prostatitis 19
K. Familial Aggregation 21
L. Marital Status and Fertility 22
M. Discussion and Conclusions 23
III. Animal Models for Prostatic Cancer 28
IV. Environmental Factors: Life-Style 31
A. Diet and Nutrition 31
B. Sexual Factors 55
C. Other Life-Style Factors 58
D. Discussion and Conclusions 58
V. Non-Life-Style Environmental Factors 68
A. Occupational Factors 68
B. Air Pollution 76
C. Other Non-Life-Style Environmental Factors 77
D. Discussion and Conclusions 79
VI. Endogenous Factors: The Hormonal System 82
VII. Concluding Remarks 87
References 94

I. Introduction

Prostatic cancer is one of the most commonly found cancers in the Western world. It is the second most frequent cause of death from cancer in men

ADVANCES IN CANCER RESEARCH, VOLUME 51

in such countries as the United States, Sweden, Germany, and the Netherlands (Page and Asire, 1985). Prostatic cancer is characteristically a disease of old age, i.e., it occurs primarily in men over 65–70 years of age (Mandel and Schuman, 1980). The disease is essentially incurable beyond stage B, and only 10% of all cases have a life expectancy comparable to that of age-matched men without prostatic cancer (Scott, 1983). Still, survival is relatively good, and survival rates have actually improved from a 5-year survival of 35–45% in 1950–1954 to 50–60% in 1965–1969 for all stages of the disease in US Whites (Schuman and Mandel, 1980). This improvement may, however, be artificial, because incidence rates (in US Whites) have increased, probably due to better detection, whereas death rates have remained fairly stable as recently pointed out by Cairns (1985) and Doll and Peto (1981). Between 1970 and 1979, no further improvement of survival has occurred in the United States (Page and Asire, 1985), but more recently (1977–1982) 5-year survival has improved to some 70% (Silverberg and Lubero, 1986). Long disease histories are a common feature of prostatic cancer patients, and many of them die from intercurrent disease. Only about 30% actually die of the disease (Gleason, 1977). Since the introduction of estrogen treatment by Huggins and associates (Huggins and Hodges, 1941; Huggins *et al.*, 1941), no major improvements in prostatic cancer therapy have occurred. Efforts to prolong survival by chemotherapy have not (yet) resulted in major gains (Schmidt, 1983). The use of antiandrogens, such as cyproterone acetate, has reduced some of the serious side effects of estrogen therapy (Schroeder, 1984). Exciting new developments are the use of agonists of gonadotropin releasing hormone (GnH-RH) as an alternative for estrogen treatment or (chemical) castration (Tolis *et al.*, 1982; Wenderoth and Jacobi, 1983) and the use of a combination of GnH-RH agonists and an antiandrogen to achieve complete androgen withdrawal (Labrie *et al.*, 1983). Whether these new treatments will result in improved survival is still unknown. Combinations of hormonal manipulation and chemotherapy may be more promising but are still in an experimental phase (Servadio, 1985).

Notwithstanding the importance of the disease, both in terms of mortality and morbidity, the etiology of prostatic cancer is essentially unknown. Basic research has led to a better understanding of the biology of the tumor, its behavior, and especially its endocrinology (Griffiths *et al.*, 1979). These research efforts have resulted in improved diagnostic and therapeutic procedures, prolonging survival and improving the quality of life, as pointed out earlier. Little information on the etiology, however, has resulted from experimental studies. The epidemiology of the disease, on the other hand, has provided a number of etiological clues, implicating as probably important factors those of dietary, sexual, occupational, genetic and racial origin (Bosland, 1985; Greenwald, 1982; Piscator, 1981; Schuman and Mandel, 1980; Winkelstein and Ernster, 1979).

The purpose of this article is 3-fold. First, the information available to date pertinent to the possible role of environmental factors in the etiology of human prostatic cancer is reviewed in detail. Other recent reviews on prostatic cancer etiology primarily dealt with epidemiological studies in general (Greenwald, 1982; Mandel and Schuman, 1980; Winkelstein and Ernster, 1979) or focused on specific aspects of human prostatic carcinogenesis (Bosland, 1985; Griffiths *et al.*, 1979; Piscator, 1981; Reddy *et al.*, 1980; Rose, 1986; Schuman and Mandel, 1980). An overview of the role of environmental factors in human prostatic carcinogensis as such has not been presented elsewhere. Second, the evidence for an environmental etiology of prostatic cancer is critically evaluated on the basis of epidemiological and experimental data from both human and animal studies, and the importance of environmental factors in human prostatic carcinogenesis relative to that of other factors is estimated. Third, an attempt is made to develop an etiological hypothesis of human prostatic carcinogenesis and to identify promising areas for future research efforts to further elucidate the etiopathogenesis of prostatic cancer in man.

The first and major indications that environmental factors are involved in prostatic carcinogenesis were derived from descriptive epidemiologic studies. Therefore, the descriptive epidemiology of prostatic cancer is reviewed first in some depth. Then, animal systems that may be helpful in studying prostatic carcinogenesis are briefly discussed. There follows an extensive overview of environmental factors in prostatic carcinogenesis that are related to life-style. Other environmental factors are summarized and discussed separately. The involvement of the endocrine system in prostatic carcinogenesis is briefly reviewed with emphasis on studies in healthy populations that differ in risk for prostatic cancer and on animal studies. Finally, an attempt is made to integrate all this information and to develop a hypothesis of the etiopathogenesis of human prostatic cancer.

II. Descriptive Epidemiology

A. Geographic Variation

The mortality and incidence of cancer of the prostate shows considerable variation worldwide (Segi, 1978, 1981; Waterhouse *et al.*, 1976, 1982). Rates are generally high in the United States, Canada, and countries in northwestern Europe. Lower rates are found in eastern and southern Europe, and in some Asiatic and most South American countries. Extremely low rates are found in Japan and some Central American and southeastern Asiatic countries. The limited data from Africa indicate that prostatic cancer is infrequent in Black populations in this continent (Kovi and Heshmat, 1973; Bradshaw and Harington, 1981). However, very recent data indicate that Black rates in some African countries are higher than was previously assumed

(Parkin, 1986). In Tables I and II, these intriguing differences are illustrated. In general, rates are higher in countries with a high degree of economic development and affluence and lower in less developed countries. There are, however, important exceptions. Rates are extremely low in Japan (Tables I and II), a highly developed country. Another example is the Caribbean, where countries such as Martinique, Trinidad–Tobago, Cuba, and Barbados exhibit death rates that are equal to or higher than those in the United

TABLE I
AGE-ADJUSTED DEATH RATES FOR CANCER OF THE PROSTATE IN DIFFERENT COUNTRIES AND GEOGRAPHICAL AREAS

	Death rates[a]	
Location	1973	1976
Switzerland	19.84	18.73
Sweden	19.53	21.03
Norway	15.41	19.33
Federal Republic of Germany	14.74	15.28
Netherlands	14.50	16.15
France	14.41	14.83
Hungary	14.23	15.43
United States	14.18	14.50
Cuba	14.13	—
Finland	13.94	—
Canada	13.65	13.43
Trinidad and Tobago	13.42	—
Denmark	13.15	13.66
England and Wales	11.53	11.98
Chile	11.43	11.45
Spain	11.38	12.48
Puerto Rico	10.85	—
Venezuela	9.76	11.24
Paraguay	9.20	8.81
Poland	8.00	8.31
Romania	7.92	8.12
Costa Rica	7.65	9.58
Yugoslavia	7.10	9.20
Greece	6.90	6.17
Bulgaria	5.99	5.89
Dominican Republic	5.73	—
Mexico	5.07	—
Ecuador	4.82	—
Japan	2.18	2.28

[a]Rates per 100,000, adjusted to "world population." From Segi (1978, 1981).

TABLE II

AGE-ADJUSTED INCIDENCE OF CANCER OF THE PROSTATE IN DIFFERENT COUNTRIES AND GEOGRAPHIC AREAS

Location[a]	Incidence[b]	
	1968–1972	1973–1977
Switzerland (Geneva)	29.9	36.3
Sweden	38.8	44.4
Norway	33.1	38.9
Urban	36.3	42.4
Rural	31.0	36.4
Federal Republic of Germany (Hamburg)	22.9	28.5
France (Bas-rhin)	—	23.0
Urban (Bas-rhin)	—	25.7
Rural (Bas-rhin)	—	20.9
Hungary (Szabolcs)	9.1	10.1
Urban (Szabolcs)	—	8.9
Rural (Szabolcs)	—	10.4
Cuba	18.0	19.9
Finland	22.7	27.2
Urban	—	32.1
Rural	—	23.2
Canada (Alberta)	32.4	38.1
Denmark	23.0	23.6
England & Wales (N. Western)	—	19.2
Urban (N. Western)	—	20.8
Rural (N. Western)	—	12.8
Spain (Zaragoza)	17.7	20.7
Urban (Zaragoza)	—	22.3
Rural (Zaragoza)	—	19.2
Puerto Rico	21.4	25.0
Jamaica (Kingston)	20.7	28.6
Poland		
Urban (Warsaw, city)	14.6	15.6
Rural (Warsaw, rural)	9.4	11.7
Yugoslavia (Slovenia)	16.8	15.8
Japan (Osaka)	2.7	3.4
Japan (Miyagi)	2.7	4.9

[a]The area for which the incidences are presented are given in parentheses.
[b]Rates per 100,000, adjusted to "world population." From Waterhouse *et al.* (1976, 1982).

States, while the Dominican Republic, Jamaica, and Puerto Rico show distinctly lower rates (Correa and Londono, 1982; Hamilton and Persaud, 1981; Segi, 1978, 1981; Waterhouse *et al.*, 1976, 1982). Still, all these Caribbean islands are less affluent than the United States.

Differences in medical care, diagnostic procedures, and registration are generally considered to be responsible for only a minor part of the reported geographic differences (Mandel and Schuman, 1980; Waterhouse *et al.*, 1982). Differences in life expectancy are not important, because all comparisons are based on age-adjusted data. Geographical differences in mortality parallel those in incidence in general (Tables I and II). Therefore, differences in survival between areas do not account for the geographical variation.

B. Migrant Studies

Large-scale migration from low-risk to high-risk areas, in particular from Asiatic and eastern European countries to the United States, created a unique natural experiment. Mortality and morbidity patterns in these migrant populations can be compared with those of the populations of their homeland and their host country. Thus, it is possible to discriminate between environmental and genetic factors in the etiology of the disease (Lilienfeld *et al.*, 1980). Among all populations that have migrated from a low-risk area to the United States, death and incidence rates are significantly higher than in their homelands. However, these rates are with no exception slightly to markedly lower than the rates found in native US Whites (Fraumeni and Mason, 1974; Haenszel and Kurihara, 1968; Kolonel, 1980; Lilienfeld *et al.*, 1972; Mandel and Schuman, 1980; Staszewski and Haenszel, 1965; Waterhouse *et al.*, 1976, 1982). This is true for eastern European Caucasians as well as for Japanese and Chinese migrants (Tables III and IV).

Prostatic cancer mortality rates among United States-born Chinese (King and Haenszel, 1973) and Japanese (Thomas, 1979), as well as incidence in United States-born Mexicans (Menck *et al.*, 1975; Thomas, 1979) seem higher than for their foreign-born counterparts, but still somewhat lower than the rates for US Whites. More recent data confirm this pattern for Chinese migrants (King and Locke, 1980) but show an opposite pattern for Japanese migrants (Locke and King, 1980). These data, however, are based on too few cases to be fully reliable. Nevertheless, this phenomenon may be the cause of the much more pronounced increase over time of incidence rates among Japanese in Hawaii in comparison with those among Caucasians in that part of the United States (Table IV) (Wynder and Hirayama, 1977). Over time, an increasing proportion of Japanese born in Hawaii is contributing to these mortality figures.

Interestingly, immigrants from Sweden have a risk that is equal to that of native US Whites (Tables I–III), whereas Swedish men in Sweden are at higher risk (Lilienfeld *et al.*, 1972). Apparently, in migrants from both low- and high-risk areas, adaptation occurs to the risk for prostatic cancer that is prevalent in their new environment.

TABLE III

AGE-ADJUSTED INCIDENCE OF PROSTATIC CANCER IN DIFFERENT ETHNIC GROUPS IN VARIOUS REGIONS OF THE UNITED STATES

Location	Incidence[a]	
	1968–1972	1973–1977
Bay Area (San Francisco–Oakland, CA)		
White	44.6	47.4
Black	77.0	92.2
Chinese	18.2	18.6
Japanese	12.7	—
New Mexico		
Hispanic	34.3	38.7
Other White	50.1	54.6
American Indian	27.5	31.6
Detroit		
White	36.1	41.4
Black	67.1	73.2
Hawaii		
Hawaiian	19.8	42.5
White	42.3	59.7
Chinese	17.8	25.8
Filipino	14.0	30.5
Japanese	24.6	35.9

[a]Rates per 100,000, adjusted to "world population." From Waterhouse *et al.* (1976, 1982).

C. Racial Differences

Mortality and morbidity patterns in different ethnic groups in the United States have been studied more extensively than in any other "melting pot" country. In comparison with Caucasians living in the United States, significantly lower death and incidence rates are found among almost all ethnic minorities, e.g., American Indians, Alaskan natives, Mexicans, Japanese, Chinese, Polynesians, and Filipinos (Tables III and IV) (Fraumeni and Mason, 1974; Haenszel and Kurihara, 1968; King and Haenszel, 1973; Kolonel, 1980; Mandel and Schuman, 1980; Menck *et al.*, 1975; Thomas, 1979; Waterhouse *et al.*, 1976, 1982; Wynder and Hirayama, 1977).

Black men in the United States, however, have a considerably higher risk for prostatic cancer than US Whites (Kovi and Heshmat, 1973; Mettlin and Natarajan, 1983; Schuman and Mandel, 1980). Incidence and mortality are higher in Blacks than in Whites in all states and counties studied in the United States, with the exception of the Rocky Mountain region (Hoover *et al.*, 1975; Lilienfeld *et al.*, 1972; Schuman and Mandel, 1980). Area-to-area

TABLE IV

AGE-ADJUSTED INCIDENCE OF PROSTATIC CANCER FOR NATIVE JAPANESE, JAPANESE MIGRANTS IN HAWAII, AND HAWAIIAN CAUCASIANS, FOR TWO TIME PERIODS

	Incidence[a]	
	1962–1964	1972–1973
Japanese in Japan	3.1	3.8
Japanese in Hawaii	11.8	21.5
Caucasians in Hawaii	27.4	30.1

[a]Rates per 100,000, adjusted to "world population." From Wynder and Hirayama (1977).

variation in incidence in the United States is more pronounced for Blacks than for Whites and does not clearly correlate between the two populations (Hoover *et al.*, 1975; Schuman and Mandel, 1980). Age at diagnosis is approximately the same in Blacks and Whites. The stage of the disease at the time of diagnosis, however, is more advanced in black patients than in white men in the United States (Levine and Wilchinsky, 1979; Mettlin and Natarjan, 1983; Schuman and Mandel, 1980). Lower 5-year survival rates have generally been found for black than for white patients, particularly for stages B and C of the disease (Dayal *et al.*, 1985; Mettlin and Natarajan, 1983; Schuman and Mandel, 1980). However, no differences in survival rates have also been reported (Levine and Wilchinsky, 1979; Page and Kuntz, 1980). Mettlin and Natarajan (1983) show that there are no differences in the diagnostic and therapeutic procedures used for black and white patients. On the basis of these findings and of the fact that black patients usually have a more advanced stage of the disease at the time of diagnosis, Mettlin and Natarajan suggest that differences in accessibility of medical services are responsible for the differences in survival. Dayal and co-workers (1985) investigated differences in survival between Blacks and Whites in relation to differences in socioeconomic status, using the level of education as a criterion. They found that the lower survival and the more advanced stage at diagnosis in Blacks was significantly correlated with lower socioeconomic status. They also found that once socioeconomic was taken into account, there were no racial differences in survival. Data from a study in black and white prostatic cancer patients from the US Veterans Administration cancer registry (Page and Kuntz, 1980) corroborate the latter observation (Page, 1986). The lower accessibility of medical services for Blacks may be causally related to these findings as suggested by Mettlin and Natarajan (1983).

Interestingly, for Blacks living in Africa, incidence and mortality are very low in comparison with those for US Blacks (Bradshaw and Harington, 1981;

Hutt, 1981; Jackson *et al.*, 1975, 1977; Kovi and Heshmat, 1973; Schuman and Mandel, 1980; Waterhouse *et al.*, 1976, 1982). Recent data, however, suggest that there is considerable variation in prostatic cancer mortality rates among various black African populations (Parkin, 1986). Further research is needed to fully establish prostatic cancer rates in African Blacks. On some of the Caribbean islands with a large black population, however, cancer of the prostate is the leading cause of death due to cancer (Hamilton and Persaud, 1981). In Jamaica and most other Caribbean islands, approximately 65% of the population is of African origin and about 30% of mixed race (Hamilton and Persaud, 1981). In Trinidad–Tobago, 40% of the population is of African descent and 40% from the East Indies, whereas the Dominican Republic, Cuba, and Puerto Rico have only small black populations (Hamilton and Persaud, 1981). As pointed out earlier, prostate cancer mortality and/or incidence rates are higher than those in the United States on some of these islands but lower on others (Correa and Londono, 1982; Hamilton and Persaud, 1981; Segi, 1981). There seems, however, not to be a relation between prostatic cancer rates and the percentage of the population that is black on these islands.

D. Geographic Pathology of Latent Carcinoma of the Prostate

In remarkably high frequency, careful histological examination reveals carcinoma of the prostate in tissue from routine autopsies and in surgical specimens from patients with benign hyperplasia of the prostate (Hirst and Bergman, 1954; Lundberg and Berge, 1970; Sheldon *et al.*, 1980; Tannenbaum, 1977; Whitmore, 1963). Its prevalence can be as high as 80% in men of 80 years and over, but the rates are heavily influenced by the extensiveness of the histological examination (Hirst and Bergman, 1954; Lundberg and Berge, 1970). The occurrence of latent prostatic cancer is roughly 1000 times higher than that of clinical cancer of the prostate in Western countries (Breslow *et al.*, 1977; Tulinius, 1982; Yatani *et al.*, 1982). Latent prostate cancer cannot be detected clinically and is asymptomatic (Sheldon *et al.*, 1980). It is comparable to stage A disease and should be distinguished from occult prostatic cancer, which is basically stage D disease, in which only the metastases can be detected clinically but not the primary tumor (Sheldon *et al.*, 1980).

Akazaki and Stemmermann (1973) were the first to study the frequency of latent prostatic cancer in populations at different risk for clinical prostate cancer: Japanese living in Japan (239 autopsies) and in Hawaii (158 autopsies). The prevalence of latent cancer was about equal in the two populations, being slightly higher in Japanese in Hawaii than in Japanese in Japan (Table V). Latent cancers with a high degree of atypia and more extensive invasive growth (proliferative type; or LIT, latent infiltrative type) were distinguished from tumors with little atypia and little invasion

TABLE V

AGE-ADJUSTED PREVALENCE OF LATENT CARCINOMA OF THE PROSTATE[a]

Study group	Number of autopsies	Prevalence (%)		
		All latent cancers	Proliferative type	Nonproliferative type
Japanese in Japan	239	20.5	8.7	11.8
Japanese in Hawaii	158	26.7	19.1	7.6

[a]Prevalence figures are adjusted to the age distribution of the two populations together. Adapted from Akazaki and Stemmermann (1973).

(nonproliferative type; or LNT, latent noninfiltrative type). The prevalence of the proliferative type was significantly ($p < 0.05$; test not indicated) higher in the Japanese living in Hawaii, but the nonproliferative type occurred at slightly higher rates in Japanese in Japan (Table V). No differences were found in the size of the lesions between the two populations.

Blacks (207 autopsies) and Whites (293 autopsies) from New Orleans, Louisiana, were compared with regard to the frequency of latent cancer by Guileyardo *et al.* (1980). The Blacks to Whites ratio for the incidence rates of clinical prostatic cancer in New Orleans is about 1.8. In this study, LNT and LIT tumors were also distinguished, as well as the size of the tumors, and the age of the cases was taken into account. The prevalence of LNT and LIT tumors together was similar in the two populations. Blacks had a somewhat higher frequency of LIT tumors than Whites. This difference was statistically significant for the 60- to 69-year age group. LNT tumors tended to occur less frequently in Blacks than in Whites, especially in the 60- to 69-year age group, but their size was equal in both racial groups (Table VI). The size of LIT tumors in Blacks was larger than in Whites, but this difference was not statistically significant (Table VI). When size was plotted against age, this size difference seemed to be due to the presence of a subgroup of large LIT tumors in Blacks that was not present in Whites of comparable age.

Breslow and co-workers (1977) studied the frequency and morphological characteristics of latent prostatic cancer at autopsy (a total of 1327 autopsies) in seven areas that differed in the risk for clinical prostatic cancer (Table VII): Singapore, Hong Kong, Uganda, Israel, Jamaica, the Federal Republic of Germany, and Sweden. They distinguished LNT from LIT tumors and small from large tumors. With increasing risk for clinical prostatic cancer among these populations, the prevalence of latent carcinoma increased significantly ($p < 0.05$; logistic regression analysis), as did the frequency of large latent tumors and of infiltrative tumors (Table VII). The differences

TABLE VI

CRUDE PREVALENCE AND MEAN SIZE OF LATENT PROSTATIC CANCER IN BLACKS AND WHITES IN NEW ORLEANS[a]

Study group	Number of autopsies	Prevalence (%) All latent cancers	Prevalence (%) LIT tumors	Prevalence (%) LNT tumors	Size (cm^2) LIT tumors	Size (cm^2) LNT tumors
Blacks						
All ages	207	31.4	19.8	11.6	5.40[b]	0.38
60–69 years	64	34.4	21.9[c]	12.5	—	—
Whites						
All ages	293	29.0	14.7	14.3	2.99	0.40
60–69 years	98	31.6	11.2	20.3	—	—

[a]Adapted from Guileyardo *et al.* (1980).
[b]$p = 0.08$ for differences with value for Whites (χ^2 test).
[c]$p < 0.05$ for differences with value for Whites (χ^2 test).

for the incidence of clinical cancer, however, were much greater than those for the occurrence of the latent tumors (Table VII). The frequency of noninfiltrative tumors and particularly of small tumors, on the other hand, did not differ as much from area to area as did the frequency of LIT and large tumors (Table VII).

More recently, Yatani *et al.* (1982) reported on latent prostatic cancer in five other populations (a total of 1606 autopsies): US Blacks, US Whites, Colombians, Japanese in Hawaii, and Japanese in Japan, thus combining the scopes of the three studies just reviewed. Also in this study, with increasing risk for clinical cancer, the prevalence of latent prostatic cancer and that of LIT tumors increased significantly and the size of LIT tumors also tended to be somewhat larger (Table VIII). The occurrence of LNT tumors and their size was about equal among the five populations (Table VIII).

Results from an incompletely reported autopsy study by Jackson and coworkers (1977) among Blacks in Washington, D.C. (249 autopsies), and Ibadan, Nigeria (243 autopsies), show an equal rate of latent carcinoma and a higher incidence of invasive cancer in the prostates of Americans than in those of Africans.

It is important to note that in most of the studies summarized earlier, standardized step sections of each prostate were examined by a team of pathologists, using standardized morphological criteria. Furthermore, all comparisons were based on age-adjusted data, ruling out differences in life expectancy and age at diagnosis as confounding factors.

In summary, the prevalence of latent carcinoma of the prostate appears to be somewhat higher in populations at high risk for clinical prostatic cancer

TABLE VII

AGE-ADJUSTED PREVALENCE OF LATENT CARCINOMA AND INCIDENCE (MORTALITY) OF CLINICAL PROSTATIC CANCER IN SEVEN POPULATIONS[a]

	Number of autopsies	Incidence (mortality)[b] of clinical prostatic cancer	Prevalence of latent prostatic cancer	Percentage of latent cancers with perineural invasion	Percentage of latent cancers without perineural invasion	Frequency (%) of large latent cancers	Frequency (%) of small latent cancers
Singapore	242	3.6	13.2	2.9	11.6	5.0	9.5
Hong Kong	173	(2.2)	15.8	5.8	9.2	6.9	8.1
Uganda	150	4.4	19.5	7.3	16.7	10.0	14.0
Israel	143	14.3	22.0	5.6	16.8	5.6	16.8
Jamaica	168	20.7	29.8	13.1	19.6	18.5	14.3
Federal Republic of Germany	145	21.1	28.4	13.1	16.6	17.9	11.7
Sweden	306	38.8	31.6	17.6	22.5	26.8	13.4

[a]Rates per 100,000, adjusted to "world population" (Waterhouse *et al.*, 1976). Adapted from Breslow *et al.* (1977).
[b]The mortality rate is given in parentheses where incidence figures were not available.

TABLE VIII

AGE-ADJUSTED INCIDENCE OF CLINICAL PROSTATIC CANCER AND AGE-ADJUSTED PREVALENCE AND MEAN SIZES OF LATENT PROSTATIC CANCER IN FIVE POPULATIONS[a]

Study group	Number of autopsies	Incidence of clinical prostatic cancer[b]	Prevalence of all latent cancer[c]	LIT Tumors		LNT Tumors	
				Prevalence (%)[c]	Size (mm)[c]	Prevalence (%)[c]	Size (mm)[c]
US Blacks	178	67.1–77.0	36.9	23.5	15.5	13.4	4.8
US Whites	253	36.1–44.6	34.6	18.2	15.7	16.4	6.1
Colombians	182	19.8	31.5	19.8	10.6	11.7	3.2
Japanese in Hawaii	417	24.6	25.6	13.8	9.7	11.8	4.8
Japanese in Japan	576	2.7–2.8	20.6	8.8	12.9	11.7	4.7

[a]Adapted from Yatani *et al.* (1982).
[b]Incidence per 100,000; adjusted to "world population." From Waterhouse *et al.* (1976).
[c]Prevalence (%) and mean size (diameter) adjusted to the age distribution of the five populations combined.

than in low-risk populations. This situation appears to be due to the fact that the prevalence of infiltratively growing, large latent tumors is clearly higher in these high-risk populations. Noninfiltrative, smaller tumors occur equally or even slightly less frequently in high-risk populations than in low-risk groups.

It is attractive to hypothesize that the factors responsible for differences in prostatic cancer risk act primarily at the phase of progression from small, noninfiltrative tumor to larger, infiltratively growing cancer (Akazaki and Stemmermann, 1973). This view presupposes the assumption that LNT lesions are precursors of LIT tumors. Whether this is true is not known and difficult to investigate. Some support for this assumption can be derived from the finding in some studies (Akazaki and Stemmermann, 1973; Guileyardo *et al.*, 1980) that, while the prevalence of LIT tumors increases with increasing risk for clinical prostate cancer, the prevalence of LNT lesions seems to decrease. On the other hand, LNT and LIT tumors could represent different biological entities. Or only a certain proportion of the LNT lesions, morphologically indistinguishable from other LNT lesions, could be precursors for LIT lesions. The finding of a subset of LIT lesions in US Blacks that are appreciably larger than those found in US Whites could point to a certain proportion of the LIT lesions in high-risk populations that have a high potential for aggressive and fast growth (Guileyardo *et al.*, 1980). Finally, the significance of LIT tumors for the development of clinically detectable prostatic carcinomas is not clear. Clinical cancer can arise from LIT lesions but may also develop as a separate process. Strong support for the former, however, comes from the comparable geographical variation in the occurrence of clinical cancer and the prevalence of large, infiltrative latent tumors (Akazaki and Stemmermann, 1973; Breslow *et al.*, 1977; Guileyardo *et al.*, 1980; Yatani *et al.*, 1982).

E. Special Populations

Cancer patterns in populations that differ in life-style from populations living in the same area may provide useful information on etiological factors. In this respect, Seventh Day Adventists (SDA) in California and Mormons in Utah (The Church of Jesus Christ of Latter Day Saints, LDS) have been investigated extensively. Both groups have rather strict life-style rules and habits (Lyon *et al.*, 1980a; Phillips, 1975).

In the initial study by Phillips (1975), covering cancer mortality in Californian SDA and non-SDA in the period 1958 to 1965, standardized mortality ratios (SMR) were found for prostatic cancer in SDA that varied from 65 to 81, depending on the population used for comparison and the type of adjustments made. In later studies (Phillips *et al.*, 1980a,b) over the periods 1960 to 1965, and 1960 to 1972 or 1976, mortality ratios of 83 and 87–91, respectively, were reported comparing SDA and non-SDA rates in California with overall US Whites' rates. In comparison with non-SDA Californians, mortality ratios of 106 and 92–103 were found, respectively. In Danish SDA, the standarized incidence ratio (SIR) for prostatic cancer was 106, using the Copenhagen male population as reference (Jensen, 1983). Thus, prostatic cancer mortality among SDA is equal to that in the general population or slightly lower.

Lyon and co-workers (1976, 1980a,b) studied LDS in Utah. In LDS they found an SIR for prostatic cancer of 111, compared with the Third National Cancer Survey (TNCS), and SIRs of 108 for urbanized areas and 111 for rural regions. These ratios were slightly but significantly higher ($p < 0.01$, $p < 0.05$, and $p < 0.01$ respectively) than those for US Whites (TNCS). Interestingly, non-LDS Utah males showed an SIR of 90 (not significantly different from TNCS data) and an SIR of 145 in urban areas ($p < 0.01$, when compared with US Whites in the TNCS) and a rural SIR of 98. The difference in SIR between LDS (111) and non-LDS (90) was statistically significant ($p = 0.0002$). The rural–urban difference was significant ($p = 0.03$) for non-LDS but not for LDS. Urban SIRs for non-LDS and LDS were different ($p < 0.01$), whereas rural SIRs did not differ significantly. Taken together, Utah LDS exhibit an excess incidence of prostatic cancer over the US white male population, rural non-LDS in Utah do not, and urban non-LDS in Utah have an increased risk compared with that of both all US white men and urban and rural LDS in Utah. Enstrom (1980a,b) studied prostatic cancer mortality among active LDS in California and Utah and found SMRs of 79 and 105–107, respectively, in comparison with the total US white male population. Active and nonactive Californian LDS taken together had an SMR of 75–77.

In conclusion, both SDA and LDS males may have somewhat lower prostate cancer rates than the average male population in certain regions of the United States but not in others, and LDS may even show slightly higher rates in some regions. Overall, no marked differences in prostatic cancer risk are apparent between LDS, SDA, and the total US white male population.

F. Socioeconomic Status

Socioeconomic status may be associated with a number of different environmental variables. A relation of cancer mortality or incidence with socioeconomic status may therefore suggest that any of these variables are important (Lilienfeld *et al.*, 1980; Mandel and Schuman, 1980). The reliability of such studies, however, may be severely influenced by a number of factors such as accessibility of medical care, accuracy of death certificates, and the method of assessment of socioeconomic status. Ernster *et al.* (1978a) Logan (1982), and Mandel and Schuman (1980) have summarized information on the relationship between prostatic cancer and socioeconomic status. Mandel and Schuman (1980) concluded that when occupation, as indicated on the death certificate, or area of residence were taken as an index of socioeconomic status, death rates appeared to be slightly to markedly higher in higher socioeconomic classes than in lower. When some measure of education or income was used, however, the rates tended to be higher in the groups with lower socioeconomic status. On the other hand, Ernster *et al.* (1978a) did not find any relation with social class, as defined by the level of education in the census tract of residence, for prostatic cancer mortality and incidence in both Whites and Blacks in California. They concluded from their results and those of other studies they reviewed that there is no consistent association between prostatic cancer and socioeconomic status. This conclusion is rather significant, given the considerable variation among the studies that Ernster and co-workers (1978a) reviewed, for the definition of socioeconomic status, racial groupings, and the time periods covered. Logan (1982) reported that in Britain a shift occurred between 1911 and 1971 for the relation between prostatic cancer mortality and socioeconomic status, as defined by occupation. In 1911 there was a gradient from low to high mortality, going from the lowest (unskilled worker) to the highest (professional) class. In 1931, there was no such gradient, and in 1971, the gradient had reversed. This finding indicates that differences in the time period studied may well be responsible for some of the inconsistencies between studies found by Ernster *et al.* (1978a). Non-British studies reviewed by Logan (1982) also indicate inconsistent results. In some United States studies there are indications that prostatic cancer risk is higher among me who are college educated or higher or who are professionals/managers (Jackson *et al.*, 1981; Lilienfeld *et al.*, 1972; Ross *et al.*, 1979, 1983). Although there is no consistency for this association (Ernster *et al.*, 1978a; Krain, 1974; Wynder *et al.*, 1971), it is the only one that has appeared with some regularity in the literature.

In conclusion, in some populations associations may be present between prostatic cancer risk and certain indicators of socioeconomic status during certain time periods, such as the higher risk reported among highly educated men in the United States in the past few decades. Overall, however, in Western countries there is no consistent relationship between socioeconomic status and prostatic cancer mortality or incidence, probably irrespective of race.

G. Urban–Rural Differences

There is a worldwide, though not fully consistent, tendency for populations of urban areas to show higher prostatic cancer rates than populations of rural regions (Table II) (Mandel and Schuman, 1980; Waterhouse *et al.*, 1976, 1982). This difference is generally not present in the United States total or white male population (Blair and Fraumeni, 1978; Hoover *et al.*,

1975; King *et al.*, 1963; Lilienfeld *et al.*, 1972; Mandel and Schuman, 1980). Levin and co-workers (1960), on the other hand, reported a slight excess incidence in urban over rural areas in three states in the United States. This study was based on data from 1949 to 1951, whereas the other United States studies are more recent. There seems to be, however, a consistent excess prostatic cancer mortality rate in US Blacks living in urban areas (Blair and Fraumeni, 1978; King *et al.*, 1963; Schuman and Mandel, 1980). Also, in the non-Mormon (white) Utah population, a distinct urban excess in incidence has been reported, whereas in Utah Mormons there is no such difference (Lyon *et al.*, 1980a,b). The reliability of urban–rural differences may be influenced by factors such as availability and quality of medical care and the accuracy of death certificates. Nevertheless, a high degree of urbanization seems positively associated with prostatic cancer risk in many geographical areas. In the United States, however, this association has only been found for Blacks and, with some exceptions, generally not for Whites.

H. Time Trends and Cohort and Age Effects

Worldwide age-specific and age-adjusted prostatic cancer death rates and incidence figures have, with only very few exceptions, increased over time, and there is a tendency for the disease to occur at a later age (Mandel and Schuman, 1980). This shift is even apparent over relatively short time intervals (Tables I, II, and IV) (Segi, 1978, 1981; Waterhouse *et al.*, 1976, 1982; Wynder and Hirayama, 1977). Noteworthy in this respect are prostatic cancer rates in US Blacks (Schuman and Mandel, 1980). Black death rates were approximately 60% of white death rates in 1930. They increased steadily, but more than the rates in US white men, crossing white death rates between 1945 and 1950, and reaching a Black:White ratio of 1.8 in about 1970 (Correa and Londono, 1982; Schuman and Mandel, 1980). The change in death rates for the 1930–1974 period was about 34% for white men and a dramatic 322% for black men. Differences in survival or accessibility of medical care cannot explain this huge Black–White difference (Mettlin and Natarajan, 1983; Schuman and Mandel, 1980). Another interesting group is the native Japanese population. Prostatic cancer rates have considerably increased in this population in recent years (Tables II and III) (Waterhouse *et al.*, 1976, 1982; Wynder and Hirayama, 1977).

Prostatic cancer is characteristically a disease of old age, more so than any other type of cancer (Waterhouse *et al.*, 1976, 1982). Also, its incidence increases more rapidly with age than any other cancer (Cook *et al.*, 1969). Notwithstanding the very large geographical and racial differences in mortality and morbidity, the age-specific incidence and mortality curves of populations that differ in prostatic cancer risk are remarkably parallel (Waterhouse *et al.*, 1976, 1982; Mandel and Schuman, 1980; Ross *et al.*, 1983).

Only a few studies have examined trends in relation to birth cohorts. Only trends in mortality for successive birth cohorts have been reported. In most populations studied, mortality rates increased for cohorts born just before the end of the last century (Gordon *et al.*, 1961; Holman *et al.*, 1981). Not in all studies, however, have such cohort effects been found (Mandel and Schuman, 1980). Most interesting is the finding of Ernster and co-workers (1978b) of peak mortality rates for non-Whites (mainly Blacks) of the birth cohort of 1896–1900, and declining rates for later cohorts. They speculate that the excess mortality among Blacks as compared with that among Whites will eventually lessen if this declining trend continues. Consequently, the explanation for the high Black:White prostatic cancer ratio should be investigated in the birth cohorts from the turn of the century (Ernster *et al.*, 1978b), notwithstanding the difficulties in doing so (Schuman and Mandel, 1980). A similar decrease in birth cohorts born after 1900 has been observed in Italy (La Rosa *et al.*, 1985).

In summary, age-adjusted prostatic cancer rates have increased worldwide over the past 50 years in most, if not all, populations. Mortality rates seem to have increased for cohorts born just before the end of the nineteenth century, and to have decreased since, particularly in US Blacks.

I. Correlations with Other Sites and Multiple Primary Tumors

The geographical patterns in the occurrence of prostatic cancer parallel those of, among others, female breast cancer and colon cancer in both sexes (Segi, 1978, 1981; Waterhouse *et al.*, 1976, 1982). On an international basis, mortality (Schrauzer, 1976a; Wynder *et al.*, 1967) and incidence (Berg, 1975) for colon and breast cancer correlate very well with those for prostatic cancer. Also, migrant studies reveal similar trends for these three sites, and comparable patterns are found among most ethnic minorities in the United States for breast and prostate cancer, but not so much for colon cancer (Fraumeni and Mason, 1974; Haenszel and Kurihara, 1968; Staszewski and Haenszel, 1965; Thomas, 1979). There are, however, important exceptions to this general pattern. In Hawaii, Caucasians have twice the prostate cancer incidence of the other ethnic groups, whereas Hawaiian natives have breast cancer rates equal to those of Caucasians, but lower colon cancer rates (Kolonel, *et al.*, 1981b; Menck and Henderson, 1985). Chinese and Japanese in Hawaii have lower breast (females) and prostate cancer rates than Caucasians, but equal colon cancer rates (both sexes). Filipinos in Hawaii, however, have lower rates than Caucasians for all three sites. In US Blacks, colon and breast cancer occur as frequently as in US Whites or slightly less frequently, even though Blacks are at twice the risk for prostatic cancer (White *et al.*, 1981). Breast and, in particular, colon cancer rates are clearly lower in Californian SDA (mortality) and Utah LDS (incidencc) than in the general US white population, while this is not true for prostate cancer

(Lyon *et al.*, 1980a,b; Phillips *et al.*, 1980a,b). Finally, an interesting correlation has been reported between prostate cancer and male breast cancer based on international incidence data (Sobin and Sherif, 1980).

Prostatic cancer patients are likely to have a second primary tumor slightly more often than expected (Lynch *et al.*, 1966; Schoenberg, 1975). Specifically, bladder cancer and leukemia have been reported to occur significantly more often than expected, both before and after the diagnosis of prostatic cancer has been made (Greene and Wilson, 1985; Jensen *et al.*, 1985; Kantor and McLaughlin, 1985; Kleinerman *et al.*, 1985; Osterlind *et al.*, 1985; Storm and Prener, 1985; Wynder *et al.*, 1971). Liskow *et al.* (1987) reported from a cohort study that US black prostatic cancer cases were more likely than expected to have bladder cancer as a second primary cancer, while Whites were more likely to have leukemia as second primary. Black and white cases combined were more likely to have colon cancer as a second primary. Because most of these relationships are bidirectional, a common risk factor may be present (Kleinerman *et al.*, 1985). The observed:expected ratios in these studies, however, are not very high, and the bidirectionality is not completely consistent.

J. Relations with Benign Prostatic Hyperplasia and Prostatitis

1. *Benign Prostatic Hyperplasia*

A number of investigators and clinicians have speculated in the past that a relation may exist between prostatic cancer and benign hyperplasia of the prostate (BHP) (Mandel and Schuman, 1980; Rotkin, 1983; Wynder *et al.*, 1971). It has been suggested that the benign disease is a precursor of the carcinoma, or that both processes have a similar etiology. There have only been two studies in which an attempt was made to address this question in a systematic manner (Armenian *et al.*, 1974; Greenwald *et al.*, 1974b). Armenian and co-workers (1974) found that BHP patients were at higher risk for prostatic cancer than controls in a follow-up mortality study on 338 cases of BHP, initially free of prostatic cancer. Of these, 296 were followed for the duration of the study, and 237 of them died during the follow-up period. Thirty-five of these 237 men died of prostatic cancer. Controls, matched for age and year of admission, were initially clinically free of BHP or prostatic cancer. Of the 299 controls, 258 died, 10 of prostatic cancer. The age-adjusted death rate per 1000 person-years of follow-up from prostatic cancer was 3.7 times higher in BHP cases than in the control group. To adjust for prostatic cancers that were present at the time of BHP diagnosis or selection as control but not clinically recognized, they did not include prostatic cancer cases that were found during the first 6 years. The relative risk for developing prostatic cancer in BHP patients (<20 cases, exact number not presented) as compared with that in controls (<9 cases, exact number not given) was 2.7 ($p < 0.05$). Some of the patients had (probably subtotal) prostatectomies, which may have influenced the results. Therefore, these BHP cases ($n = 77$) were distinguished from patients who did not undergo this treatment ($n = 229$). The death rate among the prostatectomized men (5.1/1000 person-years) was substantially lower than that among the other BHP patients (11.3), but still higher than that of the controls (2.7).

Greenwald and co-workers (1974b) followed a cohort of 838 BHP cases for an average of 10.7 years and did not find a higher risk for prostatic cancer in these patients. They studied incidence and found 24 prostatic cancer cases among BHP cases and 26 cases in 802 controls matched for age and year of hospitalization. The incidence rate in the BHP group was 3.0/1000 person-years of follow-up, and the rate in the control group was 3.1/1000 person-years. Interestingly, in the 78 controls who developed BHP during the follow-up period, 3 (3.8%) developed prostatic cancer, as compared with 23 (3.2%) of the remaining controls and 2.9% of the men in the original BHP group. All BHP patients in this study underwent subtotal prostatectomy. One might expect that removal of a substantial portion of the prostate would decrease the likelihood of prostatic cancer developing in the remainder. There was, however, no apparent relation between prostatic cancer risk and the weight of the tissue removed.

The results of the two studies summarized earlier are contradictory. They are, however, difficult to compare. The study by Greenwald and co-workers (1974b) determined incidence, whereas the study by Armenian and colleagues (1974) dealt with mortality resulting from prostatic cancer. The mean follow-up time was 10.7 years in the former study, whereas it was not specifically indicated in the latter, but must have been somewhere between 5 and 9 years. The exact age distribution is not given in either report, but the first study indicated that the average age at entry into the study was 63 years. Greenwald and co-workers (1974b) found 24 prostatic cancer cases out of 838 BHP cases (2.9%) and 26 cases per 802 control patients (3.2), whereas Armenian and colleagues (1974) found 35 cases per 296 BHP patients (11.8%) and 10 cases per 299 control patients (3.3%). Thus, the crude rates are very comparable except for the BHP group in the study by Armenian *et al.* (1974). This difference suggests that there is a possibility that the association found by Armenian and co-workers (1974) was due to chance. There are no marked differences in the methods used for the diagnosis of prostatic cancer in these studies. In fact, in neither study were detailed autopsy and histology data available, which rules out the possibility that latent cancers have contributed to the results. Increased probability of detecting prostatic cancer in BHP patients because of more attention paid to prostatic disease in that group cannot explain the high rates among BHP cases in the study by Armenian *et al.* (1974). Mortality from prostatic cancer as ascertained from the death certificates was recorded and not incidence as in the study by Greenwald *et al.* (1974b). The number of prostatic cancer cases is rather low in both studies, which lessens their reliability.

There are some other indications that BHP and prostatic cancer are not related. There are distinct differences in the epidemiology of the two diseases (Araki *et al.*, 1980; Mishina *et al.*, 1985; Rotkin, 1983). For example, the incidence of BHP is similar in Blacks and Whites in the United States (Lytton, 1983). Most important, prostatic cancer and BHP originate from different parts of the prostate: BHP develops in the periurethral zone, whereas carcinoma originates, possibly exclusively, from the peripheral zone (Breslow *et al.*, 1977; Franks, 1983; Hodges and Wan, 1983; McNeal, 1983). Furthermore, the two processes are morphologically very different in that the fibromuscular component of the prostate is intimately involved in BHP, whereas there is only secondary fibromuscular involvement in prostatic carcinoma (Franks, 1983; McNeal, 1983; Mostofi and Price, 1973; Tannenbaum, 1977). In conclusion, there are some contradictory epidemiological suggestions that BHP and prostatic carcinoma are somehow interrelated. All other epidemiological and biological data, however, indicate that they are two separate diseases that develop independently from one another in different parts of the prostate.

2. *Prostatitis*

A possible relation between prostatic cancer and prostatitis has been suggested in two case-control studies in the United States, but the information was either not convincing (Wynder *et al.*, 1971) or only a preliminary report was available (Jackson *et al.*, 1981). In a Japanese case-control study, no association was found. It is of interest that venereal diseases such as gonorrhea seem to be related to prostatic cancer (see Section IV,B), and prostatitis is frequent in these diseases (Drach and Kohnen, 1977). Another interesting similarity is the finding that prostatic cancer arises from the peripheral zone of the prostate gland (see earlier), which is also the preferential site for prostatitis (Drach and Kohnen, 1977). In conclusion, there are some suggestions for an association between prostatic cancer and prostatitis, but conclusive evidence is lacking.

K. Familial Aggregation

Cancer of the prostate appears to occur more frequently in fathers, sons, and brothers of prostatic cancer patients than in unrelated men. Studies on this have been summarized by Mandel and Schuman (1980). A significant 3- to 4-fold increase in risk was found for male relatives of white Utah prostate cancer patients in a death certificate study by Woolf (1960), who compared 355 fathers and brothers of 228 patients with controls, matched for age, county of residence, and year of death, and in a clinical study by Meikle and co-workers (Meikle and Stanish, 1982; Meikle *et al.*, 1982), who compared 257 brothers of 150 patients, less than 62 years old at diagnosis, with 202 brothers-in-law and with the Utah male population. This increased risk in Utah white males with a family history of prostatic cancer was confirmed by Cannon *et al.* (1982) in a retrospective study of Utah Mormons. In addition, there are three case-control studies reporting that prostatic cancer patients, significantly more frequently than controls, have a family history of prostatic cancer. Steele and co-workers (1971) found a family history (father or brother) of prostatic cancer in 5 of 39 (12.8%) prostatic cancer patients and in 2 of 39 controls (5.1%). In a preliminary report, Krain (1973) also indicated an increased risk for blood relatives of prostatic cancer cases. In his final report, Krain (1974) indicated that 12 of 210 (5.7%) cases had a family history of prostatic cancer versus 2 of 215 (0.9%) controls. Jackson *et al.* (1981) indicated in a preliminary report on a case-control study that US black prostatic cancer patients also more frequently had a family history of prostatic cancer than did the controls.

There are two studies that did not find an increased risk for prostatic cancer in relatives of prostatic cancer patients. Albert and Child (1977) found slightly more prostatic cancer cases ($n = 28$) among men with a family history of prostatic cancer than among controls; this difference was not statistically significant, however. Mishina *et al.* (1981, 1985) did not find any indication of familial aggregation in a case-control study on 100 cases and 100 age–residence matched controls in Japan. Thus, familial aggregation is a common but not perfectly consistent finding for cancer of the prostate.

L. Marital Status and Fertility

Generally, married men have a higher risk for prostate cancer than single men, and widowed and divorced men a higher risk than married men (Cannon *et al.*, 1982; Duffield and Jacobson, 1945; Ernster *et al.*, 1979a; King *et al.*, 1963; Lilienfeld *et al.*, 1972; Mandel and Schuman, 1980; Swanson *et al.*, 1985). There is no significant difference for this pattern between mortality studies (King *et al.*, 1963; Lilienfeld *et al.*, 1972) and incidence studies (Ernster *et al.*, 1979a; Swanson *et al.*, 1985). For black men in the United States, a different pattern was found: single Blacks showed the highest risk and divorced Blacks the lowest, with married and widowed in between. In these studies by Ernster *et al.* (1979a) and Swanson *et al.* (1985), the incidence data that were used were derived from the TNCS from 1969 to 1971, and the Metropolitan Detroit Cancer Surveillance System from 1978 to 1982, respectively. In older studies in the United States by King *et al.* (1963) and Lilienfeld *et al.* (1972), Blacks showed the same pattern as Whites, singles having the lowest risk and widowed and particularly divorced men having the highest risk. These studies used mortality data from national surveys covering 1949 to 1951 and 1959 to 1961, respectively. From these studies it appears that in US Whites no changes have occurred in the past three to four decades in the relation between prostatic cancer risk and marital status. In Blacks, however, a shift has taken place from widowed and divorced men being at highest risk to single men being the highest risk group. In fact, single Blacks are probably the population at highest risk for prostatic cancer worldwide at the present time.

Preliminary information from a case-control study on US Blacks by Jackson *et al.* (1981) supports the aforementioned observations, whereas in a Japanese case-control study, risk tended to be somewhat lower in married than in divorced men (Mishina *et al.*, 1981). There are, however, also case-control studies that did not indicate a relation between marital status and prostatic cancer risk (Greenwald *et al.*, 1974; Talamini *et al.*, 1986; Wynder *et al.*, 1971) Interestingly, no significant excess or deficit in mortality was found in a cohort study among US Catholic priests (Ross *et al.*, 1981).

No difference for age at first marriage has been found in most studies conducted in the United States (Armenian *et al.*, 1975; Greenwald *et al.*, 1974a; Ross *et al.*, 1987; Schuman *et al.*, 1977), but one (Cannon *et al.*, 1982) found an increased risk for men who first married at over 21 years of age as compared with men who first married at a younger age. However, in a Japanese case-control study (Mishina *et al.*, 1981, 1985), patients married at a younger age than the controls and the duration of their marriages was longer. Both Japanese observations were statistically significant. In an American case-control study by Armenian and co-workers (1975), a significantly larger number of patients were married much longer (>35 years) than the controls. In a case-control study conducted in the United States, Greenwald and co-workers (1979) did not find a relation between risk for prostatic cancer and the duration of widowerhood or multiple marriages.

Married men with children appear to be at higher risk than childless married men. Armenian *et al.* (1975) reported a relative risk of 2.69 for married men with children as compared to men without children, and Cannon *et al.* (1982) reported a significant ($p < 0.001$) odds ratio of 1.2. In general, patients have more children or have induced more pregnancies (Armenian *et al.*, 1975; Greenwald *et al.*, 1974a). This association is possibly independent of race and environment, because Mishina and co-workers (1981, 1985) reported similar findings in a Japanese case-control study. However, in some studies this association was not found (Ross *et al.*, 1987; Wynder *et al.*, 1971) or slightly present (Schuman *et al.*, 1977). Age at the birth of the first or last child does not seem to be associated with prostatic cancer risk (Greenwald *et al.*, 1974a).

M. Discussion and Conclusions

There is an enormous variation among countries in the occurrence of cancer of the prostate, both in terms of mortality and morbidity. Populations migrating from a low-risk area to a high-risk area tend to acquire the high risk for prostatic cancer of their new environment. This finding indicates that differences between these areas exist in the presence of environmental factors that cause prostatic cancer or critically modify prostatic carcinogenesis. Endogenous factors, i.e., genetically or constitutionally determined differences in susceptibility, thus appear to be clearly less important than environmental (exogenous) determinants. The increasing time trends in prostatic cancer mortality and incidence suggest that the presence and influence of these environmental factors have increased over time worldwide.

Although there are many factors that influence the reliability of mortality and incidence figures (Doll and Peto, 1981), the international variation in prostatic cancer rates is probably reliable because of the following reasons: (1) The variation in mortality and incidence rates is remarkably similar. (2) The data are sufficiently consistent to group Asiatic countries in the low-rate range, eastern European countries in the intermediate-rate range, and northwestern European countries, Canada, and the United States in the high-rate range. (3) In each of these groups there are at least some countries with quite reliable registries (Waterhouse *et al.*, 1976, 1982). Increasing time trends for prostatic cancer incidence and mortality reported worldwide are probably also rather reliable, particularly the figures from the United States, Japan, and western European countries. Increased autopsy rates most likely do not account for the increases in incidence and mortality, because (in the US) only 3–7% of the cases are detected at autopsy, a figure that has remained rather constant over the past several decades (Devesa, 1980; Devesa *et al.*, 1984; Heston *et al.*, 1985). In addition, the rate of detection of latent carcinoma of the prostate on routine autopsy is probably very small and therefore does not significantly contribute to the increases in rates (Harbitz and Haugen, 1972). The number of cases that have been derived from death certificates only decreased steadily in the United States until 1965, and it has remained at 1–2% since. Increases in incidence have, however, continued. Also, the accuracy of death certificates is high for prostatic cancer (Percy *et al.*, 1981), while the number of cases that are histologically confirmed has increased and has been over 90% in the United States since the end of the 1960s (Devesa, 1980; Heston *et al.*, 1985). On the other hand, a major contributing factor to the fact that incidence has increased more than mortality is probably the improvement of clinical diagnosis in the past few decades (Devesa *et al.*, 1984). Also, improved survival rates may well explain why mortality has not increased as much as incidence (Cairns, 1985; Mettlin and Natarajan, 1983; Mandel and Schuman, 1980). None of the preceding factors can explain the differences in rates and trends between Blacks and Whites in the United States, and therefore these intriguing differences should be considered as real (Devesa, 1980; Mettlin and Natarajan, 1983; Schuman and Mandel, 1980).

From the studies on the prevalence of different types of latent carcinoma of the prostate in populations that differ in risk (see Section II,D), it can be deduced that the environmental factors enhancing prostatic cancer risk act primarily at the phase of progression from small noninfiltrative cancer to large, invasive latent tumors. As outlined earlier, this view is based on the assumption that the small noninvasive lesion is the precursor of the larger, invasively growing lesion, and the larger lesion precedes the phase of clinically detectable cancer. Another possiblility is that environmental factors act at earlier phases of prostatic carcinogenesis, i.e., promotion or initiation, by influencing the potential of the developing lesions to progress, or even by affecting the susceptibility of normal prostatic epithelium at a young age to later carcinogenic events. Some support for the latter view is offered by the observation by Breslow *et al.* (1977) and Yatani *et al.* (1982) that noninfiltrative latent tumors occur slightly more frequently in populations at high risk for clinical prostate cancer than in low-risk areas (Tables VII and VIII). Other studies (Akazaki and Stemmermann, 1973; Guileyardo *et al.*, 1980), however, do not show such an association (Tables V and VI).

In US black men and perhaps also other male populations, certain environmental factors favoring the development of prostatic cancer seem to have been prevalent in birth cohorts from around the turn of the century (see Section II, H). Prostatic cancer death rates show a peak for these cohorts and have declined for later cohorts (Ernster *et al.*, 1978b). Interestingly, a large rural to urban migration took place in the black community in the United States in the early and middle twentieth century (White *et al.*, 1981). Currently, 70% of US Blacks live in urbanized areas, whereas 57% of the white population lives in urbanized areas. This migration has created major changes in life-style and other environmental conditions for the great majority of the US black population (White *et al.*, 1981). One might speculate that, although factors prevalent among male Blacks at the turn of this century may have caused an increased level of initiation of prostatic cancer, the major change in environment for most US Blacks in the first half of this century is responsible for the dramatic increase in prostatic cancer incidence and mortality among US Blacks over the past 50 years. An additional indication that environmental changes (life-style) are involved in the increase in risk in US Blacks is the shift in the relation of prostatic cancer risk with marital status: From singles having the lowest risk to singles having the highest risk (see Section II,L).

Although environment is probably the prime determinant of prostatic cancer risk, genetic factors may nevertheless be of some importance. Familial aggregation of prostatic cancer risk is a consistent finding, as pointed out in Section II,K. The studies on familial aggregation are, however, with one exception (Meikle and Stanish, 1982; Meikle *et al.*, 1985), not very thorough. Familial aggregation may be heavily influenced by common environmental exposure of such close relatives as brothers, sons, and fathers (Greenwald, 1982; Winkelstein and Ernster, 1979). As controls, Meikle and co-workers (Meikle and Stanish, 1982; Meikle *et al.*, 1985) used brothers-in-law of the patients because they possibly have more environmental variables in common with the patients than those chosen from the general population. Still, they found a 4-fold increased risk for the blood relatives of the patients. The differences in risk between the black and the white male population in the United States may in part be based on genetically controlled differences in susceptibility for the disease. This view is somewhat supported by the confusing prostatic cancer patterns in the Caribbean region, where risk among some primarily black populations does not seem to follow the general pattern of risk increasing with increasing degree of affluence (see Section II,C; Hamilton and Persaud, 1981). However, the aforementioned peak in prostatic cancer death rates in black birth cohorts from around 1900 (Ernster *et al.*, 1978b), the recent changes in the relation between prostatic cancer risk and marital status in US Blacks, and the low rates among Blacks living in Africa (Kovi and Heshmat, 1973; Bradshaw and Harington, 1981) can be regarded as arguments in favor of an environmental hypothesis (Schuman and Mandel, 1980). Whether the low prostatic cancer risk of most of the ethnic minorities in the United States (except Blacks), including migrants from Asiatic countries, is totally or in part based on differences in genetic make-up is not clear because there is little, if any reliable information about their life-styles, which constitutes one of the major environmental variables. In conclusion, although genetic factors may influence prostatic cancer risk to some extent in certain individuals or ethnic entities, it is not likely that genetic mechanisms account for a substantial proportion of the cases in the Western world (Winkelstein and Ernster, 1979).

Environmental factors that may relate to prostate cancer risk in men include (1) life-style: diet, smoking, alcohol use, and factors associated with various aspects of behavior such as sexual and transmissible factors; (2) the chemical environment: pollution of air, water, or food, occupational exposures, and exposure to various chemicals such as household chemicals and cosmetics; and (3) the psychosocial environment. The last category has hardly been investigated and is estimated to be of no major importance for human cancer in general (Doll and Peto, 1981). Nevertheless, psychosocial environment may severely affect aspects of life-style.

Exposure to chemicals from environmental pollution and occupational and other sources is generally regarded as a minor contributor to the total cancer burden (Doll and Peto, 1981). It may, nevertheless, be a major factor in certain subpopulations (such as workers exposed to asbestos or vinyl chloride) or in the genesis of specific cancers (such as mesothelioma of the pleura or angiosarcoma of the liver). Some support for chemical environment as a factor in prostatic carcinogenesis in men comes from the consistent finding (see Section II,G) of slightly higher rates in urbanized areas than in rural regions. An urban environment is more likely to be associated with exposure to pollution or occupational chemicals (Goldsmith, 1980). Rural and urban areas may, however, also differ greatly in cultural patterns (Doll and Peto, 1981; Lilienfeld *et al.*, 1972), which are reflected in differences in sexual behavior and dietary habits, for example. For Blacks in the United States, an urban:rural ratio of rates greater than 1 is consistently found (see Section II,G). However, chemical factors are probably less important in explaining this urban:rural difference than life-style factors, because there seems to be no difference in incidence for Blacks in urban areas with and without heavy industry (Demoupolos and Gutman, 1980). An indication that chemical exposure is perhaps important is that second primary tumors in prostatic cancer patients often are either bladder carcinomas or leukemias. For both tumors, occupational exposure to certain chemical carcinogens is a known risk factor (Doll and Peto, 1981). The inconsistency in studies on socioeconomic status and prostatic cancer risk hinders an evaluation of the possible importance of factors related to the work environment, such as chemical factors. On the other hand, Blacks in the United States are at higher risk for prostatic cancer than Whites, and they generally have a lower socioeconomic level than Whites and are, in general, more likely to have jobs with high exposures to disease-producing agents (Davis, 1980; Michaels, 1983; White *et al.*, 1981), and to live in communities with commercial hazardous waste facilities and uncontrolled toxic waste sites (Commission for Racial Justice, 1987). An indication that the chemical environment is not very important is the considerable difference in the occurrence of prostatic cancer in Japan and the United States, although both countries show a comparable degree of industrial development. There are, however, great differences in life-style, in particular dietary habits, between the two countries (Wynder and Hirayama, 1977). In Section V, the evidence available for the involvement of specific occupational factors or air pollution in prostatic carcinogenesis will be surveyed.

Breast and colon cancer rates are higher in second- than in first-generation migrants from low-risk areas to the United States. This is generally considered an indication that life-style factors that act throughout life are more important determinants of risk for these cancers than chemical factors in the environment (Reddy *et al.*, 1980; Wynder and Hirayama, 1977). For prostatic cancer, this so-called second-generation effect also seems to be present, a finding that supports the view that life-style is a major factor in prostatic carcinogenesis (Greenwald, 1982; Reddy *et al.*, 1980; Schuman and Mandel, 1980; Winkelstein and Ernster, 1979). Life-style is a composite of cultural (i.e., group behavioral patterns) and individual characteristics that may change considerably in relatively short periods of time, or, in some cases, remain remarkably constant. In general, smoking and dietary habits are regarded as the major life-style-related factors in human carcinogenesis (Doll and Peto, 1981). Dietary factors, first indicated by Wynder *et al.* (1971) as of possible importance in prostatic cancer, have recently received more and more attention (Bosland, 1985; Greenwald, 1982; Mandel and Schuman, 1980; N.A.S., 1982; Reddy *et al.*, 1980; Winkelstein and Ernster, 1979). The international correlation between prostatic cancer mortality and occurrence of cancer of the colon and the female breast, both strongly related to dietary factors (N.A.S., 1982; Reddy *et al.*, 1980), supports a dietary association. The aforementioned exceptions to these correlations—Californian SDA, Utah LDS, US Blacks and some ethnic groups in Hawaii (see Section II,I)—may indicate that dietary factors are not as important in prostatic carcinogenesis as they are for breast and colon cancer and that there are also other major determinants of prostatic cancer risk. The similar prostate cancer patterns in United States SDA and LDS in comparison with the general white population in the United States may also indicate that smoking and alcohol are not very important in prostatic cancer. Smoking and use of alcoholic beverages are proscribed for both religious groups (Phillips, 1975; Lyon *et al.*, 1980a). In addition, coffee and tea use are also proscribed for LDS, and SDA tend to avoid drinking them, and rather strict sexual mores pertain to both groups (Phillips, 1975; Lyon *et al.*, 1980a). A more detailed discussion of the relation of diet and nutrition and prostatic carcinogenesis will be presented in Section IV,A and will be followed by a discussion of that topic in Section IV,D.1. The use of alcohol, coffee, and tea will also be dealt with in those sections.

In general, married men seem to have a higher prostatic cancer risk than single men, and widowed and divorced men have an even higher risk than married men. In addition, there seems to be a positive association between risk for prostatic cancer and fertility. This association with marital status may be related to differences in life-style among the various categories of men. Differences in dietary habits, for example, are conceivable. On the other hand, differences in sexual habits or exposure to sex-related factors may be important. The apparent association between risk and fertility may be related to this. A further discussion on these aspects can be found in Sections IV,B and D,2.

In the following sections, a comprehensive overview will be given of the data available on the role of environmental factors in prostatic carcinogenesis. In addition, some atention will be given to endogenous factors, specifically the role of the endocrine system, and to animal studies on prostatic carcinogenesis.

III. Animal Models for Prostatic Cancer

Prostatic cancer is rare in almost all small laboratory animals. The occurence of cancer of the prostate in laboratory animals and the available animal models for prostatic cancer have been reviewed elsewhere (Bosland,

1986; Coffey *et al.*, 1979; Rivenson and Silverman, 1979). As indicated earlier, events that occur in the late stages of the promotion phase are likely to be of crucial importance in prostatic carcinogenesis in man, i.e., events taking place during the progression from noninvasive, small microcarcinoma to invasively growing larger microcarcinomas. Still, the possibility also exists that processes that take place during the early stage of the promotion phase, in the initiation phase, or even before initiation occurs may be important. Environmental factors that are of major importance in prostatic carcinogenesis in man are most likely operant at one or more of the later stages. Therefore, it is essential to study the influence of environmental factors in an animal model that comprises these stages. Thus, of the few transplantable prostatic tumor systems developed and characterized thus far, the Dunning tumor lines, the Pollard tumor lines, and the Nb rat tumor lines, (Coffey *et al.*, 1979; Smolev *et al.*, 1977; Pollard and Luckert, 1975; Noble, 1982) are not relevant in this respect. Spontaneously occuring prostatic carcinomas in the ACI/segHapBR rat (Ward *et al.*, 1980) have the major disadvantage of very long latency periods (>30 months), a condition that precludes practical experiments. Spontanous prostatic carcinomas found in aged germfree Lobund Wistar rats (Pollard, 1973) have the additional disadvantage of requiring germfree conditions. Induction of prostate cancer by hormonal manipulation has been achieved in the Nb rat (Noble, 1982) and in the Lobund Wistar rat (Pollard *et al.*, 1982). These approaches imply a profound alteration of the hormonal milieu. Therefore, they are not suitable for studying the influence of environmental factors on prostatic carcinogenesis, because that may be mediated by the endocrine system, as will be pointed out later. Many attempts in the past to induce prostatic adenocarcinomas in laboratory animals have failed (Bosland, 1987; Rivenson and Silverman, 1979). Recently, the successful induction of prostatic tumors in rats by systemic administration of chemical carcinogens has been described by some investigators (Bosland *et al.*, 1983; Katayama *et al.*, 1982; Pour, 1983). Pour (1983) induced squamous cell carcinomas, which are rarely seen in men, in the ventral prostate in 33% of his animals by repeated subcutaneous administration of nitroso bis-(2-oxopropyl)amine. Katayama *et al.* (1982) reported the induction of microscopic-size adenocarcinomas, which were probably carcinomas *in situ*, in the ventral prostate by repeated subcutaneous administration of 3,2′-dimethyl-4-aminobiphenyl with an incidence of 28%. They also found intraalveolar cribriform hyperplasias in 23% of their animals. One out of 293 rats showed a clinically manifest pelvic adenocarcinoma of undetermined origin involving the dorsal lobe of the prostate. The induction of carcinomas *in situ* in the ventral prostate by 3,2′-dimethyl-4-aminobiphenyl has recently been confirmed by Shirai and co-workers (1985). In the laboratory of the author, invasively growing, metastasizing adenocarcinomas were induced in the dorsolateral region of the prostate of Wistar rats (Cpb: WU) in a 25% incidence (5 out of 20 rats) by a single intravenous injection of *N*-methyl-*N*-nitrosourea (MNU) (Bosland *et al.*, 1983). In an additional 10% of the rats, microscopic-size adenocarcinomas were found, both types resulting in a total incidence of prostate cancer of 35%. The average latency was 64 weeks, and metastases were found in liver and lung. Prior to the MNU injection, the animals were treated with the antiandrogen cyproterone acetate, daily for 3 weeks, followed by three daily injections of testosterone. This treatment induces a synchronization of cell proliferation, and results in a peak in cell proliferation at the time of the MNU injection (Bosland *et al.*, 1986; Tuohimaa, 1980). This enhancement of cell proliferation is most likely responsible for the effectiveness of the MNU treatment by causing fixation of the promutagenic DNA lesions caused by MNU. When only cyproterone acetate was given, but no testosterone before MNU, thus actually depressing cell proliferation, no tumors were observed (Bosland *et al.*, 1984). In addition, other carcinogens—notably 7,12-dimethylbenz[*a*]anthracene or 3,2′-dimethyl-4-aminobiphenyl—could induce prostatic cancer after pretreatment with cyproterone acetate and testosterone, but they were less efficient than MNU. To date this is the only induction model for prostatic cancer available that seems relevant for the human disease for the following reasons: (1) Adenocarcinomas (and not squamous cell carcinomas) are induced. (2) The tumors originate in the dorsolateral region of the prostate and not in the ventral lobes. From an embryological point of view, there is no homologue in man for the rodent ventral prostate (Price, 1963; Sandberg *et al.*, 1980). (3) The latency period is rather long, and the tumors are thus relatively slow growing. (4) The tumors are invasively growing and give rise to metastases. Further characteristics of the tumors—notably, androgen dependence and histogenesis—have not yet been reported. Preliminary data (M. C. Bosland, unpublished observations) indicate that the tumors develop from the dorsal and/or the lateral lobes and that their development depends on the presence of androgens. The incidence of prostatic carcinomas in these further studies, however, was low (5–20%). Nevertheless, this approach may prove to be suitable for studying environmental influences on prostatic carcinogenesis beyond the initiation phase. The requirement of a high level of cell proliferation in the prostate for the chemical induction of prostatic epithelial proliferative lesions was recently also demonstrated by Shirai *et al.* (1985, 1986, 1987a). They showed that 3,2′-dimethyl-4-aminobiphenyl induces a high incidence of ventral prostatic carcinomas *in situ* in rats on repeated treatment, following enhancement of prostatic cell turnover by sequential treatment with ethinyl estradiol and methyltestosterone, or by ethinyl estradiol alone followed by a 3-day recovery from this chemical castration. Shirai *et al.* (1987b) did not produce prostatic neoplasia in F344 rats by MNU injected during stimulation of cell proliferation. This failure to reproduce the findings of Bosland *et al.* (1983) may have been due to the difference in the procedure followed to stimulate cell proliferation in the prostate (sequential administration via feed of ethinyl estradiol and methyltestosterone), or to strain differences in susceptibility from chemical induction of prostatic cancer. Preliminary data from my laboratory seem to indicate that the F344 strain is indeed refractory to MNU-induced prostatic carcinogenesis, unlike Wistar or Sprague Dawley rats. A recent report by Pollard and Luckert (1986b) indicates that a single intravenous injection with MNU (without any pretreatment) may be able to greatly enhance the formation of dorsolateral prostatic carcinomas induced by long-term administration of high doses of testosterone propionate. This study needs confirmation, but it suggests that a combination of chemical and hormonal carcinogenesis may be required for the development of rat dorsolateral prostatic carcinomas. Pour and Stephan (1987) recently confirmed that the combination of treatment with a chemical carcinogen [nitrosobis(2-oxopropyl)amine] and subsequent long-term androgen exposure enhances prostatic carcinogenesis in MRC rats. They also confirmed the need for enhanced prostatic cell proliferation at the time of carcinogen administration for the successful induction of prostatic cancer. Interestingly, they found that stimulation of cell proliferation during carcinogen treatment followed by long-term androgen administration causes adenocarcinomas predominantly located in the dorsolateral prostate in addition to the squamous cell carcinomas in the ventral prostate that can be induced by this carcinogen without the androgen treatment. If confirmed, these findings would have important implications for our views on prostatic carcinogenesis in general.

IV. Environmental Factors: Life-Style

A. Diet and Nutrition

1. *Introduction*

The possible role of diet and nutrition in prostatic carcinogenesis in man has recently been reviewed in depth (Bosland, 1985). The evidence for the involvement of dietary factors in prostatic carcinogenesis was evaluated, preceded by a comprehensive survey of the various studies on this topic. This review will be summarized here from the viewpoint of dietary variables rather than from that of the type of study, as done originally (Bosland, 1985). In addition, the studies on diet and prostatic cancer that have recently appeared in the literature, particularly those on vitamin A, will be discussed. Finally, an evaluation will be made of the information on diet, nutrition, and prostatic carcinogenesis available to date.

2. *Recent Studies*

In the review by Bosland (1985),* the following epidemiologic studies were discussed.

1. *International correlation studies.* Armstrong and Doll (1975), Carroll and Khor (1975), Correa (1981), Howell (1974), Schrauzer (1976b), Stocks (1970), and Takahashi (1964).
2. *Within-country correlation studies.* Blair and Fraumeni (1978), Breslow and Enstrom (1974), Gaskill *et al.* (1979), Kolonel *et al.* (1981a,b, 1983), and Schrauzer *et al.* (1977a,b).
3. *Case-control studies.* Graham *et al.* (1983), Kaul *et al.* (1981), Kolonel *et al.* (1983), Mishina *et al.* (1981), Ross *et al.* (1983), Rotkin (1979), Schuman *et al.* (1982), Williams and Horms (1977), and Wynder *et al.* (1971).
4. *Prospective (cohort) studies.* Hirayama (1979), Kark *et al.* (1981), and Phillips and Snowdon (1983).

There are nine new reports on cohort studies (Heilbrun, *et al.*, 1986; Hirayama, 1985; Jacobson *et al.*, 1986; Middleton *et al.*, 1987; Nomura *et al.*, 1986; Paganini *et al.*, 1985, 1987; Snowdon *et al.*, 1984; Whittemore *et al.*, 1986), and eight new case-control study reports (Heshmat *et al.*, 1985; Kaul *et al.*, 1987; Kolonel *et al.*, 1985, 1987; Ross *et al.*, 1987; Talamini *et al.*, 1986; Willett *et al.*, 1983, 1984). One international correlation study was reported (Rose *et al.*, 1986). A report has appeared in an American journal on a Japanese case-control study by Mishina *et al.* (1985) containing the same information as the previous report that was in Japanese (Mishina *et al.*, 1981). There are two reports of animal studies on the effect of dietary fat on hormonally induced prostatic cancer (Pollard and Luckert, 1985, 1986) and one study on the effect of vitamin A on the growth of prostatic cancer (Clinton *et al.*, 1985). These studies are summarized below.

Rose and colleagues (1986) recalculated international correlations between prostatic cancer mortality rates and food consumption data. They used 1978–79 mortality rates and 1979–81 food availability data. The following positive associations with prostatic cancer rates found in previous studies (Bosland, 1985) were confirmed: all meats ($r = 0.39$), milk ($r = 0.69$), total fat ($r = 0.61$), animal fat ($r = 0.69$), animal protein ($r = 0.55$), total calories ($r = 0.34$) and animal source calories ($r = 0.68$); the associations for meats, total fat and calories were, however, weaker than those previously reported.

*In the review by Bosland (1985), there are a few errors in some of the tables: In Table 1, the incidence rate in Denmark in 1968–1972 should read 23.0. In Table 2, the reference numbers presented in the column indicated by "Ref." should read as follows: 58 = 18, 85 = 35, 87 = 37, 88 = 38, 89 = 39, 90 = 40, and the correct last reference indicated for "Total Fat" is 36 and not 87. In Tables 4a and 4b, the study by Kolonel *et al.* (1983) is reference number 44, not 31.

A negative association for cereals ($r = -0.75$), and an absence of an association for fruits ($r = -0.09$) were also confirmed. For vegetables, a negative trend was found ($r = -0.38$), confirming one previous study, but contradicting one other that found no association (see Bosland, 1985). Other studies have found a weak positive association ($r = 0.30$–0.50) for egg consumption (see Bosland, 1985). Rose *et al.* (1986), however, found no such relation ($r = 0.01$). For the consumption of vegetable fat and vegetable source calories (not previously studied) correlation coefficients were found of 0.07 and −0.44, respectively.

Results from a case-control study in US Blacks were reported by Heshmat *et al.* (1985). A preliminary report (Kaul *et al.*, 1981) of the same study was discussed before (Bosland, 1985). The study involved 181 age-matched case-control pairs. In interviews lasting 30–45 min, questions were asked about diet and several other items. A food-frequency questionnaire that was used addressed serving size to estimate the actual amounts consumed more accurately. Information on food consumption for two age periods, 30–49 years and >50 years, was obtained from every participant. From these data, the average daily intake of 18 nutrients and food components was calculated. No difference between cases and controls was found for the consumption of carbohydrates, crude fiber, calcium, phosphorus, sodium, potassium, iron, thiamin, riboflavin, niacin, vitamin C, linoleic acid, and cholesterol. Average daily intake of protein, total fats, saturated fatty acids, and oleic acid was higher in patients than in controls. These differences were not statistically significant ($p < 0.08$–0.09) and they were found only for the 30–49 period, and not for the 50+ period. Vitamin A intake was significantly higher in patients than in controls for the 30–49 age period and tended to be higher for the >50 period. A follow-up study in 55 additional case-control pairs (Kaul *et al.*, 1987), found a nonsignificant higher vitamin A intake in cases than in controls for the 30–49 years of age period, but no such tendency for the >50 years period. In this latter study, a lower average daily intake was found in cases than in controls for iron and thiamin in the 30–49 years period, and for linoleic acid and riboflavin in the 50+ period.

Kolonel and co-workers (1987) presented a final report of an ongoing case-control study among the various ethnic groups in Hawaii (Kolonel *et al.*, 1983, 1985). The 1987 report is the final report on vitamin A and carotenes; this report is summarized here. Data on vitamin C were only presented in the 1985 report. For each of the 452 cases, 2 controls matched for age were selected; 58 of these subjects were at least 70 years old. In interviews, data were collected on frequency and amount of comsumption of more than 100 food items. This selection of foods represented approximately 85–90% of the food sources for vitamins A and C (Kolonel *et al.*, 1985); in addition, vitamin supplements were included in the study. There was a positive association between fat intake and prostatic cancer risk (Kolonel *et al.*, 1987; data not shown), but there was no indication that vitamin C consumption differed between cases and controls (Kolonel *et al.*, 1985). The data for vitamin A are detailed in Section IV,A,6,a.

A case-control study in US Blacks and Whites involved 142 age–residence matched pairs per racial group (Ross *et al.*, 1987). Frequency-of-use data on 20 food categories were collected by interview. Significantly elevated relative risks were found for the use of eggs and, in Blacks only, pork and kidney. Significantly reduced risk was found for use of poultry and carrots (in Whites) or cooked greens (in Blacks). Intakes of fat, protein, vitamin A and β-carotene were estimated and divided in tertiles. There was no association between risk and protein or vitamin A comsumption. Risk decreased monotonously, but not significantly, with increasing consumption of β-carotene in Blacks only. Risk increased with increasing fat consumption in both racial groups. Risk in the highest fat intake tertile was significantly elevated in Blacks ($p < 0.05$). Lower risk seemed associated with high intake of β-carotene especially in persons with low fat intake.

Talamini *et al.* (1986) conducted a case-control study in Italian men. A total of 166 cases and 202 hospital controls were included. Cases and controls were not age-matched and therefore relative risks were obtained from age-stratified data by multiple logistic regression analysis, controlling for all variables. Frequency-of-consumption data (<5 or >4 days/week) were obtained from a questionnaire on meat, milk/cheese, and green vegetables (not otherwise specified). There was a significant positive relation to risk for the consumption of milk and cheese together (relative risk 2.5; 95% confidence interval 1.3–4.7), and a borderline significant relation for meat consumption (relative risk 1.7; 95% confidence interval 1.0–2.8). There was no significant relation for the consumption of green vegetables. The authors also state that wine and coffee consumption were unrelated to prostatic cancer risk, but actual data were not given.

Willett and co-workers (1983, 1984) collected blood samples from 4480 subjects from 1973 to 1974. In this cohort, 111 cases of cancer were identified, 11 of which were prostatic cancer. For each case, two controls were selected who were matched for age, race, time of blood collection, and a number of health-related variables. Serum levels of retinol, retinol-binding protein (RBP), total carotenoids, vitamin E, and selenium were measured and adjusted for the level of total serum lipids, because there was a more or less strong association with lipid levels for all variables. There was no difference between cases (all cancer as well as prostatic cancer) and controls for serum levels of retinol, RBP, carotenoids and vitamin E. For selenium, however, cancer cases had significantly ($p = 0.02$) lower serum levels (0.129 μg/ml) than controls (0.136 μg/ml) (Willett *et al.*, 1983). For the 11 prostatic cancer cases specifically, a similar difference (0.128 versus 0.139 μg/ml) was observed, but it was not statistically significant ($p = 0.12$).

In a further report on an ongoing cohort study (Hirayama, 1979) in Japan, Hirayama (1985) presented more recent data on smoking, the use of alcohol, and the consumption of meat and green–yellow vegetables. The results are from the 16-year follow-up period of a cohort of 122,261 men. The number of prostatic cancer cases is not indicated in this report. In the report on the 10-year follow-up (Hirayama, 1979), there were 63 deaths from prostatic cancer. A negative association of the intake of green–yellow vegetables was reported in the 10-year follow-up, and no association was found for smoking and alcohol and meat consumption. In the more recent report, however, no relation between risk and the consumption of green–yellow vegetables (or meat and alcohol or smoking) was present.

Paganini-Hill *et al.* (1985, 1987) studied the association between the use of vitamin A supplements and 59 foods (including major vitamin A- and β-carotene-rich foods) and prostatic cancer risk in a cohort of mainly white subjects (median age, 75 years), 4280 of whom were male. After 5 years of follow-up, 92 prostatic cancer cases were identified. Age-adjusted incidence rates were reported. There was no relation between prostatic cancer risk and dietary vitamin A, β-carotene, or total vitamin A (dietary plus supplemental) intake (Paganini-Hill *et al.*, 1987). For vitamin A supplement use, however, incidence rates increased from 4.17 per 1000 for nonusers to 4.88 and 6.85 per 1000 for men using little or much supplementation, respectively. The latter rate was significantly higher ($p < 0.05$) than that for nonusers, and the trend for increasing rates with increasing supplement use was also significant ($p < 0.05$). In an earlier 2.5 year follow-up (70 cases), no relation between risk and supplement use was found, but mean serum retinol concentration in a random sample of 8 supplement users was significantly higher than in 18 nonusers (86 μg/100 ml versus 74 μg/100 ml; $p = 0.038$) (Paganini-Hill *et al.*, 1985).

Middleton *et al.* (1987) most likely studied the same patient-control population as Graham *et al.* (1983). There was a nonsignificant increase in risk with increasing vitamin A consumption (see Section IV,A,6,a).

In a preliminary report, Phillips and Snowdon (1983) presented the results of the 21-year follow-up of a cohort study among 21,295 white Californian Seventh Day Adventists. They indicated a nonsignificant tendency of a positive association for prostatic cancer mortality with the frequency of meat consumption, and a negative association with the frequency of use of coffee (see Bosland, 1985). A more recent report (Snowdon *et al.*, 1984) was restricted to 6763 men who reached the age of 60 in the 21-year period; 99 prostatic cancer deaths occurred among them. Data on the frequency of the use of milk, meat and poultry together, cheese, and eggs were collected from a questionnaire at the start of the study. No data on the consumption of coffee were presented in this report, but information on body weight was included. The consumption of the food items was divided into three frequency categories and relative risks were calculated. For the use of meat, cheese, and particularly eggs, there was a tendency for the age-adjusted risk relative to that of the lowest frequency tertile to increase with increasing frequency of use. Using a test for linear trend, a borderline significance was found for eggs, with a two-tailed p value of 0.09. For meat and cheese, the trend was not statistically significant. For the consumption of milk, on the other hand, the relative risk for the highest frequency tertile (2.4) was significantly elevated ($p < 0.05$). There was a clear dose-related increase in relative risk with a two-tailed P value of 0.005 for linear trend. The relative risk for men who were markedly overweight (130–249% of desirable weight) at the start of the study (2.4) was statistically significantly elevated ($p < 0.05$) in comparison with men within 10% of their desirable weight. Multivariate analysis (Cox proportional hazards regression) to evaluate the possiblility that interrelationships between the variables were responsible for the associations found was performed on the five aforementioned variables and age and level of education. The multivariate-adjusted relative risk (130–249% overweight versus normal weight) for obesity (2.5) was significant ($p < 0.01$), the relative risk (highest frequency tertile versus lowest tertile) for milk (1.5) was borderline significant ($p <$ 0.1), and relative risks for meat and poultry, cheese and eggs were not significant ($p > 0.1$). When all four animal product variables were grouped together in this analysis, the relative risk was 3.6.

A Norwegian cohort study (Jacobson *et al.*, 1986) investigated cancer risk and coffee drinking. A cohort of 13,664 men was followed for 11.5 years, during which 260 men died of prostatic cancer. There was no association with risk for prostatic cancer for the number of cups of coffee that were consumed per day at the start of the study.

Heilbrun *et al.* (1986) studied a cohort of 8006 Japanese men from the Hawaiian island of Oahu. At the time of the start of the study (1965–68) their tea consumption (black tea only) was recorded as the number of times of consumption per week. In 1985, there were 7833 men available for analysis, of which 48.6% were tea consumers; there were 149 prostatic cancer deaths. The relative risk (adjusted for age at entry) decreased significantly ($p = 0.020$; linear trend test) with increasing tea consumption (from almost never to daily). Since tea consumption decreased with increasing age, the influence of age at entry and the time interval between age at entry and age at the time of diagnosis were studied. The negative association with prostatic cancer risk for tea consumption was stronger for men that were 58+ years at entry and/or had an interval between entry and diagnosis of 10 years or longer than for men under 58 years or with a shorter interval. Thus the negative association appeared essentially independent of age as potential confounder.

A cohort study conducted in the United States (Whittemore *et al.*, 1985) followed over 29,000 male and female subjects for approximately 10–15 years from the time a questionnaire was mailed to them requesting information on personal habits. A total of 243 men developed prostatic cancer. There was no significant ($p > 0.05$) association between risk for prostatic cancer and the consumption of coffee, tea, and alcohol.

Nomura and colleagues (1986) conducted a cohort study in Hawaii on 7355 Japanese men, who were followed for 10 years. At the start of the study, in 1965–1968, the men were asked about the number of cups of coffee they were drinking daily. A total of 108 newly diagnosed cases of prostatic cancer occurred in this period. There was no relation between the number of cups of coffee that were consumed per day and the incidence of prostatic cancer.

Pollard and Luckert (1986a) reported data on the effects of fat on hormonally induced prostatic cancer in rats. A preliminary report of the same study (Pollard and Luckert, 1985) essentially contained the same data. They treated 3- to 4-month-old male rats of the Lobund-Wistar strain with testosterone propionate to induce prostatic cancer. Each rat, in groups of 40, was given two silastic implants, each of which contained 40–50 mg testosterone propionate, which were replaced twice at 3-month intervals. One testosterone-treated group was fed a powdered natural ingredient diet (indicated as L-485) that contained 5% fat, to which 15% corn oil was added, making the total fat content 20%. It is not clear from their publication whether the total fat content of this diet was 20% by weight or 20% of energy control. Furthermore, the high-fat diet was not isocaloric with the low-fat diet. Also, it is not completely clear when the feeding of the high-fat diet was started; most likely it started at the time of the first testosterone implantation. Another group was also treated with testosterone and fed the L-485 diet without extra fat added. Both groups had *ad libitum* access to the food. There was a control group of 18 rats that were fed the high-fat diet and were not treated with testosterone propionate. In other experiments, rats that were treated with testosterone propionate or that received empty implants and were fed the low-fat diet were followed for longer than 12 months. In the high-fat, testosterone-treated group 26 of 40 rats (65%) has prostatic cancer, 7 of which had grossly observed tumors of the prostate and 19 microscopic cancer. In the low-fat, testosterone-treated group 14 of 40 rats (35%) had prostatic cancer, 2 of which had gross prostatic tumors and 12 microscopic-size cancer. The difference in incidence is statistically significant ($p < 0.02$; X^2 test, two-tailed; *analysis done by the author*). The average latency time was 11.3 months in the high-fat group and 12.4 months in the low-fat group; and the average survival time was 11.7 and 12.8 months, respectively (no significant differences for latency time and survival; $p > 0.05$; t test, two-tailed; *analysis done by the author*).

The results for the testosterone-treated rats on low fat were similar to those in previous experiments. Very few details were given on the gross tumors: They were adenocarcinomas, often poorly differentiated, located in the dorsolateral region of the prostate. No details were given on the microscopic cancers. In the group fed a high-fat diet without testosterone treatment and in the group on low fat with empty silastic implants, no gross or microscopic prostatic cancer was seen. In control animals (untreated, on a low-fat diet), one prostatic tumor was found at 22 months (number of animals was not indicated; Pollard and Luckert, 1985). These results seem to indicate that the inclusion of a substantial amount of corn oil in a natural-ingredient diet accelerates the development of prostatic carcinomas induced by testosterone propionate in Lobund-Wistar rats. It is not at all clear whether this is an effect of the fat or a consequence of the dietary imbalances that certainly occurred in this experiment, because no isocaloric diets were used. The groups may have differed as much as 20–25% in intake of some essential nutrients as a result of the unadjusted differences in energy density of the high- and low-fat diets. Nevertheless, this study adds more weight to the epidemiological indications that a high intake of dietary fat is positively related to a high risk for prostatic cancer.

In a preliminary report, the results of the effects of vitamin A deficiency or supplementation (as retinyl acetate) on the growth of the transplantable Dunning prostatic carcinomas R3327H and R3327HI were summarized (Clinton *et al.*, 1985). No effects on growth of the androgen-dependent line R3327H or the androgen-independent line R3327HI were found.

3. *Foods and Foodstuffs*

Positive or negative associations of the consumption of certain foods with risk for prostatic cancer have been mainly derived from international correlation studies and case-control studies. In the first category of studies, the correlation between prostatic cancer mortality/incidence and the estimated gross per capita consumption of these foods is determined. The latter studies compare the consumption of these items in prostatic cancer cases and controls. Usually the frequency of consumption has been studied, and only occasionally the amounts consumed, which is more accurate. There are also some data from cohort studies and within-country correlation studies. The main findings reported in the literature are summarized below:

a. Meats. In four international correlation studies, consumption with meats in general correlated moderately with prostatic cancer rates, with correlation coefficients of 0.56–0.74 (Armstrong and Doll, 1975; Correa, 1981; Howell, 1974; Schrauzer, 1976b). Rose *et al.* (1986) was the only group that found a lower correlation coefficient (0.39). Cattle meat particularly showed this association (Correa, 1981; Howell, 1974); pork meat did not correlate as well (Correa, 1981; Howell, 1974), and poultry not at all (Howell, 1974). In one case-control study (Talamini *et al.*, 1986), a borderline-significant positive association for meat consumption was found. In three other case-control studies (Mishina *et al.*, 1981, 1985; Rotkin, 1979; Schuman *et al.*, 1982) and two cohort studies (Hirayama, 1979, 1985; Phillips and Snowdon, 1983; Snowdon *et al.*, 1984), no association with meat consumption was found. In a case-control study, Ross *et al.* (1987) found a positive association for pork (in Blacks, but not in Whites), and a negative association for poultry, as did Schuman *et al.* (1983). Because there are no studies that indicate a negative association between prostatic cancer risk and meat consumption and because the positive associations found in the correlation studies were moderately strong, it seems justified to conclude that there are limited indications that meat consumption (but not poultry) is positively related with risk for prostatic cancer.

b. Edible Fats and Oils. A strong positive correlation with prostatic cancer rates was found for edible fats and oils in two international correlation studies, with correlation coefficients of 0.70–0.73 (Armstrong and Doll, 1975; Howell, 1974). In preliminary reports of two case-control studies, a positive association was found for prostatic cancer risk and the consumption of butter and/or margarines (Kaul *et al.*, 1981; Rotkin, 1979). Thus, although the number of studies on the consumption of edible fats and oils is limited, there is consistency in finding a positive relationship with risk, and the correlation coefficients in the correlation studies are high.

c. Eggs. A positive relation of risk for prostatic cancer and egg consumption was found in three case-control studies (Ross *et al.*, 1987; Rotkin, 1979; Schuman *et al.*, 1982). A weak positive association was found in three international correlation studies (Armstrong and Doll, 1975; Correa, 1981; Schrauzer, 1976b), while no association ($r = 0.01$) was found by Rose *et al.* (1986). A prospective study showed only a borderline-significant positive association (Snowdon *et al.*, 1984). Hence, there are limited indications that egg consumption is positively associated with prostatic cancer risk.

d. Milk. The results of epidemiological studies on milk consumption and prostatic cancer risk are contradictory and do not permit a conclusion. In international correlation studies, correlation coefficients varied between a nonsignificant 0.35 to a highly significant 0.70 (Armstrong and Doll, 1975; Correa, 1981; Howell, 1974; Rose *et al.*, 1986; Schrauzer, 1976b). On the other hand, a negative relationship was found in one within-country correlation study (Gaskill *et al.*, 1979), while there was no association in two case-control studies (Mishina *et al.*, 1981, 1985; Schuman *et al.*, 1982) and one cohort study (Hirayama, 1979). In another cohort study, however, there was a slight tendency for a positive relationship (Snowden *et al.*, 1984), and in one case-control study (Talamini *et al.*, 1986), a significant positive association was found for the consumption of milk and cheese together.

e. Fish and Seafood. A significant negative association with prostatic cancer risk was found in two case-control studies for the consumption of fish and/or seafood (Mishina *et al.*, 1981, 1985; Schuman *et al.*, 1982). No such relationship, however, was found in three international correlation studies (Armstrong and Doll, 1975; Howell, 1974; Schrauzer, 1976b) and one prospective study (Hirayama, 1979). Therefore, the indications that fish/seafood consumption is negatively associated with prostatic cancer risk are very limited.

f. Animal Products and Fatty Foods. In one prospective study (Snowdon *et al.*, 1984), a significant positive association was found between risk and the consumption of animal products (milk, cheese, meat, and eggs together). The results of one within-country correlation study (Blair and Fraumeni, 1978) and one case-control study (Rotkin, 1979) suggested that the consumption of fatty foods in general is positively associated with prostatic cancer risk. In two other case-control studies, however, no indications for such an association were found (Mishina *et al.*, 1981, 1985; Schuman *et al.*, 1982). One within-country correlation study investigated various sources of fats separately, and in a preliminary report no association was indicated for meat, fish, or dairy fat and cholesterol consumption (Kolonel *et al.*, 1981b, 1983). In one case-control study (Talamini *et al.*, 1986), a significant positive association was found for dairy products. Thus, there are limited indications that the consumption of fatty foods and/or animal products is positively related with prostatic cancer risk.

g. Sugar. In three international correlation studies, a moderately strong correlation was reported for prostatic cancer rates and per capita sugar consumption (Armstrong and Doll, 1975; Howell, 1974; Schrauzer, 1976b). Correlation coefficients varied from 0.62 to 0.67. There are no other studies that included data on consumption of sugars, and, therefore, the evidence for a positive association with prostatic cancer risk should be regarded as limited.

h. Vitamins A- and C-Rich Foods. Because of the contradictory data on the possible relationship of vitamin A consumption and prostatic carcinogenesis (see Section IV,A,2 and 6), foods that are presumably high in vitamin A are summarized together here. Some of these foods are also rich in vitamin C and carotenoids. This group consists of vegetables in general, green–yellow vegetables, carrots, (citrus) fruits, and liver. A negative association with prostatic cancer risk was found in three case-control studies for carrots and/or liver (Ross *et al.*, 1983; Schuman *et al.*, 1982). One case-control study did not show an association for cruciferous vegetables (Graham *et al.*, 1983). A negative association for green vegetables was found in one case-control study (Ross et al., 1987), but not in another (Talamini *et al.*, 1986). In a Japanese prospective study (Hirayama, 1979), a significant negative relation was found between risk and consumption of green–yellow vegetables. In a later report (Hirayama, 1985), however, such an association seemed to be absent. It is not clear at present whether the first observation was valid. In a Japanese case-control study (Mishina *et al.*, 1981, 1985), a significant negative association was also reported for the consumption of green–yellow vegetables. In a United States cohort study, no association was found for the consumption of carrots (Paganini-Hill *et al.*, 1985). No association to a weakly negative association between prostatic cancer rates and the consumption of vegetables and/or fruits was found in four international correlation studies (Armstrong and Doll, 1975; Howell, 1974; Rose *et al.*, 1986; Schrauzer, 1976b). A consistent, moderately strong negative relation has been reported for pulses in three international correlation studies with correlation coefficients of −0.59 to −0.66 (Armstrong and Doll, 1975; Correa, 1981; Howell, 1974) and in one case-control study for peas (Schuman *et al.*, 1982). The indications that the consumption of vitamin A- and vitamin C-rich foods is negatively related to prostatic cancer risk are thus limited. A negative association with the consumption of green–yellow vegetables in Japan and with the consumption of pulses is more consistently found, but conclusive evidence is not present.

i. Fiber-Rich Foods. The consumption of cereals showed a rather strong and consistent negative correlation with prostatic cancer rates in four international correlation studies; correlation coefficients varied from −0.60 to −0.77 (Armstrong and Doll, 1975; Howell, 1974; Rose *et al.*, 1986; Schrauzer, 1976b). On the other hand, bread-cereals and wheat, which are major sources of dietary fiber, did not show an association with prostatic cancer risk in international correlation studies (Howell, 1974; Schrauzer, 1976b). There are no data on these foods from other types of studies. Other sources of dietary fiber, various vegetables, and fruits, showed a negative association in some studies and none in others, as indicated earlier. In summary, there are limited indications that dietary fiber is negatively associated with prostatic cancer risk.

4. *Alcoholic and Nonalcoholic Beverages*

a. Alcoholic Beverages. For alcohol use in general, three case-control studies in the United States showed no association with prostatic cancer risk (Ross *et al.*, 1987; Williams and Horms, 1977; Wynder *et al.*, 1971). A preliminary report on a case-control study in US Blacks (Jackson *et al.*, 1981) indicates a positive association, whereas a Japanese case-control study (Mishina *et al.*, 1981, 1985) found a borderline-significant negative association. A Japanese and a United States cohort study did not show an association between alcohol use and risk (Hirayama, 1979, 1985; Whittemore *et al.*, 1985).

For specific alcoholic beverages, few significant associations with prostatic cancer risk have been reported. In two international correlation studies, a marginally positive correlation for beer (correlation coefficients of 0.42 and 0.44) has been reported (Correa, 1981; Schrauzer, 1976b). There are a within-country correlation study (Breslow and Enstrom, 1974) and a case-control study (Williams and Horms, 1977) that did not show an association between beer consumption and prostatic cancer risk. Williams and Horms (1977) found a significant ($p < 0.01$) positive association with risk for wine in their case-control study, whereas Kaul and co-workers (1981) indicated a significant ($p < 0.01$) negative association for wine in a preliminary report from a case-control study in US Blacks. No relation between wine consumption and risk was found in an Italian case-control study (Talamini *et al.*, 1986). Also, no association for wine was found in an international correlation study (Schrauzer, 1976b) and in a within-country correlation study (Breslow and Enstrom, 1974). For the consumption of hard liquor, no association with prostatic cancer risk was found in three different types of studies (Breslow and Enstrom, 1974; Schrauzer, 1976b; Williams and Horms, 1977).

Studies of prostatic cancer mortality among alcoholics have not indicated a clear relation between the two disorders. There are two studies that indicated a slight excess mortality from prostatic cancer for alcoholics (Pell and D'Alonzo, 1973; Schmidt and De Lint, 1972), but in two other studies no such association was found (Lowenfels, 1974; Monson and Lyon, 1975). However, the number of cases in all these studies was very low, which markedly lessens the significance of the findings. Interestingly, prostatic cancer risk is lower than in the general population in men suffering from cirrhosis, which is often a consequence of alcohol abuse (Glantz, 1964; Robson, 1966).

In conclusion, most likely there is no association between the use of alcohol in general or of specific alcohol-containing beverages and risk for prostatic cancer. For beer and wine consumption, however, there are some conflicting data, and thus the evidence that there is no association with prostatic cancer risk is limited.

b. Nonalcoholic Beverages. For the per capita consumption of coffee, a statistically significant positive association with prostatic cancer rates has consistently been reported in international correlation studies (Armstrong and Doll, 1975; Schrauzer, 1976b; Stocks, 1970; Takahashi, 1964). Correlation coefficients varied from 0.57 to 0.70. No association for coffee, however, was found in three case-control studies (Jackson *et al.*, 1981; Mishina *et al.*, 1981, 1985; Talamini *et al.*, 1986) and three cohort studies (Jacobson *et al.*, 1986; Nomura *et al.*, 1986; Whittemore *et al.*, 1985). A nonsignificant tendency for a negative association was reported by Philips and Snowdon (1983) from another cohort study. The positive relation with prostatic cancer found for coffee in the international correlation studies is perhaps artificial. The per capita consumption of coffee correlates positively with that of fat, which in turn correlates very well with prostatic cancer rates (Armstrong and Doll, 1975; Schrauzer, 1976b). When Armstrong and Doll (1975) controlled for the consumption of fat, the correlation coefficient dropped from 0.57 (uncontrolled) to a nonsignificant 0.31.

No association with prostatic cancer was found for the consumption of tea in international correlation studies (Armstrong and Doll, 1975; Schrauzer, 1976b; Stocks, 1970), in case-control studies (Jackson *et al.*, 1981; Mishina *et al.*, 1981, 1985), or in one Japanese cohort study (Hirayama, 1979). In another cohort study among Japanese men in Hawaii (Heilbrun *et al.*, 1986), however, a significant negative association between black tea consumption and prostatic cancer risk was found.

In conclusion, the consumption of tea and coffee does not appear to be related with risk for prostatic cancer. This conclusion is limited because of some conflicting data.

5. *Macronutrients and Dietary Fiber*

In a number of epidemiological studies and in a few animal studies, the relation between prostatic cancer risk and specific nutrients has been investigated. As indicated elsewhere (Bosland, 1985), in the epidemiological studies, the total intake of specific nutrients has been estimated from food frequency data and sometimes from more accurate information on amounts of food consumed. These data were obtained by questionnaires and/or interviews. Using various data banks on the nutrient composition of the foods studied, estimated intakes were subsequently calculated. Macronutrients will be discussed in the following paragraphs and micronutrients in subsequent sections.

a. Fat. A positive association with prostatic cancer risk has consistently been found for total fat intake and for the consumption of animal fat. In four international correlation studies, highly significant correlation coefficients were found for total fat, varying between 0.70 and 0.89 (Armstrong and Doll, 1975; Carroll and Khor, 1975; Correa, 1981; Schrauzer, 1976b). In a fifth such study, a somewhat lower correlation coefficient was found (Rose *et al.*, 1986). For animal fat consumption data, correlation coefficients of 0.51 and 0.69 were reported (Correa, 1981; Rose *et al.*, 1986). More or less positive relationships with total, saturated, and/or animal fats were found in four case-control studies (Kolonel *et al.*, 1983; Graham *et al.*, 1983; Heshmat *et al.*, 1985; Ross *et al.*, 1987). In a within-country correlation study, animal fat consumption correlated highly significantly with risk, even though total fat intake did not (Kolonel *et al.*, 1981a, b, 1983). Thus, animal fat and, with one exception, total fat intake are consistently and rather strongly associated with prostatic cancer risk. The data for (poly)unsaturated fats, which have been less well studied, on the other hand, are somewhat contradictory. No association between prostatic cancer mortality and vegetable fat consumption (r = 0.07) was found in an international correlation study by Rose *et al.* (1986). In one within-country correlation study (Kolonel *et al.*, 1981b, 1983) and one case-control study (Heshmat *et al.*, 1985), no association was found for unsaturated fat and linoleic acid, respectively. One other case-control study, however, showed a tendency toward a positive relationship with prostatic cancer risk for unsaturated fat (Kolonel *et al.*, 1983). There are no data from cohort studies available. Hence, for (poly)unsaturated fat, sufficient information is lacking. There have been very few animal studies on the effects of dietary fat on prostatic cancer. Two preliminary reports indicate that fat does not affect the growth of transplantable prostatic carcinomas (Kross *et al.*, 1986; Spriggs *et al.*, 1983). Another preliminary report indicated that the feeding of high levels of ω3 fatty acids in the diet inhibits the growth of DU-145 human prostatic cancer cells in nude mice as compared with mice fed high levels of corn oil (Karmali *et al.*, 1986). These studies are, however, not pertinent to the *genesis* of prostatic cancer. Preliminary data from my laboratory indicate that neither saturated nor polyunsaturated fat influences the development of chemically induced prostatic cancer in rats (Kroes *et al.*, 1986). Results from a recent study by Pollard and Luckert (1985, 1986a), however, suggest that fat can enhance the development of testosterone-induced prostatic cancer in rats. Thus, there is some support from animal studies for a positive association between dietary fat and prostatic cancer risk in man.

b. Protein. In two international correlation studies, total and animal protein consumption correlated moderately strongly with prostatic cancer rates (Armstrong and Doll, 1975; Correa, 1981). Correlation coefficients between 0.50 and 0.67 were reported. A similar positive association was found for animal protein in two such studies (Armstrong and Doll, 1975; Rose *et al.*, 1986), with correlation coefficients of 0.55 and 0.67. Total and animal protein consumption were also found to be positively correlated with risk in one within-country correlation study (Kolonel *et al.*, 1981b, 1983), and a tendency of a positive association with risk was found for total protein intake in one case-control study (Heshmat *et al.*, 1985), but not in another (Ross *et al.*, 1987). There are no data on total or animal protein from cohort studies. Information on proteins from vegetable sources is not available and there are no data on protein from animal studies. Thus, a moderately strong positive association of prostatic cancer risk and the consumption of total or animal protein is a somewhat consistent finding.

c. Carbohydrate. A moderately strong positive association (correlation coefficients of 0.62 to 0.64) has been reported in three international correlation studies for sugar(s) (Armstrong and Doll, 1975; Howell, 1974; Schrauzer, 1976b). In one case-control study, carbohydrates were included, and no relation between risk and the intake of total carbohydrates was found (Heshmat *et al.*, 1985). Thus, there are very limited indications that the consumption of oligosaccharides is positively associated with prostatic cancer risk. No conclusion is possible for the intake of polysaccharides and for total carbohydrate intake. No data from animal studies are available.

d. Dietary Fiber. In one case-control study, dietary fiber was investigated (Heshmat *et al.*, 1985). Total intake was not associated with risk for prostatic cancer. No other data are available on dietary fiber and prostatic carcinogenesis.

6. *Vitamins*

a. Vitamin A and Carotenoids. A positive relationship between prostatic cancer risk and the intake of vitamin A was found in three case-control studies (Graham *et al.*, 1983; Heshmat *et al.*, 1985; Raul *et al.*, 1987; Kolonel *et al.*, 1985, 1987), but not in two others (Middleton *et al.*, 1987; Ross *et al.*, 1987). A positive association was found in a cohort study conducted in the United States for the consumption of vitamin A supplements, but no association for dietary Vitamin A or β-carotene (Paganini-Hill *et al.*, 1987). Serum retinol levels were significantly higher in users of vitamin A supplements than among nonusers (Paganini-Hill *et al.*, 1985). In a within-country correlation study done in Hawaii, no association with risk was found for the estimated intake of total vitamin A (Kolonel *et al.*, 1981b). In two United States cohort-based, case-control studies, serum levels of retinol in prostatic cancer cases were compared with control values. In one study there ws a slight tendency for retinol levels to be lower in patients than in controls (Kark *et al.*, 1981). In a further follow-up of this study, including 14 prostatic cancer cases, this tendency virtually disappeared (Peleg *et al.*, 1984). In the other study, there was no association with risk for serum levels of retinol, retinol-binding protein, or carotenoids (Willett *et al.*, 1983, 1984).

The results from the case-control studies need some further detailing. In the study by Graham and co-workers (1983) on US Whites, vitamin A intake was calculated and divided in quartiles. Cases and controls of 70 years and older and younger than 70 years were also distinguished. Relative risks for each quartile relative to the lowest intake quartile were calculated for the two age groups and for all ages together. For all ages and for the group of 70 years and older, relative risk increased significantly as tested with a test for linear trend (see Table IX). For the younger than 70 group, there was a nonsignificant ($p > 0.05$) tendency for such an increase. There was, however, no perfect dose-response relationship for any of the age groups. In each of the three age groups, risk was highest in the second highest intake quartile and it went down in the highest intake quartile (Table IX). Middleton *et al.* (1987), probably using part of the same study population as Graham *et al.* (1983), divided vitamin A intake in tertiles. They found age-adjusted relative risks of 1.00, 1.10 and 1.27 for the low, intermediate, and high intake tertiles, respectively. The increase of the latter two relative risks was not significant, nor was the increasing trend. In the study by Heshmat *et al.* (1985) on US Blacks, the mean intake of vitamin A per 1000 calories was calculated from dietary information obtained from each subject for two age periods, the 30–49 and 50 years and over. The mean difference between cases and controls was 875 international units (IU) for 30–49, which was

TABLE IX

PROSTATIC CANCER RISK AND VITAMIN A INTAKE[a]

Vitamin A intake[b]	Relative risk		
	All ages[c]	69 years and younger[d]	70 years and older[d,e]
<50,500	1.00	1.00	1.00
50,500–100,499	1.40	1.20	1.59
100,500–150,499	2.38	2.05	2.74
>150,499	1.80	1.64	1.97

[a]Adapted from Graham *et al.* (1983); calculated from 262 prostatic cancer cases and 259 controls.

[b]Subjects were divided into approximate quartiles. Vitamin A intake is given in international units/month as calculated from food-frequency data.

[c]$p < 0.01$ for linear trend.

[d]Forty-eight percent of the subjects were 69 years and younger, and 52% were 70 years and older.

[e]$p > 0.05$ for linear trend.

highly significant, and 703 IU for >49 years, which was borderline-significant (see Table X). In an extension of this study (Kaul *et al.*, 1987), a similar but nonsignificant ($p > 0.05$) difference was found between cases and controls for the 30–49 years age period (856 IU; see Table X). For the 50+ years period, however, cases reported a somewhat lower intake of vitamin A than controls (difference 620 IU; see Table X). The third study, by Kolonel and co-workers (1987), conducted in Hawaii, seems to be the most reliable one in terms of the estimation of the intake of vitamin A (see Section IV,A,2). Two other studies (Heshmat *et al.*, 1985; Graham *et al.*,

TABLE X

AVERAGE INTAKE OF VITAMIN A FROM FOOD SOURCES IN PROSTATIC CANCER PATIENTS AND CONTROLS FOR TWO AGE PERIODS[a]

	30–49 years		50 years and older	
Study	A[b]	B[c]	A[b]	B[c]
Cases	5,228[d]	5,030	6,035[e]	6,176[e]
Controls	4,353	4,174	5,332	6,769

[a]Vitamin A intake is given in international units/1000 calories per day and was calculated from food frequency data and serving size data.

[b]Adapted from Heshmat *et al.* (1985); 180 case-control pairs.

[c]Adapted from Kaul *et al.* (1987); 55 case-control pairs.

[d]$p < 0.007$ for difference with controls (paired t test).

[e]$p < 0.069$ for difference with controls (paired t test).

1983) did not indicate how many or which food items were covered whereas frequency of use of only 20–22 food categories was obtained by Middleton *et al.* (1987) and by Ross *et al.* (1987); all these studies were based on rather short interviews. In the Hawaiian study, mean weekly intakes as well as quartiles of vitamin A intake were distinguished and odds ratios were calculated relative to the lowest intake quartile. Also in this study, as in the study by Graham *et al.* (1983), subjects of younger than 70 years and subjects of 70 years and older were distinguished, as well as vitamin A from all sources, total retinol and total carotenes, β-carotene, and carotenes other than β-carotene. Data for all ages together were not presented. No association was found with any of the indices of vitamin A intake for the younger than 70 group (Tables XIA and XIB). For the 70 years and older group, the average weekly intake of total vitamin A, total carotenes and β-carotene were significantly higher in cases than in controls, and intake of retinol and carotenes other than β-carotene tended to be higher (Table XIA). The odds ratio for the highest quartile of intake for total vitamin A and total retinol was also significantly elevated (Table XIB). The odds ratio for the intake of total carotenes was increased significantly for all three quartiles higher than the lowest (Table XIB). This latter finding was further analyzed in the various ethnic groups in the cohort, and a similar significant elevated odds ratio was found for Caucasian and Japanese men separately (Table XIB). Significant trends for the odds ratios to increase with increasing intake were found for total vitamin A and, for Caucasians only, total carotenes (Table XIB). Trends for total retinol and, in all races and Japanese, total carotenes were borderline significant.

Thus, the finding of increased risk for prostatic cancer with increasing intake of vitamin A is somewhat consistent among these studies, which

TABLE XIA

AVERAGE WEEKLY INTAKE OF VITAMIN A IN PROSTATIC CANCER CASES AND CONTROLS[a]

Vitamin A component	Younger than 70 years		70 years and older	
	Cases (n = 189)	Controls (n = 391)	Cases (n = 267)	Controls (n = 508)
Total vitamin A (IU)	77,200	83,500	87,900[c]	78,200
Retinol (μg)[b]	9,600	10,500	9,800	8,600
Total carotenes (μg)	32,300	34,600	39,200[c]	35,200
β-carotene (μg)	22,100	23,700	27,200[c]	24,300
Carotenes other than β-carotene (μg)	10,200	10,900	12,000	10,900

[a]Adapted from Kolonel *et al.* (1987).
[b]Includes supplement use.
[c]$p < 0.05$ (multiple analysis of covariance, adjusted for age and ethnicity).

TABLE XIB

PROSTATIC CANCER RISK AND VITAMIN A INTAKE PROSTATIC CANCER CASES AND CONTROLS[a]

	Odds ratio[b]				
			Total carotenes		
Intake quartile	Total vitamin A[c]	Total retinol[c]	All races	Caucasians	Japanese
69 years and younger					
1 (lowest)	1.0	1.0	1.0	NP[d]	NP
2	1.3	0.8	1.2	NP	NP
3	1.0	1.1	1.1	NP	NP
4 (highest)	0.8	0.9	0.9	NP	NP
Linear trend	$P = 0.16$	$P = 0.82$	$P = 0.48$		
70 years and older					
1 (lowest)	1.0	1.0	1.0	1.0	1.0
2	1.4	1.0	1.5[e]	1.0	1.8
3	1.3	1.2	1.6[e]	1.1	1.6
4 (highest)	2.0[e]	1.4	1.6[e]	2.5[e]	2.1[e]
Linear trend	$P < 0.01$	$P = 0.10$	$P = 0.08$	$P = 0.03$	$P = 0.10$

[a]Adapted from Kolonel *et al.* (1987).
[b]Calculated using multiple logistic regression analysis adjusting for age and ethnicity.
[c]Includes vitamin A supplements.
[d]NP = not presented.
[e]$P = 0.05$ for difference with lowest intake quartile (logistic regression analysis).

were all based on vitamin A intake estimated from food consumption data. The study by Kolonel *et al.* (1987) suggests particularly carotene intake to be positively related with risk. Also consistent is the observation that this was particularly true for men of 70 years and over, and less so or not at all for men who were younger than 70 (Kolonel *et al.*, 1985, 1987; Graham *et al.*, 1983). The finding by Heshmat *et al.* (1985) that vitamin A intake between 30 and 49 years of age correlates better with risk than does the estimated intake for the period beyond 50 years is not comparable with the results of the two other studies. The results of the follow-up study by Kaul *et al.* (1987) were similar to those of Heshmat *et al.*, and those of Middleton *et al.* (1987) were comparable to those of Graham *et al.* (1983), but in neither case was statistical significance reached. Ross *et al.* (1987) was the only case-control study that found no association between risk and vitamin A intake, but it suggested a protective effect of β-carotene in men consuming little fat. The studies that did not find a (significant) positive association did not distinguish between younger and older cases. The studies that made this distinction, howver, all found a positive association particularly for older (70^{+} years) men. This difference may explain discrepancies between studies.

The results of these case-control studies contrast sharply with *in vitro* studies on the effects of vitamin A on carcinogen-induced effects in rodent prostate (see Bosland, 1985). Treatment of mouse ventral prostate explant cultures with chemical carcinogens for 7 to 10 days results in the development of hyperplastic, squamous metaplastic and dysplastic changes and enhancement of cellular proliferation in the prostatic epithelium (Chopra and Wilkoff, 1976, 1979; Lasnitski, 1955, 1974, 1976; Lasnitski and Goodman, 1974). Both indirect-acting carcinogens, benzo[*a*]pyrene, and 3-methylcholanthrene and the direct-acting agent *N*-methyl-*N'*-nitro-*N*-nitrosoguanidine have this effect. Vitamin A counteracts these effects when it is added to the medium with the carcinogens, and it reverses these effects when it is administered to the explants after carcinogen exposure. Both all-*trans*-retinol and β-retinoic acid, which are naturally occurring retinoids, have this protective effect, retinoic acid being more potent. Thus, in mouse ventral prostatic explants, vitamin A inhibits the induction of morphological changes by chemical carcinogens and it reverses these changes once they are induced.

Vitamin A deficiency or vitamin A supplementation of the diet did not effect growth of the transplantable Dunning prostatic carcinomas R3327H and R3327HI (Clinton *et al.*, 1985).

Most of the data from case-control studies discussed earlier suggest a positive relation between vitamin A/β-carotene intake and human prostatic cancer risk, but there are conflicting data from some case-control studies and from a prospective and a within-country correlation study. Furthermore, data from *in vitro* studies would support a protective role of vitamin A. Therefore, a definitive conclusion as to whether vitamin A and/or β-carotene intake is positively related with prostatic cancer risk is not possible at present.*

b. Vitamin C. In one of the three case-control studies that showed positive relation between prostatic cancer risk and vitamin A intake (Graham *et al.*, 1983), there was also a positive relation with vitamin C intake. In the highest intake quartile, the relative risk was significantly elevated in comparison with the lowest intake quartile in the 70+ group, while there was a nonsignificant elevation in the highest and second highest quartile in the younger-than-70 group. However, in the two other case-control studies that showed a positive relation between risk and vitamin A intake, no relation with vitamin C intake was reported (Heshmat *et al.*, 1985; Kaul *et al.*, 1987; Kolonel *et al.*, 1985). Also, no association between risk and vitamin C intake was found in a within-country correlation study (Kolonel *et al.*, 1981b). In

Note added in proof*: A Japanese case-control study [Ohno, Y. *et al.* (1988) *Cancer Res.* **48, 1331–1336] found a *decreased* risk for increasing β-carotene and vitamin A intake in men of all ages and of 70–79 years, but not in younger men. This strongly supports the conclusions above.

summary, most information on vitamin C indicates no relation to prostatic cancer risk, but there are some conflicting data.

c. Other Vitamins. There are few studies in which vitamins other than A and C have been investigated. Without showing the actual data, Heshmat and co-workers (1985) reported that there was no association with risk for prostatic cancer for riboflavin, niacin, and thiamine in their case-control study in US Blacks. In a follow-up study (Kaul *et al.*, 1987), a significant negative association was found for thiamin and riboflavin, but not for niacin. Willett *et al.* (1983, 1984) found no difference between prostatic cancer cases and controls for serum levels of vitamin E and total carotenoids.

7. *Trace Elements and Contaminants*

This section will be limited to a discussion of the trace elements selenium and zinc and the contaminant cadmium. There are no data on other trace elements, except one report on iron intake in a case-control study indicating that there were no differences between cases and controls (Heshmat *et al.*, 1985). In a follow-up study (Kaul *et al.*, 1987) a negative association was found for iron. There are no data for other environmental contaminants in foods than cadmium, and its relation to prostatic cancer.

a. Selenium. Schrauzer and co-workers (1977a,b) calculated per capita selenium intake figures from known data on the average selenium content of different foods and food consumption data from the FAO for 1964–1966. They did not take into account regional differences in selenium content, bbut they did exclude New Zealand, which is a known selenium-deficient area, from their analysis. A highly significant ($p < 0.0001$) correlation coefficient of -0.65 was found for the estimated selenium intake and prostatic cancer mortality for 1964–1966 for 27 (Schrauzer *et al.*, 1977a) or 28 countries (Schrauzer *et al.*, 1977b). They also measured the selenium content in whole blood obtained from blood banks in 22 different countries and found a significant ($p < 0.001$) negative correlation (-0.72) with prostatic cancer mortality (Schrauzer *et al.*, 1977a). The same investigators also measured whole blood selenium concentrations in pooled blood from blood banks in 19 states in the United States. No association, however, was found with prostatic cancer mortality in these states for 1959–1961 (Schrauzer *et al.*, 1977a,b). Willett and co-workers (1983) measured selenium in serum from 11 prostatic cancer patients and age-matched control subjects. Patients had lower serum selenium levels (0.128 μg/ml) than controls (0.139 μg/ml), but this difference was not statistically significant ($p = 0.12$). In conclusion, there are very limited epidemiological indications that selenium intake is negatively associated with the risk for prostatic cancer.

b. Zinc. An international correlation study by Schrauzer and colleagues (1977b) showed a significant ($p < 0.001$) positive correlation (0.52) between prostatic cancer mortality in 27 different countries (1964–1965) and the estimated daily intake of zinc (1964–1966). No association was found between whole blood levels of zinc and prostatic cancer mortality in 19 states in the United States in a study by the same group (Schrauzer *et al.*, 1977b) using pooled blood samples obtained from local blood banks. There is one case-control study that compared serum levels of zinc in prostatic cancer patients with those in patients with benign prostatic hyperplasia (BHP) (Whelan *et al.*, 1983). Cancer patients had significantly lower serum zinc levels than BHP patients. There were no control subjects included in this study, which severely limits its value. Because there are no other data that are directly concerned with dietary zinc and prostatic cancer risk, a conclusion on whether zinc may be related to prostatic cancer risk is not possible. Other information, however, supports the suggestion that zinc is somehow related to the development of prostatic cancer. This is further detailed in the discussion in Section IV,D,1.c.

c. Cadmium. For nonsmokers, the main source of exposure to cadmium is through contaminated food, resulting in an average daily intake of 20 μg in the United States and western Europe (Piscator, 1981). Schrauzer and co-workers (1977b) reported a positive international asssociation (correlation coefficient, 0.52; $p < 0.001$) between prostatic cancer mortality and exposure to cadmium through food products, as estimated from cadmium concentration data and food consumption data from the FAO Food Balance Sheets from 1964–1966, including data on Japan and the United States. In Japan, food levels were half that of the levels in the United States. These findings are at variance with other data indicating that the food levels in Japan are more than twice those in the United States (Piscator, 1981). Schrauzer *et al.* (1977b) did not find an association in the United States between prostatic cancer mortality and cadmium levels in pooled blood from blood banks in 19 states. Berg and Burbank (1972) studied correlations between concentrations of trace metals in water supplies and cancer mortality in 16 areas in the United States. They did not find a correlation between cadmium levels in the drinking water and prostatic cancer mortality. For the various studies concerning occupational exposure to cadmium and prostatic cancer, the reader is referred to Section V,A,3.

Cadmium is carcinogenic to rats by inhalation exposure and subcutaneous injection. Lifetime observation in an inhalation experiment on exposure of male rats to aerosols containing cadmium chloride at levels of 12.5–50 $\mu g/m^3$ for 18 months showed the induction of lung tumors (predominantly adeno- and squamous-cell carcinomas) in 15–71% of the animals (Takenaka *et al.*, 1983). Subcutaneous injection, either single or repeated, of several cadmium compounds has long been known to cause sarcomas at the site of injection and Leydig cell tumors of the testes (Gunn *et al.*, 1963, 1964; Haddow *et al.*, 1964; Levy *et al.*, 1973). Levy and colleagues (1973) specifically examined histologically the accessory sex glands of rats that had been exposed to 0.022,

0.044, and 0.087 mg cadmium (as cadmium sulfate) by subcutaneous injection, once a week for 2 years. No specific lesions were found in the prostate. Kidney cadmium levels were approximately 140, 250, and 475 μg/g for the three dosed groups, respectively. Scott and Aughey (1978) reported "a possible early adenocarcinoma" in 1 out of 50 rats that were injected with cadmium chloride. The vagueness of this report and the extremely high doses of cadmium (more than lethal) that were reportedly given make this study of very limited significance (Piscator, 1981). A preliminary report by Waalkes *et al.* (1987) indicates that cadmium administration in Wistar rats at very low doses (subcutaneous or intramuscular injection of 0.25 μmol/kg), that lack testicular toxicity, enhances the formation of naturally occurring ventral prostatic proliferative lesions. Their incidence increased from 11% in controls to 28–36% in treated animals after 2 years of observation. The lesions were predominantly atypical hyperlasias and adenomas (M.P. Waalkes, personal communication). Zinc prevented testicular toxicity of a higher dose of cadmium (30 μmol/kg) and the combined treatment also enhanced the formation of the prostatic lesions. These data were interpreted as indicating that cadmium exposure in rats with intact testicular function (androgens ?) enhances prostatic carcinogenesis. Interestingly, a deficiency of metallothionein was observed in the rat ventral prostrate.

There are several reports of the effects of oral treatment of experimental animals with various cadmium compounds. Cadmium is not carcinogenic to rats when administered to groups of 50 animals of each sex at each dose level, mixed through the diet at a level of 10 or 50 ppm cadmium (as cadmium chloride) for 2 years (Loser, 1980). At the highest dose level, a slight but significant ($P < 0.01$) growth depression was observed in males. When administered to rats and mice (50 animals of each sex per group) via drinking water at a level of 5 ppm (probably as cadmium acetate; there is no explicit information about this in the publication) for life, no carcinogenicity was detected (Schroeder *et al.*, 1964, 1965). In male rats there was a lower final body weight and an increased mortality in the dosed animals. Administration of cadmium (as sulfate) once weekly by gavage to male rats for 2 years and to male mice for 18 months did not result in detectable carcinogenicity (Levy and Clack, 1975; Levy *et al.*, 1975). The dose levels were 0.087, 0.18, and 0.35 mg/kg per week for rats, and 0.44, 0.88, and 1.75 mg/kg per week for mice. There were 30 rats and 50 mice per dose level. No effects were observed on growth. It has been argued (IARC, 1976; Piscator, 1981) that the levels in these experiments were too low. However, in the studies by Loser (1980) and Schroeder and co-workers (1964, 1965), there was some evidence of toxicity indicated by growth depression at the highest dose levels. On the other hand, kidney cadmium levels, which are good indicators of exposure (Friberg *et al.*, 1974), were low to very low in the studies in which they were measured. Levy and Clack (1975) found an average of 5.2 μg/g (range, 2.8–10.1) in rats of the highest dose group (0.35 mg/kg per week) at the end of 2 years of exposure. In the experiments by Schroeder and co-workers (1964, 1965), levels of 2.94 and 0.71 μg/g were found for mice and rats after 1.5 and 2 years of exposure to 5 ppm in the drinking water, respectively. In the study by Loser (1980), no tissue levels of cadmium were reported, but in a short-term study by the same group (Loser and Lorcke, 1977), kidney cadmium levels of approximately 5 and 12 μg/g were found after 3 weeks of feeding 10 and 30 ppm cadmium, respectively. In men, however, renal cortex cadmium levels increase steadily with age until levels of 10–100 μg/g are reached at age 50–60 (Friberg *et al.*, 1974). Smokers have levels that are about three times higher than those of nonsmokers, while men who are occupationally exposed to cadmium can have renal cadmium levels as high as 300 μg/g (Friberg *et al.*, 1974). In nonsmokers, levels are between 10 and 25 μg/g for men between 40 and 60 years of age (Friberg *et al.*, 1974). Thus, only in the study by Loser (1980) were renal cadmium levels possibly present that were comparable to those found in lightly exposed humans. In conclusion, the exposure levels that were applied in the oral dosing studies with cadmium in rats and mice were, with one possible exception, too low to result in a body burden that is comparable to that of nonsmokers with a "normal" exposure to cadmium (Piscator, 1981). In addition, with the exception of the studies by Schroeder *et al.* (1964, 1965), the maximum study duration was 2 years or less. Thus, although in some studies slight signs of toxicity were reported, the preceding experiments should be considered as inadequate to assess oral cadmium carcinogenicity properly, because the dosages of cadmium used were rather low, and because their duration was too short given the fact that prostatic tumors in rodents do not develop spotaneously until very old age. The prostate was not routinely examined in the studies by Schroeder and co-workers (1964, 1965). In the study by Loser (1980), the male accessory sex glands were examined histologically, and the studies by Levy and Clack (1975) and Levy *et al.* (1975) were specifically designed to assess the possible carcinogenicity of cadmium for the prostate, and a careful histological examination of the accessory sex gland complex was carried out.

There are three studies in which cadmium was injected into the prostate of rats (Gunn *et al.*, 1967; Hoffmann *et al.*, 1985; Scott and Aughey, 1978). The results are conflicting. Hoffman and co-workers (1985) injected 0.04 ml of a 0.1 *M* cadmium chloride solution (0.44 mg cadmium) into the right ventral lobe. The animals were 12 months old at the time of injection, and they were followed for at most 270 days after treatment. Invasive carcinomas were reported in 5 of 100 rats, dysplastic lesions in 11 of 100 rats, and atypical hyperplasia in 29 of 100 rats. In controls (saline treated) and rats that were treated with zinc chloride, no carcinomas or dysplasias were found and atypical hyperplasia in 5 and 20%, respectively. The lesions were found in both the right and left ventral lobes, although cadmium was injected only into the right lobe. In 16 of 100 animals, the right lobe was excised 200 days after cadmium injection. Still, in 3 of these rats invasive carcinomas developed, while in the 84 nonexcised rats 2 carcinomas developed, resulting in the total incidence of 5 of 100. The carcinomas did not have the typical appearance of spontaneous ventral prostatic tumors, i.e., cribriform-comedo type adenocarcinomas, but they were poorly differentiated solid carcinomas. No other tumors were reported in the prostate—specifically, no mesenchymal tumors. Scott and Aughey (1978), however, reported mainly "supportive tissue tumors," i.e., mesenchymal tumors, after injection of cadmium chloride (0.05 ml of a 1 *M* solution) into the dorsal and ventral prostate in a total of 207 rats that were 6 weeks old at the time of the injection. No (adeno)carcinomas were reported, and the study duration was not indicated. Both studies have severe weaknesses that limit their significance. The fact that Hoffmann and co-workers (1985) found proliferative lesions in both right and left ventral lobes, although cadmium was injected only in the right lobes and that they found carcinomas even though the site of injection (right lobe) was excised 200 days after the experiment sheds doubt on the reliability of their observations. Moreover, their microphotographs are not convincing. The study by Scott and Aughey (1978) is not convincing, because the doses they reportedly used are lethal (Piscator, 1981; Hoffmann *et al.*, 1985), and their report is very sketchy. Gunn and co-workers (1967) injected 0.17–0.34 mg cadmium (as cadmium chloride) into the ventral prostate of an unspecified number of rats. No tumors were found at that site. In conclusion, studies on the local injection of cadmium into the prostate have yielded contradictory results.

A very interesting *in vitro* study of the effects of cadmium chloride on primary cultures of epithelial and mesenchymal prostatic cells from rat (ventral lobe), baboon, dog, and man was recently reported by Terracio and Nachtigal (1986). Cytotoxicity and transforming effects were studied separately. Fibroblasts were more susceptible to cadmium cytotoxicity than epithelial cells in all four species. Human cells were least susceptible, and rat cells most susceptible to cadmium cytotoxicity, rat cells being some 200 times more sensitive. Baboon cells and dog cells were more sensitive than human cells but less sensitive than rat cells. Interestingly, Webber (1985) reported that cadmium at low concentrations stimulates the *in vitro* growth of normal human prostatic epithelial cells, and that this effect of cadmium is inhibited by nontoxic levels of selenium. Terracio and Nachtigal (1986) reported further that subculturing after treatment with the approximate LC_{50} of cadmium resulted in immortalization of only rat cells. Cells of the other species could not be immortalized with this cadmium treatment. Two epithelial rat cell lines and two fibroblastic rat cell lines were thus derived. These lines were characterized using immunohistochemistry (keratin), electron microscopy and karyotyping. All four lines had an abnormal karyotype.

Thus, it appears that there are distinct species differences in the *in vitro* effects of cadmium on prostatic cells. The most important observation is that human cells could not be transformed, while rat cells could. This has some bearing on the evaluation of cadmium as a carcinogenic hazard for man. In addition, if there are species differences, there may well be strain differences that could explain the contradictory results of Scott and Aughey (1978) and Hoffmann *et al.* (1985) discussed earlier. Also, it would be very interesting to know whether there are differences between the different lobes of the rat prostate in sensitivity to the cytotoxic and transforming effects of cadmium.

In conclusion, there are very limited indications—from one epidemiological study—that cadmium intake from food sources may be positively associated with prostatic cancer risk. Some other epidemiological data and results from most animal studies do not support any such relation. However, the animal studies on oral exposure to cadmium are probably inadequate to properly assess the carcinogenicity of cadmium. In animal studies with parenteral administration of low doses of cadmium that lack testicular toxicity, enhancement of naturally occurring proliferative lesions in the ventral prostate were found (Waalkes *et al.*, 1987). The findings of Hoffmann *et al.* (1985) (that ventral prostatic carcinomas can be induced by local injection of cadmium) support the observations of Waalkes and co-workers. Mechanisms underlying this possible carcinogenic effect of cadmium include direct carcinogenic activity towards the prostatic epithelium and a lack of metallothionein defense systems in the prostate. Cadmium may also act as cocarcinogen, since it enhances the mutagenic activity of MNU, a known initiator of prostatic carcinogenesis (Bosland *et al.*, 1983) in the *Salmonella*-microsome test of Ames (Mandel and Ryser, 1987). *In vitro* experiments have indicated that, unlike rat prostatic epithelial cells, human prostatic epithelium cannot be transformed by cadmium exposure as determined by the development of immortalization. Thus, overall there is very limited, if any, evidence that cadmium exposuure is related to prostatic carcinogenesis in man (see also Section V,A,3). Lifetime oral dosing studies in rodents with appropriate levels of cadmium (sufficiently low to avoid testicular toxicity, but high enough to result in prolonged exposure at levels comparable to or higher than those in humans, as determined by tissue concentrations) are highly warranted.

B. Sexual Factors

The possible relation of prostatic cancer risk with various sexual factors has been investigated in ten case-control studies I know of (Banerjee, 1986; Jackson *et al.*, 1975, 1981; Krain, 1973, 1974; Lees *et al.*, 1985; Mishina *et al.*, 1981, 1985; Ross *et al.*, 1987; Rotkin, 1977, 1980, 1983; Rotkin *et al.*, 1979; Schuman *et al.*, 1977, 1982; Steele *et al.*, 1971). Several of the reports are preliminary (Jackson *et al.*, 1975, 1981; Schuman *et al.*, 1982) or are of limited significance due to the small number (39–40) of cases involved (Schuman *et al.*, 1977; Steele *et al.*, 1971). The other studies involved 100 (Mishina *et al.*, 1981, 1985), 111 (Rotkin, 1977), 205 (Rotkin *et al.*, 1979), and 136 and 221 age/race-matched case-control pairs (Krain, 1973, 1974), while Banerjee (1986) studied 149 cases and 274 age/race/weight-matched controls. Ross *et al.* (1987) studied 142 Black and 142 White age–residence-matched pairs. Lees *et al.* (1985) used 83 cases and for each case two age-matched controls, one BHP patient and one hospital control. The study by Schuman *et al.* (1975, 1982) had neighborhood controls in addition to the hospital controls used in other studies, while Ross *et al.* (1987) used only neighborhood controls. The study by Mishina *et al.* (1981, 1985) was conducted among Japanese in Japan. The other studies were all done in the United States. The study by Jackson *et al.* (1975, 1981) involved only US Blacks.

A consistent finding was that the prostatic cancer patients had a higher sexual drive than the controls, as indicated by a greater interest in intercourse (Steele *et al.*, 1971), more frequent use of prostitutes (Schuman *et al.*, 1975, 1982), younger age at first coitus (Mishina *et al.*, 1981, 1985; Rotkin, 1977; Rotkin *et al.*, 1979), earlier onset of masturbation (Rotkin, 1977; Rotkin *et al.*, 1979), and higher frequency of masturbation (Schuman *et al.*, 1982).

Other studies found that these patients had a lower frequency of intercourse than the controls (Rotkin, 1977; Rotkin *et al.*, 1979; Schuman *et al.*, 1977, 1982; Steele *et al.*, 1971), particularly at older age (Mishina *et al.*, 1981, 1985; Rotkin, 1977; Rotkin *et al.*, 1979). However, Mishina and co-workers (1981, 1985) reported that prostatic cancer patients had a higher frequency of coitus than controls at a younger age, particularly during adolescence, and showed a lower frequency only at ages over 60 years. Krain (1974) reported a higher frequency in prostatic cancer patients than in controls at older ages. Ross *et al.* (1987) found no difference between cases and controls in US Blacks and Whites for frequency of intercourse at any age. Age at first ejaculation was younger for the patients than for controls in some United States studies (Rotkin, 1977; Rotkin *et al.*, 1979; Schuman *et al.*, 1977, 1982), while Japanese were older at first ejaculation (Mishina *et al.*, 1981, 1985). Prostatic cancer patients have been reported to have a higher average frequency of ejaculation (by intercourse or other means) than controls over their entire sexually active life (Banerjee, 1986).

Contradictory findings were reported for the number of sexual partners, coitus frequency at young ages, and age at first nocturnal emission. Some studies included other variables that were not covered by any of the other studies (Mishina *et al.*, 1981, 1985; Rotkin, 1977; Rotkin *et al.*, 1979). They are not discussed here because it is not possible to properly interpret them.

In general, the findings of the various studies are difficult to compare, because slight to marked differences between studies exist in the definition of the variables investigated. Furthermore, it should be realized that generally answers to questions about sexual life, and in particular questions about sex at younger ages, are probably not very reliable, in part due to the old age of the patients. Nevertheless, a general pattern seems to evolve from these studies, implicating sexual factors in prostatic cancer risk. In comparison with controls, prostatic cancer patients have (1) an earlier onset of sexual activity in any sense, (2) show a higher sexual drive, especially at a young age, (3) have, notwithstanding their high sexual drive, a lower frequency of intercourse, especially at older ages, or have a higher frequency until about 50 years of age and a lower frequency thereafter. Interesting is a report that prostate cancer mortality among United States Catholic priests is somewhat higher than expected but not significantly higher (Ross *et al.*, 1981).

Holman and co-workers (1981) reported a continued decrease in prostatic cancer risk for successive cohorts born after the end of the last century in Australia and England and Wales, with the exception of middle-aged (50 to 64 or 69 years) men born shortly after 1910. They suggested as an explanation for this cohort phenomenon a lowered sexual activity during the Great Depression of the 1930s, as indicated by the low birth rate during that period. This would imply, if their suggestion is correct, that lowered sexual activity between the ages of 20 and 30 would increase risk. This is not inconsistent with the results of case-control studies discussed earlier.

A consistent finding is that in these cases there is more often a history of venereal disease (Krain, 1974; Schuman *et al.*, 1977, 1982; Steele *et al.*, 1971). Only in the study by Mishina and co-workers (1981, 1985) in Japan was no such association found. Heshmat *et al.* (1975) showed that prostatic cancer patients more often have a history of gonorrhea than controls. Lees and co-workers (1985) found a higher occurrence of syphilis but not gonorrhea in prostatic cancer patients than in controls. Heshmat *et al.* (1973, 1975) suggest a causal relationship between the peak in prostate cancer mortality that occurred in 1964–1965 in Denmark and a similar peak in the incidence of gonorrhea 45 years earlier, from 1915 to 1920. Actually, they show that the curve for the gonorrhea incidence rates from 1895 to 1932 almost exactly parallels that for the death rates from prostatic cancer from 1940 to 1970. Heshmat and co-workers (1973) speculated that complications of preantibiotic treatment of gonorrhea may have played a role in the development of prostatic cancer in those years. A peak in prostatic cancer mortality for cohorts born at the end of the nineteenth century has occurred in several populations, as pointed out earlier (see Section II, H; Ernster *et al.*, 1987b; Gordon *et al.*, 1961; Holman *et al.*, 1981). Therefore, the association found by Heshmat and co-workers (1973) between prostatic cancer mortality in Denmark in the early 1960s and a peak in the incidence of gonorrhea 45 years earlier may be purely coincidental. On the other hand, a causal relation between prechemotherapy gonorrhea and prostatic cancer may in fact exist in many populations and may explain the high risk among birth cohorts from the end of the last century found in various studies.

C. Other Life-Style Factors

Smoking is a risk factor for several major human cancers (Doll and Peto, 1981). Therefore, it seems relevant to review the studies that have examined the possible association between smoking and prostatic cancer. In the Dorn study, a prospective study on smoking and mortality in about 249,000 US veterans, smokers showed an increased risk for prostatic cancer (Kahn, 1966). The mortality ratio for smokers versus nonsmokers was 1.71 for cigarette smoking ($p < 0.01$), based on 582 prostatic cancer deaths out of a total of 49,270 deaths. There was, however, no dose–response relationship with regard to the number of cigarettes smoked per day. Stocks (1970) found a significant ($p < 0.05$) negative correlation between prostatic cancer mortality and the annual consumption of cigarettes per adult in 20 countries.

No association between smoking and prostatic cancer risk has been reported in a large number of other studies: A prospective study in the United States (Hammond, 1966), a cohort study in the United States (Whittemore *et al.*, 1985), a geographical correlation study on tobacco use in the United States (Breslow and Enstrom, 1974), a prospective study among British doctors (Doll and Peto, 1976), a patient interview study (TNCS) in the United States (Williams and Horms, 1977), and three case-control studies in the United States (Jackson *et al.*, 1981; Ross *et al.*, 1987; Schuman *et al.*, 1977, 1982), one in Japan (Mishina *et al.*, 1981, 1985), and one in Italy (Talamini *et al.*, 1986). In conclusion, although some studies suggest a relation between smoking and prostatic cancer, their results are contradictory, and a large number of other studies of various types indicate that there is no evidence that smoking influences risk for cancer of the prostate.

D. Discussion and Conclusions

Diet and nutrition as well as certain sexual factors appear to be associated with human prostatic cancer risk, whereas no such association has been found for smoking, a life-style factor that is related to several other human cancers. These associations have largely been derived from epidemiological studies. Therefore, the evidence for these is circumstantial rather than direct, as would be obtained from controlled human intervention studies and animal experiments. Associations between dietary and nutritional factors and prostatic cancer risk have been found in a variety of epidemiological studies, such as international and within-country correlation studies, case-control studies, and prospective studies. These dietary associations are therefore probably more reliable than those found for certain sexual factors, which have only been derived from case-control studies. In the following sections, dietary and sexual factors will be discussed separately and will include some speculation about possible mechanisms of action.

1. *Diet and Nutrition*

An evaluation of the epidemiological evidence for dietary associations with prostatic cancer risk have been presented in a previous review on this issue (Bosland, 1985). Some important epidemiological reports on diet and prostatic cancer have recently been published, particularly concerning vitamin A, and there is some information on dietary fat from animal studies. A reevaluation of the associations between diet and prostatic cancer, taking into account these recent reports, is summarized in Table XII. This evaluation is primarily based on the consistency of the results among studies and on the degree of the associations found. If available, information is also taken into account on "dose–effect" relations, on coherence between different types of studies (epidemiological studies versus animal and *in vitro* experiments), and, in the case of vitamin A, biological plausibility. Fat and protein intake

TABLE XII

SUMMARY OF THE EVIDENCE FOR ASSOCIATIONS BETWEEN DIETARY FACTORS AND PROSTATIC CANCER RISK

Association	Foods	Nutrients
Consistently strongly positive	—	Animal/saturated fats
Moderately strongly/not fully consistently positive	Edible fats/oils	Total fat; total protein; animal protein
Weakly/not consistently positive	Meat(s); eggs; animal products; sugar(s)	Oligosaccharides
Weakly/not consistently negative	Vitamin A- and C-rich foods; fiber-rich foods; fish/seafood	Selenium
No association (some conflicting data)	Alcoholic beverages; wine/beer; tea; coffee	—
No association	—	Vitamin C
Inconclusive/unknown	Milk	(Poly)unsaturated fat; vegetable protein; total carbohydrate; polysaccharide(s); dietary fiber; vitamin E; zinc; vitamin A; carotenes

are most strongly and consistently associated with prostatic cancer risk. These two variables therefore will be discussed in some detail. In addition, zinc and vitamin A will be discussed further: Zinc because of its important role in prostatic physiology and vitamin A because it is currently the center of controversy because of the contradictory results of a number of studies.

a. Fat, Protein, and Energy Intake. Fat and protein consumption are rather consistently found to be positively associated with prostatic cancer risk. The association is most consistent and strong for fat from animal sources and for saturated fat, and somewhat less consistent and strong for total fat and for total and animal protein. The data for (poly)unsaturated fat and vegetable protein, on the other hand, are inconclusive. Foods that are moderately strongly and consistently associated with risk are edible fats and oils and, to a lesser degree of consistency and strength, animal products that are sources of animal fat and animal protein, i.e., meat(s) and eggs. The stronger association for fats and oils than for animal products could be regarded as support for the indications (see earlier) that fat is more strongly related to prostatic cancer than protein is. Actually, the fact that no vegetable foods other than edible oils are positively associated with risk, while all animal products, which are a good source of both fat and protein, are positively associated with risk, would suggest that only fat is related to prostatic cancer risk and not protein. Nevertheless, because of the high intercorrelation between fat and protein, particularly from animal sources (Armstrong and Doll, 1975; Schrauzer, 1976b), it is not possible to ascertain whether the relation with prostatic cancer risk is indeed much stronger for fat than for protein. In general, great caution is warranted in the interpretation of epidemiological data as evidence for a causal relationship (N.A.S., 1982). Only if animal data, mechanistic studies, and, ideally, intervention studies, which are all largely lacking at present, would support the observed associations, could a causal relation be regarded as very likely.

Interestingly, the intake of calories particularly from animal sources is, internationally, highly correlated with prostatic cancer mortality or incidence (Armstrong and Doll, 1975; Correa, 1981; Rose *et al.*, 1986). Obesity, which may be related to overconsumption of calories, has been found to be positively associated with prostatic cancer risk in two large-scale prospective studies (Lew and Garfinkel, 1979; Snowdon *et al.*, 1984) and in one recent case-control study (Talamini *et al.*, 1986). In four other case-control studies (Greenwald *et al.*, 1974a; Kolonel *et al.*, 1987; Ross *et al.*, 1987; Wynder *et al.*, 1971), and one cohort study (Whittemore *et al.*, 1986), however, there was no such association. Nevertheless, the studies that indicated an association between prostatic cancer risk and caloric intake or obesity give some support for the positive relation found between risk and the intake of fat, which may contribute as much as 40–45% of the total caloric intake of humans in the Western world.

b. Vitamin A. The results of epidemiological research on the relation between the intake of vitamin A and prostatic cancer risk are contradictory and confusing. Some studies show a significant positive relation, others a significant negative relation, and in still other studies, no association was found. There seems, however, to be a certain pattern to the results of specific groups of studies. A positive relationship between prostatic cancer risk was found in case-control studies only for older cases when these were distinguished from younger (two studies), and only when intake of vitamin A and carotenes was estimated from food consumption data. No relation or a negative relation was found in case-control studies (five studies) that did not distinguish between younger and older cases and/or investigated only one or a few specific vitamin A-rich and/or β-carotene-rich foods, such as carrots, liver, and (Japanese) green–yellow vegetables. The 10-year follow-up of a Japanese cohort study also showed a significant negative relationship between prostatic cancer risk and the consumption of green–yellow vegetables, but the results of the 16-year follow-up did not confirm this finding. In another cohort study conducted in the United States there was a positive association for the consumption of vitamin A supplements but not for vitamin A/β-carotene intake. In a within-country correlation study done in Hawaii there was no association with risk for the estimated intake of total vitamin A. The results of studies measuring serum levels of retinol in prostatic cancer patients and controls are contradictory. However, except in severe deficiency or overdose situations, serum vitamin A levels are poor indicators of vitamin A status (Olson, 1984).

Thus, vitamin A and/or carotenes may play a role in the genesis of prostatic cancer that develops at older age (70 years and over), but not when the disease develops earlier in life. This is further discussed in Section VII. Furthermore, if rather accurate measures of intake are used, vitamin A and carotenes are positively associated with prostatic cancer risk, whereas if less reliable measures are used, there seems to be no association or a negative relation. The results of some studies are inconclusive. One possible explanation for these divergent results is the following. The consumption of some vitamin A-rich foods, such as carrots or green–yellow vegetables, could be highly correlated with the exposure to one or more additional factors that can inhibit the development of prostatic cancer is some way. Many such putative cancer-inhibiting factors can be present in vitamin A-rich foods, such as protease inhibitors (Troll and Wiesner, 1983), and certain indoles, aromatic isothiocyanates, methylated flavones, and plant sterols (Wattenberg, 1983). On the other hand, the intake of vitamin A and carotenes, as calculated from food consumption data, could be highly correlated with the exposure to one or more prostatic cancer-enhancing factors. One such factor might be dietary fat. The fact that vitamin A and/or β-carotene or other carotenes indeed somehow stimulate the development of prostatic cancer cannot be excluded. This is, however, biologically rather implausible. Vitamin A is generally suspected to be an anticarcinogenic agent on the basis of both its activity in various cancer models and its cellular and biochemical actions (N.A.S., 1982; Sporn and Robberts, 1983) and carotenes are similarly regarded as anticarcinogens (Peto *et al.*, 1981). Vitamin A is required for normal differentiation (structure and function) of prostatic glandular epithelium (Sporn and Robberts, 1983), as vitamin A deficiency leads to prostatic squamous metaplasia (Lasnitski, 1974; Wolbach and Howe, 1925). In addition, there are retinol and retinoic acid binding proteins in the human prostate, an observation suggesting that vitamin A can directly affect this gland (Boyd *et al.*, 1984). *In vitro* data on the effects of vitamin A on carcinogen-induced changes in rodent prostate explant cultures (see also Bosland, 1985) would also support the notion of an inhibiting influence of vitamin A on prostatic carcinogenesis. Similar studies utilizing human prostatic tissue have not been reported, so extrapolation of the rodent *in vitro* data is difficult. Kolonel *el al.* (1987) suggested that a positive association between vitamin A intake and carcinogenesis at several sites is a common finding in animal experiments, which would support their observation of such a positive relation, and those of Heshmat *et al.* (1985) and Graham *et al.* (1983). This is, however, not so; inhibition of carcinogenesis by vitamin A or other retinoids is the rule, no observed effects are less common, and enhancement is the exception (N.A.S., 1982; Reddy *et al.*, 1980; Welsch, *et al.*, 1985). In conclusion, it is not clear whether vitamin A and carotenes are at all related to prostatic cancer risk, and, if it were, whether such a relation would involve inhibiting or enhancing properties of this micronutrient toward human prostatic carcinogenesis. Much more research of various types will be needed to clarify this issue.

c. Zinc and Other Trace Elements. In one international correlation study, a weak positive association was found between zinc intake and prostatic cancer rates. Because there are no other data available, it is not possible to assess the relation between zinc and prostatic cancer risk. There are, however, a number of indirect indications that zinc may play a role in prostatic carcinogenesis (see also Bosland, 1985). Zinc accumulates to a greater extent in the prostate than in any other tissue, both in man and rats (Daniel *et al.*, 1956; Gunn and Gould, 1956), and there is a zinc binding protein in the rat prostate (Thomas *et al.*, 1981). Zinc levels in prostatic carcinoma tissue are lower than in the normal human prostate (Habib *et al.*, 1976a, 1979). Zinc is essential for prostatic function in man and rats (Schenk, 1975), but not for the normal growth and development of the rat prostate (Chandler *et al.*, 1981). Zinc alters androgen metabolism and prolactin binding in the human prostate *in vitro* (Habib *et al.*, 1979; Leake *et al.*, 1984a,b). In rats zinc modulates plasma levels of pituitary hormones such as prolactin and luteinizing hormone (Root *et al.*, 1979), and a variety of hormonal manipulations can affect zinc uptake in the dorsolateral prostate (Muntzing *et al.*,

1977). On the basis of these data, it seems conceivable that zinc plays some role in the development of prostatic cancer, but this is only speculation.

A role for cadmium and selenium in prostatic carcinogenesis is equally speculative, and in fact it is more likely that cadmium plays no such role as indicated earlier. On the other hand, selenium is a powerful inhibitor of mammary carcinogenesis and of the development of a number of other experimental tumors in rodents (Thompson *et al.*, 1981; Medina, 1985). A small number of epidemiologic studies suggests a negative association between prostatic cancer risk and selenium intake. Thus, more research effort with respect to a possible protective role of selenium in prostatic carcinogenesis is certainly warranted. Interestingly, zinc, cadmium, and selenium as well as vitamin A have been shown to interact in a number of ways as indicated previously (see Bosland, 1985). Most notably, zinc inhibits cadmium carcinogenicity on subcutaneous administration of both together (Gunn *et al.*, 1964). It may well be that such interactions are of crucial importance with respect to prostatic carcinogenesis, and they should be taken into account in future research. The recent data of Waalkes *et al.* (1987) (see Section IV,A,7,b) suggest that is indeed the case.

d. Possible Mechanisms. The only specific dietary factors that are rather consistently associated with human prostatic cancer risk, both in a positive manner, are fat and protein (see Table XII). These two nutritional variables can, in theory, affect a variety of physiological and pathological processes that are related to carcinogenesis in general. However, there is no information available that is pertinent to the possible mechanisms of the role of fat and protein in prostatic carcinogenesis specifically.

The endocrine system has been implicated as a mediator of dietary influences on prostatic carcinogenesis (Reddy *et al.*, 1980). This hypothesis has been systematically explored by Hill and co-workers (Hill and Wynder, 1979; Hill *et al.*, 1979, 1980a,b, 1982). They investigated the endocrine effects of drastic changes in total diet for 2–3 weeks in a number of controlled studies in healthy men. An initial study (Hill and Wynder, 1979) involved four men of unspecified ethnic backgroud, under 45 years of age, with customary Western dietary habits. They consumed a standardized, high-fat Western diet for 2 weeks, followed by 2 weeks on a strictly vegetarian, low-fat diet. Overnight blood samples were taken via indwelling catheters at the end of each diet period. Nocturnal release of prolactin, testosterone, and luteinizing hormone were significantly lower after the vegetarian diet period than after the Western diet. This was also found in a group of 11 men subjected to the same experimental protocol for morning testosterone levels. In other studies by Hill *et al.* (1979, 1980a,b, 1982), the endocrine effects of dietary changes were compared in populations at high and low risk for prostatic cancer. High-risk North American Blacks and Whites with Western dietary habits consumed a standardized, high-fat Western diet for 2 weeks, followed by a 3-week period on a strictly vegetarian, low-fat diet. South African

Blacks, who normally consumed a very consistent, strictly vegetarian diet, were the low-risk population. They were transferred to a high-fat Western diet for 3 weeks. When white and black North American men were transferred from the Western diet to the vegetarian diet, urinary excretion of androgens and estrogens decreased (Hill *et al.*, 1979, 1980b). Plasma levels of testosterone and total androgens also decreased, but plasma concentrations of total estrogens remained unchanged (Hill *et al.*, 1980a,b). These changes in endocrine profiles were statistically significant in Blacks, but, except for plasma and urinary testosterone, not in Whites. In contrast, when South African Blacks were transferred from a vegetarian to a Western diet, urinary excretion of androgens and estrogens increased significantly (Hill *et al.*, 1979, 1980b). Plasma levels of testosterone and total androgens, however, decreased, while, as was found in North Americans, plasma concentrations of total estrogens did not change (Hill *et al.*, 1980a,b). These studies were performed in 40- to 55-year-old men. When a similar experiment was done in older (60–73 years old) South African men, however, urinary sex steroid excretion and plasma levels of testosterone and total androgens decreased, while plasma estrogens remained unchanged (Hill *et al.*, 1979, 1980a,b, 1982). This was also found in 60- to 73-year-old black prostatic cancer patients in South Africa (Hill *et al.*, 1982). In these aged South African subjects, this diet change also increased the ratio of androsterone to etiocholanolone and decreased the ratio of estrogens to androgens in the urine, while no changes in these ratios were found in any of the younger groups (Hill *et al.*, 1979, 1980b).

As summarized previously (Bosland, 1985), these data indicate that an abrupt 2- to 3-week change from a Western to a vegetarian diet, and vice versa, is related to changes in testosterone production and in the metabolism and clearance of androgens and estrogens. Furthermore, older men (over 55 years) respond differently than younger men, which may be related to changes in the control of hormone levels that occur around 50 to 60 years of age (Hill *et al.*, 1980b; see also Section VI).

Similar dietary changes appear to affect plasma prolactin levels (see above; Hill and Wynder, 1979). Interestingly, prolactin release is stimulated by consuming a meal, as shown by Carlson *et al.* (1983); the duration of this response is a few hours. Their studies indicated that this postprandial response is triggered by meals of high protein content and not by meals that have a high fat or high carbohydrate (glucose) content. On the basis of these observations it might be speculated that it was primarily the protein level in the diet that affected plasma prolactin in the study by Hill and Wynder (1979) and not fat or other dietary variables. This speculation is supported by preliminary data from my laboratory concerning studies in male rats. Differences in dietary fat levels or restriction of the intake of carbohydrates affected plasma prolactin levels less consistently and strongly than did variation in the level of protein (Bosland *et al.*, 1985; Bunnik *et al.*, 1985a,b). Preliminary results from studies by Clinton *et al.* (1982) and by Mulloy *et al.* (1983) indicate a complete absence of an effect of dietary fat level on plasma prolactin and prolactin clearance in male rats. Cohen (1979), on the other hand, reported that feeding a high-fat diet elevated plasma prolactin levels in male rats, as compared with rats on a low-fat diet. This apparent discrepancy, which also seems to occur in female rats (Bosland and Wilbrink, 1985), may be explained as an artifact due to Cohen's method of blood sampling, using ether anesthesia. Preliminary data from my laboratory (Bosland *et al.*, 1985; Bunnik *et al.*, 1983a,b; Kroes *et al.*, 1986) further suggest that complex interactions exist between type and amount of macronutrients (fat, protein, and carbohydrates) as they influence plasma levels of—besides prolactin—androgenic and estrogenic steroid hormones, as summarized previously (Bosland, 1985). It is not possible to compare these rodent data with the findings of Hill and co-workers, because individual nutrients were varied in the diets and no total diet changes were studied as was done by Hill and colleagues.

In a study of ten vegetarian Seventh Day Adventists (SDA), ten nonvegetarian SDA, and eight non-SDA omnivoric men, Howie and Schultz (1985) found that testosterone and estradiol-17β were significantly lower in the vegetarian than in the omnivoric men. Very interesting is their observation that of all macronutrient intakes that were calculated from 3-day recall data, it was only the intake of dietary fiber that correlated with plasma levels of these two hormones. These correlations were negative and quite significant when all three groups combined were analyzed ($r = -0.48$, $p < 0.005$ for estradiol-17β; $r = -0.31$, $p < 0.05$ for testosterone).

Rosenthal *et al.* (1985) studied endocrine effects of the Pritikin diet. Twenty-one men with a history of cardiovascular disease or diabetes (mean age 51 years) were fed for 21 days a very low-fat (< 10% of calories), high fiber/complex carbohydrate diet. The plasma level of estradiol decreased significantly (from 47.2 ± 4.6 pg/ml before the diet period started to 23.8 ± 2.5 pg/ml after the 21 days on the diet), while plasma testosterone levels did not change significantly.

Interestingly, obesity and overweight, which are perhaps related to prostatic cancer risk and to diet (see Section IV,D,1,a), are known to be associated with lower plasma levels of testosterone (Glass *et al.*, 1977) and sex-hormone-binding globulin (SHBG) (Glass *et al.*, 1977; Semmens *et al.*, 1983; Siiteri *et al.*, 1982), and with higher levels of estradiol-17β and estrone (Kley *et al.*, 1980; Schneider *et al.*, 1979; Siiteri *et al.*, 1982; Zumoff *et al.*, 1981). These data would support the view that obesity leads to increased peripheral conversion of androgens to estrogens by aromatization in the fat tissue. Meikle *et al.* (1982), on the other hand, did not find a correlation between body weight and plasma levels of either testosterone or SHBG.

In conclusion, it is evident that in both man and experimental animals diet and diet-associated variables, such as obesity, can affect a variety of endocrine parameters that may be related to prostatic cancer (see Section VI). Some of these variables—fat, protein and obesity—are more or less strongly associated with human prostatic cancer risk. Other variables—carbohydrates, dietary fiber, and vitamin E, that affects plasma testosterone in men and rats (Umeda *et al.*, 1982), do not seem to be related to prostatic cancer. It is attractive to hypothesize that diet affects prostatic carcinogenesis chiefly mediated by the endocrine system. This is, however, not very likely, because diet can theoretically affect several other processes in the human body that are conceivably related to the development of prostatic cancer. Furthermore, it is not clear from the data available which diet–endocrine relations are associated with prostatic cancer risk.

2. *Sexual and Transmissible Factors*

Prostatic cancer risk seems in some respects related to sexual factors such as sexual drive and ejaculatory activity through intercourse or masturbation. Risk is clearly associated with the occurrence of venereal diseases. It is conceivable that the development of prostatic cancer has indeed some relation to the functional activity of the gland, perhaps mediated via endocrine factors that are involved in the regulation of prostatic glandular function. One could speculate that, if high plasma levels of testosterone were associated with a high risk for prostatic cancer (see Section VI), such high levels might be either the cause or the consequence of a higher sexual drive and/or activity. There are to date no data available from human studies that could prove or disprove this speculation.

Some animal studies indicate that sexual activity can indeed influence the prostate. Rats that have the opportunity to be sexually active in the sense of mating have larger and heavier accessory sex glands than rats that are kept without females (Aumuller *et al.*, 1985; Braun *et al.*, 1982; Sodersten *et al.*, 1977). This effect appeared more likely to be mediated by nervous control of prostatic activity than by increased hormonal sensitivity of the gland; sexually active rats had lower prostatic androgen receptor concentrations, but a higher norepinephrine content and more numerous adrenergic nerve fibers in the prostate (Aumuller *et al.*, 1985; Braun *et al.*, 1982). Unfortunately, no plasma or tissue hormone levels were measured in these studies, and the observations were limited to the ventral prostate. In studies on aging ACI/segHapBR rats, Ward *et al.* (1980) found that there was no difference between retired breeders and virgin males in the incidence of ventral prostatic epithelial hyperplasia and adenocarcinomas. These lesions occur spontaneously in high rates in this rat strain at old age. Thus, animal studies demonstrate that sexual activity can affect the prostate gland, but they do not indicate a relation between sexual activity and prostatic cancer development. In a review of the literature on prostatic glandular function and prostatic cancer, Isaacs (1983) demonstrated that it is quite conceivable that modulation of functional activity of the human prostate by ejaculatory frequency can influence the concentration of a variety of chemical constituents in the prostatic fluid, as well as the flow of the fluid through the glandular lumina and ducts. These two factors, in turn, will determine the duration of exposure of the glandular epithelium to prostatic fluid constituents. Some of these constituents, such as proteases and polyamines (Zaneveld and Tauber, 1981), and a variety of chemical carcinogens (Smith and Hagiopan, 1981) may well have initiating and/or promoting or cocarcinogenic activity, and thus be involved in prostatic carcinogenesis. It is also conceivable that enhancement of functional activity of the gland by increased sexual activity can affect (1) androgen sensitivity of the epithelium (Braun *et al.*, 1982), (2) the capability of the glandular cells to take up and metabolize chemical carcinogens, and (3) the rate of cell turnover, which is a critical factor in chemical carcinogenesis in the rat prostate (see Section III).

The observation of an association between venereal disease and prostatic cancer risk has led to a number of speculations about other possible sex-related mechanisms of prostatic carcinogenesis. Heshmat and co-workers (1973) have suggested that the iatrogenic complications of preantibiotic management of gonorrhea is a factor in the etiology of prostatic cancer. Lees *et al.* (1985), however, did not find an association between prostatic cancer risk and (preantibiotic) treatment with arsenic drugs. As alternative explanations Heshmat *et al.* (1975) suggested that gonococcal infections may act as a vector that facilitates the entry of viruses into prostatic epithelium or that chronic inflammation and irritation are causally related to prostatic cancer. Indeed, with some frequency, reports have been published that demonstrate the presence of virus particles in human prostatic carcinomas or a higher frequency of sero-positivity for specific viruses in prostatic cancer cases than in control subjects (Zeigel, 1979). The presence of virus particles in prostatic tumor tissue or increased sero-positivity among cases has specifically been shown for Herpes simplex virus – 2, cytomegalovirus and Simian virus 40 (Rapp and Geder, 1980; Mickey and Paulson, 1980; Schuman *et al.*, 1977). There is, however, no consistency in these findings, as summarized by Mandel and Schuman (1980) and Zeigel (1979). A report on increased risk of cervical cancer among wives of prostatic cancer patients also suggests a viral etiology (Feminella and Lattimer, 1974). However, a later case-control study did not confirm this finding (Greenwald *et al.*, 1979). In addition, patterns of cervical cancer, for which a viral etiology is suspected, and of prostatic cancer in various ethnic groups in the Los Angeles area were found to be quite different by Ross *et al.* (1983). There is also no consistent relation between prostatic cancer risk and circumcision, a factor associated with decreased risk for cervical cancer (Mandel and Schuman, 1980; Ross *et al.*, 1987; Wynder *et al.*, 1971). In conclusion, the evidence for a viral etiology of prostatic cancer is at best suggestive, but the possibility that viruses play some role in this respect cannot be excluded (Mandel and Schuman, 1980; Winkelstein and Ernster, 1979; Zeigel, 1979).

Prostatitis is another factor that may be related to prostatic cancer risk, venereal disease and, perhaps, sexual activity. Prostatitis can conceivably cause chronic irritation of the prostate gland and consequently stimulate cell proliferation and affect functional activity. Particularly chronic cell stimulation of cell proliferation might be an enhancing factor in human prostatic carcinogenesis as it appears to be in chemical induction of prostatic cancer in the rat (see Section III). Venereal diseases, such as trichomoniasis and gonorrhea, often can cause prostatitis (Drach and Kohnen, 1977; Gardner *et al.*, 1986; Pfau and Caine, 1980; Vandenbroecke-Grauls *et al.*, 1982). The cause of a large proportion of chronic prostatitis cases is nonbacterial. Some of these cases can be attributed to nonbacterial microorganisms such as *Trichomonas* or *Chlamydia* (Drach and Kohnen, 1977; Pfau and Caine, 1980). For many others, the cause remains unclear. A causative relation between prostatic cancer and prostatic schistosomiasis has been suggested based on a case of prostatic adenocarcinoma coincident with heavy prostatic infestation with *Schistosoma mansoni* (Alexis and Domingo, 1986). Aseptic prostatitis can perhaps result from over- or underutilization of the gland, i.e., increased or suppressed ejaculatory activity. This speculation and the association of venereal diseases with both prostatic cancer risk and prostatitis are attractive explanations for the relation of sexual activity and venereal disease to prostatic cancer. However, there is only suggestive evidence from case-control studies for a relation between prostatic cancer risk and prostatitis, and only few studies have addressed this question. Clearly, this should be regarded as an important area for future research, as should the relationship between sexual activity and prostatic cancer risk.

V. Non-Life-Style Environmental Factors

A. Occupational Factors

A large number of very different occupations have been reported as associated with prostatic cancer risk, but for only a few occupations have prostatic cancer rates been consistently reported to be higher than expected (Dubrow and Wegman, 1983; Ernster *et al.*, 1979b; Logan, 1982; Williams *et al.*, 1977).

1. *Farmers and Farmworkers*

Farmers and farmworkers consistently show an increased risk (Burmeister, 1981; Dubrow and Wegman, 1983; Gallagher *et al.*, 1984; Logan, 1982; Wiklund and Holm, 1986; Williams *et al.*, 1977). There is only one study that did not observe this (Pearce *et al.*, 1987) using 1979 data from the New

Zealand cancer registry (617 cases). In a Swedish cohort study (size: 254,417 men; 5,922 cases) between 1961–1966 and 1974–1979 (Wiklund and Holm, 1986) there was a significant ($p < 0.01$) increase of relative risk for agricultural workers. The authors related this increase to the drastically increased potential exposure to artificial fertilizers and pesticides during the last decades. Burmeister (1981) found a standardized mortality ratio (SMR) of 141 ($p < 0.01$) in a retrospective death certificate study in Iowa involving 1138 prostatic cancer cases among farmers and 1460 cases among nonfarmers. He reported that increased risk was found particularly in ranchers working with cattle and sheep. In another death certificate study on 300 cases and 1380 controls, Siemiatycki *et al.* (1986) found an increased risk related to exposure to grain dusts (odds ratio, 1.9; $p < 0.05$). Alavanja *et al.* (1987) found a nonsignificant proportionate mortality ratio (PMR) of 111 (23 cases) in a similar study on grain industry workers, but for the subcategory ("unidentified grain industries") with the largest number of cases (15) a significantly elevated PMR of 173 ($p < 0.05$) was found. Exposure to fertilizers was significantly ($p < 0.02$) more often reported in cases than in controls in a study by Rotkin (1977) on 111 case-control pairs. It is not clear whether these exposures are at all causally related to prostatic cancer risk, or whether they are coincidentally found because farmers are more likely to be exposed to grain dust and fertilizers. Alavanja *et al.* (1987) point out that grain industry workers are likely to be exposed to a variety of pesticides.

2. *Workers in the Rubber Industry*

a. Epidemiology. An increased risk for prostatic cancer in workers in the rubber industry has been found in some studies in the United States but not in many other investigations. An SMR of 142 was reported by McMichael and co-workers (1974) for all jobs in a rubber plant in Akron, Ohio, using the 1968 United States male population as standard. This SMR was based on 49 cases out of a cohort of 6678 mainly white men (10–14% were Blacks), and it was significantly elevated ($p < 0.05$). However, when this cohort study was expanded to include workers from three other plants, two of which were also located in Akron, to a total cohort size of 18,903, the SMR was 119, based on 103 cases (McMichael *et al.*, 1976a). This is probably not significantly different from 100 (no statistical analysis was presented by the authors). For two of the four plants, SMRs were reported that probably are significantly elevated. Both studies covered the period between 1964 and 1972/1973. Since this initial report on prostatic cancer risk for workers in the rubber industry, a number of other cohort studies have been reported in the literature. In only one study (Bernadelli *et al.*, 1987) a significantly elevated SMR (518; $p < 0.05$) was found in a cohort of 4917 men in an Italian plant, but this report was based on only two cases. In none of the other studies was an increased risk for prostatic cancer found when all jobs were included in the cohorts. SMRs between 66 and 105 were reported on the basis of between 21 and 121 cases in cohorts of 8418 to 40,867 mainly white men in the United States, England and Sweden (Andjelkovich *et al.*, 1976, 1977; Baxter and Werner, 1980; Dezell and Monson, 1981; Gustavsson *et al.*, 1986; Monson and Nakano, 1976; Parkes *et al.*, 1982; Sorahan *et al.*, 1986). These studies covered different periods between 1940 and 1978. Hakama and Kilpikari (1980) summarized the results of four of these studies and one from Finland. They calculated an overall SMR of 102 for a total cohort size of 80,966, based on 204 cases. When tire manufacturing industries were distinguished from nontire rubber industries, no increased risk was found in either (Baxter and Werner, 1980; Dezell *et al.*, 1982, cited in IARC, 1982a). It is noteworthy that Williams *et al.* (1977), using data from the TNCS, also found a somewhat elevated risk for rubber production workers in the United States in general. They reported a relative odds ratio of 1.60, but this was not significantly increased. In a British cohort study (36,445 males), on the other hand, a statistically significant ($p < 0.05$) deficit in risk (SMR, 74) was found by Sorahan *et al.* (1986).

In a number of cohort studies and in two case-control studies, risk for prostatic cancer was assessed for specific job categories. In the two case-control studies (McMichael *et al.*, 1976b; Goldsmith *et al.*, 1980), increased risk was found for workers in batch preparation/mixing and calendering divisions. In these divisions, particularly the first one, exposure to the various chemicals that are used in rubber production is potentially high (Goldsmith *et al.*, 1980; IARC, 1982a; McMichael *et al.*, 1976b). In one study (McMichael *et al.*, 1976b) a relative risk of 1.6 ($p < 0.01$) was found, based on less than 30 cases (IARC, 1982a). In the other study of the same research group (Goldsmith *et al.*, 1980), involving a total of 88 cases and 258 controls, odds ratios of 2.8 to 3.0 ($p < 0.025$) were found for the 11 to 17 cases working in these divisions, depending on the duration of exposure. In a cohort study on 2666 men from the same job categories ("processing division"), however, no increased risk was found by Dezell and Monson (1982). An SMR of 99 was reported and was based on 19 cases. In the only other cohort study on men from specific job categories (Monson and Nakano, 1976; Monson and Fine, 1978), no increased risk was reported for this division. In this latter study an SMR of 140 (12 cases) was found for men from a group of jobs indicated as "miscellaneous tire" and an SMR (*calculated by IARC, 1982a*) of 180 (22 cases) for those from "materials maintenance." No statistical evaluation of these data was reported by the authors. The increased risk for maintenance workers is somewhat consistent with the increased risk that has been found for workers in the "general services" in general, as indicated above. Andjelkovich and co-workers (1977) reported an SMR of 212 ($p < 0.05$) for this category based on 10 cases in a cohort study of 8418 workers.

McMichael and colleagues (1976b) found a relative risk of 3.5 (number of cases unreported) for this group. Goldsmith *et al.* (1980), however, did not find an increased risk for this category in their case-control study. Dezell and Monson (1984a,b, 1985) did not find an excess risk for aerospace products workers (cohort size: 3161 men; 14 cases), industrial products workers (cohort size: 6533 men; 39 cases) and reclaim workers (cohort size: 1352 men; 6 cases) in United States rubber plants. In an attempt to relate cancer mortality to specific exposures in the rubber industry, Wilcosky *et al.* (1984) classified jobs in a large rubber plant on the basis of potential exposures to 20 different solvents. No relation was found for prostatic cancer mortality (33 cases in a cohort of 6678 men) with specific exposures (the number of cases per solvent was between 0 and 20).

The IARC (1982a) has extensively reviewed all existing data on carcinogenic hazards in the rubber industry. They concluded that there is "limited evidence for an excess occurrence of prostate cancer in rubber workers and inadequate evidence for causal associations with occupational exposures." On the basis of the preceding summary, however, one can justifiably conclude that there is no evidence for an increased risk for prostatic cancer in the rubber industry as a whole. It is quite remarkable that a significant increased risk for all job categories together has only been reported by the group of McMichael. And they have only found an increased occurrence of prostatic cancer in two plants, both probably located in Akron, Ohio (McMichael *et al.*, 1976a). Thus, it seems that in these plants a risk factor or combination of risk factors is present that is unique and leads to increased risk for prostatic cancer in the workers in these plants specifically. Therefore, it seems warranted to study in a retrospective manner the differences and similarities between the work environment in these plants and the plants studied by other researchers.

For some specific job categories in some plants, there is perhaps an excess occurrence of prostatic cancer. There are studies indicating that workers in the general services, including maintenance, are at increased risk. This may, however, be an incorrect interpretation of the results because of the very diverse nature of the jobs in this category, the small number of cases, and the lack of information on specific exposures. For workers in the mixing/batch preparation divisions, and perhaps also the calendering division, exposure to the many chemicals used in rubber manufacture (IARC, 1982a; Spiegelhalder and Preussmann, 1983) is likely. For these groups there is no consistency in the observation of increased risk for prostatic cancer, and the reliability of reports of an increased risk for these workers is lessened by the small number of cases in these studies. It is noteworthy that increased risk for the latter job categories was only reported by McMichael and co-workers, and not by Monson's group and others. It may be that this excess risk is limited to the same two plants mentioned above. In conclusion, there are very limited indications for increased risk for prostatic cancer in workers that are involved in mixing and batch preparation in the rubber industry.

b. Animal Studies. Very interesting findings were recently reported by a research group from the People's Republic of China (Wang *et al.*, 1984a). They housed groups of 62–68 male albino rats (otherwise unspecified) at different locations in a rubber plant in Shanghai where cancer incidence (stomach, liver, lung, and esophagus) had been shown to be higher than in control Shanghainese, the areas where compounding, mixing, and milling was done. A control group was housed in a clean animal facility. After 1.5 years of "exposure," the rats were kept for another half year before the experiment was terminated. Besides various other tumors, genital carcinomas, in both prostate and seminal vesicle, were found in 9 of 68 (13.2%), 4 of 65 (6.2%), and 4 of 62 (6.5%) of the rats in the milling, mixing, and compounding areas, respectively. In the control rats, the incidence of such tumors was 1 of 62 (1.6%). The difference between the control group and the group with the highest incidence is statistically significant ($p < 0.05$; χ^2 test, one-tailed; *analysis done by the author*). These findings are very significant, because prostate and seminal vesicle carcinomas are very rare in most rat strains, particularly invasively growing carcinomas as were apparently found in this study (Bosland, 1987).

In a separate experiment (Wang *et al.*, 1981), male rats were exposed to one of the major chemicals used in the rubber production process in this plant, *N*-phenyl-2-napthylamine (PBNA). The rats were orally dosed with 40, 100, or 160 mg/kg by gavage, 5 days per week, for 1.5 years. The experiment was terminated at 2 years. Genital carcinomas, predominantly from the prostate (no further details were presented), were found in 11 of 57 (19.3%) PBNA-exposed rats (total incidence), versus 0 of 43 and 1 of 62 (1.6%) in vehicle-treated and untreated controls, respectively ($p < 0.05$). No information was given on the incidences in the separate dose groups. In this experiment, a PBNA preparation was used that contained more than 85% PBNA, some *N*-phenyl-1-naphthylamine and no 2-naphthylamine. In another experiment, partially purified PBNA (no details given) was administered to male Wistar rats by gavage at dosages of 160 or 320 mg/kg, 5 times per week, for 1 year (Wang and Wang, 1981). This experiment was terminated at 1.5 years. No excess of prostatic or genital carcinomas were found. The incidences were 2 of 35, 0 of 22, 0 of 25, and 1 of 26 for the 160 mg, 320 mg, vehicle controls, and untreated controls, respectively. The purification may have removed the factor causing the prostatic carcinomas, the study duration may have been too short for prostatic tumors to develop, or perhaps strain differences were responsible for the negative findings in this study. The reports do not provide sufficient detail to fully judge the relevance of these findings. For example, it was not indicated whether all prostates were examined histologically, from which part of the prostate the tumors originated, and what purification was applied to the PBNA in the last experiment. However, in the first experiment, the *in situ* animal exposure, the air concentrations of PBNA were measured. They varied from 0.404 to 0.535 mg/m^3 in the mixing area and were between 0.085 and 0.385 mg/m^3 in the other areas (Wang *et al.*, 1984a). It is noteworthy that Wang and colleagues (1984a) do not report an increased occurrence of prostatic cancer in their epidemiological studies involving cohorts of 18,852 and 6183 (males and females together) in two different Shanghai rubber plants.

From various experiments with PBNA administered to mice, no prostatic tumors were reported by Wang and co-workers (1984a,b). This is in line with earlier studies done with PBNA in mice (IARC, 1976). However, some seminal vesicle carcinomas were reported by Wang *et al.* (1984b), which are very rare in mice. Their incidence did not exceed 7.6% and the duration of these experiments was 9–10 months. All prostates and seminal vesicles were examined histologically.

A draft technical report (N.T.P., 1987) of a carcinogenicity study with PBNA in F344 rats and B6C3F$_1$ mice carried out by the US National Toxicology Program indicates that no accessory sex gland neoplasia is produced upon feeding of as much as 5,000 ppm (approximately 225 mg/kg/day) in the diet. The PBNA used in this study was 98% pure and contained less than 1 ppm 2-naphthylamine.

On the basis of the Chinese animal data, one might conclude that the increased occurrence of prostatic cancer that has been reported in certain plants and in certain work sites in the rubber industry is related to exposure to aromatic amines used as antioxidants. However, an N.T.P. carcinogenicity bioassay with purified PBNA in rats and mice was negative with respect to the production of accessory sex gland neoplasia in males, as were Chinese studies with partially purified PBNA. Therefore it is conceivable that a contaminant in the unpurified Chinese PBNA was responsible for the prostatic tumor response in the studies of Wang and colleagues. Furthermore, the large number of other (potentially) carcinogenic substances found in the rubber industry, such as *N*-nitroso compounds (Spiegelhalder and Preussmann, 1983), make it likely that exposure to combinations of chemicals rather than to a single substance are involved in any carcinogenic hazard in the production of rubber (IARC, 1982a).

3. *Cadmium Exposure*

Occupational exposure to cadmium has repeatedly been suggested to be related to prostatic cancer risk (Piscator, 1981). This belief was triggered in the 1960s by a report by Potts (1965) of three cases of prostatic cancer found among 70 men who had been occupationally exposed to cadmium for more than 10 years. Before 1950, they were potentially exposed to large amounts of cadmium; air concentrations varied between 0.6 and 236 mg/m³. After 1950 the maximal air concentration was mostly below 0.5 mg/m³. The IARC (1982b) found limited evidence in the literature for carcinogenicity to humans of cadmium and certain cadmium compounds, with the prostate as one of the possible target sites. Piscator (1981) concluded in his comprehensive review of cadmium and prostatic carcinogenesis that if there were at all an excess occurrence of prostatic cancer among cadmium-exposed workers, the increased risk would be limited to those who are heavily exposed.

The epidemiologic basis for these conclusions is very weak. The number of prostatic cancer cases in most of the epidemiological studies was small: between 1 and 8. There is only one study with more cases: 23 (Armstrong and Kazantis, 1983). In that study, an SMR of 99 was found in a cohort of 6995 men working in 17 plants in England using cadmium. All cases were found among men who had always had low exposure to cadmium (80% of the cohort), resulting in an SMR of 113 for that group. No cases were found among men who were ever at moderate or high exposure (20% of the cohort). In a more recent report of this study (Armstrong and Kazantis, 1985), 39 cases were found and the SMR for prostatic cancer was 118. For the always-low-exposure group (24 cases) the SMR was 109, and for the groups that were ever-at-moderate- (9 cases) or ever-at-high-exposure (4 cases) the SMRs were 132 and 154, respectively; both were not significantly elevated. In another British study on a cohort of 3625 workers, from plants other than those studied by Armstrong and Kazantis (1983), an SMR of 121 was reported which was based on 8 cases; this figure is not statistically significant (Sorahan and Waterhouse, 1983). An update of this study including a total of 15 cases confirms this (Sorahan and Waterhouse, 1985). Doll (1984) summarized the results of these two studies and those from a third British study. He calculated that a total of 31 cases of prostatic cancer were observed in these studies as a whole (9902 men), and that 30.9 cases were to be expected, which amounts to an SMR of 100.

Studies conducted in the United States (Lemen *et al.*, 1976; Thun *et al.*, 1985) involved 3–4 cases, and SMRs of 347 and 213 were calculated, but these were not statistically significant. In a study performed in Sweden (Kjellstrom *et al.*, 1979) in two different plants, relative risks of 1.67 (2 cases) and 1.49 (4 cases) were found. Neither of these was significantly elevated. In this study, however, the average cadmium air concentrations in the workplace have been documented: > 1 mg/m³ before 1947, 0.2 mg/m³ in the 1950s, and 0.05 mg/m³ since 1962. A more recent report of this study (Elinder *et al.*, 1985) includes no further cases, but demonstrates an incrase of prostatic cancer SMR from 108 for all workers to 148 (not significantly elevated) for workers with at least 5 years of exposure and a 20-year latency period (from the start of exposure) for the cancer.

Only in two studies was an attempt made to investigate the duration and/or the extent of the exposure in relation to prostatic cancer risk. Lemen *et al.* (1976) found that cases had been exposed to cadmium for an average of 13 years and that the average time between the beginning of the exposure and the occurrence of prostatic cancer was 28 years. Sorahan and Waterhouse (1983) distinguished between workers who had been exposed for a period when air concentrations were high (0.6–2.6 mg/m^3) and workers who were exposed after 1950, when concentrations were brought down to about 0.5 mg/m^3. The SMRs they found were 112 (5 cases) and 142 (3 cases), respectively. They also distinguished between jobs with high, moderate, and low exposures. When a life-table regression analysis was performed on these data, risk appeared to be significantly ($p < 0.05$) higher for high-exposure jobs than for the others. The reliability of this assessment is low because of the small total number of cases (8).

In summary, increased risk for prostatic cancer among cadmium workers has only been found in studies involving a small number of cases. In studies on more cases (23–31), no increased risk was found (Armstrong and Kazantis, 1983, 1985; Doll, 1984). The only studies that have related the level of exposure to cadmium with prostatic cancer risk suggested a positive dose–response relationship, but the number of cases (8) was too low in one study (Sorahan and Waterhouse, 1983) to attach significance to the finding, while in the other study (Armstrong and Kazantis, 1985) no statistical significance was found for the elevated risks. In addition, it is important to note that workers in cadmium-using industries, battery and alloy plants and cadmium smelters, are also exposed to a number of other substances, such as nickel, arsenic, zinc, and copper (Kjellstrom *et al.*, 1979; Piscator, 1981; Sorahan and Waterhouse, 1983; Thun *et al.*, 1985), that may pose a health hazard.

Among men who are not occupationally exposed to cadmium and who are nonsmokers, the major source of exposure to cadmium is through food contaminated with cadmium (Piscator, 1981). Therefore, additional information concerning cadmium and prostatic cancer is given in Section IV,A,7,c on dietary factors. Animal studies and other experimental data on the effects of cadmium are also summarized in that section.

4. *Iron and Steel Foundry Workers*

There are some indications that iron and steel foundry workers are at increased risk for prostatic cancer. In a single study in United States steel workers, relative risks of 1.91–2.20 for prostatic cancer, depending on duration of employment in the job, were found in white foundry workers (Redmond *et al.*, 1981). This elevation in risk was statistically significant ($p < 0.05$). In this study a total of 58,821 steelworkers were followed from 1953 to 1975. The number of prostatic cancer cases in the group of foundry workers and the size of this group were not indicated in this report. The total number of prostatic cancer cases in all job categories in the study population was 278. In a number of other studies on foundry workers, this increased risk was not found (Decoufle and Wood, 1979; Egan-Baum *et al.*, 1981; Egan *et al.*, 1979; IARC, 1984; Koskela *et al.*, 1976). For example, Egan-Baum and co-workers (1981) studied a United States cohort of 2990 foundry workers, of which 339 were Blacks. A proportionate mortality ratio (PMR) of 88 was found for Whites (47 cases), and Blacks showed a PMR of 110 (10 cases). There are no animal data on exposure to the foundry environment available. These data led the IARC (1984) to conclude that 'there is inadequate evidence that exposures in iron and steel founding result in cancers of the genito-urinary system," including the prostate.

5. *Miscellaneous Occupations and Occupational Exposures*

In England, SMRs of 194–340 have been found for jobs in the armed forces (Logan, 1982). Also, in the United States, members of the armed forces seem to be at increased risk for prostatic cancer (Mandel and Schuman, 1980). It is not known whether specific occupational exposures are associated with this high risk or whether life-style factors are involved. Further epidemiologic studies on this occupational group seem warranted, and dietary variables, sexual factors (venereal diseases?), specific occupational exposures, and, in the United States, racial differences are likely to be of interest for such investigations.

For a large number of other occupations or jobs, an elevated risk has been reported in some studies but not in others (Hoar and Blair, 1984; Howe and Lindsay, 1983; Mandel and Schuman, 1980; Pearce *et al.*, 1987). An increased occurrence of prostatic cancer has been found in at least two studies, with no association found in only one other study for: higher administration/management/professionals (Adelstein, 1972; Howe and Lindsay, 1983; Mandel and Schuman, 1980; Logan, 1982; Pearce *et al.*, 1987), food/drinks/tobacco workers (Logan, 1982; Williams *et al.*, 1977), and for paper/printing workers (Logan, 1982; Ernster *et al.*, 1979b). Interestingly, Siemiatycki and co-workers (1986) reported an odds ratio for prostatic cancer of 1.9 ($p < 0.05$) for exposure to paper dust in their case-control study on cancer risk from organic dusts (300 cases and 1380 controls). This seems to support the finding of increased prostatic cancer risk among paper and printing workers.

B. Air Pollution

Two independent studies conducted in the United States indicated that prostatic cancer rates are highest in areas with a high level of pollution (Hagstrom *et al.*, 1967; Winkelstein and Kantor, 1969). A positive relation to the level of air pollution, measured as suspended particulate levels (Hagstrom *et al.*, 1967; Winkelstein and Kantor, 1969) or dustfall and sulfoxide levels (Hagstrom *et al.*, 1967) was found. This association was independent of age (Winkelstein and Kantor, 1969) or socioeconomic status (Hagstrom *et al.*, 1967; Winkelstein and Kantor, 1969). In both studies, prostatic cancer risk increased with increasing level of air pollution for Whites. For Blacks, risk did not seem to be related to the level of air pollution, but this observation was based on just a few cases (Hagstrom *et al.*, 1967). Interestingly, in a United States case-control study (111 age-matched pairs) patients significantly ($p < 0.02$) more often reported exposure to automobile exhaust as part of a consistent occupational pattern (Rotkin, 1977). A preliminary report of a case-control study in US Blacks presents a similar finding (Jackson *et al.*, 1981).

The association between the level of air pollution and prostatic cancer risk seems consistent with the higher risk found in urban areas than in rural areas (see Section II,G). However, these associations could be coincidental, because areas with high levels of air pollution, usually in urban regions, may, for example, have life-style patterns related to prostatic cancer risk that are different from (more rural) areas with low levels of pollution.

C. Other Non-Life-Style Environmental Factors

1. *Ionizing Radiation*

In studies (1959–1970) on survivors of the atomic bomb explosions in Hiroshima and Nagasaki, no increased occurrence of prostatic cancer was found (Beebe *et al.*, 1978; Mandel and Schuman, 1980). A detailed autopsy study on the prevalence of prostatic carcinoma in Japanese men from Hiroshima and Nagasaki was reported by Bean and co-workers (1973). Multiple sections of the prostate were examined in three groups of 71 age-matched men. One group was estimated to have received more than 100 rad, a second group was in Hiroshima or Nagasaki at the time the atomic bombs exploded, but did not receive radiation, while a third group was not in either of the two cities at the time of the explosions. Prostatic carcinomas (clinical plus latent) were found in 19, 20, and 19 men, respectively. An update of the data from Nagasaki for the period 1959–1978, however, suggests a slight excess of prostatic cancer in men exposed to heavy radiation (Wakabayashi *et al.*, 1983). Thus, there are some indications that ionizing radiation resulting from atomic bomb explosions may be related to prostatic cancer development in men. From experiments with mice that were exposed to atomic bomb-originated radiation, Upton and colleagues (1960) concluded that irradiation did not cause prostatic neoplasms under the conditions of their experiments. Only one prostatic carcinoma was found among the many hundreds of mice exposed to different types and intensities of irradiation.

In some studies with X ray exposure in rodents, however, prostatic carcinomas have been reported. Five out of 135 mice (3.7%), exposed to 8 times 1000 rad delivered to the pelvic region only, developed prostatic cancer (Hirose *et al.*, 1976). In further experiments with rats, it seemed that testosterone administration enhanced the development of X-ray-induced prostatic carcinomas, and castration had an inhibitory effect (Takizawa and Hirose, 1978). The carcinomas were found between 7 and 14 months after the start of the exposures. Control animals did not develop prostatic cancer. The latter experiments, however, are not convincing, because rats receiving X rays only did not develop prostatic carcinomas, and there was no group that received testosterone treatment only. Therefore, it is impossible to distinguish between the enhancement of the effect of irradiation by testosterone and the effects of testosterone alone. In other studies from the same group, Wistar, but not Sprague Dawley rats, did develop prostatic carcinomas upon repeated X-irradiation (Watanabe *et al.*, 1986). Another indication that X-ray exposure can cause prostatic cancer in rats was found in studies by Brown and Warren (1978) with parabiosed male rats, one of which received a single total body X-ray dose of 1000 rad. The incidence in the radiated rats was 25 of 1120 (2.2%), whereas in control rats 1 of 586 (0.2%) showed carcinomas of the prostate. The animals that died with tumors survived for an average of 16 months (range, 8 to 24 months) after irradiation. In men exposed to X rays for the treatment of spondylitis, no excess mortality due to prostatic cancer has been observed, but this was based on only a small number (9) of cases (Smith and Doll, 1982).

A few recent studies have addressed cancer mortality among workers in the nuclear industry. Beral *et al.* (1985) studied workers for the United Kingdom Atomic Energy Authority, and reported an SMR of 115, based on 15 cases. For workers with 10 or more years of employment, the SMR was 145 (12 cases). Significant positive associations were found between prostatic cancer rates and cumulative radiation exposure ($p < 0.001$ or, for a 15-year lagged analysis, $p <$ *0.01; linear trend test), exposure to tritium (SMR 5 889;* $p < 0.05$; 6 cases), other unspecified radiation (SMR = 254; $p < 0.05$; 9 cases), or any dosimeter reading exceeding 1 rem (SMR = 594; $p < 0.05$; 4 cases). The SMR for plutonium exposure was not significantly elevated (SMR = 152; 3 cases). Smith and Douglas (1986) studied a cohort of 11,402 men (60% were 'industrial" workers) employed at the UK Shellafield nuclear fuels plant. They found a nonsignificantly elevated SMR of 120 (19 cases) for prostatic cancer. Nonsignificantly elevated risks were also reported by Wilkinson *et al.*, (1987) for a cohort of 5413 white male plutonium and other radiation workers at a United States plutonium weapons facility. They found an SMR of 142, based on 8 prostatic cancer cases. They reported a relative risk of 3.74 for men with an overall estimated body burden of 2 nCi or more, which increased to 4.90 and 10.62 if an induction time was assumed of 5 and 10 years, respectively. Slight excesses in prostatic cancer risk have also been observed for uranium miners and radiologists (see Wilkinson *et al.*, 1987).

In conclusion, there are indications that exposure to ionizing radiation is related to the development of prostatic cancer in man but conclusive evidence is lacking. In rodents, X-ray irradiation can cause prostatic carcinomas. The relevance of the latter finding to human risk is not clear.

2. *Water Hardness*

From British studies it appears that a slight increase in prostatic cancer occurs in areas with hard water over that occurring in regions with soft water (Mandel and Schuman, 1980). This association is weak, however, and additional studies confirming or disproving a relation between prostatic cancer risk and water hardness are not available.

D. Discussion and Conclusions

Occupational factors that have most often been implicated in human prostatic carcinogenesis in the past are cadmium exposure and unspecified exposures in the rubber industry (IARC, 1982a,b; Piscator, 1981). From the preceding overview of occupational factors and prostatic cancer, however, it seems that these associations are more mythical than based on hard epidemiologic evidence. On the other hand, it cannot be completely ruled out that cadmium plays some role in prostatic carcinogenesis, as indicated in the discussion on dietary factors and prostatic cancer (Sections IV,A,7,c and D,1,c). A link between prostatic cancer risk and the rubber industry in general seems to be limited to a few specific plants in the United States studied by McMichael and co-workers. Workers who are involved in mixing and batch preparation procedures may be at increased risk for prostatic cancer, but the evidence for this is very limited. Animal studies have shown that prostatic cancer in rats can result from exposure to *N*-phenyl-2-naphthylamine (technical grade, but not purified), a widely used antioxidant in the rubber manufacturing process (IARC, 1982a). These studies support the view that exposure to some of the chemicals used in the rubber industry is a potential risk factor for prostatic cancer.

The increased risk found for farmers and farmworkers and for members of the armed forces seems more consistent than the elevated risk for cadmium exposure and rubber workers. There is, however, no information on specific chemical exposures in these groups that can be related to prostatic cancer. Furthermore, it is conceivable that their occupations can profoundly affect their life-style, and thus life-style factors may well be related to the increased risk for farmers and military employees. It is remarkable that farmers and farmworkers seem to be at increased risk, whereas men living in rural areas are generally at lower risk (see Section II,G). Further epidemiologic studies on prostatic cancer in farmers, farmworkers, and armed forces employees are clearly warranted. Particularly studies on chemical exposures and lifestyle in farmers and farmworkers are of interest, as are studies comparing different job categories in the armed forces, because there is such a great variation in jobs in the military.

The associations between prostatic cancer risk and the aforementioned occupational groups are rather weak. Reported relative risks or odds ratios and SMRs or SIRs were often distinctly lower than 2 and 200, respectively. In conclusion, there are indications for weak associations between prostatic cancer and a number of very different job categories. In addition, there are indications that prostatic cancer risk is positively related to the level of particulate air pollution and that risk is higher in urban areas than in rural areas. Thus, in general, it seems that exposure to potentially carcinogenic chemical factors, either from occupational or environmental sources, is a weak risk factor for prostatic cancer. However, no specific chemical exposures have been identified as being related to prostatic cancer risk in man. In addition, there are data indicating that exposure to ionizing radiation (in any form) is a risk factor for prostatic cancer as well.

The prostate gland is probably capable of metabolizing a wide variety of chemicals, including chemical carcinogens. Studies in the rat ventral prostate indicate the presence of a number of drug-metabolizing enzymes that are probably cytochrome P-450-associated, enzymes that can activate chemical carcinogens—aryl hydrocarbon hydroxylase, 7-ethoxyresorufin-*O*-deethylase and epoxide hydratase—and detoxifying enzymes—epoxide hydrolase, glutathione-*S*-transferase, and UDP-glucuronosyltransferase (Lee *et al.*, 1981; Soderkvist *et al.*, 1982; Suzuki and Lee, 1981). These enzymes can be induced, sometimes to a remarkable extent, by compounds such as β-naphthoflavone, 1,2-dibromo-3-chloropropane, Arochlor 1254, and 2,3,7,8-tetrachlorodibenzo-*p*-dioxin (TCDD) (Lee *et al.*, 1981; Soderkvist *et al.*, 1982; Suzuki and Lee, 1981). The same enzymes are present in a 5000 g supernatant from the rat ventral prostate, and they are capable of metabolizing benzo[*a*]pyrene (BaP) (Soderkvist *et al.*, 1983). The 5000 *g* fraction of rat ventral prostate is also capable of activating aflatoxin B_1, 2-acetylaminofluorene (2-AAF), and BaP in the Ames' *Salmonella*/microsome assay (Soderkvist *et al.*, 1983). A variety of chemical carcinogens can be taken up by the rat and the dog prostate, as shown by Smith and co-workers (Smith and Hagopian, 1977, 1981; Smith *et al.*, 1977): 3-methylcholanthrene, 7,12-dimethylbenz[*a*]anthracene (DMBA), aflatoxin B_1, *N*-hydroxyurethane, 2-AAF, 3-amino-1,2,4-triazole, *N*-methyl-*N'*-nitro-*N*-nitrosoguanidine (MNNG), and cadmium. Most of these compounds were more readily taken up by the rat dorsolateral prostate than by the ventral prostate; only DMBA and *N*-hydroxyurethane were taken up in higher concentrations in the ventral than in the dorsolateral lobe. With the exception of cadmium, all compounds were also secreted by the rat and canine prostate, as determined by their appearance in the prostatic fluid. This may be a route of exposure of the prostatic epithelium to such compounds. Interestingly, an androgen-dependent protein in the rat ventral prostate (prostatic binding protein) capable of binding DMBA and BaP has been described by McKeehan and Fast (1981). Organochlorine insecticides, such as DDT and dieldrin, also are capable of binding to proteins in the rat ventral prostate (Visek, 1981). This protein is similar or perhaps identical to prostatic secretory protein identified some time ago in the rat ventral prostate (Forsgren *et al.*, 1979a,b) as indicated by studies by Soderkvist *et al.* (1986). These authors also found binding of TCDD to this protein, but another TCDD-binding protein was also identified in the ventral prostate with characteristics of the TCDD receptor. Further studies (Soderkvist and Poellinger, 1987) suggested that the carcinogen-binding protein may be involved in the intracellular transfer of TCDD-like ligands to the TCDD receptor protein, resulting in a receptor-mediated toxic response in the prostate. DDT and dieldrin can also interfere with androgen uptake and metabolism in the rat ventral prostate and the mouse coagulating gland (= anterior prostate) (Schein and Thomas, 1975, 1976; Thomas *et al.*, 1973) and with the binding of 5α-dihydrotestosterone to the ventral prostatic androgen receptor, probably in a noncompetitive manner (Visek, 1981).

Unfortunately, very few studies have been done on drug metabolism in the human prostate. Kahng *et al.* (1981a,b) reported studies with explants and explant-derived cell lines from human prostatic tissue obtained from one young adult without prostatic pathology and 4–8 BHP patients, as well as from one carcinomatous prostate. Both cells and explants demonstrated aryl hydrocarbon hydroxylase activity that was inducible *in vitro* by BaP and, to a lesser degree, DMBA, but not by MNNG. Cells from BHP patients were more susceptible to enzyme induction than the cell line from the normal subject, whereas the explants from the carcinomatous prostate were much less susceptible to induction than the BHP explants were. DMBA was able to bind to the DNA of cells from three different normal subjects (Kahng *et al.*, 1981b). In studies by Sinquin and co-workers (1984) using homogenates from 6 BHP prostates, cadmium addition to the homogenates significantly increased the 5α-reduction of testosterone and inhibited the formation of the 3α- and 3β-reduced metabolites of 5α-dihydrotestosterone. In accordance with these observations, the V_m of 5α-reductase was increased and the V_m of 3α-/3β-hydroxysteroid dehydrogenase was decreased. This probably resulted in increased levels of 5α-dihydrotestosterone in the prostate. Favino *et al.* (1968) studied the urinary excretion of androgens in ten men occupationally exposed to cadmium. There was no difference with ten age-matched controls. However, one of the ten exposed men appeared to be impotent and showed a distinctly lower urinary androgen excretion than the other men. It was not clear whether this was related to the cadmium exposure in that man.

All these studies indicate that the rat ventral prostate and also, perhaps, the human prostate are capable of accumulating, secreting, metabolizing, and binding a wide variety of chemical carcinogens and noncarcinogenic chemicals, and that some of these chemicals can affect hormonal processes in the prostate and, perhaps, at the level of the entire organism. This supports the earlier conclusion that exposure to a wide variety of chemical carcinogens can be regarded as a risk factor for prostatic cancer.

VI. Endogenous Factors: The Hormonal System

The prostate is a hormone-dependent gland. Androgenic and estrogenic steroids, prolactin, growth hormone, and possibly also insulin, corticosteroids, and others play a role in the normal development and function of the prostate gland (Coffey, 1979; Griffiths *et al.*, 1979). Castration or estrogen treatment causes temporary regression of many prostatic carcinomas and their metastases (see Section I). There is anecdotal information that prostatic cancer does not occur in eunuchs (Lipsett, 1979). There are, however, some reports that in castrated dogs prostatic cancer can ocasionally develop (Dube *et al.*, 1984; Evans *et al.*, 1985). Liver cirrhosis is associated with a decreased risk for prostatic cancer (see Section IV,A,4,a). This is possibly related to impaired estrogen clearance and altered androgen metabolism in cirrhotic patients. The resulting estrogen/androgen imbalances may be causally related to the development of prostatic cancer (Chopra *et al.*, 1973; Gordon *et al.*, 1975; Robson, 1966; Southren *et al.*, 1973). Studies on the endocrine status of prostatic cancer patients in comparison with healthy controls have have not yielded a clear insight in the etiological importance of hormones (Flanders, 1986; Griffiths *et al.*, 1979, Rose, 1986). Differences have been reported in the urinary excretion of sex-steroid metabolites (Marmorston *et al.*, 1965a,b) in plasma levels of these steroids and of prolactin and luteinizing hormone (Bartsch *et al.*, 1977; Ghanadian and Puah, 1981; Ghanadian *et al.*, 1979; Habib *et al.*, 1976b, 1979; Hammond *et al.*, 1978; Hill *et al.*, 1982; Rannikko *et al.*, 1981; Rannikko and Adlercreutz, 1983; Saroff *et al.*, 1980), in levels of these hormones in prostatic fluid (Rose *et al.*, 1984), and in the metabolism and binding of androgens in prostatic carcinomas as compared with normal or BHP tissue (Bruchovsky *et al.*, 1980; Krieg *et al.*, 1979). These data are difficult to interpret, and they provide no information that is pertinent to the *genesis* of prostatic cancer as such. Moreover, the disease and its treatment may well influence the endocrine parameters measured in these studies (Habib *et al.*, 1976b; Saroff *et al.*, 1980) and there are a number of other potential sources of bias as summarized by Flanders (1986). The selection of proper controls for these studies is very difficult and may be the greatest sources of variation among studies as discussed by Rose (1986).

Because prostatic cancer is a disease of old age, several investigators have postulated a relation between the development of prostatic cancer and changes in endocrine patterns with aging. Griffiths and coworkers (1979) and Rose (1986) have summarized most of these studies. With few exceptions, plasma levels of testosterone, particularly free testosterone, seem to decline with aging, especially after age 50 (Vermeulen *et al.*, 1972). There are, however, conflicting data and most studies do not indicate large differences (Griffiths *et al.*, 1979: Rose, 1986). Although steroid metabolism in the prostate seems to decrease with aging (Griffiths *et al.*, 1979), tissue levels of testosterone and 5α-dihydrotestosterone in the prostate remain remarkably stable during life (Hammond, 1978). Serum levels of sex-hormone-binding protein and 17β-estradiol, on the other hand, increase with aging (Griffiths *et al.*, 1979), but conflicting data have also been reported (Rose, 1986). Griffiths and colleagues (1979) suggested that there is individual variation in the decline of testosterone levels, which may be related to interindividual variation in prostatic cancer risk. On the other hand, because tissue testosterone levels seem to remain constant with aging, other factors may play a more important role, such as increasing estradiol levels, leading to an estrogen/androgen imbalance.

There are some studies that have investigated endocrine differences in populations that differ in risk for prostatic cancer. Urinary excretion of androgens and estrogens is lower in low-risk (South) African Blacks than in high-risk populations, North American Blacks or Whites (Hill *et al.*, 1979, 1980b, 1981) and European Whites (Clifford and Bulbrook, 1966). The ratio of urinary estrogens to androgens has been reported to be higher and the androsterone:etiocholanolone ratio to be lower in low-risk populations (Jamaicans and South African Blacks) than in North American Blacks and Whites (Hill *et al.*, 1979; Vestergaard, 1978). Plasma estrogens, particularly estrone, were higher in South African Blacks than in North American Blacks of comparable age (40–55 years), whereas plasma testosterone and dehydroepiandrosterone levels were similar (Hill *et al.*, 1980a,b). Plasma levels of androstenedione were higher in South African Blacks than in North American Blacks, as were levels of follicle-stimulating hormone but not levels of luteinizing hormone. In black Nigerian prostatic cancer patients and healthy controls, however, plasma testosterone levels were lower than black United States prostatic cancer patients and controls, whereas there were no differences in plasma levels of estrogens and prolactin (Ahluwalia *et al.*, 1981; Jackson *et al.*, 1977).

Black and white North American men have been compared endocrinologically in a number of studies by Hill and co-workers (Hill *et al.*, 1979a, 1980a,b, 1984) and in a study by Ross and colleagues (1986). Hill and co-workers studied men between 40 and 55 years of age and boys between 12 and 15 years. The differences in plasma hormone levels between Whites and Blacks were somewhat different in the two age groups. Androstenedione was higher in Blacks than in Whites at 12 to 13 years, but not different at older ages. Dehydroepiandrosterone, a precursor of androstenedione, on the other hand, was lower in Blacks than in Whites at ages 13 and 40–55, but not different at ages 12 and 14–15. Testosterone, which can be formed from both aforementioned androgenic steroids, was not different at ages 12–15, and tended to be somewhat higher in Blacks than Whites at ages 40–55. Plasma levels of luteinizing hormone were consistently higher in Blacks than in Whites in all age groups, whereas there were no differences for follicle-stimulating hormone. Plasma levels of 17β-estradiol were lower in Blacks than in Whites at ages 12–14, higher at age 15, and there was no Black–White difference at ages 40–55. Estrone, on the other hand, and prolactin were higher in Blacks than in Whites at ages 40–55 (not measured at ages 12–15). In men of 40–55 years old, urinary steroid excretion was also measured (Hill *et al.*, 1979). Blacks had a higher urinary output of estrogens than Whites, but lower excretion of androgens. Their urinary ratio of estrogens to androgens was also lower than in Whites, but the ratio of androsterone to etiocholanolone was comparable.

Ross *et al.* (1986) took blood samples from 20-year-old US Blacks and Whites. Plasma levels of testosterone, both total and free, and of estrone were significantly higher in Blacks than in Whites. There were no differences for 17β-estradiol. These observations are consistent with the findings by Hill and colleagues for 40- to 55-year-old men. It is of interest that some of the endocrine dissimilarities between low-risk and high-risk populations were different when South African Blacks were compared with North American Whites and Blacks than for the comparison between North American Blacks and Whites. Urinary excretion of androgenic steroids was higher in North American Whites than Blacks, but lower in South African Blacks than in North American men. Plasma levels of estrone were lower in North American Whites than in Blacks, but higher in South African Blacks than in North American men. Plasma levels of luteinizing hormone were lower in North American white men than in either black group and similar in North American and South African Blacks. Follicle-stimulating hormone and androstenedione levels, on the other hand, were higher in South African Blacks than in both North American groups and not different in Whites and Blacks in the United States (Hill et al., 1980b, 1984). These apparent inconsistencies seem to suggest that the factors or endocrine mechanisms that determine the differences in risk between African Blacks and North American Blacks and Whites, on the one hand, and between North American Blacks and Whites, on the other, are dissimilar. The only more or less consistent finding is that in high-risk populations plasma levels of testosterone and luteinizing hormone are somewhat higher than in low-risk populations and they are never lower. These findings suggest that a higher pituitary luteinizing hormone secretion and a resulting higher testosterone production are associated with higher risk for prostatic cancer.

Interestingly, the endocrine differences that have been found between US Blacks and Whites in these studies are smaller than the differences that Hill and co-workers (1980b, 1984) found between North American men and South African Blacks, both at the ages of 40–55 and 12–15. This finding correlates with the difference in risk for prostatic cancer that is much larger between South African black men and North American men (3- to 4-fold) than between Blacks and Whites in the United States (1.5- to 2-fold). Unfortunately, there are no endocrine data from migrant studies (e.g., on Japanese) available.

Meikle and co-workers (Meikle and Stanish, 1982; Meikle *et al.*, 1985) determined an endocrinological profile of prostatic cancer cases, their brothers and sons, and of controls matched for age and a large number of other variables. No data, however, were available on a possible family history of prostatic cancer from the controls. Patients and their brothers and their controls were approximately 45–75 (mean, 58) years old, their sons were 24–42 (mean, 32) years old, and their controls 22–43 (mean, 36) years. Plasma levels of testosterone were significantly ($p < 0.025$–0.001) lower in the patients and their brothers and sons than in the controls. Its direct metabolite, 5α-dihydrotestosterone, however, was higher in patients and their relatives, but this was only significant for the sons ($p < 0.02$). No differences were found for estrone and 17β-estradiol. These data suggest that endocrine mechanisms may underlie a genetic predisposition for prostatic cancer in men with a family history of prostatic cancer. These data are, however, contrary to those found in the preceding studies in various black and white populations, in which high levels of plasma testosterone seemed to be associated with higher risk. This may suggest that the endocrine factors related to familial aggregation of prostatic cancer risk are different from those associated with differences in risk between populations that differ in life-style and/or ethnic background.

Animal studies on hormonal induction of prostatic cancer support a hypothesis that hormones are involved in prostatic carcinogenesis. Long-term, high-dose treatment with testosterone propionate (Noble, 1977, 1982; Pollard and Luckert, 1985, 1986; Pollard *et al.*, 1982), a combination of testosterone propionate and estrone (Noble, 1977, 1982) and a combination of testosterone and 17β-estradiol (Drago, 1984) resulted in the formation of prostatic carcinomas in the dorsolateral prostate in rats. It may be that this response is limited to only the Nb strain and the Lobund-Wistar strain (Pollard and Luckert, 1985; Pollard *et al.*, 1982), but definite evidence for such strain specificity is, in my opinion, lacking at present. The response in the Nb rat has been shown by two laboratories, whereas the studies with the other rat strain have only been reported by one research group. In the studies by Pollard and co-workers and by Drago, a prostatic cancer incidence of approximately 40% was found, while Noble (1977, 1982) found incidences between 15 and 20%. However, when a 1-year treatment with testosterone propionate was followed by treatment with estrone, Noble (1982) found an incidence of 50% prostatic cancer. When he gave estrone first and then testosterone, the incidence was below 10%. These studies indicate that in rats, testosterone administration can induce prostatic cancer and that subsequent estrogen treatment can enhance this effect. From studies in dogs, it appears that in addition to androgens, estrogens are involved in the regulation of cellular differentiation of the prostatic epithelium (Leav *et al.*, 1978; Merk *et al.*, 1982, 1986). Although a role for estrogen in the physiology and pathology of the prostate is currently undefined, it has long been known that circulating pharmacological levels of the hormone will induce a proliferative epithelial change termed squamous metaplasia. It has been shown that squamous metaplastic changes result from a direct estrogen effect on the prostate as the lesion can be induced in hypophysectomized dogs treated with pharmacological doses of the hormone (Leav *et al.*, 1978). Direct effects of estrogens on rodent prostatic explant cultures have been described (Lasnitski, 1974), and there are estrogen receptors in the human prostate (Coffey, 1979; Griffiths *et al.*, 1979). Ofner *et al.* (1979) and Isaacs and Coffey (1981) have shown that estrogen inhibits hydroxylation reactions which represent the terminal component of the catabolic 3β-hydroxysteroid egress pathway that generates biologically inactive androgen metabolites. Similarly, Isaacs and Coffey (1981) have reported that 17β-estradiol, administered together with biologically potent 5α-reduced 17β-hydroxysteroids to castrated or intact dogs, can alter the activities of key enzymes involved in prostatic 5α-dihydrotestosterone catabolism so as to favor the net intraglandular formation of this androgen. Studies by Merk *et al.* (1982, 1986) have shown that combinations of androgens and estrogens administered to castrated dogs caused marked proliferation of both basal-reserve and glandular cells (as assessed by the mitotic arrest method), which greatly exceeded the response due to either hormone given separately, and induced the formation of a new epithelial cell type. On the other hand, Barrack and Berry (1987) found that in the dog prostate, estrogen alone can cause a higher level of *in vitro* incorporation of tritiated thymidine into total prostatic DNA than did testosterone alone, while the combined treatment with both hormones reduced the incorporation of thymidine. The explanation for these contradictory results is not clear. Merk *et al.* (1982, 1986) further reported that other prostatic responses to this dual hormone treatment were increased testosterone metabolism and changes in some biochemical measures of androgen activation, which reflected separate actions of the sex hormones.

In conclusion, there are some indications that elevated circulating levels of androgens are associated with increased risk for prostatic cancer. However, the evidence for this is limited, and there are no data available on endocrine events at the level of the prostatic epithelial cell that can be related to prostatic cancer risk. There is, on the other hand, strong circumstantial evidence that hormones are somehow involved in prostatic carcinogenesis, because it is a hormonally sensitive cancer that develops from a hormonally dependent tissue. Animal studies and other experimental data strongly support a hormonal hypothesis and seem to point to a role for estrogens as well as androgens. It is, however, obscure which hormones are critically involved, and how and when during the carcinogenic process they are important. There is clearly a need for more information, particularly from studies in high-risk populations and from whole animal and *in vitro experiments, both at the level of the target cell and at the level of the entire organism.*

VII. Concluding Remarks

In this review of the epidemiological and experimental data on prostatic carcinogenesis, a number of factors have been identified as positively associated with human prostatic cancer risk. They are summarized in Table XIII in decreasing order of probable importance. These factors can be regarded as risk factors in the sense that they are positively associated with human prostatic cancer risk, but for none of them has a causative relationship been established. Hormones are not indicated as a risk factor in Table XIII. Although, as demonstrated in Section VI, it is very likely that hormones do play an important if not crucial role in human prostatic

TABLE XIII

SUMMARY OF FACTORS AND CONDITIONS ASSOCIATED WITH ELEVATED RISK FOR PROSTATIC CANCER IN DECREASING ORDER OF IMPORTANCE

Being Black and living in the United States (particularly when unmarried)
Living in a Western country and having a Western life-style
A high intake of dietary fat, protein, and energy (calories)
A family history of prostatic cancer
A history of venereal disease
Being a farmer or farmworker or an employee of the armed forces
Exposure to potentially carcinogenic chemicals and perhaps ionizing radiation
Being overweight or obese

carcinogenesis, it is not clear which hormones are critically involved, and how they act. Elevated plasma and perhaps tissue levels of testosterone, and, at older ages, elevated estrogen levels are the most likely candidates among the hormonal factors to be possibly involved. Endocrine factors are potential mediators of the various life-style variables that influence prostatic carcinogenesis (see Section IV.D). Particularly, diet appears to be capable of modifying endocrine patterns in healthy male subjects.

Environmental factors almost certainly play a much more prominent role in prostatic carcinogenesis than endogenous factors, such as genetic predisposition (see Section II). In fact, as indicated above, endocrine factors and possibly even familial aggregation of prostatic cancer can in part be modified by the environment. A Western environment, particularly a Western life-style, appears to be associated with increased risk for prostatic cancer. Overconsumption of dietary fat, protein, and energy are rather strongly associated with this increased risk as indicated by epidemiological studies and, in the case of fat, some animal exeriments. The possible positive association between risk and obesity may be related to this overconsumption pattern. Occupational exposure to chemicals and exposure to pollution and ionizing radiation may also be involved in the higher risk found in Western countries than in less affluent areas. Specific chemical factors, however, have as yet not been identified. Venereal disease and perhaps also prostatitis, which is often related to sex-induced infections, are specifically associated with increased risk. Other factors related to sexual behavior, such as sexual drive and activity, have also been implicated (see Section IV.B).

Prostatic cancer is unique in that it is known at which stage of the carcinogenic process the majority of the aforementioned environmental determinants probably act. The studies on the prevalence of latent carcinoma of the prostate in populations that differ in risk for clinical prostatic cancer clearly indicate that the environment probably acts at the stage of progression from early, small, noninvasive cancers (LNT) to more advanced, larger, and invasively growing carcinomas (LIT). Detailed studies of the age-specific prevalence of these two types of latent prostatic cancer in populations at different risk for clinical cancer should enable one to determine whether this is so. The age-specific prevalence curves of LNT tumors in low- and high-risk populations should be similar at younger ages and at older ages perhaps start to diverge, whereas the curves for LIT tumors should be very different from the beginning. The data presented by Yatani *et al.* (1982) and particularly those reported by Akazaki and Stemmermann (1973) suggest that this is probably indeed the case. Very interesting is also the observation that the age distribution for latent prostatic cancer is very similar to that of most other male and female cancers, but that the age distribution of clinical prostatic cancer, as also indicated in Section II,H, is very different in that it starts at a later age, and progresses much more rapidly (Cohen and Dix, 1985). This may suggest that the environmental determinants of prostatic cancer are increasingly effective in enhancing the progression from latent cancer to invasive clinical cancer with increasing duration of "exposure" to them. Alternatively, the lag phase between the development of latent cancer and the development of clinical cancer can be the explanation for this unique age distribution as argued by Cohen and Dix (1985). Perhaps the very high prevalence of latent prostatic cancer, that displays the same age distribution as most other cancers, is related to this peculiar age distribution of clinical prostatic cancer. If the latent cancer is the precursor of the clinical prostatic cancer, the latent cancer has to develop first, and then additional steps in the carcinogenic process, assumably not required for the genesis of most human cancers, have to occur leading to progression to invasive, metastasizing cancer.

US Blacks have the highest risk for prostatic cancer worldwide. It is not understood at present why this is so. Interestingly, US Blacks are in fact a migrant population. They were forcefully brought from Africa to the United States. To date, as most likely also in the days of the slave trade, African Blacks have a very low risk for prostatic cancer, although this has not been documented very well. A second migration, from rural areas to the big cities, took place in the first half of this century. This migration was accompanied by a dramatic increase in prostatic cancer rates in the black population. Thus, environmental determinants of prostatic cancer risk almost certainly play a major role in the extremely high rates among US Blacks today. The shift in the relation between marital status and risk in Blacks during the last decades, from singles having the lowest risk to singles having the highest risk, supports this. However, it is also possible that Blacks are by genetic predisposition more susceptible to risk-enhancing factors than Caucasians.

It is not known what the critical factors are that enhance prostatic cancer risk in US Blacks 2-fold over the risk in US Whites. Differences in life-style between US Blacks and Whites have unfortunately not been well studied; more research on this topic is highly warranted. Blacks in the United States differ environmentally from Whites in terms of economic factors. Unemployment among Blacks is at least twice as high as in Whites, and consequently poverty is more common in the black population; in fact between 1973 and 1983, three times as many Blacks as Whites were living below the official poverty level (Bread for the World, 1985), and Blacks constitute an even more disproportionally large fraction of the poor in United States cities (Shotland, 1986). Still, Blacks only make up some 10–11% of the United States population. Poverty is clearly a causative factor in under- and malnutrition in the United States (Bread for the World, 1985; Blaxter, 1983; Physicians Task Force on Hunger in America, 1985; Shotland, 1986). Infant mortality and low birth weight rates are twice as high among US Blacks as among US Whites; both are clearly related to under- or malnutrition (Physicians Task Force on Hunger in America, 1985). The rural poor in the United States have a deteriorated nutritional status, both Blacks and Whites as shown by Shotland (1986). In this study based on data from the Second National Health and Nurition Examination Survey (NHANES II), rural Blacks in general (poor and nonpoor) distinctly more often than Whites consumed less than two-thirds of the recommended daily allowance of calcium, iron, niacin, riboflavin, and phosphorus, and they had more often than Whites low serum levels of zinc. Similar data on urban Blacks have not been reported to my knowledge, but it has been observed that the zinc status in elderly low-income urban Blacks is often suboptimal (Wagner *et al.*, 1980). Mettlin (1980) reported that, based on data taken from NHANES I, Blacks, regardless of their age, less frequently consume fats and oils and fruits and vegetables than do Whites, and approximately equally frequently meats and poultry and eggs. This all strongly suggests that, on the average, US Blacks differ in some ways in dietary habits from US Whites, resulting in a higher frequency of poor nutritional status, and that this is related to their deprived economic situation. One hypothetical explanation of the higher prostatic cancer rate in Blacks than in Whites in the United States could be that their generally higher frequency of suboptimal or poor nutritional status is somehow causally related to their higher risk. This speculation seems in contradiction to the lower risk observed in countries that are less affluent than the United States and to the lower consumption of fats and oils by US Blacks (see earlier). However, one should realize that undernutrition in a developing country is likely to be of quite a different nature from undernutrition in the poor in an otherwise highly affluent country. Furthermore, a lower consumption of fats and oils does not mean a lower intake of total fat—very likely a risk factor for prostatic cancer—because this is largely determined by the consumption of fatty foods.

Another difference between Blacks and Whites in the United States is that, as indicated earlier, Blacks are more likely than Whites to live in communities with hazardous waste facilities of uncontrolled toxic waste sites (Commission for Racial Justice, 1987), and are much more likely to have jobs with a high exposure to potentially carcinogenic chemicals (Davis, 1980; Michaels, 1983). In the studies by McMichael and co-workers (1976b) on cancer mortality among rubber workers, only 3% of the Whites were employed in mixing and compounding, whereas 27% of the Blacks worked there. These processes are the only ones in the rubber industry that were associated in some studies with an elevated risk for prostatic cancer (see Section V,A,2). Blacks are also highly represented in agriculture and foundries, both perhaps associated with increased risk (see Section V,A). It is at present not clear whether the exposures in these worksites and industries contribute to the high prostatic cancer rates among Blacks or whether the higher risks observed in these worksites and industries are due to the large presence of black workers, who are already at high risk for prostatic cancer. Given the indications that in general, exposure to potential carcinogens is related to increased risk for prostatic cancer (see Section V), the former reasoning is more likely than the latter. Furthermore, increased risk has been found among some predominantly or exclusively white populations of foundry and agricultural workers (Burmeister, 1981; Redmond *et al.*, 1981). Clearly this is an area that deserves more research.

As suggested previously (Bosland, 1985; Zumoff *et al.*, 1982), it may be that there are two types of prostatic cancer, as has been demonstrated for breast cancer (De Waard, 1979). The two types would probably differ primarily in their etiology rather than in their clinical behavior or morphology. This "two-disease" hypothesis is based on the following observations. In case-control studies that distinguished between younger (<70 years) and older patients (>70 years), dietary associations with prostatic cancer were found only for the older age group, primarily with respect to the intake of fat and Vitamin A (Graham *et al.*, 1983; Kolonel *et al.*, 1983, 1987). Endocrine effects of dietary changes in healthy South African black men were different for a 40–55 year age group than for men of 70 years and older (see Section VI,D,1,d; Hill *et al.*, 1982). Plasma levels of testosterone and 5α-dihydrotestosterone were lower in 55- to 64-year-old patients than in age-matched controls, but equal to control values in 65- to 80-year-old patients in a study by Zumoff and associates (1982). In this study, plasma testosterone levels increased significantly with age ($p < 0.01$) in prostatic cancer patients, whereas they decreased with age in control subjects ($p < 0.025$). Studies that attempted to estimate the latency period for prostatic cancer, i.e., the time between the beginning of exposure to a hypothetical causative agent and the clinical detection of the disease, also indicate that there may be different etiologies of prostatic cancer that are associated with different latency times. Cook and co-workers (1969) calculated a latent period for prostatic cancer of 45 years after the beginning of exposure to a hypothetical carcinogenic agent, which would, as they estimated, start at approximately age 32. The association between a gonorrhea epidemic in Denmark and peak prostatic cancer rates some 45 years later suggested by Heshmat *et al.* (1973, 1975) also points to a latent period of 45 years. Goldsmith *et al.* (1980), on the other hand, calculated a latent period of "only" 29 years for rubber workers employed in batch preparation and Lemen *et al.* (1976) estimated a latency of time of 28 years for 4 prostatic cancer cases among cadmium smelter workers. These two quite different estimates could suggest that depending on whether there is a specific continued heavy chemical exposure contributing to the development of prostatic cancer or whether development of the cancers primarily depends on enhancement by life-style factors, as might be assumed to occur in the general population, the latent period is shorter or longer, respectively. These interesting observations all suggest the possibility that the etiology of prostatic cancers that occur at younger ages can be different from what might occur at older ages.

Meikle and colleagues (Meikle and Stanish, 1982; Meikle *et al.*, 1985) found a relation between familial aggregation of prostatic cancer and lower testosterone plasma levels than in controls. A number of other studies (see Section VI), on the other hand, strongly suggest a relation between increased risk and testosterone levels that are higher than expected. This would suggest that genetic predisposition for prostatic cancer involves mechanisms that are different from those that are related to development of prostatic cancer in men that are not genetically predisposed.

In conclusion, environmental factors are related to prostatic cancer risk. They are likely to act as enhancers of the progression of prostatic cancer. Specific causative factors have not been identified. It is, in my opinion, unlikely that none of the observed positive associations is causatively related to prostatic cancer risk, either in a direct or an indirect manner. Attractive candidates for a causative relation are nutritional variables (particularly intake of fat, protein, and energy), certain endocrine patterns (involving particularly androgens), and sex-related factors (for example, venereal disease). There are many intriguing observations with respect to prostatic cancer, most notably the extremely high incidence in US Blacks, the possible positive association between risk and vitamin A intake, and the indications for a "two-disease" theory. In Fig. 1, an etiological hypothesis is presented, which is based on the assumption that there is a sequence of events starting with initiation, and leading to the formation of first LNT and then LIT tumors, and finally clinical prostatic cancer. It shows that both the normal prostate and most prostatic carcinomas are hormone dependent. It also shows that a variety of factors can (potentially) cause or influence initiation and promotion of prostatic cancer, but that life-style factors, particularly diet and nutrition, and, probably to a lesser extent, sexual factors are critical determinants of the progression of early cancers to carcinomas that will develop into clinical prostatic cancer. Genetic factors that may predispose the gland to neoplastic derangement and endocrine factors that may be the mediators of some or several of the etiological factors are also indicated. The data that form the basis for this hypothesis, however, are not very definitive or detailed, as indicated earlier. Also this hypothesis is—necessarily—an oversimplification and does not include the "two-disease" theory.

Much more research is needed to further understand the etiopathogenesis of human prostatic cancer. Studies regarding diet and nutrition, sexual factors, and endocrine variables have particular potential. Also, comparative studies in US Blacks and Whites, especially case-control studies, as well as prospective studies using latent prostatic cancer as an end point (autopsy), rather than clinical prostatic cancer, would be very fruitful. The extremely

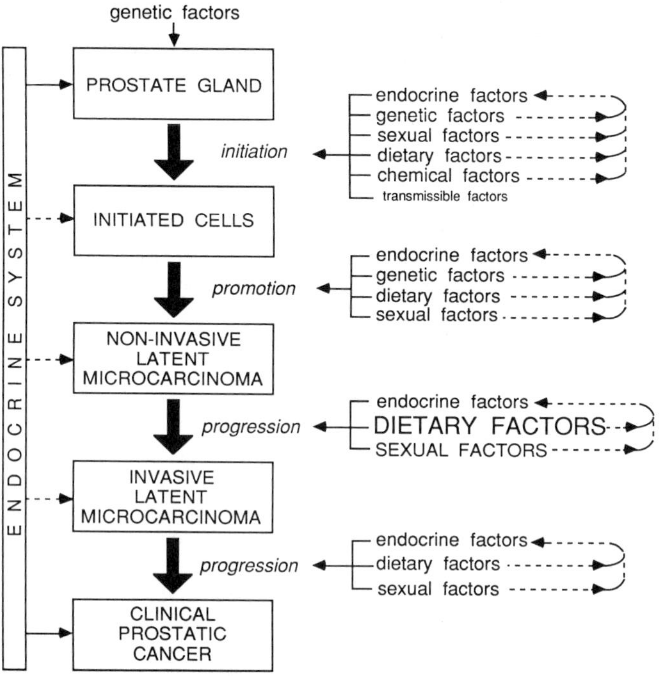

FIG. 1. Hypothesis of the etiopathogenesis of human prostatic cancer and of the contribution of environmental factors to prostatic carcinogenesis. The more important a particular factor is assumed to be, the larger the letter size is in this figure. Relations that are more speculative are indicated with interrupted lines.

high risk of US black males highly warrants further detailed epidemiological research on this population. Future research should not be restricted to known or heavily suspected risk factors, such as dietary fat and vitamin A, and to epidemiology. It should also explore newer avenues such as the possible influence of zinc, and the use of tissue culture of human prostatic tissue. Also, future investigations should include factors that were only weakly associated with prostatic cancer risk in previous investigations but may nevertheless be important in specific subpopulations, such as exposures to ionizing radiation and to chemicals in the rubber industry and other occupational situations. Further development of animal models for prostatic carcinogenesis is needed to enable testing of hypotheses derived from epidemiology. Only when more is known about the etiology of prostatic cancer will it be possible to develop a useful preventive strategy. Prevention may be particularly effective for prostatic cancer. Preventive measures against cancer in general are likely to shift the age distribution toward older ages, as has been shown for colorectal cancer (Phillips, 1980). Because prostatic cancer occurs chiefly in the very aged, such a shift in age distribution brought about by preventive measures might well result in an absolute decrease in mortality and morbidity due to this important human cancer.

Acknowledgments

I want to thank M. Freitag for secretarial assistance. This work was supported in part by grants from the Netherlands Cancer Foundation, "Koningin Wilhelmina Fonds," by Grant No. CA 43151 and Center Grant No. CA 13343, both from the National Cancer Institute, and by Center Grant No. ES 00260, from the National Institute of Environmental Health Sciences.

References

Alavanja, M. C. R., Rush, G. A., Stewart, P., and Blair, A. (1987) *J. Natl. Cancer Inst.* **78**, 247–252.

Adelstein, A. M. (1972). *Ann. Occup. Hyg.* **15**, 53–57.

Ahluwalia, B., Jackson, M. A., Jones, G. W., Williams, A. O., Rao, M. S., and Rajguru, S. (1981). *Cancer* **48**, 2267–2273.

Akazaki, K., and Stemmermann, G. M. (1973). *J. Natl. Cancer Inst.* **50**, 1137–1144.

Alexis, R., and Domingo, J. (1986). *Hum. Pathol.* **17**, 757–760.

Albert, S., and Child, M. (1977). *Cancer* **40**, 1674–1679.

Armstrong, B. G., and Kazantis, G. (1985). *Br. J. Indust. Med.* **42**, 540–545.

Andjelkovich, D., Taulbee, J., and Symons, M. (1976). *J. Occup. Med.* **18**, 387–394.

Andjelkovich, D., Taulbee, J., Symons, M., and Williams, T. (1977). *J. Occup. Med.* **19**, 397–403.

Araki, H., Mishina, T., Miyakoda, K., Fujiwara, T., and Kobayashi, T. (1980). *Tohuku J. Exp. Med.* **130**, 159–164.

Armenian, H. K., Lilienfeld, A. M., Diamond, D. L., and Bross, I. D. J. (1974). *Lancet* **2**, 115–117.

Armenian, H. K., Lilienfeld, A. M., Diamond, E. L., and Bross, I. D. J. (1975). *Am. J. Epidemiol.* **102**, 47–54.

Armstrong, B., and Doll, R. (1975). *Int. J. Cancer* **15**, 617–631.

Armstrong, B. G., and Kazantis, G. (1983). *Lancet* **1**, 1425–1427.

Aumuller, G. A., Braun, B. E., Seitz, J., Muller, T., Heyns, W., and Krieg, M. (1985). *Anat. Rec.* **212**, 345–352.

Banerjee, A. K. (1986). *Urology* **28**, 159.

Barrack, E. R., and Berry, S. J. (1987). *Prostate* **10**, 45–56.

Bartsch, N., Horst, H.-J., Becker, H., and Nehse, G. (1977). *Acta Endocrinol.* **85**, 650–664.

Baxter, P. J., and Werner, J. B. (1980). "Mortality in the British Rubber Industries 1967–1976." H.M.S.O., London.

Bean, M. A., Yatani, R., Liu, P. L., Fukazawa, K., Ashley, F. W., and Fujita, S. (1973). *Cancer* **32**, 498–506.

Beebe, G. W., Kato, H., and Land, C. E. (1978). *Radiat. Res.* **75**, 138–201.

Beral, V., Inskip, H., Fraser, P., Booth, M., Coleman, D., and Rose, G. (1985). *Br. Med. J.* **291**, 440–447.

Berg, J. W. (1975). *Cancer Res.* **35**, 3345–3350.

Berg, J. W., and Burbank, F. (1972). *Ann. N.Y. Acad. Sci.* **199**, 249–262.

Bernadelli, L., De Marco, R., and Tinelli, C. (1987). *Br. J. Indust. Med.* **44**, 187–191.

Blair, A., and Fraumeni, J. F. (1978). *J. Natl. Cancer Inst.* **61**, 1379–1384.

Blaxter, M. (1983). *In* "Food and People" (M. R. Turner, ed.) pp. 25–41. Libbey, London.

Bosland, M. C. (1985). *In* "Diet, Nutrition, and Cancer: A Critical Evaluation" (B. S. Reddy and L. A. Cohen, eds.), Vol. I, pp. 125–149. CRC Press, Boca Raton, Florida.

Bosland, M. C. (1987). *In* "Monographs on Pathology of Laboratory Animals: Genital System" (T. C. Jones, U. Mohr, and R. D. Hunt, eds.), pp. 252–260. Springer, New York.
Bosland, M. C., and Wilbrink, B. (1985). *Proc. Eur. Nutr. Conf., 4th* pp. 167–168.
Bosland, M. C., Prinsen, M. K., and Kroes, R. (1983). *Cancer Lett.* **18**, 69–78.
Bosland, M. C., Prinsen, M. K., and Kroes, R. (1984). *Proc. Am. Assoc. Cancer Res.* **25**, 103.
Bosland, M. C., Bunnik, G. S. J., Prinsen, M., and Hidajat, E. (1985). *Proc. Eur. Nutr. Conf., 4th* pp. 169–170.
Bosland, M. C., Prinsen, M. K., and Kroes, R. (1986). *Proc. Am. Assoc. Cancer Res.* **27**, 92.
Boyd, D., Beynon, L., Chisholm, G. D., and Habib, F. K. (1984). *Cancer Res.* **44**, 5532–5537.
Bradshaw, E., and Harington, J. S. (1981). *In* "Cancer Among Black Populations" (C. Mettlin and G. P. Murphy, eds.), pp. 17–33. Liss, New York.
Braun, B.-E., Krieg, M., Smith, K., and Lammel, A. (1982). *Mol. Cell. Endocrinol.* **26**, 177–188.
Bread for the World (1985). "Hunger in a Land of Plenty." Bread for the World Educational Fund, Washington, D.C.
Breslow, N. E., and Enstrom, J. E. (1974). *J. Natl. Cancer Inst.* **53**, 631–639.
Breslow, N., Chan, C. W., Dhom, G., Drury, R. A. B., Franks, L. M., Gellei, B., Lee, Y. S., Lundberg, S., Sparke, B., Sternby, N. H., and Tulinius, H. (1977). *Int. J. Cancer* **20**, 680–688.
Brown, C. E., and Warren, S. (1978). *Cancer Res.* **38**, 159–162.
Bruchovsky, N., Rennie, P. S., and Shnitka, T. K. (1980). *In* "Hormones and Cancer" (S. Iacobeli, R. J. B. King, and H. R. Lindner, eds.), pp. 457–487. Raven, New York.
Bunnik, G. S. J., Bosland, M. C., Prinsen, M. K., and Hidajat, E. (1982). *J. Steroid Biochem.* **17**, lxxxiii.
Bunnik, G. S. J., Bosland, M. C., Prinsen, M. K., and Floor, B. (1985a). *Proc. Eur. Nutr. Conf., 4th* p. 170.
Bunnik, G. S. J., Bosland, M. C., Prinsen, M. K., and van den Berg, H. (1985b). *Proc. Eur. Nutr. Conf., 4th* p. 167.
Burmeister, L. F. (1981). *J. Natl. Cancer Inst.* **66**, 461–464.
Cairns, J. (1985). *Sci. Am.* **253**, 51–59.
Cannon, L., Bishop, D. T., Skolnick, M., Hunt, S., Lyon, J. L., and Smart, C. R. (1982). *Cancer Surv.* **1**, 47–69.
Carlson, H. E., Wasser, H. L., Levin, S. L., and Wilkins, J. N. (1983). *J. Clin. Endocrinol. Metab.* **57**, 334–338.
Carroll, K. K., and Khor, H. T. (1975). *Prog. Biochem. Pharmacol.* **10**, 308–353.
Chandler, J. A., Timms, B. G., and Battersby, S. (1981). *In* "The Prostatic Cell" (G. P. Murphy, A. A. Sandberg, and J. P. Karr, eds.), Part A, pp. 475–490. Liss, New York.
Chopra, D. P., and Wilkoff, L. J. (1976). *J. Natl. Cancer Inst.* **56**, 583–589.
Chopra, D. P., and Wilkoff, L. J. (1979). *Eur. J. Cancer* **15**, 1417–1423.
Chopra, I. J., Tulchinsky, S., and Greenway, F. L. (1973). *Ann. Intern. Med.* **79**, 198–203.
Clifford, P., and Bulbrook, R. D. (1966). *Lancet* **1**, 1228–1230.
Clinton, S. K., Mulloy, A. L., and Visek, W. J. (1982). *Fed. Proc. Fed. Am. Soc. Exp. Biol.* **41**, 357.
Clinton, S. K., Mulloy, A. L., and Visek, W. J. (1985). *Fed. Proc. Fed. Am. Soc. Exp. Biol.* **44**, 770.
Coffey, D. S. (1979). *In* "Prostate Cancer" (D. S. Coffey and J. T. Isaacs, eds.), Vol. 48, pp. 4–23. U.I.C.C., Geneva.
Coffey, D. S., Isaacs, J. T., and Weisman, R. M. (1979). *In* "Prostatic Cancer" (G. P. Murphy, ed.), pp. 89–109. PSG Publ., Littleton.
Cohen, L. A. (1979). *Proc. Annu. Meet. Endocrinol. Soc., 61th, Anaheim*, p. 291.
Cohen, P., and Dix, D. (1985). *Prostate* **6**, 437–443.
Commission for Racial Justice (1987). "Toxic Wastes and Races in the United States." United Church of Christ, New York.
Cook, P. J., Doll, R., and Fellingham, S. A. (1969). *Int. J. Cancer* **4**, 93–112.

Correa, P. (1981). *Cancer Res.* **41**, 3685–3690.
Correa, P., and Londono, J. L. (1982). *In* "Trends in Cancer Incidence" (K. Magnus, ed.), pp. 335–344. Hemisphere Publ., Washington, D.C.
Daniel, O., Haddad, F., Prout, G. and Whitmore, W. F. (1956). *Br. J. Urol.* **28**, 271–278.
Davis, M. E. (1980). *Labor Law J.* **31**, 723–732.
Dayal, H. H., Polissar, L., and Dahlberg, S. (1985). *J. Natl. Cancer Inst.* **74**, 1001–1006.
Decoufle, P., and Wood, D. J. (1979). *Am. J. Epidemiol.* **109**, 667–675.
Demopoulos, H. B., and Gutman, E. G. (1980). *J. Environ. Pathol. Toxicol.* **3**, 219–235.
Devesa, S. S. (1980). *Prev. Med.* **9**, 589–600.
Devesa, S. S., Pollack, E. S., and Young, J. L., Jr. (1984). *Am. J. Epidemiol.* **119**, 274–289.
De Waard, F. (1979). *J. Natl. Cancer Inst.* **63**, 549–552.
Dezell, E., and Monson, R. R. (1981). *J. Occup. Med.* **23**, 677–684.
Dezell, E., and Monson, R. R. (1982). *J. Occup. Med.* **24**, 539–545.
Dezell, E., and Monson, R. R. (1984). *Am. J. Indust. Med.* **6**, 273–279.
Dezell, E., and Monson, R. R. (1985). *Am. J. Indust. Med.* **7**, 307–313.
Doll, R. (1984). *Ann. Occup. Hyg.* **28**, 291–305.
Doll, R., and Peto, R. (1976). *Br. Med. J.* **2**, 1525–1536.
Doll, R., and Peto, R. (1981). *J. Natl. Cancer Inst.* **66**, 1191–1308.
Drach, G. W., and Kohnen, P. W. (1977). *In* "Urologic Pathology: The Prostate" (M. Tannenbaum, ed.), pp. 157–170. Lea & Febiger, Philadelphia.
Drago, J. R. (1984). *Anticancer Res.* **4**, 255–256.
Dube, J. Y., Frenette, G., Tremblay, Y., Belanger, A., and Tremblay, R. R. (1984). *Prostate* **5**, 495–501.
Dubrow, R., and Wegman, D. H. (1983). *J. Natl. Cancer Inst.* **71**, 1123–1142.
Duffield, T. J., and Jacobson, P. H. (1945). *J. Natl. Cancer Inst.* **6**, 103–112.
Egan, B., Waxweiler, R. J., Blade, L., Wolfe, J., and Wagoner, J. K. (1979). *J. Environ. Pathol. Toxicol.* **2**, 259–272.
Egan-Baum, E., Miller, B. A., and Waxweiler, R. J. (1981). *Scand. J. Work Environ. Health* **7**, 147–155.
Elinder, C.-G., Kjellstrom, T., Hogstedt, C., Andersson, K., and Spang, G. (1985). *Br. J. Indust. Med.* **42**, 651–655.
Enstrom, J. E. (1980a). *In* "Cancer Incidence in Defined Populations" (J. Cairns, J. L. Lyon, and M. Skolnick, eds.), pp. 69–90. Cold Spring Harbor Laboratory, Cold Spring Harbor, New York.
Enstrom, J. E. (1980b). *J. Natl. Cancer Inst.* **65**, 1073–1082.
Ernster, V. L., Selvin, S., Sacks, S. T., Austin, D. F., Brown, S. M., and Winkelstein, W. (1978a). *Am. J. Epidemiol.* **107**, 311–320.
Ernster, V. L., Selvin, S., and Winkelstein, W. (1978b). *Science* **200**, 1165–1166.
Ernster, V. L., Sacks, S. T., Selvin, S., and Petrakis, N. L. (1979a). *J. Natl. Cancer Inst.* **63**, 567–585.
Ernster, V. L., Selvin, S., Brown, S. M., Sacks, S. T., Winkelstein, W., and Austin, D. F. (1979b). *J. Occup. Med.* **21**, 175–183.
Evans, J. E., Zontine, W., and Grain, E. (1985). *J. Am. Vet. Med. Assoc.* **186**, 78–80.
Favino, A., Candura, F., Chiappino, G., and Cavalleri, A. (1968). *Med. Lavoro* **59**, 105–110.
Feminella, J. G., and Lattimer, J. K. (1974). *Pirquet Bull. Clin. Med.* **20**, 3–10.
Flanders, W. D. (1986). *Alabama J. Med. Sci.* **23**, 439–443.
Franks, L. M. (1983). *In* "Benign Prostatic Hypertrophy" (F. Hinman, ed.), pp. 139–144. Springer, New York.
Fraumeni, J. F., and Mason, T. J. (1974). *J. Natl. Cancer Inst.* **52**, 659–665.
Friberg, L., Piscator, M., Nordberg, G. F., and Kjellstrom, T. (1974). "Cadmium in the Environment." CRC Press, Boca Raton, Florida.
Gallagher, R. P., Threllfall, W. J., Jeffries, E., Band, P. R., Spinelli, J., and Coldman, A. J. (1984). *J. Natl. Cancer Inst.* **72**, 1311–1315.

Gardner, W. A., Culberson, D. E., and Bennett, B. D. (1986). *Arch. Pathol. Lab. Med.* **110**, 430–432.
Gaskill, S. P., McGuire, W. L., Osborne, C. K., and Stern, M. P. (1979). *Cancer Res.* **39**, 3628–3637.
Gesell, M. S., Brandes, M. J., Arnold, E. A., Isaacs, J. T., Keda, H., Millau, J. C., and Brandes, D. (1982). *Prostate* **3**, 131–138.
Ghanadian, R., and Puah, C. M. (1981). *J. Endocrinol.* **88**, 255–262.
Ghanadian, R., Puah, C. M., and O'Donoghue, E. P. N. (1979). *Br. J. Cancer* **39**, 696–699.
Glantz, G. M. (1964). *J. Urol.* **91**, 291–293.
Glass, A. R., Swerdloff, R. S., Bray, G. A., Dahms, W. T., and Atkinson, R. L. (1977). *J. Clin. Endocrinol. Metabol.* **45**, 1211–1219.
Gleason, D. F. (1977). *In* "Urologic Pathology: The Prostate" (M. Tannenbaun, ed), pp. 171–197. Lea & Febiger, Philadelphia.
Goldsmith, D. F., Smith, A. H., and McMichael, A. J. (1980). *J. Occup. Med.* **22**, 533–541.
Goldsmith, J. R. (1980). *J. Environ. Pathol. Toxicol.* **3**, 205–217.
Gordon, G. G., Olivo, J., Rafii, F., and Southren, A. L. (1975). *J. Clin. Endocrinol. Metab.* **40**, 1018–1026.
Gordon, T., Crittenden, M., and Haenszel, W. (1961). *Natl. Cancer Inst. Monogr.* **6**, 131–350.
Graham, S., Harighey, B., Marshall, J., Priore, R., Byers, T., Rzepka, T., Mettlin, C., and Pontes, J. E. (1983). *J. Natl. Cancer Inst.* **70**, 687–692.
Greene, M. H., and Wilson, J. (1985). *Natl. Cancer Inst. Monogr.* **68**, 191–217.
Greenwald, P. (1982). *In* "Cancer Epidemiology and Prevention" (D. Schottenfeld and J. F. Fraumeni, eds.), pp. 938–946. Saunders, Philadelphia.
Greenwald, P., Damon, A., Kirmss, V., and Polan, A. K. (1974a). *J. Natl. Cancer Inst.* **53**, 341–346.
Greenwald, P., Kirmss, V., Polan, A. K., and Dick, V. S. (1974b). *J. Natl. Cancer Inst.* **53**, 335–340.
Greenwald, P., Kirmss, V., and Burnett, W. S. (1979). *J. Natl. Cancer Inst.* **62**, 1131–1136.
Griffiths, K., Daries, P., Harper, M. E., Peeling, W. B., and Pierrepoint, C. G. (1979). *In* "Endocrinology of Cancer" (D. P. Rose, ed.), pp. 1–55. CRC Press, Boca Raton, Florida.
Guileyardo, J. M., Johnson, W. D., Welsh, R. A., Akazaki, K., and Correa, P. (1980). *J. Natl. Cancer Inst.* **65**, 311–316.
Gunn, S. A., and Gould, T. C. (1956). *Proc. Soc. Exp. Biol. Med.* **92**, 17–20.
Gunn, S.A., Gould, T. C., and Anderson, W. A. D. (1963). *J. Natl. Cancer Inst.* **31**, 745–759.
Gunn, S. A., Gould, T. C., and Anderson, W. A. D. (1964). *Proc. Soc. Exp. Biol. Med.* **115**, 653–657.
Gunn, S. A., Gould, T. C., and Anderson, W. A. D. (1967). *Arch. Pathol.* **83**, 493–499.
Gustavsson, P., Hogstedt, C., and Holmberg, B. (1986). *Scand. J. Work Environ. Health* **12**, 538–544.
Habib, F. K., Hammond, G. L., Lee, I. R., Dawson, J. B., Mason, M. K., Smith, P. H., and Stitch, S. R. (1976a). *J. Endocrincol.* **71**, 133–141.
Habib, F. K., Lee, I. R., Stitch, S. R., and Smith, P. H. (1976b). *J. Endocrinol.* **71**, 99–107.
Habib, F. K., Mason, M. K., Smith, P. H., and Stitch, S. R.(1979). *Br. J. Cancer* **39**, 700–704.
Haddow, A., Roe, F. J. C., Dukes, C. E., and Mitchley, B. C. V. (1964). *Br. J. Cancer* **18**, 667–673.
Haenszel, W., and Kurihara, M. (1968). *J. Natl. Cancer Inst.* **40**, 43–68.
Hagstrom, R. M., Sprague, H. A., and Landau, E. (1967). *Arch. Environ. Health* **15**, 237–248.
Hakama, M., and Kilpikari, L. (1980). *J. Toxicol. Environ. Health* **6**, 1211–1218.
Halverson, A. W., Palmer, I. S., and Guss, P. L. (1966). *Toxicol. Appl. Pharmocol.* **9**, 477–484.
Hamilton, P. J. S., and Persaud, V. (1981). *In* "Cancer Among Black Populations" (C. Mettlin and G. P. Murphy, eds.), pp. 1–15. Liss, New York.
Hammond, E. C. (1966). *Natl. Cancer Inst. Monogr.* **19**, 127–204.
Hammond, G. L. (1978). *J. Endocrinol.* **78**, 7–19.
Hammond, G. L., Vihko, K. P., and Vihko, R. (1978). *Clin. Endocrinol.* **9**, 113–121.

Harbitz, T. B., and Haugen, O. A. (1972). *Acta Pathol. Microbiol. Scand.* **80**, 756–768.
Heilbrun, L. K., Nomura, A., and Stemmermann, G. N. (1986). *Br. J. Cancer* **54**, 677–683.
Heshmat, M. Y., Herson, J., Kovi, J., and Niles, R. (1973). *Med. Ann. D. C.* **42**, 378–383.
Heshmat, M. Y., Kovi, J., Herson, J., Jones, G. W., and Jackson, M. A. (1975). *Urology* **6**, 457–460.
Heshmat, M. Y., Kaul, L., Kovi, J., Jackson, M. A., Jackson, A. G., Jones, G. W., Edson, M., Enterline, J. P., Worrell, R. G., and Perry, S. L. (1985). *Prostate* **6**, 7–17.
Heston, J. F., Kelly, J. B., Meigs, J. W., and Flannery, J. T. (1985). *Natl. Cancer Inst. Monogr.* **70**, 18–28.
Hill, P. B., and Wynder, E. L. (1979). *Cancer Lett.* **7**, 273–282.
Hill, P., Wynder, E. L., Garbaczewski, L., Garnes, H., and Walker, A. R. P. (1979). *Cancer Res.* **39**, 5101–5105.
Hill, P., Wynder, E. L., Garbaczewski, L., and Garnes, H. (1980a). *Am. J. Clin. Nutr.* **33**, 1010–1018.
Hill, P., Wynder, E. L., Garnes, H., and Walker, A. R. P. (1980b). *Prev. Med.* **9**, 657–666.
Hill, P., Wynder, E. L., Garbaczewski, L., and Walker, A. R. P. (1982). *Cancer Res.* **42**, 3864–3869.
Hill, P., Garbaczewski, L., and Walker, A. R. P. (1984). *Med. Hypotheses* **14**, 29–39.
Hirayama, T. (1979). *Natl. Cancer Inst. Monogr.* **53**, 149–155.
Hirayama, T. (1985). *Natl. Cancer Inst. Monogr.* **69**, 143–153.
Hirose, F., Takizawa, S., Watanabe, H., and Takeichi, N. (1976). *Gann* **67**, 407–411.
Hirst, A. E., Jr., and Bergman, R. T. (1954). *Cancer* **7**, 136–141.
Hoar, S. K., and Blair, A. (1984). *Arch. Environ. Health.* **39**, 280–283.
Hodges, C. V., and Wan, S. P. (1983). *In* "Benign Prostatic Hypertrophy" (F. Hinman, ed), pp. 167–173. Springer, New York.
Hoffman, L., Putzke, H. P., Kampehl, H. J., Russbult, R. R., Gase, P., Simonn, C., Erdmann, S. T., and Huckstorf, C. (1985). *J. Cancer Res. Clin. Oncol.* **109**, 193–199.
Hoisaeter, P. A., Haukass, S., Bakke, A., Hoiem, L., Segadel, E., and Thorsen, T., (1982). *Prostate* **3**, 375–381.
Holman, C. D. J., James, I. R., Segal, M. R., and Armstrong, B. K. (1981). *Br. J. Cancer* **44**, 340–348.
Hoover, R., Mason, T. J., McKay, F. W., and Fraumeni, J. F., (1975). *In* "Persons at High Risk of Cancer" (J. F. Fraumeni, ed.), pp. 343–360, Academic Press, New York.
Howe, G. R., and Landsay, J. P. (1983). *J. Natl. Cancer Inst.* **70**, 37–44.
Howell, M. A. (1974). *Br. J. Cancer* **29**, 328–336.
Howie, B. J., and Shultz, T. D. (1985). *Am. J. Clin. Nutr.* **42**, 127–134.
Huggins, C., and Hodges, C. V. (1941). *Cancer Res.* **1**, 293–297.
Huggins, C., Stevens, R. E., and Hodges, C. V. (1941). *Arch. Surg.* **43**, 209–223.
Hutt, M. S. R. (1981). *In* "Cancer Among Black Populations" (C. Mettlin and G. P. Murphy, eds.), pp. 55–66. Liss, New York.
IARC (1976). "Monographs on the Evaluation of Carcinogenic Risk of Chemicals to Humans," Vol. 11, "Cadmium, Nickel, Some Epoxides, Miscellaneous Industrial Chemicals and General Considerations on Volatile Anaesthetics." IARC, Lyon.
IARC (1978). "Monographs on the Evaluation of Carcinogenic Risk of Chemicals to Humans," Vol. 16, "Some Aromatic Amines and Related Nitro Compounds—Hair Dyes, Coloring Agents and Miscellaneous Industrial Chemicals." IARC, Lyon.
IARC (1982a). "Monographs on the Evaluation of Carcinogenic Risk of Chemicals to Humans," Vol. 28, "The Rubber Industry." IARC, Lyon.
IARC (1982b). "Monographs on the Evaluation of Carcinogenic Risk of Chemicals to Humans," Suppl. 4, "Chemicals, Industrial Processes, and Industries Associated with Cancer in Humans." IARC, Lyon.
IARC (1984). "Monographs on the Evaluation of Carcinogenic Risk of Chemicals to Humans," Vol. 34, "Polynuclear Aromatic Compounds, Part 3, Industrial Exposures in Aluminum

Production, Coal Gasification, Coke Production, and Iron and Steel Founding." IARC, Lyon.
Isaacs, J. T. (1983). *Prostate* **4**, 351–366.
Jackson, M. A., Ahluwalia, B. S., Attah, E. B., Connally, C. A., Herson, J., Heshmat, M. Y., Jackson, A. G., Jones, G. W., Kapoor, S. K., Kennedy, J., Kovi, J., Lucas, A., Nkposong, E. O., Olisa, E., and Williams, A. O. (1975). *Cancer Chemother. Rep.* **59**, 3–15.
Jackson, M. A., Ahluwalia, B. S., Herson, J., Heshmat, M. Y., Jackson, A. G., Jones, G. W., Kapoor, S. K., Kennedy, J., Kovi, J., Lucas, A. O.,, Nkposong, E. O., Olisa, E., and Williams, A. O. (1977). *Cancer Treat. Rep.* **61**, 167–172.
Jackson, M. A., Kovi, J., Heshmat, M. Y., Jones, G. W., Rao, M. S., and Ahluwalia, B. S., (1981). *In* "Cancer Among Black Populations" (C. Mettlin and G. P. Murphy, eds.), pp. 111–132. Liss, New York.
Jacobsen, B. K., Bjelke, E., Kvale, G., and Heuch, I. (1986). *J. Natl. Cancer Inst.* **76**, 823–831.
Jensen, O. M. (1983). *J. Natl. Cancer Inst.* **69**, 1011–1014.
Jensen, O. M., Knudsen, J. B., and Sorensen, B. L. (1985). *Natl. Cancer Inst. Monogr.* **68**, 349–360.
Kahn, H. A. (1966). *Natl. Cancer Inst. Monogr.* **19**, 1–125.
Karmali, R. A., Reichel, P., and Cohen, L. A. (1986). *Fed. Proc. Fed. Am. Soc. Exp. Biol.* **45**, 236.
Kahng, M. W., Liu, W., Sanefuji, H., Resau, J. H., Heatfield, B. M., and Trump, B. F. (1981a). *Chem. Biol. Interact.* **34**, 249–256.
Kahng, M. W., Smith, M. W., and Trump, B. F. (1981b). *In* "The Prostatic Cell" (G. P. Murphy, A. A. Sandberg, and J. P. Karr, eds.), Part B, pp. 183–190. Liss, New York.
Kantor, A. F., and McLaughlin, J. K. (1985). *Natl. Cancer Inst. Monogr.* **68**, 149–159.
Kark, J. D., Smith, A. H., Switzer, B. R., and Hames, C. G. (1981). *J. Natl. Cancer Inst.* **66**, 7–16.
Katayama, S., Fiala, E., Reddy, B. S., Rivenson, A., Silverman, J., Williams, G. M., and Weisburger, J. H. (1982). *J. Natl. Cancer Inst.* **68**, 867–873.
Kaul, L., Rao, M. S., Heshmat, M. Y., and Kovi, J. (1981). *Proc. Int. Conf. Nutr., 12th, San Diego*, p. 164.
Kaul, L., Heshmat, M. Y., Kovi, J., Jackson, M. A., Jackson, A. G., Jones, G. W., Edson, M., Enterline, J. P., Worrell, R. G., and Perry, S. L. (1987). *Nutr. Cancer* **9**, 123–128.
King, H., and Haenszel, W. (1973). *J. Chron. Dis.* **26**, 623–646.
King, H., and Locke, F. B., (1980). *J. Natl. Cancer Inst.* **65**, 1141–1148.
King, H., Diamond, E., and Lilienfeld, A. M. (1963). *J. Chron. Dis.* **16**, 117–153.
Kinlen, L. J., Hermon, C., and Smith, P. G. (1983). *Br. J. Cancer* **48**, 355–361.
Kjellstrom, T., Friberg, L., and Rahnster, B. (1979). *Environ. Health Perspect.* **28**, 199–204.
Kleinerman, R. A., Liebermann, J. V., and Li, F. P. (1985). *Natl. Cancer Inst. Monogr.* **68**, 139–147.
Kley, H. K., Edelmann, P., and Kruskemper, H. L. (1980). *Metabolism* **29**, 1041–1045.
Kolonel, L. N. (1980). *J. Natl. Cancer Inst.* **65**, 1127–1139.
Kolonel, L. N., Hankin, J. H., Nomura, A. M. Y., and Chu, S. Y. (1981a). *Cancer Res.* **41**, 3727–3728.
Kolonel, L. N., Hankin, J. H., Lee, J., Chu, S. Y., Nomura, A. M. Y., and Hinds, M. W. (1981b). *Br. J. Cancer* **44**, 332–339.
Kolonel, L. N., Nomura, A. M. Y., Hinds, M. W., Hirohata, T., Hankin, J. H., and Lee, J. (1983). *Cancer Res.* **43**, 2397s–2402s..
Kolonel, L. N., Hinds, M. W., Nomura, A. M. Y., Hankin, J. H., and Lee, J. (1985). *Natl. Cancer Inst. Monogr.* **69**, 137–142.
Kolonel, L. N., Hankin, J. H., and Yoshizawa, C. N. (1987) *Cancer Res.* **47**, 2982–2985.
Koskela, R.-S., Hernberg, S., Karava, R., Yarvineu, E., and Nurminen, M. (1976). *Scand. J. Work Environ. Health* **2** (Suppl. 1), 73–89.
Kovi, J., and Heshmat, M. Y. (1973). *Am. J. Epidemiol.* **96**, 401–413.
Krain, S. (1973). *Geriatrics* **28**, 93–98.
Krain, L. S. (1974). *Prev. Med.* **3**, 154–159.

Krieg, M., Bartsch, W., and Janssen, W. (1979). *J. Steroid Biochem.* **11**, 615–624.

Kroes, R., Beems, R. B., Bosland, M. C., Bunnik, G. S. J., and Sinkeldam, E. J. (1986). *Fed. Proc., Fed. Am. Soc. Exp. Biol.* **45**, 136–141.

Labrie, F., Dupont. A., Belanger, A., Lavcoursierse, Y., Rayhand, J., Husson, J. M., Gareau, J., Fazelhas, A. T. A., Sandow, J., Monfette, G., Girard, J. G., Emond, J., and Houle, J. G. (1983). *Prostate* **4**, 579–594.

La Rosa, F., Cresci, A., Orpianesi, C., and Saltalamacchia, G. (1985). *Eur. J. Epidemiol.* **1**, 145–149.

Lasnitski, I. (1955). *Br. J. Cancer* **9**, 434–441.

Lasnitski, I. (1974). *In* "Male Accessory Sex Organs" (D. Brandes, ed.), pp. 348–382. Academic Press, New York.

Lasnitski, I. (1976). *Br. J. Cancer* **34**, 239–248.

Lasnitzki, I., and Goodman, D. S. (1974). *Cancer Res.* **34**, 1564–1571.

Leake, A., Chisholm, G. D., and Habib, F. K. (1984a). *J. Endocrinol.* **102**, 73–76.

Leake, A., Chisholm, G. D., and Habib, F. K. (1984b). *J. Steroid Biochem.* **20**, 651–655.

Leav, I., Merk, F., Ofner, P., Goodrich, G., Kwan, W. L., Stein, B. M., Sar, M., and Stumpf, W. F. (1978). *Am. J. Pathol.* **93**, 69–92.

Lee, I. P., Suzuki, K., and Nagayama, J. (1981). *Carcinogenesis* **2**, 823–831.

Lees, R. E.M., Steele, R., and Wardle, D. (1985). *J. Epidemiol. Commun. Health* **39**, 227–230.

Lemen, R. A., Lee, J. S., Wagoner, J. K., and Blejer, H. P. (1976). *Ann. N.Y. Acad. Sci.* **271**, 273–279.

Levin, M. L., Haenszel, W. A., Carroll, B. E., Gerhardt, P. R., Handy, V. H., and Ingraham, S. C. (1960). *J. Natl. Cancer Inst.* **24**, 1243–1257.

Levine, R. L., and Wilchinsky, M. (1979). *J. Urol.* **121**, 761–762.

Levy, L. S., and Clack, J. (1975). *Ann. Occup. Hyg.* **17**, 205–211.

Levy, L. S., Roe, F. J. C., Malcolm, D., Kazantzis, G., Clack, J., and Platt, H. S. (1973). *Ann. Occup. Hyg.* **16**, 111–118.

Levy, L. S., Clack, J., and Roe, F. J. C. (1975). *Ann. Occup. Hyg.* **17**, 213–220.

Lew, E. A., and Garfinkel, L. (1979). *J. Chron. Dis.* **32**, 563–576.

Lilienfeld, A. M., Levin, M. L., and Kessler, I. I. (1972). "Cancer in the United States." Harvard Univ. Press, Cambridge, Massachusetts.

Lilienfeld, A. M., Lilienfeld, D. E., and Eng, A. B. (1980). "Foundations of Epidemiology." Oxford Univ. Press, Oxford.

Lipsett, M. B. (1979). *Cancer* **43**, 1967–1981.

Liskow, A. S., Neugut, A. I., Benson, M., Olsson, C. A., Birkhoff, J., and Chang, C. H. (1987). *Cancer* **59**, 380–384.

Locke, F. B., and King, H. (1980). *J. Natl. Cancer Inst.* **65**, 1149–1156.

Logan, W. P. D. (1982). "Cancer Mortality by Occupational and Social Class, 1851-1971." IARC Publ. No. 36/Studies on Medical and Population Subjects No. 44., H.M.S.O., London/IARC, Lyon.

Loser, E. (1980). *Cancer Lett.* **9**, 191–198.

Loser, E., and Lorke, D. (1977). *Toxicology* **7**, 215–224.

Lowenfels, A. B., (1974). *N.Y. State J. Med.* **1**, 56–59.

Lundberg, S., and Berge, T. (1970). *Scand. J. Urol. Nephrol.* **4**, 93–97.

Lynch, H. T., Larsen, A. L., Magnuson, C. W., and Krush, A. J. (1966). *Cancer* **19**, 1891–1897.

Lyon, J. L., Klauber, M. R., Gardner, J. W., and Smart, C. R. (1976). *N. Engl. J. Med.* **294**, 129–133.

Lyon, J. L., Gardner, J. W., and West, D. W. (1980a). *In* "Cancer Incidence in Defined Populations" (J. Cairns, J. L. Lyon, and M. Skolnick, eds.), pp. 3–28. Cold Spring Harbor Laboratory, Cold Spring Harbor, New York.

Lyon, J. L., Gardner, J. W., and West, D. W. (1986). *J. Natl. Cancer Inst.* **65**, 1063–1071.

Lytton, B. (1983). *In* "Benign Prostatic Hypertrophy" (F. Hinman, ed.), pp. 22–26. Springer, New York.

Mandel, R. and Ryser, H. J.-P. (1987). *Mutation Res.* **176**, 1–10.
McKeehan, W. L., and Fast, D. (1981). *Cell Biol. Int. Rep.* **5**, 2.
McMichael, A. J., Spirtas, R., and Kupper, L. L. (1974). *J. Occup. Med.* **16**, 458–464.
McMichael, A. J., Andjelkovic, D. A., and Tyroler, H. A. (1976a). *Ann. N.Y. Acad. Sci.* **271**, 125–137.
McMichael, A. J., Spirtas, R., Gamble, J. F., and Tousey, P. M. (1976b). *J. Occup. Med.* **18**, 178–185.
McNeal, J. E. (1983). *In* "Benign Prostastic Hypertrophy" (F. Hinman, ed.), pp. 150–166. Springer, New York.
Mandel, J. S., and Schuman, L. M. (1980). *In* "Reviews in Cancer Epidemiology" (E. M. Lilienfeld, ed.), Vol. I, pp. 1–83. Elsevier, Amsterdam.
Marmorston, J., Lombardo, L. J., Jr., Meyers, S. M., Gierson, H., Stern, E., and Hopkins, C. E. (1965a). *J. Urol.* **93**, 287–295.
Marmorston, J., Lombardo, L. J., Jr., Meyers, S. M., Gierson, H., Stern, E., and Hopkins, C. E. (1965b). *J. Urol.* **93**, 287–295.
Medina, D. (1985). *In* "Diet, Nutrition, and Cancer: A Critical Evaluation"(B. S. Reddy and L. A. Cohen, eds.), Vol. II, pp. 23–41. CRC Press, Boca Raton, Florida.
Meikle, A. W., and Stanish, W. M. (1982). *J. Clin. Endocrinol. Metab.* **54**, 1104–1108.
Meikle, A. W., and Stanish, W. M., Taylor, N., Edwards, C. Q., and Bishop, C. T. (1982). *Metabolism* **31**, 6–9.
Meikle, W. A., Smith, J. A., and West, D. W. (1985). *Prostate* **6**, 121–128.
Menck, H. R., and Henderson, B. E. (1985). *J. Natl. Cancer Inst. Monogr.* **69**, 105–111.
Menck, H. R., Henderson, B. E., Pike, M. C., Mack, T., Martin, S. P., and Soohoo, J. (1975). *J. Natl. Cancer Inst.* **55**, 531–536.
Merk, F. B., Ofner, P., Kwan, P. W. L., Leav, I., and Vena, R. L. (1982). *Lab. Invest.* **47**, 437–450.
Merk, F. B., Warhol, M. J., Kwan, P. W. L., Leav, I., Alroy, J., Ofner, P., and Pinkus, G. S. (1986). *Lab. Invest.* **54**, 442–456.
Mettlin, C. (1980). *Prev. Med.* **9**, 601–606.
Mettlin, C., and Natarajan, N. (1983). *Prostate* **4**, 323–331.
Michaels, D. (1983). *J. Natl. Med. Assoc.* **75**, 1014–1018.
Mickey, D. D., and Paulson, D. F. (1980). *In* "Male Accessory Sex Glands" (E. Spring-Mills and E. S. E. Hafez, eds.), pp. 341–355. Elsevier, Amsterdam.
Middleton, B., Byers, T., Marshall, J., and Graham, S. (1987). *Nutr. Cancer* **8**, 107–116.
Mishina, T., Watanabe, H., Araki, H., Miyakoda, K., Fujiwara, T., Kobayshi, T., and Maegawa, M. (1981). *Nippon Hinyokika Gakkai Zasshi* **72**, 1256–1279.
Mishina, T., Watanabe, H., Araki, H., and Nakao, M. (1985). *Prostate* **6**, 423–436.
Monson, R. R., and Fine, L. J. (1978). *J. Natl. Cancer Inst.* **61**, 1047–1053.
Monson, R. R., and Lyon, J. L. (1975). *Cancer* **36**, 1077–1079.
Monson, R. R., and Nakano, K. (1976). *Am. J. Epidemiol.* **103**, 284–296.
Mostofi, F. K., and Price, E. B. (1973). "Tumors of the Male Genital System." AFIP, Washington, D.C..
Mulloy, A. L., Li, P. S., Clinton, S. K., and Visek, W. J., (1983). *Fed. Proc., Fed. Am. Soc. Exp. Biol.* **42**, 1313.
Muntzing, J., Kirdam, R., Murphy, G. P., and Sandberg, A. A. (1977). *Invest. Urol.* **14**, 492–495.
N. A. S. (1982). "Diet, Nutrition, and Cancer." National Academy Press, Washington, D.C..
Noble, R. L. (1977). *Cancer Res.* **37**, 1929–1933.
Noble, R. L. (1982). *Int. Rev. Exp. Pathol.* **23**, 113–159.
Nomura, A., Heilbrun, L. K., and Stemmermann, G. N. (1986). *J. Natl. Cancer Inst.* **76**, 587–590.
N.T.P. (1987). "N.T.P. Technical Report on the Toxicology and Carcinogenesis Studies of *N*-Phenyl-*N*-Naphthylamine (CAS No. 135–88–6) in F344/N Rats and B6C3F$_1$ Mice (Feed Studies), Board Draft Version," NRP TR 333, NIH Publication No. 87–2589, National Toxicology Program, Research Triangle Park, North Carolina.

Ofner, P., Vena, R. L., Leav, I., and Hamilton, D. W. (1979). *J. Steroid Biochem.* **11**, 1367–1379.
Olson, J. A. (1984). *J. Natl. Cancer Inst.* **73**, 1439–1444.
Osterlind, A., Rorth, M., and Prener, A. (1985). *Natl. Cancer Inst. Monogr.* **68**, 341–347.
Paganini–Hill, A., Ross, R. K., Gray, G. A., and Henderson, B. E. (1985). *Natl. Cancer Inst. Monogr.* **69**, 133–135.
Paganini-Hill, A., Chao, A., Ross, R. K., and Henderson, B. E. (1987). *J. Natl. Cancer Inst.* **79**, 443–448.
Page, H. S., and Asire, A. J. (1985). "Cancer Rates and Risks." USDHHS, NIH Publ. No. 85–691.
Page, W. F. (1986). *J. Natl. Cancer Inst.* **76**, 1259.
Page, W. F., and Kuntz, A. J. (1980). *Cancer* **45**, 1029–1040.
Parkes, H. G., Veys, C. A., Waterhouse, J. A. H., and Peters, A. (1982). *Br. J. Ind. Med.* **39**, 209–220.
Parkin, D. M. (1986). "Cancer Occurrence in Developing Countries", IARC Sci. Publ. No. 75. LARC, Lyon.
Peleg, I., Heyden, S., Knowles, M., and Hames, C. G. (1984). *J. Natl. Cancer Inst.* **73**, 1455–1458.
Pell, S., and D'Alonzo, C. A. (1973). *J. Occup. Med.* **15**, 120–125.
Percy, C., Stanek, E., and Gloeckler, L. (1981). *Am. J. Public Health* **71**, 242–250.
Peto, R., Doll, R., and Buckley, J. D. (1981). *Nature (London)* **290**, 201–208.
Pfau, A., and Caine, M. (1980). *In* "Male Accessory Sex Glands" (E. Spring–Mills and E. S. E. Hafez, eds.), pp. 357–372. Elsevier, Amsterdam.
Phillips, R. L. (1975). *Cancer Res.* **35**, 3513–3522.
Phillips, R. L. (1980). *J. Environ. Pathol. Toxicol.* **3**, 157–169.
Phillips, R. L., and Snowdon, D. A. (1983). *Cancer Res.* **43**, 2403s–2408s.
Phillips, R. L., Kuzma, J. W., and Lotz, T. M. (1980a). *In* "Cancer Incidence in Defined Population" (J. Cairns, J. L. Lyon, and M. Skolnick, eds.), pp. 93–102. Cold Spring Harbor Laboratory, Cold Spring Harbor, New York.
Phillips, R. L., Garfinkel, L., Kuzma, J. W., Beeson, W. L., Lotz, T., and Brin, B. (1980b). *J. Natl. Cancer Inst.* **65**, 1097–1107.
Physicians Task Force on Hunger in America (1985). "Hunger in America." Harvard Medical School of Public Health, Boston.
Piscator, M. (1981). *Environ. Health Persp.* **40**, 107–130.
Pollard, M. (1973). *J. Natl. Cancer Inst.* **51**, 1235–1241.
Pollard, M., and Luckert, P. H. (1975). *J. Natl. Cancer Inst.* **54**, 643–649.
Pollard, M., and Luckert, P. H. (1985). *Prostate* **6**, 1–5.
Pollard, M., and Luckert, P. H. (1986a). *Cancer Lett.* **32**, 223–227.
Pollard, M., and Luckert, P. H. (1986b). *J. Natl. Cancer Inst.* **77**, 583–587.
Pollard, M., Luckert, P. H., and Schmidt, M. A. (1982). *Prostate* **4**, 563–568.
Potts, C. L. (1965). *Ann. Occup. Hyg.* **8**, 55–61.
Pour, P. M. (1983). *Carcinogenesis* **4**, 49–55.
Pour, P. M., and Stephan, K. (1987). *Cancer Res.* **47**, 5699–5706.
Price, D. (1963). *Natl. Cancer Inst. Monogr.* **12**, 1–25.
Rannikko, S., and Adlercreutz, H. (1983). *Prostate* **4**, 223–229.
Rannikko, S., Kairento, A., Karonen, S., and Adlercreutz, H. (1981). *Acta Endocrinol.* **98**, 625–633.
Rapp, F., and Geder, L. (1980). *In* "Male Accessory Sex Glands" (E. Spring-Mills and E. S. E. Hafez, eds.), pp. 327–340. Elsevier, Amsterdam.
Reddy, B. S., Cohen, L. A., McCoy, G. D., Hill, P., Weisburger, J. H., and Wynder, E. L. (1980). *Adv. Cancer Res.* **32**, 237–245.
Redmond, C. K., Wieand, H. S., Rockette, H. E., Sass, R., and Weinberg, G. (1981). "Long-term Mortality Experience of Steelworkers." U.S.D.H.H.S. (N.I.O.S.H.) Publ. No. 81–120.
Rivenson, A., and Silverman, J. S. (1979). *Invest. Urol.* **16**, 468–472.
Robson, M. C. (1966). *Geriatrics* **21**, 150–154.

Root, A. W., Duckett, G., Sweetland, M., and Reiter, E. O. (1979). *J. Nutr.* **109**, 958–964.
Rose, D. P., Laakso, K., Sotarauta, M., and Wynder, E. L. (1984). *Eur. J. Cancer Clin. Oncol.* **20**, 1317–1319.
Rose, D. P. (1986). *In* "Dietary Fat and Cancer" (C. Ip, D. F. Birt, A. E. Rogers, and C. Mettlin, eds.), pp. 43–68. Liss, New York.
Rose, D. P., Boyar, A. P., and Wynder, E. L. (1986). *Cancer* **58**, 2363–2371.
Rosenthal, M. B., Barnard, R. J., Rose, D. P., Inkeles, S., Hall, J., and Pritikin, N. (1985). *Am. J. Med.* **78**, 23–27.
Ross, R. K., McCurtis, J. W., Henderson, B. E., Menck, H. R., Mack, T. M., and Martin, S. P. (1979). *Br. J. Cancer* **39**, 284–289.
Ross, R. K., Deapen, D. M., Casagrande, J. T., Paganini-Hill, A., and Henderson, B. E. (1981). *Br. J. Cancer* **43**, 233–235.
Ross, R. K., Paganini-Hill, A., and Henderson, B. E. (1983). *Prostate* **4**, 333–334.
Ross, R., Bernstein, L., Judd, H., Hanisch, R., Pike, M., and Henderson, B. (1986). *J. Natl. Cancer Inst.* **76**, 45–48.
Ross, R. K., Shimizu, H., Paganini-Hill, A., Honda, G., and Henderson, B. E. (1987). *J. Natl. Cancer Inst.* **78**, 869–874.
Rotkin, I. D. (1977). *Cancer Treat. Rep.* **61**, 173–180.
Rotkin, I. D. (1980). *In* "Male Accessory Sex Glands" (E. Spring-Mills and E. S. E. Hafez, eds.), pp. 290–309. Elsevier, Amsterdam.
Rotkin, I. D. (1983). *In* "Benign Prostatic Hypertrophy" (F. Hinman, ed.), pp. 9–21. Springer, New York.
Rotkin, I. D., Moses, V. K., Kaushal, D., Cooper, J. F., Osburn, W. C., and Benjamin, J. A. (1979). *Cancer Detect. Prev.* **2**, 517–529.
Sandberg, A. A., Karr, J. P., and Muntzing, J. (1980). *In* "Male Accessory Sex Glands" (E. Spring-Mills and E. S. E. Hafez, eds.), pp. 566–608. Elsevier, Amsterdam.
Saroff, J., Kirdani, R. Y., Chu, T. M., Wajsman, Z., and Murphy, G. P. (1980). *Oncology* **37**, 46–52.
Schein, L. G., and Thomas, J. A. (1975). *Environ. Res.* **9**, 26–31.
Schein, L. G., and Thomas, J. A. (1976). *J. Toxicol. Environ. Health* **1**, 829–838.
Schenk, B. (1975). *In* "Physiologie und Pathophysiologie der Prostata" (T. Senge, F. Neumann, and K. D. Richter, eds.), pp. 11–24. Thieme, Stuttgart.
Schmidt, J. D. (1983). *Prostate* **5**, 493–501.
Schmidt, W., and de Lint, J. (1972). *Q. J. Stud. Alcohol* **33**, 171–185.
Schneider, G., Kirschner, M. A., Berkowitz, R., and Ertel, N. H. (1979). *J. Clin. Endocrinol. Metabol.* **48**, 633–638.
Schoenberg, B. S. (1975). *In* "Persons at High Risk of Cancer" (J. F. Fraumeni, ed.), pp. 103–118. Academic Press, New York.
Schrauzer, G. N. (1976a). *Med. Hypotheses* **2**, 31–36.
Schrauzer, G. N. (1976b). *Med. Hypotheses* **2**, 39–49.
Schrauzer, G. N., White, D. A., and Schneider, C. J. (1977a). *Bioinorg. Chem.* **7**, 23–33.
Schrauzer, G. N., White, D. A., and Schneider, C. J. (1977b). *Bioinorg. Chem.* **7**, 35–56.
Schroeder, F. H. (1984). *Prostate* **5**, 193–198.
Schroeder, H. A., Balassa, J. J., and Vinton, W. H., Jr. (1964). *J. Nutr.* **83**, 239–250.
Schroeder, H. A., Balassa, J. J., and Vinton, W. H., Jr. (1965). *J. Nutr.* **86**, 51–66.
Schuman, L. M., and Mandel, J. S. (1980). *Prev. Med.* **9**, 630–649.
Schuman, L. M., Mandel, J., Blackard, C., Bauer, H., Scarlet, J., and McHugh, R. (1977). *Cancer Treat. Rep.* **61**, 181–186.
Schuman, L. M., Mandel, J. S., Radke, A., Seal, U., and Halberg, F. (1982). *In* "Trends in Cancer Incidence" (K. Magnus, ed.), pp. 345–353. Hemisphere, Washington, D.C..
Scott, R., and Aughey, E. (1978). *Br. J. Urol.* **50**, 25–28.
Scott, W. W. (1983). *Prostate* **4**, 435–440.

Segi, M. (1978). "Age-Adjusted Death Rates for Cancer for Selected Sites (A-Classification) in 52 Countries in 1973." Segi Inst. Cancer Epidemiol., Nagoya.
Segi, M. (1981). "Age-Adjusted Death Rates for Cancer for Selected Sites (A-Classification) in 40 Countries in 1976." Segi Inst. Cancer Epidemiol., Nagoya.
Semmens, J. B., Rouse, I. L., Beilen, L. J., and Masarei, J. R. L., (1983). *Clin. Chim. Acta* **133**, 295–300.
Servadio, R. (1985). *In* "Therapeutic Principles in Metastatic Prostatic Cancer" (F. H. Schroeder and B. Richards, eds.), pp. 407–426. Liss, New York.
Sheldon, C. A., Williams, R. D., and Fraley, E. E. (1980). *J. Urol.* **124**, 626–631.
Shirai, T., Sakata, T., Fukushima, S., Ikawa, E., and Ito, N. (1985). *Jpn. J. Cancer Res. (Gann)* **76**, 803–808.
Shirai, T., Fukushima, S., Ikawa, E., Tagawa, Y., and Ito, N. (1986). *Cancer Res.* **46**, 6423–6426.
Shirai, T., Tagawa, Y., Fukushima, S., Asamoto, M., and Ito, N. (1987a). *Cancer Lett.* **35**, 1–6.
Shirai, T., Ikawa, E., Tagawa, Y., and Ito, N. (1987b). *Cancer Lett.* **35**, 7–15.
Shotland, J. (1986). "Rising Poverty, Declining Health: The Nutritional Status of the Rural Poor." Public Voice for Food and Health Policy, Washington, D.C..
Siemiatycki, J., Richardson, L., Gerin, M., Goldberg, M., Dewar, R., Des, M., Campbell, S., and Wacholder, S. (1986). *Am. J. Epidemiol.* **123**, 235–249.
Siiteri, P. K., Murai, J. T., Hammond, G. L., Nisker, J. A., Raymoure, W. J., and Kuhn, R. W. (1982). *Rec. Prog. Horm. Res.* **38**, 457–507.
Silverberg, E., and Lubera, J. (1986). "Cancer Statistics, 1986." American Cancer Society, New York.
Sinquin, G., Morfin, R. F., Charles, J.-F., and Floch, H. H. (1984). *J. Steroid Biochem.* **20**, 773–780.
Smith, E. R., and Hagiopan, M. (1977). *J. Natl. Cancer Inst.* **59**, 119–122.
Smith, E. R., and Hagiopan, M. (1981). *In* "The Prostatic Cell" (G. P. Murphy, A. A. Sandberg, and J. P. Karr, eds.), Part B, pp. 131–163. Liss, New York.
Smith, E. R., Hagiopan, M., and Reister, H. C. (1977). *Toxicol. Appl. Pharmacol* **40**, 185–191.
Smith, P. G., and Doll, R. (1982). *Br. Med. J.* **284**, 449–460.
Smith, P. G., and Douglas, A. J. (1986). *Br. Med. J.* **293**, 845–854.
Smolev, J. K., Heston, W. D. W., Scott, W. W., and Coffey, D. S. (1977). *Cancer Treat. Rep.* **61**, 273–287.
Snowdon, D. A., Phillips, R. L., and Choi, W. (1984). *Am. J. Epidemiol.* **120**, 244–250.
Sobin, L. H., and Sherif, M. (1980). *Br. J. Cancer* **42**, 787–790.
Soderkvist, P. and Poelliger, L. (1987). *Carcinogenesis* **8**, 1287–1290.
Soderkvist, P., Toftgard, R., and Gustafsson, J.-A. (1982). *Toxicol. Lett.* **10**, 61–69.
Soderkvist, P., Busk, L., Toftgard, R., and Gustafsson, J.-A. (1983). *Chem. Biol. Interact.* **46**, 151–163.
Soderkvist, P., Poelliger, L., and Gustafsson, J.-A. (1986). *Cancer Res.* **46**, 651–657.
Sodersten, P., Damassa, D., and Smith. (1977). *Horm. Behav.* **8**, 320–341.
Sorahan, T., and Waterhouse, J. A. (1983). *Br. J. Ind. Med.* **40**, 293–300.
Sorahan, T., and Waterhoue, J. A. H. (1985). *Lancet* **1**, 459.
Sorahan, T., Parkes, H. G., Veys, C. A., and Waterhouse, J. A. H. (1986). *Br. J. Indust. Med.* **43**, 363–373.
Southren, A. L., Gordon, G. G., Olivo, S., Raffii, F., and Rosenthal, W. S. (1973). *Metabolism* **22**, 695–702.
Spiegelhalder, B., and Preussmann, R. (1983). *Carcinogenesis* **4**, 1147–1152.
Sporn, M. B., and Roberts, A. B. (1983). *Cancer Res.* **43**, 3034–3040.
Spriggs, C. E., Clinton, S. K., and Visek, W. J. (1983). *Fed. Proc., Fed. Am. Soc. Exp. Biol.* **42**, 1313.
Staszewski, W., and Haenszel, W. (1965). *J. Natl. Cancer Inst.* **35**, 291–297.

Steele, R. (1972). *Med. Aspects Hum. Sex* **6**, 70–81.
Steele, R., Lee, R. E. M., Kraus, A. S., and Rao, C. (1971). *J. Chron. Dis.* **24**, 29–37.
Stocks, P. (1970). *Br. J. Cancer* **24**, 215–225.
Storm, H. H., and Prener, A. (1985). *Natl. Cancer Inst. Monogr.* **68**, 389–410.
Sugawara, C., Sugawara, N., and Miyake, H. (1981). *Toxicol. Lett.* **8**, 323.
Suzuki, K., and Lee, I. P. (1981). *Toxicol. Appl. Pharmacol.* **58**, 151–155.
Swanson, G. M., Belle, S. H., and Satariano, W. A. (1985). *Cancer Res.* **45**, 5883–5889.
Takahashi, E. (1964). *Tohoku J. Exp. Med.* **82**, 218–223.
Takenaka, S., Oldiges, H., Konig, H., Hochrainer, D., and Oberdoerster, G. (1983). *J. Natl. Cancer Inst.* **70**, 367–373.
Takizawa, S., and Hirose, F. (1978). *Gann* **69**, 723–726.
Talamini, R., LaVecchia, C., Decarli, A., Negri, E., and Franceschi, S. (1986). *Br. J. Cancer* **53**, 817–821.
Tannenbaum, M. (1977). *In* "Urologic Pathology: The Prostate" (M. Tannenbaum, ed.), pp. 303–397. Lea & Febiger, Philadelphia.
Terracio, L., and Nachtigal, M. (1986). *Arch. Toxicol.* **58**, 141–151.
Thomas, D. B. (1979). *Natl. Cancer Inst. Monogr.* **53**, 103–113.
Thomas, J. A., Lloyd, J. W., Smith, M. T., Mawhinney, M. G., and Smith, C. G. (1973). *Toxicol. Appl. Pharmacol.* **26**, 523–531.
Thomas, J. A., Donovan, M. P., Waalkes, M. P., and Curto, K. A. (1981). *In* "The Prostatic Cell" (G. P. Murphy, A. A. Sandberg, and J. P. Karr, eds.), Part A, pp. 459–474. Liss, New York.
Thompson, H. J., Meeker, L. D., and Becci, P. J. (1981). *Cancer Res.* **41**, 1413–1416.
Thun, M. J., Schnorr, T. M., Blair Smith, A., Holperin, W. E., and Lemen, R. A. (1985). *J. Natl. Cancer Inst.* **74**, 325–333.
Tolis, G., Ackman, D., Stellos, A., Mehta, A., Labrie, F., Fazakas, A. T. A., Comarin-Schally, A. M., and Sehall, A. V. (1982). *Proc. Natl. Acad. Sci. U.S.A.* **79**, 1658–1662.
Troll, W., and Wiesner, R. (1983). *Prostate* **4**, 345–349.
Tulinius, H. (1982). *In* "Cancer Campaign, Vol. 6, Cancer Epidemiology" (E. Grundman, ed.), pp. 129–137. Fischer, Stuttgart.
Tuohimaa, P. (1980). *In* "Male Accessory Sex Glands" (E. Spring-Mills and E. S. E. Hafez, eds.), pp. 131–153. Elsevier, Amsterdam.
Umeda, F., Kato, K., Muta, K., and Ibayashi, H. (1982). *Endocrinol. Jpn.* **29**, 287–292.
Upton, A. C., Kimball, A. W., Furth, S., Christenberry, K. W., and Benedict, W. H. (1960). *Cancer Res.* **20**, 1–60.
Vandenbroecke-Grauls, C. M. J. E., Rozenberg-Arska, M., Denhengst, C. W., and Verhoef, J. (1982). *Br. J. Vener. Dis.* **58**, 311–313.
Vermeulen, A., Rubens, R., and Verdonck, L. (1972). *J. Clin. Endocrinol.* **34**, 730–736.
Vestergaard, P. (1978). *Acta Endocrinol.* **217**, (Suppl.), 157–189.
Visek, W. J., (1981). *In* "The Prostatic Cell" (G. P. Murphy, A. A. Sandberg, and J. P. Karr, eds.), Part B, pp. 165–182. Liss, New York.
Waalkes, M. P., Rehm, S., and Perantoni, A. (1987). *Proc. Am. Assoc. Cancer Res.* **28**, 25.
Wagner, P. A., Krista, M. L., Baily, L. B., Christakis, G. J., Jernigan, J. A., Aranjo, P. E., Appledorf, H., Davis, C. G., and Dinning, J. S. (1980). *Am. J. Clin. Nutr.* **33**, 1771–1777.
Wakabayashi, T., Kato, H., Ikeda, T., and Schull, W. J., (1983). *Radiat. Res.* **93**, 112–146.
Wang, D., and Wang, H.-W. (1981). *Tumor (Shanghai)* **1**, 1–2.
Wang, H.-W., Wang, D., Tang, P.-X., Shen, R.-J., and Zhang, R.-W (1981). *Acta Biol. Exp. Sin.* **14**, 77–85.
Wang, H., Wang, D., and Dzeng, R. (1984a). *Cancer Res.* **44**, 3098–3100.
Wang, H., You, X., Qu, Y., Wang, W., Wang, D., Long, Y., and Ni, J. (1984b). *Cancer Res.* **44**, 3101–3105.

Ward, J. M., Reznik, G., Stinson, S. F., Lattirada, C. P., Longfellow, D. G., and Cameron, T. P. (1980). *Lab. Invest.* **43**, 517–522.

Watanabe, H., Ito, A., and Hirose, F. (1986). *In* "Radiation Carcinogenesis" (A. C. Upton, R. E. Albert, F. J. Burns, and R. E. Shore, eds.), pp. 237–244. Elsevier, New York.

Waterhouse, J., Muir, C., Correa, P., and Powell, J. (1976). "Cancer Incidence in Five Continents," Vol. III. IARC, Lyon.

Waterhouse, J., Muir, C., Correa, P., and Powell, J. (1982). "Cancer Incidence in Five Continents," Vol. IV. IARC, Lyon.

Wattenberg, L. W. (1983). *Cancer Res.* **43**, 2448s–2453s.

Webber, M. M. (1985). *Biochem. Biophys. Res. Comm.* **127**, 871–877.

Welsch, C. W., Zile, M. H., and Cullum, M. E. (1985). *In* "Diet, Nutrition, and Cancer: A Critical Evaluation. Vol. II" (B. S. Reddy and L. A. Cohen, eds.), pp. 1–21. CRC Press, Boca Raton, Florida.

Wenderoth, U. K., and Jacobi, G. H. (1983). *World J. Urol.* **1**, 40–48.

Whelan, P., Walker, B. E., and Kelleher, J. (1983). *Br. J. Urol.* **55**, 525–528.

White, J. E., Enterline, J. P., Alam, Z., and Moore, R. M., Jr., (1981). *In* "Cancer Among Black Populations" (C. Mettlin and G. P. Murphy, eds.), pp. 35–53. Liss, New York.

Whitmore, W. F., (1963). *Cancer* **16**, 1119–1132.

Whittemore, A. S., Paffenbarger, R. S., Anderson, K., and Lee, S. E. (1986). *J. Natl. Cancer Inst.* **74**, 43–51.

Wiklund, K., and Holm, L.-E (1986). *J. Natl. Cancer Inst.* **77**, 657–664.

Wilcosky, T. C., Checkoway, H., Marshall, E. G., and Tyroler, H. A. (1984). *Am. Ind. Hyg. Assoc. J.* **45**, 809–811.

Wilkinson, G. S., Tietjen, G. L., Wiggs, L. D., Galke, W. A., Acquavella, J. F., Reyes, M., Voelz, G. L., and Waxweiler, R. J. (1987). *Am. J. Epidemiol.* **125**, 231–250.

Willett, W. C., Morris, J. S., Pressel, S., Taylor, J. O., Polk, B. F., Stampfer, M. J., Rosner, B., Schneider, K., and Hames, C. G. (1983). *Lancet* **2** 130–134.

Willett, W. C., Polk, B. F., Underwood, B. A., Stampfer, M. J., Pressel, S., Rosner, B., Taylor, J. O., Schneider, K., and Hames, C. G. (1984). *N. Engl. J. Med.* **310**, 430–434.

Williams, R. R., and Horms, J. W. (1977). *J. Natl. Cancer Inst.* **58**, 525–547.

Williams, R. R., Stegens, M. L., and Goldsmith, J. R. (1977). *J. Natl. Cancer Inst.* **59**, 1147–1185.

Winkelstein, W., and Ernster, V. L. (1979). *In* "Prostatic Cancer" (G. P. Murphy, ed.), pp. 1–17. PSG Publ., Littleton.

Winkelstein, W., and Kantor, S, (1969). *Am. J. Publ. Health* **59**, 1134–1138.

Wolbach, S., and Howe, P. R. (1925). *J. Exp. Med.* **42**, 753–769.

Woolf, C. M. (1960). *Cancer* **13**, 739–743.

Wynder, E. L., and Hirayama, T. (1977). *Prev. Med.* **6**, 567–594.

Wynder, E. L., Hyams, L., and Shigematsu, T. (1967). *Cancer* **20**, 113–126.

Wynder, E. L., Mabuchi, K., and Whitmore, W. F. (1971). *Cancer* **28**, 344–360.

Yatani, R., Chigusa, I., Akazaki, K., Stemmermann, G. N., Welsh, R. A., and Correa, P. (1982). *Int. J. Cancer* **29**, 611–616.

Zaneveld, L. J. D., and Tauber, P. F. (1981). *In* "The Prostatic Cell" (G. P. Murphy, A. A. Sandberg, and J. P. Karr, eds.), Part A, pp. 265–277. Liss, New York.

Zeigel, R. F. (1979). *In* "Prostatic Cancer" (G. P. Murphy, ed.), pp. 19–33. PSG Publ., Littleton.

Zumoff, B., Strain, G. W., Kream, J., O'Connor, J., Levin, J., and Fukushima, D. K. (1981). *Metabolism* **30**, 1011–1014.

Zumoff, B., Levin, J., Strain, G. W., Rosenfeld, R. S., O'Connor, J., Freed, S. Z., Kream, J., Whitmore, W. S., Fukushima, D. K., and Hellman, L. (1982). *Prostate* **3**, 579–588.

TRANSFORMING GROWTH FACTOR β

Anita B. Roberts and Michael B. Sporn

Laboratory of Chemoprevention, National Cancer Institute, Besthesda, Maryland 20892

I. Introduction 107
II. TGF-α and Its Relationship to EGF 110
A. Structure of TGF-α 110
B. Biological Activity of TGF-α 112
III. TGF-β 113
A. Assays Employed for the Isolation of TGF-β 113
B. Purification of TGF-β 115
C. Physical Properties of Type β TGFs 116
D. Structure of the TGF-β Precursor 119
E. Other Peptides Related to the TGF-β Family 121
F. Membrane Receptors for TGF-β 123
G. The "Latent" or Inactive Form of TGF-β 128
H. Biological Actions of TGF-β *in Vitro* 130
I. Actions of TGF-β *in Vivo* and Potential Therapeutic Uses 136

I. Introduction

Transforming growth factors α and β owe their shared nomenclature to the nature of the assay by which they were first discovered and which was later used to purify these peptides to homogeneity. In 1978 De Larco and Todaro reported that mouse 3T3 cells transformed by Moloney sarcoma virus produced polypeptide growth factors, called sarcoma growth factors (SGFs), which were secreted into the extracellular medium and had the unusual property of being able to induce a "transformed" phenotype in a non-neoplastic "reader" cell, such as the rat NRK 49F fibroblast. This transformed phenotype was operationally characterized by the loss of density-dependent growth in monolayer culture, overgrowth in monolayer, the characteristic change in cellular morphology, and most important, the acquisition of anchorage independence and the resultant ability of the NRK 49F cells to grow in soft agar, a property with a strong correlation to tumorigenicity of fibroblasts *in vivo* (Kahn and Shin, 1979; Cifone and Fidler, 1980). The transforming activity of SGF on NRK cells was only phenotypic; upon removal of SGF from the NRK cells, they reverted back to their normal morphology and normal growth properties. Shortly

ADVANCES IN CANCER RESEARCH, VOLUME 51

thereafter, Todaro *et al.* (1980) and Ozanne *et al.* (1980) reported similar transforming activity in the conditioned medium of several human cancer cells and a variety of mouse and rat cells transformed by Kirsten sarcoma virus. All of these transforming activities were also characterized by their ability to compete with epidermal growth factor (EGF) for binding to its cell surface receptor.

At the same time Roberts *et al.* (1980) introduced the use of acid-ethanol to extract the transforming peptides from tumor cells themselves, and the term *transforming growth factor* (TGF) was coined, because it was realized that peptides with similar activities could be extracted from a very wide variety of tumor cells. Surprisingly, it was found that TGF activity could also be extracted from almost every normal tissue of the mouse, particularly if one added EGF to the transformation assay (Roberts *et al.*, 1981), although EGF itself could not induce transformation. It was suggested that these peptides, extractable from nonneoplastic tissues and requiring EGF to potentiate the growth of NRK 49F cells in soft agar, represented a new class of transforming growth factor. Shortly thereafter, peptides with similar properties were found in normal serum and blood platelets (Childs *et al.*, 1982).

At this point it became essential to achieve a chemical, as well as a functional definition of the term *TGF*; and the use of high-pressure liquid chromatography (HPLC) rapidly clarified many of the ambiguities that existed in the early experiments. Using the NRK 49F cell as the assay cell, two principal types of TGFs were isolated and defined (Anzano *et al.*, 1982; Roberts *et al.*, 1983b): peptides that competed with EGF for receptor binding but did not require additional EGF for promotion of growth of cells in soft agar were defined as TGF-α, and peptides that did not compete with EGF for receptor binding but did require EGF (or TGF-α) for promotion of growth in soft agar were defined as TGF-β (see Fig. 1). Furthermore, it was found that in this NRK system neither TGF-α nor EGF promoted growth of colonies in soft agar by themselves, but that they were dependent on the concomitant presence of TGF-β for eliciting this biological activity (Anzano *et al.*, 1982). Thus the original transforming activity of SGF was shown to be the result of the presence of both TGF-α and TGF-β in the conditioned medium of the cells transformed by Moloney sarcoma virus; when these two peptides were separated, biological activity in the NRK system was lost, whereas recombination of the separated peptides restored activity (Anzano *et al.*, 1983).

With the aid of HPLC and the demonstration that two peptides—rather than just a single transforming peptide—were required for phenotypic transformation of NRK cells, it was then possible to achieve total purification and characterization of TGF-β. This was achieved almost simultaneously from three tissue sources, namely, human platelets (Assoian *et al.*, 1983), human placenta (Frolik *et al.*, 1983), and bovine kidney (Roberts *et al.*,

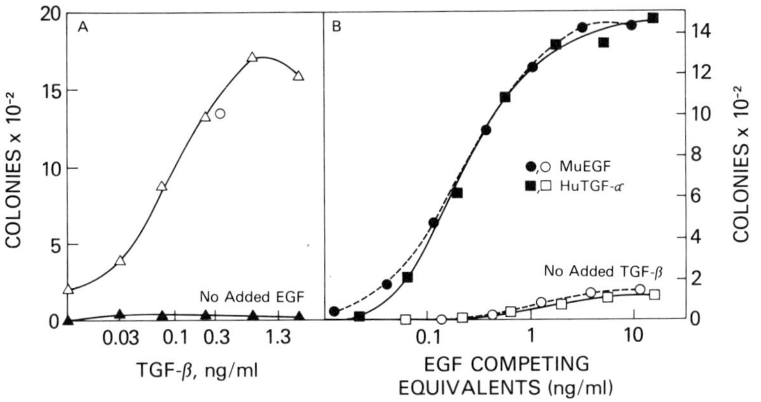

FIG. 1. Colony formation of NRK 49F cells in soft agar requires the combined action of both EGF (or TGF-α) and TGF-β. A. TGF-β alone (▲) has no effect on colony formation but can stimulate colony formation in a dose-dependent fashion when assayed in the presence of 0.8 n*M* EGF (△) or TGF-α (○). B. EGF (○) or TGF-α (□) alone induces the formation of only a small number of colonies (probably resulting from the TGF-β in the 10% serum used in the assay); in the presence of 10 p*M* TGF-β, these peptides induce optimal colony formation (closed symbols). Under these assay conditions, the ED_{50}s for TGF-β and EGF/TGF-α are 3 and 50 p*M*, respectively. Recombinant TGF-α (Derynck *et al.*, 1984) and EGF are interchangeable in this assay.

1983a). A homodimeric peptide of M_r 25,000 (giving two monomeric subunits of M_r 12,500 upon reduction) with identical amino-terminal amino acid sequences was defined from these three tissues.

This article will focus on the structure and function of TGF-β; TGF-α will be dealt with only briefly. Current interest in TGF-β is very different from the context in which this peptide was originally discovered. Like many other peptide growth factors, TGF-β is multifunctional, and many of its most important activities have little to do with the transformation system in which it was first discovered. It is now very clear that there is no intrinsic chemical or biological relationship between TGF-α and TGF-β and that they are indeed two entirely separate peptides, which may act synergistically, may act antagonistically, or may have separate actions that have little to do with one another. Much of the current interest in TGF-β research reflects its importance as a mediator of inflammation, repair, and angiogenesis (Sporn and Roberts, 1986), as well as its importance as a negative growth regulator for many epithelial cells (Moses *et al.*, 1985) and for both T and B lymphocytes (Kehrl *et al.*, 1986a,b). Because essentially all cells have receptors for TGF-β (Frolik *et al.*, 1984; Tucker *et al.*, 1984a; Massagué and Like, 1985; Wakefield *et al.*, 1987b), TGF-β has the potential to regulate physiological function in almost all tissues of the body; many of its actions have little to do with control of cell proliferation itself. Rather, TGF-β appears to be a fundamental autocrine or paracrine regulator of many disparate activities in many different types of cells; its action is often directly related to the specialized function of individual cells or tissues.

II. TGF-α and Its Relationship to EGF

Now that both TGF-α and TGF-β have been purified to homogeneity, sequenced, and cloned, it is clear that they represent distinct families of peptides; their amino acid sequences, secondary structures, cell membrane receptors, and mRNAs are unique. TGF-α and TGF-β share *only* a common nomenclature, based on their discovery as synergistic effectors of the "transformation" of NRK fibroblasts (Fig. 1). This is not unlike the interleukins, which share a common nomenclature based on their secretion by leukocytes but are all distinct peptides with distinct biological activities. A brief overview of the structure and biology of TGF-α illustrates the differences between it and TGF-β.

A. Structure of TGF-α

The amino acid sequences of both human (Derynck *et al.*, 1984) and rat TGF-α (Marquardt *et al.*, 1983, 1984; Lee *et al.*, 1985b) have been determined and show that both peptides are monomeric and 50 amino acids in length, with six cysteine residues in positions homologous to those in the three disulfide bonds of EGF (Fig. 2A and B). Two protein products of members of the poxvirus family—vaccinia virus protein (Blomquist *et al.*, 1984; Brown *et al.*, 1985) and Shope fibroma virus protein (Chang *et al.*, 1987)—also have significant homology in their amino acid sequences to EGF and TGF-α sequences, again showing positional conservation of all three disulfide bonds.

The structural relatedness of TGF-α and EGF is the basis for the EGF receptor binding activity of TGF-α, a property used to achieve its purification. Vaccinia virus protein also binds to the EGF receptor and stimulates its autophosphorylation (Twardzik *et al.*, 1985; Stroobant *et al.*, 1985), and the infectivity of the virus can be blocked by pretreatment of susceptible cells with EGF (Eppstein *et al.*, 1985). Comparison of the amino acid sequences of rat and human TGF-αs, mouse and human EGFs, and the two viral proteins suggests that the loop between the fifth and sixth cysteine residues might play an important role in receptor recognition (Todaro *et al.*, 1985). Six of ten amino acids in this loop are conserved among all members of this EGF family (Fig. 2A and B).

Cloning of the cDNAs corresponding to human (Derynck *et al.*, 1984) and rat TGF-α (Lee *et al.*, 1985a) has shown that TGF-α, like EGF (Gray *et al.*, 1983; Scott *et al.*, 1983), is encoded by a relatively large mRNA of

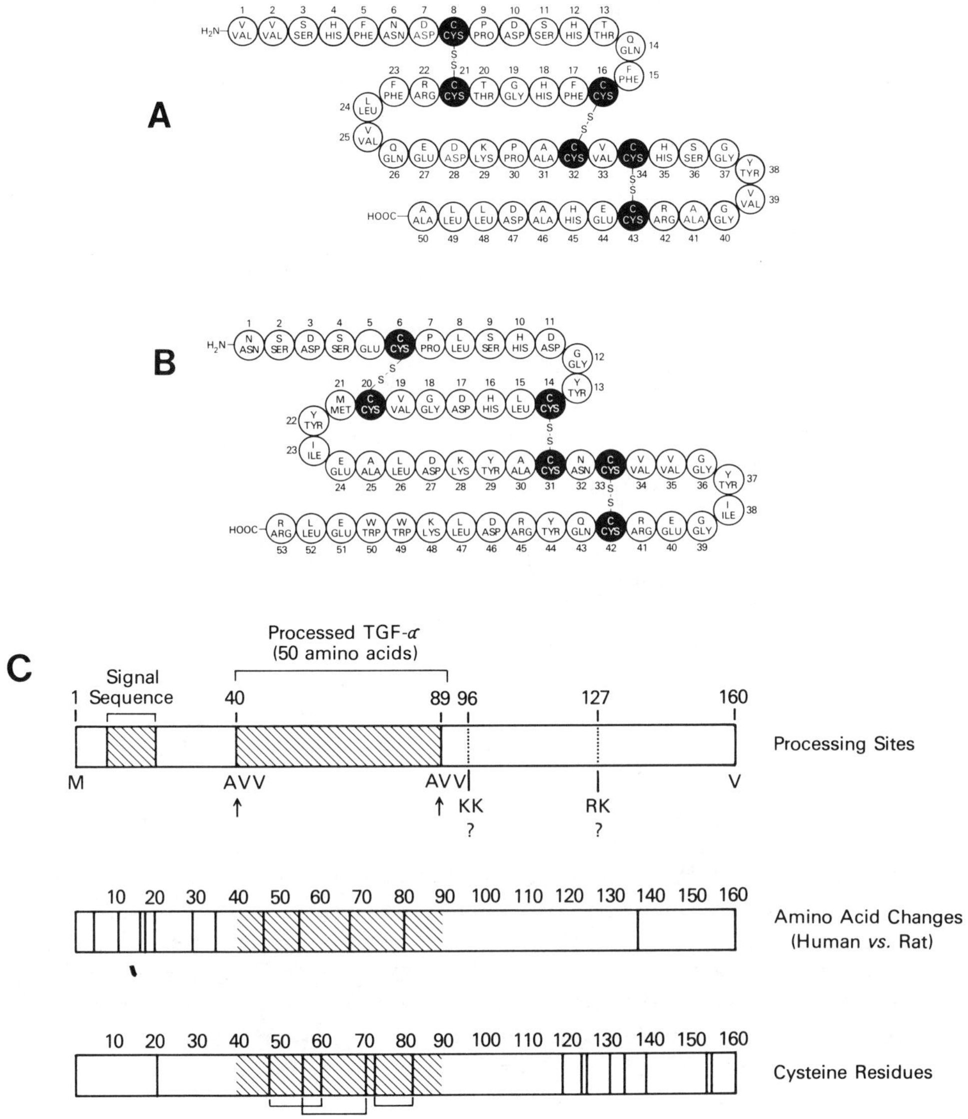

FIG. 2. Structures of human TGF-α and EGF. A. Deduced sequence of the 50-amino acid, processed human TGF-α (Derynck *et al.*, 1984). B. Amino acid sequence of human EGF (Gregory, 1975). C. Features of the deduced 160-amino acid TGF-α precursor, including processing sites (Derynck *et al.*, 1984; Todaro *et al.*, 1985; Bringman *et al.*, 1987). Note the high degree of conservation in the cysteine-rich carboxyl-terminal portion of the precursor.

approximately 4800 nucleotides. In humans, the gene has been localized to chromosome 2 (Brissenden *et al.*, 1985). The processed 50-amino acid TGF-α is contained within a 160-amino acid precursor with both amino-terminal (39 amino acids) and carboxyl-terminal (71 amino acids) extensions from which it is proteolytically cleaved by a novel protease that cleaves between alanine and valine residues (Fig. 2C). Recent experiments suggest that previously observed larger TGF-α species of approximately 18 kDa (De Larco and Todaro, 1978; Todaro *et al.*, 1980; Dart *et al.*, 1985; Linsley *et al.*, 1985) arise from partial processing of the precursor to glycosylated peptides, which start after the signal peptide at the amino-terminus and end at either the carboxyl-terminus of the processed peptide or at residue 97 (Ignotz *et al.*, 1986; Bringman *et al.*, 1987). Regardless, processing leaves a transmembrane carboxyl-terminal portion of the precursor with a cytoplasmic extension that is cysteine rich and has been found to be palmitoylated (Bringman *et al.*, 1987). This carboxyl-terminal portion of the precursor is even more highly conserved between rodents and man than the processed 50-amino acid peptide (1 change out of 71 amino acids, and 4 changes out of 50 amino acids, respectively; see Fig. 2C) a finding suggesting that it must serve an important, though presently unknown, function (Todaro *et al.*, 1985).

B. Biological Activity of TGF-α

The hallmark of TGF-α activity has always been its ability to compete for binding to the EGF receptor. Recent experiments using natural TGF-α (Massagué, 1983) or chemically synthesized TGF-α (Tam *et al.*, 1984) have shown its binding to the EGF receptor to be on an approximately equimolar basis with EGF; recombinant TGF-α reportedly is only 55% as effective in EGF binding competition assays (Winkler *et al.*, 1986). It should then not be surprising that most of the biological activities of TGF-α are identical to those described for EGF. Among these shared activities are several *in vitro* effects such as stimulation of mitogenesis (Carpenter *et al.*, 1983), dissolution of actin fibers (Ozanne *et al.*, 1980), and transformation of NRK cells (Anzano *et al.*, 1982; see also Fig. 1), as well as two *in vivo* assays; induction of precocious eyelid opening in newborn mice (Smith *et al.*, 1985) and inhibition of gastric acid secretion (Rhodes *et al.*, 1986).

There are reports suggesting that TGF-α has greater activity than EGF. These include induction of angiogenesis in a hamster cheek pouch model (Schreiber *et al.*, 1986), promotion of calcium release from fetal long bones (P. H. Stern *et al.*, 1986), enhancement of osteoclast activity (Takahashi *et al.*, 1986), healing of epithelial wounds (Schultz *et al.*, 1987), and promotion of growth of human epithelial cell clones in culture (Barrandon and Green, 1987). Each of these experimental systems, with the exception of the last one, is complex, and it cannot yet be ruled out that the enhanced activity of TGF-α might be due to differential stability or pharmacokinetic properties. On the other hand, it must also be considered that there might exist a distinct receptor with preference for TGF-α; experiments to date investigating receptor binding of TGF-α and EGF have relied on the use of established cell lines, which might express only the EGF receptor.

Although TGF-α is expressed by a variety of tumor cells, with the exception of cells of hematopoietic origin (Derynck *et al.*, 1987), there is growing evidence that TGF-α might also play a role in normal physiology. Transcriptional activity of TGF-α is high in the early mouse embryo (Lee *et al.*, 1985a), and it is secreted by normal untransformed bovine anterior pituitary cells in culture (Samsoondar *et al.*, 1986; Kobrin *et al.*, 1986). The present availability of specific antibodies and cDNA probes for both EGF and TGF-α should serve to elucidate possible unique roles of each of these peptides in both nonneoplastic and neoplastic processes.

III. TGF-β

TGF-β belongs to a new gene family clearly distinct from that of the EGF-related peptides. We will describe in detail the unique distribution, structure, gene, cell membrane receptor, and biological activity of this peptide.

A. Assays Employed for the Isolation of TGF-β

1. *Stimulation of Anchorage-Independent Growth of Cells*

As noted earlier, the discovery that the ability of NRK 49F cells to grow to form large colonies in soft agar medium was dependent upon the action of two distinct peptides, TGF-α/EGF and TGF-β (Anzano *et al.*, 1982, 1983), formed the basis for the assay used for purification of TGF-β. As shown in Fig. 1A, colony formation by NRK cells assayed in 10% serum in the presence of approximately 1 n*M* EGF was dose-dependent upon the concentration of added TGF-β. This assay was utilized for purification of TGF-βs from human, bovine, and rodent sources (Roberts *et al.*, 1984b). Under the conditions described, the assay has an absolute dependence on TGF-β; no other peptide has been shown to elicit this response, although TGF-βs from all species work equally well in the assay.

Moses and co-workers have used a mouse embryo fibroblast cell line—AKR–2B—to assay for TGF-β activity (Moses *et al.*, 1984). Unlike NRK cells, AKR–2B cells form colonies in soft agar in the presence of TGF-β alone, thereby demonstrating that the requirement of both EGF and TGF-β for transformation of NRK cells is a function of the indicator cell itself rather than an obligatory mechanism of TGF-β action.

Although anchorage-independent growth of either NRK or AKR-2B cells in the presence of serum is absolutely dependent on TGF-β, anchorage-independent growth of other cells is not specific for TGFs. Kaplan and Ozanne (1983) have shown that subclones of the rat fibroblast line F2408 can be induced to grow in soft agar by EGF and platelet-derived growth factor (PDGF). The spectrum of "transforming" growth factors is extended yet further by the finding that insulin-like growth factor II (IGF-II) (Massagué *et al.*, 1985) and PDGF (Assoian *et al.*, 1984b) are also required for transformation of NRK cells; these two growth factors are provided by the 10% serum used in the initial description of the assay (De Larco and Todaro, 1978). BALB/c 3T3 cells can also be induced to grow in soft agar and require both TGF-β and IGF-II (Massagué *et al.*, 1985).

Use of serum-free conditions alters the response of NRK cells to growth factors. Rizzino *et al.* (1986) have shown that neither EGF/TGF-α nor TGF-β are essential for the colony-forming response of the cells under serum-free conditions and that various combinatons of EGF, PDGF, TGF-β, and fibroblast growth factor (FGF) can induce a response. A similar conclusion has been reached by van Zoelen *et al.* (1986), who have shown that NRK cells assayed in serum in which the growth factors have been chemically inactivated can form large colonies in the presence of either EGF and retinoic acid or the combination of PDGF, TGF-β, and retinoic acid. In both of these studies it is clear that the cellular response is determined by the *entire set* of growth factors acting on the cells and not by an intrinsic "transforming" activity associated with any particular growth factor.

2. *Inhibition of Growth*

A growth inhibitor isolated from the conditioned medium of the BSC−1 monkey kidney cell line (Holley *et al.*, 1980) has been found to be similar, if not identical to TGF-β (Tucker *et al.*, 1984b). Purification of this peptide was monitored by assay of its ability to inhibit the growth of BSC−1 cells in monolayer culture. TGF-β has subsequently been found to inhibit the growth of many different cell lines, both neoplastic and nonneoplastic (Tucker *et al.*, 1984b; Roberts *et al.*, 1985a), as will be discussed in greater detail later in this article. However, given that other peptides can also inhibit the growth of the some of the same cells, such as A549 human lung carcinoma cells and A375 and SK-MEL−28 human melanoma cells (Iwata *et al.*, 1985; Zarling *et al.*, 1986; Fryling *et al.*, 1985), this assay is likely to be less specific than the assay for colony growth in soft agar described earlier.

3. *Induction of Cartilage*

Two cartilage-inducing factors—CIF-A and CIF-B—isolated from bovine demineralized bone and purified to homogeneity based on their ability to induce embryonic rat mesenchymal cells in culture to assume a cartilage morphology and synthesize cartilage-specific proteoglycan and type II collagen (Seyedin *et al.*, 1985) have now been found to be identical to TGF-β (Seyedin *et al.*, 1986) and to a second form of TGF-β, TGF-β2, respectively (Cheifetz *et al.*, 1987; Seyedin *et al.*, 1987). As in the colony-forming assays, the rat mesenchymal cells were grown under anchorage-independent conditions; proteoglycan and type II collagen levels were monitored by ELISA assays and shown to be dependent on the concentration of added TGF-β. Chondrogenic induction by TGF-β was specific to embryonic rat mesenchymal cells, much as colony-forming activity was specific to NRK or AKR–2B cells as previously described.

B. Purification of TGF-β

Type β TGFs have been purified to homogeneity from several nonneoplastic tissues, from transformed cells, and from conditioned medium. Sources include human placenta (Frolik *et al.*, 1983), human platelets (Assoian *et al.*, 1983), human A673 cells (Dart *et al.*, 1985), bovine kidney (Roberts *et al.*, 1983a), conditioned medium of virally transformed rat embryo cells (Massagué, 1984) or transformed murine L–929 cells (Fernandez-Pol *et al.*, 1986), and, most recently, porcine platelets (Cheifetz *et al.*, 1987) and bovine bone (Seyedin *et al.*, 1985, 1986). Of these tissues, platelets represent the most concentrated source of TGF-β, with a final yield of approximately 2–3 mg TGF-β/kg wet weight human platelets. Bone, however, represents the greatest reservoir of TGF-β in the body; the yield of TGF-β from bovine bone is approximatley 200 μg/kg demineralized bone powder, or 10% that of platelets. Soft tissues such as placenta or kidney have only 1% the TGF-β content of bone, yielding approximately 2–3 μg TGF-β/kg, whereas the final yield of TGF-β from conditioned medium of transformed cells in culture has ranged from 14 ng to about 2 μg/liter. Thus, platelets clearly represent the best and most practical source of the peptide at the present time.

Each of the published purification schemes takes advantage of the stability of TGF-β at low pH and under denaturing conditions such as alcohol, urea, or guanidine. Purification of TGF-β from either human or porcine platelets, the major sources of TGF-β used in research, is based on the procedure of Assoian *et al.* (1983; see also Assoian, 1987). This method involves extensive washing of fresh platelets followed by extraction with acidic ethanol and precipitation with ether. The peptide is then purified by two chromatographic steps on BioGel P–60. On the first column, which is eluted with 1 *M* acetic acid, TGF-β migrates at an aberrantly low molecular weight, presumably as a result of hydrophobic interactions with the acrylamide gel matrix, and coelutes with contaminating proteins of approximately

13,000 Da. The second column is eluted with 1 *M* acetic acid–8 *M* urea; under these conditions TGF-β (M_r, 25,000) is separated from the low-molecular-weight impurities. Final purification and desalting is accomplished by reverse-phase HPLC using an acetonitrile gradient in 0.1% trifluoroacetic acid. Human platelet TGF-β purified by this procedure is at least 95% pure as determined by silver staining of samples run on nonreducing sodium dodecyl sulfate (SDS) gels.

Unlike the purification of human platelet TGF-β, which yields only a single species of TGF-β, porcine platelet TGF-β purified by a minor modification of this method can be resolved into three forms called TGF-β1, TGF-β2, and TGF-β1.2 (Cheifetz *et al.*, 1987). Final separation of these three forms is accomplished by two more HPLC purification steps.

The only other quantitatively significant method for TGF-β purification is its isolation from demineralized bone powder as described by Seyedin *et al.* (1985). Briefly, this method involves demineralizaton of bone in 0.5 *M* HCl followed by extraction with 4 *M* guanidine•HCl, pH 6.8, gel filtration in the same solvent, ion exchange on CM-cellulose, and reverse-phase HPLC using an acetonitrile gradient in 0.1% trifluoroacetic acid. CIF-A and CIF-B (identical to TGF-β1 and TGF-β2, respectively) are separated by chromatography on CM-cellulose and chromatographed individually on HPLC.

C. Physical Properties of Type β TGFs

TGF-β purified from cells, tissues, or platelets is a 25,000-Da homodimeric peptide that, upon reduction, yields two identical peptides of approximately 12,500 Da (Fig. 3A). Each chain contains nine half-cystine residues (Fig. 4A); which of these is involved in inter- or intrachain disulfide bridges is not known. Only the nonreduced dimeric form of the peptide is known to be biologically active (Fig. 3B). Amino-terminal amino acid sequence analysis shows TGF-β from human (Derynck *et al.*, 1985), murine (Derynck *et al.*, 1986), rat (Massagué, 1984), bovine (Seyedin *et al.*, 1986), and porcine sources (Cheifetz *et al.*, 1987) to have identical sequences up to residue 30. Total amino acid sequence deduced from the cDNA clones shows that the processed human (Derynck *et al.*, 1985) and bovine TGF-βs (Van Obberghen-Schilling *et al.*, 1987) are identical, whereas the murine peptide differs from human TGF-β in one amino acid at position 75 (Derynck *et al.*, 1985; see Fig. 4B); the alanine at that position of the human or bovine sequence is replaced with a serine residue in the murine sequence. The complete amino acid sequences of porcine and chicken TGF-β are currently being deduced from cDNA clones. This remarkable conservation of amino acid sequence shows extreme evolutionary pressures operating to preserve the specific structure and function of this peptide.

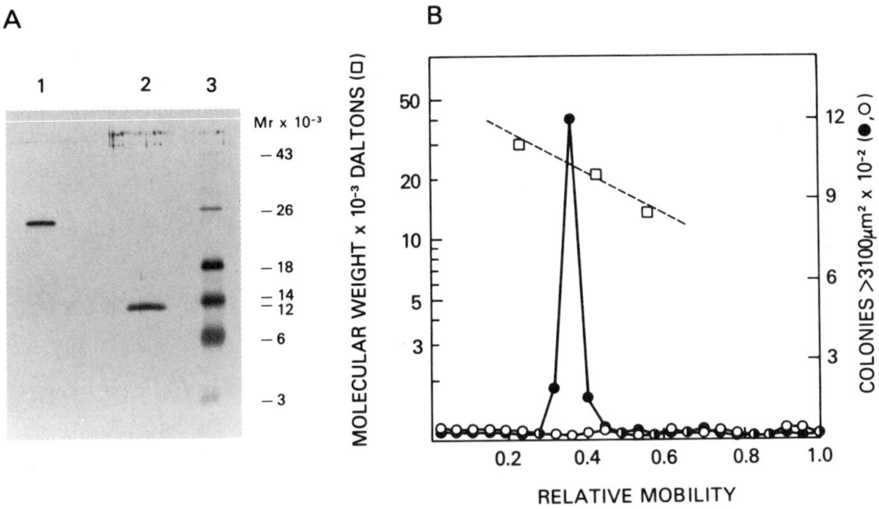

FIG. 3. Sodium dodecyl sulfate-polyacrylamide gel electrophoresis of TGF-β purified from bovine kidney (Roberts *et al.*, 1983a). A. TGF-β (50 ng) was chromatographed under nonreducing conditions (lane 1) or in the presence of β-mercaptoethanol (lane 2) and stained with silver. Molecular weight markers (lane 3) are indicated on the left. B. TGF-β was eluted from the gel as described (Roberts *et al.*, 1984b) and assayed for colony-forming activity of NRK cells in soft agar. Note that only 25,000-Da, nonreduced TGF-β (●) had biological activity in this assay; reduced TGF-β (○) was inactive.

Recently, the discoveries of chromatographically distinct forms of TGF-β in bovine bone (Seyedin *et al.*, 1985, 1987) and porcine platelets (Cheifetz *et al.*, 1987) have led to the identification of a second form of homodimeric TGF-β (TGF-β2) and a heterodimeric TGF-β composed of one chain of each type (TGF-β1.2). These variant forms of the peptide are less abundant than TGF-β1 in the sources examined thus far; TGF-β2 represents approximately 1/6 to 1/4 the amount of TGF-β1 in either bovine bone or porcine platelets, and TGF-β1.2 is a minor form characterized thus far only in porcine platelets. Remarkably, the amino-terminal amino acid sequences of bovine TGF-β2 (CIF-B; Seyedin *et al.*, 1987) and of porcine TGF-β2 (Cheifetz *et al.*, 1987) are identical, a similarity suggesting high evolutionary pressure on this less abundant form of the peptide as well as on the major species of peptide. TGF-β1 and TGF-β2 differ by over 50% in the first 20 residues, but are conserved approximately 85% in the region of residues 21–36 (Fig. 5). No data are yet available on the sequence of the carboxyl-terminal half of the peptide; antibodies raised to amino acids 64–91 of TGF-β1 do not detect TGF-β2 on Western blots (Cheifetz *et al.*, 1987), but antibodies raised to

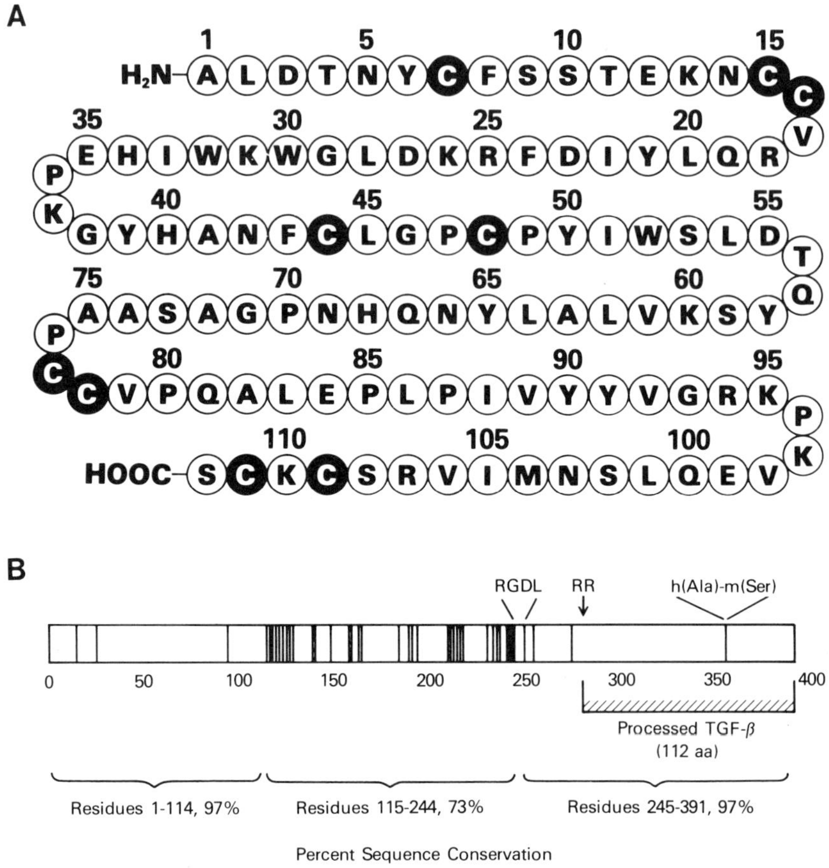

FIG. 4. Structure of human TGF-β and its precursor. A. Deduced sequence of the processed 112-amino acid monomer unit of human TGF-β (Derynck *et al.*, 1985). B. Homology between the deduced sequence of the entire 390-amino acid precursor of mouse (Derynck *et al.*, 1986) and human TGF-β. Substituted amino acids are indicated by a line. Note the high degree of sequence conservation in the amino-terminal region of the precursor as well as in the processed region. Although its importance is not known, the fibronectin binding site, Arg-Gly-Asp-(Leu) (Ruoslahti and Pierschbacher, 1986), is also conserved between mouse and man.

amino acids 50–75 and amino acids 78–109 of TGF-β1 do recognize TGF-β2 in an ELISA assay, and the latter antibodies recognize reduced TGF-β2 on Western blots as well (Flanders *et al.*, 1988).

The three forms of TGF-β are indistinguishable on SDS gels and have apparently identical biological activities in many of the various assay systems previously described, including induction of colony formation in soft agar, inhibition of cell growth, and induction of a chondrogenic phenotype

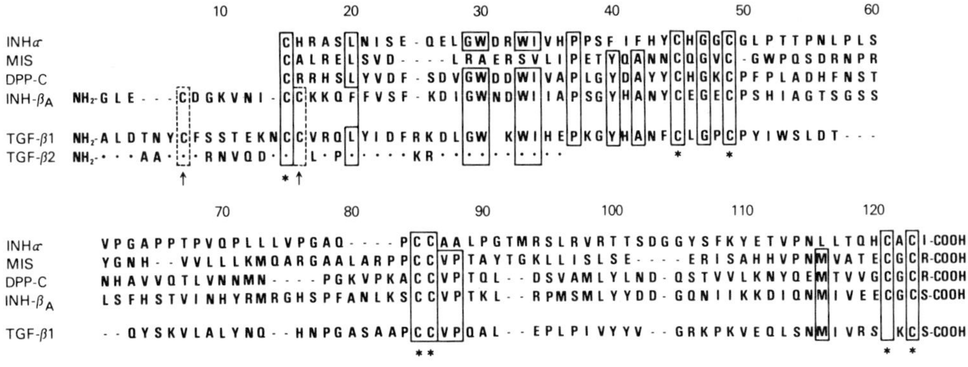

FIG. 5. Homologies among members of the TGF-β family. Representatives of each of the peptides related to TGF-β are aligned with the best fit: the α and β_A chains of porcine inhibin (INHα, INH-β_A) (Mason *et al.*, 1985); human Müllerian inhibitory substance (MIS) (Cate *et al.*, 1986); the product of the decapentaplegic gene complex of *Drosophila* (DPP-C) (Padgett *et al.*, 1987); human TGF-β (TGF-β1), and porcine or bovine TGF-β2 (Cheifetz *et al.*, 1987; Seyedin *et al.*, 1987). Cysteine residues conserved in all family members are marked with an asterisk; cysteine residues conserved only in the TGF-βs and the β chain of inhibin are marked with an arrow. Other residues shared by TGF-β and at least three other family members are boxed in. Note that the carboxyl termini of all family members are identical. The amino termini of INHα, MIS, and DPP-C do not align with the amino terminus of TGF-β and show no homology to TGF-β prior to the second cysteine residue; for that reason, they have not been included in this diagram.

(Cheifetz *et al.*, 1987; Seyedin *et al.*, 1987; Segarini *et al.*, 1987). Differences are found, however, in the binding patterns of each of these peptides to cellular receptors, as will be discussed later (Cheifetz *et al.*, 1987; Segarini *et al.*, 1987). The existence of specific cellular receptors and the high degree of conservation of this second form of TGF-β suggests that the alternate forms of this peptide might play unique roles in some as yet unidentified biological processes and might differ from form 1 in either cellular localization or mechanisms of cellular induction, secretion, or activation.

D. Structure of the TGF-β Precursor

The cDNA encoding TGF-β1 was isolated from a library derived from human term placenta (Derynck *et al.*, 1985); the gene was subsequently localized to the long arm of human chromosome 19 and to mouse chromosome 7 (Fujii *et al.*, 1986). Northern hybridization showed that the mRNA encoding TGF-β is approximately 2500 base pairs long. The transcriptional start signal begins about 840 base pairs from the 5′ end, and the open reading frame goes on for 1173 nucleotides, encoding a 390-amino acid precursor form of the peptide that begins with an amino-terminal signal peptide sequence of 16 amino acids (Fig. 4B). There is a proteolytic processing site (Arg-Arg) immediately before the amino-terminal alanine residue of the processed 112-amino acid form of TGF-β that had previously been determined by amino-terminal sequencing of the purified human platelet TGF-β. Both a 60-nucleotide segment of the 5′ untranslated region and a 75-nucleotide segment just 3′ of the termination codon consist almost entirely of purines. The latter is also found in the transcript endoding the β chain of inhibin (Mason *et al.*, 1985), which is related to the TGF-β gene family (see later). It has been suggested that these regions might play a role in RNA stability or in regulation of RNA transcription (Derynck *et al.*, 1985).

The gene encoding murine TGF-β has also been cloned (Derynck *et al.*, 1986), its sequence confirming a 390-amino acid precursor form of the peptide. Interestingly, not only the sequence of the processed peptides of these species (see earlier), but also the sequences of the precursor peptides show remarkable homologies. There are only 3 amino acid differences in the 117 amino-terminal amino acids of the human and murine precursor peptides and a 75% conservation in the rest of the precursor peptide; the tripeptide recognition sequence of the cellular fibronectin binding site (Ruoslahti and Pierschbacher, 1986) is also conserved (Fig. 4B). This suggests that there might be separate functional activities associated with portions of the cleaved precursor peptide, as appears to occur in the latent form of TGF-β (see following discussion).

The gene encoding TGF-β2 has not yet been cloned.[1] Because TGF-β2 is less abundant than TGF-β1 in both bone and platelets, there must be differential control of the transcriptional or translational activity of these two genes. Also, because peptides more distantly related to the TGF-β family all have precursor forms that are proteolytically cleaved to the processed dimer (see following), it is highly likely that the TGF-β2 mRNA also encodes a larger precursor form of the peptide. This precursor might, however, differ significantly from that of TGF-β1 and result in differential rates of processing or activation of TGF-β2.

Northern hybridization using the TGF-β cDNA probes has shown that many cells and tissues, both neoplastic and nonneoplastic, express a single TGF-β mRNA of 2.5 kb (Derynck *et al.*, 1985, 1987; Kehrl *et al.*, 1986a,b; Robey *et al.*, 1987). In RNA isolated from selected paired samples from malignant and surrounding noninvolved tissues, it could be shown that there was frequently a striking increase in TGF-β mRNA levels associated with the tumor tissues (Derynck *et al.*, 1987), as had been found in pairs of fibroblast cell lines and their retrovirus-transformed counterparts (Derynck *et al.*, 1986; Jakowlew *et al.*, 1987). Induction could also be demonstrated in nonneoplastic tissues; mitogenic activation of peripheral blood human lymphocytes leads to significant elevation of TGF-β mRNA levels, which is sustained for several days (Derynck *et al.*, 1985; Kehrl *et al.*, 1986b; discussed in greater detail later).

E. Other Peptides Related to the TGF-β Family

In the past year, several other peptides have been shown to have partial amino acid sequence homology to TGF-β (Figs. 5 and 6). These include two inhibins, which are heterodimeric proteins (M_r, 32,000) of gonadal origin (inhibin A and B are each comprised of a common α subunit and a different β subunit) that act on the pituitary to suppress follicle-stimulating hormone (FSH) secretion (Ling *et al.*, 1985; Mason *et al.*, 1985; Forage *et al.*, 1986); three activins, which are dimeric peptides (M_r, ~24,000) also of gonadal origin, are formed by combinations of the β_A and β_B subunits of inhibin, and are potent stimulators of pituitary FSH secretion (Ling *et al.*, 1986; Vale *et al.*, 1986); Müllerian inhibitory substance (MIS), which is a homodimeric testicular glycoprotein (M_r, 140,000) that causes regression of the Müllerian duct during development of the male embryo (Cate *et al.*, 1986); and, most recently, the product of the decapentaplegic gene complex (DPP-C), which is involved in pattern formation and dorsal–ventral specification during *Drosophila* development (Padgett *et al.*, 1987). The relatedness of the amino acid sequences of these peptides, and especially the strong positional conservation of the cysteine residues, suggest that all

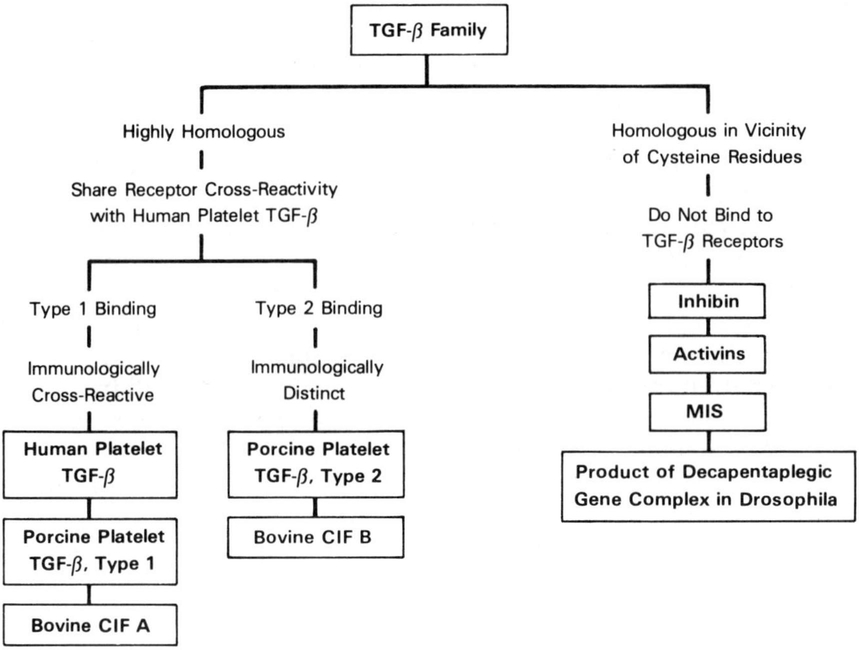

FIG. 6. Diagrammatic representation of the TGF-β gene family, with emphasis on receptor binding and immunological characteristics.

of these peptides belong to a single gene family (Fig. 5). Padgett *et al.* (1987) propose that the homology between the DPP-C and the mammalian TGF-β gene family demonstrates that an ancestral gene existed before the evolutionary divergence of arthropods and vertebrates and, moreover, that the closer relationship between TGF-β, DPP-C, and the β chains of inhibin than any of these three to either MIS or the α chain of inhibin suggests that the family had at least two members at that time in evolution.

The known dimeric structure of TGF-β, the inhibins, and the activins, as well as MIS, together with the conservation of cysteine residues throughout the TGF-β family suggest that the product of DPP-C is probably also a secreted dimeric peptide that acts through cellular receptors. Whether this gene product is biologically active as a homodimer or as part of a heterodimer is not yet known. The rather new discovery of the family of TGF-β peptides appears to be yet another demonstration of the ability of nature to repeatedly utilize a limited number of three-dimensional structures (as dictated by the positioning of the cysteine residues) but yet to attain diversity of function by altering specific amino acid sequences important for receptor binding (Doolittle, 1985). An example of this is found in the insulin family of peptides, where it has been shown that insulin, IGF-I and IGF-II, and relaxin all have a similar configuration of disulfide bridges and similar three-dimensional structures, yet interact through specific receptors to elicit distinct biological effects (Blundell and Humbel, 1980). Given the newness of the discoveries of TGF-β family members, it is likely that additonal members will yet be found.

Yet another similarity among members of the TGF-β gene family is that all of the peptides are encoded as larger precursor peptides (300–575 amino acids) and all contain signal peptide sequences near their aminotermini (summarized in Padgett *et al.*, 1987). The homologous cysteine-rich region of each of these peptides lies at the carboxyl-terminal end of the precursor, which, with the exception of MIS, is proteolytically cleaved from the precursor at a dibasic amino acid site (Arg-Arg for all peptides except the β_A chain of inhibin, where the site is Lys-Arg). In all family members, the carboxyl-terminal amino acid of the processed peptide is followed by a stop codon. It is interesting that whereas TGF-β and the β chains of inhibin have all nine cysteine residues in homologous positions, the homologies between TGF-β and MIS, inhibin-α, and the DPP-C begin only at the second cysteine (residue 15) and cover just seven of the nine cysteines (see Fig. 5). This amino-terminal region of amino acids 1–15 is also the region of least homology (only 50%) between TGF-β1 and the known partial sequence of TGF-β2 (see Fig. 5)[1], an observation suggesting that the divergence may have resulted in part from an alternative splicing pattern or from exon shuffling.

[1]Since the writing of this article, the complete amino acid (Marquardt *et al.*, 1987) and cDNA (de Martin *et al.*, 1987) sequences of human TGF-β2 have been published. The mature 112 amino acid TGF-β 1 and 2 chains are 71% homologous, whereas the precursors are much less highly conserved.

At the present time, not enough is known about possible biological activities of the inhibins, the activins, MIS, or the DPP-C product in diverse systems to discuss whether members of this family share similar biological functions. TGF-β, the inhibins, and the activins all act on pituitary cells. TGF-β (Ying *et al.*, 1986a) and the activins (Ling *et al.*, 1986) both stimulate FSH release, whereas inhibin acts to inhibit its release by pituitary cells (Ling *et al.*, 1985), yet neither inhibin nor activin is able to compete for binding of TGF-β to these cells, a finding suggesting that the two peptides act through distinct receptors (unpublished data, Fig. 6). Support for this observation comes from the report that the homodimer of the β_A chains of inhibin can stimulate differentiation of Friend erythroleukemia cells and suppress growth of these cells in soft agar, whereas TGF-β at more than 100 times greater concentration has no effect (Eto *et al.*, 1987). Thus, although there might be some shared actions, many of the specific functions and specific target cells of the various members of this gene family will probably be distinct.

F. Membrane Receptors for TGF-β

1. *General Features*

The action of TGF-β on cells is mediated through specific cell membrane receptors. Early studies showed that iodinated TGF-β bound with high affinity (K_d's in the range of 20 to 30 pM) to saturable, specific receptors on a variety of cells of both mesenchymal and epithelial origin (Frolik *et al.*, 1984; Tucker *et al.*, 1984a; Massagué and Like, 1985; Wakefield *et al.*, 1987b). Various methods based on use of chloramine T (Frolik *et al.*, 1984), the Bolton-Hunter reagent (Tucker *et al.*, 1984a), or lactoperoxidase–glucose oxidase (Massagué and Like, 1985) have been used for the radioiodination of TGF-β; none of these procedures compromise the biological activity of TGF-β, and all give equivalent results. The very high affinity of TGF-β for its receptors is consistent with the ED_{50}'s of TGF-β action on cells that are typically in the range of 1 to 20 pM. However, comparison of binding parameters and biological response parameters for any particular cell line suggests that only about 10 to 20% occupancy of TGF-β receptors is required for maximal biological effect (Massagué and Like, 1985). This concept of 'spare" receptors has been previously observed for binding of other growth factors such as insulin to its receptor (Freychet *et al.*, 1971).

TGF-β receptors are distinguished from other known growth factor receptors in several aspects. First, depending on the particular cell line, receptors for TGF-β are either refractory to any down-regulation (Massagué and Like, 1985; Massagué, 1985b) or are downregulated only 50 to 70% by exposure to high concentrations of ligand (Frolik *et al.*, 1984; Wakefield *et al.*, 1987b), by chemical transformation (Tucker *et al.*, 1984a), or in retrovirally transformed cells that secrete high levels of TGF-β (Anzano *et al.*, 1985; Massagué, 1985b). This response is in striking contrast to the ability of cells to acutely downregulate receptors for EGF or PDGF upon exposure to high ligand concentrations or following transformation (De Larco and Todaro, 1978; Carpenter and Cohen, 1979; Bowen-Pope and Ross, 1984). Second, treatment of cells with a variety of factors known to modulate TGF-β action on cells including phorbol myristate acetate, retinoic acid, other growth factors, or epinephrine, has no appreciable effect on TGF-β binding (Wakefield *et al.*, 1987b; Roberts *et al.*, 1984a, 1985b). This finding again contrasts with the modulation of the EGF receptor by either phorbol esters or retinoic acid (Magun *et al.*, 1980; Jetten, 1981; Roberts *et al.*, 1984a).

Analysis of the binding of TGF-β to a wide variety of cell types, including nonneoplastic cells of fibroblastic, epithelial, endothelial, or hemopoietic origin as well as tumor cells and cells transformed by chemical carcinogens or by either DNA or RNA tumor viruses, showed that all cell types examined bound TGF-β, with the number of receptors per cell ranging from only 600 on human tonsillar T lymphocytes to about 80,000 on Swiss 3T3 cells (Table I) (Wakefield *et al.*, 1987b). Receptor affinity, but not receptor number, was decreased in quiescent cells relative to actively growing cells. The apparent universality and resistance to modulation of the TGF-β receptor and the high degree of evolutionary conservation of the ligand itself suggest that this growth factor and its receptor have a more fundamental role in cellular physiology than do other mitogenic growth factors such as

TABLE I
PROPERTIES OF THE TGF-β RECEPTOR ON REPRESENTATIVE CELLS[a]

	Receptor parameters	
Cell type	K_d (p*M*)	No./cell
Nonneoplastic		
NRK-49F, rat kidney	40	25,000
NIH 3T3, mouse embryonic	26	36,000
Swiss 3T3, mouse embryonic	45	81,000
Bovine pulmonary artery	26	9,000
NHBE 555, human bronchial	10	10,000
Human tonsillar T lymphocyte	2	600
Transformed		
A673, human rhabdomyosarcoma	10	3,000
HT1080, human fibrosarcoma	6	7,000
T24, human bladder carcinoma	9	9,000
HaSV-NIH 3T3	31	17,000
MoSV-NRK	36	21,000

[a]Data represent the results of Scatchard analysis of the binding of radiolabeled human platelet TGF-β to cells at 22°C (selected from Wakefield *et al.* 1987b).

PDGF or EGF and that assurance of a response to TGF-β is essential for survival of cells.

2. *Structural and Functional Properties of TGF-β Receptors*

Although the TGF-β receptor has not yet been purified to permit sequencing and eventual cloning, the use of receptor affinity cross-linking methodology has resulted in the identification of several species of membrane components that bind TGF-β with high affinity. Massagué and Like (1985), using the cross-linking agent disuccinimidyl suberate, first described a 280-kDa cell membrane component that appears to be the major membrane binding species for TGF-β in most cells. The native form of this binding protein is a 600-kDa protein consisting of two subunits cross-linked by disulfide bonds; the 280-kDa subunit of this dimeric protein binds TGF-β (Massagué, 1985a,b; Fanger *et al.*, 1985). The native protein binds TGF-β with high affinity and is the major species of binding protein in mammalian and avian fibroblasts and epithelial cells. Its binding to wheat germ agglutinin suggests that it, like the receptors for many other growth factors, is a glycoprotein containing *N*-acetylglucosamine or sialic acid residues (Massagué, 1985a).

Other less abundant species of TGF-β binding proteins have also been identified by cross-linking experiments. Most prominent are a 65- and an 85-kDa species, both of which are present in most cells examined (Cheifetz *et al.*, 1986). Limited proteolysis of these cross-linked complexes suggests that these binding proteins can be separated into two groups; the affinity-labeled binding domains of the 65- and the 280-kDa species are similar, but the binding domain of the 85-kDa protein is unrelated to that of the other two. Binding affinities for the 280- and 65-kDa species range from 50 to 500 p*M* in different cells, whereas TGF-β binds to the 85-kDa species with an affinity of about 50 p*M*. It is noteworthy that rat skeletal muscle myoblast cell lines have no detectable 280-kDa labeled component, but only 65- and 85-kDa species (Cheifetz *et al.*, 1986), yet the cells are sensitive to 2–10 p*M* TGF-β responding with an inhibition of differentiation and a stimulation of matrix protein synthesis (Massagué *et al.*, 1986; Florini *et al.*, 1986). Thus, although it cannot be said with certainty that any of these proteins is a signaling receptor that mediates transmembrane effects of TGF-β, they are all glycosylated integral cell membrane proteins that bind TGF-β with affinities consistent with the effective biological activity concentration range for TGF-β-mediated effects (Cheifetz *et al.*, 1986).

3. *Membrane Binding Characteristics of TGF-β2*

The discovery of alternative forms of TGF-β with identical biological effects on cells raises the question of possible specificity of binding of these variants. Examples of related peptides that have identical biological effects and bind to a single receptor type are found in the binding of the two forms of interleukin 1 (IL−1) (Bird and Saklatvala, 1986; Dower *et al.*, 1986) and in the binding of many peptides belonging to the EGF family (Marquardt *et al.*, 1984; Stroobant *et al.*, 1985). On the other hand, insulin IGF-I and IGF-II have both shared and specific biological effects; each binds to specific receptors with a complex pattern of cross-reactivity (Czech, 1982). Scatchard analysis of the binding of TGF-β1 and TGF-β2 to both NRK and A549 human lung carcinoma cells shows that there are fewer receptor for TGF-β2 on both cell types, but that the binding affinities of each ligand are comparable (Segarini *et al.*, 1987). In support of differential binding of these two peptides, experiments in which the binding of radiolabeled TGF-β1 or TGF-β2 to these two cell types was compared with that of the native ligands suggest that NRK cells have specific sites for TGF-β2 that cannot bind TGF-β1 and that A549 cells have specific sites for TGF-β1 that cannot bind TGF-β2 (Segarini *et al.*, 1987; see also Fig. 7). The binding of these two forms to several other cell types examined generally fits one of these two patterns.

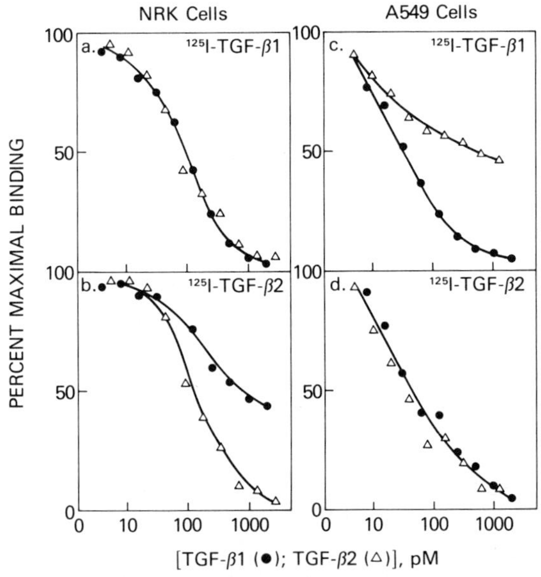

FIG. 7. Distinct patterns of binding of TGF-β1 and TGF-β2 to cellular receptors. The binding of radioiodinated human TGF-β1 and bovine TGF-β2 to rat NRK fibroblasts (a,b) and to human A549 lung carcinoma cells (c,d) was compared with that of native TGF-β1 (●) and TGF-β2 (△). The data suggest that NRK cells have a subset of binding sites specific for TGF-β2, whereas A549 cells have sites specific for binding of TGF-β1. (Adapted from Segarini *et al.*, 1987.)

Affinity cross-linking of TGF-β1 and TGF-β2 to cell membrane proteins has produced discrepant results. Cheifetz *et al.* (1987) report that TGF-β1 and TGF-β2 bind to the 280-kDa component with equal affinity, but that TGF-β1 binds with higher affinity than TGF-β2 to the 65- and 85-kDa species. In contrast to these findings, Segarini *et al.* (1987), using different cell lines, proposed that there are two distinct species of 280-kDa affinity-labeled proteins, one that binds both TGF-β1 and TGF-β2 and another that preferentially binds TGF-β2. Several less abundant labeled species were also identified, among them a 120- to 150-kDa protein that also showed preferential labeling with TGF-β2. Although final conclusions cannot yet be made, the results at hand demonstrate that binding patterns for TGF-β1 and TGF-β2 differ from cell to cell and strongly suggest that specific receptors will be identified and that cells will be found that perhaps exclusively bind one or the other TGF-β species.

4. *Signaling Mechanisms of TGF-β Receptors*

The receptors for EGF/TGF-α (Carpenter *et al.*, 1979; Pike *et al.*, 1982), PDGF (Ek *et al.*, 1982), FGF (Huang and Huang, 1986), insulin (Kasuga *et al.*, 1983), and IGF-I (Jacobs *et al.*, 1983) all have associated with them a tyrosine kinase activity that can be stimulated by binding of the respective ligands. Attempts to demonstrate tyrosine kinase activity of the TGF-β receptor have been negative (Fanger *et al.*, 1985; Libby *et al.*, 1986). Indirectly supporting these findings are two sets of observations on cells in which TGF-β inhibits the mitogenic effects of other growth factors. First, Like and Massagué (1986) have observed that although TGF-β blocks the mitogenic effects of EGF and insulin on Mv1Lu mink lung epithelial cells, it does not block the elevation of S6 kinase activity induced by either mitogen. Second, Chambard and Pouysségur (1988) have observed that, although mitogenic stimulation of Chinese hamster lung fibroblasts by thrombin or FGF is completely blocked by TGF-β, the various signals induced by binding of these mitogens to their receptors are not blocked: phospholipid turnover and activation of protein kinase C, Na^+/H^+ antiport activity, expression of *myc* and *fos* in the nucleus, ornithine decarboxylase activity, and thymidine kinase activity. In separate experiments, it has been shown that neither the basal levels of *fos* expression nor the induction of *fos* expression in rat fibroblasts by either serum, EGF, or FGF is affected by TGF-β treatment (T. Curran, personal communication). Together these data suggest that signals from the TGF-β receptor probably do not involve pathways common to receptors with tyrosine kinase activity but rather novel pathways yet to be discovered that converge in the nucleus to block DNA synthesis at some step distal to those already examined.

G. THE "LATENT" OR INACTIVE FORM OF TGF-β

1. *Description and Properties*

Although TGF-β purified from platelets and from tissue extracts or conditioned medium is active in a variety of biological assays, it was found that unprocessed, neutral, conditioned medium of cells known to secrete TGF-β activity was inactive in these assays, unless the medium was first acidified to approximately pH 3 and then reneutralized before assay (Lawrence *et al.*, 1984; Pircher *et al.*, 1984). This observation led to the concept of "latent" TGF-β activity. Most preparations of purified TGF-β have been exposed to acid during purification process and therefore are permanently activated. Further investigations have shown that TGF-β from neutral, conditioned media of many different cell lines (Wakefield *et al.*, 1987a,b) and of primary cells such as T lymphocytes (Roberts *et al.*, 1986), macrophages (Assoian *et al.*, 1987), platelets (Pircher *et al.*, 1986), and fetal bovine osteoblasts (Robey *et al.*, 1987) and from wound fluid (Cromack *et al.*, 1987) is in a latent form.

Investigations into methods for unmasking the latent activity showed that TGF-β could be acivated by a variety of nonenzymatic procedures including acidification, alkalinization, exposure to denaturing agents such as urea, or boiling for 3 min (Lawrence *et al.*, 1985). These same authors obsered that after chromatography of neutral, conditioned medium on BioGel P−60, TGF-β activity could be assayed in high-molecular-weight fractions only after acidification; no activity was found in low-molecular-weight fractions. Upon rechromatography of the high-molecular-weight activity under acid conditions, TGF-β activity could be found in low-molecular-weight fractions. Similar behavior was found for TGF-β activity released from platelets under neutral conditions (Pircher *et al.*, 1986). This result suggested that TGF-β released from cells or from platelets was complexed with a carrier protein and that this complex could not reassociate after denaturation. The nonenzymatic conditions employed for activation made it unlikely that activation involved cleavage of TGF-β from its precursor form.

Using several different antibodies raised to synthetic peptides in the amino-terminal precursor portion of TGF-β, it has now been possible to show that the remaining amino-terminal portion of the processed precursor, beginning after the signal peptide sequence (amino acids 8–23; Derynck *et al.*, 1985; 1986) and continuing to the Arg-Ala bond in position 279 (see Fig. 4B), is associated with TGF-β in the latent complex (Wakefield *et al.*, 1987a). Both use of these precursor antibodies and chromatography of latent TGF-β on SDS gels under denaturing conditions suggest that the latent form is complex with 2-fold symmetry formed from the association of one molecule of mature, dimeric TGF-β with the resulting two molecules of the cleaved amino terminus of the precursor, processed as previously described, and two molecules of a third, as yet unidentified, component of approximately 70,000 M_r. Whether the larger protein might have protease activity as has been found for the γ subunit of the nerve growth factor (NGF) complex (Greene *et al.*, 1968) as well as the binding protein of the high-molecular-weight form of the EGF (Server and Shooter, 1976) is currently under investigation.

Recently it has been found that TGF-β can be partially activated by proteases such as plasmin and cathepsin D (Keski-Oja *et al.*, 1987). This finding suggests that although latent TGF-β may be activated by nonenzymatic means, mechanisms of activation *in vitro* may involve enzymatic pathways. Indeed, acid proteinase activity is elevated in a healing wound (Im and Hoopes,1983). In certain situations, however, acidification may also play an activating role *in vivo*, such as in a healing wound where hypoxic conditions would be expected to locally lower pH (Knighton *et al.*, 1981). The data of Lawrence *et al.* (1985), showing that there is a progressive increase in the rate of activation with lowered pH, imply that moderate acidity in the range of pH 3 to 5 could serve to slowly activate TGF-β from a reserve of the latent form.

2. *Potential Significance of Latent TGF-β*

Wakefield *et al.* (1987a,b) have found that the latent form of TGF-β is unable to bind to TGF-β receptors, nor is it recognizable by anti-TGF-β antibodies (O'Connor-McCourt and Wakefield, 1987; Flanders *et al.*, 1988). A549 human lung carcinoma cells are exquisitely sensitive to inhibition by TGF-β, both in monolayer culture and in soft agar. Therefore, it was postulated that the uncontrolled growth of the cells might have resulted from loss of the ability to make a TGF-β-like growth regulator (Roberts *et al.*, 1985a). It was subsequently found that these cells secreted sufficient quantities of TGF-β for optimal inhibition of growth, but that this TGF-β was secreted in latent form (Wakefield *et al.*, 1987b). Exposure of the cells to their own acidified, conditioned medium resulted in inhibition of growth and in partial down-regulation of TGF-β receptors. This result suggests as an alternative hypothesis that one aspect of the uncontrolled growth characteristic of tumorigenic transformation may be the loss of mechanisms of activation of TGF-β, a loss that might be responsible for maintenance of the normal growth-inhibited phenotype. Moreover, because there appears to be little regulation of TGF-β activity at the level of its receptor, it must be considered that activation of latent TGF-β could constitute a major regulatory step in control of TGF-β action on cells (Wakefield *et al.*, 1987b). Thus, the secretion of a *latent* form of TGF-β by many cells that also have receptors for this ligand, might be a mechanism to prevent continual autocrine action of TGF-β; conversely, such a system would always be in a state of readiness, requiring only activation of the ligand. In support of this, Knabbe *et al.* (1987) have shown that treatment of human breast cancer

MCF−7 cells with tamoxifen, an antiestrogen, results in growth inhibition that apparently is due to an increase in the degree of activation of the TGF-β secreted by the cells.

3. *Latent TGF-β in Serum: A Specific Complex with α_2-Macroglobulin*

Assay of TGF-β following acid-ethanol extraction of serum shows that TGF-β levels in serum range from 0.2 to 1 n*M*. Yet assays carried out in the presence of 10% serum, such as colony formation by NRK cells or inhibition of colony formation by A549 cells, have ED_{50}'s of approximately 8 and 0.4 p*M* for added TGF-β, respectively. This finding suggests that the TGF-β in serum is latent (Pircher *et al.*, 1986; O'Connor-McCourt and Wakefield, 1987). A similar conclusion can be reached by direct assay of serum in a binding competition assay; serum is unable to compete for binding without prior acid activation (unpublished data).

O'Connor-McCourt and Wakefield (1987) have identified α_2-macroglobulin (α_2M) as the serum carrier of TGF-β and have shown that this complex has all the properties ascribed to the latent form of TGF-β. The major conclusions follow: (1) iodinated TGF-β affinity cross-linked to serum proteins binds to a single species identified immunologically as α_2M; (2) α_2M decreases binding of TGF-β to its receptor; (3) the majority of endogenous serum TGF-β is bound to α_2M in such a way that it is not dissociated on SDS gels, even in the absence of cross-linking agent; this complex migrates as a high-molecular-weight complex on gel filtration, and assay of TGF-β activity requires acid activation. The physiological role of this complex remains to be determined. However, because α_2M has now been identified as a carrier of both TGF-β and PDGF (Huang *et al.*, 1984; Raines *et al.*, 1984)—the two major platelet growth factors—it may serve an important function at sites of healing or inflammation by scavenging excess growth factors as well as proteases, irreversibly earmarking them for destruction.

H. Biological Actions of TGF-β *in Vitro*

Any attempt to classify the biological actions of TGF-β must of necessity be arbitrary, because TGF-β is a multifunctional agent. When this multifunctionality of TGF-β was first discovered, it was thought that this was a somewhat unique property of this particular peptide; however, it is now realized that many peptide growth factors are multifunctional and are capable of eliciting a very broad range of unrelated responses in many different types of cells (Sporn and Roberts, 1988). In general the highly specific fit of a peptide ligand with a glycoprotein cell membrane receptor provides a modular regulatory element that can be used in a wide variety of cells for many different purposes, such as to alter their growth, their differentiation, or yet other functions that are associated with neither growth nor differentiation; the numerous and varied actions of TGF-β should be viewed from this perspective. For the purposes of this article, we will arbitrarily divide the actions of TGF-β into three main categories, namely, (1) proliferative effects, (2) antiproliferative effects, and (3) effects unrelated to proliferation.

1. *Proliferative Effects of TGF-β*

Nowhere is the multifunctional nature of TGF-β more evident than in analysis of its effects on cellular proliferation. Effects of TGF-β can be growth stimulatory or growth inhibitory, depending on whether cells are grown as attached monolayers or under anchorage-independent conditions, depending on the particular set of growth factors acting together with TGF-β, or depending on the developmental stage of the cell. TGF-β was originally discovered in an assay that measured its ability to cause a proliferative effect, namely, its ability to stimulate the anchorage-independent growth of nonneoplastic NRK 49F fibroblasts in soft agar (Roberts *et al.*, 1981). This assay clearly identifies TGF-β as a *bona fide* growth factor. In the case of the NRK 49F cell, EGF (or TGF-α, as well as PDGF (Assoian *et al.*, 1984b) and IGF-II (Massagué *et al.*, 1985), are also required for anchorage-independent growth, whereas other cells, such as the mouse AKR – 2B fibroblast (Moses *et al.*, 1984), can be stimulated to grow in soft agar with TGF-β alone. Still other cells are stimulated to grow in soft agar by TGF-β; human foreskin fibroblasts are stimulated to grow by TGF-β alone (Moses *et al.*, 1985), whereas BALB/c – 3T3 cells require both IGF-II and TGF-β (Massagué *et al.*, 1985). However, in the case of NRK and AKR – 2B cells, concentrations of TGF-β identical to those that stimulate the growth of the cells under anchorage-independent conditions, inhibit or slow the growth of the same cells in monolayer culture. In NRK cells in monolayer culture, TGF-β inhibits the mitogenic effect of EGF, whereas TGF-β and EGF act synergistically under anchorage-independent conditions (Roberts *et al.*, 1985a). In AKR – 2B cells, TGF-β stimulates growth in monolayer culture, but with a delayed replication time (Shipley *et al.*, 1985). In these cells, the mitogenic action of TGF-β is postulated to be indirect and to be mediated by its induction of the c-*sis* gene, followed by autocrine action of PDGF and the resultant induction of expression of the *fos* and *myc* genes (Leof *et al.*, 1986).

For some fibroblasts, bifunctional activity of TGF-β has been demonstrated under the same assay conditions, but in the presence of different growth factors. Thus, TGF-β promotes anchorage-independent growth of *myc*-transfected Fischer rat 3T3 cells in the presence of PDGF, but it inhibits the growth of the same cells in the presence of EGF (Roberts *et al.*, 1985a).

A related phenomenon has been observed in human embryonic fibroblasts, where the action of TGF-β is a function of the developmental state of the cells. TGF-β stimulates thymidine incorporation and growth of fibroblasts derived from very early human fetuses, while it is a growth inhibitor for fibroblasts derived from late gestational stage embryos (Hill *et al.*, 1986). This is in agreement with the findings of Anzano *et al.* (1986), who showed that TGF-β was growth inhibitory for late gestational stage rat embryo fibroblasts, regardless of whether the cells were cultured under anchorage-dependent or anchorage-independent conditions.

An important cell type for which TGF-β is mitogenic in monolayer culture is the osteoblast (Centrella *et al.*, 1987; Robey *et al.*, 1987); not only do these cells respond to TGF-β with a growth response, but they themselves also produce high levels of TGF-β, a finding suggesting that this peptide might exert some type of autocrine growth control in bone. With respect to the functional role of TGF-β in bone, its ability to stimulate the formation of various matrix proteins, which will be discussed later, also is undoubtedly of major significance.

Finally, very recently it has been shown (N. Ratner, personal communication) that TGF-β has strong mitogenic activity for Schwann cells of the peripheral nervous system, a cell type for which there are few known mitogens. Because the Schwann cell is believed to play an important role in regeneration of peripheral nerves after injury, this finding raises the intriguing possibility that TGF-β might function as an intrinsic mediator of repair of peripheral neuronal damage. Other data, which strongly implicate TGF-β in promotion of wound healing and connective tissue repair will be discussed later.

2. *Antiproliferative Effects of TGF-β*

TGF-β is a potent inhibitor of the growth of many cells. This is particularly true of epithelial cells, although there are also cells of mesenchymal origin in which strong growth suppressive effects are seen. The first indication that TGF-β was a growth inhibitor came from studies of BSC−1 monkey kidney cells. A previously known growth inhibitor produced by these cells (Holley *et al.*, 1980) was identified as TGF-β or a closely related peptide (Tucker *et al.*, 1984a). Further studies have revealed that BSC−1 cells have high affinity receptors for TGF-β (Tucker *et al.*, 1984a), a finding suggesting an autocrine mode of growth inhibition by TGF-β in these cells.

Subsequent to these initial studies, potent inhibitory effects on many other epithelial cells have been demonstrated; these include cells derived from bronchus (Masui *et al.*, 1986), liver (Hayashi and Carr, 1985; Nakamura *et al.*, 1985; Carr *et al.*, 1986; McMahon *et al.*, 1986; Fausto *et al.*, 1987), skin (Shipley *et al.*, 1986; Bertolero *et al.*, 1986), and intestine (Kurokowa *et al.*, 1987). Interestingly, in three of these tissues—namely, bronchus, liver, and skin—nonneoplastic epithelial cells are sensitive to growth inhibition by TGF-β, but neoplastic cells may have lost this sensitivity (see Lechner *et al.*, 1983; McMahon *et al.*, 1986; Shipley *et al.*, 1986). On kidney epithelial cells, TGF-β inhibits the mitogenic action of insulin and hydrocortisone without blocking the protein synthesis induced by these agents; the net result of this action is to stablize the differentiated state induced by these hormones and to cause cellular hypertrophy (Fine *et al.*, 1985). TGF-β thus may play an important role in the compensatory hypertrophy of the contraleteral kidney, whch occurs after unilateral nephrectomy.

There are several cells of mesenchymal origin in which TGF-β has strong antiproliferative actions, most notably T and B lymphocytes (Kehrl *et al.*, 1986a,b; Ristow, 1986) and vascular endothelial cells (Baird and Durkin, 1985; Fràter-Schröder *et al.*, 1986; Heimark *et al.*, 1986). In the case of both T and B lymphocytes, it has been shown that these cells synthesize and secrete TGF-β and express receptors for the peptide (Kehrl *et al.*, 1986a,b); it has thus been suggested that TGF-β in lymphocytes may function as an autocrine growth inhibitor, preventing excessive clonal expansion and immunoglobulin synthesis. Similarly, the antiproliferative action of TGF-β on vascular endothelium may facilitate orderly regeneration of capillaries at sites of vascular injury (Baird and Durkin, 1986; Heimark *et al.*, 1986).

Finally there are many tumor cells that are highly sensitive to the antiproliferative actions of TGF-β (Roberts *et al.*, 1985a; Moses *et al.*, 1985; Knabbe *et al.*, 1987). In two experimental systems, the growth of the tumor cells can be correlated with the cells' ability to activate latent TGF-β as discussed earlier. In the case of human MCF−7 breast cancer cells, which possess receptors for TGF-β, only small amounts of TGF-β are secreted in a biologically active form; this secretion of active TGF-β can be increased up to 20-fold by treatment of the MCF−7 cells with growth-inhibitory concentrations of antiestrogens such as tamoxifen and its metabolite, hydroxytamoxifen. TGF-β is thus a hormonally regulated growth inhibitor with a negative autocrine action in its producer cell. In the case of human A−549 lung cancer cells, large amounts of TGF-β are secreted in an inactive, latent form. However, as discussed previously, the A−549 cell cannot activate the latent TGF-β that it secretes (Wakefield *et al.*, 1987b). Activation of the TGF-β in the conditioned medium from these cells or addition of exogenous (activated) TGF-β from platelets results in potent inhibition of A−549 tumor cell proliferation (Roberts *et al.*, 1985a; Wakefield *et al.*, 1987b). These findings suggest that the inability of the A−549 cell to activate latent, secreted TGF-β may contribute to the uncontrolled proliferation of these cells.

3. *Effects Unrelated to Proliferation*

TGF-β has many effects, unrelated to proliferation, on many different cell types; this is hardly surprising considering the almost universal occurence of TGF-β receptors on all types of cells (Wakefield *et al.*, 1987b). These effects are so numerous and varied that they do not appear to fit into any particular pattern; rather, it would seem that TGF-β has a significant role in many cells that is uniquely related to the regulation of the specialized, critical function of an individual cell type.

This phenomenon is particularly striking in fibroblasts and other cells of connective tissue, in which TGF-β is an important regulator of the synthesis of collagen, fibronectin, proteoglycans, and other components of the extracellular matrix. Thus, it has been shown that within as little as 6 hr, fibroblasts of human, rat, mouse, and chicken origin all respond to addition of TGF-β with a significant increase in collagen and fibronectin synthesis (Ignotz and Massagué, 1986; Roberts *et al.*, 1986; Wrana *et al.*, 1986); in NRK cells, effects are seen at concentrations of TGF-β less than 100 pg/ml (4 p*M*). Recent studies have shown that TGF-β can increase the level of mRNA for types I, III, and V collagen (Rossi *et al.*, 1988) and fibronectin in NRK cells (Ignotz *et al.*, 1987); this increase in collagen mRNA or fibronectin mRNA would appear, in part, to be the result of a respective activation by TGF-β of the promoter for the gene for type I collagen (Rossi *et al.*, 1988) or the promoter for the fibronectin gene (S. Bourgeois, personal communication). In embryonic rat mesenchymal cells, TGF-β induces the synthesis of specific matrix proteins characteristic of cartilage, namely, type II collagen and certain proteoglycans (Seyedin *et al.*, 1985, 1987).

Another action of TGF-β that appears related to its ability to enhance formation of extracellular matrix is its ability to induce the formation of specific proteins that are inhibitors of plasminogen activator (Laiho *et al.*, 1986; Thalacker and Nilsen-Hamilton, 1987). Several cell types, including fibroblasts, have been shown to synthesize large amounts of plasminogen activator inhibitors (PAIs) in response to TGF-β and it has been suggested that a principal action of these PAIs is to stabilize newly synthesized matrix proteins by preventing their proteolytic degradation (Bergman *et al.*, 1986). TGF-β has also been shown to increase synthesis of a tissue inhibitor of metalloproteinases (TIMP), another well-characterized protease inhibitor (Edwards *et al.*, 1987). Concomitant with this increase in secretion of protease inhibitors, TGF-β has also been shown to decrease the secretion by fibroblasts of several proteases themselves, including the serine protease, plasminogen activator (Laiho *et al.*, 1986), as well as a thiol protease (Chiang and Nilsen-Hamilton, 1986). Furthermore, it has been shown that TGF-β suppresses the induction by EGF of increased levels of mRNA for the metalloproteinase, transin/stromelysin, a major proteolytic enzyme of broad specificity produced in large quantities by various fibroblasts (Chin *et al.*, 1985; Matrisian *et al.*, 1986a,b; Whitham *et al.*, 1986; Frisch *et al.*, 1987; Fini *et al.*, 1987). These effects of TGF-β on increased synthesis of protease inhibitors and decreased synthesis of proteases both serve to further augment the accumulation of matrix proteins by TGF-β.

In glandular cells, such as ovarian granulosa cells or adrenocortical cells, TGF-β can control synthesis or release of a principal secreted product, such as estrogen or cortisol. Thus, TGF-β markedly potentiates the ability of FSH to stimulate estrogen secretion in granulosa cells (Ying *et al.*, 1986b; Adashi *et al.*, 1987), whereas its effects on adrenocortical cells are just the opposite: in this case, TGF-β strongly antagonizes the ability of adrenocorticotropic hormone to stimulate the secretion of cortisol (Hotta and Baird, 1986; Feige *et al.*, 1987a). In neither of these instances was there any significant effect of TGF-β on cell proliferation. Still another related effect is the enhancement of basal FSH secretion in pituitary cells by TGF-β (Ying *et al.*, 1986a), although in this case the principal peptides involved in physiological control of FHS release appear to be substances that are structurally related to TGF-β; namely, activin and inhibin, rather than TGF-β itself (Ling *et al.*, 1985, 1986; Vale *et al.*, 1986).

In cells of the immune system, TGF-β also has significant effects that are not related to proliferation. Thus, secretion of immunoglobulins is suppressed in B lymphocytes by very low concentrations of TGF-β, which have no effect on DNA synthesis (Kehrl *et al.*, 1986a). Cytotoxic activity is blocked in both natural killer lymphocytes (Rook *et al.*, 1986), in lymphokine-activated killer (LAK) lymphocytes, as well as in the mixed lymphocyte reaction (Mulé *et al.*, 1988). In general, TGF-β appears to have actions that strongly antagonize many of the effects of interleukin 2 (IL – 2) on various T lymphocytes, such as its ability to upregulate its own receptor. In monocytes, however, TGF-β may activate certain functions that are involved in tissue repair. Thus, not only is TGF-β extremely potent as a chemotactic agent for monocytes (concentrations as low as 1 pg/ml [40 f*M*] are active in this regard), it also increases mRNA levels for interleukin 1 (Wahl *et al.*, 1987). Chemotactic activity of TGF-β for fibroblasts has also been reported, which again is relevant to tissue repair (Postlethwaite *et al.*, 1987).

Several reports demonstrate that TGF-β can also control the direction of cellular differentiation. Thus, three groups have shown that low concentrations of TGF-β, which have no effect on cell proliferation, block the fusion of various types of myoblasts, so that they do not form myotubes; the expression of muscle-specific proteins, such as creatine kinase and the acetylcholine receptor is also blocked by this action (Florini *et al.*, 1986; Massagué *et al.*, 1986; Olson *et al.*, 1986). The adipogenic differentiation of 3T3-L1 cells, induced by insulin and dexamethasone, is also blocked by TGF-β without affecting mitosis (Ignotz and Massagué, 1985).

4. *Cellular Mechanisms of TGF-β Action*

TGF-β has several effects on cellular metabolism that are shared with other growth factors and are thus unlikely to account for the specific actions of TGF-β on cells. These include stimulation of glucose uptake (Inman and Colowick, 1985), increased amino acid transport (Boerner *et al.*, 1985; Racker *et al.*, 1985), and stimulation of prostaglandin synthesis in cultured mouse calvaria (Tashjian *et al.*, 1985).

The ability of TGF-β to modulate cellular receptors for other growth factors appears to be cell specific and is therefore more likely to be related to the mode of action of TGF-β on those cells. In this regard, TGF-β increases synthesis of EGF receptors in NRK cells (Assoian *et al.*, 1984a; Assoian, 1985) and in cultured rat granulosa cells (Feng *et al.*, 1986); in both cases these effects correlate well with the modulation by TGF-β of the effects of EGF on the cells. Treatment of T lymphocytes with TGF-β in the presence of IL−2 blocks the ability of IL−2 to upregulate its own receptor as well as the transferrin receptor (Kehrl *et al.*, 1986b); this interference with the action of IL−2 on the T cells supports a role for TGF-β in the regulation of T cell growth. In ovarian granulosa cells, TGF-β both increases and decreases the effects of FSH on receptors for luteinizing hormone, depending on the particular concentrations of TGF-β and FSH (Knecht *et al.*, 1987; Dodson and Schomberg, 1987).

Finally, the ability of TGF-β to interfere with the actions of other specific mitogens is probably central to many of the antiproliferative effects of TGF-β on cells. As examples, TGF-β antagonizes the effects of both PDGF and EGF on growth of established cell lines as well as primary fibroblast cultures (Roberts *et al.*, 1985a; Anzano *et al.*, 1986; D. F. Stern *et al.*, 1986); it also blocks the effects of FGF on endothelial cells (Fràter-Schröder *et al.*, 1986; Baird and Durkin, 1986), the effects of IL-2 on both T and B lymphocytes as well as LAK cells (Kehrl *et al.*, 1985a,b; Mulé *et al.*, 1988), the effects of insulin on mink lung epithelial cells (Like and Massagué, 1986) and of IGF-I on embryonic fibroblasts (Hill *et al.*, 1986), as well as the effects of neuroleukin on growth of sensory neurons (M. Gurney, personal communication). As discussed earlier, in the specific cases studied in detail, these blocking effects on TGF-β occur without interference with the generation of many of the early intracellular signals resulting from action of mitogenic peptides on their target cells (Like and Massagué, 1986; Chambard and Pouysségur, 1988). It is likely therefore that TGF-β blocks initiation of DNA synthesis at some step distal to these early signaling events.

I. Actions of TGF-β *in Vivo* and Potential Therapeutic Uses

Although there is now an immense literature on the effects of TGF-β on various cells in culture, much less information is presently available on the actions of this peptide *in vivo*. This is primarily the result of the relatively inadequate supplies of TGF-β that currently exist for animal studies and the paucity of knowledge regarding appropriate methods for stabilization and delivery of the peptide to a target site. As of the start of 1987, all *in vivo* studies have been performed with material that has been extracted from tissues such as platelets, bone, or kidney; such studies have been very expensive to perform. However, the availability of recombinant TGF-β at some time in the future should make this peptide more readily available for many animal and clinical studies that are clearly implicated as potentially important by the actions of TGF-β in cell culture. In spite of these limitations, several animal studies that have already been performed indicate that TGF-β does have significant biological activity *in vivo*, and these will be summarized below.

The first report of any biological action of TGF-β *in vivo* involved its administration to rats in which wire-mesh wound healing chambers were implanted subcutaneously (Sporn *et al.*, 1983). Treatment with TGF-β accelerated the accumulation of total protein, collagen, and DNA within the chambers; in addition, there was a marked fibrotic reaction around the chambers treated with TGF-β. The ability of TGF-β to stimulate collagen formation in wound-healing chambers has also been seen in rats treated with Adriamycin, a drug that impairs wound healing (Lawrence *et al.*, 1986). More recently, it has been shown that TGF-β, when injected subcutaneously in newborn mice, causes formation of granulation tissue (induction of angiogenesis and activation of fibroblasts to produce collagen) at the site of injection (Roberts *et al*, 1986). These effects occur within 2–3 days at dose levels of less than 1 μg. The *in vivo* effects of TGF-β on collagen synthesis directly correspond to its *in vitro* actions on this process; however, the stimulation of angiogenesis *in vivo* at first seems somewhat paradoxical, because it has been found in several laboratories that TGF-β strongly blocks the mitogenic action of FGF on vascular endothelial cells. Thus, it has been suggested that the angiogenic action of TGF-β may be indirect and may be mediated by its chemotactic effects on monocytes and macrophages (Wahl *et al.*, 1987) and the resultant activation of these cells to produce angiogenic peptides.

Based on the above findings, the first studies to show that TGF-β can accelerate healing of incisional wounds in rats have recently been performed (Mustoe *et al.*, 1987). TGF-β was applied directly, as a single dose, to linear incisions made through the dorsal skin of the rat. It caused a significant increase in healing of the wound, as measured by breaking strength of the repaired tissue; this was accompanied by a marked increase of mononuclear cells and fibroblasts and enhanced collagen deposition at the wound site.

The preceding studies, demonstrating that TGF-β can enhance wound healing when added as an exogenous agent, are of definite relevance to intrinsic, physiological wound healing, because it is known that TGF-β is released from platelets when they are induced to degranulate by thrombin (Assoian and Sporn, 1986) and that TGF-β is found intrinsically in wound fluid in biologically significant concentrations (Cromack *et al.*, 1987), most likely as a result of its secretion by activated macrophages that are present in wound fluid (Assoian *et al.*, 1987). The demonstration that it is possible to enhance wound healing by exogenous administration of an endogenous mediator has obvious therapeutic implications. There are many clinical situations in which it is desirable to enhance the formation of collagen and other extracellular matrix proteins, as well as the formation of new blood vessels; these include surgical wounds, as well as decubitus, diabetic, and stasis ulcers. Successful clinical results have already been reported, using crude platelet extracts, for treatment of patients with diabetic ulcers, ulcers resulting from vascular insufficiency, and ulcers resulting from spinal cord injury (Knighton *et al.*, 1986). The results that have been obtained in experimental animals with pure preparations of TGF-β suggest that it may be equivalently useful in human patients, although further studies will be required to determine whether other peptide growth factors will be administered with TGF-β to achieve optimal therapeutic effects.

Two other situations in which TGF-β has significant actions in cell culture, namely, stimulation of osteoblasts and suppression of T and B lymphocytes, also have important *in vivo* applications, but investigations along these lines are still in a preliminary state. The progress that has been made in stimulation of wound healing has benefited greatly from the ability to apply TGF-β directly at a wound site. Although one can theoretically conceive of potential therapeutic usefulness of TGF-β as an immunosuppressive agent or as an agent to stimulate bone formation, experimental studies in these areas are currently hampered by difficulties in administering TGF-β to target cells. The half-life of TGF-β after intravenous administration is only a few minutes, and further progress in developing sustained-release forms of TGF-β will be required before its potential use in many *in vivo* applications can be fully explored.

Acknowledgments

We thank Drs. Kathleen Flanders, Ellen Van Obberghen, Sonia Jakowlew, Tom Curran, Jean-Claude Chambard, Jacques Pouysségur, Mark Gurney, James Mulé, Steven Rosenberg, George Stricklin, Arnold Postlethwaite, Pellegrino Rossi, Benoit deCrombrugghe, Suzanne Bourgeois, and Nancy Ratner for sharing their experimental results prior to publication.

References

Adashi, E. Y., Hernandez, E. R., Resnick, C. E., and May, J. (1987). *Endocrinology*, in press.

Anzano, M. A., Roberts, A. B., Meyers, C. A., Komoriya, A., Lamb, L. C., Smith, J. M., and Sporn, M. B. (1982). *Cancer Res.* **42**, 4776–4778.

Anzano, M. A., Roberts, A. B., Smith, J. M., Sporn, M. B., and De Larco, J. E. (1983). *Proc. Natl. Acad. Sci. U.S.A.* **80**, 6264–6268.

Anzano, M. A., Roberts, A. B., De Larco, J. E., Wakefield, L. M., Assoian, R. K., Roche, N. S., Smith, J. M., Lazarus, J. E., and Sporn, M. B. (1985). *Mol. Cell. Biol.* **5**, 242–247.

Anzano, M. A., Roberts, A. B., and Sporn, M. B. (1986). *J. Cell. Physiol.* **126**, 312–318.

Assoian, R. K. (1985). *J. Biol. Chem.* **260**, 9613–9617.
Assoian, R. K. (1987). *In* "Methods in Enzymology" (D. Barnes and D. A. Sirbasku, eds.), Vol. 146, pp. 153–163. Academic Press, Orlando.
Assoian, R. K., and Sporn, M. B. (1986). *J. Cell Biol.* **102**, 1217–1223.
Assoian, R. K., Komoriya, A., Meyers, C. A., Miller, D. M., and Sporn, M. B. (1983). *J. Biol. Chem.* **258**, 7155–7160.
Assoian, R. K., Frolik, C. A., Roberts, A. B., Miller, D. M., and Sporn, M. B. (1984a). *Cell* **36**, 35–41.
Assoian, R. K., Grotendorst, G. R., Miller, D. M., and Sporn, M. B. (1984b). *Nature (London)* **309**, 804–806.
Assoian, R. K., Fleurdelys, B. E., Stevenson, H. C., Miller, P. J., Madtes, D. K., Raines, E. W., Ross, R., and Sporn, M. B. (1987). *Proc. Nat. Acad. Sci. U.S.A.* **84**, 6020–6024.
Baird, A., and Durkin, T. (1986). *Biochem. Biophys. Res. Commun.* **138**, 476–482.
Barrandon, Y., and Green, H. (1987). *Cell* **50**, 1131–1137.
Bergman, B. L., Scott, R. W., Bajpai, A., Watts, S., and Baker, J. B. (1986). *Proc. Natl. Acad. Sci. U.S.A.* **83**, 996–1000.
Bertolero, F., Kaighn, M. E., Camalier, R. F., and Saffiotti, U. (1986). *In Vitro* **22**, 423–428.
Bird, T. A., and Saklatvala, J. (1986). *Nature (London)* **324**, 263–266.
Blomquist, M. C., Hunt, L. T., and Barker, W. C. (1984). *Proc. Natl. Acad. Sci. U.S.A.* **81**, 7363–7367.
Blundell, T. L., and Humbel, R. E. (1980). *Nature (London)* **287**, 781–787.
Boerner, P., Resnick, R. J., and Racker, E. (1985). *Proc. Natl. Acad. Sci. U.S.A.* **82**, 1350–1353.
Bowen-Pope, D., and Ross, R. (1984). *In* "Methods in Enzymology" (L. Birnbaumer and B. W. O'Malley, eds.), Vol. 109, pp. 69–100. Academic Press, New York.
Bringman, T. S., Lindquist, P. B., and Derynck, R. (1987). *Cell* **48**, 429–440.
Brissenden, J. E., Derynck, R., and Franke, U. (1985). *Cancer Res.* **45**, 5593–5597.
Brown, J. P., Twardzik, D. R., Marquardt, H., and Todaro, G. J. (1985). *Nature (London)* **313**, 491–492.
Carpenter, G., and Cohen, S. (1979). *Annu. Rev. Biochem.* **48**, 193–216.
Carpenter, G., King, Jr., L., and Cohen, S. (1979). *J. Biol Chem.* **254**, 4884–4891.
Carpenter, G., Stoscheck, C. M., Preston, Y. A., and De Larco, J. E. (1983). *Proc. Natl. Acad. Sci. U.S.A.* **80**, 5627–5630.
Carr, B. I., Hayashi, I., Branum, E. L., and Moses, H. L. (1986). *Cancer Res.* **46**, 2330–2334.
Cate, R. L., Mattaliano, R. J., Hession, C., Tizard, R., Farber, N. M., Cheung, A., Ninfa, E. G., Frey, A. Z., Gash, D. J., Chow, E. P., Fisher, R. A., Bertonis, J. M., Torres, G., Wallnew, B. P., Ramachandran, K. L., Ragin, R. C., Manganaro, T. F., MacLaughlin, D. T., and Donahoe, P. K. (1986). *Cell* **45**, 685–698.
Centrella, M., McCarthy, T. L., and Canalis, E. (1987). *J. Biol. Chem.* **262**, 2869–2874.
Chambard, J.-C., and Pouysségur, J. (1988). *J. Cell. Phsyiol.*, in press.
Chang, W., Upton, C., Hu, S.-L., Purchio, A. F., and McFadden, G. (1987). *Mol. Cell. Biol.* **7**, 535–540.
Cheifetz, S., Like, B., and Massagué, J. (1986). *J. Biol. Chem.* **261**, 9972–9978.
Cheifetz, S., Weatherbee, J. A., Tsang, M. L.-S., Anderson, J. K., Molé, J. E., Lucas, R., and Massagué. (1987). *Cell* **48**, 409–415.
Chiang, C. P., and Nilsen-Hamilton, M. (1986). *J. Biol. Chem.* **261**, 10478–10481.
Childs, C. B., Proper, J. A., Tucker, R. F., and Moses, H. L. (1982). *Proc. Natl. Acad. Sci. U.S.A.* **79**, 5312–5316.
Chin, J. R., Murphy, G., and Werb, Z. (1985). *J. Biol. Chem.* **260**, 12367–12376.
Cifone, M. A., and Fidler, I. J. (1980). *Proc. Natl. Acad. Sci. U.S.A.* **77**, 1039–1043.
Cromack, D. T., Sporn, M. B., Roberts, A. B., Merino, M. J., Dart, L. L., and Norton, J. A. (1987). *J. Surg. Res.* **42**, 622–628.

Czech, M. P. (1982). *Cell* **31**, 8–10.
Dart, L. L., Smith, D. M., Meyers, C. A., Sporn, M. B., and Frolik, C. A. (1985). *Biochemistry* **24**, 5925–5931.
De Larco, J. E., and Todaro, G. J. (1978). *Proc. Natl. Acad. Sci. U.S.A.* **75**, 4001–4005.
de Martin, R., Haendler, B., Hofer-Warbinek, R., Gaugitsch, H., Wrann, M., Schlüsener, H., Seifert, J. M., Bodmer, S., Fontana, A., and Hofer, E. (1987). *EMBO J.* **6**, 3673–3677.
Derynck, R., Roberts, A. B., Winkler, M. E., Chen, E. Y., and Goeddel, D. V. (1984). *Cell* **38**, 287–297.
Derynck, R., Jarrett, J. A., Chen, E. Y., Eaton, D. H., Bell, J. R., Assoian, R. K., Roberts, A. B., Sporn, M. B., and Goeddel, D. V. (1985). *Nature (London)* **316**, 701–705.
Derynck, R., Jarrett, J. A., Chen, E. Y., and Goeddel, D. V. (1986). *J. Biol. Chem.* **261**, 4377–4379.
Derynck, R., Goeddel, D. V., Ullrich, A., Gutterman, J. U., Williams, R. D., Bringman, T. S., and Berger, W. H. (1987). *Cancer Res.* **47**, 707–712.
Dodson, W. C., and Schomberg, D. W. (1987). *Endocrinologgy* **120**, 512–516.
Doolittle, R. F. (1985). *Trends Biochem. Sci.* **10**, 233–237.
Dower, S. K., Kronheim, S. R., Hopp, T. P., Cantrell, M., Deeley, M., Gillis, S., Henney, C. S., and Urdal, D. L. (1986). *Nature (London)* **324**, 266–268.
Edwards, D. R., Murphy, G., Reynolds, J. J., Whitham, S. E., Docherty, A. J. P., Angel, P., and Heath, J. K. (1987). *EMBO J.* **6**, 1899–1904.
Ek, B., Westermark, B., Wasteson, A., and Heldin, C.-H. (1982). *Nature (London)* **294**, 419–420.
Eppstein, D. A., Marsh, Y. V., Schreiber, A. B., Newman, S. R., Todaro, G. J., and Nestor, S. J. (1985). *Nature (London)* **318**, 663–665.
Eto, Y., Tsuji, T., Takezawa, M., Takano, S., Yokogawa, Y., and Shibai, H. (1987). *Biochem. Biophys. Res. Commun.* **142**, 1095–1103.
Fanger, B. O., Wakefield, L. M., and Sporn, M. B. (1985). *Biochemistry* **25**, 3083–3091.
Fausto, N., Mead, J. E., Braun, L., Thompson, N. L., Panzica, M., Goyette, M., Bell, G. I., and Shank, P. R. (1987). *Symp. Fundam. Cancer Res.* **39**, 69–86.
Feige, J. J., Cochet, C., and Chambaz, E. M. (1987a). *Biochem. Biophys. Res. Commun.* **139**, 693–700.
Feige, J. J., Cochet, C., Rainey, W. E., Madani, C., and Chambaz, E. M. (1987b). *J. Biol. Chem.* **262**, 13491–13495.
Feng, P., Catt, K. J., and Knecht, M. (1986). *J. Biol. Chem.* **261**, 14167–14170.
Fernandez-Pol, J. A., Klos, D. J., and Grant, G. A. (1986). *Cancer Res.* **46**, 5153–5161.
Fine, L. G., Holley, R. W., Nasri, H., and Badie-Dezfooly, B. (1985). *Proc. Natl. Acad. Sci. U.S.A.* **82**, 6163–6166.
Fini, M. E., Karmilowicz, M. J., Ruby, P. L., Beeman, A. M., Borges, K. A., and Brinckerhoff, C. E. (1987). *Arthritis Rheum.* **30**, 1255–1264.
Flanders, K. C., Roberts, A. B., Ling, N., Fleurdelys, B. E., and Sporn, M. B. (1988). *Biochemistry*, **27**, 739–746.
Florini, J. R., Roberts, A. B., Ewton, D. Z., Falen, S. L., Flanders, K. C., and Sporn, M. B. (1986). *J. Biol. Chem.* **261**, 16509–16513.
Forage, R. G., Ring, J. M., Brown, R. W., McInerney, B. V., Cobon, G. S., Gregson, R. P., Robertson, D. M., Morgan, F. J., Hearn, M. T. W., Findlay, J. K., Wettenhall, R. E. H., Burger, H. G., and de Kretser, D. M. (1986). *Proc. Natl. Acad. Sci. U.S.A.* **83**, 3091–3095.
Fràter-Schröder, M., Müller, G., Birchmeier, W., and Böhlen, P. (1986). *Biochem. Biophys. Res. Commun.* **137**, 295–302.
Freychet, P., Roth, J., and Neville, D. M. (1971). *Proc. Natl. Acad. Sci. U.S.A.* **68**, 1833–1837.
Frisch, S. M., Clark, E. J., and Werb, Z. (1987). *Proc. Natl. Acad. Sci. U.S.A.* **84**, 2600–2604.
Frolik, C. A., Dart, L. L., Meyers, C. A., Smith, D. M., and Sporn, M. B. (1983). *Proc. Natl. Acad. Sci. U.S.A.* **80**, 3676–3680.

Frolik, C. A., Wakefield, L. A., Smith, D. M., and Sporn, M. B. (1984). *J. Biol. Chem.* **259**, 10995–11000.
Fryling, C. M., Iwata, K. K., Johnson, P. A., Knott, W. B., and Todaro, G. J. (1985). *Cancer Res.* **45**, 2695–2699.
Fujii, D., Brissenden, J. E., Derynck, R., and Franke, U. (1986). *Somatic Cell Mol. Genet.* **12**, 281–288.
Gray, A., Dull, T. J., and Ullrich, A. (1983). *Nature (London)* **303**, 722–725.
Greene, L. A., Shooter, E. M., and Varon, S. (1968). *Proc. Natl. Acad. Sci. U.S.A.* **60**, 1383–1388.
Gregory, H. (1975). *Nature (London)* **257**, 325–327.
Hayashi, I., and Carr, B. (1985). *J. Cell. Physiol.* **125**, 82–90.
Heimark, R. L., Twardzik, D. R., and Schwartz, S. M. (1986). *Science* **233**, 1078–1080.
Hill, D. J., Strain, A. J., Elstow, S. F., Swenne, I., and Milner, R. D. G. (1986). *J. Cell. Physiol.* **128**, 322–328.
Holley, R. W., Böhlen, P., Fava, R., Baldwin, J. H., Kleeman, G., and Armour, R. (1980). *Proc. Natl. Acad. Sci. U.S.A.* **77**, 5989-5992.
Hotta, M., and Baird, A. (1986). *Proc. Natl. Acad. Sci. U.S.A.* **83**, 7795–7799.
Huang, J. S., Huang, S. S., and Deuel, T. F. (1984). *Proc. Natl. Acad. Sci. U.S.A.* **81**, 342–346.
Huang, S. S., and Huang, J. S. (1986). *J. Biol. Chem.* **261**, 9568–9571.
Hunt, T. K., Knighton, D. R., Thakral, K. K., Goodson, W. H., and Andrews, W. S. (1984). *Surgery* **96**, 48–54.
Ibbotson, K. J., Twardzik, D. R., D'Sousa, S. M., Hargreaves, W. R., Todaro, G. J., and Mundy, G. R. (1985). *Science* **228**, 1007–1009.
Ignotz, R., and Massagué, J. (1985). *Proc. Natl. Acad. Sci. U.S.A.* **82**, 8530–8534.
Ignotz, R., and Masasgué, J. (1986). *J. Biol. Chem.* **261**, 4337–4345.
Ignotz, R., Kelly, B., Davis, R., and Massagué, J. (1986). *Proc. Natl. Acad. Sci. U.S.A.* **83**, 6307–6311.
Ignotz, R. A., Endo, T., and Massagué, J. (1987). *J. Biol. Chem.* **262**, 6443–6446.
Im, M. J., and Hoopes, J. E. (1983). *J. Surg. Res.* **35**, 159–162.
Inman, W. H., and Colowick, S. P. (1985). *Proc. Natl. Acad. Sci. U.S.A.* **82**, 1346–1349.
Iwata, K. K., Fryling, C. M., Knott, W. B., and Todaro, G. J. (1985). *Cancer Res.* **45**, 2689–2694.
Jacobs, S., Kull, F. C., Earp, H. S., Svoboda, M. E., Van Wyck, J. J., and Cuatrecasas, P. (1983). *J. Biol. Chem.* **258**, 9581–9584.
Jakowlew, S. B., Kondaiah, P., Flanders, K. C., Thompson, N. L., Dillard, P. J., Sporn, M. B. and Roberts, A. B. (1988). *Oncogene Res.* **2**, 135–148.
Jetten, A. M. (1981). *Ann. N.Y. Acad. Sci* **359**, 200–217.
Kahn, P., and Shin, S. (1979). *J. Cell. Biol.* **82**, 1–16.
Kaplan, P. L., and Ozanne, B. (1983). *Cell* **33**, 931–938.
Kasuga, M., Fujita-Yamaguchi, Y., Blithe, D. L., White, M. F., and Kahn, C. R. (1983). *J. Biol. Chem.* **258**, 10973–10980.
Kehrl, J. H., Roberts, A. B., Wakefield, L. M., Jakowlew, S., Sporn, M. B., and Fauci, A. S. (1986a). *J. Immunol.* **137**, 3855–3860.
Kehrl, J. H., Wakefield, L. M., Roberts, A. B., Jakowlew, A., Alvarez-Mon, M., Derynck, R., Sporn, M. B., and Fauci, A. S. (1986b). *J. Exp. Med.* **163**, 1037–1050.
Keski-Oja, J., Lyons, R. M., and Moses, H. L. (1987). *J. Cell. Biochem. Suppl.* **11A**, 60.
Knabbe, C., Lippman, M. E., Wakefield, A. M., Flanders, K. C., Kasid, A., Derynck, R., and Dickson, R. B. (1987). *Cell* **48**, 417–428.
Knecht, M., Feng, P., and Catt, K. J. (1987). *Biochem. Biophys. Res. Commun.* **139**, 800–807.
Knighton, D. R., Silver, I. A., and Hunt, T. K. (1981). *Surgery* **90**, 262–270.
Knighton, D. R., Fiegel, V. D., Austin, L. L., Ciresi, K. F., and Butler, E. L. (1986). *Ann. Surg.* **204**, 322–330.
Kobrin, M. S., Samsoondar, J., and Kudlow, J. E. (1986). *J. Biol. Chem.* **261**, 14414–14419.

Kurokowa, M., Lynch, K., and Podolsky, D. K. (1987). *Biochem. Biophys. Res. Commun.* **142**, 775–782.
Laiho, M., Saksela, O., Andreasen, P. A., and Keski-Oja, J. (1986). *J. Cell. Biol.* **103**, 2403–2410.
Lawrence, D. A., Pircher, R., Kryceve-Martinerie, C., and Jullien, P. (1984). *J. Cell. Physiol.* **121**, 184–188.
Lawrence, D. A., Pircher, R., and Jullien, P. (1985). *Biochem. Biophys. Res. Commun.* **133**, 1026–1034.
Lawrence, W. T., Sporn, M. B., Gorschboth, C., Norton, J. A., and Grotendorst, G. R. (1986). *Ann. Surg.* **203**, 142–147.
Lechner, J. F., McClendon, I. A., LaVeck, M. A., Shamsuddin, A. M., and Harris, C. C. (1983). *Cancer Res.* **43**, 5915–5921.
Lee, D. C., Rochford, R., Todaro, G. J., and Villarreal, L. P. (1985a). *Mol. Cell. Biol.* **5**, 3644–3636.
Lee, D. C., Rose, T. M., Webb, N. R., and Todaro, G. J. (1985b). *Nature (London)* **313**, 489–491.
Leof, E. B., Proper, J. A., Goustin, A. S., Shipley, G. D., DiCorleto, P. E., and Moses, H. L. (1986). *Proc. Natl. Acad. Sci. U.S.A.* **83**, 2453–2457.
Libby, J., Martinez, R., and Weber, M. J. (1986). *J. Cell. Physiol.* **129**, 159–166.
Like, B., and Massagué, J. (1986). *J. Biol. Chem.* **261**, 13426–13429.
Ling, N., Ying, S.-Y., Ueno, N., Esch, F., Denoroy, L., and Guillemin, R. (1985). *Proc. Natl. Acad. Sci. U.S.A.* **82**, 7217–7221.
Ling, N., Ying, S.-Y., Ueno, N., Shimasaki, S., Esch, F., Hotta, M., and Guilleman, R. (1986). *Nature (London)* **321**, 779–782.
Linsley, P. S., Hargreaves, W. R., Twardzik, D. R., and Todaro, G. J. (1985). *Proc. Natl. Acad. Sci. U.S.A.* **82**, 356–360.
McMahon, J. B., Richards, W. L., del Campo, A. A., Song, M.-K., and Thorgiersson, S. S. (1986). *Cancer Res.* **46**, 4665–4671.
Magun, B. E., Matrisian, L. M., and Bowden, G. T. (1980). *J. Biol. Chem.* **255**, 6373–6381.
Marquardt, H., Hunkapiller, M. W., Hood, L. E., Twardzik, D. R., De Larco, J. E., Stephenson, J. R., and Todaro, G. J. (1983). *Proc. Natl. Acad. Sci. U.S.A.* **80**, 4684–4688.
Marquardt, H., Hunkapiller, M. W., Hood, L., and Todaro, G. J. (1984). *Science* **223**, 1079–1082.
Marquardt, H., Lioubin, M. N., and Ikeda, T. (1987). *J. Biol. Chem.* **262**, 12127–12131.
Mason, A. J., Hayflick, J. S., Ling, N., Esch, F., Ueno, N., Ying, S.-Y., Guillemin, R., Niall, H., and Seeburg, P. H. (1985). *Nature (London)* **318**, 659–663.
Massagué, J. (1983). *J. Biol. Chem.* **258**, 13614–13620.
Massagué, J. (1984). *J. Biol. Chem.* **259**, 9756–9761.
Massagué, J. (1985a). *J. Biol. Chem.* **260**, 7059–7066.
Massagué, J. (1985b). *In* "Cancer Cells" Vol 3 (J. Feramisco, B. Ozanne, and C. Stiles, eds.) pp. 73–78. Cold Spring Harbor Laboratory, Cold Spring Harbor, New York.
Massagué, J., and Like, B. (1985). *J. Biol. Chem.* **260**, 2636–2645.
Massagué, J., Kelly, B., and Mottola, C. (1985). *J. Biol. Chem.* **260**, 4551–4554.
Massagué, J. Cheifetz, S., Endo, T., and Nadal-Ginard, B. (1986). *Proc. Natl. Acad. Sci. U.S.A.* **83**, 8206–8210.
Masui, T., Wakefield, L. M., Lechner, J. F., LaVeck, M. A., Sporn, M. B., and Harris, C. C. (1986). *Proc. Natl. Acad. Sci. U.S.A.* **83**, 2438–2442.
Matrisian, L. M., Bowden, G. T., Krieg, P., Furstenberger, G., Briand, J.-P., LeRoy, P., and Breathnach, R. (1986a). *Proc. Natl. Acad. Sci. U.S.A.* **83**, 9413–9417.
Matrisian, L. M., Leroy, P., Ruhlmann, C., Gesnel, M.-C., and Breathnach, R. (1986b). *Mol. Cell. Biol.* **6**, 1679–1686.
Moses, H. L., Childs, C.B., Halper, J., Shipley, G.D., and Tucker, R. F. (1984). *In* "Control of Cell Growth and Proliferation" (C. M. Veneziale, ed.), pp. 147–167. Van Nostrand-Reinhold, Princeton, New Jersey.

Moses, H. L., Tucker, R. F., Leof, E. B., Coffey, R. J., Halper, J., and Shipley, G. D. (1985). *In* "Cancer Cells" Vol. 3, (J. Feramisco, B. Ozanne, and C. Stiles, eds.), pp. 65–71. Cold Spring Harbor Laboratory, Cold Spring Harbor, New York.

Mulé, J. J., Schwarz, S. L., Roberts, A. B., Sporn, M. B., and Rosenberg, S. A. (1988). *Cancer Immunol. Immunother.*, in press.

Mustoe, T. A., Pierce, G. F., Thomason, A., Gramates, P., Sporn, M. B., and Deuel, T. F. (1987). *Science* **237**, 1333–1336.

Nakamura, T., Tomita, Y., Hirai, R., Yamaoka, K., Kaji, K., and Ichihara, A. (1985). *Biochem. Biophys. Res. Commun.* **133**, 1042–1060.

O'Connor-McCourt, M. D., and Wakefield, L. M. (1987). *J. Biol. Chem.* **262**, 14090–14099.

Olson, E. N., Sternberg, E., Hu, J. S., Spizz, G., and Wilcox, C. (1986). *J. Cell Biol.* **103**, 1799–1805.

Ozanne, B., Fulton, R. J., and Kaplan, P. L. (1980). *J. Cell Physiol.* **105**, 168–180.

Padgett, R. W., St. Johnston, R. D., and Gelbart, W. M. (1987). *Nature (London)* **325**, 81–84.

Pike, L. J., Marquardt, H., Todaro, G. J., Gallis, B., Casnellie, J. E., Bornstein, P., and Krebs, E. G. (1982). *J. Biol. Chem.* **257**, 14628–14631.

Pircher, R., Lawrence, D. A., and Jullien, P. (1984). *Cancer Res.* **44**, 5538–5543.

Pircher, R., Jullien, P., and Lawrence, D. A. (1986). *Biochem. Biophys. Res. Commun.* **136**, 30–37.

Postlethwaite, A. E., Keski-Oja, J., Moses, H. L., and Kang, A. H. (1987). *J. Exp. Med.* **165**, 251–256.

Racker, E., Resnick, R. J., and Feldman (1985). *Proc. Natl. Acad. Sci. U.S.A.* **82**, 3535–3538.

Raines, E. W., Bowen-Pope, D. F., and Ross, R. (1984). *Proc. Natl. Acad. Sci. U.S.A.* **81**, 3424–3428.

Rhodes, J. A., Tam, J. P., Finke, U., Saunders, M., Bernanke, J., Silen, W., and Murphy, R. A. (1986). *Proc. Natl. Acad. Sci. U.S.A.* **83**, 3844–3846.

Ristow, H.-J. (1986). *Proc. Natl. Acad. Sci. U.S.A.* **83**, 5531–5533.

Rizzino, A., Ruff, E., and Rizzino, H. (1986). *Cancer Res.* **46**, 2816–2820.

Roberts, A. B., Lamb, L. C., Newton, D. L., Sporn, M. B., De Larco, J. E., and Todaro, G. J. (1980). *Proc. Natl. Acad. Sci. U.S.A.* **77**, 3493–3498.

Roberts, A. B., Anzano, M. A., Lamb, L. C., Smith, J. M., and Sporn, M. B. (1981). *Proc. Natl. Acad. Sci. U.S.A.* **78**, 5339–5343.

Roberts, A. B., Anzano, M. A., Meyers, C. A., Wideman, J., Blacher, R., Pan, Y.-C., Stein, S., Lehrman, R., Smith, J. M., Lamb, L. C., and Sporn, M. B. (1983a). *Biochemistry* **22**, 5692–5698.

Roberts, A. B., Frolik, C. A., Anzano, M. A., and Sporn, M. B. (1983b). *Fed. Proc., Fed. Am. Soc. Exp. Biol.* **42**, 2621–2626.

Roberts, A. B., Anzano, M. A., Lamb, L. C., Smith, J. M., and Sporn, M. B. (1984a). *Cancer Res.* **44**, 1635–1641.

Roberts, A. B., Frolik, C. A., Anzano, M. A., Assoian, R. K., and Sporn, M. B. (1984b). *In* "Methods for Preparation of Media, Supplements, and Substrata for Serum-free Animal Cell Culture" (D. Barnes, G. Sato, and D. Sirbasku, eds.), pp. 181–194. Liss, New York.

Roberts, A. B., Anzano, M. A., Wakefield, L. M., Roche, N. S., Stern, D. F., and Sporn, M. B. (1985a). *Proc. Natl. Acad. Sci. U.S.A.* **82**, 119–123.

Roberts, A. B., Roche, N. S., and Sporn, M. B. (1985b). *Nature (London)* **315**, 237–239.

Roberts, A. B., Sporn, M. B., Assoian, R. K., Smith, J. M., Roche, N. S., Wakefield, L. M., Heine, U. I., Liotta, L. A., Falanga, V., Kehrl, J. H., and Fauci, A. S. (1986). *Proc. Natl. Acad. Sci. U.S.A.* **83**, 4167–4171.

Robey, P. G., Young, M. F., Flanders, K. C., Roche, N. S., Kondaiah, P., Reddi, A. H., Termine, J. D., Sporn, M. B., and Roberts, A. B. (1987). *J. Cell Biol.* **105**, 457–463.

Rook, A. H., Kehrl, J. H., Wakefield, L. M., Roberts, A. B., Burlington, D. B., Lane, H. C., Sporn, M. B., and Fauci, A. S. (1986). *J. Immunol.* **136**, 3916–3920.
Rossi, P., Karsenty, G., Roberts, A. B., Roche, N. S., Sporn, M. B., and de Crombrugghe, B. (1988). *Cell*, **52**, 405–414.
Ruoslahti, E., and Pierschbacher, M. D. (1986). *Cell* **44**, 517–518.
Samsoondar, J., Kobrin, M. S., and Kudlow, J. E. (1986). *J. Biol. Chem.* **261**, 14408–14413.
Schreiber, A. B., Winkler, M. E., and Derynck, R. (1986). *Science* **232**, 1250–1253.
Schultz, G. S., White, M., Mitchell, R., Brown, G., Lynch, J., Twardzik, D. R., and Todaro, G. J. (1987). *Science* **235**, 350–352.
Scott, J., Urdea, M., Quiroga, M., Sanchez-Pescador, R., Fong, N., Selby, M., Rutter, W. J., and Bell, G. I. (1983). *Science* **221**, 236–240.
Segarini, P. R., Roberts, A. B., Rosen, D. M., and Seyedin, S. M. (1987). *J. Biol. Chem.* **262**, 14655–14662.
Server, A. C., and Shooter, E. M. (1976). *J. Biol. Chem.* **251**, 165–173.
Seyedin, S. M., Thomas, T. C., Thompson, A. Y., Rosen, D. M., and Piez, K. A. (1985). *Proc. Natl. Acad. Sci. U.S.A.* **82**, 2267–2271.
Seyedin, S. M., Thompson, A. Y., Bentz, H., Rosen, D. M., McPherson, J. M., Conti, A., Siegel, N. R., Galluppi, G. R., and Piez, K. A. (1986). *J. Biol. Chem.* **261**, 5693–5695.
Seyedin, P. R., Segarini, P. R., Rosen, D. M., Thompson, A. Y., Bentz, H., and Graycar, J. (1987). *J. Biol. Chem.* **262**, 1946–1949.
Shipley, G. D., Tucker, R. F., and Moses, H. L. (1985). *Proc. Natl. Acad. Sci. U.S.A.* **82**, 4147–4151.
Shipley, G. D., Pittelkow, M. R., Wille, J. J., Scott, R. E., and Moses, H. L. (1986). *Cancer Res.* **46**, 2068–2071.
Smith, J. M., Sporn, M. B., Roberts, A. B., Derynck, R., Winkler, M. E., and Gregory, H. (1985). *Nature (London)* **315**, 515–516.
Sporn, M. B., and Roberts, A. B. (1986). *J. Clin. Invest.* **78**, 329–332.
Sporn, M. B., and Roberts, A. B. (1988). *Nature (London)* **332**, 217–219.
Sporn, M. B., Roberts, A. B., Shull, J. H., Smith, J. M., Ward, J. M., and Sodek, J. (1983). *Science* **219**, 1329–1331.
Stern, D. F., Roberts, A. B., Roche, N. S., Sporn, M. B., and Weinberg, R. A. (1986). *Mol. Cell. Biol.* **6**, 870–877.
Stern, P. H., Krieger, N. S., Nissenson, R. A., Williams, R. D., Winkler, M. E., Derynck, R., and Strewler, G. J. (1986). *J. Clin. Invest.* **76**, 2016–2019.
Stroobant, P., Rice, A. P., Gullick, W. J., Cheng, D. J., Kerr, I. M., and Waterfield, M. D. (1985). *Cell* **42**, 383–393.
Takahashi, N., MacDonald, B. R., Hon, J., Winkler, M. E., Derynck, R., Mundy, G. R., and Roodman, G. D. (1986). *J. Clin. Invest.* **78**, 894–898.
Tam, J. P. (1985). *Science* **229**, 673–675.
Tam, J. P., Marquardt, H., Rosberger, D. F., Wong, T. W., and Todaro, G. J. (1984). *Nature (London)* **309**, 376–378.
Tashjian, A. H., Voelkel, E. F., Lazzaro, M., Singer, F. R., Roberts, A. B., Derynck, R., Winkler, M. E., and Levine, L. (1985). *Proc. Natl. Acad. Sci. U.S.A.* **82**, 4535–4538.
Thalacker, F. W., and Nilsen-Hamilton, M. (1987). *J. Biol. Chem.* **262**, 2283–2290.
Todaro, G. J., Fryling, C., and De Larco, J. E. (1980). *Proc. Natl. Acad. Sci. U.S.A.* **77**, 5258–5262.
Todaro, G. J., Lee, D. C., Webb, N. R., Rose, T. M., and Brown, J. P. (1985). *In* "Cancer Cells (J. Feramisco, B. Ozanne, and C. Stiles, eds.), Vol. 3, pp. 51–58. Cold Spring Harbor Laboratory, Cold Spring Harbor, New York.
Tucker, R. F., Branum, E. L., Shipley, G. D., Ryan, R. J., and Mos, H. L. (1984a). *Proc. Natl. Acad. Sci. U.S.A.* **81**, 6757–6761.

Tucker, R. F., Shipley, G. D., Moses, H. L., and Holley, R. W. (1984b). *Science* **226**, 705–707.
Twardzik, D. R., Brown, J. P., Ranchalis, J. E., and Todaro, G. J. (1985). *Proc. Natl. Acad. Sci. U.S.A.* **82**, 5300–5304.
Vale, W., Rivier, J., Vaughan, J., McClintock, R., Corrigan, A., Woo, W., Karr, D., and Spiess, J. (1986). *Nature (London)* **321**, 776–779.
Van Obberghen-Schilling, E., Kondaiah, P., Ludwig, R. L., Sporn, M. B., and Baker, C. C. (1987). *Molec. Endocrinol.* **1**, 693–698.
Van Zoelen, E. J. J., van Oostwaard, T. M. J., and de Laat, S. W. (1986). *J. Biol. Chem.* **261**, 5003–5009.
Wahl, S. M., Hunt, D. A., Wakefield, L. M., McCartney-Francis, N., Wahl, L. M., Roberts, A. B., and Sporn, M. B. (1987). *Proc. Natl. Acad. Sci. U.S.A.* **84**, 5788–5792.
Wakefield, L. M., Smith, D. M., Flanders, K. C., and Sporn, M. B. (1987a). *J. Cell. Biochem. Suppl.* **11A**, 46.
Wakefield, L. M., Smith, D. M., Masui, T., Harris, C. C., and Sporn, M. B. (1987b). *J. Cell Biol.* **105**, 965–975.
Whitham, S. E., Murphy, G., Angel, P., Rahmsdorf, H.-J., Smith, B. J., Lyons, A., Harris, T. J. R., Reynolds, J. J., Herrlich, P., and Docherty, A. J. P. (1986). *Biochem. J.* **240**, 913–916.
Winkler, M. E., Bringman, T., and Marks, B. J. (1986). *J. Biol. Chem.* **261**, 13838–13843.
Wrana, J. L., Sodek, J., Ber, R. L., and Bellows, C. G. (1986). *Eur. J. Biochem.* **159**, 69–76.
Ying, S.-Y., Becker, A., Baird, A., Ling, N., Ueno, N., Esch, F., and Guillemin, R. (1986a). *Biochem. Biophys. Res. Commun.* **135**, 950–956.
Ying, S.-Y., Becker, A., Ling, N., Ueno, N., and Guillemin, R. (1986b). *Biochem. Biophys. Res. Commun.* **136**, 969–975.
Zarling, J. M., Shoyab, M., Marquardt, H., Hanson, M. B., Lioubin, M. N., and Todaro, G. J. (1986). *Proc. Natl. Acad. Sci. U.S.A.* **83**, 9739–9743.

ONCOGENE ACTIVATION IN CHEMICAL CARCINOGENESIS

Allan Balmain and Ken Brown

Beatson Institute for Cancer Research, Garscube Estate, Switchback Road, Bearsden, Glasgow G61 1BD, Scotland

I. Introduction 000
II. Activation of Oncogenes during Carcinogenesis *in Vivo* 000
  A. *ras* Gene Activation
  B. Function of *ras* Genes
  C. Tissue-Specific Gene Activation
  D. Oncogene Activation by Carcinogens: Direct or Indirect?
  E. The Role of Oncogenes in Tumor Promotion
  F. The Role of Oncogenes in Tumor Progression
III. The Role of Oncogenes in Carcinogenesis *in Vitro* 000
  A. Activated Oncogenes in Cells Transformed *in Vitro* by Carcinogens
  B. Stage-Specific Oncogene Activation *in Vitro*
  C. Comparison of Stages of Carcinogenesis *in Vivo* and *in Vitro*
IV. Conclusions 000
  References 000

I. Introduction

The emergence of oncogenes as major factors in the control of normal cell proliferation and differentiation has had far-reaching consequences for studies in chemical carcinogenesis. It has been appreciated for many years that chemical carcinogens interact with DNA to form specific adducts, some of which can lead to the introduction of single base mutations, deletions, or rearrangements in the genetic material. One of the major dilemmas in studies of this kind has been the identification of the critical adduct and indeed the critical target gene that, when altered, leads to the induction of the transformed state. Although many adducts resulting from treatment of DNA or cells with chemical carcinogens have been identified, the biological significance of specific adduct formation has not been clear. Some of the major adducts may be particularly easily repaired, whereas minor adducts could be those that are most biologically relevant. One of the main advances stemming from the research on oncogenes is that this group of genes provides at least potential targets for activation by carcinogens. Indeed, the full spectrum of changes that have been noted in DNA of cells treated

ADVANCES IN CANCER RESEARCH, VOLUME 51

by chemical carcinogens—i.e., point mutations, translocations, gene amplification—has been implicated in the activation of protooncogenes to an oncogenic state (Balmain, 1985; Barbacid, 1987; Klein and Klein, 1985; Alitalo and Schwab, 1986). It is therefore logical to expect that some oncogenes can be activated directly by interaction between the target genes and chemical carcinogens. Others may be activated indirectly during the progression of tumorigenesis by nontargeted genetic events in somatic cells.

The purpose of this article is to discuss the advances made in understanding mechanisms of action of chemical carcinogens in the light of the recent evidence that oncogenes are directly implicated in the process of tumor development. Various model systems that have been used to address the question of cell transformation *in vivo* will be considered with respect to oncogene activation, and the process of carcinogenesis in cell culture will be compared with the various stages of tumor development *in vivo*.

II. Activation of Oncogenes during Carcinogenesis *in Vivo*

Animal model systems have been invaluable in establishing the accepted concepts of tumor initiation, promotion, and progression (Hecker *et al.*, 1982). The value of such model systems lies in the fact that the etiology of tumor development can be carefully controlled, in contrast to the situation in most human tumors, for which the causative agents are completely unknown. The reproducible induction of specific types of tumors in animals by particular chemical or physical carcinogens therefore provides an ideal opportunity to investigate the sequential molecular events associated with the different stages of carcinogenesis. The activation of oncogenes in a number of such animal model systems has now been investigated in some detail. The results are summarized in Table I.

A. *ras* GENE ACTIVATION

The most noticeable feature of Table I is the very high prevalence of activation of *ras* protooncogenes. This may be due to the highly selective nature of the assay system, which involves transfection of high-molecular-weight DNA from tumors into NIH 3T3 cells. These cells are particularly efficient in taking up exogenous DNA and are also highly susceptible to transformation by members of the *ras* gene family. *ras* genes were originally identified as the transforming principles of retroviruses isolated from rodent tumors (Bishop, 1983; Barbacid, 1987). One of the major advances in recent years was the demonstration in 1982 that the same genes could be detected by transfection of human tumor DNA samples into NIH 3T3 cells (Parada *et al.*, 1982; Santos *et al.*, 1982; Der *et al.*, 1982). It has now been firmly established that the individual members of the *ras* gene family comprising the Harvey, Kirsten, and N-*ras* genes can be activated in a very wide variety of both human and animal tumor types. The mechanism of activation of the genes is normally by point mutations at one of several possible activating positions within the coding sequence (Balmain *et al.*, 1986; Barbacid, 1987), but examples of activation by promoter insertion have also been reported (Westaway *et al.*, 1986; George *et al.*, 1986). The latter experiments are consistent with earlier observations that elevated expression of the normal *ras* gene can under certain circumstances lead to transformation of cells in culture (Chang *et al.*, 1982; Spandidos and Wilkie, 1984). These results in turn suggest that the elevated expression levels of normal *ras* proteins seen in a number of both human and animal turmors can play at least a permissive role in the induction of tumors (Tanaka *et al.*, 1986; Spandidos and Kerr, 1984).

B. Function of *ras* Genes

The strong evidence linking *ras* gene activation to tumor formation has led to an intensification of the efforts to find a biological role for this gene family. Much of the research in this area has recently been comprehensively reviewed by Barbacid (1987). The evidence to date indicates that the *ras* proteins are GTP-binding proteins with intrinsic GTPase activity. As such, they are similar to a family of "G proteins" known to be involved in the transduction of growth or differentiation signals through cellular membranes. Not surprisingly, the search for a biological role for *ras* has been concentrated in this area.

The emerging consensus on a possible function is that *ras* proteins act as tranducers of signals from growth factor receptors to the interior of the cell (Gibbs *et al.*, 1984; McGrath *et al.*, 1984; Sweet *et al.*, 1984). Recent work has shown that the N-*ras* P21 appears to be linked to the bombesin receptor. Treatment of cells expressing elevated levels of N-*ras* P21 with bombesin leads to stimulation of phospholipase C and an increased turnover of phosphatidylinositol (Wakelam *et al.*, 1986). Other, similar results have linked the H-*ras* P21 to the PDGF receptor (M. Wakelam, C. Marshall, and A. Hall, personal communication). The subsequent generation of intracellular second messengers is then thought to mediate the cellular response, i.e., increased cell proliferation or differentiation according to the particular target cell being studied.

Evidence that growth factors can have positive or negative effects on target cells has been available for some considerable period (Moses and Leof, 1986). It is therefore interesting that expression of mutated *ras* genes in particular cell types can have similarly disparate effects (Stacey and Kung, 1984; Feramisco *et al.*, 1984; Noda *et al.*, 1985; Bar-Sagi and Feramisco, 1985). This reinforces the idea that the *ras* genes themselves may be linked up to the growth factor response. The perturbation of this growth signal transduction mechanism by mutations in *ras* genes is not at present clear. However,

TABLE I

ACTIVATION OF ONCOGENES IN CARCINOGEN-INDUCED ANIMAL TUMORS

Tumor	Carcinogen[a]	Oncogene[b]	Incidence	Mutation[b]	Reference
I. Mouse					
Skin pap./carc.	DMBA	H-*ras*	45/50	$A^{182} \rightarrow T$	Quintanilla *et al.* (1986)
Skin pap./carc.	DMBA	H-*ras*	1/50	Codon 61	Balmain and Brown, unpub. results
Skin pap./carc.	DMBA	H-*ras*	1/50	$G^{35} \rightarrow T$	Balmain and Brown, unpub. results
Skin carcinoma	DMBA	H-*ras*	3/4	$A^{182} \rightarrow T$	Bizub *et al.* (1986)
Skin carcinoma	DBACR	H-*ras*	3/4	$A^{182} \rightarrow T$	Bizub *et al.* (1986)
Skin papilloma	DMBA	H-*ras*	—	N.D.	Storer *et al.* (1986a)
Skin papilloma	MCA	H-*ras*	2/6	$A^{182} \rightarrow T$	Balmain and Brown (unpub. results)
Skin papilloma	MNNG	H-*ras*	4/4	$G^{35} \rightarrow A$	Balmain and Brown (unpub. results)
Skin pap./carc.[c]	BP	H-*ras*	2/5	$G^{35} \rightarrow T$	Balmain and Brown (unpub. results)
Skin pap./carc.[c]	BP	K- or N-*ras*	1/5	N.D.	Balmain and Brown (unpub. results)
Skin carcinoma	Urethane	H-*ras*	4/6	$A^{182} \rightarrow T$	T. Bowden, personal communication
Skin carcinoma	Urethane	H-*ras*	1/6	$G^{35} \rightarrow C$	T. Bowden, personal communication
Skin pap./carc.	*cis*-Platin	H-*ras*	2/3	N.D.	T. Bowden, personal communication
Fibrosarcoma	MCA	K-*ras*	2/4	N.D.	Eva and Aaronson (1983)
Fibrosarcoma	BP	K-*ras*	—	N.D.	Vousden and Marshall (1984)
Skin carcinoma	β-PL	H-*ras*	1/2	$A^{182} \rightarrow T$	Garte *et al.* (1985); S. J. Garte (personal communication)
Mammary carcinoma	DMBA	H-*ras*	75%	$A^{182} \rightarrow T$	Dandekar *et al.* (1986)
Lung carcinoma	TNM	K-*ras*	100%	$G^{35} \rightarrow A$	Barbacid (1987)
Plasmacytoma	Mineral oil	*mos*	—	LTR insertion	Cohen *et al.* (1983)
Plasmacytoma	Mineral oil	c-*myc*	—	Translocation	Shen-Ong *et al.* (1982)
Macrophage tumor	MCA	K-*ras*	—	N.D.	Vousden and Marshall (1984)
T lymphoma	MCA	K-*ras*	—	N.D.	Vousden and Marshall (1984)
T lymphoma	NMU	N-*ras*	85%	$G^{35} \rightarrow A$	Guerrero and Pellicer (1987)
T lymphoma	NMU	N-*ras*	—	$G^{38} \rightarrow A$	Guerrero and Pellicer (1987)
T lymphoma	NMU	N-*ras*	—	$C^{181} \rightarrow A$	Guerrero and Pellicer (1987)
T lymphoma	NMU	N-*ras*	—	$A^{182} \rightarrow T$	Guerrero and Pellicer (1987)
T lymphoma	NMU	K-*ras*	—	$G^{35} \rightarrow A$	Guerrero and Pellicer (1987)

T lymphoma	γ rays	K-*ras*	57%	$G^{35} \rightarrow A$	Guerrero and Pellicer (1987)
T lymphoma	γ rays	N-*ras*	—	$G^{35} \rightarrow A$	Guerrero and Pellicer (1987)
T lymphoma	MCA	K-*ras*	83%	N.D.	Eva and Trimmer (1986)
T lymphoma	NMU	K-*ras*	3/4	N.D.	Warren *et al.* (1987)
Hepatocellular	None	H-*ras*	77%	$C^{181} \rightarrow A$	Reynolds *et al.* (1986)
Carc./adenoma	None	H-*ras*	—	$A^{182} \rightarrow T/G$	
Hepatoma	HO-DHE	H-*ras*	5/11	$A^{182} \rightarrow T$	Wiseman *et al.* (1986)
Hepatoma	HO-DHE	H-*ras*	5/11	$A^{182} \rightarrow G$	
Hepatoma	HO-DHE	K-*ras*	1/11	N.D.	
Hepatoma	HO-AAF	H-*ras*	7/10	$C^{181} \rightarrow A$	Wiseman *et al.* (1986); R. W. Wiseman (personal communication)
Hepatoma	HO-AAF	H-*ras*	2/10	$A^{182} \rightarrow T$	
Hepatoma	HO-AAF	H-*ras*	1/10	N.D.	
Hepatoma	VC	H-*ras*	8/10	$A^{182} \rightarrow T$	Wiseman *et al.* (1986); R. W. Wiseman (personal communication)
Hepatoma	VC	H-*ras*	1/10	$A^{182} \rightarrow G$	
Hepatoma	VC	H-*ras*	1/10	N.D.	
Hepatoma	HO-AAB	H-*ras*	9/10	$C^{181} \rightarrow A$	R. W. Wiseman (personal communication)
Hepatoma	EC	H-*ras*	5/7	$A^{182} \rightarrow T$	
Hepatoma	EC	H-*ras*	1/7	$A^{182} \rightarrow G$	
Hepatoma	Estragole	H-*ras*	3/6	$A^{182} \rightarrow T$	R. W. Wiseman (personal communication)
Hepatoma	Estragole	H-*ras*	1/6	$A^{182} \rightarrow G$	
Hepatoma	Estragole	H-*ras*	1/6	N.D.	
Hepatoma	Estragole	K-*ras*	1/6	N.D.	
Hepatoma	Safrole	H-*ras*	4/6	$A^{182} \rightarrow T$	R. W. Wiseman (personal communication)
Hepatoma	Safrole	H-*ras*	2/6	$A^{182} \rightarrow G$	
Hepatoma	DMBA	H-*ras*	10/10	$A^{18} \rightarrow T$	R. W. Wiseman (personal communication)

TABLE I (*continued*)

ACTIVATION OF ONCOGENES IN CARCINOGEN-INDUCED ANIMAL TUMORS

Tumor	Carcinogen[a]	Oncogene[b]	Incidence	Mutation[b,c]	Reference
Hepatoma	BP	H-*ras*	1/10	$C^{181} \rightarrow A$	R. W. Wiseman (personal communication)
Hepatoma	BP	H-*ras*	5/10	$A^{182} \rightarrow T$	
Hepatoma	BP	K-*ras*	3/10	N.D.	
Hepatoma	BP	N.D.	1/10	N.D.	
Hepatoma	AFB_1	H-*ras*	1/10	$C^{181} \rightarrow A$	R. W. Wiseman (personal communication)
Hepatoma	AFB_1	H-*ras*	6/10	$A^{182} \rightarrow T$	
Hepatoma	AFB_1	K-*ras*	1/10	N.D.	
Hepatoma	AFB_1	N.D.	1/10	N.D.	
Hepatoma	DEN	H-*ras*	6/16	$C^{181} \rightarrow A$	R. W. Wiseman (personal communication)
Hepatoma	DEN	H-*ras*	4/16	$A^{182} \rightarrow T$	
Hepatoma	DEN	H-*ras*	3/16	$A^{182} \rightarrow G$	
Hepatoma	DEN	H-*ras*	1/16	N.D.	
Hepatoma	DEN	K-*ras*	2/16	N.D.	
Hepatocellular	Furan	H-*ras*	4/29	$C^{181} \rightarrow A$	Reynolds *et al.* (1987)
carc./adenoma	Furan	H-*ras*	1/29	$A^{182} \rightarrow G$	Reynolds *et al.* (1987)
Hepatocellular	Furan	H-*ras*	2/29	$G^{351} \rightarrow C$	
carc./adenoma	Furan	H-*ras*	2/29	$G^{351} \rightarrow T$	
Hepatocellular	Furan	H-*ras*	1/29	N.D.	
carc./adenoma	Furan	K-*ras*	2/29	N.D.	
Hepatocellular	Furfural	H-*ras*	1/16	$A^{182} \rightarrow G$	
carc./adenoma	Furfural	H-*ras*	5/16	$C^{181} \rightarrow G$	Reynolds *et al.* (1987)

Hepatocellular	Furfural	H-*ras*	1/16	$G^{37} \rightarrow C$	
carc./adenoma	Furfural	H-*ras*	1/16	$G^{38} \rightarrow T$	
Hepatocellular	Furfural	H-*ras*	1/16	$G^{351} \rightarrow T$	
carc./adenoma	Furfural	K-*ras*	1/16	Codon 12	
Hepatocellular carc./adenoma	Furfural	Unknown	3/16	—	
II. Rat					
Fibrosarcoma	DNP	K-*ras*	1/7	$G^{35} \rightarrow T$	Tahira *et al.* (1986)
Mammary carcinoma	NMU	H-*ras*	86%	$G^{35} \rightarrow A$	Zarbl *et al.* (1985)
Mammary carcinoma	DMBA	H-*ras*	23%	$A^{182}/A^{183} \rightarrow N$	Zarbl *et al.* (1985)
Lung carcinoma	TNM	K-*ras*	74%	$G^{35} \rightarrow A$	Barbacid (1987)
Hepatocellular carcinoma	AFB_1	K-*ras*	2/10	N.D.	McMahon *et al.* (1986)
Renal carcinoma	DMN-OMe	K-*ras*	10/25	N.D.	Sukumar *et al.* (1986)
Renal carcinoma	DMN-OMe	N-*ras*	1/25	N.D.	
Neuroblastoma or glioblastoma	ENU	*neu*	4/6	T → A	Bargmann *et al.* (1986)
Neuroblastoma	NMU	*neu*	—	T → A	Barbacid (1986)
Glioblastoma	NMU	*neu*	—	T → A	Barbacid (1986)
Schwannoma	NMU	*neu*	—	T → A	Barbacid (1987)
Nasopharyngeal carcinoma	MMS	N.D.	—	N.D.	Garte *et al.* (1985)

[a]DMBA, dimethylbenzanthracene; DBACR, dibenzacridine; MCA, methylcholanthrene; MNNG, *N*-methyl-*N'*-nitro-*N*-nitrosoguanidine; BP, benzypyrene; β-PL, β-propiolactone; TNM, tetranitromethane; NMU, nitrosomethylurea; HO-DHE, hydroxydehydroestragole; HO-AAF, hydroxyacetylaminofluorene; VC, vinylcarbamate; DNP, dinitropyrene; AFB_1, aflatoxin B_1; DMN-OMe, methyl(methoxymethyl)nitrosamine; MMS, methylmethanesulfonate; HO-AAB, hydroxyaminoazobenzene; EC, ethyl carbamate; DEN, diethylnitrosamine.

[b]N.D., not determined.

[c]Mutations were analyzed using cell lines derived from tumors.

it is possible that the mutation, which is known to induce a substantial conformational change in the protein product, can lead to an alteration in the specificity of interaction between the *ras* P21 and its appropriate receptor or effector molecules. This may lead to constitutive production of the second messengers without necessarily requiring binding of the external ligand.

C. Tissue-Specific Gene Activation

It can be seen from Table I that the various animal model systems used show prevalent activation of one particular type of oncogene. For example, the skin papillomas and carcinomas induced by treatment with the initiator dimethylbenzanthracene (DMBA), followed by multiple applications of the tumor promoter 12-*O*-tetradecanoylphorbol-13-acetate (TPA) have a very high frequency (over 90%) of activation of the H-*ras* gene (Quintanilla *et al.*, 1986). Similar results have been obtained with the mammary gland system of Barbacid and colleagues; in this system, mammary carcinomas are induced by treatment of pregnant rats with nitrosomethylurea (NMU) (Zarbl *et al.*, 1985). In contrast, thymic lymphomas induced by the carcinogen NMU have predominantly the N-*ras* gene activated (Guerrero *et al.*, 1984a, 1985), whereas those induced by radiation (Guerrero *et al.*, 1984b) or by methylcholanthrene (MCA) (Eva and Trimmer, 1986) and fibrosarcomas induced by MCA treatment (Eva and Aaronson, 1983) frequently show activation of a K-*ras* gene. Yet another situation is observed in gliomas and schwannomas induced in rats by treatment with alkylating agents, in which the *neu* gene is activated (Schechter *et al.*, 1984; Barbacid, 1986).

1. *The Role of Chromatin Structure*

One rationale for tissue-specific activation is that the genes may have a different susceptibility to mutation in particular cell types. For example, the H-*ras* gene has been shown to be less methylated in mouse epidermal cells than in cells of other lineages (Ramsden *et al.*, 1985). This tissue-specific methylation pattern may determine the degree of binding of nuclear proteins to the chromatin of these cells, thereby leading to an increased or a decreased susceptibility to mutagenesis by chemical carcinogens. It is noteworthy that fibroblast cells have a highly methylated H-*ras* gene, and these cells, when transformed by chemical carcinogens either *in vivo* or *in vitro*, give rise to tumors with an activated K-*ras* gene (Eva and Aaronson, 1983; Parada and Weinberg, 1983). Hence one factor in determining tissue preference for activation may be the overall chromosome structure surrounding the individual gene family members.

In this context, it is interesting that binding of the ultimate carcinogen from benzo[*a*]pyrene (BP) has been located to specific polytene chromosome bands in *Drosophila* cells, presumably as a consequence of some variation in chromatin structure (Kurth and Bustin, 1985). Binding to the DNA of mammalian cells has also been reported to be nonrandom (Boles and Hogan, 1984; Kootstra, 1987). In addition, alkylation of DNA by ethylnitrosourea (ENU) takes place predominantly in a very small proportion of the genome (Nehls *et al.*, 1984), although the nature of the sequences within this fraction is not presently known. This nonrandom interaction between carcinogens and DNA may be an important factor in the determination of specific gene mutations.

2. *Tissue-Specific Signal Transduction*

An attractive alternative explanation is based on recent evidence showing that *ras* gene products may be linked to different growth factor receptors (Wakelam *et al.*, 1986). Although *ras* genes are apparently ubiquitously expressed in virtually all cell types (Müller *et al.*, 1983; Slamon and Cline, 1984), possibly as a consequence of having a promoter structure resembling that of housekeeping genes (Ishii *et al.*, 1985), this finding does not necessarily mean that all growth induction pathways are functional at the same time. In other words, even if a particular cell is producing the H-*ras* P21, the growth factor receptor to which this P21 is linked may not be stimulated by interaction with its specific ligand. This could in turn mean that a mutation in the H-*ras* in that cell type would be "silent" and not lead to any phenotypic changes. Similar mutations in other family members that are active in signal transduction could lead to cell transformation.

3. *The Role of Hormones and Tissue Differentiation*

Another example of specificity in oncogene activation comes from the results of Barbacid and colleagues on rat tumors induced by treatment with NMU. When rats are treated during sexual development with a single dose of this carcinogen, mammary carcinomas that develop have a high proportion of activated H-*ras* genes (Zarbl *et al.*, 1985). However, when the treatment is carried out during fetal development, the subsequent adult rats develop gliomas and schwannomas that have an activated *neu* gene (Barbacid, 1986). This gene had previously been shown to be activated in rat gliomas induced by ENU (Schechter *et al.*, 1984). This variation in tumor type and pattern of oncogene activation as a function of the time of carcinogen treatment clearly indicates that other factors, e.g., hormonal status or the particular differentiation state of the target tissue, are important in determining the specificity. These questions will be discussed in more detail in the section on tumor promotion (Section II,E).

D. Oncogene Activation by Carcinogens: Direct or Indirect?

When members of the *ras* family were first found to be mutated in human and animal tumors, it was assumed that the mutation probably took place at a late stage of carcinogenesis. This assumption was based on the fact that the recipient cells in transfection assays, NIH 3T3 cells, were already thought to be in a premalignant state and as such required only one additional (late) event in order to progress to malignancy. More recent evidence from animal model systems showed that mutations in *ras* genes can be found in premalignant tumors (Balmain *et al.*, 1984a; Reynolds *et al.*, 1986) and consequently might take place during the initiation stage of carcinogenesis, by direct interaction between the carcinogen and the target gene. The relevance of these observations to human cancer is supported by recent observations that mutated *ras* genes are found in a substantial proportion of premalignant tumors of the colon (Bos *et al.*, 1987).

1. *Carcinogen-Specific Mutations*

Because of the difficulties in isolating "initiated cells," several groups have used indirect methods to demonstrate that mutations in *ras* genes take place concomitantly with initiation. The strategy is based on the assumption that if the mutations are directly caused by interaction with the carcinogen, the type of mutation introduced should correlate with the known metabolism and DNA-binding characteristics of each initiator. The first example of such an analysis involved the induction of rat mammary carcinomas by the methylating agent NMU (Sukumar *et al.*, 1983; Zarbl *et al.*, 1985). These carcinoma cells were found to contain an activated H-*ras* oncogene with a G:C → A:T transition at the second position of codon 12. This particular mutation would indeed be that predicted for the methylating agent NMU and would result from the generation of O^6-methylguanosine, which is known to mispair with thymidine during DNA replication (Eadie *et al.*, 1984; Loechler *et al.*, 1984). When DMBA was substituted for NMU in this animal system, no G:C → A:T mutations were obtained (Zarbl *et al.*, 1985).

In the mouse skin system, initiation with DMBA and promotion with phorbol esters induced papillomas and carcinomas in which the H-*ras* gene was consistently activated by an A:T → T:A transversion at the second base of codon 61 (Quintanilla *et al.*, 1986). This mutation was not seen if *N*-methyl-*N*′-nitro-*N*-nitrosoguanidine (MNNG), a carcinogen similar in action to NMU, was substituted for DMBA. In this case, 40% of the skin tumors investigated showed a G:C → A:T transition at the second nucleotide of codon 12 (K. Brown and A. Balmain, unpublished results). The predominance of A:T → T:A mutations after initiation with DMBA is consistent with previous results on the metabolism and binding of this carcinogen to DNA in mouse skin (Dipple *et al.*, 1983). These studies indicated that although DMBA forms adducts with both dG and dA residues, there appears to exist a clear correlation between the formation of specific aromatic hydrocarbon-dA adducts and tumor initiation (Biggar *et al.*, 1983; DiGiovanni *et al.*, 1986), a result implying that the dA adduct is the critical lesion involved in the action of these carcinogens in mouse skin. Similar results involving A:T → T:A transversions have been obtained for the carcinogen dibenz[c,h]acridine (DBACR) (Bizub *et al.*, 1986).

An extensive study has been carried out using a wide variety of chemicals to induce hepatomas in B6C3F1 mice (Wiseman *et al.*, 1986). Treatment with the arylhydroxamic acids *N*-hydroxy-2-acetylaminofluorene (N-OH-AAF) and *N*-hydroxyaminoazobenzene, the metabolic products of the respective aromatic amines, resulted predominantly in C:G → A:T mutations at codon 61 of H-*ras* (Table I). Studies in *Escherichia coli* (Bichara and Fuchs, 1985) and cultured hamster cells (Carothers *et al.*, 1986) have shown that the major point mutation induced by N-OH-AAF is a G:C → T:A transversion, presumably via the deacetylated C−8 dG adduct. This would correspond to a C:G → A:T transversion on the other strand, in agreement with the results of the *in vivo* experiments. A different spectrum of mutations was seen in tumors induced by other carcinogens (Table I). Interestingly, Reynolds *et al.* (1987) have found a similar pattern of specific H-*ras* gene mutations in B6C3F1 mouse liver tumors induced by furan and furfural, both of which are nonmutagenic in the standard Ames test.

The demonstration from these three independent animal model systems that varying the carcinogen leads frequently to a change in the type of *ras* mutation observed provides very strong evidence that at least in certain cases a direct interaction can take place between the carcinogen and the *ras* gene.

However, the situation is less clear for some polycyclic aromatic hydrocarbons such as MCA or BP. Studies in *E. coli* on mutations induced in the *lac I* gene have shown that BP preferentially induces G:C → T:A transversions (Eisenstadt *et al.*, 1982). Other workers have found that benzo[a]pyrene-7,8-diol 9,10-epoxide (BPDE), the ultimate carcinogen obtained by metabolic activation of BP, induces nucleotide deletions at GC cluster regions in *E. coli* (Lobanenkov *et al.*, 1986; Wei *et al.*, 1984). Experiments involving the transfection of BPDE-treated plasmids containing *ras*-protooncogenes into 3T3 cells resulted in a variety of transversion mutations (Vousden *et al.*, 1986). An A:T → T:A transversion at codon 61 of the H-*ras* gene was also found to be the predominant mutational event in BP-induced hepatomas in B6C3F1 mice (Table I) (R. Wiseman, personal communication). Bizub *et al.* (1986) have reported that BP-induced mouse skin carcinomas did not have any activated transforming genes, whereas in our laboratory, three of five cell lines derived from skin papillomas or carcinomas induced with BP (Pera and Gorman, 1984) were found to have *ras* genes containing mutations at codon 12 (K. Brown, M. Quintanilla, S. Young, M. Pera, and A. Balmain, unpublished results). Preliminary results on tumors initiated with MCA indicate that only about 20% of these have the A:T → T:A transversion induced with high frequency by DMBA (Table I). These disparate results emphasize the heterogeneous pattern obtained using polycyclic aromatic hydrocarbon carcinogens other than DMBA. Some tumors contain activated *ras* genes but with no consistent mutations, whereas others have either unidentified transforming genes or lack dominant transforming activity in transfection assays.

Some tumors induced by NMU also show an interesting spectrum of *ras* gene alterations, a pattern that is not readily explicable in terms of a simple mutational mechanism. Guerrero, Pellicer, and co-workers have shown that thymic lymphomas induced by this carcinogen have N-*ras* genes activated by either G:C → A:T, C:G → A:T, or A:T → T:A mutations (Guerrero *et al.*, 1985; Guerrero and Pellicer, 1987). Similar tumors induced by radiation treatment, which is not normally considered to be a potent inducer of point mutations, have predominantly K-*ras* genes activated by G:C → A:T transitions at codon 12 (Guerrero and Pellicer, 1987). It is not yet possible to say whether these mutations are all directly induced by the carcinogenic agent or arise at a later stage of tumor development. The observation that G:C → A:T transitions occur in the *lac I* gene after treatment of DNA with ionizing radiation, followed by transfection into *E. coli* (Ayaki *et al.*, 1986), raises the possibility that the *ras* mutations may indeed by directly induced *in vivo*. However, the interpretation is complicated by the fact that G:C → A:T transitions are also fairly frequent "spontaneous" mutations in eukaryotic cells (Hauser *et al.*, 1987).

It should be pointed out that any attempt to correlate mutations found in activated *ras* genes with the known chemical modifications of macromolecules by carcinogens must of necessity be limited. A tumor induced *in vivo* is the end result of multiple biological events. In the initial adduct formation, the heterogeneity of the DNA structure is likely to lead to nonrandom distribution of these adducts (Kurth and Bustin, 1985; Boles and Hogan, 1984; Kootstra, 1987). The carcinogenic species may be biased toward or against certain bases because of the stereoelectronic effects of neighboring bases or the stereochemistry of the ultimate carcinogen. Targeting of mutations may also result from the bias of repair mechanisms for or against certain sites. One such example has been obtained by analysis of the role of repair of O^6-methyl dG residues in the ampicillinase gene of a bacteriophage F1-pBR322 chimera (Topal *et al.*, 1986). This study has revealed a consensus sequence around unrepaired dG residues. The sequence 5′ GCTGGTCGCCA<u>GGA</u>GG 3′ is 75% homologous to the H-*ras1* sequence around codon 12 (underlined). The observation that O^6-Me dG is more easily repaired when located at the first nucleotide of this codon (Topal *et al.*, 1986; Burns *et al.*, 1987) may explain the prevalence of mutations at the secod base of codon 12 in the *ras* genes of tumors induced by alkylating agents (Zarbl *et al.*, 1985) (Table I). A combination of adduct formation and repair parameters may also explain the apparent selectivity for mutations at the second base (dA) of codon 61 in preference to the third base, which is also dA, in tumors induced by DMBA.

2. *Mutated* ras *Genes: Cause or Effect?*

In the mouse skin system it has been possible to directly test the hypothesis that activation of *ras* genes can initiate tumorigenesis (Brown *et al.*, 1986). The results have shown that when retroviruses containing activated H-*ras* genes are applied directly to mouse skin, some cells within the epidermis become stably infected but do not give rise to any tumors in the absence of treatment with the tumor promoter TPA. When promotion is carried out, premalignant papillomas develop with a relatively short latent period (four weeks), and a proportion of these subsequently progress to carcinomas. Analysis by Southern blotting showed that the papillomas that arose were polyclonal in origin but the carcinomas were monoclonal, a result suggesting that they had arisen after additional events taking place in a single papilloma cell. These results therefore demonstrate the causal nature of mutations in *ras* genes in initiating carcinogenesis.

3. *Activation of the* neu *Oncogene*

An interesting example of oncogene activation *in vivo* comes from studies on the induction of gliomas and schwannomas by the carinogens ENU and NMU, respectively. Transfection with DNA from these tumors led to the identification of a novel oncogene, designated *neu* (Schechter *et al.*, 1984; Barbacid, 1985). This gene encodes a growth factor receptor, the ligand for which is presently unknown. Activation takes place by a specific T:A → A:T transversion mutation within the transmembrane domain of the *neu* proto-oncogene, leading to an alteration in receptor specificity and/or affinity for the external ligand in such a way that cell transformation results (Bargmann *et al.*, 1986). Mutations of this type, i.e., T:A → A:T transversion mutations, have not previously been thought to be part of the repertoire of these alkylating carcinogens. Model studies have suggested that O^4-alkylated thymidine could be a premutagenic lesion (Hu and Guttenplan, 1985), but this should lead to T:A → C:G transitions by mispairing with deoxyguanosine residues (Singer *et al.*, 1986). Consequently, either the *neu* gene mutations must arise by misrepairs of very minor adducts giving rise to T:A → A:T transversions or the mutation is not targeted at all to the *neu* gene but arises at a later stage of tumor development. At present it is not possible to distinguish between these possibilities, because premalignant stages of this particular tumor type have not been identified and studied. It is interesting that similar T:A → A:T transversions have been noted in the germ line cells of mice mutagenized by treatment with ENU (Popp *et al.*, 1983; Lewis *et al.*, 1985), a result indicating that mutations of this kind may be a relatively frequent consequence of treatment with alkylating carcinogens and may possibly be due to the presence of minor adducts in the DNA that are biologically important.

4. *Alternative Routes to Initiation*

Another major school of thought argues that initiation of carcinogenesis cannot be accomplished by a single point mutation in one target gene. This opinion is based mainly on the results of *in vitro* cell transformation experiments in which the frequency of transformation was seen to be much higher than could be explained by a simple mutational mechanism (Reznikoff *et al.*, 1973). It was shown that treatment of 10T.1/2 cells with chemical carcinogens or with various forms of ionizing radiation induced a high-frequency event leading to an increased susceptibility of essentially each treated cell to subsequent morphological transformation by what was presumed to be a somatic mutation (Kennedy *et al.*, 1980, 1984). Other authors have noted, however, that transformation of the same cells with ENU occurs as a single, low-frequency event similar to a point mutation (de Kok *et al.*, 1986). A relatively high frequency change has been described for Syrian hamster cells in culture (Barrett and Ts'o, 1978) and for rat tracheal epithelial cells after carcinogen treatment (Nettesheim and Marchok, 1983). In these systems early morphological changes that occur in approximately 1% of treated cells appear to precede the development of immortalized lines from the cultures (Barrett ad Fletcher, 1986). However, substantial differences may exist between the routes to tumorigenesis *in vivo* and *in vitro* (see later), and, even though convincing evidence exists that high-frequency events take place in cell culture, their relevance to tumorigenesis *in vivo* remains unclear.

An approach to this problem has been made by Mulcahy *et al.* (1984), who concluded that initiation of thyroid cancer *in vivo* by ionizing radiation may be a relatively frequent event. Whether this is a specific feature of radiation carcinogenesis or reflects a more general mechanism remains to be established by a detailed molecular analysis of the tumors induced.

One of the explanations proposed to account for the differences between frequencies of transformation and mutation at specific gene loci is that the target size for the carcinogen could be much larger than a typical single gene. It has been postulated that families of genes, e.g., those encoding the endogenous murine retroviruses, may constitute a possible target for carcinogens (Kirschmeier *et al.*, 1982). Rearrangement of an endogenous retrovirus element with insertion adjacent to the *mos* protooncogene has been observed in mouse myelomas (Cohen *et al.*, 1983), but no examples exist of similar events in tumors induced by chemical mutagens. The c-*myc* gene is frequently rearranged by aberrant recombination with immunoglobulin genes in mouse plasmacytomas induced by intraperitoneal injection of mineral oil (Shen-Ong *et al.*, 1982). However, the rearrangement probably takes place as a consequence of the development of a foreign body granuloma (Klein and Klein, 1986) rather than being directly induced in B lymphocytes by mineral oil treatment.

It is also possible that carcinogens induce a more general destabilization of the genome, leading to amplification of protooncogenes as an initiation step. Carcinogen-induced gene amplification has been noted in SV40-transformed cells in culture (Lavi, 1981), but amplification of protooncogenes in tumors is generally associated with later stages of tumor development (see Section II,F,1) rather than initiation.

In conclusion, it appears self-evident that initiation of carcinogenesis can take place by several different routes. In some animal model systems the most logical candidate for an initiating event is a *ras* gene mutation. However, this is not the mechanism of initiation in the substantial proportion of animal tumors, which have no obvious transforming gene, and in the majority of cases of cell transformation *in vitro* (see Section III,B).

E. The Role of Oncogenes in Tumor Promotion

Tumor promoters appear to be essential components of the process of carcinogenesis in many *in vivo* systems (Hecker *et al.*, 1982). Initiation of mouse skin carcinogenesis does not lead to tumor formation unless the skin is subsequently treated repeatedly with a tumor-promoting agent. More recent experiments have shown that even when initiation is accomplished using a viral *ras* gene linked to a transcriptional enhancer, no tumors develop at all in the absence of promoter treatment (Brown *et al.*, 1986). Similarly, transplacental initiation of carcinogenesis in mice with DMBA demonstrates that cells harboring mutations in oncogenes can lie dormant within the growing organism, but the malignant phenotype is only expressed when the appropriate tumor promoter is applied (M. Hollstein, personal communication). A promoter may be exogenously applied as is when used to treat mouse skin, or it may be an endogenous growth-promoting stimulus, such as a steroid hormone. A good example of this is the mammary gland system of Barbacid and colleagues, where the tumors containing activated *ras* oncogenes develop only after the animals reach sexual maturity, after a phase of active proliferation and differentiation of the maturing mammary glands (Barbacid, 1986). Similarly, transgenic mice carrying specific oncogenes linked to a hormone-inducible promoter, such as the MMTV LTR, develop tumors predominantly in those tissues that respond *in vivo* to glucocorticoid hormones (Stewart *et al.*, 1984). In such cases the increased expression of the gene in response to the steroid hormone is not the sole determining factor of tumorigenicity, because expression of a transgenic MMTV-*myc* gene can also be detected in other tissues that do not develop tumors (Leder *et al.*, 1986). Presumably, the induction of other events by the hormones in the target tissue must be important determinants in promoting the development of visible tumors. These studies emphasize the need for further investigations on the basic mechanism of tumor promotion and the possible role of promoters in the development of human tumors.

In considering the way in which tumor promoters exert their effects, one can envisage mechanisms at either the cellular or the molecular level. Recent results give some cause for hope that in the near future the explanations of tumor promotion at these two levels might begin to converge.

1. *The Role of Cell Selection*

Cell selection has long been thought to be a major factor in tumor promotion. This notion has been most clearly documented using the mouse skin model system. Studies using hybrid mice have shown that the papillomas that arise by an initiation and promotion scheme are clonal in origin and hence thought to arise by initiation of a single cell (Reddy and Fialkow, 1983; Taguchi *et al.*, 1984). Yuspa and colleagues have previously shown that epidermal cells can be isolated from skin initiated *in vivo* with a chemical carcinogen and that these cells have an altered program of terminal differentiation (Yuspa and Morgan, 1981). They postulated that papillomas arise by clonal expansion of cells with a terminal differentiation defect allowing them to proliferate in an area of epidermis that is no longer in contact with the basement membrane. Repeated exposure to the promoter eventually results in the accumulation of a critical cell mass of initiated cells that progress by continued proliferation to form a benign tumor (Yuspa *et al.*, 1982).

It is not immediately clear what role activation of oncogenes in the initiated cell may play in this process. If, as argued earlier, mutations in *ras* genes are important in the initiation process—at least in tumors initiated with the carcinogen DMBA—it might be expected that the introduction of mutated *ras* genes into primary epidermal cells would lead to the induction of a phenotype similar to that described (Yuspa and Morgan, 1981; Kulesz-Martin *et al.*, 1983) for initiated cells with a terminal differentiation block. This, however, appears not to be the case, because some important differences exist between the chemically initiated cells and those derived by infection with retroviruses containing *ras* genes (Yuspa *et al.*, 1983; see also discussion in Section III,C). Further experiments are required in order to fully investigate the effects of activated *ras* genes in primary cells.

2. *Tumor Promoters, Oncogenes, and Cell Communication*

Another mechanism of cell selection that has been discussed by various authors concerns the role of cell–cell communication in the control of proliferation and differentiation. It has been appreciated for a long time that the tumorigenic phenotype can be inhibited when individual tumor cells are surrounded by a population of normal cells (Stoker, 1964). One explanation of this phenomenon is that the normal cells communicate through gap junctions with the tumor cells in such a way as to suppress the transformed phenotype (Yotti *et al.*, 1979; Mehta *et al.*, 1986; Paul, 1987). Early experiments by Sivak and Van Duuren (1967) showed that TPA treatment of mixed cultures containing small numbers of tumor cells and larger numbers of the equivalent normal cell population allowed selection of the cells with transformed characteristics. This demonstration led to the emergence of theories based on a block in gap-junctional communication induced by tumor promoters. Such theories were attractive, because they could also provide a framework for the mechanism of tumor promotion *in vivo*. Clonal selection could proceed only after the elimination of junctional communication between the initiated cell in the basal area of the epidermis and its surrounding normal counterparts.

The recent evidence implicating specific oncogenes in the initiation process now provides us with a new basis upon which to consider these hypotheses. The transfection of *ras* genes into primary fibroblast cells derived from rodents does not lead to full transformation (Land *et al.*, 1983; Ruley, 1983; Newbold and Overell, 1983; Weinberg, 1985). Normally a second oncogene has to be supplied, e.g., one of the oncogenes known to encode nuclear proteins such as *myc* or *myb*, or the cells have to be immortalized first, either spontaneously or by prior treatment with a chemical carcinogen. Recent studies, however, indicate that the frequency of transformation by a single oncogene can be substantially increased by treating the cells with the tumor promoter TPA. Synergism between the promoter TPA and an activated *ras* gene was shown by Weinstein and colleagues using 10T.1/2 cells transfected with the mutated EJ H-*ras* gene (Hsiao *et al.*, 1984). Subsequent experiments by Dotto *et al.* (1985) demonstrated that similar phenomenon is observed when primary rat embryo fibroblasts are treated with TPA after transfection with the same *ras* oncogene.

These experiments may in fact mimic the sequence of events seen during initiation and promotion of mouse skin tumors *in vivo*. Activation of the *ras* genes is accomplished by a single treatment with a carcinogen, with expression of the transformed phenotype being dependent upon subsequent treatment with the tumor promoter. TPA may exert its promoting effects either by repeated transcriptional activation of genes of the *myc/fos* class, with effects similar to those obtained by transfection of an activated *myc* gene, or by directly influencing the suppressive effect exerted by normal cells on the transformed phenotype. These two possibilities are of course not mutually exclusive.

It is interesting that the transformed phenotype can also be manifest *in vitro* if the primary cells are cotransfected with the H-*ras* gene and a gene containing a selectable marker, e.g., that conferring neomycin resistance (*neo*^{R}) (Land *et al.*, 1986). Under these circumstances, the normal cells are eliminated by biochemical selection, and the resultant cell clones that emerge can be seen to have a transformed phenotype. Similar results were also reported after cotransfection of activated *myc* and *neo*^{R} genes (Land *et al.*, 1986). This would appear to indicate that the role of TPA in promotion of neoplastic transformation *in vitro* is simply to remove the effects of the normal cells rather than to induce some particular phenotypic change in the *ras*-transfected cell. Experiments by Mehta *et al.* (1986) were designed to directly demonstrate the effects of TPA on junctional communication between transformed cells and surrounding normal cells. These studies provide support for the idea that clonal selection is attributable to disruption of communication between initiated cells and their normal counterparts. Transfection of the v-*src* gene into fibroblast cells can also lead to a block in the ability to communicate with the surrounding normal cells, a result suggesting that some oncogenes may be able to directly affect cell–cell communication (Chang *et al.*, 1985).

3. *Transforming Growth Factors*

DeLarco and Todaro (1978) first demonstrated that one of the effects of transformation oncogenes is the induction of transforming growth factor (TGF) synthesis and secretion. It is only in more recent years that the biological effects of these growth factors have been investigated in more detail (Kahn and Graf, 1986). TGF-α binds to the receptor for epidermal growth factor and can induce the transformed phenotype in cells in culture (Derynck, 1986). TGF-β appears to have multiple effects on cells, influencing both proliferation and/or differentiation depending on the particular target cell (Moses and Leof, 1986). For epidermis, TGF-β appears to have an inhibitory effect on cell growth, whereas fibroblasts are stimulated to grow by the same factor. An interesting finding was that the inhibitory effect on normal epithelial cells is not always observed in some transformed epithelial cells (Moses and Leof, 1986). One could therefore envisage that continued exposure to a factor like TGF-β could lead to the selection of transformed or initiated cells, as previously discussed by Parkinson (1985). The possible role of TGFs in the process of tumor promotion is obviously an important area for future research.

4. *Tumor Promoters, Signal Transduction, and Gene Activation*

Some exciting advances have been made recently in understanding the molecular basis for the diverse effects of TPA on cell proliferation and differentiation. TPA is known to bind directly to protein kinase C, the pleiotropic activator that phosphorylates a variety of substrates within the cell (Nishizuka, 1984). Early speculation that protein kinase C might turn out to be a known member of the family of protooncogenes has turned out to be unfounded. Recent sequence data has demonstrated that the protein product has no homology with any previously characterized gene (Parker and Ullrich, 1986). However, the same molecular analysis showed that there are several different types of protein kinase C molecules, and it remains to be determined whether any of these genes can under suitable circumstances be active as oncogenes. Additional questions that remain to be answered concern the relative binding affinity of TPA for the various forms of protein kinase C and whether these independently mediate the specific cellular responses. It would appear highly unlikely that one single biochemical pathway could account for all of the phenotypic consequences of TPA treatment in many different cell types.

In terms of specific gene activation, TPA has been shown to induce sequential transcription of the *fos* and *myc* protooncogenes in a variety of cell systems *in vitro* (Greenberg and Ziff, 1984; Bravo *et al.*, 1985; Skouv *et al*, 1986). As such the tumor promoter can mimic the effects of certain growth factors in influencing gene expresion. A number of other genes appear to respond to TPA either *in vivo* or *in vitro*. A particularly interesting group of sequences has been isolated by differential screening of cDNA libraries obtained from mouse skin papillomas and carcinomas (Melber *et al.*, 1986). These investigators identified cDNA clones termed pmal 1 to pmal 6, which were highly expressed in papillomas and carcinomas but essentially absent from normal mouse skin. Interestingly, some of these clones could be induced by treatment of mouse skin *in vivo* with TPA, whereas others appeared to show different transcriptional patterns in papillomas and carcinomas, results that suggest that they could be used as markers for the malignant state (Melber *et al.*, 1986; P. Krieg, personal communication). Sequencing of these clones is presently in progress, and it remains to be determined whether any of them have homology with known protooncogenes. Preliminary results indicate that one of the sequences has some homology with a lipid-binding protein (P. Krieg and G. T. Bowden, personal communication).

Colburn *et al.* (1985) have also isolated genes that are induced by TPA in cell culture systems. JB6 cells are cells of epidermal origin that respond to TPA by becoming irreversibly anchorage-independent. Colburn *et al.* used sib selection to isolate two genes that appeared to mediate this response, these genes being termed *pro1* and *pro2*. The role of these genes in tumor promotion *in vivo* remains to be clarified, however, because as yet no experiments have been carried out to demonstrate the induction of *pro1* and *pro2* transcription by tumor promoters in mouse skin.

The pleiotropic response of cells to TPA treatment, in which many different genes have been reported to be transcriptionally activated (Angel *et al.*, 1985; Melber *et al.*, 1986), suggested that there may be a group of genes that can respond to the stimulus of TPA by virtue of having common promoter elements within their controlling regions. It has recently been demonstrated that specific, relatively short nucleotide sequences can mediate the effects of TPA in the induction of gene transcription (Comb *et al.*, 1986; Imbra and Karin, 1986). The number of genes that have such promoter elements and the nature of the induction process remain to be determined. However, such inroads into the mechanisms of TPA action could eventually lead to the identification of the "master switch" that mediates a number of cellular responses involved in growth control.

5. *Possible Genetic Mechanisms in Tumor Promotion*

On the basis of observations that TPA could induce sister chromatid exchanges in Chinese hamster cells, Kinsella and Radman (1978) proposed that one mechanism of tumor promotion might be the induction of homozygosity at a mutated site that was recessive in the initiated cell, thereby leading to the expression of malignancy. However, TPA is known to be non-mutagenic, and these chromosomal effects have been the subject of some controversy. The induction of mitotic aneuploidy has been demonstrated in yeast (Parry *et al.*, 1981), but several groups have failed to show that TPA causes sister chromatid exchange (Thomson *et al.*, 1980; Loveday and Latt, 1979). Most of these studies have been carried out using cell systems in which tumor promotion itself has not been demonstrated. More recently Fusenig and coworkers have shown that TPA can induce chromosome aberrations in cell lines derived directly from mouse keratinocytes and have postulated an important role for genetic changes in the mechanism of tumor promotion (Dzarlieva-Petrusevska and Fusenig, 1985). A wide variety of chromosomal changes was observed in the treated cells, including the induction of gaps, chromatid and isochromatid breaks, inter- and intrachromosomal exchanges. No similar effects were observed in control cultures. More recently the induction of similar chromosomal changes in mouse skin *in vivo* has been directly demonstrated by examination of mitotic figures in trypsinized cell preparations obtained from TPA-treated mouse epidermis (N. E. Fusenig, personal communication).

It is interesting to speculate as to how such results might relate to the recent evidence on activation of *ras* oncogenes during mouse skin carcinogenesis. As described earlier, the most likely explanation of initiation by the carcinogen DMBA is that a single point mutation is induced in one allele of the mouse H-*ras* gene. This mutation gives rise to a polymorphism because it induces a new recognition site for the restriction endonuclease *Xba*I. Using this assay, Quintanilla *et al.* (1986) demonstrated that the vast majority of mouse skin papillomas initiated with DMBA and promoted with TPA have a heterozygous mutation in one allele of the H-*ras* gene. This mutation became homozygous or amplified in a substantial proportion (over 50%) of mouse skin carcinomas induced in the same mouse strain. Subsequent investigation of a larger number of papillomas indicated that a subpopulation of these already contained the amplified or homozygous mutated gene (Quintanilla *et al.*, unpublished results). While the role of the promoter appears not to be related to the induction of the specific mutation observed, it could nevertheless be involved at an early stage in the generation of homozygosity or amplification. A subpopulation of the initiated cells with homozygous mutations may develop into papillomas that have a relatively high probability of subsequent conversion to carcinomas (Hennings *et al.*, 1985). An alternative explanation is that the development of homozygosity takes place relatively late during the tumor promotion process and is not directly induced by TPA but simply a consequence of the increaseed cellular proliferation and elevated tendency to develop aneuploidy that appears to be associated with tumor progression (Balmain *et al.*, 1984b). Defined molecular studies on both very early and late papilloma stages will be required to distinguish between these possibilities. It should be noted that such additional chromosomal changes at the *ras* locus are obviously not essential per se for the mechanism of tumor promotion, because the vast majority of papillomas that develop have heterozygous mutations in the *ras* gene. Hence, some other effects of TPA, either at the chromosome level or at the cell selection level (see earlier discussion), could be responsible for the development of these papillomas.

F. The Role of Oncogenes in Tumor Progression

1. *Gene Amplification*

Most of the evidence for oncogene involvement in progression of the tumorigenic phenotype comes from studies on human tumors in which various members of the *myc* gene family have been implicated in the late stages of tumor development (Alitalo and Schwab, 1986). In human neuroblastomas, for example, the N-*myc* gene is amplified in the later stages of progression, and the degree of amplification can be correlated with prognosis (Schwab *et al.*, 1984). In animal model systems, the types of oncogene that may be involved in tumor progression during chemical carcinogenesis have not yet been extensively investigated. This investigational deficiency may be due partly to the fact that many animal systems do not lend themselves easily to a comparison of early and late stages in tumor development. In the mouse skin system, however, such a comparison is possible, and the results indicate that additional changes involving amplification at the *ras* gene locus may be involved in the generation of a more aggressive phenotype, at least in some tumor types (Quintanilla *et al.*, 1986) (see Section II,E,5). Hence, increased expression as a consequence of amplification of the mutated *ras* gene may play a role in progression, but this is not invariably necessary, because many carcinomas exhibit only heterozygous mutations in the gene. Amplification of the c-*myc* gene has also been reported in radiation-induced rat skin tumors that also showed activation of the K-*ras* gene (Sawey *et al.*, 1987), but the order in which these molecular events take place is not yet known.

2. *Loss of* ras *Alleles or Suppressor Genes*

An increasing number of cases have been reported of tumors in which mutations in *ras* genes are accompained by the loss of the corresponding normal allele. This situation was first demonstrated in tumor cells in culture. The EJ bladder carcinoma cell line was shown to contain only a mutated *ras* gene, the normal allele being absent (Taparowsky *et al.*, 1982). Other situations exist where two *ras* alleles are present but either both are mutated or there is a bias toward transcription of the mutant allele (Capon *et al.*, 1983). In cell culture systems, however, it is not possible to say whether such changes already existed in the primary tumors from which the cell lines were derived. Loss of normal *ras* alleles has also been shown in cell lines from lung or bladder carcinomas (Santos *et al.*, 1984) and in a chemically induced mouse thymic lymphoma (Guerrero *et al.*, 1985). Similar results have recently been obtained in the mouse skin system; the normal allele was absent from two carcinomas that had amplified a mutated H-*ras* allele (unpublished results from this laboratory).

A number of possible explanations can be envisaged for these results. First, the presence of the normal allele may inhibit the full expression of malignancy by competing with the mutant allele for an active site within the cell. Loss of the normal gene could then allow the complete expression of the transformed phenotype. Second, loss of the normal gene may be a consequence of the random deletions and genetic changes that frequently take place in highly tumorigenic cells (Yunis, 1983); although studies with human tumors suggest that these deletions may be nonrandom, with particular sequences being preferentially lost in certain tumor cell types (Fearon *et al.*, 1985; Koufos *et al.*, 1985; Seizinger *et al.*, 1986). Finally, the loss of a normal *ras* gene could be a consequence of linkage with a putative tumor suppressor gene locus on the same chromosome. Evidence for the existence of such suppressor genes comes from cell fusion experiments (Stanbridge *et al.*, 1982) or single chromosome transfer experiments (Saxon *et al.*, 1986), which demonstrate that the tumorigenicity of cells, even those containing activated *ras* oncogenes, may be suppressed by the introduction of specific genetic material from normal cells. Subsequent loss of a chromosome from the normal parental cell is associated with the reestablishment of tumorigenicity in the hybrid cells. The loss of such suppressor genes, or antioncogenes, may constitute a very important step in tumor development, although no evidence is presently available that allows us to determine whether this is an early or late event. An exciting prospect is that the loss of the normal *ras* allele at the transition from the benign to the malignant state in mouse skin tumors might reflect a mechanism of this type. This proposal could be tested by investigating the capacity of cell lines derived from either premalignant or malignant tumors to suppress the transformed phenotype in cell fusion experiments.

3. *Karyotypic Changes during Tumor Progression*

It is probable that mechanisms of progression are not the same in every tumor type, and alternative routes involving amplification or activation by other means of additional oncogenes could play an important role. The development of aneuploidy has long been recognized as a common feature of tumor development (Oshimura and Barrett, 1986). More detailed analyses of karyotypic changes taking place at early or late stages of tumor development indicate that the many random changes observed are accompanied in some cases by specific changes involving individual chromosomes (Oshimura and Barrett, 1986). Slaga and colleagues have demonstrated trisomy of chromosome 2 in skin carcinomas initiated with DMBA and promoted with TPA (T. Slaga, personal communication). It is intriguing that the trisomy of chromosome 2 was associated with an increase in the expression levels of the protooncogenes *src* and *abl*, both of which are located on this chromosome. It remains to be determined whether such changes are actively involved in the progression of benign to malignant tumors.

Hennings *et al.* (1983) have previously shown that progression could be induced by treatment of premalignant skin tumors with known mutagens such as MNNG or DMBA. An interesting recent development is that compounds such as benzoylperoxide are particularly efficient at inducing this stage of carcinogenesis (Rotstein *et al.*, 1986). Compounds of this type are not highly mutagenic in bacterial systems but are known to induce the formation of activated oxygen species that cause single-strand breaks in DNA. Such changes might facilitate the type of chromosomal event discussed earlier involving gene or chromosome loss or amplification. Whether changes in any of the known protooncogenes are involved in this type of induced progression remains to be established.

III. The Role of Oncogenes in Carcinogenesis *in Vitro*

The cellular and molecular mechanisms of carcinogenesis in cell culture models have recently been comprehensively reviewed (Barrett and Fletcher, 1986). The purpose of this section will be to emphasize the role of oncogenes in the multistep process of the carcinogenesis *in vitro*, but, more importantly, to underline the similarities and differences that may exist between the paths leading to cell transformation *in vitro* and *in vivo*.

A. Activated Oncogenes in Cells Transformed *in Vitro* by Carcinogens

The activation of oncogenes after treatment of cells in culture with chemical carcinogens has been studied in a number of cell types (Table II). Studies by Weinberg and colleagues showed that a dominant transforming gene identified as the K-*ras* gene was present in mouse fibroblasts treated

TABLE II

ACTIVATION OF ONCOGENES IN CHEMICALLY TRANSFORMED CELL LINES

Cell line	Carcinogen[a]	Oncogene[b]	Mutation[b]	Reference
Mouse fibroblasts (3T3 or 10T 1/2)	MCA	K-*ras*	N.D.	Parada and Weinberg (1983)
Guinea pig	MNNG	N-*ras*	N.D.	Sukumar *et al.* (1984)
Guinea pig	DEN	N-*ras*	N.D.	Sukumar *et al.* (1984)
Guinea pig	BP	N-*ras*	N.D.	Sukumar *et al.* (1984)
Guinea pig	MCA	N-*ras*	N.D.	Sukumar *et al.* (1984)
Chinese hamster	EMS	N.D.	N.D.	Smith *et al.* (1982)
CHEF/18	MNNG	N.D.	N.D.	Smith *et al.* (1986)
Human HOS	MNNG	*met*	Translocation	Cooper *et al.* (1984)
Human HOS	MCA	H-*ras*	Codon 61	Rhim *et al.* (1986)
Syrian hamster	Various	*ras*	N.D.	Barrett and Fletcher (1986)
Mouse 3T3	Spontaneous	*met*	Amplification	Cooper *et al.* (1986)
Mouse 3T3	DMBA	K-*ras*	N.D.	Small (1984)
Mouse epidermis (PDV)	DMBA	H-*ras*	$A^{182} \rightarrow T$	M. Quintanilla, K. Brown and A. Balmain (unpublished results)

[a]DEN, diethylnitrosamine; EMS, ethylmethanesulfonate; see also footnote (*a*) of Table I.
[b]N.D., not determined.

with the carcinogen MCA (Parada and Weinberg, 1983). Interestingly, fibrosarcomas induced *in vivo* by treatment of rodents with MCA frequently show activation of the same gene (Eva and Aaronson, 1983). It is not presently possible to say whether the mutations in the K-*ras* gene are directly induced by the carcinogen either *in vitro* or *in vivo*. A more complete classification of the mutations in cells transformed by different carcinogens will be necessary to resolve this question. A clear difference, however, has been demonstrated to exist between chemically transformed 3T3 cells and those that arise by spontaneous transformation in cell culture. The latter frequently show amplification of the *met* oncogene (Cooper *et al.*, 1986), which was originally identified in human osteosarcoma (HOS) cells after extensive treatment with MNNG *in vitro* (Cooper *et al.*, 1984). The mechanism of activation of the *met* gene in this case was not a point mutation but rather a translocation between the *met* gene on chromosome 7 and a previously unknown locus on chromosome 1 (Park *et al.*, 1986).

The HOS cells have also been shown to be transformed by the carcinogens DMBA and MCA. In the former case, no activated transforming gene was detected in transfection assays, but cells transformed by MCA could be shown to have a dominant H-*ras* transforming gene (Rhim *et al.*, 1986). The position of the activating mutation was determined to be at codon 61. It is not presently possible to determine whether these various genetic events in transformed human cells were directly induced by the activating carcinogen. A transforming event is apparently extremely rare, and reproducible activation of the same gene by the same mechanism has yet to be demonstrated.

Fibroblasts isolated from fetal guinea pigs can be transformed by a variety of chemical carcinogens *in vitro*. When transformed either by alkylating agents or polycyclic aromatic hydrocarbons, these cells have a transforming gene that appears to be the guinea pig equivalent of N-*ras* (Sukumar *et al.*, 1984). Initial experiments showed that the transforming gene was present only in late passage cells and was not detected in cells shortly after carcinogen treatment (Sukumar *et al.*, 1984). This finding suggested that mutation occured at a late stage of transformation *in vitro*, at a time when the carcinogen was no longer present. However, it remains possible that a small proportion of the initially treated cells did have an activating mutation in the N-*ras* gene but that this was not expressed or selected for until many cell generations had taken place.

B. Stage-Specific Oncogene Activation *in Vitro*

Cell transformation *in vitro*, like that *in vivo*, is a multistep process that proceeds in discrete stages. The main steps are thought to involve immortalization, or induction of an unlimited life span, and morphological transformation. This model is almost certainly an oversimplification, because each of these stages may involve at least two or more changes (Barrett and

Fletcher, 1986). It was initially shown by Newbold and colleagues that the immortalization step that can be induced by chemical carcinogens is an essential prerequisite for transformation by subsequent carcinogen treatment or by transfection with an activated *ras* oncogene (Newbold *et al.*, 1982; Newbold and Overell, 1983). The suggestion from these studies—that the activation of dominant transforming genes in cell culture systems should occur at the late stages of cell transformation—was subsequently borne out by investigations on the stage-specific activation of oncogenes *in vitro*. A number of investigators have now shown that immortalized fibroblast cells do not in general contain activated transforming genes but that DNA from late passage cells that have a fully transformed phenotype can induce foci when transfected into NIH 3T3 cells (Sukumar *et al.*, 1984; Tainsky *et al.*, 1984; Vousden and Marshall, 1984). *ras* gene mutations *in vitro* appear to occur at a late stage of tumorigenesis and probably are unrelated to the early immortalization step. In agreement with this hypothesis, attempts to immortalize primary rodent cells by transfection with activated *ras* genes are in general unsuccessful (Dotto *et al.*, 1985; Land *et al.*, 1986) except when the expression of the gene is elevated by fusion to transcriptional enhancers (Spandidos and Wilkie, 1984). The way in which immortalization can be induced in the latter experiments is unclear, but it may involve secondary chromosomal changes in the target cells. The nature of the genes responsible for immortalization *in vitro*, which may constitute important targets for carcinogens, is still unclear, although the *myc* oncogene has been implicated in this process. Syrian hamster cells transfected with this gene nevertheless do not have the same properties as similar cultures immortalized by chemical carcinogens (R. Newbold, personal communication). The latter have an indefinite life span in culture, whereas cells transfected with the *myc* oncogene, although they do show a somewhat extended life span, senesce at later passage levels. This finding suggests that the *myc* gene may not be a universal immortalizing gene. Cell fusion experiments have shown that the genes responsible for immortalization are recessive, because hybrids between immortal cells and primary cells enter a crisis and subsequently senesce (Pereira-Smith and Smith, 1983). Cells immortalized by different methods may have multiple immortalizing genes, which can be classified into different complementation groups. Cell proliferation can also be inhibited by direct injection of mRNA from senescent cells into fibroblasts (Lumpkin *et al.*, 1986), a finding offering some hope that genes responsible for cessation of DNA synthesis may be isolated and characterized in the near future.

Although it is clear that under certain circumstances the two steps of immortalization and morphological transformation appear to be sufficient for the induction of malignancy, other situations obviously exist where additional steps are required. It has been shown that transfection with an activated *ras* gene will not lead to transformation of certain fibroblast cell lines (Tsunokawa *et al.*, 1984; Barrett and Fletcher, 1986) or of epidermal lines immortalized by chemical carcinogen treatment (Quintanilla *et al.*, 1987), observations suggesting that immortalization together with a transforming oncogene may be a necessary but not sufficient condition for malignancy. Oshimura *et al.* (1985) have studied the cytogenetic changes taking place in Syrian hamster primary cells after transfaction with both *ras* and *myc* oncogenes. Tumors arising from the transfected cells showed, in addition to the expression of *ras* and *myc*, and consistent loss of chromosome 15. Barrett and colleagues interpret these observations as indicating that a cellular gene located on hamster chromosome 15 can exert a suppressive effect on the transformed phenotype. Loss of this gene appears to be essential for full neoplastic development. Cell fusion experiments further support the existence of a suppressor gene in this system and indicate that the loss of this gene function may be a gradual process, because some clones of immortalized cells retain only a reduced ability to suppress tumorigenicity in cell hybrids while others completely lose this function. The authors have therefore proposed that transformation *in vitro* involves at least three steps: (1) induction of immortality, (2) activation of a transforming oncogene, and (3) loss of a tumor suppression function. Furthermore, the temporal sequence of these steps may vary in different cell clones (Barrett and Fletcher, 1986).

C. COMPARISON OF STAGES OF CARCINOGENESIS *in Vivo* AND *in Vitro*

The use of cell culture models to study carcinogenesis has been invaluable in the elucidation of the many cellular and molecular changes that can contribute to the transformed phenotype. It must be borne in mind, however, that the sequence of events observed *in vitro* may not necessarily be the same as that taking place during tumor development in the whole animal. The particular requirements of cell growth in culture may impose specific selection mechanisms that lead to the emergence of phenotypes not normally encountered *in vivo*. For this reason it is important in the light of recent evidence on the molecular events taking place during carcinogenesis *in vivo* to see whether similar changes can be identified at appropriate stages of transformation *in vitro*. The mouse skin model system would appear to constitute an ideal vehicle for such a comparison, because extensive studies have been carried out both *in vivo* and *in vitro* on the biological and molecular events associated with tumor initiation, promotion, and progression.

The evidence described in Section II,D points to a critical role for the *ras* gene in initiation of carcinogenesis *in vivo* after treatment of mouse skin with DMBA. Over 90% of DMBA-initiated papillomas exhibit the same point mutation in the H-*ras* gene. Yuspa and colleagues have demonstrated that primary cultures established from newborn mouse epidermis can be initiated by treatment with a carcinogen *in vitro*, giving rise to foci of cells that have altered growth and differentiation characteristics (Kulesz-Martin *et al.*, 1983). Foci with similar properties can also be isolated from adult mouse skin after initiation *in vivo* (Yuspa and Morgan, 1981), a result suggesting that initiating events *in vivo* and *in vitro* are the same. The assay system upon which the detection of initiated cells depends is based upon the fact that normal mouse epidermal cells proliferate in medium containing low levels of calcium but switch to a pathway of terminal differentiation when calcium is restored to the medium (Hennings *et al.*, 1980). A carcinogen-induced change in the initiated cells allows them to survive this calcium switch and continue to proliferate under high-calcium conditions. The observation has been interpreted in terms of a block in the terminal differentiation pattern of the initiated cell that can allow it to proliferate even when detached from the basement membrane, a situation in which normal epidermal cells are committed to differentiation (Yuspa *et al.*, 1982). Epidermal cells that are initiated in this way are immortalized and nontumorigenic when injected into syngeneic animals but can become tumorigenic when passaged extensively *in vitro*. Because papillomas are thought to arise by clonal expansion of such initiated cells (Yuspa *et al.*, 1982), it might be expected by analogy with the results discussed earlier that the epidermal cells initiated *in vitro* might already exhibit a carcinogen-specific mutation in the H-*ras* gene. Experiments carried out in this laboratory, however, indicate that this is not the case. Initiated cell lines derived from mouse epidermis after treatment *in vitro* with DMBA or MNNG have been tested for the presence of an activated *ras* gene both by transfection analysis in NIH 3T3 cells and by direct investigation of the *ras* P21 synthesized *in vitro* by immunoprecipitation using *ras*-specific monoclonal antibodies (Quintanilla *et al.*, 1987). These studies indicated that the initiated cell lines synthesized an apparently normal H-*ras* P21; and in addition, DNA from these cells did not have the capacity to induce foci of transformation in the NIH 3T3 assay. Transfection of an activated human *ras* gene into a cell line initiated with DMBA did, however, lead to morphological changes and the induction of tumorigenic properties. The transfected cells gave rise to undifferentiated carcinomas after subcutaneous inoculation into nude mice (M. Quintanilla and A. Balmain, unpublished results). These results using *in vitro*-initiated epidermal cells are entirely analogous to the conclusions that were reached using fibroblast cells in culture and indicated that the first stage of transformation involves immortalization without concomitant mutation of a member of the *ras* gene family. Similar results have also been obtained recently using preneoplastic hamster epidermal cell lines (Storer *et al.*, 1986b).

Our interpretation of this apparent discrepancy is as follows. When mouse skin is initiated *in vivo* with DMBA, a specific mutation is induced in the H-*ras* gene. Whether this is the sole event in initiation or is accompanied by an additional general event taking place in a high proportion of the treated cells remains to be established. If a *ras* gene mutation were to take place *in vitro*, such an event would probably not lead to immortalization (see Section III,B) or selection by the calcium switch technique. The critical point in this analysis is that the *in vitro* selection procedure dictates that the cells that survive must have a terminal differentiation defect and either be immortalized or have an extended life span. The genetic events that take place during *in vitro* initiation may therefore involve genes similar to those implicated in immortilization of fibroblast cells by chemicals (Newbold *et al.*, 1982) rather than members of the *ras* protooncogene family. Evidence in favor of this interpretation comes from critical comparison of the properties of cells either initiated by treatment with carcinogens *in vitro* or after infection with retroviruses containing activated *ras* genes. Although it appears clear that *ras*-containing retroviruses can initiate *in vivo* (Brown *et al.*, 1986), primary epidermal cells infected *in vitro* do not have properties that are identical to those of the chemically initiated cell lines (Yuspa *et al.*, 1983). Whereas the latter are completely blocked in their program of terminal differentiation in high-calcium medium, virus-infected cells appear to show only limited changes in the differentiation pattern, which, furthermore, can be overcome by treatment with the tumor promoter TPA (Yuspa *et al.*, 1985). This property is exactly that expected of an initiated cell *in vivo* that responds to TPA teatment by clonal expansion and selection to form a papilloma. Indeed, Roop *et al.* (1986) have shown that grafting of primary cells after infection with helper-free Harvey sarcoma virus onto nude mice results in the appearance of tumors that are morphologically similar to papillomas.

These results confirm the evidence that *ras* genes can initiate *in vivo*, but a number of questions remain to be answered. The first concerns the nature of the genetic alteration in cells that are chemically initiated *in vitro* and the relevance of such changes to carcinogenesis *in vivo*. It is undoubtedly true that cells initiated *in vitro* have an altered pattern of terminal differentiation, but this may be more relevant to changes taking place at later stages of tumorigenesis *in vivo*. Papillomas are composed of cells with an apparently normal differentiation pattern, whereas carcinomas show evidence of changes in specific differentiation markers (Klein-Szanto *et al.*, 1983; Toftgard *et al.*, 1985). The molecular changes taking place *in vitro* and *in vivo* may be similar, but their particular sequence may be substantially different. Elucidation of the events leading to altered differentiation is an important goal; but because the genes responsible do not appear to be amenable to detection or analysis using presently available transfection assays, alternative approaches will have to be developed to facilitate their characterization.

Recent experiments on cell lines obtained directly from mouse skin papillomas suggest that the culture conditions are critical in determining which cell populations are selected. Yuspa *et al.* (1986) have isolated cell lines from papillomas initiated with DMBA and promoted with TPA. Of the six cell lines developed, it would be expected that at least five would demonstrate the presence of an activated H-*ras* gene, because the proportion of tumors with this mutation *in vivo* is approximately 90% (Quintanilla *et al.*, 1986). Harper *et al.* (1986) demonstrated that none of the isolated lines contained a *ras* mutation, a finding suggesting that either the immortalized cells obtained did not in fact derive from the (presumably clonal) papillomas used or that the mutated gene had been lost during establishment in cell culture.

When different culture conditions are used, it does appear to be possible to derive cell lines from papillomas that contain activated *ras* genes and express the mutated form of the *ras* P21 but are nevertheless nontumorigenic when injected into syngeneic hosts. Some of the skin tumor cell lines derived by Pera and Gorman (1984) using a 3T3 feeder layer culture system have these characteristics (M. Quintanilla and A. Balmain, unpublished results). Similar conclusions have recently been reported in preliminary form by Storer *et al.* (1986a). Consequently, it can be concluded that the particular selective pressures that are applied to cells in culture can determine whether cells with the desired characteristics reflecting genetic events taking place *in vivo* are allowed to grow.

Treatment of epidermal cells *in vitro* with the carcinogen DMBA can, however, under certain circumstances lead to the isolation of cell lines that have the same type of *ras* mutation as that seen after DMBA initiation *in vivo*. Such a cell line is represented by the PDV cells originally described by Fusenig *et al.* (1973). The PDV cells were derived from newborn mouse epidermal cultures after treatment with DMBA. They have a mutated H-*ras* gene and exhibit the *XbaI* polymorphism characteristic of DMBA-initiated papillomas (Quintanilla *et al.*, 1986). These cells are weakly tumorigenic in adult syngeneic hosts, but a more malignant phenotype can be selected by *in vivo* transplantation. Under these conditions, a selective increase is observed in the number of copies of the mutated *ras* allele and in the expression of the mutant *ras* P21 (M. Quintanilla and A. Balmain, unpublished results). Hence, these cells do reflect some of the characteristics seen during initiation and progression of tumors initiated by DMBA treatment *in vivo*.

Comparison of carcinogenesis *in vivo* and *in vitro* therefore suggests that important differences may exist in the sequence of events leading to transformation. Generally, *in vitro* systems show immortalization as an early step, with *ras* gene activation taking place at a late stage. This two-stage process may be a reflection of the selection pressure placed on cells in culture. Tumor development in animals frequently involves *ras* activation as an early event, and it may now be possible to design culture conditions that will yield cell lines representing the various stages of transformation *in vivo*.

IV. Conclusions

The discovery of oncogenes has led to a major advance in our understanding of carcinogenesis at the molecular level. Studies carried out on the mechanism of transformation by chemicals have concentrated on the possible roles of only a relatively small number of protooncogenes. This has largely been dictated by the types of available assay systems, which bias the types of genes detected either toward those that can transform 3T3 cells as a consequence of point mutations or toward those that can be readily detected by virtue of amplification or rearrangement in tumor cells. The complexity of the relationships between different families of oncogenes is only beginning to be understood. Cell growth is obviously controlled by a complex network of pathways involving different gene families, each member of which is potentially capable of activation by chemical carcinogens. Some chemically induced tumors or transformed cell lines show specific genetic changes involving growth factor receptors (*neu*), signal transducing systems (*ras*), or nuclear DNA-binding proteins (*myc*). It is to be expected that further work will reveal examples of activating mutations or rearrangements in many other types of protooncogenes. The information obtained will have relevance to studies on mutagenesis, in particular in identifying critical adducts or mutations that contribute to the transformed phenotype, to the control of cell growth and differentiation, and finally to the elucidation of the role of environmental carcinogens in the development of human cancers.

Acknowledgments

The Beatson Institute is supported by grants from the Cancer Research Campaign of Great Britain. We are grateful to Dr. John Paul for discussions to Drs. M. Quintanilla, G. T. Bowden, R. Wiseman, I. Guerrero, S. Garte, and C. Barrett for permission to quote unpublished work.

References

Alitalo, K., and Schwab, M. (1986). *Adv. Cancer Res.* **47**, 235–281.

Angel, P., Rahmsdorf, H. J., Poting, A., Lucke-Huhle, C., and Herrlich, P. (1985). *J. Cell. Biochem.* **29**, 351–360.

Ayaki, H., Higo, K., and Yamamoto, O. (1986). *Nucleic Acids Res.* **14**, 5013–5018.

Balmain, A. (1985). *Br. J. Cancer* **51**, 1–7.

Balmain, A., and Pragnell, I. B. (1983). *Nature (London)* **303**, 72–74.

Balmain, A., Ramsden, M., Bowden, G. T., and Smith, J. (1984a). *Nature (London)* **307**, 658–660.

Balmain, A., Sauerborn, R., Ramsden, M., Pragnell, I. B., Bowden, G. T., Smith, J., and Cole, G. (1984b). *In* "Genetic Variability in Responses to Chemical Exposure" (G. Omenn, C. Harris, and H. Gelboin, eds.), pp. 243–255. Cold Spring Harbor Laboratory, Cold Springs Harbor, New York.

Balmain, A., Quintanilla, M., Brown, K., and Ramsden, M. (1986). *J. Pathol.* **149**, 3–8.

Barbacid, M. (1986). *Trends Genet.* **2**, 188–192.

Barbacid, M. (1987). *Annu. Rev. Biochem.* **56**, 779–827.

Bargmann, C. I., Hung, M.-C., and Weinberg, R. A. (1986). *Cell* **45**, 649–657.

Barrett, J. C., and Fletcher, W. F. (1986). *In* "Mechanism of Environmental Carcinogenesis, Vol. II—Multistep Models of Carcinogenesis" (J. C. Barrett, ed.), in press. CRC Press, Boca Raton, Florida.

Barrett, J. C., and Ts'o, P. O. P. (1978). *Proc. Natl. Acad. Sci. U.S.A.* **75**, 3297–3301.

Bar-Sagi, D., and Feramisco, J. R. (1985). *Cell* **42**, 841–848.

Bichara, M., and Fuchs, R. P. P. (1985). *J. Mol. Biol.* **183**, 341–351.

Biggar, C. A. H., Sawicki, J. T., Blake, D. M., Raymond, L. G., and Dipple, A. (1983). *Cancer Res.* **43**, 5647–5651.

Bishop, J. M. (1983). *Annu. Rev. Biochem.* **52**, 301–354.

Bizub, D., Wood, A. W., and Skalka, A. M. (1986). *Proc. Natl. Acad. Sci. U.S.A.* **83**, 6048–6052.

Boles, T. C., and Hogan, M. E. (1984). *Proc. Natl. Acad. Sci. U.S.A.* **81**, 5623–5627.

Bos, J. L., Fearon, E. R., Hamilton, S. R., Verlaan-de Vries, M., van Boom, J. H., van der Eb, A. J., and Vogelstein, B. (1987). In press.

Bravo, R., Burckhardt, J., Curran, T., and Muller, R. (1985). *EMBO J.* **4**, 1193–1197.

Brown, K., Quintanilla, M., Ramsden, M., Kerr, I. B., Young, S., and Balmain, A. (1986). *Cell* **46**, 447–457.

Burns, P. A., Gordon, A. J. E., and Glickman, B. W. (1987). *J. Mol. Biol.* **194**, 385–390.

Capon, D. J., Seeburg, P. H., McGrath, J. P., Hayflick, J. S., Edman, U., Levinson, A. D., and Goeddel, D. V. (1983). *Nature (London)* **304**, 507–513.

Carothers, A. M., Urlaub, G., Steigerwalt, R. W., Chasin, L. A., and Grunberger, D. (1986). *Proc. Natl. Acad. Sci. U.S.A.* **83**, 6519–6523.

Chang, C.-C., Trosko, J. E., King, H.-J., Bombick, D., and Matsumara, F. (1985). *Proc. Natl. Acad. Sci. U.S.A.* **82**, 5360–5364.

Chang, E. H., Furth, M. E., Scolnick, E. M., and Lowy, D. R. (1982). *Nature (London)* **297**, 479–483.

Cohen, J. B., Unger, T., Rechavi, G., Canaani, E., and Givol, D. (1983). *Nature (London)* **306**, 797–799.

Colburn, N. H., Lerman, M. I., Hegamyer, G. A., and Gindhart, T. D. (1985). *Mol. Cell. Biol.* **5**, 890–893.

Comb, M., Birnberg, N. C., Seasholtz, A., Herbert, E., and Goodman, H. (1986). *Nature (London)* **323**, 353–355.

Cooper, C. S., Park, M., Blair, D. G., Tainsky, M. A., Huebner, K., Croce, C. M., and Vande Woude, G. F. (1984). *Nature (London)* **311**, 29–33.

Cooper, C. S., Tempest, P. R., Beckman, M. P., Heldin, C.-H., and Brookes, P. (1986). *EMBO J.* **5**, 2623–2628.

Dandekar, S., Sukumar, S., Zarbl, H., Young, L. J., and Cardiff, R. D. (1986). *Mol. Cell. Biol.* **6**, 4104.

de Kok, A. J., Sips, H., den Engelse, L., and Simons, J. W. I. M. (1986). *Carcinogenesis* **7**, 1387–1392.

DeLarco, J. E., and Todaro, G. (1978). *Proc. Natl. Acad. Sci. U.S.A.* **75**, 4001–4005.

Der, C. J., Kontiris, T. G., and Cooper, G. M. (1982). *Proc. Natl. Acad. Sci. U.S.A.* **79**, 3637–3640.

Derynck, R. (1986). *In* "Oncogenes and Growth Control" (P. Kahn and T. Graf, eds.), pp. 58–64. Springer-Verlag, Heidelberg.

DiGiovanni, J., Sawyer, T. W., and Fisher, E. P. (1986). *Cancer Res.* **46**, 4336–4341.

Dipple, A., Piggot, M., Moschel, R. C., and Constantino, N. (1983). *Cancer Res.* **43**, 4132–4135.

Dotto, G. P., Parada, L. F., and Weinberg, R. A. (1985). *Nature (London)* **318**, 472–475.

Dzarlieva-Petrusevska, R. T., and Fusenig, N. E. (1985). *Carcinogenesis* **6**, 1447–1456.

Eadie, J. S., Conrad, M., Toorchen, D., and Topal, M. D. (1984). *Nature (London)* **308**, 201–203.

Eisenstadt, E., Warren, A. J., Porter, J., Atkins, D., and Miller, J. H. (1982). *Proc. Natl. Acad. Sci. U.S.A.* **79**, 1945–1949.

Eva, A., and Aaronson, S. A. (1983). *Science* **220**, 955–956.

Eva, A., and Trimmer, R. W. (1986). *Carcinogenesis* **7**, 1931–1933.

Fearon, E. R., Feinberg, A. P., Hamilton, S. H., and Vogelstein, B. (1985). *Nature (London)* **318**, 377–380.

Feramisco, J. R., Gross, M., Kamata, T., Rosenberg, M., and Sweet, R. W. (1984). *Cell* **38**, 109–117.

Fusenig, N. E., Samsel, W., Thon, W., and Worst, P. K. M. (1973). *INSERM* **19**, 219–228.

Garte, S. J., Hood, A. T., Hochwalt, A. E., D'Eustachio, P., Snyder, C. A., Segal, A., and Albert, R. E. (1985). *Carcinogenesis* **6**, 1709–1712.

George, D. L., Glick, B., Trusko, S., and Freeman, N. (1986). *Proc. Natl. Acad. Sci. U.S.A.* **83**, 1651–1655.

Gibbs, J. B., Sigal, I. S., Poe, M., and Scolnick, E. M. (1984). *Proc. Natl. Acad. Sci. U.S.A.* **81**, 5704–5708.

Greenberg, M. E., and Ziff, E. B. (1984). *Nature (London)* **311**, 433–438.

Guerrero, I., and Pellicer, A. (1987). *Mutat. Res.* **185**, 293–308.

Guerrero, I., Calzada, P., Mayer, A., and Pellicer, A. (1984a). *Proc. Natl. Acad. Sci. U.S.A.* **81**, 202–205.

Guerrero, I., Villasante, A., Corces, V., and Pellicer, A. (1984b). *Science* **225**, 1159–1162.

Gurerrero, I., Villasante, A., Corces, V., and Pellicer, A. (1985). *Proc. Natl. Acad. Sci. U.S.A.* **82**, 7810–7814.

Harper, J. R., Roop, D. R., and Yuspa, S. H. (1986). *Mol. Cell. Biol.* **6**, 3144–3149.

Hauser, J., Levine, A. S., and Dixon, K. (1987). *EMBO J.* **6**, 63–67.

Hecker, E., Fusenig, N. E., Kung, W., Marks, F., and Thielman, H. W., eds. (1982). "Carcinogenesis—A Comprehensive Survey, Vol. 7. Raven, New York.

Hennings, H., Michael, D., Cheng, C., Steinert, P., Holbrook, K., and Yuspa, S. H. (1980). *Cell* **19**, 245–254.

Hennings, H., Shores, R., Wenk, M. L., Spangler, E. F., Tarone, R., and Yuspa, S. H. (1983). *Nature (London)* **304**, 67–69.

Hennings, H., Shores, R., Mitchell, P., Spangler, E. F., and Yuspa, S. H. (1985). *Carcinogenesis* **6**, 1607–1610.

Hsiao, W.-L. W., Gattoni-Celli, S., and Weinstein, I. B. (1984). *Nature (London)* **226**, 552–555.

Hu, Y. C., and Guttenplan, J. B. (1985). *Carcinogenesis* **6**, 1513–1516.

Imbra, R. J., and Karin, M. (1986). *Nature (London)* **323**, 555–558.

Ishii, S., Merlino, G. T., and Pastan, I. (1985). *Science* **230**, 1378–1381.

Kahn, P., and Graf, T., eds. (1986). "Oncogenes and Growth Control." Springer-Verlag, Heidelberg.

Kennedy, A. R., Fox, M., Murphy, G., and Little, J. B. (1980). *Proc. Natl. Acad. Sci. U.S.A.* **77**, 7262–7266.

Kennedy, A. R., Cairns, J., and Little, J. B. (1984). *Nature (London)* **307**, 85–86.

Kinsella, A., and Radman, M. (1978). *Proc. Natl. Acad. Sci. U.S.A.* **75**, 6149–6153.

Kirschmeier, P., Gattoni-Celli, S., Dina, D., and Weinstein, I. B. (1982). *Proc. Natl. Acad. Sci. U.S.A.* **79**, 2773–2777.

Klein, G., and Klein, E. (1985). *Nature (London)* **315**, 190–195.

Klein, G., and Klein, E. (1986). *Cancer Res.* **46**, 3211–3224.

Klein-Szanto, A. J. P., Nelson, K. G., Shah, Y., and Slaga, T. J. (1983). *J. Natl. Cancer Inst.* **70**, 161–168.

Kootstra, A. (1986). *Nucleic Acids Res.* **14**, 9897–9909.

Koufos, A., Hausen, M. F., Copeland, N. G., Jenkins, N. A., Lampkin, B. C., and Cavanee, W. K. (1985). *Nature (London)* **316**, 330–334.

Kulesz-Martin, M., Kilkenny, A. E., Holbrook, K. A., Digernes, V., and Yuspa, S. H. (1983). *Carcinogenesis* **4**, 1367–1377.

Kurth, P. D., and Bustin, M. (1985). *Proc. Natl. Acad. Sci. U.S.A.* **82**, 7076–7080.
Land, H., Parada, L. F., and Weinberg, R. A. (1983). *Nature (London)* **304**, 596–602.
Land, H., Chen, A., Morgenstern, A. P., Parada, L. F., and Weinberg, R. A. (1986). *Mol. Cell. Biol.* **6**, 1917–1925.
Lavi, S. (1981). *Proc. Natl. Acad. Sci. U.S.A.* **78**, 6144–6148.
Leder, A., Pattengale, P. K., Kuo, A., Stewart, T. A., and Leder, P. (1986). *Cell* **45**, 485–495.
Lewis, S. E., Johnson, F. M., Skow, L. C., Popp, D., Barnett, L. B., and Popp, R. A. (1985). *Proc. Natl. Acad. Sci. U.S.A.* **82**, 5829–5831.
Lobanenkov, V. V., Plumb, M., Goodwin, G. H., and Grover, P. L. (1986). *Carcinogenesis* **7**, 1689–1695.
Loechler, E. L., Green, C. L., and Essigmann, J. M. (1984). *Proc. Natl. Acad. Sci. U.S.A.* **81**, 6271–6275.
Loveday, K. S., and Latt, S. A. (1979). *Mutat. Res.* **67**, 343–348.
Lumpkin, C. K., Jr., McClung, J. K., Pereira-Smith, O. M., and Smith, J. R. (1986). *Science* **232**, 393–395.
McGrath, J. P., Capon, D. J., Goeddel, D. V., and Levinson, A. D. (1984). *Nature (London)* **310**, 644–649.
McMahon, G., Hanson, L., Lee, J.-J., and Wogan, G. N. (1986). *Proc. Natl. Acad. Sci. U.S.A.* **83**, 9418–9422.
Mehta, P. P., Bertram, J. S., and Loewenstein, W. R. (1986). *Cell* **44**, 187–196.
Melber, K., Krieg, P., Furstenberger, G., and Marks, F. (1986). *Carcinogenesis* **7**, 317–322.
Moses, H., and Leof, E. B. (1986). *In* "Oncogenes and Growth Control" (P. Kahn and T. Graf, eds.), pp. 51–57. Springer-Verlag, Heidelberg.
Mulcahy, R. T., Gould, M. N., and Clifton, K. H. (1984). *Int. J. Radiat. Biol.* **45**, 419.
Müller, R., Slamon, D. J., Adamson, E. D., Tremblay, J. M., Muller, D., Cline, M. J., and Verma, I. M. (1983). *Mol. Cell. Biol.* **3**, 1062–1069.
Nehls, P., Rajewsky, M. F., Spiers, E., and Werner, D. (1984). *EMBO J.* **3**, 327–332.
Nettesheim, P., and Marchok, A. (1983). *Adv. Cancer Res.* **39**, 1–70.
Newbold, R. F., and Overell, R. W. (1983). *Nature (London)* **304**, 648–651.
Newbold, R. F., Overell, R. W., and Connell, J. R. (1982). *Nature (London)* **299**, 633–635.
Nishizuka, Y. (1984). *Nature (London)* **308**, 693–698.
Noda, M., Ko, M., Ogura, A., Liu, D. G., Amano, T., Takano, T., and Ikawa, Y. (1985). *Nature (London)* **318**, 73–75.
Oshimura, M., and Barrett, J. C. (1986). *Environ. Mutagen.* **8**, 129–159.
Oshimura, M., Gilmer, T. M., and Barrett, J. C. (1985). *Nature (London)* **316**, 636–639.
Parada, L. F., and Weinberg, R. A. (1983). *Mol. Cell. Biol.* **3**, 2298–2301.
Parada, L. F., Tabin, C. J., Shih, C., and Weinberg, R. A. (1982). *Nature (London)* **297**, 474–478.
Park, M., Dean, M., Cooper, C. S., Schmidt, M., O'Brien, S. J., Blair, D. G., and Vande Woude, G. F. (1986). *Cell* **45**, 895–904.
Parker, P., and Ullrich, A. (1986). *In* "Oncogenes and Growth Control" (P. Kahn and T. Graf, eds.), pp. 154–162. Springer-Verlag, Heidelberg.
Parkinson, E. K. (1985). *Br. J. Cancer* **52**, 479–493.
Parry, J., Parry, E. M., and Barrett, J. C. (1984). *Nature (London)* **294**, 263–265.
Paul, J. (1987). *Proc. Int. Conf. Cancer Res.*, in press.
Pera, M. F., and Gorman, P. A. (1984). *Carcinogenesis* **5**, 671–682.
Pereira-Smith, O. M., and Smith, J. R. (1983). *Science* **221**, 963–966.
Popp, R. A., Bailiff, E. G., Skow, L. C., Johnson, F. M., and Lewis, S. E. (1983). *Genetics* **105**, 157–167.
Quintanilla, M., Brown, K., Ramsden, M., and Balmain, A. (1986). *Nature (London)* **322**, 78–80.
Ramsden, M., Cole, G., Smith, J., and Balmain, A. (1985). *EMBO J.* **4**, 1449–1454.

Reddy, A. L., and Fialkow, P. J. (1983). *Nature (London)* **304**, 69–71.

Reynolds, S. H., Stowers, S. J., Maronpot, R. R., Anderson, M. W., and Aaronson, S. A. (1986). *Proc. Natl. Acad. Sci. U.S.A.* **83**, 33–37.

Reynolds, S. H., Stowers, S. J., Patterson, R. M., Maronpot, R. R., Aaronson, S. A., and Anderson, M. W. (1987). *Science* **237**, 1309–1316.

Reznikoff, C. A., Bertram, J. S., Brankow, D. W., and Heidelberger, C. (1973). *Cancer Res.* **33**, 3239–3249.

Rhim, J. S., Fujita, J., and Park, J. B. (1986). *Proc. Am. Assoc. Cancer Res.* **27**, 137 (Abstr. No. 543).

Roop, D. R., Lowy, D. R., Tambourin, P. E., Strickland, J., Harper, J. R., Balaschak, M., Spangler, E. F., and Yuspa, S. H. (1986). *Nature (London)* **323**, 822–824.

Rotstein, J., O'Connell, J., and Slaga, T. (1986). *Proc. Am. Assoc. Cancer Res.* **27**, 143 (Abstr. No. 567).

Ruley, H. E. (1983). *Nature (London)* **304**, 602–606.

Santos, E., Tronick, S. R., Aaronson, S. A., Pulciani, S., and Barbacid, M. (1982). *Nature (London)* **298**, 343–347.

Santos, E., Martin-Zanca, D., Reddy, E. P., Pierotti, M. A., Della Porta, G., and Barbacid, M. (1984). *Science* **223**, 661–664.

Sawey, M. J., Hood, A. T., Burns, F. J., and Garte, S. J. (1987). *Mol. Cell. Biol.* **7**, 932–935.

Saxon, P. J., Srivatsan, E. S., and Stanbridge, E. J. (1986). *EMBO J.* **5**, 3461–3466.

Schechter, A. L., Stern, D. F., Vaidyanathan, L., Decker, S. J., Drebin, J. A., Green, M. I., and Weinberg, R. A. (1984). *Nature (London)* **312**, 513–516.

Schwab, M., Ellison, J., Busch, M., Rosenau, W., Varmus, H. E., and Bishop, J. M. (1984). *Proc. Natl. Acad. Sci. U.S.A.* **81**, 4940–4944.

Seizinger, B. R., Martuza, R. L., and Gusella, J. F. (1986). *Nature (London)* **322**, 644–647.

Shen-Ong, G. L. C., Keath, E. J., Piccoli, S. P., and Cole, M. E. (1982). *Cell* **31**, 443–452.

Singer, B., Spangler, S. J., Fraenkel-Conrat, H., and Kusmierek, J. T. (1986). *Proc. Natl. Acad. Sci. U.S.A.* **83**, 28–32.

Sivak, A., and Van Duuren, B. (1967). *Science* **157**, 1443–1444.

Skouv, J., Christensen, B., Skibshoj, I., and Autrup, H. (1986). *Carcinogenesis* **7**, 331–333.

Slamon, D. J., and Cline, M. J. (1984). *Proc. Natl. Acad. Sci. U.S.A.* **81**, 7141–7145.

Small, M. B. (1984). *Diss. Abstr. Int. (B)* **45**, 2053B.

Smith, B. L., Anisowicz, A., Chodosh, L. A., and Sager, R. (1982). *Proc. Natl. Acad. Sci. U.S.A.* **79**, 1964–1968.

Spandidos, D., and Kerr, I. B. (1984). *Br. J. Cancer* **49**, 681–688.

Spandidos, D. A., and Wilkie, N. M. (1984). *Nature (London)* **310**, 469–475.

Stacey, D. W., and Kung, H. F. (1984). *Nature (London)* **310**, 508–511.

Stanbridge, E. J., Der, C. J., Doersen, C.-J., Nishima, R. Y., Peehl, D. M., Weissman, B. E., and Wilkinson, J. E. (1982). *Science* **215**, 252–259.

Stewart, T. A., Pattengale, P. K., and Leder, P. (1984). *Cell* **38**, 627–637.

Stoker, M. G. P. (1964). *Virology* **24**, 165–174.

Storer, R. D., Sina, J. F., Stein, R. B., and Bradley, M. O. (1986a). *Proc. Am. Assoc. Cancer Res.* **27**, 145 (Abstr. No. 573).

Storer, R. D., Stein, R. B., Sina, J. F., DeLuca, J. G., Allen, H. L., and Bradley, M. O. (1986b). *Cancer Res.* **46**, 1458–1464.

Sukumar, S., Notario, V., Martin-Zanca, D., and Barbacid, M. (1983). *Nature (London)* **306**, 658–661.

Sukumar, S., Pulciani, S., Doniger, J., DiPaulo, J. A., Evans, C. H., Zbar, B., and Barbacid, M. (1984). *Science* **223**, 1197–1199.

Sukumar, S., Peratoni, A., Reed, C., Rice, J. M., and Wenk, M. L. (1986). *Mol. Cell. Biol.* **6** 2716–2720.

Sweet, R. W., Yokoyama, S., Kamata, T., Feramisco, J. R., Rosenberg, M., and Gross, M. (1984). *Nature (London)* **311**, 273–275.

Taguchi, T., Yokoyama, M., and Kitamura, Y. (1984). *Cancer Res.* **44**, 3779–3782.

Tahira, T., Hayashi, K., Ochiai, M., Tsuchida, N., Nagao, M., and Sugimara, T. (1986). *Mol. Cell. Biol.* **6**, 1349–1351.

Tainsky, M. A., Cooper, C. S., Giovanella, B. C. and Vande Woude, G. F. (1984). *225*, 643–645.

Tanaka, T., Slamon, D. J., Battifora, H., and Cline, M. J. (1986). *Cancer Res.* **46**, 1465–1470.

Taparowsky, E., Suard, Y., Fasano, D., Shimizu, K., Goldfarb, M., and Wigler, M. (1982). *Nature (London)* **300**, 762–765.

Thomson, L. M., Baker, R. M., Carrano, A. V., and Brookman, K. W. (1980). *Cancer Res.* **40**, 3245–3251.

Toftgard, R., Yuspa, S. H., and Roop, D. R. (1985). *Cancer Res.* **45**, 5845–5850.

Topal, M. D., Eadie, J. S., and Conrad, M. (1986). *J. Biol. Chem.* **261**, 9879–9885.

Tsunokawa, Y., Hiroyasu, E., Susaki, M. S., Mori, M., Sakamoto, H., Terada, M., and Sugimara, T. (1984). *Gann* **75**, 732–736.

Vousden, K. H., and Marshall, C. J. (1984). *EMBO J.* **3**, 913–917.

Vousden, K. H., Bos, J. L., Marshall, C. L., and Phillips, D. H. (1986). *Proc. Natl. Acad. Sci. U.S.A.* **83**, 1222–1226.

Wakelam, M. J. D., Davies, S. A., Houslay, M. D., McKay, I., Marshall, C. J., and Hall, A. (1986). *Nature (London)* **323**, 173–176.

Warren, W., Lawley, P. D., Gardner, E., Harris, G., Ball, J. K., and Cooper, C. S. (1987). *Carcinogenesis* **8**, 163–172.

Wei, S-J. C., Desai, S. M., Harvey, R. G., and Weiss, S. B. (1984). *Proc. Natl. Acad. Sci. U.S.A.* **81**, 5936–5940.

Weinberg, R. A. (1985). *Science* **230**, 770–776.

Westaway, D., Papkoff, J., Moscovici, C., and Varmus, H. E. (1986). *EMBO J.* **5**, 301–309.

Wiseman, R. W., Stowers, S. J., Miller, E. C., Anderson, M. W., and Miller, J. A. (1986). *Proc. Natl. Acad. Sci. U.S.A.* **83**, 5825–5829.

Yotti, L. P., Chang, C. C., and Trosko, J. E. (1979). *Science* **206**, 1089–1091.

Yunis, J. J. (1983). *221*, 227–236.

Yuspa, S. H., and Morgan, D. L. (1981). *Nature (London)* **293**, 72–74.

Yuspa, S. H., Hennings, H., Kulesz-Martin, M., and Lichti, H. (1982). *In* "Carcinogenesis" (E. Hecker *et al.*, eds.), Vol. 7, pp. 217–230. Raven, New York.

Yuspa, S. H., Vass, W., and Scolnick, E. (1983). *Cancer Res.* **43**, 6021–6030.

Yuspa, S. H., Kilkenny, A. E., Stanley, J., and Lichti, U. (1985). *Nature (London)* **314**, 459–462.

Yuspa, S. H., Morgan, D., Lichti, U., Spangler, E. F., Michael, D., Kilkenny, A., and Hennings, H. (1986). *Carcinogenesis* **7**, 949–958.

Zarbl, H., Sukumar, S., Arthur, A. V., Martin-Zanca, D., and Barbacid, M., (1985). *Nature (London)* **315**, 382–386.

THE INTRACISTERNAL A-PARTICLE GENE FAMILY: STRUCTURE AND FUNCTIONAL ASPECTS

Edward L. Kuff and Kira K. Lueders

Laboratory of Biochemistry, National Cancer Institute, National Institutes of Health, Bethesda, Maryland 20892

I. Introduction ... 184
II. Structural and Genomic Organization of *Mus musculus* IAP Sequences ... 185
A. Type I Elements ... 187
B. Deleted Type I Elements ... 188
C. Type II IAP Elements ... 189
D. Mouse IAP-Element LTRs ... 190
E. Internal Structure of the 5′ End ... 190
III. Relationships between IAPs and Other Retroviruses ... 191
A. IAPs and *Mus musculus* Extracellular Retroviruses ... 191
B. Relationships between IAPs and Other *Mus* Retroviruses ... 192
C. IAP-Related Elements in Genomic DNA of Species Other Than Mouse ... 193
D. Relationships with Other Viral Genomes from Sequence Analysis ... 197
IV. Chromosomal Distribution of IAP-Related Sequences: Association with Other Repetitive Sequence Elements ... 201
V. IAP Component Proteins ... 203
A. GAG Proteins ... 204
B. Reverse Transcriptase ... 208
C. Integrase ... 212
D. Envelope ... 212
VI. Transmission ... 212
VII. IAP-Related RNAs ... 214
A. A-Particle-Associated RNAs ... 214
B. Transcription of IAP Genes ... 217
VIII. Regulation ... 219
A. DNA Methylation ... 221
B. Oncogene Effects ... 224
C. Cell Proliferation ... 225
D. Halogenated Pyrimidines ... 226
E. Interferon Effects ... 227
IX. IAP Gene Expression in Normal Somatic Cells ... 227
X. IAP Expression in Early Development ... 230
A. Intracisternal Particles in Embryos of Laboratory Mice ... 230
B. Intracisternal Particles in Embryos of Wild Mice and Other Species ... 235
C. General Comments ... 235
XI. IAP Expression in Mouse Teratocarcinoma Cells ... 236
XII. IAP Element Transpositions ... 243
XIII. IAP Gene Products as Immunoglobulin Regulatory Factors ... 249
XIV. IAP Gene Expression in Genetically Determined Mouse Diabetes ... 252

ADVANCES IN CANCER RESEARCH, VOLUME 51

XV. Type-R Particles 253
XVI. Occurrence of IAPs in Other Species 257
XVII. IAP Expression in Relation to Neoplastic Transformation 259
A. Possible Basis for Enhanced IAP Expression in Transformed Cells 264
B. Possible Role of IAP Elements in Tumor Induction and/or Progression 266
References 267

I. Introduction*

Murine intracisternal type A particles (intracisternal A-particles, IAPs) are defective retrovirions encoded by members of a large family of endogenous proviral elements. The particles assemble on membranes of the endoplasmic reticulum and bud into the cisternae. They are not known to leave the cell. Horizontal transmission via free particles has not been achieved.

A low level of IAP gene transcription is constitutive in many adult mouse tissues, and IAPs appear transiently in preimplantation embryos. However, IAPs are most abundantly expressed in neoplastic cells. Many, perhaps most, types of mouse tumor cells contain at least a few IAPs; and in some cases, such as the transplantable plasmacytomas of BALB/c and C3H mice, particles may accumulate to the extent of several thousand per cell. IAPs can be isolated from these sources in biochemically usable quantities.

A number of mouse IAP genetic elements have been cloned, from both genomic and cDNA libraries; and several—including one full-size, 7-kb* genomic element—have been sequenced. The sequence of a homologous element in the Syrian hamster is also known. These data show that the IAP genome is evolutionarily related to the type B mouse mammary tumor virus (MMTV), the type D simian retroviruses (SRV), and most distantly to the type C avian sarcoma virus. The organization of the IAP genome being known, it has been possible to correlate the deduced protein structure with certain known properties of the particle components. Interestingly, various IAP-encoded proteins appear to act as immunoregulatory factors and neoantigens in the mouse.

IAP genetic elements have been shown to transpose in the genome of mouse tumor cells and also in the germ line of several mouse strains. Most of the tranpositions were found because they affected the function of genes at the target sites. Among the various effects of IAP proviral insertions has been the constitutive activation of c-*mos* and interleukin 3 genes. IAP transpositions are a source of genetic variability and as such may contribute to the process of neoplastic transformation.

*Abbreviations: kb, kilobase(s); bp, base pair(s); aa, amino acid(s); kDa, kilodalton(s); nt, nucleotide(s); HAT, hypoxanthine-aminopterine-thymidine.

Various aspects of research on IAPs have been reviewed: expression in early development (Kelly and Condamine, 1982; Yotsuyanagi and Szöllösi, 1984); genomic sequences as chromosomal genes (Kozak, 1985) and as transposable elements (Finnegan, 1985); general molecular biology (Stoye and Coffin, 1985); proteins as neoantigen in autoimmune diabetes (Leiter and Wilson, 1987). However, the body of information on IAPs has not previously been collated. We hope that a comprehensive review will be useful to investigators who encounter IAP-related proteins or genetic elements in the course of their studies or who are concerned directly with the role of endogenous transposable elements in normal development or neoplasia.

II. Structural and Genomic Organization of *Mus musculus* IAP Sequences

The nuclear DNAs of *Mus musculus*, *Mus domesticus*, and closely related species contain about 1000 IAP-related proviral elements per haploid genome. The majority of IAP elements exhibit structural features generally associated with integrated retroviruses, i.e., colinearity with the 7.2-kb IAP genomic RNA and the presence of terminal repeated sequences (long terminal repeats, LTRs) (Lueders and Kuff, 1980; Kuff *et al.*, 1981; Cole *et al.*, 1981). Six such elements isolated from a BALB/c mouse embryo DNA library in phage Charon4A showed individual variations in some restriction sites. One element containing a major deletion was also cloned (Kuff *et al.*, 1981). Additional structural variants were isolated by Ono *et al.* (1980) from a neonatal Swiss mouse DNA library using as probe poly(A) RNA from MOPC-315 myeloma enriched for species about 2 kb in size. Of the seven IAP elements selected this way, only one was full size. The heterogeneity of this gene population, which included major deletions and substitutions, was in striking contrast to that observed with the 7.2-kb elements. More recently Pikó *et al.* (1984) have isolated elements representative of the previously described variants using a single probe, a cDNA to MOPC-104E poly(A) RNA. Four of ten clones contained deleted elements, whereas six of the ten contained full-size elements.

Different subclasses of IAP elements were defined by Shen-Ong and Cole (1982) primarily by analysis of restriction digests of genomic DNA using the enzymes *Eco*RI and *Hin*dIII, which recognize conserved sites within the elements, and by isolation of representatives from a mouse genomic library. The genomic digests contain a diagnostic array of fragments of 5.8, 5.3, 4.2, 3.9, 3.5, and 2.8 kb, which arise from a variety of full-size and deleted elements. The structure of the various classes of IAP elements is shown in Fig. 1, and a brief description of their properties follows.

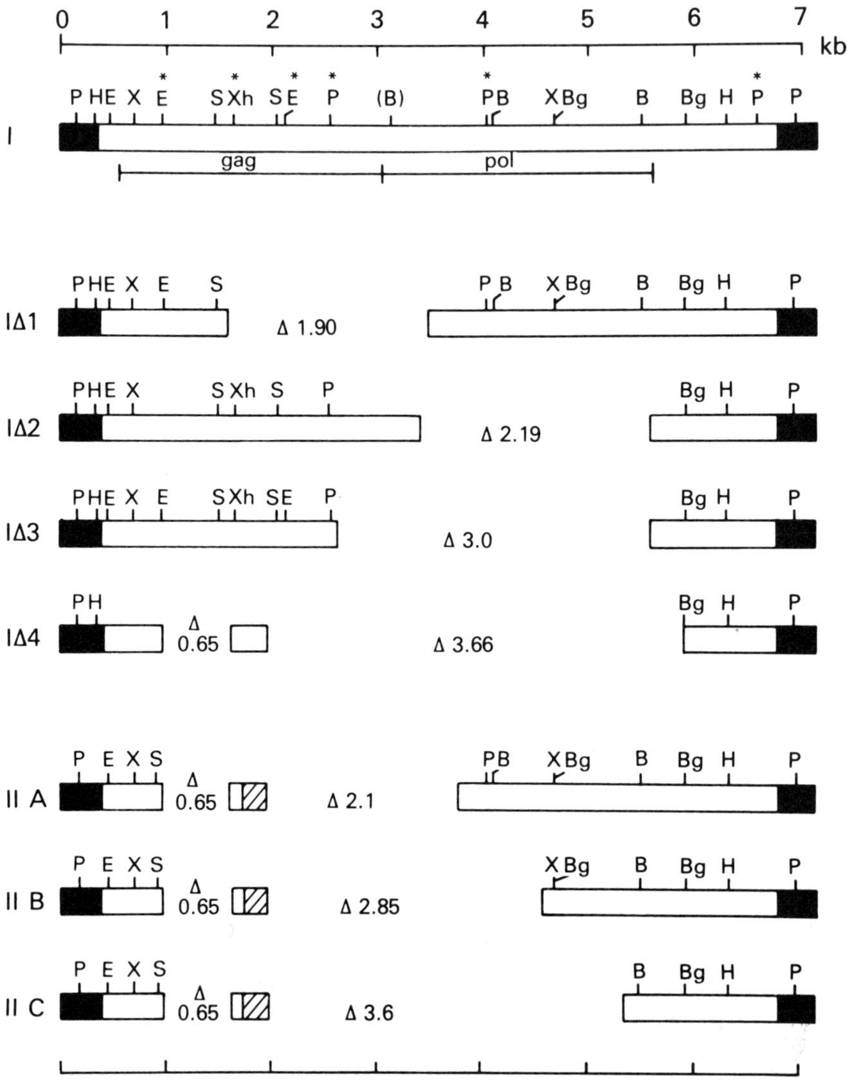

FIG. 1. Structure of mouse IAP elements. The restriction map and major genetic regions of a representative full-size type I IAP element (MIA4) are shown at the top. IAP internal sequences are represented by open boxes, LTRs by solid boxes. Restriction sites are P, *Pst*I; H, *Hin*dIII; E, *Eco*RI; X, *Xba*I; S, *Sac*I; Xh, *Xho*I; B, *Bam*HI; Bg, *Bgl*II. Asterisks indicate sites that are variable among many copies; parentheses a site variable in some copies. Four classes of type I deleted elements are shown beneath, with Δ indicating the size in kilobases of the missing sequence. Three classes of type II IAP elements are shown; the type II-specific insertion, AIIins, is indicated by ▨.

A. Type I Elements

The 7.1-kb elements that are colinear with the 7.2-kb IAP genomic RNA make up the major class of IAP sequences. One such element, MIA14, was randomly selected from a BALB/c mouse genomic library (Lueders and Kuff, 1980) and has been completely sequenced (Mietz *et al.*, 1987). IAP 81 (Ono *et al.*, 1980) is another example of a cloned type I element. There are estimated to be about 700 full-size elements per haploid genome in the BALB/c mouse (Shen-Ong and Cole, 1982). These elements are relatively homogeneous and contain many highly conserved restriction sites, but they do differ in the occurrence of certain characteristic restriction sites (Kuff *et al.*, 1981). These characteristic sites include a variable number of *Eco*RI sites at the 5′ end, internal *Pst*I sites, and *Hin*dIII sites at the 3′ ends of the LTRs. This variation divides the large family of elements into a number of overlapping subgroups that contribute to and can be identified in the complex restriction patterns derived from total mouse DNA (Lueders and Kuff, 1980; Kuff *et al.*, 1981).

The sequenced mouse IAP element, MIA14 (Mietz *et al.*, 1987), is 7095 bp long, including LTRs of 338 bp. MIA14 contains four open reading frames (ORFs); ORF 1 begins at nt 555 and extends to nt 3075. It is likely that translation begins at an AUG codon at position 594. Three distinct regions of *gag* were recognizable by homology with the functional retroviruses simian retrovirus 1 (SRV-1) and Rous sarcoma virus (RSV)(see Section III,D); these were p27 (223 aa), p12 (139 aa), and protease (248 aa). The total coding capacity of the *gag* ORF is 93 kDa, whereas the size of the *gag* product determined chromatographically and electrophoretically was 73 kDa (Marciani and Kuff, 1973). *In vitro* translation of the *gag* ORF yielded a main product of 73 kDa and a minor product of about 90 kDa, a finding demonstrating that p73 can be produced from ORF 1. From the predicted sequence, p73 appears to include 7–8 kDa of protease coding sequence. This may account for the lack of processing of p73 (see Section V,A,2). There was generally good agreement between the amino acid composition of p73 predicted from the nucleic acid sequence of MIA14 and that determined biochemically for p73 isolated from myeloma IAPs (Marciani and Kuff, 1973). However, some differences were found, consistent with the variation in sequence among different IAP elements.

The *pol* reading frame begins at nt 3041 with a frame shift of −1 relative to ORF 1 and contains 3 ORFs due to a frame shift at nt 4628 and an in-frame stop at nt 4782. Other IAP elements that have been sequenced (Ymer *et al.*, 1986; M. Trounstine, personal communication) have a continous ORF in this region. The intact *pol* ORF contains 867 codons with 590 aa in reverse transcriptase and 277 aa in the endonuclease; these numbers have been deduced by homology with the respective proteins in SRV-1 (See Section III,D).

The *env* region of 1100 bp contains multiple stops in all reading frames in MIA14 and six other mouse IAP elements that have been sequenced in this region (IL-3, Ymer *et al.*, 1985; clone 8.3, Martens *et al.*, 1985; clones p3A67 and L31, Aota *et al.*, 1987; clone 10.2, M. Trounstine, personal communication; pMIA1, J. Mietz, unpublished). These stops are highly conserved among different elements.

Some characteristic properties of mouse IAPs are undoubtedly determined by the peptide encoded in the 5′ *gag* domain (Mietz *et al.*, 1987). Secondary structure analysis shows that the product of this region includes an amino-terminal hydrophobic signal peptide that could account for association of the *gag* protein with the endoplasmic reticulum membrane. No sequence resembling a myristylation site is present. The amino-terminal hydrophobic domain is followed by a helix-rich, predominantly hydrophilic polypeptide segment with localized regions of marked charge asymmetry and a cluster of four cysteine residues. These cysteines could contribute to the known insolubility of p73 and the disulfide cross-linking of p73 in the IAPs (Kuff *et al.*, 1972; Wivel *et al.*, 1973).

B. Deleted Type I Elements

Four distinct subclasses of deleted IAP elements with at least three examples for each one have been defined (Fig. 1). The IΔ1 class is the most abundant deleted-element class in the mouse genome and contributes to a major 4-kb *Hin*dIII fragment on Southern blots (Kuff *et al.*, 1981, 1986b). Shen-Ong and Cole (1982) estimated that there are 130 such deleted type I IAP elements in the haploid BALB/c genome and none in *M. molossinus*. Type IΔ1 elements contain a 1.9-kb deletion that results in fusion of the *gag* and *pol* regions. Two such deleted IAP elements have been involved in transpositions (see Section XII). cDNA clones isolated from a T cell hybridoma (Martens *et al.*, 1985; Kuff *et al.*, 1986b) and from normal thymus (Grossman *et al.*, 1987) have also represented type IΔ1 elements. The deletions in three cloned and sequenced type IΔ1 elements—the IL-3 element, clone 10.2, and clone D20—occur at precisely the same position (nt 1575–3475) in the MIA14 genome. The deletion is in frame and results in an ORF with coding potential for a 120-kDa *gag–pol* fusion product. In MIA14, a partially related sequence precedes each of the two sites that define the deletion, a finding suggesting that homologous recombination may have been involved in creating this class of deleted elements (Mietz *et al.*, 1987). The presence of homologous sequences at the deletion points is also consistent with an alternative mechanism involving recognition of such sequences in the template by reverse transcriptase, as postulated by Xu and Boeke (1987) on the basis of their observations with Ty elements.

A second, less abundant, class of deleted type I IAP elements—designated IΔ2—contains a 2.2-kb deletion that is located further downstream than that in IΔ1; this deletion results in the absence of virtually all of the *pol* region. An example of such an element, MIA48, has been isolated from the mouse library and has been described (Kuff *et al.*, 1981). We have also found such an element 3′ to a VL30 gene (unpublished observation). A T cell hybridoma cDNA (clone 9.5) also had this structure (Martens *et al.*, 1985), and the position of the deletion (aa 131 to 860 in *pol*) has been precisely determined by sequencing this element (Mietz *et al.*, 1987). Common nucleotide sequences again precede the two sites that define the deletion.

Another class of deleted type I elements—IΔ3—has a 3-kb deletion. The position of this deletion has been determined by heteroduplex analysis of the element inserted downstream from the pseudo α-globin gene (Lueders *et al.*, 1982) and by restriction mapping of clones containing two independent insertions in the c-*mos* genes in myelomas (Canaani *et al.*, 1983). A genomic IAP element clone, L31, from BALB/c myeloma cells which was recently sequenced (Aota *et al.*, 1987) appears to be an example of an IΔ3 element. The deletion includes nucleotides 2919 to 5674 on the MIA14 sequence.

The final class of deleted type I elements—IΔ4—has two deletions that add up to approximately 4 kb. A number of such elements have been isolated as genomic clones (Ono *et al.*, 1980; Pikó *et al.*, 1984). One such element has been involved in a transposition in germ-line DNA of the DBA/2 mouse downstream of the renin gene. This IAP element—designated MIARN (Burt *et al.*, 1984)—has been sequenced. In addition to a large 3.7-kb deletion resulting in a *gag*–*"env"* fusion, there is also a deletion of 0.65 kb and an insertion of 116 bp.

C. Type II IAP Elements

Shen-Ong and Cole (1982) determined that approximately 10% of the IAP sequences in the BALB/c mouse genome have a characteristic 0.5-kb insertion not present in type I elements as well as internal deletions of various sizes; these elements were designated type II IAP elements. They were further subdivided into three classes IIA, IIB, and IIC on the basis of the sizes of the deletions they contain relative to the type I elements (Shen-Ong and Cole, 1984). A fragment carrying the type II insertion sequence was cloned and used as probe to select a number of type II IAP clones from a genomic library of mouse myeloma MOPC-315 and to demonstrate that the type IIB subclass was amplified in this tumor by multiple insertions of the same (or very similar) proviral elements (Section XII).

The type II probe provided by Michael Cole was subsequently used to select 12 genomic clones from a mouse embryo gene library (Lueders and Mietz, 1987). When the probe clone was sequenced, an appreciable portion of it was found to consist of type I sequences. The insertion specific for type II IAP elements—designated AIIins—had sizes of 272, 268, and 264 bp in three examples. It had at its ends the inverted repeats TA. . . AT and generated a 9-bp target site duplication TACAGGTCT in the surrounding IAP sequence. AIIins is inserted at IAP map position 1741. Sequencing of several type II elements upstream of AIIins revealed a complicated arrangement of type I IAP sequences interrupted by multiple small deletions that had not been obvious from heteroduplex analysis (Ono *et al.*, 1980; Pikó *et al.*, 1984; our observations) as well as the large deletions shown in Fig. 1. Their sequence organization suggests that type II IAP elements were derived by a series of complex events.

Using a probe containing primarily AIIins, we estimated that there are 200 copies of IIA and 100 copies each of IIB and IIC elements in the normal mouse genome; these numbers are 3- to 5-fold greater than those reported by Shen-Ong and Cole (1982), who used a less specific probe to estimate the reiteration frequencies.

D. Mouse IAP-Element LTRs

Over 20 LTRs, including samples from a variety of different IAP classes, have been completely sequenced, and partial sequences are available for several more. For six elements, both LTRs have been sequenced; five were bracketed by 6-bp target site duplications in the genomic DNA. Multiple differences have been found between the 5′ and 3′ LTRs of these elements, even in cases where transposition has been demonstrated—except for the IL-3 insertion, in which the two LTRs were identical (Ymer *et al.*, 1986). Both the size and sequence of the LTRs varied considerably, with the major size differences occurring in the R region (Christy *et al.*, 1985). The smaller of the LTRs had sizes in the range of 350 bp. The U5 regions were all between 53 and 58 bp, making them unusually short relative to other retroviral U5 regions. The U3 regions were also relatively constant, with lengths of 208 to 217 bp—except for the 5′ LTR of MIARN, which was 245 bp long (Burt *et al.*, 1984). The R regions, on the other hand, varied from 48 to 222 bp. This variability is primarily due to duplication of a CT stretch downstream from the start site. Overall LTR length does not appear to correlate with the element class, although two of the longest LTRs were found in type II elements (Christy *et al.*, 1985). Although sequence variations are found throughout the LTRs, some regions appeared to be hypervariable, and it was in these regions that the majority of differences between 5′ and 3′ LTRs were located. IAP LTRs contain the usual retroviral set of transcriptional signal sequences (Kuff *et al.*, 1983b; Christy *et al.*, 1985; Lueders *et al.*, 1984), and several cloned examples have been shown to be active in promoting transcription (see Section VII,B).

E. Internal Structure of the 5′ End

The primer binding site for mouse IAP elements is homologous to the 3′ region of phenylalanine tRNA (Ono and Ohishi, 1983). Only three of nine mouse elements for which this sequence has been determined have a perfect 18/18 match (the igk-1 insertion, DNAX 10.2 cDNA clone, and MIA3.2 genomic clone) (Hawley *et al*, 1984a; Martens *et al.*, 1985; Canaani *et al.*, 1983). In the others, there are 2- to 3-bp mismatches, some of which result in marked reduction of binding affinity for $tRNA^{phe}$.

An unusual feature of IAP element structure is the duplication of various regions downstream from the 5′ LTR. These include part of the tRNA binding site which is imperfectly repeated a variable number of times—for instance, seven times in MIARN (Burt *et al.*, 1984). Regions at the 5′ non-translated end that contribute to length heterogeneity of the IAP elements include a 75-bp repeat (Lueders and Mietz, 1986) and a 87-bp repeat (Mietz *et al.*, 1987), which occur a variable number of times in different elements. A packaging sequence has not yet been identified.

III. Relationships between IAPs and Other Retroviruses

A. IAPs and *Mus musculus* Extracellular Retroviruses

It is now clear from nucleotide sequence analysis of their respective genomes that IAP elements (Ono *et al.*, 1985; Mietz *et al.*, 1987) and various murine leukemia virus (MuLV) isolates are essentially unrelated. The frequent expression of both IAPs and type C viruses by the same tumor cell occasioned much early speculation and some work on the possible relationship between the two, particularly whether the IAPs represented a defective intracellular form of the secreted viruses. A thorough study of cloned cell culture lines with various proportions of IAPs and type C viruses showed complete dissociation between the two types of expression and led to the conclusion, since amply confirmed, that IAPs and type C viruses were essentially unrelated (Hall *et al.*, 1968). Antisera against IAP proteins fail to react with purified MuLV and MMTV (Kuff *et al.*, 1972).

Thach and co-workers investigated the relationship between IAPs and an extracellular noninfectious retroviral particle ("myeloma-associated virus," or MAV) produced by MOPC-460 myeloma cells in ascites form or adapted to tissue culture (Robertson *et al.*, 1976, 1979; Ramabhadran *et al.*, 1979). MOPC-460 cells produce, in addition to IAPs and MAV, intracytoplasmic A-particles (MMTV precursors) and infectious MuLV. The authors adduced evidence from protein comparisons, immunological cross-reactivity, and nucleic acid hybridization that IAPs and MAV were closely related. The multiplicity of retroviral forms in this cell line and the possibility of cross-contamination in the various particle preparations raise questions about this interpretation. It is conceivable, however, that MAV contains a recombinant genome with some IAP sequence.

Wong-Staal *et al.* (1975) showed that products of the endogenous reverse-transcriptase reaction in myeloma- and neuroblastoma-derived IAPs did not hybridize significantly to MuLV RNA. Nucleic acid sequence relationships between IAPs and type B and C viruses were later examined in detail by reciprocal cDNA:RNA hybridizations (Lueders and Kuff, 1979). No major sequence homologies were found between IAP RNA and the RNA of representative members of the type B and C viruses of *M. musculus*. However, as will be seen later, sequence analysis of cloned viral genomes has revealed distant relationships between IAPs and type B and D retroviruses that could not be detected by hybridization.

B. Relationships between IAP Elements and Other *Mus* Retroviruses

The IAPs of *Mus musculus* showed partial homology (30%) with the endogenous M432 retrovirus (Kuff *et al.*, 1978) originally derived from the Asian mouse *Mus cervicolor* (Callahan *et al.*, 1976). The hybrids between M432 cDNA and IAP RNAs had lower thermal stabilities (ΔT_m, -6 to $-8°C$) than those formed with the homologous RNA. Immunological cross-reactivity between the IAP and M432 structural proteins was also detectable (Kuff *et al.*, 1980).

Molecular cloning of IAP elements and the M432 viral genome made it possible to define more precisely the relationship between these genomes by heteroduplex and restriction enzyme analyses. Two regions of homology were defined in this way (Callahan *et al.*, 1981): A major homology of 3.7 kb spanned a region including the 3′ end of the M432 *gag* gene and extending through *pol*. A second 0.6-kb region of weak homology was observed adjacent to the 3′ LTRs of the respective genomes. Although no homology was detected between the LTRs, we have recently found by inspection of an LTR sequence of M432 (provided by R. Callahan) 59% homology with the MIA14 LTR. Sequences at the 5′ end of the M432 genome, which are unrelated to the *Mus musculus* IAP sequences, were found only in cellular DNA of *M. cervicolor* and the closely related species *M. cooki*. Thus, the infectious M432 retroviral genome appears to represent a recombination event between an IAP genome and another class of retroviral or cellular sequences in *M. cervicolor*.

Liquid hybridization of a *Mus musculus* IAP cDNA probe to *M. cervicolor* and *M. caroli* genomic DNAs showed that divergent sequences representing the entire IAP element were present in these mice (Kuff *et al.*, 1978). The ΔT_m of these hybrids ($-7°$ C) was commensurate with the evolutionary distance between *M. musculus* and the two Asian species. The copy number of sequences with this ΔT_m in *M. cervicolor* was estimated at 25–30 per haploid genome; a similar number had been determined earlier for M432 virus-related sequences in this species (Callahan *et al.*, 1976). Hybridization of a cloned IAP probe to Southern blots of genomic DNAs from a variety of *Mus* species and subspecies, shown in Fig. 2, confirms the amplification of IAP sequences in mice closely related to *M. musculus* and suggests that much smaller numbers of sequences are present in the more distantly related Southeast Asian species *cervicolor*, *cooki*, and *caroli*. It was therefore surprising when copy numbers nearly 10 times those previously described were reported by Ono *et al.* (1984) who used both cloned *M. musculus* and *M. caroli* IAP elements as probes and determined copy numbers of 230–400 for *M. caroli* and 390–570 for *M. cervicolor*.

Using a representative *Mus musculus* IAP probe under conditions of relaxed stringency (ΔT_m = 22.5°C) to hybridize dot blots of genomic DNAs, we obtained copy numbers between 1050 and 1600 for the closely related species shown in Fig. 2, and 120, 225, and 250 copies per haploid genome for *M. cervicolor*, *caroli*, and *cooki*, respectively. We suggest that the latter species contain a high proportion of very heterodisperse IAP-related sequences that do not contribute to the discrete genomic restriction fragments in Fig. 2 but account for the high copy numbers obtained by other methods of assay.

IAP elements isolated from the genome of the Southeast Asian wild mouse *Mus caroli* are 6.5 kb long, have LTRs of 345 bp, and are bracketed by a 6-bp target site duplication (Ono *et al.*, 1984). The primer binding site is homologous to phenylalanine tRNA. Sequencing of the LTR showed that it was 80% homologous to the *Mus musculus* IAP LTRs. The restriction map of the *Mus caroli* IAP elements resembles that of the *Mus musculus* type I elements, although it is shorter in two regions. A number of characteristic restriction sites are conserved.

C. IAP-Related Elements in Genomic DNA of Species Other Than Mouse

Cloned mouse IAP elements have been used as probes to study related sequences in the DNAs of other species. In one study (Lueders and Kuff, 1981), heterologous DNAs were bound to nitrocellulose filters and hybridized with labeled probes representing the entire 7-kb IAP element, using conditions designed to permit association of divergent sequences (T_m 27.5°C below that of the homologous hybrids). After the least stringent wash (ΔT_m, −27.5°C), strong reactions were seen with all *Mus* DNAs. The only other DNA with a comparable reaction was from Syrian hamster. Weaker reactions were seen with DNAs from gerbil, rat, guinea pig, monkey, cat, deer mouse, and mink, and still weaker reactions with DNAs from bat, raccoon, and Chinese hamster. No reaction was detected with DNA from human placenta. The filters were washed at increasing temperatures to evaluate the degree of base matching in the hybrids; for the most part the reactions were weak, as expected from the evolutionary distance between the species tested and mouse. However, the persistent reactions of Syrian hamster and rat DNAs after stringent washing (ΔT_m, −4°C) suggested the presence of relatively well conserved and/or repetitive IAP-related sequences in these species.

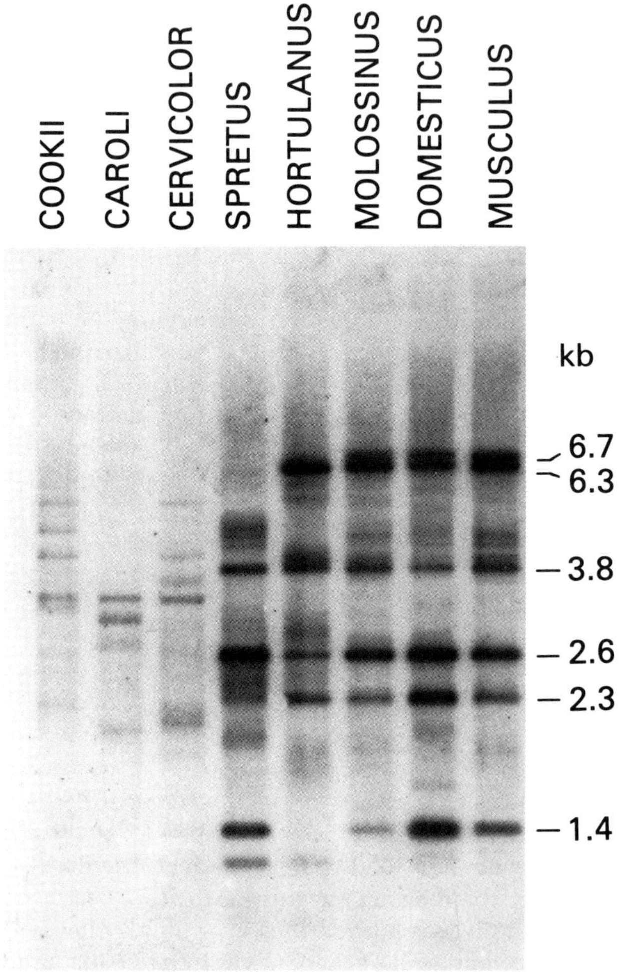

FIG. 2. Analysis of genomic DNAs from *Mus* species and subspecies. DNAs (5 μg) were cut with *Pst*I, fractionated by electrophoresis in agarose gels, and hybridized with a representative IAP element probe pMIA1, a clone containing sequences from the *Eco*RI site near 1 kb to the *Hin*dIII site at 6.3 kb on the MIA14 map in Fig. 1. Hybridization and washing were carried out a lowered stringency (ΔT_m = $-20°C$), to permit visualization of divergent sequences. The common progenitor of the Asian species *M. cooki*, *caroli*, and *cervicolor* diverged from the progenitor of the other species between 2 and 4 million years ago.

The stability of hybrids formed between hamster and rat DNAs and a cloned mouse IAP probe was determined by temperature elution of the hybrids from hydroxylapatite columns. The T_m's were virtually identical (T_m, 61–62°C), and similar to those found earlier for the hybrids formed between a mouse IAP-specific cDNA and hamster DNAs (Lueders and Kuff, 1977).

A Syrian hamster DNA genomic library was screened with a mouse IAP *pol* region probe (Suzuki *et al.*, 1982); and from the frequencies of positive clones, it was calculated that there are 700 copies of IAP sequences per mouse and 950 copies of IAP-related copies per hamster haploid genome. A similar number of copies was estimated for the Syrian hamster genome using a different gene library and a mouse IAP element probe (Lueders and Kuff, 1983).

Syrian hamster IAP elements have been cloned from these two gene libraries (Suzuki *et al.*, 1982; Lueders and Kuff, 1983), and one 7951-bp element (H18) has been completely sequenced (Ono *et al.*, 1985). These elements have a structure very much like the type I mouse IAP elements; no deleted forms have been observed among eight clones isolated by Suzuki *et al.* and six clones isolated in our laboratory. Both LTRs from two elements have been sequenced (Ono and Ohishi, 1983). Those of clone H10 (350 bp) differed by a single base pair, whereas those of clone H18 (376 bp) were identical. Overall homology between the hamster and mouse IAP LTRs was 60%, but some regions showed much higher homology over short stretches.

The gene order in H18 was established by Ono *et al.* by comparison of the deduced amino acid sequence with that of known retrovirus gene products. They showed that the sequence organization of the IAP elements was similar to that in RSV in which the 5′ to 3′ order of viral polypeptides is p19, p10, p27 (*gag*), p12 (nucleic acid binding), p15 (protease), *pol*, and *env*. Limited homology between H18 and RSV was found in parts of p27 and p15, and throughout *pol*, but multiple frame shifts were necessary in H18, a finding indicating that this hamster IAP element is a pseudogene.

Comparison of the restriction patterns of cloned Syrian hamster elements with those given by genomic DNA indicated that the IAP-related sequences in this species represented a family of relatively homogeneous, well-conserved units (Lueders and Kuff, 1983); in this they resemble mouse IAP elements. The Chinese hamster genome has a much lower number of IAP-related sequences that were quite divergent from those in the Syrian hamster.

About 500 IAP-related sequences were estimated to be present in the rat genome from the fraction of positive plaques in a genomic library that reacted with the mouse IAP probe, and a number of such elements have been cloned (Lueders and Kuff, 1983). In contrast to the mouse and Syrian hamster IAP elements, the rat IAP-related sequences were heterogeneous. Heteroduplexes formed between rat and mouse clones showed short regions of homology interspersed with regions of nonhomology. None of the recombinants appeared to be a "typical" unit as judged by comparison of the restriction patterns of cloned sequences and genomic DNA. Regions of homology between individual rat IAP elements were interrupted by regions of nonhomology, a finding suggesting that they are made up of a patchwork of different subsets of sequences. The length of the rat IAP elements and whether they are bounded by LTRs has not been determined. These elements are clearly much more heterogeneous and divergent from one another than the IAP elements of the mouse and the Syrian hamster.

The extent of divergence between IAP elements in the mouse, Syrian hamster, and rat genomes has been estimated by measurements of the thermal stability of hybrids formed between individual cloned elements and their respective genomic DNAs (Lueders and Kuff, 1983). The "self-hybrids" in all cases had a T_m of 84.5°C. Hybrids formed between mouse probe and mouse genomic DNA melted only 1° below that of the self-hybrid, a result indicating that the average sequence divergence within the family of mouse IAP elements is small. Hybrids formed between the hamster probe and hamster genomic DNA had a T_m only 1.5°C below that of the self-hybrid, showing a homogeneity similar to that of the IAP sequences in mouse. Hybrids between the rat probe and rat genomic DNA, on the other hand, had a T_m of 6°C below that of the self-hybrid, a result indicating a large degree of divergence among rat IAP family members. Similarly low T_m's were found for hybrids between the rat probe and several other cloned rat IAP sequences.

Amplification of IAP-related sequences seems to have occurred independently and at different times in the evolutionary lineage of at least three genera (*Mus*, *Rattus*, and *Mesocricetus*). The genomic patterns for gerbil (*Gerbillus*) showed a moderate number of relatively homogeneous fragments reacting with a mouse IAP probe (Lueders and Kuff, 1983), a finding perhaps indicating an intermediate amplification. There appears to be no recent amplification of homologous sequences in the genome of Chinese hamster (*Cricetulus*).

Hawley *et al.* (1984c) detected IAP-related sequences in human DNA with probes derived primarily from the *pol* gene. Hybridization was done under conditions that represent a T_m of -46°C and permit formation of hybrids with 33% mismatch. Discrete bands were seen in samples of DNA cut with a number of enzymes. The sizes of the fragments were consistent with the restriction maps of clones subsequently isolated from the human genome (Ono, 1986). IAP-related sequences had not been detectable in human DNA under similar conditions of stringency when the entire IAP element was used as probe (Lueders and Kuff, 1981). It is now clear that the polymerase region represented in the probes used by both Hawley *et al.* and Ono *et al.* is the most highly conserved among IAP elements in different species (see Section III,D). It is also the region that shares the greatest homology with other retroviruses in its evolutionary lineage (Chiu *et al.*, 1984, 1985).

The majority of the human IAP-related elements cloned by Ono (1986) were 9.1- or 9.4-kb units—designated HERV-K genes. Recently Ono *et al.* (1986) have published a composite sequence representing an entire HERV-K element—designated HERV-K10(+). HERV-K10, which was chosen as an element most likely to be capable of coding for protein on the basis of the almost identical LTRs, had a number of ORFs in positions corresponding to those of known retroviral genes.

A family of retrovirus-like elements similar to the HERV-K family had earlier been characterized in the human genome by Callahan *et al.* (1984, 1985), using as probe a region of the MMTV polymerase gene. One such element—designated HLM-2—was isolated from a human gene library and is 90% homologous to HERV-K in the endonuclease gene (Ono *et al.*, 1986). A similar group of clones was isolated by Deen and Sweet (1986) using a MMTV *pol* probe and designated the HM family. The HM and HLM elements contain a large number of restriction site polymorphisms (Callahan *et al.*, 1985) as well as multiple termination signals and rearrangements in the *pol* coding region (Deen and Sweet, 1986) and are thus probably pseudogenes. Heterologous transcripts detected with a mouse IAP *pol* probe in human color carcinomas may represent expression of these elements (Moshier *et al.*, 1986). A 426-bp probe from just upstream of the HERV-K element 3′ LTR detected discrete 8.8-kb poly(A) RNAs in human larynx carcinoma and malignant melanoma cells; these could represent full-size transcripts of the HERV-K genome (Ono *et al.*, 1987). HLM-2 elements had a reiteration frequency of 30–50 copies per haploid genome, but the LTRs were much more highly reiterated at 1000 copies (Horn *et al.*, 1986).

D. Relationships with Other Viral Genomes from Sequence Analysis

In a comparison of the amino acid sequences of the Syrian hamster IAP element H18 and of RSV, Ono *et al.* (1985) showed that with the exception of one region of protease (which in RSV is shorter than that in H18), the homologous regions are essentially colinear over about 1400 codons. The upstream homology between H18 and RSV ends near the 5′ end of p27; p19 and p10 of RSV are apparently nonhomologous to the equivalent sequences in H18. The extent of homology between H18 and RSV is shown in Fig. 3. On the basis of homologies within a short region of the putative endonuclease domain of *pol* (180 aa; Chiu *et al.*, 1984), H18 was more closely related to MMTV and squirrel monkey retrovirus (SMRV) than any other retroviral type for which sequence in this region was available (namely,

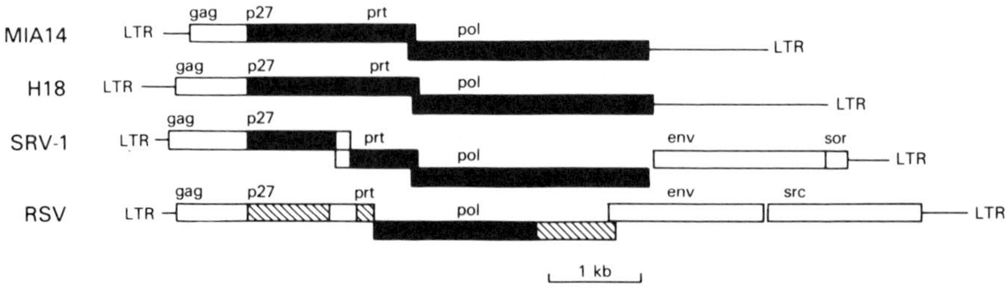

FIG. 3. Conserved regions of two IAP elements, SRV-1, and RSV. Regions with greater than 50% amino acid homology are shown as solid blocks, those with greater than 40% homology (from Ono *et al.*, 1985) as shaded blocks, and those with no detectable homology as open blocks. Open reading frames and frame shifts are shown. Introduction of three insertions of 5, 9, and 4 amino acids near the 3′ end of the RSV *gag* sequence relative to H18 eliminates the short region of apparent nonhomology.

avian C, mammalian A, B, D, and human T lymphocyte virus [HTLV]). These relationships were entirely consistent with retroviral phylogeny established by Chiu *et al.*, (1984) and others (Callahan *et al.*, 1984, 1985).

A high degree of nucleotide sequence homology exists between the mouse MIA14 element and Syrian hamster H18 element (Mietz *et al.*, 1987), making it apparent that the gene order in mouse and Syrian hamster IAP elements is the same. At the amino acid level, homology in p27 and *pol* is 88% over a total of 1077 codons (Fig. 4). Homology in p12 and protease, although lower, is still more than 72%. There is no homology between MIA14 and H18 upstream of p27. The envelope regions, which are closed in all three reading frames in both elements, share 74% homology at the nucleotide level.

Recently, Power *et al.* (1986) published the complete nucleotide sequence of SRV-1, a type D retrovirus implicated in an outbreak of acquired immune deficiency syndrome in macaques. (It is now known that SRV-1 and Mason-Pfizer monkey virus (MPMV) are strains of the same virus [Sonigo *et al.*, 1986].) Power *et al.* showed that the SRV-1 and H18 proteases are homologous and noted that some homology existed between the *pol* genes as well. This report reinforced the earlier suggestions, based on hybridization data, that IAP genetic elements are members of a lineage of retroviruses that share limited regions of homology between the genes for their magnesium-dependent polymerases (Chiu *et al.*, 1984, 1985).

The region of homology shared by representatives of this retroviral lineage is much more extensive than suggested by the above studies. For instance, as shown in Figs. 3 and 4, we found by inspection of the sequences of MIA14, H18, and SRV-1 that virtually continuous amino acid homology exists over a region that includes p27, p12, p15, and all of *pol*. In several localities, homology exceeds 90%. Sizes of the coding regions are essentially identical in the three genomes, and most of the differences involve single amino acid changes. Highly conserved regions that have been found in other retroviruses and retrotransposons are indicated in Fig. 4a–h. A short region at the p14/protease junction in SRV-1 has no counterpart in the p12/protease junctions in MIA14 and H18; and in contrast to SRV-1, there is no frame shift for protease in MIA14 and H18 (Fig. 3). A frame shift occurs in all three genomes between protease and *pol*. H18 required one frame shift in the *pol* gene to maintain homology with the SRV-1 *pol* and MIA14 required two. Homology between the three genomes ends abruptly slightly upstream of the 5′ end of p27; the polypeptides upstream of this position are apparently unrelated.

Within the limits of error of heteroduplex measurements, *M. musculus* IAP elements and the M432 retrovirus of *Mus cervicolor* share major homology over the same region as the hamster IAP elements, the mouse IAP elements, SRV-1, and RSV. Mouse IAP elements and the M432 retrovirus also share partial nucleotide homology in the *env* region just inside the 3′ LTR (Callahan *et al.*, 1981).

The gene order on the human IAP-related element HERV-K was determined by Ono *et al.* (1986) by comparison with H18, MMTV, and SRV-1 sequences. This element shared about 55% amino acid homology with the *pol* gene of SRV-1 and slightly lower homology with that of H18. Other human putative IAP-related elements, for which only partial *pol* sequences are available (Deen and Sweet, 1986; Callahan *et al.*, 1985), were 89% (HM16) and 88% (HLM2) related to HERV-K *pol* at the amino acid level (Ono *et al.*, 1986). We have found that amino acid homology between MIA14 and HERV-K is close to 60% from p27 through *pol* over the same region shared between MIA14, H18, and SRV-1. Once again, no significant homology was found 5′ to p27.

The IAP-related elements in hamster, mouse, monkey, and human have strongly conserved a block of coding information, or "cassette," which includes two structural proteins and three characteristic retroviral enzymes used by this group of phylogenetically related retroviruses (Fig. 3). It is likely that this cassette has participated in recombinational events to generate a diverse group of retroviruses which are characterized by distinctive 5′ ends upstream of p27 in each virus. The cassette encodes polypeptides essential for the viral life cycle, which is apparently consistent with considerable variation at the 5′ ends. In the case of the rodent IAP elements, conservation of these polypeptide domains could reflect selective pressure imposed by an amplification process that involves the intracellular generation and reintegration of new IAP-related proviral copies. This pressure would be analogous

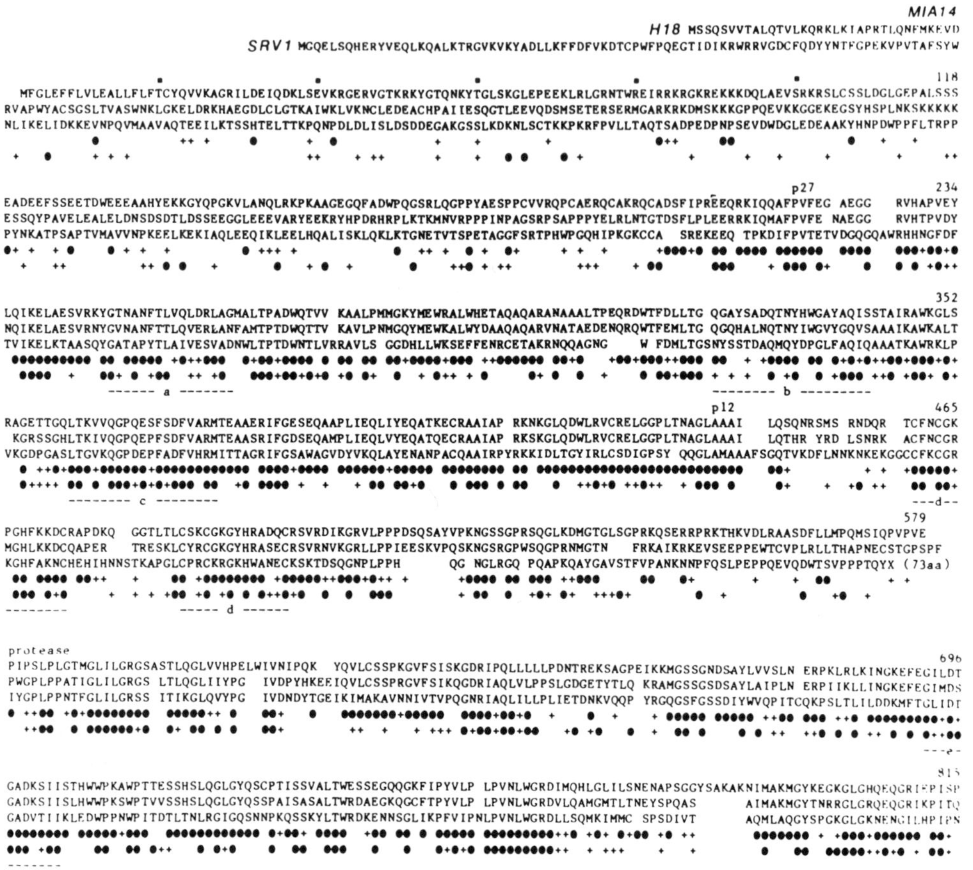

FIG. 4. Amino acid sequence homologies between mouse and Syrian hamster IAP elements (MIA14 and H18, respectively), and a simian type D retrovirus (SRV1). Amino acids are represented by the standard one-letter abbreviations. Numbering is with respect to the MIA14 deduced amino acid sequence of Mietz *et al.* (1987). X indicates a stop codon. The H18 sequence is from the data of Ono *et al.* (1985) and includes some regions that were not translated by these authors. The SRV1 sequence is from Power *et al.* (1986). The first 73 amino acids of the SRV1 protease ORF, which is longer than that in the IAPs, are indicated by (73 aa). Solid circles below the sequences indicate amino acids which are identical to those in MIA14 for H18 (top line) and SRV1 (bottom line); conservative changes are indicated by +. Regions conserved in a variety of retroviruses and retrotransposons are designated *a–h* as follows: *a–c*, homologies to erythroid-potentiating activity factor or tissue inhibitor of metalloproteinases (Patarca and Haseltine, 1985); *d*, nucleic acid binding domains [2 copies] (Copeland *et al.*, 1984; Mount and Rubin, 1985); *e*, homology to acid proteases (Toh *et al.*, 1985a); *f*, reverse transcriptase homologies (Patarca and Haseltine, 1984); g, potential zinc binding finger (Johnson *et al.*, 1986); *h*, endonuclease "core" sequence (Chiu *et al.*, 1984).

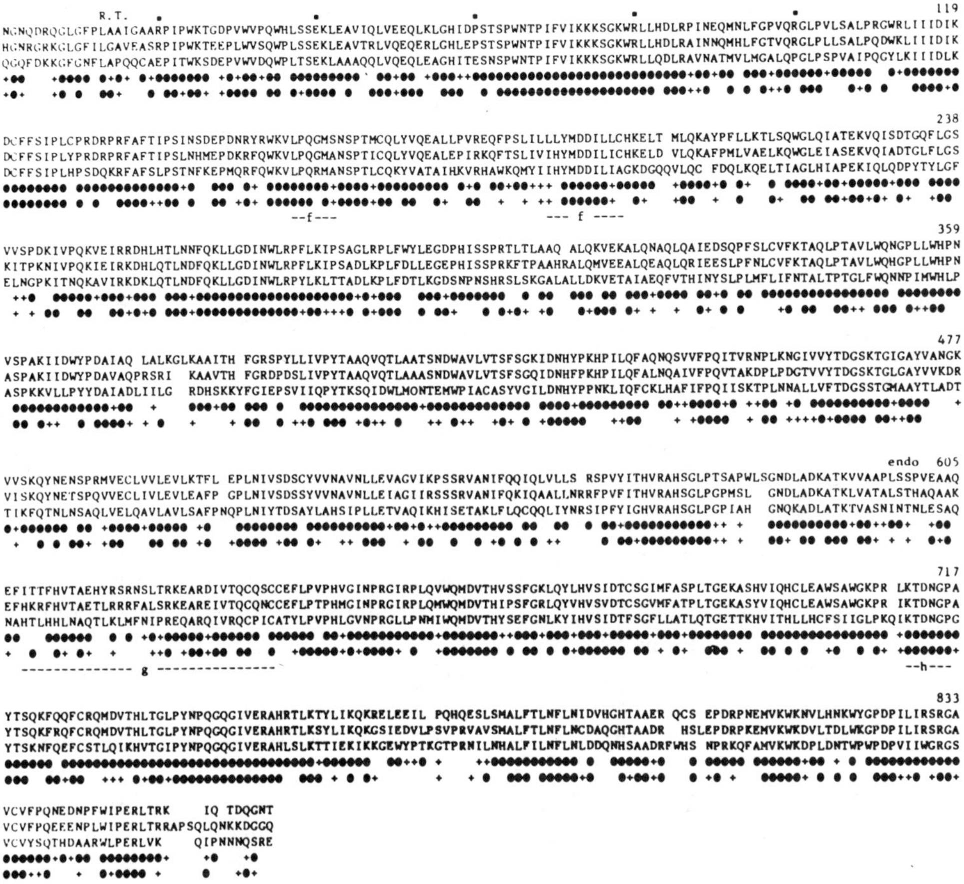

FIG. 4. (*continued*)

to the demands imposed on conventional virus genomes by the need for successful extracellular transmission.

IV. Chromosomal Distribution of IAP-Related Sequences: Association with Other Repetitive Sequence Elements

IAP sequences were demonstrated on mouse L-cell chromosomes by *in situ* hybridization with the specific cDNA prepared from myeloma IAP poly(A) RNA (Lueders *et al.*, 1977). Grains appeared over many chromosomes. There was no evidence of preferential localization of grains in centromeric areas. Because L cells have many chromosomal rearrangements, an analysis of the grain distribution was not made.

The distribution of IAP-related sequences in both mouse and Syrian hamster chromosomes has more recently been determined by *in situ* hybridization with radiolabeled probes derived from cloned IAP genes of the corresponding species (Kuff *et al.*, 1986a). Multiple IAP sequences were found on all chromosomes of both species. Because of the favorable organization of heterochromatic and euchromatic regions in hamster chromosomes, it was possible to show that over 50% of the IAP sequences in the hamster genome are in large blocks of noncentromeric, constitutive heterochromatin. The average concentration of IAP sequences per unit chromosome length in these regions was 5-fold greater than in euchromatic regions. The other dispersed IAP sequences showed marked local variations in concentration, and both discrete foci and large grain clusters were observed as well as regions apparently lacking IAP sequences.

The distribution of IAP-related sequences in Syrian hamster chromosomes resembles that of certain middle repetitive transposable elements, including *copia*, in *Drosophila* chromosomes. *In situ* hybridization has shown that many of these elements are concentrated in the chromocentric heterochromatin, with other individual members dispersed at discrete polymorphic loci on the chromosome arms (Pardue and Dawid, 1981; Spradling and Rubin, 1981; Dowsett and Young, 1982). *Drosophila* chromosomes also have regions of interstitial or intercalary heterochromatin, and these too contain clustered assortments of mobile repetitive elements (Ananiev *et al.*, 1978; Tchurikov *et al.*, 1980). The sequestering of mobile elements in heterochromatin may reflect a biological selection favoring the fixation of newly inserted elements in regions containing relatively few active genetic loci (see Hilliker *et al.*, 1980).

IAP sequences appeared to be more evenly distributed over the mouse chromosomes, although some prominent variations in grain concentrations were observed (Kuff *et al.*, 1986a). Mouse chromosomes do not have large blocks of noncentromeric heterochromatin favorable for *in situ* localization. However, there is other evidence that many IAP elements in this species are also localized in clusters of repetitive sequences and that the number of potentially active IAP elements may thus be restricted by the preferential location of the sequences in genetically inert regions of the genome.

Most mouse genomic clones that contain type II IAP elements also have other repetitive sequences (Lueders, 1987). Eleven of twelve type II IAP clones contained the 3′ ends of L1 elements (Voliva *et al.*, 1983). In addition, 14 of 51 genomic clones containing type I IAP elements reacted with a probe from the 3′ end of the L1 element. The repeats are found in both the 5′ and 3′ flanking regions (Lueders, 1987).

Five of seven clones containing a newly identified mouse repetitive sequence present at approximately 200 copies per haploid genome also contained type II IAP sequences, a finding suggesting a specific association between type II elements and this repeat as well (Lueders, 1987).

Sequences from the 3′ region of an L1 element were also found by Yang *et al.* (1986) in the region between two IAP elements in a genomic clone originally selected by Ono *et al.* (1980). The unsuspected presence of the L1 sequence in this position had led to an earlier report of homology between the IAP LTR and a mouse "*Eco*RI satellite" (Brown and Hwang, 1982).

V. IAP Component Proteins

IAPs assemble at the endoplasmic reticulum membranes and bud into the cisternal cavities; they remain within the microsomal vesicles when cells are disrupted by homogenization. Efficient liberation of particles was achieved by subjecting microsome suspensions to mechanical shear in the presence of a carefully controlled amount of Triton X-100 (Kuff *et al.*, 1968); the particles were then purified by two cycles of sedimentation and isopycnic banding (ϱ = 1.22 g/cm^3) in sucrose density gradients. A-particles extracted by this method retained their characteristic inner and outer shells (Kuff *et al.*, 1968; Wivel *et al.*, 1973). The isolated fraction consisted of 80% protein, 14% phospholipid, and 5–6% RNA. Yields of 100–300 μg of IAP protein can be obtained per gram wet weight of particle-rich tissue such as the MOPC-104E myeloma.

Liberation of IAPs has also been achieved with nitrogen cavitation (Nissen-Meyer *et al.*, 1979). The latter procedure offers the advantages of avoiding any possible effects of detergent exposure on the IAPs. The proportion of IAP-specific high-molecular-weight RNA in particles liberated by nitrogen cavitation was as good as or somewhat better than in particles obtained with the detergent technique. Sonication of microsomes (10 kc at 0–5°C in a well-type sonicator) was also used to release IAPs for assay of reverse transcriptase activity in particles prepared without detergent (Wilson and Kuff, 1972).

The outer IAP shell is formed by the endoplasmic reticulum membrane during assembly of the particle. No IAP-specific envelope protein has been detected, and there is no evidence that IAP-encoded proteins contribute to this shell. The electron-dense inner IAP shell is composed of a 73-kDa *gag*-equivalent protein, with minor amounts of other structurally related polypeptides (Wivel *et al.*, 1973; Marciani and Kuff, 1973). A reverse transcriptase activity is tightly associated with the inner shell (Wilson and Kuff, 1972). Myeloma-derived IAPs may be treated with sodium dodecyl sulfate (SDS) to remove the outer membrane, leaving a still-particulate inner shell in which the proteins are held together by inter-molecular disulfide bonds (Wivel *et al.*, 1973). These "SDS cores" are easily solubilized in the presence of SDS by sulfhydryl compounds such as 2-mercaptoethanol or dithiothreitol and provide a convenient source of IAP structural proteins.

A. Gag Proteins

1. *Biochemical Properties*

A 73-kDa protein (p73) was identified as the major structural protein in the inner cores isolated from three myelomas and a neuroblastoma tissue culture line (Wivel *et al.*, 1973). Polyvalent rabbit antisera prepared against myeloma particles that had been treated with deoxycholate to remove most of the outer shell fixed complement and reacted in immunodiffusion assays with IAP proteins that had been solubilized by disulfide reduction in the presence of SDS (Kuff *et al.*, 1972). Antigenic activity was shown to be associated with p73; and the antisera reacted with IAPs prepared from other mouse tumors and with crude extracts of IAP-producing but not IAP-negative cells. Subsequently, rabbit antisera have been prepared by injection of chromatographically or electrophoretically purified p73 prepared from SDS-washed particles. These antisera have been useful in radioimmunoassays (Kuff *et al.*, 1980), immunoprecipitation of labeled cell extracts (Kuff and Fewell, 1985), immunoblotting, and immunocytochemistry at both the light and electron microscopic levels (Leiter and Kuff, 1984). Attempts to obtain monoclonal antibodies against p73 in mouse or rat-mouse hybridomas have been unsuccessful, possibly because the simultaneous production of IAPs and antibodies against the major IAP protein present some difficulties for the cells (IAPs are abundantly produced in mouse hybridomas).

Antisera against IAPs do not react with purified Rauscher or Moloney MuLV, with MMTV, or with extracts of mouse JLS-V9 cells productively infected with Rauscher MuLV (Kuff *et al.*, 1972).

IAP inner shell proteins are difficultly soluble: SDS or guanidine thiocyanate are required to overcome the self-associative properties of p73. Triton X-100, NP-40, or deoxycholate are ineffective in this respect. The IAP proteins from two mouse myelomas (MOPC-104E and RPC-20) and a neuroblastoma cell line (F1007) were fractionated by gel chromatography in the presence of SDS (Marciani and Kuff, 1973). The main component in each core had an apparent molecular weight of 73,000 in SDS–polyacrylamide gel electrophoresis (SDS–PAGE). The amino acid compositions of p73 from the two myelomas were essentially identical. A total residue number of 663 was calculated, corresponding to a molecular weight of 73,660. Chemical assays for sialic acid and reducing sugars were negative under conditions that would detect one residue per molecule of p73. A small amount of glucosamine comigrated with p73 on SDS–PAGE after metabolic labeling for 24 hr.

The amino-terminal group of p73 was identified as arginine by dansylation and analysis on silica-gel thin-layer chromatography (Marciani and Kuff, 1974). The yield was not calculated, and it is possible that blocked amino-terminal groups were also present. Myristylation of p73 was not detected (Schultz, Fewell, and Kuff, unpublished observation), a result consistent with the absence of glycine in the penultimate amino acid position. p73 is phosphorylated on both serine and threonine residues, with serine predominating: no phosphotyrosine was detected (our unpublished observation). Lopo and Calarco (1981) have reported phosphorylation of p73 during the stage-specific appearance of IAPs in early mouse embryos.

IAP cores contain lesser amounts of proteins with apparent molecular weights of 100,000, 45,000, and 30,000 (Marciani and Kuff, 1973, 1974). The two smaller components were heterogeneous in both SDS and phenol-urea-acetic acid PAGE (p100 was not examined). They shared all of the tryptic peptides of p73, gave reactions of immunological identity with the large protein, and contained amino-terminal arginine (Marciani and Kuff, 1974). They appear to be mixtures of fragments representing all regions of p73, but whether they are produced by a specific processing enzyme or by nonspecific proteolysis during turnover of the particles is not known. Marciani and Kuff (1974) suggested a possible repetitive structure for p73, but this has not been confirmed by sequence analysis (Mietz *et al.*, 1987).

The higher molecular weight proteins of IAPs have not been isolated in biochemically usable quantities. However, when cells such as the N4 neuroblastoma and normal thymus are labeled for 4 hr in culture with [^{35}S]methionine, protein components with molecular weights between 114,000 and 120,000 can be immunoprecipitated (together with p73) from cytoplasmic extracts and crude particle preparations with antiserum against p73 (Kuff and Fewell, 1985). In contrast to p73, which is tightly bound in the IAPs themselves, a significant proportion of the 114- to 120-kDa proteins (p114–120) can be solubilized with Triton X-100 or NP-40 (our unpublished observations), and this easily solubilized fraction turns over more rapidly than the fraction that remains associated with IAPs.

Tryptic peptide maps of [^{35}S]methionine-labeled p73 and p120 from neuroblastoma cells were compared: p120 contained most of the met-peptides of p73 plus additional peptides consistent with its higher molecular weight (Kuff and Fewell, 1985). The p114–120 group of proteins are now known to represent *gag–pol* fusion products encoded by 5.4-kb transcripts of type IΔ1 IAP elements (Pikó *et al.*, 1984; Wujcik *et al.*, 1984; Kuff and Fewell, 1985; Kuff *et al.*, 1986).

2. *Synthesis and Assembly*

IAP p73 was detected on membrane-bound polyribosomes isolated from MOPC-104E cells but not on free polyribosomes (Lueders, 1976). In cultured neuroblastoma cells, newly formed p73 became associated with the membranes in a Triton X-100:EDTA insoluble form within 2 min after addition of radioactive label to the medium, the shortest time period examined (Lueders and Kuff, 1975). The pool of soluble nonparticulate p73, if it existed, was too small to be detected by direct antigen assay or in pulse–chase experiments. Components of about 110 kDa, 46 kDa, and 35 kDa were labeled and incorporated into detergent-insoluble (particulate) form with the same kinetics as p73. Pulse–chase experiments provided no evidence these components were either precursors or products of the main protein within the time frame of the experiment (30 min).

p73 represented about 1.2% of total cell protein synthesis in both growing and near-stationary phase neuroblastoma cultures. IAP protein turned over in growing cells at a rate of 60% in 24 hr, whereas only 20% of the general cell protein was lost in this period, partly through transfer of labeled protein to the medium. No labeled IAP protein could be detected in the extracellular phase. It was concluded that the particles undergo an entirely intracellular cycle of formation and decay (Lueders and Kuff, 1975).

At the electron microscopic level, IAP proteins begin to accumulate in electron-dense patches on the cytoplasmic surfaces of rough-surfaced endoplasmic reticulum in regions that are locally devoid of ribosomes. The patches grow by lateral accretion, forming spherical buds with electron-lucent cores and intruding into the cisternae (Fig. 5). In the process, the particles acquire an outer shell composed of the reticulum unit membrane. Although the mature particles appear to be free in the cisternae, a study of serial sections from IAP-rich rhabdomyosarcoma and myeloma tumors showed that nearly all IAPs remained attached to the membranes at some point (Perk and Dahlberg, 1974). The authors regarded this attachment as

FIG. 5. Morphology of intracisternal particles observed in mouse and Syrian hamster cells. A. Intracisternal A-particles (IAPs) in the cisternae of the endoplasmic reticulum (ER) in the BALB/c myeloma RPC-20. Ribosomes are associated with some regions of the ER membrane but are characteristically absent from membranes in the immediate vicinity of budding particles. Inset: An individual IAP, showing an outer shell continuous with the ER unit membrane, a dense inner shell, and an electron-lucent core region. B. Intracisternal R-particles in the cytoplasm of an SV40-transformed Syrian hamster BHK-21 cell. Various incomplete, presumably budding forms can be seen. Very few ribosomes are associated with the ER membranes; however, a large polyribosome is located in the cytoplasmic matrix near two budding particles. Inset: An individual particle, showing the outer unit membrane, radial spokes, and an almost totally dense inner core (reprinted from Zeigel *et al.*, 1969). C. Intracisternal particles with radial configuration in cytoplasm of Ki-MSV-transformed BALB 3T3 cells treated with 5-azacytidine. These particles resemble the so-called epsilon particles found in mouse embryos. A typical IAP is seen at lower left. Photomicrograph provided by J. Lasneret (Lasneret *et al.*., 1981). D. Intracisternal epsilon particles in the cytoplasm of an early AKR mouse embryo. Inset shows general similarity in organization to the hamster R-particle, but this particle is a smaller size (reprinted from Yotsuyanagi and Szollosi, 1981). The bars indicate 100 nm; approximate magnifications are 70,000 for main panels and 180,000 for insets.

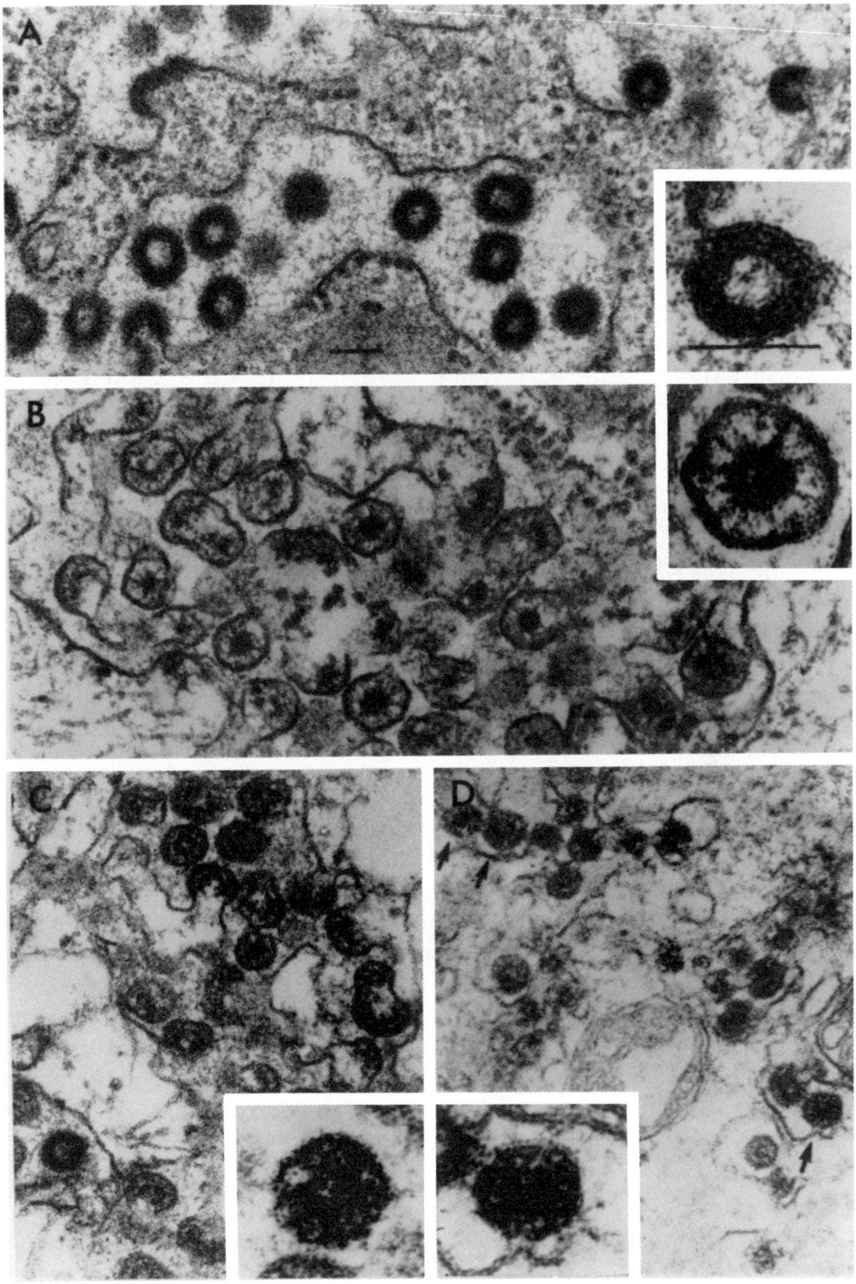
A
B
C
D

a failure to complete the budding process, which in turn reflected defectiveness in some stages of assembly or maturation. They suggested that the connection with the cisternal membrane could be related to the fact that IAPs do not appear in the extracellular phase. It is not known whether IAPs in all cell types retain this type of connection.

The structure of p73 predicted from the nucleotide sequence of both genomic and cDNA clones shows a hydrophobic amino-terminal segment followed by a strongly charged α-helical region (Mietz *et al.*, 1987). The hydrophobic leader lacks the amino-proximal positive charge characteristic of the usual secretory signal sequence peptides and has an atypical signal sequence cleavage site (von Heijne, 1983) preceding the first arginine at residue 27 (Fig. 4). We speculate that newly synthesized p73 associates with the endoplasmic reticulum through the usual pathway of signal sequence recognition but that cleavage of the signal peptide is slow relative to the process of IAP assembly. As a result, the IAP protein is anchored on the cytosolic side of the reticulum membrane and the accreting molecules self-assemble by high-affinity (salt- and detergent-resistant) interactions that are not understood in detail. The inner particle shell can be further stabilized by formation of intermolecular disulfide bonds. The outer unit membrane is tightly apposed to the inner particle shell and only incompletely removed by detergents such as Triton X-100 and sodium deoxycholate. There is no evidence for viral-specific proteins in the outer membrane; an 80-kDa protein prominent in the Triton-resistant membrane material is also detected in the microsomal membranes of tissues such as liver that are devoid of IAPs. Aspects of IAP internal structure were studied by Malech and Wivel (1976b) in IAPs prepared for electron microscopy by critical point drying.

B. Reverse Transcriptase

1. *Enzymatic Properties*

An IAP-associated DNA polymerase activity with some properties of reverse transcriptase was described by Wilson and Kuff (1972). The activity was tightly bound and resisted solubilization by nondenaturing detergents or high salt (Wilson *et al.*, 1974). The enzyme had a marked preference for Mg^{2+} over Mn^{2+}. Full activity required detergent treatment of the particles with Triton X-100 or NP-40. It was possible to develop reaction conditions that distinguished between the IAP-associated activity and other cellular DNA polymerases and to show that this activity cofractionated rigorously with IAP-specific antigen during particle purification from the myeloma MOPC-104E (Wilson *et al.*, 1973, 1974). Under ionic conditions optimal for activity toward added poly(rA)·oligo(dT)(200 m*M* KCl, 12.5 m*M* MgCl), the activity of isolated IAPs toward endogenous RNA was approximately 1000-fold less (Table I). No endogenous reaction was detected

TABLE I

REVERSE TRANSCRIPTASE ACTIVITIES OF IAP AND MuLV

Source[a]	[K+] (mM)	[Cation^{2+}] (mM)	Activity with indicated template–primers[a]: Poly(rA)·oligo(dT)	Poly(rC)·oligo(dG)	Activated DNA	None: Endogenous activity	Reference
IAP MOPC-104E	200	Mg, 12.5	300–350	1.5	0	0.2–0.6	Wilson and Kuff (1972)
	40	Mg, 12.5	65	1.5	0.5	0.2	Wilson *et al.* (1974)
	40	Mn, 1.5	13	3.5	0.7	0	Bohn and Wilson (1974)
	75	Mg, 10				0.2	Yang and Wivel (1974)
	75	Mn, 0.8	2–4.5	1.5		0.5(30°C)	Yang and Wivel (1974)
	75	?				0.2	Yang and Wivel (1976)
IAP Neuroblastoma	75	Mn, 0.8				0.3	Yang and Wivel (1974)
IAP MOPC-104E	200	Mg, 15	1	8		0.1[c]	Wong-Staal *et al.* (1975)
IAP FLOPC-1	40(Na)	Mn, 1.0	8[f]	21[f]		2	Krueger (1976)
IAP MOPC-460	200	Mg, 12				11[d]	Robertson *et al.* (1975)
	200	Mn, 0.2				17	Robertson *et al.* (1975)
	200	Mg, 10	64			5.5[e]	Robertson *et al.* (1976)
MAV	200	Mg, 10	60			5	Robertson *et al.* (1976)
MuLV Rauscher	40	Mg, 12.5	300	31	80	0	Wilson and Kuff (1972)
	50	Mn, 1.5	4900	42	16	21	Wilson and Kuff (1972)
	40	Mg, 12		1620	43	15	Spiegelman *et al.* (1970)
MuLV Kirsten	40	Mn, 1		7		8	Krueger (1976)

[a]Activities are expressed as picomoles of labeled nucleotide incorporated per minute per milligram protein at 37°C.
[b]MOPC and FLOPC are myelomas of BALB/c mice. MAV is an extracellular virus from MOPC-460.
[c,d,e]Product hybridized to MuLV RNA to the extent of 15, 50, and 30%, respectively.
[f]Calculated from ratio of exogenous to endogenous reactions.

under conditions favorable for type C MuLV activity (40 m*M* KCl, 1.5 m*M* MnCl). IAP-associated polymerase activity was not affected by an antiserum that inhibited MuLV reverse transcriptase by 75%.

IAPs purified from neuroblastoma cells had exogenous activities comparable to those of myeloma-derived IAPs (Yang and Wivel, 1974, 1976; Yang *et al.*, 1975). Very low endogenous reactions were seen with either Mg^{2+} or Mn^{2+} as the divalent cation. Mn^{2+} was preferred over Mg^{2+}. The endogenous reaction was sensitive to added ribonuclease and was dependent on detergent activation for maximal activity. The reaction products were analyzed by isopycnic banding in cesium sulfate gradients: at 5 min, incorporated radioactivity was distributed almost equally between the RNA and RNA:DNA densities; by 10 min, 75% of the label banded as single-stranded DNA, and at 30 min, the shift to this position was complete. The average size of the endogenous product was estimated at about 350 nucleotides, and 90% could be hybridized to 35 S IAP RNA. The endogenous products of IAP reverse transcriptase activity were also examined by Wong-Staal *et al.* (1975), who confirmed the association of newly formed DNA with the IAP RNA.

The enzyme activity in IAPs liberated by sonication or nitrogen cavitation has not been adequately studied. However, in one case, neither endogenous nor poly(rA)·oligo(dT)-primed activities were higher in IAPs released from myeloma microsomes by sonication rather than by the conventional detergent-facilitated shearing (Wilson and Kuff, 1972).

The endogenous activities detected by all of the preceding authors were well below 1 pmol per min per mg IAP protein, far less than the endogenous activities associated with the type C MuLV (Table I). On the other hand, considerably higher values were ascribed to IAPs isolated from cultured FLOPC-1 and MOPC-460 myeloma lines (Krueger, 1976; Robertson *et al.*, 1975, 1976). The endogenous reaction products from both IAP preparations showed significant hybridization (30–50%) to MuLV RNAs. The endogenous activity associated with the IAP fraction from MOPC-460 was the same as that of the extracellular particles produced by this tumor (Robertson *et al.*, 1976). Weimann and co-workers (Schmidt *et al.*, 1977; Weimann *et al.*, 1978; Weimann, 1985) have reported that myeloma IAPs contain a Mn^{2+}-dependent reverse transcriptase fully inhibited by antiserum against the MuLV enzyme. Particles with properties typical of type C virions were found in culture and ascites fluids from myeloma and hybridoma cells, and electron microscopy showed particles budding from the plasma membranes with the enveloped type A morphology characteristic of immature type C virions (Bernhard, 1960). We suggest that the "IAP-associated" endogenous reverse transcriptase activities above 0.5 to 1 pmol per min per mg protein at 37°C (Table I) were due to contamination of the fractions with components of MuLV and/or MMTV (in the case of MOPC-460).

The nontransforming infectious M432 retrovirus of *Mus cervicolor* contains IAP-related genetic information for the carboxyl-terminal portion of *gag* and essentially all of *pol* (Callahan *et al.*, 1981). Thus, the 70-kDa Mg^{2+}-dependent reverse transcriptase of M432 (Callahan *et al.*, 1977) is presumably structurally related to that associated with IAPs. Mice carrying an M432-producing tumor develop antibodies that inhibit the viral transcriptase; however, these antibodies did not inhibit the activity of IAPs from MOPC-104E (S. Wilson, personal communication).

The very strong physical association between reverse transcriptase activity and the IAPs is unusual among conventional retroviruses. An impaired protease function, indicated by the failure to process the IAP 73-kDa *gag* protein, might also leave the *gag–pol* precursor intact and tightly associated with the assembled particles by virtue of its *gag* domain. Further progress in characterizing the bound IAP reverse transcriptase will depend critically on the development of nondenaturing methods for solubilizing the particles.

2. *Synthesis of Provirus*

Closed circular proviral forms were not detected in extracts of the MOPC-315 myeloma, even though a specific type II IAP element was shown to have undergone major amplification in the genome of this cell line (Shen-Ong and Cole, 1984). Attempts to demonstrate free provirus in the IAP-rich N4 neuroblastoma cell line were also unsuccessful (Feenstra *et al.*, 1986). However, Grigoryan *et al.* (1985) detected small amounts of closed circular IAP-related DNA cobanding with added SV40 marker in ethidium bromide–cesium chloride gradients when they analyzed Hirt extracts (Hirt, 1969) of Ehrlich ascites carcinoma cells. Treatment of this fraction with *Eco*RI produced a single fragment of about 7 kb, which hybridized with DNA of a cloned IAP element. The *Eco*RI-digested DNA was cloned into lambda phage. One clone was extensively studied: the IAP element was 6.4 kb in length, extending from the *Eco*RI site at MIA14 map position 0.96 through the remaining body of the element and through a single LTR followed by the 5′ primer-binding site, ending at the conserved *Eco*RI site at MIA14 map position 0.48 (see Fig. 1). The presence of three internal *Eco*RI sites in the cloned sample was inconsistent with the 7-kb linear form produced by *Eco*RI digestion of the banded, closed circular DNA. This discrepancy suggests that the cloned sequence represented a minor fraction of the IAP-homologouus DNA in the banded fraction.

The difficulty in detecting free IAP-related proviral forms is consistent with the defective endogenous reverse transcriptase function noted earlier (Section V,B,1). Maturation of precursor polypeptides and generation of a fully competent enzyme may occur in a very small fraction of IAPs, which are not detected in the usual assay systems.

C. Integrase

An endonuclease function essential for integration is encoded in the carboxyl-terminal portion of the *pol* gene in conventional retroviruses. This coding region is present in the IAP genome (see Section II,A). An endonuclease activity stimulated by ATP was detected by Nissan-Meyer and Eikhom (1981) in association with IAPs from myeloma MPC-11 cells. The activity fractionated with a 40-kDa protein isolated from proteinase K-treated particles and required detergent for activation. This activity has not yet been shown to be viral-encoded.

D. Envelope

The IAP genome contains sufficient DNA between *pol* and the 3′ LTR to encode an envelope polypeptide of about 40 kDa. However, this region contains multiple conserved stop codons in all three reading frames in every IAP gene thus far sequenced. Thus, the IAP genome lacks a functional envelope gene.

VI. Transmission

IAPs are not known to have an infectious extracellular phase. Early bioassays of cell-free preparations from plasmacytomas were negative (Dalton *et al.*, 1961; Parsons *et al.*, 1961b; Merwin and Redman, 1963). After development of an isolation procedure, large numbers of myeloma-derived IAPs were injected into newborn mice without apparent effect on growth and development of the animals (Kuff *et al.*, 1968). The biological significance of this observation is questionable, however, because detergent used to facilitate particle release could have destroyed infectivity. An attempt to coinfect IAP-negative JLS-V9 cells with MuLV and sonically released myeloma IAPs was also unsuccessful (Kuff *et al.*, 1972). IAPs were taken up in phagocytic vesicles and retained for several days, as judged by electron microscopy, but no evidence of new antigen or particle formation was seen. At the same time, however, CF tests for MuLV became strongly positive in the treated cells. In another study (Minna *et al.*, 1974), JLS-V9 cells were cocultivated with IAP-rich neuroblastoma cells for 20 cell generations and then reisolated by growth in a selective medium; here again, the target cells remained IAP antigen-negative.

Malech and Wivel (1976a) undertook to transfer the IAP-positive phenotype by fusion between cytoplasts derived from IAP-producing cells and whole cells of an IAP-negative line. Cytoplasts were prepared from a chloramphenicol-resistant derivative of the MT-29240 cell line originating from a BALB/c mammary tumor. Recipient chloramphenicol-sensitive, IAP-negative cells were Swiss 3T3-4EF and a clone of feral mouse origin; the

3T3-4EF cells were also bromodeoxyuridine-resistant and HAT-sensitive. In a series of fusions followed by isolation of "cybrid" clones in appropriate selective media, from 50 to 80% of the examined clones were IAP-positive by electron microscopy after 30 to 60 cell generations. IAP numbers were low; the highest titer was one IAP per three cell sections, in contrast to the parent mammary tumor clones containing 20–40 IAP in each cell section. Cocultivation of intact MT-29240 cells with both IAP-negative lines confirmed the lack of horizontal transmission previously noted by Minna *et al.* (1974).

The results of Malech and Wivel were confirmed in a study by Shay and co-workers (1978), who prepared cybrid clones by fusion of cytoplasts of another chloramphenicol-resistant subline of MT-29240 and cells of a HAT-resistant SV40-transformed line of BALB/c 3T3. Again, expression of IAPs in small numbers was a stable phenotype of the cybrid lines.

Yang and Wivel (1979) prepared cDNA by an endogenous reverse transcriptase reaction with IAPs obtained from MT-29240 cells. This cDNA had an average size of about 350 nucleotides and was hybridized to the extent of 90% with either "IAP 35-70 S RNA" (source?) or whole RNA from MT-29240 cells. It showed a negligible reaction with MuLV RNA. Using this cDNA as probe in liquid hybridization assays with DNAs derived from the parental and cybrid clones described in the preceding paragraph (Malech and Wivel, 1976a), the authors detected only one or two copies of "IAP-specific" DNA sequences per haploid genome of the 3T3-4EF recipient cell line and about ten copies per haploid genome in both MT-29240 cells and a cybrid clone derived from fusion of MT-29240 cytoplasts and 3T3-EF cells. A second IAP-negative recipient cell II6C of feral mouse origin had four copies of "IAP-specific sequence," which were not detectably increased in a cybrid clone. A cDNA clone prepared from IAP poly(A) RNA with avian myeloblastosis virus (AMV) reverse transcriptase, as described by Lueders and Kuff (1977), showed no competition with the endogenous cDNA probe in competitive hybridization with MT-29240 cellular DNA. The authors suggested that the two cDNA probes were most likely transcribed from different regions of IAP RNA.

However, there is no evidence that any portion of the IAP genome is represented to the extent of only ten copies in mouse DNA. The endogenous cDNA used in the preceding experiments is a size (350 nucleotides) that would barely extend through the 5′ LTR were it to have initiated on IAP RNA at the usual primer binding site, and there are many hundreds of LTR copies in the mouse genome. Thus, the endogenous probe in the experiment of Yang and Wivel represents a sequence that is not part of the "standard" IAP genome. In the trivial case, the endogenous reaction may have copied an unrelated cellular sequence fortuitously encapsidated in the IAPs of MT-29240. A more interesting possibility is that the endogenous reaction in these particles was primed on a rare IAP-related retroviral variant that is effective for integration and expression in the cybrid clones. It would seem important to test this hypothesis, because an IAP variant of the type described might be a useful vector for integration of new sequences into recipient cells.

IAP expression has been observed in a human osteosarcoma tumor line serially passaged in nude mice (Tralka *et al.*, 1983). Because IAPs are otherwise not known to be produced in human cells, nor are the mouse particles known to be infectious for this species, the authors suggested that IAPs may have been introduced by fusion with mouse cells during the tumor's passage history and that particle expression then became a stable phenotypic property of the tumor cells. Although it was not formally demonstrated that the IAPs were of mouse origin, this suggestion is plausible.

VII. IAP-Related RNAs

A. A-Particle-Associated RNAs

During the initial isolation of IAPs from MOPC-104E solid myeloma tissue (Kuff *et al.*, 1968), the particle preparation was found to contain approximately 5% RNA, of which about half was shown by appropriate reconstruction experiments to represent contamination by microsomal components. The IAP-associated RNA sedimented in sucrose gradients as a broad 29 S peak. Yang and Wivel (1973; see also Yang *et al.*, 1975) examined the RNAs of IAPs isolated from both MOPC-104E and a neuroblastoma cell line N18 and detected minute amounts of 70 S RNA mixed with ribosomal and 4 S species. Wong-Staal *et al.* (1975) found that 30–40% of the RNA in IAPs from the N18 cell line was polyadenylated, with tracts approximately 220 nucleotides in length. The whole particle RNA sedimented in heterodisperse fashion with a peak at 28 S; but the polyadenylated fraction contained a major heat-stable 30–35 S component when analyzed by gel electrophoresis. Robertson *et al.* (1975) examined the RNA in IAPs isolated from the MOPC-460 myeloma. Most of the RNA was small (5–15 S), but minute amounts of 70 S and 35 S components were detected. Krueger (1976) found that IAPs from the FLOPC-1 myeloma also contained a heat-sensitive 60–70 S RNA demonstrable by gel electrophoresis. The IAP-associated RNA contained poly(A) tracts approximately 100 nucleotides long. Half of the DNA products of the endogenous reverse transcriptase reactions in IAPs from both MOPC-460 and FLOPC-1 hybridized with MuLV RNA, a reaction indicating that the IAP preparations from these sources were significantly contaminated with type C retroviral components.

Lueders *et al.* (1977) isolated a probe for RNA sequences specifically associated with mouse IAPs. Particles were purified from MOPC-104E tumor tissue and the particle-associated poly(A) RNA was reverse transcribed with AMV DNA polymerase. The kinetics of hybridization of the [3H]-labeled cDNA with its template RNA revealed an abundant class of sequences constituting about 55% of the total IAP-associated RNA. The fraction of cDNA representing this abundant class was isolated by selective low-C_rt hybridization and used to quantify the sequences in other RNA preparations. These sequences were manyfold more concentrated in IAP-rich tumors than in cell lines devoid of IAPs or in normal liver. In MOPC-104E, the sequences constituted nearly 8% of the total cytoplasmic poly(A) RNA and were concentrated 40-fold in the isolated IAPs as compared to the crude microsome fraction from which they were derived.

High-molecular-weight poly(A) RNAs prepared from IAPs of MOPC-104E solid tumor and cultured neuroblastoma (N4) cells were tested for their capacity to code for IAP-pecific protein in an *in vitro* translation system (Paterson *et al.*, 1978). N4 IAPs contained two major species with sizes of 35 S and 32 S (7.2 and 5.4 kb, respectively; see Fig. 6). MOPC-104E IAPs contained very small amounts of these RNAs; the major component was 28 S (4.0 kb; see Fig. 6) with lesser amounts of 4.7-kb and 3.5-kb species. The two N4 RNAs were fractionated on sucrose gradients and tested separately for their coding capacity. The 7.2-kb species directed synthesis of a 73-kDa product that had a methionine-containing tryptic peptide map identical to that of the authentic *in vivo*-labeled IAP structural protein. The 5.4-kb RNA coded for a heterogeneous group of polypeptides with a concentration of products in the region of 110–120 kDa. In subsequent experiments, the 5.4-kb RNA was shown to code for a discrete component of 120 kDa that was immunoprecipitable with antiserum prepared against myeloma p73 (see Section V,A). The 4-kb RNA fraction from MOPC-104E IAPs also encoded a 73-kDa product identified as the IAP protein by its methionine-labeled tryptic peptides (Paterson *et al.*, 1978). However, the peptide map of this product differed in several details from the map of p73 encoded by the N4 7.2-kb RNA. The genetic structure of the RNA that encodes the myeloma p73 structural protein is not yet understood. It may be a quantitatively minor component, because the 4-kb RNA fraction consists largely of transcripts from type II IAP genes (Fig. 6) from which most of the p73-coding sequences are deleted (Fig. 1; Shen-Ong and Cole, 1984).

The larger RNA species was sized at 7.2 kb by electrophoretic mobility in denaturing gels with known DNA standards. R-loop analysis showed it to be colinear with several genomic 7-kb IAP elements (Kuff *et al.*, 1981). The displacement loops averaged 6.7 ± 0.5 kb and the poly(A) tails 0.2 kb, giving a total estimated size of 6.9 ± 0.5 kb. The calculated length of a full-size transcript from the sequenced IAP element MIA14 (Mietz *et al.*, 1987) is 6810 bp, which would give a total size of about 7000 bp when the poly(A) tail is included.

Among thymus glands of various inbred mouse strains, there is a close corrrespondence between the levels of 5.4-kb IAP-related RNA and synthesis

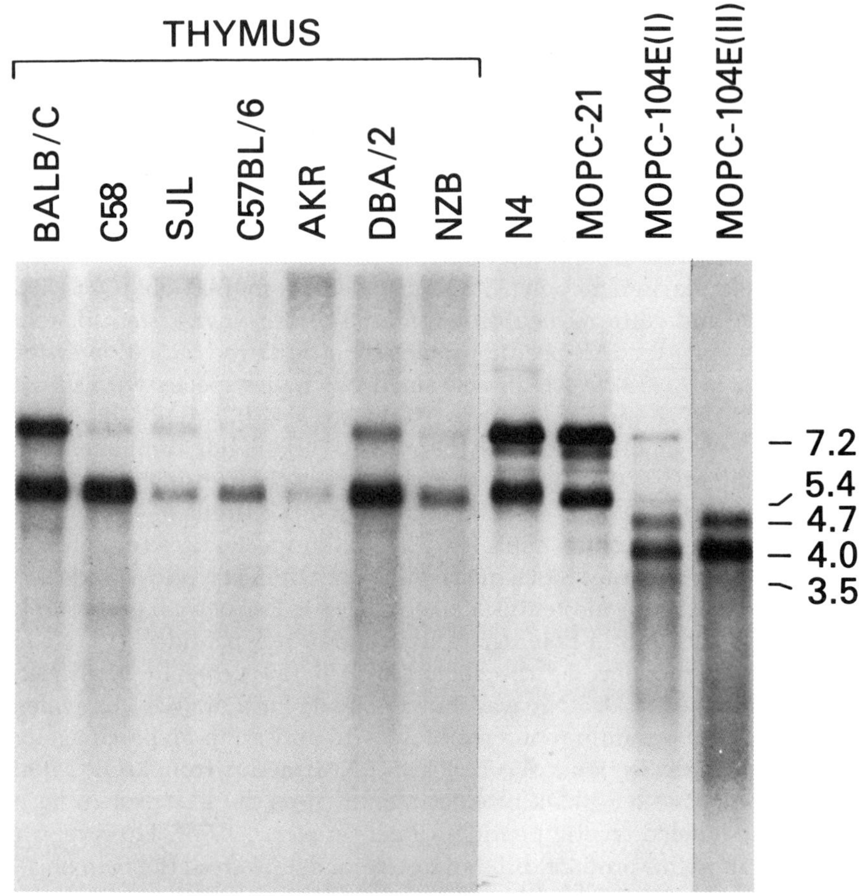

FIG. 6. IAP-specific transcripts in poly(A) RNA from mouse thymus and tumor cells. RNA (4 μg) from thymuses of 1-month-old mice of the indicated inbred strains and RNA (0.5 μg) from N4 neuroblastoma and MOPC-21 and MOPC-104E myelomas were hybridized with pMIA1 probe. MOPC-104E RNA was also hybridized with the AIIins probe specific for type II elements. Sizes of the RNAs are given in kilobases (data rearranged from Kuff and Fewell, 1985).

of immunoprecipitable protein in the size range of 115–120 kDa (Kuff and Fewell, 1985). As noted earlier, this capacity has been demonstrated directly by *in vitro* translation of the isolated RNA. The size of this RNA, about 1.8 kb less than the full-size transcripts, suggests that it may be transcribed from the most numerous type IΔ element, type IΔ1, which carries a 1.9-kb deletion encompassing the 3′ portion of *gag* and a 5′ portion of the *pol* gene regions (Fig. 1). The cDNA clone 10.2 isolated from the T cell hybridoma represents such an element: it has an open reading frame of 1057 codons that specifies a *gag–pol* fusion protein of about 116 kDa (Kuff *et al.*, 1986b).

When molecular probes for IAP sequences became available, the predominant 29 S RNA in both MOPC-104E and MOPC-315 myeloma IAPs were shown to be transcripts of deleted genomic elements (Ono *et al.*, 1980), which are now referred to as type IIB (Shen-Ong and Cole, 1982; see Section II,C). In a subsequent study, RNA from seven myelomas was analyzed using a type II-specific probe (Shen-Ong and Cole, 1984); type II RNAs of 3.8 kb were abundant in five of these myelomas. Low levels of type I transcripts were also said to be present in these cell lines. MOPC-21 is an example of a myeloma with very little if any type II RNA and abundant 7.2- and 5.4-kb type I transcripts (Fig. 6).

The IAP-related RNAs in MOPC-315 myeloma were examined by Wujcik *et al.* (1984), who detected species of 7.2, 5.3, and 3.8 kb. Using as probes fragments derived from different portions of a cloned full-size type I IAP element, they carried out a series of hybridizations, which they interpreted to indicate that the 3.8-kb RNA species might be formed by splicing from a larger transcript. Alternatively, they suggested that the 3.8-kb RNA could be derived from the type IIΔ gene (now IIB) if the estimates of LTR and poly(A) tail lengths were modified.

Our own measurements using DNA restriction fragments rather than ribosomal RNAs as size standards indicate that the major type IIB transcripts are 4.0 kb in length (see Fig. 6), precisely the size expected from the known structure of the IIB elements (Shen-Ong and Cole, 1984; Lueders and Mietz, 1986). In addition to the 4.0-kb type IIB RNA species, IAPs from MOPC-104E contain small amounts of a 4.7-kb type IIA transcript and a 3.5-kb species of unknown origin.

B. Transcription of IAP Genes

The 7.2-kb transcripts in neuroblastoma IAP were shown to initiate and terminate within the 5′ and 3′ LTRs, respectively, by heteroduplex mapping (Kuff *et al.*, 1981). Cole *et al.* (1982) confirmed this for type II transcripts in two myelomas—MOPC-315 and TEPC-15—using S1 digestion of RNA:DNA hybrids and cDNA-primed extension. RNA synthesized *in vitro* by isolated MOPC-315 nuclei using $[^{35}S]\gamma$ATP was also used as a hybridization probe against restriction digests of cloned IAP elements to localize the transcription initiation site in a 5′ LTR (Wujcik *et al.*, 1984). The studies of Cole *et al.* (1982) and Wujcik *et al.* (1984) suggested the 5′ termini of IAP RNAs were located near an invariant *Pst*I site (approximate nt 155) in the LTR. A more precise determination located the origin in a cloned transcriptionally active LTR at a G residue (nt 218) about 30 bp downstream from the TATA box (Lueders *et al.*, 1984). IAP transcripts terminate in the usual retroviral fashion in the 3′ LTR following a canonical AATAAA polyadenylation signal and have poly(A) tails of approximately 200 nucleotides (Wong-Staal *et al.*, 1975; Kuff *et al.*, 1981).

Wujcik *et al.* (1984) showed that transcription of IAP sequences in isolated myeloma nuclei was sensitive to low levels of α-amanitin (2μg/ml), an observation indicating that IAP transcription is carried out by RNA polymerase II. We have confirmed this observation (W. Kastern, E. L. Kuff, and K. K. Lueders, unpublished observation). No evidence for splicing of IAP transcripts has been obtained.

The promoter activity of cloned IAP LTRs has been studied in two laboratories. Lueders *et al.* (1984) showed that the 5′ LTR of a randomly selected type I genomic element, MIA14 (Lueders and Kuff, 1980) was active both in transiently transfected monkey and mouse cells and in permanently transformed rat cells. For the transient assay, the LTRs were linked to the chloramphenicol acetyltransferase (CAT) gene in a plasmid vector (pSVOCAT) and transfected into both monkey (CV-1 and COS7) and mouse (L and NIH 3T3) cells. The 5′ LTR promoted CAT activity in monkey cells 5–8 times more effectively than in the mouse lines. The IAP LTR was 20 and 7 times more active in CV-1 and COS7 cells, respectively, than was the MSV LTR in an equivalent plasmid construct; however, in mouse cells, the MSV LTR was 10 times more effective than the IAP LTR. IAP LTR promoter activity was greatly enhanced in monkey cells by the presence of an R-type repetitive sequence element (Lueders and Paterson, 1982) in a near upstream position. Promoter activity of the 5′ LTR in reverse orientation with respect to the CAT gene was also studied: the activity in CV-1 cells was 3% of that shown by the LTR in the proper orientation; essentially no activity was seen in COS7 cells. BRLtk$^-$ rat cells were transfected with a modified construct of MIA14 carrying the herpes *tk* gene, and transformants were selected in HAT medium. S1 analysis using RNA extracted from two clones showed expression of IAP sequences. The start site of the IAP transcripts mapped to the same position in the 5′ LTR in RNAs extracted from both permanently transformed rat cells and transiently transfected monkey cells.

Horowitz *et al.* (1984) examined the promoter activity of the 5′ LTR from an IAP element that had transposed into a c-*mos* gene in the mouse XRPC-24 myeloma. The element had entered in reverse orientation, displacing the 5′ third of the c-*mos* gene; thus, the 5′ LTR lay head to head with the remaining 3′-*mos* coding sequences (see Fig. 8). Although c-*mos* is ordinarily quiescent, the modified gene—designated 3′ rc-*mos*—was actively transcribed and capable of transforming NIH 3T3 cells (Rechavi *et al.*, 1982). The 3′ rc-*mos* mRNA in XRPC-24 was found by S1 mapping to have start sites at two positions, one at the junction of 3′ rc-*mos* and the 5′ LTR, the other ten nucleotides upstream within the LTR (Horowitz *et al.*, 1984). This LTR was cloned, inserted in both orientations into pSVOCAT, and transfected into CV-1 and HIH 3T3 cells. In contrast to the 5′ LTR from IAP element MIA14 (Lueders *et al.*, 1984), promoter activity of the 5′ LTR from the transposed IAP element was similar in both mouse and monkey cells. In CV-1 cells, the activity of the LTR in reverse orientation was 3% of the forward activity (a value in agreement with that of Lueders *et al.* for the MIA14 LTR), and in mouse cells, between 5 and 9%. Thus, two IAP LTRs have been found to have a relatively weak but significant promoter activity in the reverse direction. Horowitz *et al.* point out that a low level of promoter activity could be sufficient to activate rc-*mos in vivo*, citing a personal communication from G. Vande Woude to the effect that no more than ten molecules of *mos*-specific mRNA are present in murine sarcoma virus (MSV)-transformed cells.

Double-stranded RNA homologous to IAP elements represented about 0.004% of the heterogeneous nuclear RNA (hnRNA) of Ehrlich ascites carcinoma cells (Kramerov *et al.*, 1985). This fraction hybridized equally well to separated strands of a cloned IAP element, whereas both nuclear and cytoplasmic poly(A) RNAs reacted with only one strand. The authors examined IAP-related transcripts in the poly(A) RNAs of Ehrlich ascites cells and MOPC-21 myeloma, using probes derived from various regions of a 7-kb cloned IAP element. Their results are not easily interpretable, because they, in contrast to other investigators, described a major 9.5-kb transcript in both cell types and assigned unusual sizes to the other RNAs. The authors' conclusion that some of the RNAs are formed by transcription of a minor undescribed variant of IAP elements awaits confirmation. Questions also arise as to the size assignments of IAP-homologous poly(A) RNAs in a variety of tumor and normal tissues (Grigoryan *et al.*, 1985). It is our belief that the sizing of these components may be systematically too large and that the "9.5 kb" and "6.8 kb" poly(A) RNA species probably correspond to the commonly observed 7.2- and 5.4-kb transcripts of the type I and type IΔ1 elements, respectively (see Figs. 6 and 7).

VIII. Regulation

Various types of normal and transformed cells differ characteristically in both the overall level of IAP-related RNA and in the relative proportions of the different sized transcripts (Lueders and Kuff, 1977; Paterson *et al.*, 1978; Shen-Ong and Cole, 1984; Wujcik *et al.*, 1984; Kuff and Fewell, 1985). With the exception of the thymus in certain inbred strains (Kuff and Fewell, 1985), normal somatic cells have only low levels of IAP transcripts (Fig. 7). IAPs appear often in primary mouse tumors, usually in small numbers, but occasionally in profusion (Kakefuda *et al.*, 1970). Individual transplanted or cultured tumor cell lines often acquire characteristic levels of IAP expression that tend to persist with time. IAP expression is a dominant property

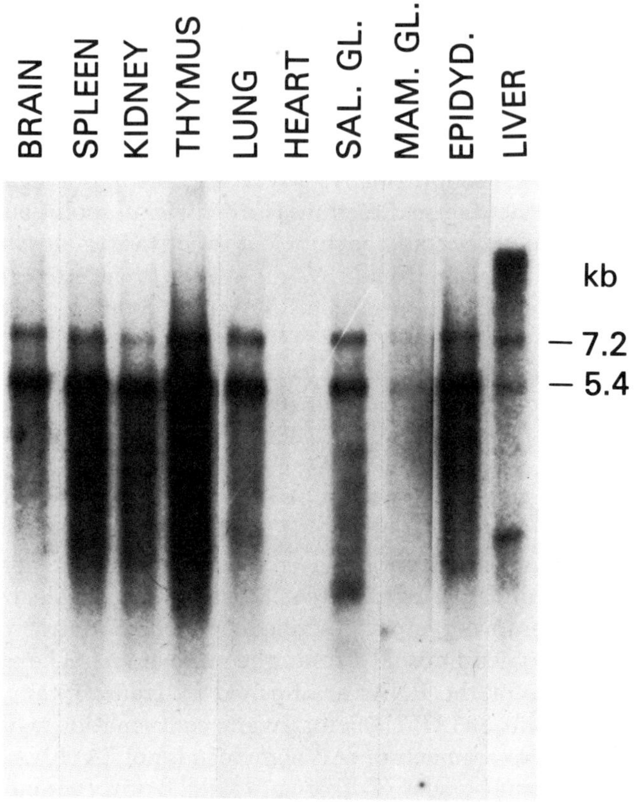

FIG. 7. IAP-transcripts in poly(A) RNAs from normal BALB/cN tissues. Poly(A) RNA (4–5 μg) from the indicated tissues was hybridized with pMIA1 as in Fig. 6. Blots were exposed for 4 days to detect low levels of hybridization (compared with 1 day for the blots in Fig. 6).

when tumor cells are fused with other transformed or normal cells. For example, high levels of IAP antigen production were dominant in cell hybrids between IAP-rich neuroblastoma cells and either IAP-negative normal cells or L-cells with low IAP expression (Minna *et al.*, 1974). IAP production was also maintained in hybrids between Syrian hamster BHK and mouse L-cells until all of the mouse chromosomes had been segregated (Yotsuyanagi and Ephrussi, 1974). The high levels of IAPs and IAP-specific RNAs characteristic of mouse plasmacytomas and many T cell lymphomas are maintained in hybridomas formed by fusions with normal B and T cells (Hawley *et al.*, 1984b; Moore *et al.*, 1986). On the other hand, individual cells within certain populations must differ heritably in their capacity for IAP expression, because it has been possible to establish subclones of cultured cell lines (Kindig and Kirsten, 1967; Hall *et al.*, 1968) or an ascites tumor (Kodama and Kodama, 1973) with different levels of IAPs. To our knowledge, no instance of conversion from an IAP-positive to an IAP-negative state has been reported, except possibly in the special case of certain differentiating embryonal carcinoma lines (see Section XI).

The regulation of IAP expression is not fully understood. We will discuss some of the factors that have been demonstrated or suggested to influence IAP expression.

A. DNA Methylation

Methylation is known to suppress the transcriptional activity of some cellular and viral genes (Razin and Riggs, 1980; Doerfler, 1983), including integrated retroviral elements (see Hsiao *et al.*, 1986, for references; also Jahner and Jaenisch, 1985). We have reviewed under a separate heading (Section XI) studies attempting to relate IAP expression and gene methylation in mouse teratocarcinoma cells. There appears to be no uniform relationship between expression and the methylation state of the IAP gene family as a whole in various embryonal carcinoma (EC) cell lines and their differentiated derivatives. However, the DNA methylation inhibitor 5-azacytidine was found to increase greatly both the fraction of IAP-positive cells and the number of particles per cell section (as counted by electron microscopy) in two EC and one differentiated cell line (Table IV; Hojman-Montes de Oca *et al.*, 1984). The effects were observed within 24 hr of treatment and were accompanied by extensive demethylation of IAP genomic sequences and an increase in IAP-specific transcripts of several size classes. Lasneret *et al.* (1983) earlier reported similarly large effects of 5-azacytidine on Kirsten sarcoma virus-transformed BALB/c fibroblasts (Ki-BALB cells). The percentage of IAP-producing cells and the number of particles per cell section were both significantly increased after only 3 hr of treatment; and by 24 hr, the cells were 100% IAP-positive and had 15–20 times as many particles per cell as the untreated controls. When the drug was removed after 24 hr treatment, IAP content fell progressively to control levels during three additional culture passages; whether this dilution was associated with loss of IAPs within the whole 5-azacytidine-treated cell population or resulted from proliferation of a minority of IAP-deficient viable cells was not reported. In untreated Ki-BALB cells, there was partial demethylation of genomic IAP sequences as judged by their relative resistance to digestion with *Msp*I and *Hpa*II (methylation-insensitive and -sensitive isoschizomers, respectively, for the sequence CCGG). IAP sequences appeared to be completely demethylated after 24 hr exposure to 5-azacytidine. The probe used in these experiments, pMIA1, contained 5.2 kb of internal IAP sequence (Lueders and Kuff, 1980).

Hsiao *et al.* (1986) obtained contrasting results when they treated the C3H10T1/2 mouse embryo fibroblast line with 5-azacytidine for 24 hr and then followed the cells through successive culture passages. Using an IAP LTR probe and the same pM1A1 probe as Lasneret *et al.* (1983), they found that the marked increase in IAP transcripts in the treated cells persisted through many generations (60 culture passages shown). Azacytidine induced a partial demethylation of genomic IAP sequences detected with the LTR probe, and this change also persisted through five passages (later generations were not shown). Demethylation and transcription of endogenous MuLV sequences behaved in a similar fashion. Although endogenous MMTV sequences were also demethylated, no transcripts were detected in the treated and passaged cells. The 10T1/2 cells treated only once with azacytidine and then serially passaged underwent progressive loss of anchorage dependence, increase in saturation density, and morphological changes indicative of transformation. The authors suggested that induction of endogenous retroviruses resulting from aberrations in DNA methylation could have a role in multistage carcinogenesis.

Mays-Hoopes *et al.* (1983) compared the methylation of IAP sequences in normal mouse liver, which is devoid of IAPs and contains very low levels of IAP RNA (Lueders *et al.*, 1977), with that in the IAP-rich MOPC-315 myeloma. A specific 0.5-kb *Msp*I fragment derived from the 3′ region of IAP proviral elements was used as indicator; this fragment was detected by hybridization in *Msp*I digests of both liver and myeloma DNAs. The fragment was detected in *Hpa*II digests of myeloma DNA in amounts suggesting minor but substantial demethylation of the relevant IAP sites in this tissue but was not seen at all in *Hpa*II digests of DNA from neonatal mice or livers of BALB/c mice up to the age of 2 years. The data were consistent with the hypothesis that DNA methylation is important in silencing transcription of IAP sequences in normal tissues.

These observations were extended by Morgan and Hwang (1984) in a study of DNA methylation and IAP gene expression in the murine myelomas TEPC-15 and MOPC-315, in NIH 3T3 fibroblasts and in normal BALB/c liver. Using probes derived from various regions of a cloned 7-kb IAP element (IAP81), hypomethylation of *Msp*I/*Hpa*II sites throughout the IAP sequence was demonstrated for the genomic elements in both myelomas and, surprisingly, in the IAP-negative 3T3 cells. Liver showed hypomethylation at several internal sites, but much less than in the other cell types. Using a specific LTR probe, the authors showed that a conserved *Hha*I site in IAP LTRs was hypomethylated in the myelomas and the 3T3 cells to a very much greater extent than in liver. Northern blots of total RNA showed abundant IAP transcripts in MOPC-315 and to a lesser extent in TEPC-15, but no IAP-specific RNA was detected in either BALB/c liver or NIH 3T3 cells. The authors suggested that while DNA methylation may be sufficient to block transcription in all cell types, expression of hypomethylated genes can be regulated by additional mechanisms in cases such as the "undifferentiated" 3T3 and EC cells (see Section XI).

The importance of examining methylation sites within the LTR rather than the body of the IAP genes was emphasized by the results of Jahner and Jaenisch (1985). These authors found that six different transgenic MuLV proviral insertions were all completely methylated at day 12 of gestation and progresively demethylated during subsequent development. Demethylation was confined exclusively to the enhancer regions of the LTRs and did not involve host flanking sequences or internal proviral sites.

Feenstra *et al.* (1986) demonstrated extensive hypomethylation of conserved *Hha*I and *Hpa*II sites in 5′ IAP LTRs of the MOPC-21 and MOPC-104E myelomas and the N4 neuroblastoma, all cells known to contain abundant IAP transcripts (Paterson *et al.*, 1978; Kuff and Fewell, 1985). The proportion of 5′ LTRs showing demethylation at these sites ranged from 10 to 30% in the myelomas to 50% in N4, values corresponding to several hundred demethylated LTRs per cell. Demethylation of these LTR sites was below the limit of detection (10–20 copies per genome) not only in BALB/c liver, as expected, but also in thymus, where IAP transcripts and protein synthesis are fairly abundant (Kuff and Fewell, 1985).

The methylation state of the type II IAP elements was examined in DNA from 14-day embryo and from two myeloma cell lines in which these sequences are transcribed (Lueders, 1987). All of the LTRs of type II elements appeared to be methylated in embryo DNA, but hypomethylation of both type IIA and IIB elements was observed in myelomas. Hypomethylation of the LTRs of type IIB elements was especially prominent, a result consistent with the preferential transcription of these elements in the myelomas (Fig. 6). No demethylation of type IIC elements, which are not transcribed, was seen.

Using a plasmid construct in which a cloned 5′ IAP LTR was linked to the CAT gene (Lueders *et al.*, 1984), Feenstra *et al.* (1986) showed that *in vitro* methylation of three *Hha*I sites located between 137 and 205 bp upstream of the RNA start site completely inactivated the promoter activity of the LTR when the construct was transfected into COS7 cells. Methylation of a single *Hpa*II site 94 bp downstream of the start site also significantly reduced promoter activity. These results provide the first direct evidence that DNA methylation within the 5′ LTR can serve to suppress IAP gene expression. The *Hha*I sites are located in a region containing two short sequences with potential for Z-DNA configuration (Nordheim and Rich, 1983) and an SV40-like enhancer sequence (Lueders *et al.*, 1984). We postulate that this region contains a methylation-sensitive binding site for *trans*-acting cellular factors. The inhibition caused by methylation of the downstream *Hpa*II site was unexpected. However, downstream regulatory sequences have been found in the LTRs of the bovine leukemia virus (Derse *et al.*, 1986) and HTLV-II (Sodroskie *et al.*, 1985).

A. Feenstra (personal communication) used fill-in reactions to label the sites generated by separate *Hpa*II and *Msp*I digestions of cellular DNAs; comparison of the incorporated radioactivities in the two digests provided a measure of the relative methylation state of the *Msp*I/*Hpa*II sites in the genome as a whole. She found a general correspondence between the proportions of demethylated sites in the IAP 5′ LTRs and in the total genomic DNAs of the tumors and normal tissues. Thus, the extensive hypomethylation of IAP genes in IAP-rich tumors is probably not a specific property of these particular genetic elements. When levels of genomic demethylation reach 30–50%, as they can in neuroblastoma and myeloma cells for example, many IAP LTRs may be randomly derepressed. Cell-specific activation of IAP elements may be most easily observed in normal tissues such as thymus, where IAP gene expression is found in the context of extensive genomic methylation.

B. Oncogene Effects

The abundance of IAP expression in myeloma led Luria and Horowitz (1986) to test whether oncogene products, particularly nuclear ones such as *myc* gene product, SV40 T antigen, p53, and adenovirus E1A gene product, might have an activating effect on genomic IAP elements. The authors used plasmids in which the CAT gene was placed under control of the subcloned 5′ LTR from the IAP element transposed into rc-*mos* (Horowitz *et al.*, 1984). CAT activities after transfection of the LTR-CAT plasmid into SV40-transformed CV-1 cells were 10-times the CAT activities observed after transfection into uninfected CV-1 cells. Cotransfection of HeLa cells with the LTR-CAT plasmid and a plasmid containing the E1a and most of E1b early region of adenovirus-2 gave CAT levels 10-times greater than those seen after transfection with the LTR-CAT construct alone. Similar results were obtained when NIH 3T3 cells were cotransfected with the LTR-CAT construct and with plasmids expressing either *myc* gene product or p53. The promoter activity of the LTR in head-to-head configuration with respect to the CAT gene was also enhanced by T-antigen and the E1A gene product. On an absolute basis, the enhanced activity was 1–2% of that provided by the LTR in head-to-tail orientation. The CAT activity induced in human embryonal kidney 293 cells that constitutively express E1a proteins was at least 100-times that induced in HeLa cells. Increase in CAT levels was accompanied by increase in CAT mRNA in cells when the LTR-CAT plasmid was transfected into cells constitutively expressing p53 or E1a gene products. Whether this resulted from increased transcription or stabilization of the mRNA in the presence of the oncogene products was not determined. The exceptional enhancement of LTR promoter activity in 293 cells has been confirmed in this laboratory, using the LTR of another genomic element, M1A14 (K. K. Lueders, unpublished observations).

Luria and Horowitz (1986) suggested that the elevated IAP expression in certain mouse tumors could be related to transactivation (direct or indirect) by oncogene products, noting for example that IAP formation and c-*myc* expression are both characteristically elevated in mouse myelomas. They further suggested that IAP expression might be a useful indication of cellular oncogene activity in situations such as early embryonic development, and also that the IAP LTR could serve as a convenient general model system to test the activation of cellular promoters mediated by nucler oncogene products.

Dragani *et al.* (1986) observed a considerable increase in the levels of transcripts from IAP, VL30, and endogenous MuLV sequences in liver adenomas and carcinomas induced in B6C3F1 mice by a single treatment with nitrosodiethylamine. Increases of a similar degree were also seen in spontaneous liver carcinomas in C3Hf mice. Of three oncogenes studied (c-*myc*, c-Ha-*ras*, and c-*fos*), only c-*myc* was expressed at consistently higher levels in the chemically induced tumors than in normal liver. (In this and a subsequent study [Dragani *et al.*, 1987], the predominant IAP transcript on Northern blots was assigned a size of 6 kb and the larger species seen in some samples a size of 8 kb. We suggest that these values are too high, possibly because they are derived with the use of rRNA standards, and that the transcripts observed by these authors are the usual 5.4- and 7.2-kb species, respectively [see Fig. 6 and 7]).

C. Cell Proliferation

Augenlicht *et al.* (1984) examined a cDNA library of sequences whose expression was enhanced in a chemically induced BALB/c mouse colon carcinoma relative to normal colon, and they identified a clone, pMCT-1, that contained most of an IAP 3′ LTR and several hundred base pairs of upstream IAP sequence. Cells of the Friend erythroleukemia line DS-19 contained a high level of homologous transcripts, consistent with the known IAP expression in these cells (Table VI). *In situ* hybridization of biotin-substituted pMCT-1 to frozen sections of colon tumor and normal colon showed related RNA sequences throughout the tumor but not in normal colon epithelium (Royston and Augenlicht, 1983). The reaction within the tumor tissue was very heterogeneous on a cellular basis; it was prominent in cell doublets (presumably paired daughter cells) and hardly detectable in the rest of the tumor cells. This observation raised the possibility that IAP expression was cell-cycle regulated in the tumor.

In a subsequent study, Augenlicht and Halsey (1985) replated confluent DS-19 cells at low density and found that the concentration of IAP-related

RNA, probed with labeled pMCT-1, fell within a period of 3 hr to 10% of its original value, then increased to a constant level of about 30% in logarithmically growing cells. After cells attained confluence on day 3, the IAP RNA level continued to increase over the next 3 days while cell number was approximately constant. We calculate from the data in this experiment that the rate of IAP RNA synthesis per cell did not vary by a factor of more than about 1.5 during log growth and confluency. The authors fractionated DS-19 cells at mid-logarithmic growth by centrifugal elutriation and found that the content of IAP-related RNA was 3–4 times greater in early G1 cells than in any later stage of the cell cycle. They suggested that changes in RNA stabilization as well as in gene transcription might be involved in the rather rapid changes in levels of IAP transcripts that followed dilution of the cells or passage from early to later G1. The authors did not attempt to show whether the sequences they assayed by hybridization were localized within IAP themselves or eleswhere in the cell. Minna *et al.* (1974) measured IAP antigen levels by complement fixation throughout the growth of mouse L-cell fibroblasts and several neuroblastoma lines. IAP antigen was the same in log and confluent L-cells (B82 line) and one neuroblastoma line (N4), but doubled in confluent cultures of N18 and NL1, a hybrid line of N4 and B82 cells.

D. Halogenated Pyrimidines

Mouse neuroblastoma cells treated with iododeoxyuridine (IdUr) and dexamethasone showed a strong burst of type C virus production as evidenced by release of type C DNA polymerase activity and p30 antigen into the medium and confirmed by electron microscopy of pelleted extracellular particulate material (Kuff *et al.*, 1976). Intracellular levels of p30 antigen rose 20- to 30-fold. In contrast, no IAP antigen, DNA polymerase activity, or free particles were found in the extracellular phase and intracellular A-particle antigen increased only about 2-fold. The rate of IAP protein synthesis was also unchanged. Thus, in these already IAP-rich cells, IdUr treatment had little detectable effect on IAP expression.

A contrasting situation was observed by Lasneret *et al.* (1978, 1981), who found that IAP production was activated in a Ki-BALB line (BALB/c fibrobasts transformed by Kirsten MSV) on treatment with IdUr. About 20% of untreated cells displayed sparse IAPs and no other virus-like structure. Cells treated with IdUr alone or with IdUr plus dexamethasone for 24 and 48 hr showed numerous budding and extracellular type C virus and a significant increase in IAPs. In addition, a minority of the cells contained both IAPs and many intracisternal 75- to 85-nm particles of the type seen in preimplantation mouse embryos (Fig. 5) and referred to as epsilon- (ϵ) particles by Yotsuyanagi and Szöllösi (1980). To our knoweldge, this is the only report of ϵ-particle expression in somatic cells.

E. Interferon Effects

Billiau *et al.* (1973) studied the effects of mouse interferon on production of murine type C viruses and IAPs in several mouse cell lines. Interferon was obtained from L-929 cells infected with Newcastle disease virus. Replication of integrated sarcoma or leukemia viruses was as sensitive to interferon as the replication of newly infecting vesicular stomatitis virus (VSV). In a line of MSV-transformed fibroblastic cells constitutively producing small numbers of IAPs, interferon did not prevent the 4-fold increase in IAP number observed by electron microscopy after treatment with bromodeoxyuridine and dimethylsulfoxide, whereas VSV replication was blocked by interferon to the usual extent. In a second paper on the subject, Billiau *et al.* (1975) confirmed that type C virus production was as sensitive to interferon inhibition as VSV and showed that release of B-type MMTV and synthesis of IAP were both interferon-resistant in a methylcholanthrene transformed fibroblast line that showed good sensitivity to the anti-VSV effect of this agent.

The effect of mouse interferon on IAP number was studied in several clonal lines from a Friend virus-induced leukemia (Krieg *et al.*, 1978). IAPs increased 20-fold in interferon-treated erythroleukemia cells at the same time that release of Friend virus (helper plus spleen focus-forming virus) was inhibited. IAPs did not increase, however, on interferon inhibition of Friend or Moloney helper virus production in a fibroblastic line or in Friend cells with marginal Friend virus production. Speculation that IAPs represent expression of the spleen focus-forming component of Friend virus has been superseded by more recent genetic evidence to the contrary.

Six months of treatment of an MSV-transformed fibroblast line (Ki-BALB) with mouse interferon at 50 units/ml was accompanied by a significant increase in levels of both the 5.4- and 7.2-kb IAP transcripts. A 7.2-kb Ki-*ras* transcript was similarly increased, whereas a 2.5-kb c-*myc* RNA species was reduced about 4-fold (Emanoil-Ravier *et al.*, 1985).

The studies summarized above do not provide sufficient basis for judging whether interferon has any direct effect on IAP expression. It seems clear at the least that established IAP-production is not inhibited by this agent.

IX. IAP Gene Expression in Normal Somatic Cells

Although overt IAP expression is commonly associated with the transformed state, a low level of IAP gene activity is found in most normal mouse tissues that have been examined (Table II and Fig. 7). IAP-related transcripts of 7.2 and 5.4 kb are typically observed, with the 5.4-kb species generally predominant on Northern blots (Fig. 7). IAPs are observed rarely but consistently in many normal tissues (Wivel and Smith, 1971), as if the

TABLE II
IAP GENE EXPRESSION IN MOUSE SOMATIC CELLS

Tissue	Strain	Electron microscopy	Antigen	RNA
Spleen	BALB/c	+[1]		++[2,3]
Small lymphocyte	BALB/c	+[1]		
Plasma cell	BALB/c	+[1]		
Thymus	BALB/cJ	+[1,4]	++[2]	+++[2]
	C57BL/6J	−[4]	+[2]	+[2]
	C57BL/KsJ	+[4]	++[5]	
	C58/J		++[2]	+++[2]
	DBA/2J		+[2]	++[2]
	AKR/J		±[2]	±[2]
	NZB/J		+[2]	+[2]
	SJL/J		+[2]	+[2]
	SWR/J		−[2]	
	C57L	−[8]		
Macrophage	BALB/c	+[1]		
Fibroblast	BALB/c	+[1]		
Skeletal muscle	BALB/c	+[1]		
Heart	BALB/c	−[1]		−[6]
Epidermis	BALB/c	+[7]		
	C57L	−[8]		
Brain	C57BL			+[3]
	C3H			+[3]
	BALB/c			+[6]
Trigeminal ganglion	NMRI	++[9]		
Cerebellum				
Purkinje cells[a]	C57BL/6J	+[10]		+[11]
Stellate cells	BALB/c	+[12]		
Stellate cells	C57BL/6	−[12]		
Liver	BALB/c		−[13]	±[2,14]
	?			+[3]
	C3Hf			+[15,16]
	C57BL/6 × C3HfF1			+[15,16]
Salivary gland	BALB/c			+[6]
Pancreas B cells	C57BL/KsJ	+[17]	++[5]	
	C57BL/6J	−[17]	+[5]	
	CBA/LtJ	+[17]	+[5]	+[5]
	CD-1[b]	++[18]		
Lung	BALB/c			+[6]
Kidney	BALB/c			+[2,6]
Seminal vesicle	C3H	+[1]		
Epididymus	C3H	+[7]		
	BALB/c			+[6]
Leydig cell	C3H	+[1]		
Ovary	C3H	+[1]		
	BALB/c	+[1]		

[a]*pcd-pcd* mutant mice.
[b]Streptozotocin-treated animals; ε-particle morphology.
[1]Wivel and Smith (1971); [2]Kuff and Fewell (1985); [3]Grigoryan *et al.* (1985); [4]E. Leiter (personal communication); [5]Leiter *et al.* (1986b); [6]E. L. Kuff (unpublished observations; see Fig. 7); [7]Bibby and Smith (1975); [8]Kakefuda *et al.* (1970); [9]Herrlinger *et al.* (1975); [10]Landis and Mullen (1978); [11]M. Brilliant (personal communication); [12]Larramendi (1969); [13]Kuff *et al.* (1972); [14]Lueders and Kuff (1977); [15]Dragani *et al.* (1986); [16]Dragani *et al.* (1987); [17]Leiter and Kuff (1984); [18]Appel *et al.* (1978).

level of IAP protein synthesis in some cells occasionally reached a threshold level for particle formation.

Among normal tissues thus far examined, IAP expression is greatest in the thymus of young mice (Kuff and Fewell, 1985). Here, expression is clearly strain-related with respect to both the absolute amount and the relative proportions of the two main IAP transcripts (Fig. 6). Relatively high levels of both 7.2- and 5.4-kb RNA species are found in thymus of BALB/cJ mice. In contrast, 7.2-kb transcripts are not detected in C57BL/6J thymus, which also contains lower levels of 5.4-kb RNA. The two tissues show corresponding differences in synthesis of IAP-related proteins: BALB/cJ thymus makes products of the 7.2-kb and 5.4-kb transcripts (p73 and p114–120, respectively) in almost equal amounts, whereas C57BL/6J thymus makes small amounts of p117 and no p73 (Kuff and Fewell, 1985). IAPs have been observed by electron microscopy in thymocytes of BALB/cJ but not C57BL/6 animals (E. Leiter, personal communication). The genetic control of IAP expression in thymus does not follow simple Mendelian rules, because p73 synthesis is generally suppressed in F1 progeny of BALB/cJ and C57BL/6J crosses, although p117 synthesis is not.

We have found that IAP protein synthesis is strongly activated in splenic cells stimulated for 72 hr with bacterial lipopolysaccharide (LPS), a material that induces polyclonal B cell activation. Some activation was detected at 24 hr. Cells from spleens of C57BL/6N, DBA/2N, and BALB/cπ mice all responded. Treatment of spleen cultures with concanavalin A (Con A) to stimulate quiescent T cells produced a slower and less marked induction of IAP protein synthesis.

Both c-*myc* and c-*myb* protooncogenes are known to be expressed at relatively high levels in BALB/c mouse thymus, and to a much lower extent in the spleen (Mushinski *et al.*, 1983a,b). Mountz *et al.* (1984) found that c-*myc* transcripts were markedly elevated in DBA/2 spleen cells after only 4 hr of exposure to LPS, whereas c-*myb* transcripts were still not detected after 18 hr. ConA treatment of spleen cells caused no increase in transcripts of either oncogene. The correlation between IAP protein expression and the level of c-*myc* transcripts in these situations accords with the results of Luria and Horowitz (1986) noted above.

Dragani *et al.* (1987) observed low levels of IAP transcripts in normal livers of B6C3F1 mice and markedly increased amounts during the acute proliferative response to the hepatotoxic agent CCl4. Maximum levels of IAP RNA were seen on the first day after treatment, whereas the mitotic index peaked on day 2. VL30 transcripts were also most abundant on day 1, whereas Moloney MuLV-related RNA was highest on day 2. The peak in IAP transcript level on day 1 is consistent with a response to increased c-*myc* levels, which might be expected to peak early in the proliferative response.

Basal levels of IAP transcripts were higher in livers of 7-day-old mice than in those of 15-day-old or adult animals (Dragani *et al.*, 1987). Cycloheximide administration to adult mice resulted in dramatic increases in the levels of IAP, MuLV, and VL30 transcripts within 3–6 hr, whereas RNA homologous to a control mouse genomic sequence did not change. The authors suggest the presence of labile repressor proteins that normally regulate the abundance of these endogenous retroviral transcripts, and they postulated that variations in the amounts of these putative regulatory proteins may be involved in the response to induced liver cell proliferation as well as in normal development and hepatic carcinogenesis.

The number and chromosome location of active IAP genes are not known for any tissue. Because IAP LTRs are heavily methylated in normal liver and thymus (Morgan and Hwang, 1984; Feenstra *et al.*, 1986), only a few IAP elements are presumably active in these tissues. Grossman *et al.* (1987) addressed the problem of tissue-specific activation of particular IAP elements by asking whether transcripts of the same gene could be detected in the thymus of different mouse strains. They prepared cDNA libraries in λgt11 from the poly(A) RNAs of DBA/2 and C58 thymus and detected in each a few recombinants expressing protein(s) that reacted with antiserum against IAP p73. Within this small group, one pair of cDNA clones, consisting of an isolate from each strain, had remarkably similar structural properties. The two inserts represented identical segments of the IAP genome and the degree of sequence variability between them (0.3%) was an order of magnitude less than that seen in pairwise comparisons with and among any previously isolated IAP genomic and cDNA clones. Each clone also contained an identical set of short internal sequence repeats not seen in other IAP elements. The authors suggest that these cDNAs could represent allelic IAP elements specifically activated in thymuses of the two mouse strains. Cloning of the active genomic elements from thymuses of the two strains and comparison of their flanking sequences will be required to confirm this suggestion.

One cDNA clone from brain poly(A) RNA of BALB/c mouse which contained IAP sequences has been sequenced (Aota *et al.*, 1987). This clone contained 2.2 kb of sequences from the 3′ end of the IAP genome.

X. IAP Expression in Early Development

A. Intracisternal Particles in Embryos of Laboratory Mice

Virus-like particles were observed by electron microscopy in preimplantation guinea pig embryos by Enders and Schlafke (1965) and in mouse oocytes and embryos by Calarco and Brown (1969). More detailed descriptions of IAP expression in mouse embryos appeared in 1973 (Calarco and Szöllösi; Chase and Pikó; Biczysko *et al.*). The literature, then encompassing some 25 research papers, was first reviewed by Kelly and Condamine (1982) and more recently by Yotsuyanagi and Szöllösi (1984). The latter authors, whose in-depth discussion includes a number of their own previously unpublished observations, emphasize two main points with respect to the intracisternal particles found in early mouse embryos. (1) Two morphologically distinct types of particles are expressed. Chase and Pikó (1973) distinguished a large type A particle, 85–100 nm in diameter and resembling those typically seen in mouse tumor cells, from a more abundant type of particle 75–85 nm in size. The large IAPs appeared in 8-cell embryos and increased in morula and blastocyst stages, whereas the smaller particles were maximally abundant in the 2- to 8-cell embryos. Yotsuyanagi and Szöllösi (1980, 1981) showed that the small particles differ from the "typical" IAPs in their internal organization: Instead of the closely apposed inner and outer shells found in the large IAPs, the smaller particles display an array of spokes projecting radially from the central nucleoid to the outer membrane, resembling in this respect the 100-nm intracisternal type R particle found in Syrian hamster tumor cells and embryos (Fig. 5). The authors proposed the noncommittal designation epsilon (ϵ) for the small intracisternal particle seen in mouse embryos, because their genetic relationship to the intracisternal A and R particles is unknown. Yotsuyanagi and Szöllösi observed A-particles in ovarian and tubal oocytes in a variety of inbred mice; these particles diminished in number in early zygotes, were rare or absent at the 2-cell stage and reappeared in later preimplantation embryos. The ϵ-particles followed a reciprocal course; absent in oocytes and zygotes, they appeared in greatest abundance in the 2- to 4-cell stages and then diminished throughout the remainder of preimplantation development. Epsilon particles far exceeded the IAPs in number in the 2- to 8-cell stages of all mouse strains examined and in most strains throughout subsequent preimplantation development. It is the ϵ-particle, rather than the typical IAP, that is abundant in early mouse embryos. (2) Yotsuyanagi and Szöllösi (1981) found great variation in the relative and absolute numbers of A- and ϵ-particles among embryos of different inbred mouse strains. In a quantitative electron microscopic study, Szöllösi and Yotsuyanagi (1985) found that the low-producer state was dominant in all embryos derived from matings between high- and low-producer strains of either A- or ϵ-particles. Suppression was observed when either parent carried the low-producer trait, a result indicating that both maternal and paternally introduced regulatory mechanisms can operate as early as the 2-cell stage. Strain-specific differences in the ratio of A- and ϵ-particles suggested that the respective genes were independently regulated. Biczysko *et al.* (1974) observed the appearance of intracisternal particles, primarily of the ϵ type (Yotsuyanagi and Szöllösi, 1984), in the 4- and 8-cell stages of parthenogenetically activated eggs from both ICR and AKR mice. Thus, ϵ-particle expression can be programmed entirely under maternal control.

Calarco (1975) examined the developing particles found in the 2-cell stage in cultured embryos from five inbred mouse strains and distinguished a presumptive early stage in which dense fibrillar material accumulated in patches on the ribosome-free cytoplasmic surfaces of the endoplasmic reticulum and areas of "crystalloid" material appeared in the nearby cytoplasmic matrix (see also Chase and Pikó, 1973; Yotsuyanagi and Szöllösi, 1981). The accumulation of fibrillar material was blocked in zygotes cultured to the 2-cell stage in the presence of 10 ng/ml of actinomycin D; however, when embryos were not exposed to actinomycin until the 2- to 4-cell stages, progression of the early forms to mature particles occurred to nearly the same extent as in untreated embryos. These observations seem to suggest that either the mRNA or the particle proteins themselves had accumulated by the 2-cell stage to the point that formation of particles could continue in the absence of new RNA synthesis. Calarco (1975) also reported that intracisternal particle expression in the embryos was resistant to α-amanitin, in contrast to the subsequent finding that transcription of IAP genes in tumor cells is carried out by RNA polymerase II (Wujcik *et al.*, 1984). The question needs to be reinvestigated with proper controls to show that the α-amanitin was indeed active under the conditions used. The possible utilization of stored material mRNAs (see following) and/or preformed proteins (fibrillar material and crystalloid?) must also be considered.

The synthesis of IAP-related RNA in early mouse embryos was elegantly studied by Pikó *et al.* (1984). Defined restriction fragments from a cloned IAP element were used as probes to detect and quantitate the IAP-related RNA on dot blots. The number of RNA molecules was 17,000 in the mature oocyte, but fell to only 1300 in the unfertilized egg. An increase in IAP-related RNA was detected in the late 2-cell stage and continued through the late blastocyst, by which time 99% of the total IAP RNA in the embryo had been synthesized since fertilization. A single 5.4-kb RNA species was detected on Northern blots of blastocyst RNA probed with the IAP restriction fragments. Table III presents data of Pikó *et al.* recalculated to show the numbers of RNA copies and the rates of synthesis per cell at various developmental stages. The rate of IAP-related transcription per genome was essentially constant throughout the preimplantation period. This rate, approximately 1300 RNA molecules per cell per 5 hr, is about 35% of that calculated for the IAP-rich N4 neuroblastoma cell line. Because N4 cells have approximately equal amounts of 7.2-kb and 5.4-kb IAP transcripts (Kuff and Fewell, 1985), whereas the 5.4-kb species accounts for all of the synthesis in the embryos, the rate of accumulation of 5.4-kb RNA per genome in the embryo is nearly 70% that of the comparable-sized transcript in the N4 tumor cells. Pikó *et al.* point out that the IAP-related RNA molecules per embryo may be 30–100 times more numerous than the IAPs themselves and that therefore most of the RNA molecules cannot be accommodated in this type of particle. On the other hand, at the 2-cell stage, the number of ϵ-particles per embryo, estimated at $1–2 \times 10^5$, far exceeds the number

TABLE III

IAP RNA IN PREIMPLANTATION MOUSE EMBRYOS

Embryo stage	Number of cells	IAP RNA[a]: Total number of molecules per embryo	IAP RNA[a]: Molecules per cell	IAP RNA[a]: Synthesis rate molecules/cell per 5 hr	IAP RNA *in situ* hybridization[b]: No. of cells	IAP RNA *in situ* hybridization[b]: Grains per cell	IAP RNA *in situ* hybridization[b]: Total grains per embryo
1-cell	1	—	—	—	1	19	19
2-cell	2	7,100	3,550	1300	2	24	48
8-cell	8	9,700	1,210	1200	4–8	15	60–120
Early blastocyst	32	37,900	1,180	1600	32[d]	8	256
Late blastocyst	64	156,000	2,440	1300		—	—
Neuroblastoma N4	—	—	18,000[c]	3600[c]			

[a]Calculated from data of Pikó *et al.* (1984); (C × D)F_1 embryos.

[b]From Moshier *et al.* (1985); BALB/c embryos; total grain numbers per embryo calculated from their data.

[c]Based on a doubling time of 20 hr, the presence of equal numbers of 7.2-kb and 5.4-kb transcripts, and IAP poly(A) RNA content of 16 μg per 2.6 × 10^8 cells (1 ml of packed cells) (Kuff and Fewell, 1985).

[d]Morula–blastula.

of IAP-related RNA molecules, about 7×10^3. The authors take this discrepancy, plus the fact that the synthesis of 5.4-kb RNA continues during and after the disappearance of the ϵ-particles in later embryonic stages as evidence that these particles may represent the expression of another family of retroviral elements. However, in considering this argument, it must be noted that (1) the actual particle number in the F2 hybrid embryos used for these experiments was not determined; (2) the ϵ-particles may not contain a full complement of RNA (type C retrovirus particles have been shown to assemble in the absence of high-molecular-weight viral RNA [Levin and Rosenak, 1976]); (3) the cessation of particle formation in the face of continued RNA synthesis could reflect a posttranscriptional control (cf. Morgan and Hwang, 1987). Moshier *et al.* (1985) studied the levels of IAP-related RNA in early BALB/c embryos by *in situ* hybridization and concluded that in this strain synthesis diminished sharply after the 2-cell stage. However, as shown in Table III, even though the number of grains per cell was reduced, the calculated grains per embryo increased progressively, a result indicating that IAP RNA synthesis was continuing at a significant rate.

In tumor cells and normal thymus, some 5.4-kb IAP-related transcripts code for *gag–pol* fusion proteins (p115–120) that contain less than half of the total *gag* peptide sequence (Kuff and Fewell, 1985; Kuff *et al.* 1986b). Proteins of this type may not assemble by themselves to form IAP-like structures, because particles are not seen in thymus cells containing predominantly these polypeptides. However, the structurally diverse family of IAP-related genetic elements may include other variants that could give rise to 5.4-kb transcripts encoding a 73-kDa *gag* protein in the embryo.

Hwang and Calarco (1982) studied the distribution of IAP-related antigens by immunoelectron microscopy in sectioned embryonic material. They used a polyvalent rabbit antibody prepared against whole IAPs isolated from the MOPC-104E myeloma and pre-absorbed on a mixture of membranes from normal mouse tissues (Hwang and Calarco, 1981a); the antibody was reactive with IAP major core protein(s). Antibody binding, detected with peroxidase-coupled second antibody, was localized over cisternae containing budding and complete ϵ-particles in 4- to 8-cell embryos. The reaction product appeared diffusely over the interior of the cisternae as well as over the particles themselves. Because of the diffuse localization, it is not possible to conclude that the ϵ-particles themselves share antigenic determinants with the tumor-derived IAPs, although this possibility is consistent with the data.

Hwang and Calarco (1981b) used this antiserum to immunoprecipitate IAP-related proteins from embryos cultured in the presence of [^{35}S]methionine. They detected proteins with molecular weights of 67, 69, 73, 75, and 77 kDa. Immunoprecipitation of all five species was blocked with tumor-derived IAP core protein. Labeling of the 67- to 73-kDa components was seen only in 2- to 8-cell embryos; thus their synthesis coincided with the appearance of the ϵ-particles rather than with that of the typical IAPs (Yotsuyanagi and Szöllösi, 1984). The 75- and 77-kDa proteins were labeled at all postzygotic stages. Taken as a whole, the immunological data are consistent with the hypothesis that the ϵ-particles contain 67- to 73-kDa proteins that share antigenic determinants with the 73-kDa IAP core protein(s). Confirmation of this relationship requires more precise immunocytochemical localization of IAP-related epitopes using monoclonal or affinity-purified antibodies.

The same polyvalent antibody preparation was used to probe for surface-localized IAP-related antigens in live unfertilized eggs and preimplantation embryos and in fixed and sectioned material (Hwang and Calarco, 1981b). Surface antigens were not detected on the eggs; they appeared first on the zygotes, reached peak expression at the 2- to 8-cell stages, and fell to very low levels in morulae and blastocysts. The precise nature of the reacting surface molecules has not been established; as Yotsuyanagi and Szöllösi (1984) point out, they could represent either IAP core-related proteins or cross-reactive components of the ϵ-particles. IAP-related antigens have not been detected on the surface of IAP-rich myeloma, rhabdomyosarcoma, and neuroblastoma cells (Hwang and Calarco, 1981a; J. W. Fewell and E. L. Kuff, unpublished observations).

Epsilon intracisternal particles were induced in Kirsten MSV-transformed BALB/3T3 (Ki-BALB) cells treated with iododeoxyuridine (Fig. 5c) and typical IAPs, which are constitutively produced by these cells, were also increased (Lasneret *et al.*, 1981). This cell line may provide an additional, more accessible, system for immunological comparison of the two particle types.

B. Intracisternal Particles in Embryos of Wild Mice and Other Species

Calarco (1979) reported that small intracisternal particles, (presumably ϵ-type, were absent in the zygotes of feral *Mus musculus* (Lake Casitas), abundant in 2-cell embryos and dramatically decreased at the 4-cell stage. Calarco *et al.* 1980), confirmed by Yotsuyanagi and Szöllösi (1984), observed ϵ-particles peaking in the 8-cell embryos of *Mus cervicolor* and the 2-cell stage of *Mus pahari*. A retrovirus resembling M432 was expressed in the morula stage of *Mus cervicolor* embryos (Yotsuyanagi and Szöllösi, 1984).

C. General Comments

It is difficult to imagine a programmatic role for either IAPs or ϵ-particles in early mouse development. The work of Yotsuyanagi and Szöllösi (1981) shows that levels of expression of both types of intracisternal particles are genetically determined. However, the intrastrain variations have no obvious developmental correlates. The same point may be made with regard to the marked interspecies variation in the temporal course of ϵ-particle expression. We might suggest that particle formation in itself is irrelevant to normal embryogenesis and results from activation of IAP and ϵ-particle proviral elements through fortuitous proximity to essential cellular genes or in response to stage-specific cellular factors. A possible exception might be the transient cell-surface expression of putative IAP-related proteins (Hwang and Calarco, 1981b) if their identity can be confirmed. It will be important to determine whether A-, ϵ-, (or hamster R-) particle-specific reverse transcriptase and endonuclease activities are expressed in embryos, because these activities could be instrumental in the generation and integration of new proviral copies or DNA copies of other mRNA species.

XI. IAP Expression in Mouse Teratocarcinoma Cells

Teratoma-derived cell lines have long been regarded as interesting systems for investigating mechanisms of gene regulation in early mammalian development. A number of studies have dealt with the comparative expression of IAPs in primitive and differentiated cell types. As we shall see, these studies have as yet produced little coherent information relevant to the regulation of IAP expression in differentiating systems.

Intraperitoneal implantation of minced teratoma tissue in syngeneic mice gives rise to a population of embryoid bodies in which a core of undifferentiated embryonic-like stem cells (embryonal carcinoma, or EC cells) is surrounded by a layer of cells resembling those destined to become the parietal endoderm of the trophoblast (parietal endoderm, or PE cells) (Stevens, 1970). A number of cell lines have been derived from transplantable embryoid bodies (Nicolas *et al.*, 1976; Martin, 1975). Particularly relevant to the present discussion are the lines developed at the Pasteur Institute (Nicolas *et al.*, 1976) from embryoid bodies of the OTT6050 teratoma (Stevens, 1970). Clonal derivatives have properties of EC cells (most commonly), parietal yolk sac endoderm (occasionally), and a variety of other differentiated cell types. Some EC cell lines are pluripotent, giving rise to tumors containing multiple differentiated cell types when reintroduced into syngeneic mice, whereas other, nullipotential lines produce tumors composed of EC cells alone. Pluripotent EC lines may differentiate spontaneously when maintained in culture at high density, often passing through an aggregate stage corresponding to the embryoid bodies seen *in vivo* (Martin, 1975). Nullipotent EC cells differentiate poorly if at all in culture, but some—for example, the F9 cell line used in many studies—can be transformed to PE-like cells by treatment with agents such as retinoic acid (Strickland and Mahdavi, 1978). Various biological, immunological, and biochemical properties suggest that EC cells correspond most closely in developmental capacity to the undifferentiated pluripotent cells in 4- to 6-day embryos (Martin, 1975; Mintz and Illmensee, 1975). At the outset, therefore, it is questionable whether information gained from the study of established EC lines will be relevant to the regulation of IAP expression in oocytes and in the very early preimplantation stages where the particles are ordinarily seen. Possibly related to this difference in stage-equivalence is the fact that ϵ-particles, which are more abundantly expressed in normal embryos than are the typical IAPs, are not seen in mouse teratocarcinoma cells or their differentiated derivatives. In spite of these reservations, the various teratocarcinoma lines do provide opportunities for manipulation of IAP expression and may ultimately yield insight into the response of IAP LTRs to a variety of developmental regulatory signals.

Pierce *et al.* (1967) examined by electron microscopy very early teratocarcinomas induced by transplantation of genital ridges of strain 129 mice into adult testes. They observed that EC cells contained few membranous organelles other than mitochondria. Virus-like particles were not commented on nor did they appear in the published electron micrographs. Lehman *et al.* (1974) reported a similar paucity of cytoplasmic organelles and no virus particles in EC cells of embryoid bodies derived from OTT6050 (also of strain 129 origin), whereas the surrounding endoderm contained abundant smooth and rough endoplasmic reticulum with occasional IAPs. Teresky *et al.* (1974) described IAPs in the endoderm cells of OTT6050 embryoid bodies and established by complement fixation assay their antigenic relationship to IAPs isolated from other types of mouse tumors. Nicolas *et al.* (1976) found no IAPs in several EC cell lines derived from OTT6050 enbryoid bodies nor in cells differentiated *in vitro* from the pluripotent line PCC3. Spence *et al.* (1975) confirmed the rarity of IAPs in cells of solid OTT6050 tumors, but at the same time found large numbers of IAPs in the undifferentiated stem cells of another transplanted teratocarcinoma, OTT2466, derived by Stevens (1970) from a 6-day A/He embryo. A variety of differentiated cells from the OTT6050 tumor, including primitive endoderm, were said to contain a few IAPs. IAP expression may be genetically favored in EC cells of A/He mice, because Lasneret *et al.* (1978) found numerous IAPs in the PCC6 EC line derived from this strain.

Parietal yolk sac carcinomas can develop spontaneously or during ascites conversion of teratocarcinomas (Pierce and Dixon, 1959). Neither Pierce *et al.* (1962) nor Lehman *et al.* (1974), who, respectively, examined a PYS tumor and two PYS lines developed from OTT6050 (including line PYS-2), commented on the presence of virus particles. Damjanov and Solter (1973) found relatively few IAPs in an early PYS carcinoma developed from the egg cylinder of a 7- to 8-day C3H/He embryo, even though the endoplasmic reticulum was extensively developed. However, by the tenth transplant generation, large numbers of IAPs were present in distended cisternae.

Thus, the strong IAP expression associated with the established PYS-2 line (Howe and Overton, 1986) may be a property acquired during its passage history. No general conclusions can be drawn, however, about the lack of IAP expression in primary PYS tumors, because Pierce *et al.* (1970) found rather numerous IAPs in a postpregnancy PYS carcinoma of a Swiss mouse.

Table IV summarizes recent morphological and molecular studies of IAP expression in established teratocarcinoma lines. For the F9 cell line, the results conform to expectations based on studies of the OTT6050 tumor and derived embryoid bodies; i.e., IAP expression, judged by particle number and RNA levels, is absent in EC cells but strong in PE cells obtained by retinoic acid treatment of F9, in the endoderm cells of F9-derived embryoid bodies, and in an established PE line derived from retinoic acid-differentiated F9 cells. Surprisingly, isolated nuclei from both EC and retinoic acid-induced PE cells of F9 were about equally active in transcription of IAP sequences, a finding leading Morgan and Hwang (1987) to suggest that the difference in overt IAP expression between the two cell states results from changes in posttranscriptional handling of the IAP RNA (see later discussion).

Cells of the PCC4 EC line contained only rare IAPs, consistent with the low levels of 7.2-kb IAP RNA and extensive genomic IAP sequence methylation reported by Hojman-Montes de Oca *et al.* (1983). However, Moshier *et al.* (1985) reported high levels of all sizes of IAP transcripts in these cells. This discrepancy is unresolved.

The pluripotent EC cells of the PCC3 line, initially devoid of IAPs (Nicolas *et al.*, 1976), currently express low levels of particles; in a quantitative EM study, 25–35% of the cells were positive, with an average of only 100 particles counted per 100 cell sections. Howe and Overton (1986) found no IAP transcripts in the PCC3/A/1 line (data were not presented), but two other groups, one of them using PCC3 cells obtained from Howe and Overton, observed relatively high levels of IAP RNA and active transcription of IAP sequences in isolated nuclei. Differentiation to fibroblastic cells entailed a 50% reduction in nuclear transcription and an even more drastic fall in cellular content of IAP-specific RNA. IAPs were said to be reduced in numbers (+ + + to + +).

Canivet *et al.* (1980) found that 80% of the EC cells of line PCC6 had IAPs "too numerous to count." IAP transcripts of all sizes were abundant in these cells.

As mentioned earlier, transplanted PYS cells contain IAPs. Although Canivet *et al.* (1980) found only 46% of PYS-2 cells positive for IAPs, with an average of fewer than one particle per observed cell section, Howe and Overton (1986) reported that IAPs were abundant and the isolated nuclei more active in transcription of IAP sequences than those of F9 cells. The 5.4-kb transcript was particularly abundant in PYS-2 cells. In the diferentiated cell lines PCDl (myocardial) and PCD3 (fibroblastic), 30–40% and

60%, respectively, of the cells were positive for IAPs, with an average of 1–2 particles per cell section. Low but detectable levels of RNA were found.

Much more information, as well as the resolution of currently conflicting results with the same cell lines, will be required before such factors as genetic background, potential for differentiation, and other clonal characteristics of EC cell lines can be related to IAP expression in a systematic fashion. Perhaps one can generalize that parietal endoderm is the only differentiated cell type thus far studied that supports a high level of IAP expression. No consistent relationship between the overall methylation state of genomic IAP sequences and IAP expression in the various cells lines was observed (except when general hypomethylation was induced by treatment with 5′-azacytidine). This should not be surprising in view of the large number of IAP elements in the genome and the possibility that IAP formation may result from transcription of only a small minority of competent genes. The complexity of the situation is underlined by the interesting data of Morgan and Hwang (1987). They point out that there was little change in the level of nuclear transcription in F9 cells treated with retinoic acid, even though treatment resulted in a marked demethylation of IAP genomic sequences, and they suggested that the observed increase in the amount of IAP-specific RNA in the PE cells may result from stabilization of transcripts encapsidated in newly formed IAPs. We suggest that mechanisms for facilitating assembly of particles in the treated cells might include (1) activation of particular proviral elements encoding complete structural proteins not detected as a change in the general level of IAP transcription; and (2) stabilization of IAP structural proteins through interaction with the amplified endoplasmic reticulum membrane system in PE cells.

Finally, it should be reemphasized that the relationship between the expression of IAPs in teratocarcinoma cells and in normal embryos is tenuous. Expression of both ϵ-particles and IAPs was found to be strongly strain-dependent during preimplantation development (Chase and Pikó, 1973; Yotsuyanagi and Szöllösi, 1981), but particle formation in all strains examined had fallen to minimal levels by the blastocyst stage. Biczysko *et al.* (1973) found only rare IAPs in 7-day egg cylinders of ICR/Ha (Swiss) and AKR mice. Thus, the appearance of IAPs in moderate to large numbers in the PE cells of embryoid bodies and cultures of retinoic acid-treated F9 cells probably has no counterpart in normally differentiated parietal endoderm. It must be kept in mind that EC cells are tumorigenic and may have altered patterns of expression for some genes, although major programs of differentiation can be appropriately executed. It might be of interest to study IAP expression in the normally differentiated descendants of embryonal carcinoma cells that have been incorporated into mouse embryos (Mintz and Illmensee, 1975).

Jaenisch and co-workers (Jahner *et al.*, 1982) showed that Moloney MuLV introduced into preimplantation mouse embryos (1–3 days) became

TABLE IV

IAP EXPRESSION IN TERATOCARCINOMA[a,b]

Cell line	Cell type	Treat-ment	IAPs by EM[c]	IAP RNA 7.2-kb	IAP RNA 5.4-kb	IAP RNA <5-kb	Methylation of IAP sequences	Reference
F9	EC	—	—	–	–	–	N.D.	Howe and Overton (1986)
	EC	—	N.D.	–	–	–	+++	Morgan and Huang (1987)
	PE	RA	Numerous	–	++	++	N.D.	Howe and Overton (1986)
	PE	RA	N.D.	+++	+++	++	+	Morgan and Huang (1987)
	EB	—	N.D.	+	+++	+	N.D.	Moshier *et al.* (1985)
F9AcC19	PE	—	Numerous	±	+++	+++	N.D.	Howe and Overton (1986)
PCC4	EC	—	<1		N.D.		N.D.	Lasneret *et al.* (1978)
	EC	—	<1		N.D.		N.D.	Canivet *et al.* (1980)
	EC	—	—	+	–	–	+++	Hojman-Montes de Oca *et al.* (1983)
	EC	—	—	++	+++	+++	N.D.	Moshier *et al.* (1985)
	EC	5-Ac	92% (1658)	+++	++	++	±	Hojman-Montes de Oca *et al.* (1984)
PCC3	EC	–	–		N.D.		N.D.	Nicolas *et al.* (1976)
	EC	–	35% (107)		N.D.		N.D.	Lasneret *et al.* (1978)
	EC	–	25% (107)		N.D.		N.D.	Hojman-Montes de Oca *et al.* (1984)
	EC	5-Ac	93% (1816)		N.D.		N.D.	Hojman-Montes de Oca *et al.* (1984)

	EC	–	"+++"[c]	+++	+++	++	+++	Hojman-Montes de Oca *et al.* (1983)
	EC	–	N.D.	+++	+++	++	++	Morgan and Huang (1987)
PCC3/A/1	EC	—	N.D.	Negative-data not shown			N.D.	Howe and Overton (1986)
PCC3d+	FIB	RA	"++"	–	+	+	N.D.	Hojman-Montes de Oca *et al.* (1983)
	FIB	RA	N.D.	±	+	+	+++	Morgan and Huang (1987)
	FIB	SC	27% (34)		N.D.		N.D.	Lasneret *et al.* (1978)
	FIB	SC	"++"	+	++	++	+++	Hojman-Montes de Oca *et al.* (1983)
PCC6	EC	–	80% (TNTC)		N.D.		N.D.	Lasneret *et al.* (1978)
	EC	–	"+++"	+++	+++	+	+++	Hojman-Montes de Oca *et al.* (1983)
PCD1	MYO	–	42% (94)		N.D.		N.D.	Lasneret *et al.* (1978)
	MYO	–	30% (94)		N.D.		N.D.	Hojman-Montes de Oca *et al.* (1984)
	MYO	–	"+"	±("+")	+	–	+	Hojman-Montes de Oca *et al.* (1983)
	MYO	5-Ac	68% (513)		N.D.		N.D.	Hojman-Montes de Oca *et al.* (1984)
PCD3	FIB	—	60% (196)		N.D.		N.D.	Lasneret *et al.* (1978)
	FIB	—	"–"	+			+	Hojman-Montes de Oca *et al.* (1983)
PYS-2	PYS	—	46% (94)		N.D.		N.D.	Canivet *et al.* (1980)
	PYS	—	Numerous	+	+++	±	N.D.	Howe and Overton (1986)

[a]Abbreviations: N.D., not determined; SC, stationary culture; RA, retinoic acid; 5-Ac, 5-azacytidine; EB, embryoid body; PE, parietal endoderm; PYS, parietal yolk sac; FIB, fibroblast; EC, embryonal carcinoma; MYO, myocardial.

[b]Levels: – (absent) to +++ (very numerous) are our estimates from the data. "+" to "+++" are authors' estimates.

[c]% indicates proportion of cells positive; the number in parentheses indicates the number of particles per 100 cell sections.

integrated and that the integrated provirus was inactivated by *de novo* methylation, whereas integrated proviruses formed after infection of 8-day embryos remained unmethylated and active in many cells of the embryos. A parallel study (Stewart *et al.*, 1982) showed that MuLV-infected F9 EC cells contained as many as 100 integrated copies, whose activity (measured by XC test and assay of virus-specific RNA) was largely suppressed by *de novo* methylation, whereas an established line of differentiated cells (derived from another primary teratocarcinoma) did not methylate the integrated proviruses and supported a productive infection as efficiently as did NIH 3T3 cells. Infected F9 cells subsequently differentiated with retinoic acid also failed to produce virus and contained the same low level of viral RNA. Azacytidine treatment of infected F9 EC and retinoic acid-differentiated cells also left the viral RNA levels unchanged and yielded only minute amounts of virus.

Comparison of these results with the data shown in Table IV reveals no systematic correlation in behavior between the integrated MuLV and IAP proviruses. Thus, even though both MuLV and IAP are poorly expressed in F9 EC cells, they respond quite differently to retinoic acid treatment. Furthermore, IAP expression is high in at least two of the other three EC lines studied. Finally, IAP expression is relatively low in differentiated cells other than endoderm. Although methylation is clearly an important mechanism in governing expression of both IAP and MuLV integrated elements, additional tissue-specific factors must affect the activity of the IAP genes.

Jahner and Jaenisch (1985) have emphasized the importance of integration site in determining the activity of newly inserted proviral elements. They found that the individual Moloney MuLV (MoMuLV) proviruses integrated in six different transgenic mouse substrains were each highly methylated in 12-day embryos but during subsequent development showed progressive demethylation of specific CpG sites located exclusively in the 5′ and 3′ enhancer regions of the LTRs. The extent of demethylation was tissue specific and strongly affected by chromosomal position. The methylation of flanking host and internal proviral sequences was essentially unchanged. A subsequent study (Soriano *et al.*, 1986) provided further support for the concept that expression from the LTRs of integrated proviruses is dependent on the site of integration. The authors suggested that retroviruses could be used to identify the specific loci that permit activation during development (Barklis *et al.*, 1986). These results have obvious relevance for the observed strain- and tissue-related variations in IAP expression.

In EC cells recently infected with MoMuLV, virus expression was suppressed at all times after infection, but methylation of integrated provirus was not complete until days 15–16 (Gautsch and Wilson, 1983; Niwa *et al.*, 1983; Linney *et al.*, 1984). Evidence was presented that certain MoMuLV LTR regulatory sequences are not functional in the EC cells (Linney *et al.*, 1984). Evidence for control of IAP expression by mechanisms other than DNA methylation is provided by the results of Morgan and Hwang (1984),

Morgan and Hwang (1987), and Dragani *et al.* (1987), with NIH 3T3 cells, EC cells, and B6C3 mouse liver, respectively.

XII. IAP Element Transpositions

A number of IAP element transpositions have been observed. The majority of these have occurred in mouse tumor cell lines that express IAP RNAs at high levels. The target genes have been ones whose products either confer some growth advantage to the cell or cause other detectable change in the cell properties. The precise effect on the target gene has depended on the position and orientation of the IAP element, and both activation and inactivation of gene expression have been observed. Figure 8 presents a summary

Structure of Recombinant

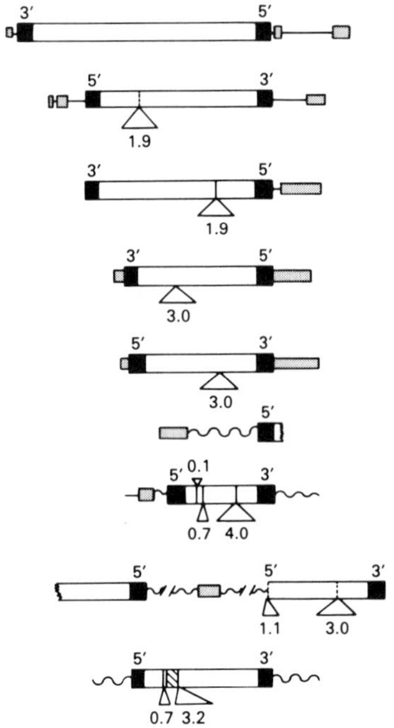

Target Gene	Cells	Effect of Insertion on Expression	IAP Element Type
κ-light chain	igk-20 (MOPC-21)	↓	I
κ-light chain	igk-1 (MOPC-21)	↓	IΔ1
interleukin-3	WEHI-3B	↑	IΔ1
c-mos	XRPC 24	↑	IΔ3
c-mos	NSI (MOPC-21)	—	IΔ3
c-myc	J558	—	?
renin	germ line DBA/2	↑	IΔ4
pseudo α-globin	germ line BALB/C	—	I I(?), IΔ3
various	MOPC-315	unknown	IIB

FIG. 8. IAP element transpositions. The structures of the IAP elements are shown on the left: open bars represent internal IPA sequences, and solid bars the IAP LTRs; stippled bars represent the target genes and lines the mouse-flanking sequences. Deletions are indicated by Δ and their sizes are given in kb. A solid vertical line shows that the position of the deletion was determined from sequence (compared with the sequence of full-size MIA14), whereas a broken vertical line indicates that the position was determined from heteroduplex analysis; absence of a vertical line indicates that the position of the deletion was deduced from a restriction map.

of the structural organization of transposed IAP elements and their target sequences. Transposition of IAP elements was first noted by Hawley *et al.* (1982) in a κ light chain-producing mouse hybridoma. Two subclones selected from the hybridoma on the basis of defective κ chain synthesis were shown to contain rearranged κ genes created by insertion of IAP elements. Each cell line contained a different IAP insertion (Kuff *et al.*, 1983b). In igk-1, a 5.2-kb IAP element was inserted in the large intron between the variable (v–j) and constant (c) regions of the κ gene and in the same transcriptional orientation. Sequencing of the LTRs revealed they were nonidentical and no target site duplication was found (Hawley *et al.*, 1984a). This insertion caused a decrease in κ light chain protein to a level 10% of that in the wild-type gene, and this level reflected the reduction in transcripts from the κ gene (Hawley *et al.*, 1984a). In the igk-20 cell line, a full-size 7.2-kb IAP element was inserted in the small intron between the hyrophobic leader (l) and v–j gene sequences in an orientation opposite that of κ gene transcription (Hawley *et al.*, 1982; Kuff *et al.*, 1983b). A target site duplication (AAAAGG) was found. In this case no κ light chain was detected, even though a slightly larger than normal RNA transcript complementary to the κ chain gene was detectable in the cells at 10–20% of the wild-type level (Hawley *et al.*, 1984a). Because both of the IAP insertions occurred in κ gene introns, they might have been expected to be spliced out without affecting gene expression. It was subsequently shown for the igk-20 line that an abnormal splice is made to a cryptic site in the l–v intron that puts the variable region sequence out of phase (Hawley *et al.*, 1984c).

Another IAP element transposition resulted in activation of the c-*mos* gene in myeloma XRPC-24 (Rechavi *et al.*, 1982). This element inserted into the c-*mos* gene at codon 88 in the opposite transcriptional orientation. Initially it was thought that an insertion element of 150 bp was involved, but subsequently it became clear that this sequence was actually part of an IAP 5′ LTR (Kuff *et al.*, 1983a). When the rearranged gene, designated 3′rc-*mos*, was cloned and transfected into 3T3 cells, transformed foci were induced, whereas the cloned unrearranged c-*mos* gene did not induce such foci (Rechavi *et al.*, 1982). Transcriptional activation of rc-*mos* was shown by Horowitz *et al.* (1984) to be due to the presence of promoters in the IAP 5′ LTR. Using CAT constructs with the LTR inserted 5′ to the CAT gene in both orientations, they showed that transcription could occur from cryptic promoters in the direction opposite to that in the IAP element, although at a much lower rate than that in the usual direction. The IAP insertion removed an upstream cis-acting transcriptional inhibitor of c-*mos* (Canaani *et al.*, 1984) in an event analogous to that which occurred when the c-*mos* gene was incorporated into MSV; in that case, Moloney MuLV sequences were joined to codon 22 of c-*mos* to produce a transformation-competent gene (Cohen *et al.*, 1983). Cloning of the 5′ c-*mos* sequences displaced by the IAP element insertion allowed construction of a restriction map, which revealed that a 4.2-kb IAP element had been inserted into the c-*mos* sequence (Canaani *et al.*, 1983). Both LTRs were sequenced and are nonidentical; a target site duplication (CACTCC) was found.

A second c-*mos* rearrangement was observed by Gattoni-Celli *et al.* (1983) in the NSI myeloma (derived from MOPC-21) on the basis of a new restriction fragment detected when Southern blots of genomic DNA were hybridized with a c-*mos* gene probe. This rearranged c-*mos* gene appeared to be amplified as well, and c-*mos* sequences were less methylated in the parental myeloma and a number of other hybridoma lines than in normal cells. There appeared to be little effect of this rearrangement on the expression of c-*mos*. The rearrangement was cloned as a 12-kb *Eco*RI fragment by Cohen *et al.* (1983) and designated rc-*mos* NSI. Sequencing of the junction between c-*mos* and the inserted DNA revealed that a 3′ IAP LTR was joined to c-*mos* at codon 30, with the LTR oriented in the same transcriptional direction as the c-*mos* gene is. When this clone was transfected into NIH 3T3 monolayers, a small but significant number of foci were induced. The most likely mechanism of activation of the c-*mos* by the IAP element insertion is in providing a viral promoter, and the low level of activity of this clone was attributed to the absence of upstream LTR regulatory regions, such as the putative enhancer sequence. Restriction mapping of the region 5′ to the rc-*mos* gene has shown that the insertion consists of an approximately 4.2-kb IAP element. The LTRs have not been sequenced.

It should be noted that the two IAP element insertions into the c-*mos* gene are distinct. Although the insertions involved similar types of IAP structural variants (Fig. 8) and occurred at nearby locations in c-*mos*, the elements were in opposite orientations with respect to c-*mos* transcription and represent independent events that occurred in unrelated mouse myeloma lines. The fact that the NSI myeloma as well as hybridoma cell lines derived from it all contained the IAP insertion in c-*mos* strongly suggests that this rearrangement occurred in the parental MOPC-21 myeloma (Gattoni-Celli *et al.*, 1983). The hybridoma lines igk-1 and igk-20 containing mutant κ genes were also isolated from cell lines derived from MOPC-21 myeloma (Hawley *et al.*, 1982).

The MOPC-315 myeloma cell line contains an increased number of genomic type II IAP elements compared with embryonic cells and some other myelomas (Shen-Ong and Cole, 1984). Type IIB elements are the major source of transcripts in these cells. Restriction analysis showed that the newly inserted copies were very similar to one another, a finding suggesting they were derived from a small number (or perhaps even one) of the active elements. The target sites were single-copy sequences or low-number repetitive sequences, but they have not been further studied, so the possible functional effects of the type II IAP element insertions in MOPC-315 are not known.

Rearrangement of the 5′ end of the c-*myc* gene is a common event in many mouse myelomas and is involved in the 15:12 chromosomal translocation and the activation of *myc* gene transcription (see references in Greenberg *et al.*, 1985). In the J558 myeloma, a secondary rearrangement involving an IAP element appears to have occurred in this region (Greenberg *et al.*, 1985). In the clone designated J558α25, an IAP 5′ LTR and some internal sequence have been found inserted approximately 2-kb downstream from c-*myc* in the same transcriptional orientation. Transcription of the c-*myc* sequences appears not to be significantly changed by this insertion, because *myc* RNA levels in this tumor and in MOPC-11 myeloma, which has the same 5′ rearrangement but not the IAP insertion, were the same.

Another IAP transposition was found in the myelomonocytic leukemia cell line WEHI-3B (Ymer *et al.*, 1985). A 5.2-kb IAP element had inserted 215 bp upstream of the putative IL-3 gene TATA box in the opposite transcriptional orientation, leading to constitutive production of IL-3 by this cell line. Transfection of the cloned rearranged IL-3 gene into NIH 3T3 and COS cells resulted in production of the factor by these cell lines. Complete sequencing of the inserted IAP element (Ymer *et al.*, 1986) has shown that the LTRs are identical and that there is a target site duplication (CACAAC). The mechanism by which activation of the IL-3 gene is achieved is not clear. Evidence suggests the LTR is not providing a cryptic promoter in this case: three IL-3 cDNA clones made from WEHI-3B cells have the same 5′ ends as full-length cDNA clones from a T cell line lacking the IAP insertion, thus making it likely that the IL-3 and not an LTR promoter is used (Ymer *et al.*, 1985). The LTR could be providing an enhancer or removing a *cis* acting regulatory sequence as for the c-*mos* gene. The enhancer model has been proposed to account for conversion of a T cell line to IL-2 independence upon insertion of a Gibbon ape endogenous retrovirus provirus 3′ to the IL-2 gene (Chen *et al.*, 1985).

The examples of IAP element transpositions thus far cited have occurred in cells that are actively expressing IAP transcripts. Several germ-line insertions have also been found. One insertion was into a renin gene of DBA/2 mice (Burt *et al.*, 1984). Mice fall into low and high submaxillary gland (SMG) renin producers depending on whether they carry only the *ren-A* gene (*Ren-1*) (low) or have a duplicated *ren-B* (*Ren-2*) gene (high) as well. Burt *et al.* found that the *ren-B* gene contains a 3-kb IAP element inserted in the 3′ flanking region in the same transcriptional orientation. Sequencing of the entire IAP element, designated MIARN, has shown it to be one of the most deleted and modified elements analyzed. Extremely dissimilar LTRs were flanked by a target site duplication (GAACAA). Although many features common to other IAP elements were present, regions that are variable among IAP elements as a result of different numbers of internal repeats are particularly variable in this element. The LTR R region contains large amplifications of pyrimidine-rich sequences, as pointed out by Burt *et al.* The number of repeats within the two LTRs was very different. Transgenic mice formed by microinjection of a cloned *Ren-2* gene, including the downstream IAP element, showed the usual high levels of SMG renin expression (Tronik *et al.*, 1987). However, it has not been shown that the IAP element has any effect on *Ren-2* gene expression, and *M. hortulanus* mice produce high SMG renin even though they lack the IAP insertion at the 3′ end of the *ren-B* gene (Dickinson *et al.*, 1984).

An association between the α-globin pseudogene and IAP elements in the BALB/c genome (Lueders *et al.*, 1982) is also probably due to a transposition event. Mice have three functional α-globin genes and two closely related pseudogenes. Whereas the functional genes are clustered on chromosome 11, the pseudogenes α-3 and α-4 are found on chromosomes 15 and 17, respectively (Leder *et al.*, 1981). One of the pseudogenes, α-3, has precisely lost the intervening sequences of the functional gene (Nishioka *et al.*, 1980) and is flanked by two IAP elements (Lueders *et al.*, 1982). The IAP element inserted upstream of the α-globin gene may be an intact 7.2-kb element truncated by cloning. The IAP element inserted about 4-kb downstream is similar in structure to the 4.2-kb element inserted in rc-*mos* X24, but it is missing the sequences at the 5′ end, including the LTR. We speculated that the loss of introns as well as transposition to another chromosomal location could have been mediated by a reverse transcription mechanism involving the inserted IAP elements. However, the topographical relationships between the sequences (Fig. 8) do not permit a straightforward mechanism to be proposed.

A solo IAP LTR was recently found inserted in a γ-actin-processed pseudogene; the original insertion was assumed to have been a complete IAP element with the LTRs subsequently undergoing unequal crossing over (Man *et al.*, 1987).

Major internal IAP sequence rearrangements have been reported to occur in normal developing and senescing tissues of BALB/c, Swiss Webster, and C57BL/6J mice (Mays-Hoopes *et al.*, 1983). We did not find comparable changes in tissues from BALB/cJ mice (E. Kuff, unpublished observations).

Although free IAP provirus has not yet been found in cells in which transpositions have occurred, it seems reasonable to propose that transposition does involve an RNA intermediate and the reverse transcriptase encoded by the IAP elements themselves. In favor of this possibility is the fact that transcripts from elements of the type that transposed are abundant in the cells in which transposition has occurred. However, a problem with this model is the fact that in many instances, the transposed elements have had nonidentical LTRs (Hawley *et al.*, 1984a; Canaani *et al.*, 1983; Burt *et al.*, 1984), whereas the accepted model of reverse transcription requires that the two LTRs be identical. In fact, among transposed elements, only the IL-3 insertion has had identical LTRs (Ymer *et al.*, 1986). In addition, for the element in igk-1 cells, no target site duplication was present and the terminal A of the 3′ LTR was missing (Hawley *et al.*, 1984a). Boeke *et al.* (1985), in order to explain a similar situation in yeast, suggested that the Ty element reverse transcriptase is error prone. Baltimore (1985), however, questioned this interpretation and pointed out that most mutations have occurred at sites in Ty previously shown to be polymorphic and could as well have resulted from recombination between elements. In fact many of the differences between the transposed IAP 5′ and 3′ LTR sequences occur at positions that are polymorphic among a large collection of sequenced LTRs associated with genomic IAP elements, cDNAs, and transposed elements. The LTR sequence TCCTTAAGAG was proposed by Hawley *et al.* (1984a) to be a hallmark of transposed elements. A number of cDNAs do have this precise sequence, but the LTRs of the MIARN element, the IAP element associated with the *myc* rearrangement, and the 3′ LTR of rc-*mos* X24 do not.

Hawley *et al.* (1984b) have since found an additional mutant line that may be due to an IAP insertion in the same position as that in igk-1. They have proposed that IAP elements prefer certain chromosomal loci for insertion. From other studies it appears that this region may be particularly prone to recombinational events (Perlmutter *et al.*, 1984). It is DNase I-hypersensitive and contains an enhancer sequence. DNase I-hypersensitive sites have recently been demonstrated to be favored sites for proviral insertions by Vijaya *et al.* (1986), who found that in seven cases of retroviral integrations the acceptor sites mapped within 500 bp of a DNase I-hypersensitive site. The positions into which the transposed elements are inserted may thus be more a reflection of the transcriptional activity of the region than of any sequence specificity.

Whatever the mechanism of transposition, the transposed IAP element has the potential to affect the target gene in a number of ways. Interruption of the sequence can inactivate a coding sequence as in the case of the κ gene insertions (Hawley *et al.*, 1982). LTRs with bidirectional promoters can affect translation levels (Horowitz *et al.*, 1984). In a fashion similar to activation of genes in yeast by upstream insertion of Ty elements (see Elder *et al.*, 1983), activation occurred when the element was inserted in a transcriptional orientation opposite to that of the target gene, in the case of both rc-*mos* X24 (Canaani *et al.*, 1983) and the IL-3 gene (Ymer *et al.*, 1985). Additionally, the LTRs can presumably provide enhancer elements to modify levels of gene expression (Lueders *et al.*, 1984). With the large number of IAP elements in the genome, homologous recombination between elements and gene conversion events might be common. Maintaining a large number of nonfunctional elements may be one level of control of transcription in IAP-containing mouse cells as well as Ty element-containing yeast cells (Boeke *et al.*, 1985). In view of the large number of IAP elements in the mouse and their varied modes of effect, it would seem that transpositions have the potential to cause considerable genetic variation at both the germ-line and somatic cell levels.

XIII. IAP Gene Products as Immunoglobulin Regulatory Factors

An unexpected recent development has been the identification of multiple IAP-related cDNA clones that encode secreted factors with regulatory effects on immunoglobulin E (IgE) production (Martens *et al.*, 1985, 1987; Moore *et al.*, 1986; Kuff *et al.*, 1986b). For several years it has been known that synthesis of IgE by B lymphocytes can be isotypically regulated by soluble T lymphocyte-derived factors that have affinity for the Fc region of IgE (IgE-binding factors or IgE-BF) (Ishizaka, 1984). IgE-BF secreted by normal cells (rat, mouse, human) have sizes ranging from 13 to 15 kDa and may selectively potentiate or suppress the IgE response. It was suggested that IgE-potentiating or IgE-suppressive factors were polypeptides of similar primary structure but differed in glycosylation state and perhaps other features of their posttranslational processing (Martens *et al.*, 1985).

Huff *et al.* (1982) described a rat–mouse T cell hybridoma that, on incubation with IgE, secreted immunosuppressive IgE-BFs with sizes of approximately 13, 26, and 60 kDa. Polyadenylated RNA from the IgE-induced hybridoma was used to prepare and isolate a series of eight cross-hybridizing cDNA clones that coded for secreted Ig-BF when transfected into COS7 (Martens *et al.*, 1985), a line of SV40-transformed monkey kidney cells. The IgE-BF produced by two of the eight clones were biologically active and potentiated IgE production in B lymphocytes. All of the clones hybridized with a probe representing a cloned mouse genomic IAP element. One clone, 8.3, which produced 60-kDa and 11-kDa potentiating IgE-BF, was sequenced in its entirety (Martens *et al.*, 1985; Moore *et al.*, 1986) and found to represent a mouse IAP gene with a 3.4-kb deletion involving the 3′ portion of the *gag* coding region and the 5′ portion of *pol*; the open reading frame of 556 aa defined a *gag–pol* fusion protein that represented the 60-kDa secretory product. The sequence contained two N-glycosylation sites in the *gag* portion. The fully active 11-kDa IgE-BF was encoded entirely within the *gag* sequences and presumably was derived by posttranslational processing of the 60-kDa product; it contained the more 3′ N-glycosylation site (Martens *et al.*, 1987). Antisera prepared against electrophoretically purified p73 from myeloma-derived IAPs reacted with both the 60- and 11-kDa IgE-BF and with two oligopeptides prepared from the predicted amino acid sequence in the 11-kDa coding region (Moore *et al.*, 1986). The antisera also reacted with the immunosupressive IgE-BF produced by the hybridoma itself and by normal mesenteric lymph nodes of immunized rats and mice. The earlier prediction was confirmed when it was shown that the IgE-BF products of clone 8.3 could act as either suppressing or potentiating factors, depending on the state of glycosylation at the downstream site (Martens *et al.*, 1987). Mutagenesis of the more 5′ N-glycosylation site was without effect on the binding or biological activity of the clone 8.3 IgE-BF (Martens *et al.*, 1987).

Clone 8.3 and four other IgE-BF-producing cDNA clones were characterized by heteroduplex and additional sequence analysis (Kuff *et al.*, 1986b). Each one was shown to represent a different structural variant of the basic IAP provirus (Fig. 1). The only coding region common to all five clones was the region of *gag* corresponding to the 11-kDa peptide of clone 8.3. One clone, 10.2, was a typical type IΔ1 IAP element, containing a 1.9-kb deletion and an open reading frame for an 11.6-kDa *gag–pol* fusion protein. This clone yielded a biologically inert IgE-BF of 60 kDa, presumably by cleavage of the primary translation product. Antisera prepared against the oligopeptides mentioned above reacted with IAP-related proteins produced in neuroblastoma and myeloma cells. The nucleotide sequences of cDNA clones 8.3 and 10.2 were 90–96% homologous with that of the full-length genomic clone MIA14 in shared regions, and amino acid homology was strongly conserved.

Murine IAPs share extensive amino acid sequence homology with the cloned hamster element H18 (Ono *et al.*, 1985; Mietz *et al.*, 1987) and primate type D retroviruses (Mietz *et al.*, 1987) over the region beginning with the p27 domain of *gag* and extending through the *pol* gene (see Fig. 3). The region that encodes the 11-kDa IgE-BF of cDNA clone 8.3 is composed partly of sequences from the conserved p27 region and partly from upstream sequences unique to mouse IAPs (Toh *et al.*, 1985a; Kuff *et al.*, 1986b); the critical N-glycosylation site is in the p27 domain and appears also in the H18 sequence.

These observations raise interesting questions about the evolution of murine IgE-BF genes. In view of conservation of sequence over the central region of IAPs, hamster elements, and type D retroviruses (see Section III,D), it seems likely that the unrelated 5′ coding regions represent recombinant events peculiar to each form. The murine IAP genome has apparently incorporated cellular genetic information that when combined with sequence contributed by the p27 *gag* coding domain, can yield polypeptides with affinity for IgE. This new genetic material has become part of the IAP *gag*-equivalent structural protein p73 and greatly amplified in the mouse genome. Although IAPs themselves are not secreted from the producing cells and IAP-related proteins have not been detected in the medium over neuroblastoma and myeloma cells, the derived amino acid sequences of MIA14 and several IAP-related cDNA clones contain a hydrophobic N-terminal segment resembling a secretory signal peptide (Mietz *et al.*, 1987). Apparently the modified proteins produced by the structurally variant IgE-BF genes are not assembled into particle form but can move through the usual secretory channels. The signals that specifically regulate expression of IgE-BF genes in the hybridoma in response to IgE stimulation are not known. However, glycosylation of the IgE-BF is determined by the same external factors that regulate this process in normal T cells (Martens *et al.*, 1987). Other IAP genes are constitutively expressed in the hybridoma cells, and these do not respond in an obvious way (Moore *et al.*, 1986). The complex factors governing IgE-BF production in the normal rodent immune response have been reviewed (Ishizaka, 1984). Whether IAP-related genes are involved in production of binding factors for other immunoglobulin isotypes is not yet known.

IgE-BF of similar size and glycosylation state are secreted by human T cells. A gene for human lymphocyte membrane-associated and soluble IgE-binding proteins (Fc_E receptor and IgE-BF, respectively) has recently been cloned and sequenced (Ikuta *et al.*, 1987). This gene shows no sequence homology with the mouse IgE-BF cDNA clones. This is not surprising, because the recombinant event that produced the murine IAP *gag* protein appears to be peculiar to that species. IgE-BF have not been studied in the Syrian hamster. It will be interesting to know whether Syrian hamster IgE-BF are coded by retroviral elements, or, as seems likely, by cellular genes that have not been coopted into a retroviral genome.

A different type of interaction between IAPs and the mouse immune system was suggested by studies on the mechanism of immunosuppression in plasmacytoma-bearing mice (Giacomoni *et al.*, 1976; Giacomoni and Katzmann, 1976; Katzmann *et al.*, 1975, 1978). Intraperitoneal injection of IAP-containing subcellular fractions or gradient-purified IAPs from several transplantable myelomas were found to suppress the primary immune response to sheep red blood cells in BALB/c mice by 50–60%, and inhibitions of 70–90% were achieved by injection of RNA prepared from whole myeloma or isolated IAPs. "Control" RNA from normal mouse liver was without effect. Inhibition was abolished by ribonuclease treatment of the RNA preparations; however, the effect of protease treatment was not reported. Tumor-derived RNA was also said to cause conversion of surface Ig on normal lymphocytes to the same idiotype as the myeloma secretory protein, and this effect also was reportedly concentrated in RNA from a crude IAP-containing tumor fraction.

Subsequently, it was found that immunosuppression of the primary immune response was mediated by soluble protein factors produced by splenic macrophages (Katzmann, 1978) and that the induction of these suppressor cells could be achieved by injection of subcellular myeloma fractions enriched in IAPs (Chen *et al.*, 1982). It apparently has not been determined whether the induction is due to the the IAP themselves or to a factor copurified with them. The conversion of lymphocyte surface Ig following exposure to extracted IAP RNA is not easily understood in the light of current knowledge.

XIV. IAP Gene Expression in Genetically Determined Mouse Diabetes

The recessive *db* gene in homozygous state induces a chronic hyperglycemia that in susceptible mouse strains is followed by pancreatic beta cell necrosis, and a non-insulin-dependent diabetes (Leiter *et al.*, 1986a; Leiter and Wilson, 1987). IAPs were detected in the beta cells of genetically diabetic mice by electron microscopy and biochemical assays (Like and Chick, 1970; Leiter and Bedigian, 1979). Leiter and Kuff (1984) used immunocytochemical methods at both the light and electron microscopic level to demonstrate p73-related antigens in beta cells of the susceptible strains C57BL/Ks and CBA/Lt. Antigenic material was widely distributed throughout the cytoplasm of beta cells from hyperglycemic *db/db* mice but not from normoglycemic *db/+* or +/+ littermate controls. In contrast to the situation in the IAP-rich MOPC-104E myeloma cells, where the immunocytochemical reagent was localized to IAPs and their sites of assembly on the endoplasmic reticulum, p73-related antigen in the beta cells of *db/db* mice was also found dispersed through other cytoplasmic organelles involved in secretion, including Golgi complex and secretory granules, and occasionally in patches at the cell surfaces. IAPs themselves were observed in beta cells of four diabetes-susceptible inbred strains (C57BL/Ks, CBA/LtJ, DBA/2J, and C3HEB/FEJ) but not in cells of resistant strains (C57BL/6J, 129/J, Ma/MyJ). IAP numbers in beta cells from the susceptible strains were further enhanced by culture in high glucose. These observations were subsequently extended to the molecular level (Leiter *et al.*, 1986b). Levels of IAP transcripts and proteins were increased 5- to 7-fold and 10- to 15-fold, respectively, in explanted CBA pancreatic islets cultured for 48 hr in high glucose, relative to levels in cells maintained in low glucose. Preproinsulin mRNA was induced to a similar relative extent in the high-glucose cells. Both 7.2- and 5.4-kb IAP transcripts were enhanced in the CBA/J cells, as were their respective 73-kDa and 114- to 120-kDa protein products. In contrast, little or no increase in the low basal IAP expression was observed when islets from C57BL/6 mice were cultured in high glucose.

Strain differences were also observed with respect to IAP protein expression in thymus cells of 1-month-old mice (Leiter *et al.*, 1986b). Whereas C57BL/6J thymocytes synthesized a 117-kDa component exclusively (Kuff and Fewell, 1985), both 73-kDa and 117-kDa proteins were produced in C57BL/Ks cells. Synthesis of p117 was maintained in thymuses of both C57BL/Ks (susceptible) and C57BL/6J (resistant) mice containing the *db/db* genes; however, synthesis of p73 was almost entirely abrogated in the

C57BL/Ks *db/db* thymus. It was suggested that the accelerated thymic involution characteristic of *db/db* mice might entail selective elimination of the p73-producing cells.

Enhanced IAP protein expression might play a part in pathogenesis of insulin-dependent diabetes by sensitizing the beta cells to autoimmune attack (Leiter *et al.*, 1986b). Antibodies to p73 appear in the sera of both *db/db* and +/+ C57BL/Ks and C57BL/6J mice at about 8 weeks of age and increase to maximum levels (ELISA titers of 1:400 or more) by 5 months (Serreze *et al.*, 1988). The onset and phase of rapid increase coincides with the development of islet cell disease in the susceptible *db/db* animals (Leiter *et al.*, 1985). Surprisingly, titers to p73 parallel those to insulin, and reciprocal absorption experiments indicate that a common epitope on the two proteins can be recognized by the autoantibodies in the diabetic mice. Insulin and p73 have no obvious regions of homology at the primary sequence level, so this "mimicry" may be based on higher order configuration. Antibody-mediated autoimmune reactions may have only a secondary or accelerating role in development of disease, because beta cell necrosis also occurs, albeit more slowly, in susceptible *db/db* mice carrying the *scid* mutation, which renders them deficient in all forms of immunoglobulin (Leiter and Wilson, 1987).

A retroviral role in induction of beta cell autoimmunity has also been suggested for the nonobese diabetic (NOD) mice, which are characterized by an early insulitis followed by insulin-dependent diabetes. In these animals, both IAPs and aberrant type-C particles are seen in the beta cells and the sera carry antibodies against both types of antigen. These and other data on the interactions of viruses with pancreatic beta cells have recently been reviewed (Leiter and Wilson, 1987).

XV. Type-R Particles

Bernhard and Tournier (1964) described a virus-like particle of novel appearance in the cytoplasm of certain Syrian hamster cells. The particles (see Fig. 5b) had a dense central core with radial spokes ending at an outer unit membrane and occurred in small or large groups within the cisternae of the endoplasmic reticulum. The particles were found in cells of the BHK21 clone 13 line derived from baby hamster kidney, in polyoma- and SV40-transformed BHK cells, and in an adenovirus 12-induced tumor, but not in normal embryonic cells. This report was followed by a number of other studies on the occurrence of these particles in Syrian hamster cell lines and tumors. The illustrations of the particles in MSV-transformed culture lines by de Petris and Harvey (1969) are particularly clear. Thomas and coworkers (1967, 1968) presented a detailed morphological study of particle formation and pointed out the occurrence of elongated forms and cleavage of these to form individual particles. They proposed the term H-particle because of the exclusive association of this entity with hamster cells. The term type R for the radial virus-like particle of hamsters was coined by Shipman *et al.* (1969). These authors estimated the numbers of R-particles in several clones of BHK-21 cells, including BHK-21/13. They found no particles in HaK and RPMI-1846, two other established hamster lines, or in embryonal hamster kidney or germinal centers from hamster Peyer's patches. Zeigel *et al.* (1969) described type R particles in cultured cells derived from hamster tumors induced by inoculation of Bryant strain RSV (see Fig. 5b). Gazzolo and De-The (1971) observed R-particles in all RSV-transformed cell lines of BHK21/13 origin, as well as in tumors induced with RSV *in vivo*. Cesarini and De Micco (1972) examined a number of Syrian hamster cell cultures and tumors induced by oncogenic viruses. Particles were not seen in primary cultures from embryos, hamster kidney and kidney cultures, and young adult hamster thymus. Differing amounts of particles were seen in BHK21/13 cells, in tumors resulting from implantation of these cells, and in 11 clones of BHK-21 transformed *in vitro* by RNA or DNA oncogenic viruses. Particles were present in largest numbers in BHK21/13-derived clones doubly transformed by RSV and polyoma virus and in tumors formed by BHK21/13 cells transformed with polyoma virus. Cesarini and De Micco reviewed all previous reports of type H(R) particle occurrence in spontaneous hamster tumors (lymphoma and melanoma), in induced tumors, and in cell lines obtained from *in vivo*-induced (RSV and MSV) tumors. They also tabulated previous studies on particle occurrence in BHK21/13 cell lines and their transformed derivatives (including a number not mentioned above). Epstein and Fukuyama (1973) subsequently examined R-particles in cultured hamster melanoma cells with varying degrees of differentiation.

Type R particles were demonstrated in normal Syrian hamster embryos by Sobis and Vandeputte (1978). In blastocysts (day 3), single particles were found in cisternae in both trophoectoderm and inner cell mass. On day 6, particles were more numerous in cells of all germ layers and budding forms were numerous. One day later, particle accumulation was at its peak, with frequent budding observed. The number of "mature" and budding forms decreased until they were no longer detectable at day 14 or thereafter in any of the tissues. R-particles were quite abundant in yolk sac carcinomas and in a sarcoma induced by *in vivo* injection of SV40.

Hamster R-particles and murine IAPs resemble one another in their intracellular location, appearance in transformed but not normal somatic cells, and temporary expression in early embryos. In hamster–mouse hybrid cells producing both particles simultaneously, the two kinds of particle cores can be encapsidated in a common outer shell acquired during budding through the endoplasmic reticulum membrane (Yotsuyanagi and Ephrussi, 1974; Yotsuyanagi, 1977). This fact suggests (a) that the respective protein components can be effectively segregated even though assembled in close proximity and (b) that any protein processing that may be involved in producing the more complex R-particle morphology does not visibly affect the IAP core.

With the demonstration that the Syrian hamster genome contains a reiterated family of proviral elements homologous to the murine IAP (Lueders and Kuff, 1981; Suzuki *et al.*, 1982) and that RNA from hamster cells containing R-particles reacted with probes derived from both mouse and hamster elements (Lesser *et al.*, 1986), the likelihood must be considered that the R-particles are in fact encoded by the IAP-related hamster genes. Lesser *et al.* (1986) demonstrated that 5-azacytidine treatment, previously shown to greatly enhance IAP expression in mouse KiBALB cells (Hojman-Montes de Oca *et al.*, 1984), produced a similarly powerful increase of R-particle number in BHK-21 clone 13 cells. The number of particle-positive cells was increased from 22% in controls to as many as 90%, and the number of particles seen by electron microscopy was increased 10- to 15-fold. Poly(A) RNA extracted from control and azacytidine-treated cells and hybridized with probes derived from cloned hamster IAP-related elements (Lueders and Kuff, 1983) showed a single band at 8.5-kb. Densitometry of the patterns indicated a 2-fold increase in the level of hybridization in RNA from the treated cells, considerably less than the apparent increase in particle number. The same 8.5-kb component was detected with a mouse IAP probe, although at a lower level of hybridization consistent with the known sequence divergence between mouse and hamster elements (Kuff and Lueders, 1981, 1983). Comparative restriction of genomic DNAs indicated extensive demethylation of the IAP-related sequence elements in the azacytidine-treated BHK-21 cells. These data provide the strongest current evidence that R-particles are encoded by the Syrian hamster IAP-homologous genomic elements. Definitive proof could be obtained by isolation of the particles and examination of the particle-associated RNA. Short of this, a positive *in situ* hybridization signal over large R-particle clusters would also be strongly indicative, as would a positive immunocytochemical reaction using a mouse IAP-specific antiserum.

An early biochemical characterization of R-particles was reported by Birkmayer *et al.* (1972), who prepared a 10,000 g cytoplasmic membrane fraction from hamster melanoma, sonicated the preparation, and then followed a sucrose density fractionation scheme much like that employed for IAPs (Kuff *et al.*, 1968). Gradient fractions were assayed for reverse transcriptase in an NP-40- and Mg-containing reaction mix. The peak of activity was located at a density of 1.21 gm/cm^3. Electron microscopy revealed that the R-particles were all contained in ribosome-stripped microsomal vesicles. The extracted RNA showed a major 70 S species on both sedimentation and gel electrophoresis. An endogenous reverse transcriptase activity of 0.2 pmol [^{3}H]TMP incorporated per min per mg protein was stimulated 6-fold by addition of poly(dT–rA) and high-molecular-weight particle RNA.

A different approach was used by Albu and Holmes (1972) to obtain R-particles from the BHK-21-F subclone of BHK-21/13. Monolayers of these cells, found by the authors to be particularly rich in R-particles, were labeled with [^{3}H]-uridine for 12 hr. The supernatant medium was then clarified, pelleted onto a 50% sucrose cushion, precipitated with polyethylene glycol (PEG), and fractionated on a 20–45% sucrose gradient. A lower band of 1.12–1.14 gm/cm^3, containing R-particles and debris, was purified by a second cycle of treatment with PEG and RNase A and gradient centrifugation. A single sharp peak of ^{3}H-labeling appeared at a density of 1.13 gm/cm^3. Electron microscopy of fixed pellets showed many 100-nm particles, often with radial spokes, and considerable background material, some of which we interpret as poorly preserved membranes. RNA from this gradient peak contained a large proportion of material sedimenting in the 70 S range on sucrose gradients or comigrating with AMV RNA on acrylamide-agarose gel electrophoresis. The authors cite a personal communication from W. P. Parks and M. Myers to the effect that no reverse transcriptase activity could be detected in BHK-21-F cells or in the isolated R-type preparations. The recovery of R-particles from the culture medium is surprising, because secretion of these particles is not known to occur. The authors pointed out that very small amounts of particles were recovered and suggested that the particles could be released by fusion of endoplasmic reticulum sacs with the plasma membrane or by lysis of a small number of cells from the otherwise intact monolayer.

Rossignol and co-workers (1975) isolated type R particles from TSV5-clone 2 cells derived from an SV40-induced tumor in newborn hamster. The cells were disrupted by nitrogen cavitation rather than by sonication, the suspension cleared at 20,000 g, and a pellet obtained from the 20,000- g supernatant fluid by centrifugation at 105,000 g. This pellet was resuspended and fractionated on a sucrose density gradient. The 105,000 g pellet and gradient fractions were assayed for reverse transcriptase activity. The pellet showed an RNase-sensitive endogenous activity of 3 pmol [^{3}H]dTMP per mg protein per min. Most of the activity was solubilized in the presence of NP-40. Total activity with poly(A)·oligo(dT) was about 250 pmol [^{3}H]dTMP per mg protein per min, and with poly(C)·oligo(dG) between 30 and 45 pmol [^{3}H]dGTP per mg per min. The maximum exogenous enzyme activity was recovered at gradient densities between 1.135 and 1.145 gm/cm^3. Electron microscopy showed a number of free R-particles together with other membrane vesicles, ribosomes, and unidentifiable material. Partial purification of reverse transcriptase was attempted from untreated TSV5 cells. Three activity peaks were eluted from a phosphocellulose column with a linear KCl gradient. A peak eluting at 0.4 *M* KC had template-primer, salt, and divalent cation responses indistinguishable from the reverse transcriptase of Rauscher MuLV. No activity could be recovered from BHK-21 cells or transformed embryo cells even through R-particles were present in both cell lines. A possible role of SV40 in activation of R-particles in the TSV5 clone 2 cells was suggested.

XVI. Occurrence of IAPs in Other Species

We have discussed the family of endogenous IAP-related genetic elements in the Syrian hamster and the intracisternal type R particles that may represent the physical expression of these elements. Reiterated elements with homology to the mouse IAP genes are also found in the DNA of rat and gerbil (Lueders and Kuff, 1981, 1983). IAPs have been observed by electron microscopy in a rat hepatoma (Novikoff and Biempica, 1966), in cell lines derived from rat hepatomas (Weinstein *et al.*, 1972; Orenstein and Weinstein, 1973; Weber *et al.*, 1978), and in a rat plasmacytoma (Burtonboy *et al.*, 1978). In the latter tumor, IAPs were much rarer than in the mouse myelomas. Weber *et al.* (1978) found that IAPs were strongly induced in HTC cells by treatment with bromodeoxyuridine (IAPs per cell section increased from 0.3 in controls to 15–20 in treated cells). In contrast, a culture line derived from Morris hepatoma 5123C showed no change in IAP content when treated with bromodeoxyuridine and dimethylsulfoxide (Orenstein and Weinstein, 1973). IAPs in rat closely resemble those of mouse in size and detailed morphology. Surprisingly, we found no information on the occurrence of virus-like entities in early rat development. As noted earlier, several rat genomic IAP-related elements have been cloned, but none were completely colinear with the mouse elements or among themselves on heteroduplex analysis (Lueders and Kuff, 1983).

Pyrinov *et al.* (1984) described an RNA-dependent (ribonuclease-sensitive) reverse transcriptase activity in Wistar rat liver postmitochondrial supernatant fractions and found that the activity was concentrated in the density region of 1.18–1.19 g/cm^3 of sucrose density gradients. This fraction contained 80- to 120-nm particles said to have both type A and type C virus-like morphologies. In a subsequent paper (Salganik *et al.*, 1985), the authors showed that the activity present in the peak density gradient fractions (1.16–1.18 g/cm^3) was enhanced 2- to 3-fold by Triton X-100. The density gradient peak contained more than 2% of the total homogenate protein. After purification by chromatography on DE-52 cellulose and phosphocellulose P11, the enzyme was shown to use poly(rC)·oligo(dG) 2–3 times more effectively than poly(rA)·oligo(dT) and poly(A) RNA·oligo(dT) and to have a very slight preference of Mg^{2+} over Mn^{2+}. About 90% of the total enzyme activity of this type was recovered in the final soluble fraction of the homogenate, i.e., not associated with particles. Poly(A) RNA from the peak gradient fraction hybridized with a 2.2-kb probe containing *gag* and *pol* sequences of mouse IAPs, but not with a MoMuLV probe. Hybridization of labeled poly(A) RNA to rat genomic digests displayed the same fragments detected with the mouse IAP probe, plus several additional bands. In evaluating these rather surprising results, it would be helpful to know whether virus-like particles are seen in sections of intact liver from the Wistar rats used for the experiments; this in itself would be an unusual observation. We note that the size and number of genomic restriction fragments hybridizing with the gradient fraction of poly(A) RNA are different from those that reacted with a cloned rat IAP element in the study of Lueders and Kuff (1983). The template–primer and divalent cation reguirements of the purified enzyme are also atypical for the mouse IAP-associated reverse transcriptase.

The literature contains two reports of IAPs in gerbil cells: Tumilowicz and Cholon (1971) described the presence of rare IAPs in cells of a continuous line originating from a fibroma in a Mongolian gerbil. Yelle and Berthiaume (1982) observed virus-like particles in some cell lines established from gerbil embryo and kidney. Both R-particles and IAPs were observed in different cell lines after multiple culture passages. Intracisternal particles with a radial structure much like the Syrian hamster R-particles were abundant in a spontaneous mammary tumor of a collared lemming (Hiraki *et al.*, 1973) but absent in normal mammary gland and other tissues. The lemming particles were somewhat larger than those of the hamster (145 nm versus 80–100 nm) but otherwise formed in identical fashion at the rough-surfaced ER. Lemmings, gerbils, and Syrian hamsters are all members of the family *Cricetidae*, whose antecedents diverged from those of Old World rats and mice (*Muridae*) about 20 million years ago. Endogenous IAP-related genetic elements have not been assessed in the lemming.

Guinea pig has little or no genomic sequence homologous to the mouse IAP elements (Lueders and Kuff, 1981). However, intracisternal particles of A-type morphology have been observed in cells of a passaged guinea pig leukemia (Nadel *et al.*, 1967; Opler, 1967; additional references in Fong and Hsiung, 1976), in a chemically induced hepatoma (Dunkel *et al.*, 1974), in normal cells of germinal centers (Ma *et al.*, 1969), and in fetal germ-line cells (Andersen and Jeppesen, 1972; Black, 1974; Fong and Hsiung, 1976). The guinea pig intracisternal particles are larger than the IAPs of mice (85–110 nm versus 70–90 nm), but otherwise bud in similar fashion at the rough-surfaced ER. Black (1974) emphasized the morphological differences between the guinea pig and mouse particles, a distinction supported by Yotsuyanagi and Szöllösi (1984). Guinea pig leukemic cells also produce an extracellular virus-like particle with a C-type morphology that can be induced in cultured cells from normal tissue by treatment with BrdUr (see Fong and Hsiung, 1976, for references). Feldman and Gross (1970) suggested that the intracisternal particles were immature forms of the extracellular virus; but no evidence to support this view has been forthcoming.

Feldman and Gross (1971) also examined by electron microscopy a variety of mammary tumors in domestic dogs and cats. Five of 11 cat tumors contained 90-nm A-particles in the cisternal spaces including perinuclear cisternae. Budding forms were observed. The particle cores varied from electron lucent to moderate density. Some cells also contained 100-nm particles resembling enveloped A-type precursors of type C particles. No particles were found in the dog tumors. The cat particles were later studied by Weijer and co-workers (Weijer *et al.*, 1974; Calafat *et al.*, 1977). They confirmed the results of Feldman and Gross, finding the 90-nm intracisternal particles in 11 of 36 feline mammary tumors. Type C particles (100-nm immature particles and/or extracellular virus) were seen in 7% of the tumors. No tumor produced both A- and C-particles. The cat intracisternal A-particles were very similar in dimensions to mouse IAPs. The authors (Calafat *et al.*, 1977) suggested that the cat IAPs may represent an endogenous virus, different from the RD-114 type C virus. Lueders and Kuff (1981) found significant hybridization of a cloned mouse IAP probe with the DNA of a feline cell line when washing was performed at a ΔT_m of $-25°C$. The reaction was barely detectable at a ΔT_m of $-14°C$. The results were consistent with the presence in the cat genome of a reiterated sequence family with distant homology to the mouse IAP.

Rare 100-nm A-particles, including budding forms, were seen in the rough-surfaced ER of an infectious pulmonary adenoma of sheep (Perk *et al.*, 1971). They closely resembled mouse IAPs. The tumor also contained other virus-like structures, including intracytoplasmic A-type and extracellular C-particles. Mussgay *et al.* (1969) observed R-type particles 100–150 nm in diameter in ER cisternae and nuclear envelope of a cell line derived from calf kidney.

Molecular hybridization shows that IAPs in rats and probably gerbils are encoded by elements related to those in the mouse (Lueders and Kuff, 1981, 1983). It remains to be shown whether this is also true for the intracisternal particles in lemming, guinea pig, and cat. The association of budding forms with the ER membranes suggests that the particle structural proteins may resemble those of the mouse IAP in having an N-terminal hydrophobic leader or internal membrane-spanning hydrophobic sequence, but tells nothing about the genetic relationships of the particle genomes.

XVII. IAP Expression in Relation to Neoplastic Transformation

The data collected in Tables V and VI illustrate the frequent association of IAP gene activity with precancerous and transformed mouse cells. The actual list of positive tumor cells is certainly longer, because IAP sightings

TABLE V

OCCURRENCE OF IAPS IN PRECANCEROUS TISSUES AND PRIMARY TUMORS

	Strain	Electron microscopy	Remarks[a]
Plasmacytomas			
Blast cells	BALB/c	+[1]	ip MO granulomas, 12 days
Tumor cells	BALB/c	++[1]	ip MO granulomas, 12 weeks
Squamous cell papillomas	C57L	+[2]	MCA-induced
	BALB/c	++[3]	MCA-induced
Squamous cell carcinomas	C57L	++++[2]	MCA-induced
	BALB/c	++++[3]	MCA-induced
	Feral	+[4]	MCA-induced 6 of 11 tumors
Mammary gland hyperplastic alveolar nodules	BALB/cAn	+[5]	Frequency not specified
Mammary tumors	BALB/cAn	+[5]	Frequency not specified
	RBR/An (RIII)	++[5]	6 of 7 tumors
	BALB/c × C3Hf	+[5]	All tumors
	BALB/c × RBR	++[5]	All tumors; RBR RIII
	RBR × C3Hf	+[5]	All tumors
Sarcomas, s.c.	CBA/H	± to +++[6]	Foreign body, 5 of 8 tumors
	C57BL/10	± to +++[6]	Foreign body
	6 inbred strains	+[7]	MCA-induced, 10 of 29 tumors
	Feral	+[4]	MCA-induced, 11 of 87 tumors
Liver	C3H, CBA, A, BALB/c	+[8]	DEN-treated, 1–3 weeks
Hepatoma	C3H × C3H/St	+[9]	Frequency not specified
Pulmonary adenoma	C57BL	+[9]	Frequency not specified
Pituitary adenoma	C57BL	+[9]	Frequency not specified
Leydig cell tumor	BALB/c × RBR	+[9]	Frequency not specified
	C3H × RBR	+[9]	Frequency not specified
Ovarian adenoma	Feral	+[9]	Frequency not specified

[a]MO, mineral oil; MCA, methylcholanthrene; DEN, diethylnitrosamine.

[1]Scholle and Foft (1970); [2]Kakefuda *et al.* (1970); [3]Bibby and Smith (1975); [4]Gardner *et al.* (1971); [5]Smith *et al.* (1970); [6]Johnson *et al.* (1973); [7]de Harven (1966); [8]Shinozuka and Estes (1977); [9]Wivel and Smith (1971).

TABLE VI

IAP OCCURRENCE IN ESTABLISHED TUMORS AND TISSUE CULTURE LINES

Cell type	Strain	Electron microscopy	Antigen	RNA	Remarks[a]
Friend erythroleukemia	DBA/2J	++ [1-4]			Friend virus-induced
Line B8	DBA/2J	+++ [1-4]			TK⁻ subline
Line B8/3	DBA/2J	− [1-4]			Spontaneous change in B8
Strain DS-19	DBA/2J			+++ [5,6]	Expression cell cycle-linked
Myelomonocytic leukemia	BALB/cAn	+++ [7]			WEHI-3B TC line
Chloroleukemia La	?			++++ [8]	
T lymphoma EL4	C57BL/6	+++ [9]			Radiation-induced
L1210	DBA/2	+++ [10]	++ [11]	++++ [8]	Ascites and solid
P1758	BALB/c			++++ [12]	Tissue culture line
5AKR13	AKR			+ [12]	Tissue culture
6C3HED	C3H	++ [13]			Estrogen-induced
BW5147	AKR			++++ [14]	
Unnamed	C57/BALB/c	++ [14a]			
Myeloma X5563	C3H/He	++++ [15-18]	++++ [11]		Ileocecal tumor
Myeloma X5563	C3H/He	++++ [19,20]			Tissue culture
X5647	C3H/He	++++ [18]			Ileocecal tumor
H86199	C3H/He	++++ [18]			Millipore chamber
MPC-1, -2, -3, -4	BALB/c	++++ [18]			Millipore chamber
H93595	BALB/c	++++ [18]			Millipore chamber
AdjPC-2, -3, -5, -6	BALB/c	++++ [18]			Adjuvant-staph
MOPC-104E	BALB/c	++++ [21]	++++ [11]	++++ [12,21,22]	Mineral oil-induced
MOPC-321	BALB/c	+ [11]	+ [11]		Mineral oil-induced
MOPC-315	BALB/c	++++ [11]		++++ [23]	Mineral oil-induced
MOPC-21, clone P3	BALB/c	++++ [20,24,25a]		++++ [12,25b,26]	Mineral oil-induced, TC line
MOPC-21, clone NSI	BALB/c	++++ [25a]			
MOPC-460	BALB/c	+++ [27,28]		+++ [27,28]	Solid & TC; also cytoplasmic A's
Various	BALB/c	? [28a]			Poorly differentiated

(*continued*)

TABLE VI (*continued*)

IAP OCCURRENCE IN ESTABLISHED TUMORS AND TISSUE CULTURE LINES

Cell type	Strain	Electron microscopy	Antigen	RNA	Remarks[a]
Hybridoma 23B6	Rat/AKR		++++[14]	++++[29]	Rat T cel/BW5147
SP603	BALB/c	++++[30]			B cell/X63Ag8
SJL/J disease	SJL/J				
Plasma cells		−[31]			Massive proliferation
Reticulum cell		+[31]			Plasma cell regression
Reticulum cell tumor		++[31]			Transplanted tumor
Reticulum cell 70429	C3H/He	±[11]	±[11]		
Sarcoma 180	Swiss			+++[8]	
L-cells, L929	C3H	+ to +++[32,33]			Ex subcut. tissue, MCA *in vitro*
B82	C3H		+[34]	++[23]	TK⁻ clone of L-929 cells
Ki-BALB clone 13	BALB/c	++[35]			25% of cells positive
clone 22	BALB/c	+[35]	+[34]		20% of cells positive
NIH-3T3	Swiss			+[8]	
Fibroblasts	C3H/He				Spontaneous transformation in TC
Lines 4953, 3069		++++[36]			Tumor-derived, TC
Line 4700		++++[36]			Strongly tumorigenic, TC
Line 2472		++[36]			Weakly tumorigenic, TC
10T1/2	C3H			+++[26]	Azacytidine treated, transformed
Rhabdomyosarcoma	?	++++[37]			Solid and TC
Osteosarcoma BF	CBA	++[38]			
Neuroblastoma C1300	A/J	++++[39]			Subcutaneous solid
		++[40]			TC lines
N4TG1		++++[14]	++++[11,34]	++++[11]	Clone from C1300, TC
N18TG2		+++[41,42]	+++[34]	+++[42]	Clone from C1300, TC
N4TG1 × B82	A × C3H		++++[34]		Stable hybrid TC line
N18TG2 × B82	A × C3H		+++[34]		Stable hybrid TC line

Melanoma S91	C × DBA F1	+[43]			
B16				–[8]	
Carcinoma D	C57L	+++[44]	++[11]		Squamous cell, MCA
Mammary adenocarcinoma					
MT-29240	BALB/c	+++[45]			TC line
Ehrlich ascites	?	+ to ++++[46-49]	+[11]	+++[8,25b]	Subclones vary in IAPs
Hepatoma 129P	C3H	±[11]	±[11]		Ascites line
Hepatocellular adenoma	BL6 × C3H			++[50]	NDEA-induced
Hepatocellular carcinoma	BL6 × C3H			++[50]	NDEA-induced
Colon tumor	BALB/c			+++[51]	DMH-induced
Preputial gland					
ESR 586	C57BL/6J	+++[52]			
Teratocarcinomas (see Table IV)					

[a]TC, tissue culture; MCA, methylcholanthrene; NDEA, nitrosodiethylamine; DMH, dimethylhydrazine.

[1]Sato *et al.* (1971); [2]deHarven and Friend (1958); [3]deHarven and Friend (1960); [4]Ostertag *et al.* (1978); [5]Augenlicht *et al.* (1984); [6]Augenlicht and Halsey (1985); [7]Sanel (1973); [8]Grigoryan *et al.* (1985); [9]Aoki *et al.* (1970); [10]E. Shelton, NCI (personal communication); [11]Kuff *et al.* (1972); [12]Kuff and Fewell (1985); [13]Sobin (1964); [14]E. L. Kuff (unpublished observations); [14a]Petrea and Gardner (1973); [15]Howatson and McCulloch (1958); [16]Parsons *et al.* (1961b); [17]Parsons *et al.* (1961a); [18]Dalton *et al.* (1961); [19]Pettingill *et al.* (1966); [20]Watson *et al.* (1970); [21]Kuff *et al.* (1968); [22]Lueders *et al.* (1977); [23]Wujcik *et al.* (1984); [24]Karpas and Cawley (1972); [25a]Bartal *et al.* (1982); [25b]Kramerov *et al.* (1985); [26]Dragani *et al.* (1987); [27]Robertson *et al.* (1975); [28]Robertson *et al.* (1976); [28a]Ebbesen and Nielsen (1970); [29]Moore *et al.* (1986); [30]Hawley *et al.* (1984c); [31]de Tkaczevski and Wanebo (1969); [32]Dales and Howatson (1961); [33]Kindig and Kirsten (1967); [34]Minna *et al.* (1974); [35]Lasneret *et al.* (1983); [36]Hall *et al.* (1968); [37]Perk and Dahlberg (1974); [38]Nakata *et al.* (1980); [39]Graham and Gonatas (1976); [40]Schubert *et al.* (1969); Augusti-Tocco *et al.* (1970); Kataoka *et al.* (1978); Ross *et al.* (1975); [41]Herrlinger *et al.* (1975); [42]Yang and Wivel (1973); [43]Dalton and Felix (1956); [44]Kakefuda *et al.* (1970); [45]Malech and Wivel (1976a); [46]Friedlander and Moore (1956); [47]Yasuzumi and Higashizawa (1956); [48]Adams and Prince (1957); [49]Kodama and Kodama (1973); [50]Dragani *et al.* (1986); [51]Royston and Augenlicht (1983); [52]Prutkin *et al.* (1977).

made incidentally to other electron microscopic finds are often only briefly noted or ignored. IAP expression is activated to some extent in many primary tumors and in premalignant situations such as squamous cell papillomas and hyperplastic mammary nodules; but with few exceptions IAP levels are more abundant in long-established tumor lines. IAP-rich cells such as the transplanted myelomas of BALB/c and C3H strain mice and subclones of the C1300 neuroblastoma of an A strain mouse may contain up to 10,000 particles per cell, and the IAP-specific RNAs, including components associated with the particles themselves, may represent from 5 to 10% of the total cytoplasmic poly(A) RNA fraction.

A. Possible Basis for Enhanced IAP Expression in Transformed Cells

We have seen that IAP gene expression is enhanced in certain normally proliferating cells (immature thymocytes) and in other somatic cells induced to divide by appropriate stimuli (hepatocytes, B lymphocytes). A general association between cell proliferation and IAP gene expression might be mediated by the enhancing action of viral or cellular oncogenes on the promoter activity of IAP LTRs. Luria and Horowitz (1986; see Section VIII,B) found that a cloned IAP LTR responded to the co-expression of all four nuclear oncogenes tested (SV40 early region, adenovirus E1a, c-*myc*, and the cellular p53 gene). c-*myc* expression has been widely linked to the proliferative state, and there is a good correlation between IAP expression and elevated levels of c-*myc* transcripts in thymus, stimulated B cells, and plasmacytomas (Mushinski *et al.*, 1983b; Marcu *et al.*, 1983). Dragani *et al.* (1986) found increased amounts of MuLV- and IAP-related transcripts in both chemically induced liver carcinomas and spontaneous hepatocellular adenoma. Transcripts of c-*myc*, but not of c-Ha-*ras* or c-*fos*, were significantly increased in all of the tumors. The possible linkage between oncogene expression and IAP transcription is an important question that deserves more extensive study.

Other factors undoubtedly have important effects on the levels of IAP expression. In particular, demethylation of sites in the IAP LTRs seems to be essential for LTR promoter activity (see Section VIII,A), possibly by permitting or enhancing the binding of soluble proteins required for transcription. Proximity to regions of activated (hypomethylated) chromatin may facilitate the transcription of individual IAP elements and determine the pattern of expression characteristic of each cell type. The presence of labile proteins that can repress the transcription of IAP genes and other endogenous retroviral elements in normal mouse liver has been suggested by Dragani *et al.* (1987).

Cell differentiation, in particular the development of the endoplasmic reticulum, may have an important influence on the apparent level of IAP gene activity. The retinoic acid-induced differentiation of F9 teratocarcinoma cells (see Table IV and Section XI) provides an interesting system in which to speculate on the complex interplay of nuclear and cytoplasmic factors in regulating IAP levels. Campisi *et al.* (1984) found that c-*myc* transcripts were drastically reduced in F9 cultures during differentiation into nonproliferating parietal endoderm (PE). The endoplasmic reticulum undergoes an extensive hypertrophy as part of this differentiation process, and there is an associated accumulation of IAPs as observed by electron microscopy (Howe and Overton, 1986). Although IAP-related RNAs were increased in the PE cells (Howe and Overton, 1986; Morgan and Hwang, 1987), transcription of genomic IAP sequences, measured in isolated nuclei, was unchanged or even slightly diminished (Morgan and Hwang, 1987). The latter authors suggested that the observed increase in IAP RNA in the face of a constant or reduced transcription rate meant that the IAP transcripts were being stabilized in the differentiated cells, possibly by encapsidation in the newly accumulating particles. It is likely that nascent IAP core protein, p73, becomes associated with the ER membrane by virtue of a hydrophobic signal sequence (Mietz *et al.*, 1987). Lack of membrane receptor sites for the signal recognition particle (Wickner and Lodish, 1985) in the undifferentiated ER-deficient embryonal carcinoma cells could result in inhibition of p73 synthesis and increased turnover of IAP transcripts. This situation could be reversed with development of the ER in differentiated PE cells. Morgan and Hwang (1984) reported a rather extensive demethylation of IAP genomic sequences in the retinoic acid-treated F9 culture. An increased number of active IAP elements generated by the DNA demethylation could have compensated for a reduced activity of individual elements associated with reduction in c-*myc* levels.

The preceding speculation seems to accord with available facts but requires experimental testing. It is interesting to compare this rather complicated set of postulated interactions with the apparently straightforward situation in transplanted myelomas, where high c-*myc* levels, widespread demethylation of IAP genomic elements, and extensive development of the ER membrane system could all favor abundant synthesis and accumulation of IAPs.

Scholle and Foft (1970; see Table V) observed IAPs in blast cells within mesenteric oil granulomas only 12 days after intraperitoneal injection of mineral oil; and particles were fairly numerous in transformed plasma cells at 12 weeks. On the other hand, Volkman *et al.* (1972) found few if any IAPs in primary tumor cells induced by an intraperitoneally implanted nitrocellulose membrane-lucite ring. The tumor, which secreted an IgG paraprotein, consisted originally of ER-deficient reticulum cells. Over successive transplant generations, the cells differentiated to a typical plasma cell morphology with extensive cytoplasmic membranes and a concomitant increase in the number of IAPs.

B. Possible Role of IAP Elements in Tumor Induction and/or Progression

Although IAP expression is a common accompaniment of transformation in mouse cells, there is no evidence for a direct causal relationship between the two phenomena. That is, IAP proviral elements are not known to have acquired cellular oncogenes or to integrate regularly at preferred sites near cellular transforming elements. On the other hand, the apparently random transposition of IAP elements within cellular genomes could occasionally have important effects on transformation or tumor progression. Precedent-setting examples are (1) the insertions of IAP proviral elements into c-*mos* genes in two different BALB/c myeloma lines (Canaani *et al.*, 1983; Gattoni-Celli *et al.*, 1983), in one case causing transcriptional activation of the recombined gene and converting it to a transformation-competent form (Rechavi *et al.*, 1982); and (2) constitutive activation of an interleukin 3 gene by adjacent upstream proviral insertion in the WEHI-3B myelomonocytic leukemia line, with consequent growth factor autonomy of these cells (Ymer *et al.*, 1985). The down-regulation of κ light chain production in subclones of the Sp602 hybridoma by two independent IAP proviral insertions in this gene (Hawley *et al.*, 1982; Kuff *et al.*, 1983b) illustrates another possible effect of IAP transposition. Abrogation of critical cell regulatory functions by insertional mutation could enhance or complement the effects of activated oncogenes. Weinstein and associates have been particularly interested in the expression of endogenous retroviral sequences during chemical carcinogenesis and have speculated on the possible intervention of the activated elements in transformation or progression (Dragani *et al.*, 1986, 1987; Hsiao *et al.*, 1986).

The mechanism(s) of IAP transposition is(are) not known. It seems likely, although it has yet to be verified experimentally, that IAP proviral elements transpose primarily through RNA intermediates, as established for analogous retrotransposons in yeast and *Drosophila* (Boeke *et al.*, 1985; see Baltimore, 1985). Grigoryan *et al.* (1985) have apparently succeeded in cloning an IAP provirus from Ehrlich ascites tumor cells. However, unintegrated closed circular intermediates seem to be rare in other IAP-rich tumor cells, because they were not detected in either the MOPC-315 myeloma (Shen-Ong and Cole, 1984) or the N4 neuroblastoma (Feenstra *et al.*, 1986). It may be recalled that many, perhaps most, of the IAP genomic elements are not competent to code for all of the necessary retroviral function because of deletions or other mutations. For example, the full-size genomic element MIA14 has a functional LTR (Lueders *et al.*, 1984) and an open reading frame for the structural protein p73 (Mietz *et al.*, 1987). However, the *pol* reading frame has two single-base mutations that would terminate translation of the reverse transcriptase and endonuclease coding domains. Thus, activation of this particular element might result in synthesis of p73 and assembly of IAPs containing viral RNA but defective in the enzymatic functions required for formation and integration of new proviral copies.

Some IAP genomic elements obviously code for functional polymerase, because particles isolated from myeloma, neuroblastoma, and squamous cell carcinoma were all active in reverse transcription of exogenous template primers. However, the activity of IAPs toward endogenous RNA is very low. We have suggested that *gag–pol* precursor proteins remain largely unprocessed in IAPs, accounting for the observed tight binding of enzyme to the particles and the atypical enzymatic properties noted earlier.

There are several reasons then why formation of new IAP provirus by reverse transcription may be restricted in frequency. On a statistical basis, the more numerous the active IAP gene copies, the greater the expectation of encountering replication-competent examples. The extensive demethylation of IAP sequences found in the DNA of long-established myeloma and neuroblastoma cells suggests that many elements are transcriptionally active. As a consequence, the likelihood of transposition and the frequency of insertional mutation may be increased in such cells. The only information on the frequency of IAP transposition has been provided by Shen-Ong and Cole (1984), who estimated that 20–30 new copies of a particular type II IAP element have been inserted into the DNA of the MOPC-315 myeloma during its transplant history. Whether these insertions occurred as a single time-limited burst or as part of an ongoing process is not known.

In summary, there is no present evidence that endogenous IAP elements have any programmed role in cell transformation. We suggest that IAP expression in tumor cells is generally the result rather than the cause of perturbed cellular regulatory mechanisms and continued proliferative activity. On the other hand, IAP elements have a demonstrated capacity to transpose in the genome of mouse cells and to cause insertional mutations that activate cellular oncogenes or alter growth properties of the cells through other means. It is likely than that IAP transpositions occasionally have a role in transformation and tumor progression. The enhanced activity of IAP genes in many tumors could increase the probability of transposition and contribute to the genetic variability of the tumor cell population. The frequency and magnitude of these effects remain to be assessed.

Acknowledgments

We thank Beverly Miller for her superb help in preparation of the manuscript. Judy Mietz generously provided the amino acid homology comparison shown in Fig. 3; and Robert Callahan, the blots of normal tissue RNAs used for the hybridization shown in Fig. 7.

References

Adams, W. R., and Prince, A. M. (1957). *J. Biophys. Biochem. Cytol.* **3**, 161–170.

Albu, E., and Holmes, K. V. (1972). *J. Virol.* **12**, 1164–1172.

Ananiev, E. V., Gvozdev, V. A., Ilyin, Y. V., Tchurikov, N. A., and Georgiev, G. P. (1978). *Chromosoma* **70**, 1–17.

Andersen, H. K., and Jeppesen, Th. (1972). *J. Natl. Cancer Inst.* **49**, 1403–1410.

Aoki, T., Stuck, B., Old, L. J., Hammerling, U., and deHarven, E. (1970). *Cancer Res.* **30**, 244–251.

Aota, S., Gojobori, T., Shigesada, K., Ozeki, H., and Ikemura, T. (1987). *Gene* **56**, 1–12.

Appel, M. C., Rossini, A. A., Williams, R. M., and Like, A. A. (1978). *Diabetologia* **15**, 327–336.

Augenlicht, L. H., and Halsey, H. (1985). *Proc. Natl. Acad. Sci. U.S.A.* **82**, 1946–1949.

Augenlicht, L. H., Korbin, D., Pavlovec, A., and Royston, M. E. (1984). *J. Biol. Chem.* **259**, 1842–1847.

Augusti-Tocco, G., Sato, G. H., Claude, P., and Potter, D. D. (1970). *In* "Control Mechanisms in the Expression of Cellular Phenotypes" (H. A. Padykula, ed.), pp. 109–120. Academic Press, New York.

Baltimore, D. (1985). *Cell* **40**, 481–482.

Barklis, E., Mulligan, R. C., and Jaenisch, R. (1986). *Cell* **47**, 391–399.

Bartal, A. H., Feit, C., Erlandson, R., and Hirshaut, Y. (1982). *N. Engl. J. Med.* **306**, 1423.

Bernhard, W. (1960). *Cancer Res.* **20**, 712–727.

Bernhard, W., and Tournier, P. (1964). *Ann. Inst. Pasteur (Paris)* **107**, 447–452.

Bibby, M. C., and Smith, G. M. (1975). *Br. J. Cancer* **32**, 660–666.

Biczysko, W., Pienkowski, M., Solter, D., and Koprowski, H. (1973). *J. Natl. Cancer Inst.* **51**, 1041–1051.

Biczysko, W., Solter, D., Graham, C., and Koprowski, H. (1974). *J. Natl. Cancer Inst.* **52**, 483–489.

Billiau, A., Sobis, H., and DeSomer, P. (1973). *Int. J. Cancer* **12**, 646–653.

Billiau, A., Edy, V. G., DeClercq, E., Heremans, H., and DeSomer, P. (1975). *Int. J. Cancer* **15**, 947–953.

Birkmayer, G. D., Miller, F., and Balda, B. -R. (1972). *Hoppe-Seyler's Z. Physiol. Chem.* **353**, 1749–1754.

Black, V. H. (1974). *J. Natl. Cancer Inst.* **52**, 545–551.

Boeke, J. D., Garfinkel, D. J., Styles, C. A., and Fink, G. R. (1985). *Cell* **40**, 491–500.

Bohn, E. W., and Wilson, S. H. (1974). *Cancer Res.* **34**, 1977–1981.

Brown, A., and Hwang, R.-C. (1982). *Proc. Natl. Acad. Sci. U.S.A.* **79**, 6123–6127.

Burt, D. W., Reith, A. D., and Brammar, W. J. (1984). *Nucleic Acids Res.* **12**, 8579–8593.

Burtonboy, G., Beckers, A., Rodhain, J., Bazin, H., and Lamy, M. E. (1978). *J. Natl. Cancer Inst.* **61**, 477–484.

Calafat, J., Weijer, K., and Daams, H. (1977). *Int. J. Cancer* **20**, 759–767.

Calarco, P. G. (1975). *Biol. Reprod.* **12**, 448–454.

Calarco, P. G. (1979). *Intervirology* **11**, 321–325.

Calarco, P. G., and Brown, E. H. (1969). *J. Exp. Zool.* **171**, 253–284.

Calarco, P., and Szöllösi, D. (1973). *Nature (London)* **243**, 91–93.

Calarco, P. G., Callahan, R., Yasamura, T., and Hwang, T. T.-F. (1980). *J. Cell Biol.* **87**, 140a.

Callahan, R., Benveniste, R. E., Sherr, C. J., Schidlovsky, G., and Todaro, G. J. (1976). *Proc. Natl. Acad. Sci. U.S.A.* **73**, 3579–3583.

Callahan, R., Sherr, C. J., and Todaro, G. J. (1977). *Virology* **80**, 401–416.

Callahan, R., Kuff, E. L., Lueders, K. K., and Birkenmeier, E. (1981). *J. Virol.* **40**, 901–911.

Callahan, R., Chiu, I.-M., Horn, T., Ali, I., Robbins, J., Aaronson, S., and Schlom, J. (1984). *In* "RNA Tumor Viruses, Oncogenes, Human Cancer and AIDS: On the Frontiers of Understanding" (P. Furmanski, J. Hager, and M. Rich, eds.), pp. 76–92, Martinus Nijhoff, Boston.

Callahan, R., Chiu, I., Wong, J. F. H., Tronick, S. R., Roe, B. A., Aaronson, S. A., and Schlom, J. (1985). *Science* **228**, 1208–1211.

Campisi, J., Gray, H. E., Pardue, H. B., Dean, M., and Sonenshein, G. (1984). *Cell* **3**, 241–247.

Canaani, E., Dreazen, O., Klar, A., Rechavi, G., Ram, D., Cohen, J. B., and Givol, D. (1983). *Proc. Natl. Acad. Sci. U.S.A.* **80**, 7118–7122.

Canaani, E., Cohen, J. B., Dreazen, O., Horowitz, M., Unger, T., Klar, A., Rechavi, G., and

Givol, D. (1984). *In* "Cancer Cells, Oncogenes and Viral Genes" (G. F. Vande Woude, A. J. Levine, W. C. Topp, and J. D. Watson, eds.), pp. 295–301. Cold Spring Harbor Laboratory, Cold Spring Harbor, New York.
Canivet, M., Lasneret, J., Dianoux, L., Roseto, A., and Peries, G. (1980). *Eur. J. Cancer* **16**, 609–615.
Cesarini, J. P., and De Micco, C. (1972). *Int. J. Cancer* **10**, 174–185.
Chase, D. G., and Pikó, L. (1973). *J. Natl. Cancer Inst.* **51**, 1971–1973.
Chen, S. J., Holbrook, N. J., Mitchell, K. F., Vallone, C. A., Greengard, J. S., Crabtree, G. R., and Lin, Y. (1985). *Proc. Natl. Acad. Sci. U.S.A.* **82**, 7284–7288.
Chen, Y., Hwang, L. T., and Heller, P. (1982). *Clin. Exp. Immunol.* **47**, 191–196.
Chiu, I.-M., Callahan, R., Tronick, S. R., Schlom, J., and Aaronson, S. A. (1984). *Science* **223**, 364–370.
Chiu, I.-M., Hwang, R. C. C., and Aaronson, S. A. (1985). *Virus Res.* **3**, 1–11.
Christy, R. J., Brown, A. R., Gourlie, B. B., and Hwang, R. C. C. (1985). *Nucleic Acids Res.* **13**, 289–302.
Cohen, J. B., Unger, T., Rechavi, G., Canaani, E., and Givol, D. (1983). *Nature (London)* **306**, 797–799.
Cole, M. D., Ono, M., and Hwang, R. C. C. (1981). *J. Virol.* **38**, 680–687.
Cole, M. D., Ono, M., and Hwang, R. C. C. (1982). *J. Virol.* **42**, 123–130.
Copeland, T. D., Morgan, M. A., and Oroszlan, S. (1984). *Virology* **133**, 137–145.
Dales, S., and Howatson, A. F. (1961). *Cancer Res.* **21**, 193–197.
Dalton, A. J., and Felix, M. D. (1956). *Ann. N.Y. Acad. Sci.* **63**, 1117–1140.
Dalton, A. J., Potter, M., and Merwin, R. M. (1961). *J. Natl. Cancer Inst.* **26**, 1221–1267.
Danjanov, I., and Solter, D. (1973). *Arch. Pathol.* **95**, 182–184.
Deen, K. C., and Sweet, R. W. (1986). *J. Virol.* **57**, 422–432.
de Harven, E. (1966). *Cong. Electron Micros., 6th* pp. 221–222.
de Harven, E., and Friend, C. (1958). *J. Biophys. Biochem. Cytol.* **4**, 151–156.
de Harven, E., and Friend, C. (1960). *J. Biophys. Biochem. Cytol.* **7**, 747–752.
de Petris, S., and Harvey, J. J. (1969). *J. Gen. Virol.* **5**, 561–564.
Derse, D., Caradonna, S. J., and Casey, J. W. (1985). *Science* **227**, 317–320.
de Tkaczevski, L. Z., and Wanebo, H. J. (1969). *Int. J. Cancer* **4**, 533–547.
Dickinson, D. P., Gross, K. W., Piccini, N., and Wilson, C. M. (1984). *Genetics* **108**, 651–667.
Doerfler, W. A. (1983). *Annu. Rev. Biochem.* **52**, 93–124.
Dowsett, A. P., and Young, M. W. (1982). *Proc. Natl. Acad. Sci. U.S.A.* **79**, 4570–4574.
Dragani, T. A., Manenti, G., Della Porta, G., Gattoni-Celli, S., and Weinstein, I. B. (1986). *Cancer Res.* **46**, 1915–1919.
Dragani, T. A., Manenti, G., Della Porta, G., and Weinstein, I. B. (1987). *Cancer Res.* **47**, 795–798.
Dunkel, V. C., Bast, R. C., Gerwin, B. I., Heine, U., Cottler-Fox, M., and Borsos, T. (1974). *J. Natl. Cancer Inst.* **53**, 591–593.
Ebbesen, P., and Nielsen, M. H. (1970). *Acta Pathol. Microbiol. Scand. Sect. B* **78**, 390–394.
Elder, R. T., Loh, E. Y., and Davis, R. W. (1983). *Proc. Natl. Acad. Sci. U.S.A.* **80**, 2432–2436.
Emanoil-Ravier, R., Pochart, F., Canivet, M., Garcette, M., Toblay-Tapiero, J., and Peries, J. (1985). *J. Interferon Res.* **5**, 613–619.
Enders, A. C., and Schlafke, S. J. (1965). *In* "Preimplantation Stages of Pregnancy" (G. E. W. Wolstenholme and M. O'Connor, eds.), pp. 29–54. Brown, Boston.
Epstein, W. L., and Fukuyama, K. (1973). *Cancer Res.* **33**, 825–831.
Feenstra, A., Fewell, J., Lueders, K., and Kuff, E. (1986). *Nucleic Acids Res.* **14**, 4343–4352.
Feldman, D. G., and Gross, L. (1970). *Cancer Res.* **30**, 2702–2711.
Feldman, D. G., and Gross, L. (1971). *Cancer Res.* **31**, 1261–1267.
Finnegan, D. J. (1985). *Int. Rev. Cytol.* **93**, 281–326.

Fong, C. K. Y., and Hsiung, G. D. (1976). *Virology* **70**, 385–398.
Friedlaender, M., and Moore, D. H. (1956). *Proc. Soc. Exp. Biol. Med.* **92**, 828–831.
Gardner, M. B., Officer, J. E., Rongery, R. W., Estes, J. D., Turner, H. C., and Huebner, R. J. (1971). *Nature (London)* **232**, 617–620.
Gattoni-Celli, S., Hsiao, W.-L. W., and Weinstein, I. B. (1983). *Nature (London)* **306**, 795–796.
Gautsch, J., and Wilson, M. (1983). *Nature (London)* **301**, 32–37.
Gazzolo, L., and De-The, G. (1971). *Int. J. Cancer* **7**, 119–130.
Georgiev, G. P., Kramerov, D. A., Ryskov, A. P., Skryabin, K. G., and Lukanidin, E. M. (1983). *Cold Springs Harbor Symp. Quant. Biol.* **47**, 1109–1121.
Giacomoni, D., and Katzmann, J. (1976). *In* "Immune RNA in Neoplasia" (M. Fink, ed.), pp. 85–93. Academic Press, New York.
Giacomoni, D., Katzmann, J., Chandra, S., and Heller, P. (1976). *In* "Tumor Virus Infections and Immunity" (R. L. Crowell, H. Friedman, and J. E. Prier, eds.), pp. 187–196. Univ. Park Press, Tokyo.
Graham, D. I., and Gonatas, N. K. (1976). *Neurophathol. Appl. Neurobiol.* **2**, 451–458.
Greenberg, R., Hawley, R., and Marcu, K. B. (1985). *Mol. Cell. Biol.* **5**, 3625–3628.
Grigoryan, M. S., Kramerov, D. A., Tulchinsky, E. M., Revasova, E. S., and Lukanidin, E. M. (1985). *EMBO J.* **4**, 2209–2215.
Grossman, Z., Mietz, J. A., and Kuff, E. L. (1987). *Nucleic Acids Res.*, **15**, 3823–3834.
Hall, W. T., Hartley, J. W., and Sanford, K. K. (1968). *J. Virol.* **2**, 238–247.
Hawley, R. G., Shulman, M. J., Murialdo, H., Gibson, D. M., and Hozumi, N. (1982). *Proc. Natl. Acad. Sci. U.S.A.* **79**, 7425–7429.
Hawley, R. G., Shulman, M. J., and Hozumi, N. (1984a). *Mol. Cell. Biol.* **4**, 2565–2572.
Hawley, R. G., Shulman, M. J., and Hozumi, N. (1984b). *In* "Cancer Cells, Oncogenes and Viral Genes" (G. F. Vande Woude, A. J. Levine, W. C. Topp, and J. D. Watson, eds.), pp. 273–279. Cold Spring Harbor Laboratory, Cold Spring Harbor, New York.
Hawley, R. G., Trimble, W. S., Shulman, M. J., and Hozumi, N. (1984c). *J. Cell. Physiol. (Suppl.)* **3**, 29–38.
Herrlinger, H., Anzil, A. P., Stavrou, D., Heumann, R., Hamprecht, B., and Blinzinger, K. (1975). *J. Natl. Cancer Inst.* **55**, 1473–1475.
Hilliker, A. J., Appel, R., and Schalet, A. (1980). *Cell* **21**, 607–619.
Hiraki, S., Van Pelt, R. W., and Dmochowski, L. (1973). *Cancer Res.* **33**, 3159–3164.
Hirt, B. (1969). *J. Mol. Biol.* **26**, 365–369.
Hojman-Montes de Oca, F., Dianoux, L., Peries, J., and Emanoil-Ravicovitch, R. (1983). *J. Virol.* **46**, 307–310.
Hojman-Montes de Oca, F., Lasneret, J., Dianoux, L., Canivet, M., Ravicovitch-Ravier, R., and Peries, J. (1984). *Biol. Cell.* **52**, 199–204.
Horn, T. M., Huebner, K., Croce, C., and Callahan, R. (1986). *J. Virol.* **58**, 955–959.
Horowitz, M., Luria, S., Rechavi, G., and Givol, D. (1984). *EMBO J.* **3**, 2937–2941.
Howatson, A. F., and McCulloch, E. A. (1958). *Nature (London)* **181**, 1213–1214.
Howe, C. C., and Overton, G. C. (1986). *Mol. Cell. Biol.* **6**, 150–157.
Hsiao, W.-L. W., Gattoni-Celli, S., and Weinstein, I. B. (1986). *J. Virol.* **57**, 1119–1126.
Hwang, T. F., and Calarco, P. G. (1981a). *J. Natl. Cancer Inst.* **67**, 1129–1133.
Hwang, T. F., and Calarco, P. G. (1981b). *Dev. Biol.* **82**, 388–392.
Hwang, T. F., and Calarco, P. G. (1982). *J. Natl. Cancer Inst.* **68**, 643–649.
Huff, T. F., Ueda, T., and Ishizaka, K. (1982). *J. Immunol.* **129**, 509–514.
Ikuta, K., Takami, M., Kim, C. W., Honjo, T., Miyoshi, T., Tagaya, Y., Kawake, T., and Yodi, J. (1987). *Proc. Natl. Acad. Sci. U.S.A.* **84**, 819–823.
Ishizaka, K. (1984). *Annu. Rev. Immunol.* **2**, 159–182.
Jahner, D., and Jaenisch, R. (1985). *Mol. Cell. Biol.* **5**, 2212–2220.
Jahner, D., Stuhlman, H., Stewart, C. L., Habers, K., Lohler, J., Simon, I., and Jaenisch, R. (1982). *Nature (London)* **298**, 623–628.

Johnson, K. H., Ghobrial, H. K. G., Buoen, L. C., Brand, I., and Brand, K. G. (1973). *Cancer Res.* **33**, 1165–1168.

Johnson, M. S., McClure, M. A., Feng, D.-F., Gray, J., and Doolittle, R. F. (1986). *Proc. Natl. Acad. Sci. U.S.A.* **83**, 7648–7652.

Kakefuda, T., Roberts, E., and Suntzeff, V. (1970). *Cancer Res.* **30**, 1011–1019.

Karpas, A., and Cawley, J. (1972). *Eur. J. Cancer* **8**, 601–604.

Kataoka, S., Williams, T. H., Sandquist, D., and Sahu, S. K. (1978). *Experientia* **34**, 879–881.

Katzmann, J. A. (1978). *J. Immunol.* **121**, 1405–1409.

Katzmann, J., Giacomoni, D., Yakulis, V., and Heller, P. (1975). *Cell. Immunol.* **18**, 98–109.

Katzmann, J., Bhoopalam, N., Heller, P., Hwang, L. T., Ostro, M., Lavelle, D., and Giacomoni, D. (1978). *Cancer Res.* **38**, 2555–2561.

Kelly, F., and Condamine, H. (1982). *Biochim. Biophys. Acta* **651**, 105–141.

Kindig, D. A., and Kirsten, W. H. (1967). *Science* **155**, 1543–1545.

Kodama, T., and Kodama, M. (1973). *J. Natl. Cancer Inst.* **50**, 707–712.

Kodama, M., Kojima, K., and Kodama, T. (1968). *J. Natl. Cancer Inst.* **41**, 565–579.

Kozak, C. A. (1985). *Adv. Cancer Res.* **44**, 295–336.

Kramerov, D. A., Bukrinsky, M. I., and Ryskov, A. P. (1985). *Biochim. Biophys. Acta* **826**, 20–29.

Krieg, C. J., Ostertag, W., Clauss, U., Pragnell, I. B., Swetly, P., Roesler, G., and Weimann, B. J. (1978). *Exp. Cell Res.* **116**, 21–29.

Krueger, R. G. (1976). *J. Virol.* **18**, 745–756.

Kuff, E. L., and Fewell, J. W. (1985). *Mol. Cell. Biol.* **5**, 474–483.

Kuff, E. L., Wivel, N. A., and Lueders, K. K. (1968). *Cancer Res.* **28**, 2137–2148.

Kuff, E. L., Lueders, K. K., Ozer, H. L., and Wivel, N. A. (1972). *Proc. Natl. Acad. Sci. U.S.A.* **69**, 218–222.

Kuff, E. L., Lueders, K. K., Orenstein, J. M., and Wilson, S. H. (1976). *J. Virol.* **19**, 709–716.

Kuff, E. L., Lueders, K. K., and Scolnick, E. M. (1978). *J. Virol.* **28**, 66–74.

Kuff, E. L., Callahan, R., and Howk, R. S. (1980). *J. Virol.* **33**, 1211–1214.

Kuff, E. L., Smith, L. A., and Lueders, K. K. (1981). *Mol. Cell. Biol.* **1**, 216–227.

Kuff, E. L., Feenstra, A., Lueders, K., Rechavi, G., Givol, D., and Canaani, E. (1983a). *Nature (London)* **302**, 547–548.

Kuff, E. L., Feenstra, A., Lueders, K., Smith, L., Hawley, R., Hozumi, N., and Shulman, M. (1983b). *Proc. Natl. Acad. Sci. U.S.A.* **80**, 1992–1996.

Kuff, E. L., Fewell, J. W., Lueders, K. K., DiPaolo, J. A., Amsbaugh, S. C., and Popescu, N. C. (1986a). *Chromosoma* **93**, 213–219.

Kuff, E. L., Mietz, J. A., Trounstine, M. L., Moore, K. W., and Martens, C. L. (1986b). *Proc. Natl. Acad. Sci. U.S.A.* **83**, 6583–6587.

Landis, S. C., and Mullen, R. J. (1978). *J. Comp. Neurol.* **177**, 125–144.

Larramendi, L. M. H. (1969). *In* "Neurobiology of Cerebellar Evolution and Development" (R. Llinas, ed.), pp. 803–843. American Medical Assoc., Chicago.

Lasneret, J., Canivet, M., Bittoun, P., Dianoux, L., and Peries, J., (1978). *C.R. Acad. Sci. Paris* **287**, 399–401.

Lasneret, J., Canivet, M., Bittoun, P., and Peries, J. (1981). *Ann. Virol. (Inst. Pasteur)* **132E**, 151–159.

Lasneret, J., Canivet, M., Hojman-Montes de Oca, F., Tobaly, J., Emanoil-Ravicovitch, R., and Peries, J. (1983). *Virology* **128**, 485–489.

Leder, A., Swan, D., Ruddle, F., D'Eustachio, P., and Leder, P. (1981). *Nature (London)* **293**, 196–200.

Lehman, J. M., Spiers, W. C., Swartzendruber, D. E., and Pierce, G. B. (1974). *J. Cell. Physiol.* **84**, 13–28.

Leiter, E. H., and Bedigian, H. G. (1979). *Diabetologia* **17**, 175–185.

Leiter, E. H., and Kuff, E. L. (1984). *Am. J. Pathol.* **114**, 46–55.

Leiter, E. H., and Wilson, G. L. (1987). *In* "The Pathology of the Endocrine Pancreas in

Diabetes" (D. Pipeleers and P. Lefebre, eds.). Springer Verlag, Berlin, in press.
Leiter, E. H., Yoon, J.-W., and Kuff, E. L. (1985). *Diabetes* **34**, (Suppl. 1), 8A (Abstr.).
Leiter, E. H., Prochazka, M., Coleman, D. L., Serreze, D. V., and Shultz, L. D. (1986a). *In* "The Immunology of Diabetes Mellitus" (M. A. Jaworski, G. D. Mollnar, R. V. Rajotte, and B. Singh, eds.), pp. 29–36. Elsevier, Amsterdam.
Leiter, E. H., Fewell, J. W., and Kuff, E. L. (1986b). *J. Exp. Med.* **163**, 87–100.
Lesser, J., Lasneret, J., Canivet, M., Emanoil-Ravier, R., and Peries, J. (1986). *Virology* **155**, 249–256.
Levin, J., and Rosenak, M. J. (1976). *Proc. Natl. Acad. Sci. U.S.A.* **73**, 1154–1158.
Like, A. A., and Chick, W. L. (1970). *Diabetologia* **6**, 216–242.
Linney, E., Davis, B., Overhauser, J., Chao, E., and Fan, H. (1984). *Nature (London)* **308**, 470–472.
Lopo, A. C., and Calarco, P. G. (1981). *Cell. Biol.* **91**, 182a.
Lueders, K. K. (1976). *J. Virol* **18**, 1088–1094.
Lueders, K. K. (1987). *Gene* **52**, 139–146.
Lueders, K. K., and Kuff, E. L. (1975). *J. Biol. Chem.* **250**, 5192–5199.
Lueders, K. K., and Kuff, E. L. (1977). *Cell* **12**, 963–972.
Lueders, K. K., and Kuff, E. L. (1979). *J. Virol.* **30**, 225–231.
Lueders, K. K., and Kuff, E. L. (1980). *Proc. Natl. Acad. Sci. U.S.A.* **77**, 3571–3575.
Lueders, K. K., and Kuff, E. L. (1981). *Nucleic Acids Res.* **9**, 5917–5930.
Lueders, K. K., and Kuff, E. L. (1983). *Nucleic Acids Res.* **11**, 4391–4408.
Lueders, K. K., and Mietz, J. A. (1986). *Nucleic Acids Res.* **14**, 1495–1510.
Lueders, K. K., and Paterson, B. M. (1982). *Nucleic Acids Res.* **10**, 7715–7729.
Lueders, K. K., Segal, S., and Kuff, E. L. (1977). *Cell* **11**, 83–94.
Lueders, K., Leder, A., Leder, P., and Kuff, E. (1982). *Nature (London)* **295**, 426–428.
Lueders, K. K., Fewell, J. W., Kuff, E. L., and Koch, T. (1984). *Mol. Cell. Biol.* **4**, 2128–2135.
Luria, S., and Horowitz, M. (1986). *J. Virol.* **57**, 998–1003.
Ma, B. I., Swartzendruber, D. C., and Murphy, W. H. (1969). *Proc. Soc. Exp. Biol. Med.* **130**, 586–590.
Malech, H. L., and Wivel, N. A. (1976a). *Cell* **9**, 383–391.
Malech, H. L., and Wivel, N. A. (1976b). *Virology* **69**, 802–809.
Man, Y. M., Delius, H., and Leader, D. P. (1987). *Nucleic Acids Res.* **15**, 3291–3304.
Marciani, D. J., and Kuff, E. L. (1973). *Biochemistry* **12**, 5075–5083.
Marciani, D. J., and Kuff, E. L. (1974). *J. Virol* **14**, 1597–1599.
Marcu, K. B., Harris, L. J., Stanton, L. W., Erickson, J., Watt, R., and Croce, C. (1983). *Proc. Natl. Acad. Sci. U.S.A.* **80**, 519–523.
Martens, C. L., Huff, T. F., Jardieu, P., Trounstine, M. L., Coffman, R. L., Ishizaka, K., and Moore, K. W. (1985). *Proc. Natl. Acad. Sci. U.S.A.* **82**, 2460–2464.
Martens, C. L., Jardieu, P., Trounstine, M. L., Stuart, S. G., Ishizaka,, K., and Moore, K. W. (1987). *Proc. Natl. Acad. Sci. U.S.A.* **84**, 809–813.
Martin, G. (1975). *Cell* **5**, 229–243.
Mays-Hoopes, L. L., Brown, A., and Hwang, R. C. C. (1983). *Mol. Cell. Biol.* **3**, 1371–1380.
Merwin, R. M., and Redman, L. W. (1963). *J. Natl. Cancer Inst.* **31**, 997–1018.
Mietz, J. A., Grossman, Z., Lueders, K. K., and Kuff, E. L. (1987). *J. Virol.* **61**, 3020–3029.
Minna, J. D., Lueders, K. K., and Kuff, E. L. (1974). *J. Natl. Cancer Inst.* **52**, 1211–1217.
Mintz, B., and Illmensee, K. (1975). *Proc. Natl. Acad. Sci. U.S.A.* **72**, 3585–3589.
Moore, K. W., Jardieu, P., Mietz, J. A., Trounstine, M. L., Kuff, E. L., Ishizaka, K., and Martens, C. L. (1986). *J. Immunol.* **136**, 4283–4290.
Morgan, R. A., and Hwang, R. C. C. (1984). *Cancer Res.* **44**, 5234–5241.
Morgan, R. A., and Hwang, R. C. C. (1987). *Dev. Genet.* **8**, 125–133.
Moshier, J. A., Morgan, R. A., and Hwang, R. C. C. (1985). *In* "Interrelationships Among Aging, Cancer and Differentiation" (B. Pullman, P. O. P. Tso, and E. L. Schneider, eds.), pp. 101–116. Reidel, Dordrecht.
Moshier, J. A., Luk, G. D., and Hwang, R. C. C. (1986). *Biochem. Biophys. Res. Commun.*

139, 1071–1077.
Mount, S. M., and Rubin, G. M. (1985). *Mol. Cell. Biol.* **5**, 1630–1638.
Mountz, J. D., Stainberg, A. D., Klinman, D. M., Smith, H. R., and Mushinski, J. F. (1984). *Science* **226**, 1087–1089.
Mushinski, J. F., Bauer, S. R., Potter, M., and Reddy, E. P. (1983a). *Proc. Natl. Acad. Sci. U.S.A.* **80**, 1073–1077.
Mushinski, J. F., Potter, M., Bauer, S. R., and Reddy, E. P. (1983b). *Science* **220**, 795–798.
Mussgay, M., Reczko, E., and Ahl, R. (1969). *J. Gen. Virol.* **4**, 445–447.
Nadel, E., Banfield, W., Burnstein, S., and Tousimis, A. J. (1967). *J. Natl. Cancer Inst.* **83**, 979–982.
Nakata, Y., Ochi, T., Kurisaki, E., Okano, H., Hamada, H., Amitani, K., Tanabe, S., Ono, K., and Sakamoto, Y. (1980). *Cancer Res.* **40**, 127–132.
Nicolas, J. F., Avner, P., Gaillard, J., Guenet, J. L., Jakob, H., and Jacob, F. (1976). *Cancer Res.* **36**, 4224–4229.
Nishioka, Y., Leder, A., and Leder, P. (1980). *Proc. Natl. Acad. Sci. U.S.A.* **77**, 2806–2809.
Nissen-Meyer, J., Abro, A., and Eikhom, T. S. (1979). *Anal. Biochem.* **97**, 85–94.
Nissen-Meyer, J., and Eikhom, T. S. (1981). *J. Virol.* **40**, 927–931.
Niwa, O., Yokota, Y., Ishida, H., and Sugahara, T. (1983). *Cell* **32**, 1105–1113.
Nordheim, A., and Rich, A. (1983). *Nature (London)* **303**, 574–678.
Novikoff, A. B., and Biempica, L. (1966). *Gann Monogr.* **1**, 65–88.
Ono, M. (1986). *J. Virol.* **58**, 937–944.
Ono, M., and Ohishi, H. (1983). *Nucleic Acids Res.* **11**, 7169–7179.
Ono, M., Cole, M. D., White, A. T., and Hwang, R. C. (1980). *Cell* **21**, 465–473.
Ono, M., Kitasato, H., Ohishi, H., and Motobayashi-Nakajima, Y. (1984). *J. Virol.* **50**, 352–358.
Ono, M., Toh, H., Miyata, T., and Awaya, T. (1985). *J. Virol.* **55**, 387–394.
Ono, M., Yasunaga, T., Miyata, T., and Ushikubo, H. (1986). *J. Virol.* **60**, 589–598.
Ono, M., Kawakami, M., and Takezawa, T. (1987). *Nucleic Acids Res.* **15**, 8725–8737.
Opler, S. R. (1967). *J. Natl. Cancer Inst.* **38**, 797–800.
Orenstein, J. M., and Weinstein, I. B. (1973). *Cancer Res.* **33**, 1998–2004.
Ostertag, W., Krieg, C. J., Cole, T., Pragnell, I. B., Swetly, P., Weimann, B. J., and Dube, S. K. (1978). *Exp. Cell Res.* **116**, 31–37.
Pardue, M. L., and Dawid, I. B. (1981). *Chromosoma* **83**, 29–43.
Parsons, D. F., Bender, M. A., Darden, E. B., Pratt, G. T., Lindsley, D. L., and Edwards, M. P. (1961a). *J. Cell Biol. (J. Biophys. Biochem. Cytol.)* **9**, 369–381.
Parsons, D. F., Darden, E. B., Lindsley, D. L., Pratt, G. T., and Edwards, M. P. (1961b). *J. Cell Biol. (J. Biophys. Biochem. Cytol.)* **9**, 353–381.
Patarca, R., and Haseltine, W. A. (1984). *Nature (London)* **309**, 728.
Patarca, R., and Haseltine, W. A. (1985). *Nature (London)* **318**, 390.
Paterson, B. M., Segal, S., Lueders, K. K., and Kuff, E. L. (1978). *J. Virol.* **27**, 118–126.
Perk, K., and Dahlberg, J. E. (1974). *J. Virol* **14**, 1304–1306.
Perk, K., Hod, I., and Nobel, T. A. (1971). *J. Natl. Cancer Inst.* **46**, 525–537.
Perlmutter, R. M., Klotz, J. L., Pravtcheva, D., Ruddle, F., and Hood, L. (1984). *Nature (London)* **307**, 473–476.
Petrea, I., and Gardner, W. U. (1973). *Cancer Res.* **33**, 2291–2299.
Pettingill, O. S., Sorenson, G. D., and Elliott, H. L. (1966). *Arch. Pathol.* **82**, 483–492.
Pierce, G. B., and Dixon, F. J. (1959). *Cancer* **12**, 584.
Pierce, G. B., Jr., Midgley, A. R., Jr., Sri Ram, J., and Feldman, J. D. (1962). *Am. J. Pathol.* **41**, 549–566.
Pierce, G. B., Stevens, L. C., and Nakane, P. K. (1967). *J. Natl. Cancer Inst.* **39**, 755–774.
Pierce, G. B., Bullock, W. H., and Huntington, R. (1970). *Cancer* **25**, 644–658.
Pikó, L., Hammons, M. D., and Taylor, K. D. (1984). *Proc. Natl. Acad. Sci. U.S.A.* **8**, 488–492.
Power, M. D., Marx, P. A., Bryant, M. L., Gardner, M. B., Barr, P. J., and Luciw, P. A. (1986). *Science* **231**, 1567–1572.
Prutkin, L., Rossman, T. G., and Wheatley, V. R. (1977). *Cancer Res.* **37**, 551–556.

Pyrinov, G. B., Korokhov, N. P., Kiseleva, E. V., Tomsons, V. P., Khristolyubova, N. B., and Salganik, R. I. (1984). *Mol. Biol.* **18**, 919–924.
Ramabhadran, T. V., Hartley, J. W., Rowe, W. P., Godefroy-Colburn, T., Jhabvala, P. S., and Thach, R. E. (1979). *J. Virol.* **32**, 123–130.
Razin, A., and Riggs, A. D. (1980). *Science* **210**, 604–610.
Rechavi, G., Givol, D., and Canaani, E. (1982). *Nature (London).* **300**, 607–611.
Robertson, D. L., Baenziger, N. L., Dobbertin, D. C., and Thach, R. E. (1975). *J. Virol.* **15**, 407–415.
Robertson, D. L., Yau, P., Dobbertin, D. C., Sweeney, T. K., Thach, S. S., Brendler, T., and Thach, R. E. (1976). *J. Virol.* **18**, 344–355.
Robertson, D. L., Jhabvala, P. S., Godefroy-Colburn, T., and Thach, R. E. (1979). *J. Virol.* **32**, 114–122.
Ross, J., Olmsted, J. B., and Rosenbaum, J. L. (1975). *Tissue Cell* **7**, 107–136.
Rossignol, J.-M., Kress, M., and de Recondo, A.-M. (1975). *Intervirology* **5**, 273–292.
Royston, M. E., and Augenlicht, L. H. (1983). *Science* **222**, 1339–1341.
Salganik, R. I., Tomsons, V. P., Pyrinova, G. B., Korokhov, N. P., Kiseleva, E. V., and Khristolyubova, N. B. (1985). *Biochem. Biophys. Res. Commun.* **131**, 492–499.
Sanel, F. T. (1973). *Cancer Res.* **33**, 671–678.
Sato, T., Friend, C., and de Harven, E. (1971). *Cancer Res.* **31**, 1402–1417.
Schmidt, J., Pragnell, I. B., and Weimann, B. J. (1977). *Eur. J. Biochem.* **73**, 493–497.
Scholle, R. H., and Foft, J. W. (1970). *Exptl. Mol. Pathol.* **13**, 147–158.
Schubert, D., Humphreys, S., Baroni, C., and Cohn, M. (1969). *Proc. Natl. Acad. Sci. U.S.A.* **64**, 316–323.
Serreze, D. V., Leiter, E. H., Kuff, E. L., Jardieu, P., and Ishizaka, K. (1988). *Diabetes* **37**, 351–358.
Shay, J. W., Peters, T. T., and Fuseler, J. W. (1978). *Cell* **14**, 835–842.
Shen-Ong, G. L. C., and Cole, M. D. (1982). *J. Virol.* **42**, 411–421.
Shen-Ong, G. L. C., and Cole, M. D. (1984). *J. Virol.* **49**, 171–177.
Shinozuka, H., and Estes, L. W. (1977). *J. Natl. Cancer Inst.* **58**, 1163–1166.
Shipman, C., Vander Weide, G. C., and Ma, B. I. (1969). *Virology* **38**, 707–710.
Smith, G. H., Andervont, H. B., and Dunn, T. B. (1970). *J. Natl. Cancer Inst.* **44**, 657–672.
Sobin, L. H. (1964). *Cancer Res.* **24**, 64–69.
Sobis, H., and Vandeputte, M. (1978). *J. Natl. Cancer Inst.* **61**, 891–895.
Sodroskie, T., Patarca, R., Rosen, C., Wong-Staal, F., and Haseltine, W. (1985). *Science* **229**, 74–77.
Sonigo, P., Barker, C., Hunter, E., and Wain-Hobson, S. (1986). *Cell* **45**, 375–385.
Soriano, P., Core, R. D., Mulligan, R. C., and Jaenisch, R. (1986). *Science* **234**, 1409–1413.
Spence, A. M., Vandenberg, S. R., and Herman, M. M. (1975). *Beitr. Pathol.* **155**, 428–434.
Spiegelman, S., Burny, A., Das, M. R., Keydar, J., Schlom, J., Tarvnicek, M., and Watson, K. (1970). *Nature (London).* **227**, 563–567.
Spradling, A. C., and Rubin, G. M. (1981). *Annu. Rev. Genet.* **15**, 219–264.
Stevens, L. C. (1970). *Dev. Biol.* **21**, 364–382.
Stewart, C., Stuhlman, H., Jahner, D., and Jaenisch, R. (1982). *Proc. Natl. Acad. Sci. U.S.A.* **79**, 4098–4102.
Stoye, J., and Coffin, J. (1985). *In* "RNA Tumor Viruses" (R. Weiss, N. Teich, H. Varmus, and J. Coffin, eds.), pp. 357–404. Cold Spring Harbor Laboratory, Cold Spring Harbor, New York.
Strickland, S., and Mahdavi, V. (1978). *Cell* **15**, 393–403.
Suzuki, A., Kitasato, H., Kawakami, M., and Ono, M. (1982). *Nucleic Acids Res.* **10**, 5733–5746.
Szöllösi, D., and Yotsuyanagi, Y. (1985). *Dev. Biol.* **111**, 256–259.
Tchurikov, N. A., Zelentsova, E. S., and Georgiev, G. P. (1980). *Nucleic Acids Res.* **8**, 1243–1258.

Teresky, A. K., Marsden, M., Kuff, E. L., and Levine, A. J. (1974). *J. Cell. Physiol.* **84**, 319–332.
Thomas J. A. (1967). *C.R. Acad. Sci. Series D (Paris)* **264**, 785–788.
Thomas, J. A., Henry, M., Hollande, E., and Vitaine, C. (1968). *C.R. Acad. Sci. (Paris)* **266**, 2129–2132.
Toh, H., Ono, M., Saigo, K., and Miyata, T. (1985a). *Nature (London)* **315**, 691.
Toh, H., Ono, M., and Miyata, T. (1985b). *Nature (London)* **318**, 388–389.
Tralka, T. S., Yee, C. L., Rabson, A. B., Wivel, N. A., Stromberg, K. J., Rabson, A. S., and Costa, J. C. (1983). *J. Natl. Cancer Inst.* **71**, 591–599.
Tronik, D., Dreyfus, M., Babinet, C., and Rougeon, F. (1987). *EMBO J.* **6**, 983–987.
Tumilowicz, J. J., and Cholon, J. J. (1971). *Proc. Soc. Exp. Biol. Med.* **136**, 1107–1110.
Vijaya, S., Steffen, D. L., and Robinson, H. L. (1986). *J. Virol.* **60**, 683–692.
Voliva, C. F., Jahn, C. L., Comer, M. B., Hutchinson, III, C. A., and Edgell, M. H. (1983). *Nucleic Acids Res.* **11**, 8847–8859.
Volkman, L. E., Smuckler, E. A., and Krueger, R. G. (1972). *J. Natl. Cancer Inst.* **46**, 953–962.
Von Heijne, G. (1983). *Eur. J. Biochem.* **133**, 17–21.
Watson, J., Ralph, P., Sarkar, S., and Cohn, M. (1970). *Proc. Natl. Acad. Sci. U.S.A.* **66**, 344–351.
Weber, H. W., Geddes, A., and Stellwagen, R. H. (1978). *J. Natl. Cancer Inst.* **60**, 919–923.
Weijer, K., Calafat, J., Daams, J. H., Hageman, Ph. C., and Misdorp, W. (1974). *J. Natl. Cancer Inst.* **52**, 673–679.
Weimann, B. J. (1985). *In* "Mechanisms of B-cell Neoplasia" (F. Melchers and M. Potter, eds.), pp. 217–222. Roche, Basel.
Weimann, B. J., Schmidt, J., and Takacs, B. (1978). *Eur. J. Biochem.* **85**, 571–579.
Weinstein, I. B., Gebert, R., Stadler, U., Orenstein, J. M., and Axel, R. (1972). *Science* **178**, 1098–1100.
Wickner, W. T., and Lodish, H. F. (1985). *Science* **230**, 400–407.
Wilson, S. H., and Kuff, E. L. (1972). *Proc. Natl. Acad. Sci. U.S.A.* **69**, 1531–1536.
Wilson, S. H., Kuff, E. L., Bohn, E. W., Lueders, K. K., and Matsukage, A. (1973). *In* "DNA Synthesis in Vitro" (R. D. Wells and R. B. Inman, eds.), pp. 361–367. Univ. Park Press, Baltimore.
Wilson, S. H., Bohn, E. W., Matsukage, A., Lueders, K. K., and Kuff, E. L. (1974). *Biochemistry* **13**, 1087–1093.
Wivel, N. A., and Smith, G. H. (1971). *Int. J. Cancer* **7**, 165–175.
Wivel, N. A., Lueders, K. K., and Kuff, E. L. (1973). *J. Virol.* **11**, 329–334.
Wong-Staal, F., Reitz, Jr., M. S., Trainor, D. D., and Gallo, R. C. (1975). *J. Virol.* **16**, 887–896.
Wujcik, K. M., Morgan, R. A., and Hwang, R. C. C. (1984). *J. Virol.* **52**, 29–36.
Xu, H., and Boeke, J. D. (1987). *Proc. Natl. Acad. Sci. U.S.A.* **84**, 8553–8557.
Yang, A. D., Gourlie, B. B., Christy, R. J., Brown, A. R., and Hwang, R. C. (1986). *Gene* 33–38.
Yang, S. S., and Wivel, N. A. (1973). *J. Virol.* **11**, 287–298.
Yang, S. S., and Wivel, N. A. (1974). *J. Virol.* **13**, 712–720.
Yang, S. S., and Wivel, N. A. (1976). *Biochim. Biophys. Acta* **447**, 167–174.
Yang, S. S., and Wivel, N. A. (1979). *Virology* **96**, 166–176.
Yang, S. S., Calarco, P. G., and Wivel, N. A. (1975). *Eur. J. Cancer* **11**, 131–138.
Yasuzumi, G., and Higashizawa, S. (1956). *Gann* **47**, 527–528.
Yelle, J., and Berthiaume, L. (1982). *Arch. Virol.* **74**, 77–83.
Ymer, S., Tucker, W. Q. J., Sanderson, C. J., Hapel, A. J., Campbell, H. D., and Young, I. G. (1985). *Nature (London)* **317**, 255–258.
Ymer, S., Tucker, W. Q., Campbell, H. D., and Young, I. G. (1986). *Nucleic Acids Res.* **14**, 5901–5918.
Yotsuyanagi, Y. (1977). *J. Ultrastruct. Res.* **60**, 71–83.
Yotsuyanagi, Y., and Ephrussi, B. (1974). *Proc. Natl. Acad. Sci. U.S.A.* **71**, 4575–4578.

Yotsuyanagi, Y., and Szöllösi, D. (1980). *Biol. Cell.* **39**, 201–204.

Yotsuyanagi, Y., and Szöllösi, D. (1981). *J. Natl. Cancer Inst.* **67**, 677–685.

Yotsuyanagi, Y., and Szöllösi, D. (1984). *In* "Ultrastructure of Reproduction" (J. Van Blerkom and P. M. Motta, eds.), pp. 218–234. Martinus Nijhoff, Boston.

Zeigel, R. F., Rabotti, G., and Smith, M. V. A. (1969). *J. Natl. Cancer Inst.* **43**, 653–669.

NOTE ADDED IN PROOF: The following papers appeared after this chapter was completed: Christy, R. J., and Hwang, R. C. C. (1988). *Mol. Cell Biol.* **8**, 1093–1102, showed that IAP LTRs differ in their promoter activity and that some are capable of bidirectional transcription. Lesser, J., Ganem, Y. J., Kupiec, J. J., Launay, J. M., and Peries, J. (1988). *Nucleic Acids Res.* **16**, 767, demonstrated the presence of IAP-related sequences in genomic DNA of *Mastomys natalensis* (Muridae). Lasneret, J., Lesser, J., Dianoux, L., Canivet, M., Bittoun, P., and Peries, J. (1988). *J. Exptl. Path.*, in press, described induction of four morphologically distinct retroviral particles in Syrian hamster cells treated with demethylating agents. In addition, we became aware of Ono, M., Kawakami, M., and Ushikubo, H. (1987). *J. Virol.* **61**, 2059–2062 in which expression of the human HERV-K sequences was shown to be stimulated by female steroid hormones in a breast cancer cell line. Dexamethasone has been shown to stimulate expression of IAP sequences in mouse cells (R. Emanoil-Ravier, personal communication).

IMMUNOLOGIC UNRESPONSIVENESS TO MURINE LEUKEMIA VIRUS ANTIGENS: MECHANISMS AND ROLE IN TUMOR DEVELOPMENT

Luigi Chieco-Bianchi, Dino Collavo, and Giovanni Biasi

Institute of Oncology, University of Padova, Padova, Italy

I. Introduction ... 277
II. Early Work on Immunological Tolerance to Murine Leukemia and Sarcoma Retroviruses ... 279
  A. Murine Leukemia Viruses ... 279
  B. Moloney Murine Sarcoma Virus ... 280
III. Immune Reactivity to Viral Antigens in Mice Carrying Endogenous M-MuLV ... 282
IV. Immune Reactivity to Viral Antigens in Mice Infected with Exogenous M-MuLV ... 287
  A. Expression of Virus-Coded Antigens on Lymphoreticular Cells ... 287
  B. Effect of Neonatal M-MuLV Infection on Nonspecific Immune Reactivity ... 289
  C. M-MSV Tumor Progression in Neonatally M-MuLV-Infected Mice ... 290
V. Lack of Virus-Specific T Lymphocyte Generation in Neonatally M-MuLV-Infected Mice ... 290
VI. Role of Antigen-Presenting Cells in Immune Reactivity to M-MuLV ... 293
VII. Role of Immune Reactivity on Lymphoma Development in Mice with Persistent M-MuLV Infection ... 296
VIII. Discussion ... 296
  References ... 301

I. Introduction

The immune system of higher vertebrates has evolved a vast repertoire of cell types to identify and eliminate infectious organisms. But despite this sophisticated defense machinery, some intracellular parasites, such as viruses, may survive and persist in the population, in the individual, and in the cell.

Retroviruses are a good example of this situation. Retrovirus genes are contained in the chromosomal DNA of most vertebrates and may be transmitted vertically from parent to offspring through the germ line, as well as congenitally or horizontally as infectious virus particles. In the individual host, retrovirus replication preferentially occurs in lymphoreticular tissue cells, thus inducing subtle or manifest immune function derangement; moreover, antigenic modulation and genetic instability of the virus may contribute in eluding the immune response. At the cellular level,

ADVANCES IN CANCER RESEARCH, VOLUME 51

where the provirus is stably integrated in the host genome, it may be completely or partly silent (albeit inducible), or fully expressed. In the latter case, a steady-state virus-cell relationship is usually established in that both virus and cell multiplication proceeds without death of the cell.

Members of the retrovirus family have been causally associated with tumor induction in host animals. These oncogenic viruses are ususally divided into two main groups (Teich *et al.*, 1984): viruses that induce rapid tumor development and transform target cells in culture (acute transforming viruses) and viruses that induce neoplasia with a prolonged latency (i.e., 2 to 12 months) and do not cause observable effects in tissue cultures despite adequate virus replication (chronic transforming viruses). Viruses in the first group contain a cell-derived gene (oncogene) whose product is held responsible for the transformed cell phenotype. No transforming protein has yet been detected for the chronic transforming viruses, however, so the mechanism underlying their oncogenic potential is still unclear.

Several hypotheses have been advanced to explain how oncogene-devoid retroviruses manage to subvert the proliferative machinery of cells. The receptor-mediated hypothesis is specifically concerned with lymphocyte malignancy induction and postulates that neoplastic transformation results from the continuous stimulation of antigen-reactive T cells by viral antigens that interact with specific receptors (McGrath and Weissman, 1979). In a related model, a similar chronic immunostimulation of antigen-specific T lymphocytes with helper phenotype results in continued production of lymphokines, which, in turn, promote differentiation and expansion of various lymphocyte subpopulations that may give rise to tumor cells by way of secondary somatic mutations (Ihle and Lee, 1982). The insertional mutagenesis hypothesis has a wider application and is based on the assumption that, because the provirus DNA is able to integrate at many sites in the host genome, it may induce mutations that either rearrange or increase the expression of adjacent potentially oncogenic genes, whose products could lead to neoplastic transformation (Teich *et al.*, 1984). Several examples of mutations by proviral insertion have been recorded. The first known instance is the activation of *myc* oncogene by avian leukemia virus promoter insertion; this phenomenon has been observed in a number of chicken B cell lymphomas (Hayward *et al.*, 1981).

More recently, a trans-acting mechanism has been proposed for human, bovine, and some simian retroviruses. A specific protein, coded by a novel viral gene designated as *tat*, appears to regulate posttranscriptionally both viral and cellular genes, the latter being possibly involved in abnormal cell proliferation (Sodroski *et al.*, 1985).

All these mechanisms are based on the assumption that definite persistent virus infection is needed to produce transformation of appropriate target cells. Host failure to rid the body of infecting virus would thus greatly increase the risk of developing a neoplastic disease.

This article will treat the immunological aspects of retrovirus oncogenesis, with particular emphasis on the mouse system and specific immune unresponsiveness, which represent the main topics of the authors' experimental research.

II. Early Work on Immunological Tolerance to Murine Leukemia and Sarcoma Retroviruses

A. Murine Leukemia Viruses

Following the classic studies with lymphocytic choriomeningitis (LMC) virus of Volkert and Hannover Larsen (1965), it was believed that perinatal infection or early activation of genetically transmitted endogenous retroviruses could render the host immunologically unresponsive to the same infecting agent later in life. In chickens congenitally infected with avian leukemia virus, no signs of humoral or cellular immune response to the virus nor clearance of the virus from the blood were detected (Rubin *et al.*, 1962).

In a similar manner, mice neonatally infected with Gross (G-) (Axelrad, 1965), Moloney (M-) (Klein and Klein, 1966), or Graffi (Gi-) (Chieco-Bianchi *et al.*, 1967) murine leukemia viruses (MuLVs) showed persistent viremia, deficient antibody production, and absence of transplantation resistance even following repeated immunizations. The lack of immune reactivity was not due to a general immune suppression, because neonatally Gi-MuLV-inoculated mice produced anti-H-2 cytotoxic antibodies in normal amounts and recognized antigens determined by a similar but antigenically distinct MuLV, such as the passage A G-MuLV (Chieco-Bianchi *et al.*, 1979).

Two factors appeared to play important roles in inducing tolerance (Chieco-Bianchi *et al.*, 1970; Chieco-Bianchi, 1972): the age of hosts at the first antigen inoculation and the dose of antigen used. Reactivity was gradually observed when Gi-MuLV was given to progressively older mice, the animals being fully immunocompetent if infected after the third week of life. When a very small dose of Gi-MuLV was injected into newborn mice, they were able to respond immunologically to it, a result indicating that the ratio between the antigen dose and the host's response is crucial in determining whether tolerance or immunity occurs in this experimental system.

Adoptive immunization, one of the typical techniques for abrogation of tolerance, was effective in the case of MuLV tolerance as well. Partial prevention of leukemia development in neonatally G-MuLV-infected mice was observed when sensitized lymphocytes were injected into young adults (Spärck and Volkert, 1965). Transfer of sensitized or even normal spleen cells from syngeneic adult donors was also effective in preventing or abolishing tolerance to Gi-MuLV (Chieco-Bianchi *et al.*, 1970). Similarly, maternal transmission of antibodies could counteract development of tolerance to MuLVs (Mirand *et al.*, 1966; Wahren, 1968; Chieco-Bianchi *et al.*, 1970).

Other findings, however, were at variance with the concept of immunological tolerance. Neonatally M-MuLV-infected BALB/c mice (Hirsch *et al.*, 1969) and leukemia-prone AKR mice (Oldstone *et al.*, 1972), which were considered tolerant to endogenous G-MuLV, produced antibodies that were not detectable in the body fluids but could be found as complexes with virus and complement along the renal glomerular basement membrane. Furthermore, antibodies to various antigenic determinants of G-MuLV were found in the kidney eluates of AKR mice (Hollis *et al.*, 1974).

On the other hand, neonatally M-MuLV-infected C57BL/6 mice failed to generate cytotoxic T lymphocytes (CTL) against M-MuLV-induced leukemic target cells (Chieco-Bianchi *et al.*, 1974b) and did not produce virus-neutralizing serum antibody, although specific immunoglobulins to M-MuLV reverse transcriptase were found in kidney eluates. Lack of T cell-mediated cytotoxicity against virus-specified cellular antigens was also reported in AKR mice (Lee and Ihle, 1977).

On the whole, these observations suggest that a state of partial or "split" tolerance exists in neonatally MuLV-infected mice or in mice carrying early activated endogenous MuLV. Thus, even though the virus-specific T cell-mediated immune response appeared undetectable, antibody synthesis against virion structural components could be demonstrated in the individual host.

B. Moloney Murine Sarcoma Virus

Even though the Moloney murine sarcoma virus (M-MSV) belongs to the group of acute transforming viruses, its replication defect can be overcome through the helper activity of chronic transforming viruses, which are able to synthesize the envelope components necessary for infection. Consequently, M-MSV particles as well as virus-infected cells possess the antigenic specificities of associated helper virus, and the vigorous host immune response evoked by the tumor tissue is directed mostly against the MuLV-coded antigens (Chieco-Bianchi and Collavo, 1977; Levy and Leclerc, 1977). Thus, tumor induction by M-MSV represents an amplified and highly reproducible experimental system for studying the immune reactivity to MuLVs.

Actually, as schematically illustrated in Fig. 1, in young adult mice of conventional strains, tumors arise 5 to 10 days following virus infection, and after a rapid increase in size, they undergo spontaneous regression. This peculiar evolution, together with other tumor features (e.g., histopathology and lack of metastatic potential) suggests a nonclonal growth pattern of tumor cells. It was then proposed that the tumors are sustained by a high constant rate of virus replication, with continuous recruitment of newly infected transformed cells (Chieco-Bianchi *et al.*, 1973). Therefore, when virus synthesis is slowed down by host immune reaction, prevention as well as tumor regression could result. Conversely, lack of regression, leading to fatal progressive tumor growth, was usually found in newborn or very aged mice, or in mice that had been immunologically depressed by a variety of treatments (Levy and Leclerc, 1977).

It soon became clear that the spontaneous tumor regression depended mostly on the T lymphocyte population, because M-MSV injection into T lymphocyte-deficient (Collavo *et al.*, 1974) or nude mice (De Clerc, 1975; Stutman, 1975) produced tumors that grew until the host's death. Extensive studies further indicated that M-MSV-immune mice are able to generate CTL specifically active against target cells bearing the relevant viral antigens (Herberman *et al.*, 1973; Plata *et al.*, 1975; Collavo *et al.*, 1978). Moreover, it was shown that the cytotoxic activity induced following *in vitro* stimulation of M-MSV-immune spleen cells with infected cells is virus-specific and H-2 restricted, because syngeneic chemically induced or H-2-incompatible M-MuLV-induced leukemic cells are not lysed (Gomard *et al.*, 1976; Plata *et al.*, 1976; Biasi *et al.*, 1979; Collavo *et al.*, 1979a,b).

On the other hand, virus-neutralizing antibodies appeared to exert only an ancillary protective role, because passive transfer of mouse immune serum, while effective in reducing the tumor incidence in conventional mice (Bubenik *et al.*, 1969), only delayed the appearance of progressing tumors in T lymphocyte-deficient mice (Collavo *et al.*, 1976).

T cell-deficient mice could be reconstituted in their capacity to resist challenge by M-MSV by the implantation of a syngeneic thymus or injection of T lymphocytes from normal or immune mice (Collavo *et al.*, 1974, 1980a,b). However, neither thymus nor peripheral lymphocytes obtained from mice infected with M-MuLV at birth conferred resistance to M-MSV tumor progression in T cell-deficient mice (Chieco-Bianchi *et al.*, 1980).

M-MSV oncogenicity was also potentiated by prior infection of newborn mice with MuLV. When mice characterized by early expression of endogenous MuLV (e.g., strains AKR and C58) or mice infected at birth with exogenous Gi- or passage A G-MuLV were challenged with M-MSV as young adults (long before lymphoma appearance), a remarkable percentage of lethal tumors was observed (Chieco-Bianchi *et al.*, 1971, 1974a, 1975). Because the MSV recovered from the progressing sarcomas possessed an antigenicity and a host range identical to that of pre-infecting helper MULV, it was evident that a phenotypic mixing phenomenon had occurred. It was therefore suggested that the progressing tumors might be sustained by the new MSV pseudotype formed *in vivo* with endogenous or exogenous MuLV, to which the host was immunologically tolerant.

During studies concerning the influence of endogenous retroviruses on tumorigenesis by M-MSV, an intriguing observation was made. Adult mice of strains characterized by early activation of endogenous ecotropic MuLV, such as C58, AKR, SJL/J(v+), Akv-2, congenic NIH, and recombinant inbred (Fig. 1), were resistant to early M-MSV oncogenesis (Colombatti *et al.*, 1976; Chieco-Bianchi *et al.*, 1979). In SJL/J(v+) mice, the resistance was almost complete, because very few tumors appeared following M-MSV injection (Colombatti *et al.*, 1978a), whereas resistance in AKR mice and their hybrids was expressed by a very long latent period of M-MSV tumor development even though, as described above, late appearing, progressing tumors were eventually seen (Colombatti *et al.*, 1977, 1978b). No clear explanation has been provided for the resistance phenomenon. That endogenous viruses interfere with M-MSV infection by competing for cell surface virus receptors appears unlikely, as no resistance was found in adult AKR mice infected as newborns with M-MuLV (Chieco-Bianchi *et al.*, 1979). Similarly, as will be reported in the following section, no obvious humoral or cell-mediated immunity seems to be at work, because neither protective antibodies, high NK cell activity, nor virus-specific CTL generation were found in mice carrying endogenous M-MuLV.

III. Immune Reactivity to Viral Antigens in Mice Carrying Endogenous M-MuLV

As described earlier, mice inoculated at birth with M-MuLV become viremic and show a high incidence of thymic lymphoma; if challenged with M-MSV at an adult age, they develop fatal, progressing tumors. These mice fail to generate virus-specific CTL despite their ability to mount a prompt CTL response against other antigens. It is noteworthy that viral DNA sequences were found only in the target organs (i.e., thymus and spleen) and in tumor tissues of mice infected after birth with M-MuLV, but not

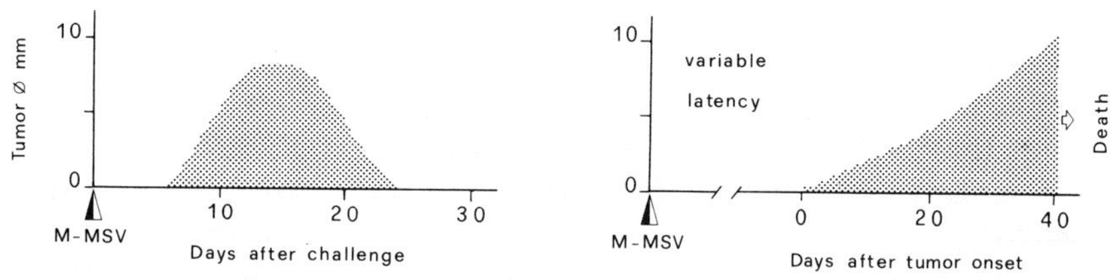

FIG. 1. Tumor behavior patterns in adult mice of different strains following M-MSV infection. *Tumor regression* (left) in conventional susceptible mice, e.g., BALB/c, C57BL/6, NIH, CBA, DBA/2. *Tumor progression* (right) in three groups of mice: (a) conventional mice immunodepressed by various treatments; (b) conventional mice neonatally infected with MuLV (tolerant mice); (c) mice expressing endogenous retroviruses and resistant to early tumor induction, e.g., AKR, C58, SJL/J(v+), Akv-2, BALB/Mo.

in the kidneys, liver, brain, testes, muscle, and lungs (Jaenisch *et al.*, 1975). Thus, nonhematopoietic tissues apparently are not susceptible to M-MuLV infection even at advanced stages of the disease when infectious virus in high titers is present in body fluids.

By exposing early mouse embryos to M-MuLV, Jaenisch *et al.* (1976, 1981) derived different mouse substrains, each of which transmitted viral DNA as endogenous proviral sequences integrated in the DNA of germ-line cells at a distinct Mendelian locus. The availability of these mouse lines offered an additional opportunity to study whether immune reactivity to M-MuLV-coded antigens could be modified by the expression of proviral sequences inherited in all somatic and germ cells. BALB/Mo mice, which carry M-MuLV DNA integrated at a single locus (*Mov-1*) on chromosome 6 (Breindl *et al.*, 1979), were particularly investigated in this sense. Activation of endogenous M-MuLV genes, as determined by molecular hybridization (Jaenisch, 1979) and by infectious virus production (D'Andrea *et al.*, 1981), is observed in BALB/Mo mice only after the first week of life and reaches peak levels at 5 to 6 weeks of age. Virus gene amplification, most likely due to cell superinfection, occurs predominantly in the hematopoietic system (Jaenisch, 1979). *In situ* hybridization and immunocytochemistry techniques have further demonstrated that viral RNA and proteins may be also detected in variable amounts in cells of nonlymphoid organs (Simon *et al.*, 1982). Heterozygosity at the *Mov-1* locus does not alter the establishment of viremia and the incidence of lymphomas: mating experiments showed that the disease develops at essentially similar rates regardless of whether the virus is genetically transmitted in one or two copies (Jaenisch, 1979; Chieco-Bianchi *et al.*, 1984).

Env-gene recombinants of M-MuLV with xenotropic viruses have been isolated from BALB/Mo lymphomas (Vogt, 1979; Bosselman *et al.*, 1979). By making use of molecular probes that recognize M-MuLV without interacting with other endogenous viruses, investigators showed that target tissues in the preleukemic stage contain multiple, randomly integrated M-MuLV proviruses. During lymphoma outgrowth, however, cell selection seems to occur, because leukemic cells harbored recombinant genomes along with the ecotropic M-MuLV (Van der Putten *et al.*, 1981).

The natural history of M-MSV-induced tumors in BALB/Mo mice parallels that observed in mice expressing high titers of endogenous MuLV in that tumors develop after a prolonged latency and are lethal in a high percentage of animals (Chieco-Bianchi *et al.*, 1983). This mouse line was derived from an M-MuLV-infected H-$2^{d/b}$ (BALB/c × 129)F_1 blastocyst, so the possible effect of a residual heterozygosity from the 129 strain on the peculiar M-MSV tumor response was also considered. However, both 129 and (BALB/c x 129)F_1 mice inoculated with M-MSV exhibited the same tumor pattern as mice of conventional strains (L. Chieco-Bianchi, unpublished observation).

Endogenous M-MuLV influence on M-MSV tumor behavior was then studied in backcross mice segregating for M-MuLV phenotype (*Mov-1* +/-) (Chieco-Bianchi *et al.*, unpublished). Although no difference was evident in tumor incidence, the percentage of mice dead from progressing tumors was by far greater in the M-MuLV$^+$ group; moreover, tumors appeared after a longer latent period in M-MuLV$^+$ Bc_1 mice. Thus, in line with observations made in the parental BALB/Mo mice, resistance to early tumor appearance followed by lethal tumor growth were noticed only in hybrid mice segregating for endogenous M-MuLV expression.

Further work to clarify the basis of this behavior revealed that NK activity in BALB/Mo mice was similar to that found in BALB/c mice (Chieco-Bianchi *et al.*, unpublished), but virus-specific CTL generation was deficient (Chieco-Bianchi *et al.*, 1983). To prevent interference from residual H-2^b heterozygosity derived from the 129 ancestor, which might diminish the generation of virus-specific H-2^d-restricted CTL, these last experiments were conducted in (BALB/c × BALB/Mo)F_1 hybrids. Spleen cells from M-MSV-infected F_1 mice, restimulated *in vitro* with H-2^d M-MuLV-induced leukemia cells (LSTRA) did not lyse H-2-compatible target cells bearing the relevant viral antigens. On the other hand, presensitized BALB/c lymphocytes restimulated with spleen cells from F_1 donors were highly effective in producing virus-specific CTL, a result indicating that M-MuLV antigens are expressed on these cells. Thus, lack of virus-specific CTL in F_1 mice (and, by inference, in their BALB/Mo parents) may explain, even if partially, the progression of M-MSV-induced tumors observed in these mice.

Another approach to the study of BALB/Mo immunoreactivity to M-MuLV-related antigens consisted in the search for natural antibody production. Indeed, natural humoral immune response against MuLVs has been reported in a variety of mouse strains (Ihle and Hanna, 1977). Using a ^{125}I-labeled *Staphylococcus* protein A binding assay, we found that sera from BALB/Mo mice exhibit a specific reactivity with M-MuLV antigens (D'Andrea *et al.*, 1981); these antibodies were detectable from the third week of life on, thus showing a direct correlation with the time course of M-MuLV activation. BALB/Mo sera also reacted specifically with M-MuLV-infected cells in an immunofluorescence test, a finding indicating that antibodies possess binding capacity for M-MuLV-induced cellular antigens as well (Chieco-Bianchi *et al.*, 1983). In BALB/c × (BALB/c × BALB/Mo) Bc_1 mice, the occurrence of natural antibodies was observed only in hybrids segregating the M-MuLV$^+$ phenotype. Moreover, when Bc_1 M-MuLV$^+$ mice were challenged with M-MSV (Fig. 2), no rise in antibody binding was observed, whereas sera from Bc_1 M-MuLV$^-$ mice showed a marked increase in binding activity (E. D'Andrea, unpublished observation). These results indicate that mice already producing natural M-MuLV antibodies are no longer susceptible to a further increase in the level of antibody synthesis.

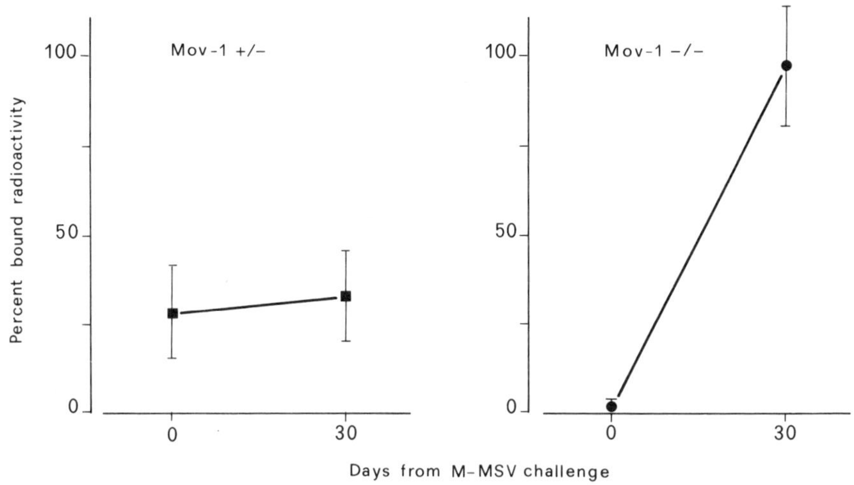

FIG. 2. M-MuLV antibody response following M-MSV inoculation in BALB/c × (BALB/c × BALB/Mo) Bc_1 mice segregating for M-MuLV phenotype (Mov-1 +/−; −/−). Sera from fifteen 6-week-old mice were individually tested on immobilized M-MuLV with radiolabeled protein A. Specific bound radioactivity is expressed as the percentage of binding referred to a hyperimmune anti-M-MSV BALB/c reference serum (for details see D'Andrea *et al.*, 1981). Typing for M-MuLV was performed at 4 weeks of age by determining presence of infectious virus in tail biopsies; the UV-XC plaque assay was used for this determination.

Despite the fact that the natural antibodies recognize the envelope gp70 and other M-MuLV structural components, protective activity in BALB/Mo mice sera was apparently absent, as shown by the inconsistent pattern of complement-dependent lysis of a panel of virus-infected cells (D'Andrea *et al.*, unpublished) and by the inability of the sera to neutralize M-MSV focus formation activity on SC-1 cells (Chieco-Bianchi *et al.*, 1983). In agreement with binding assay results, neutralization was not even found using sera from putatively immune BALB/Mo mice, which had been previously challenged with M-MSV. The possibility that natural antibodies compete with antibodies possessing neutralizing capacity was also considered (Chieco-Bianchi *et al.*, 1983); in fact, when M-MSV was preincubated with serum from BALB/Mo mice, the neutralizing activity of M-MSV immune Balb/c serum was remarkably reduced (Fig. 3). This finding is similar to that observed with monoclonal antibodies specific for gp52 of mouse mammary tumor virus (Massey and Schochetman, 1981) and suggests that the natural antibodies found in BALB/Mo mice may recognize viral antigenic determinants distinct from, but adjacent to, the target site for neutralizing antibodies. Thus, the observation that BALB/Mo serum binds to M-MuLV and yet competes with the neutralizing activity of M-MSV immune serum would indicate its potential "blocking" capability. Indeed, M-MSV tumor

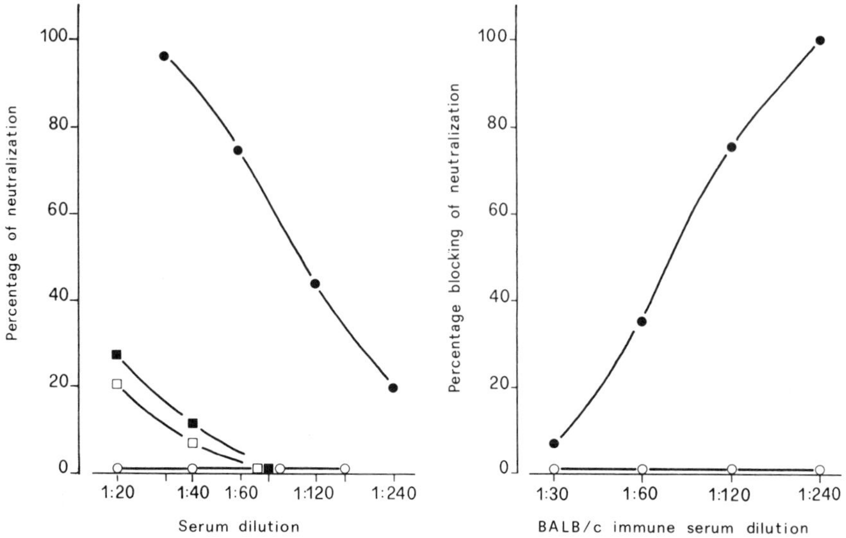

FIG. 3. Virus neutralization (left) and blocking of virus neutralization (right) by BALB/Mo mouse sera. Serum donors (left panel): BALB/Mo (□); BALB/Mo previously challenged with M-MSV (■); BALB/c (○); BALB/c M-MSV tumor regressors (●). Serum donors (right panel): BALB/c + BALB/c M-MSV tumor regressors (○) and BALB/Mo + BALB/c M-MSV tumor regressors (●). The assays were performed by M-MSV focus reduction on SC-1 cells. Blocking of neutralization was carried out by incubating the virus with heat-inactivated, pooled sera (1:20) from uninjected BALB/c or BALB/Mo donors, followed by an additional incubation with twofold serial dilutions of an immune serum from M-MSV tumor regressor BALB/c mice (for details, see Chieco-Bianchi *et al.*, 1983).

growth is facilitated in BALB/c mice following repeated injections of heat-inactivated normal BALB/Mo serum (Chieco-Bianchi *et al.*, unpublished).

Additional findings relevant to immune reactivity to endogenously carried M-MuLV have been obtained by studying *Mov-13* mice, another line produced by Jaenisch. These mice differ from BALB/Mo (*Mov-1*) in that the endogenous M-MuLV is carried with a C57BL/6 genetic background and is activated during embryogenesis; the virus is fully expressed by the sixteenth day of gestation in lymphoid and nonlymphoid organs (Jaenisch *et al.*, 1981). Because homozygosis at the *Mov-13* locus is lethal, *Mov-13* mice have been maintained by mating heterozygous *Mov-13* V^+ males with homozygous virus-negative (V^-) C57BL/6 females. Littermates were typed as V^+ and V^- at 1 month of age on the basis of infectious virus detection in tail biopsies. Using the ^{125}I-labeled protein A- binding technique, sera from V^+ and V^- mice were analyzed for M-MuLV-specific antibodies before and after challenge with M-MSV (Ronchese *et al.*, 1984). No reactivity was detected in either group before viral injection; after M-MSV inoculation, negligible binding activity was observed in V^+ mouse sera, whereas all V^- mice produced antibodies. Immunoprecipitation experiments showed that sera from immune V^- mice reacted mainly with the viral envelope gp70, and to a lesser and variable degree with some core proteins. No virus-specific bands were found with sera from V^+ mice either before or after M-MSV challenge.

These results clearly indicate that *Mov-13* V^+ mice are unable to produce antibodies against M-MuLV antigens. The discrepancy between these data and observations made in BALB/Mo is very likely related to the different pattern of M-MuLV activation, because, as already mentioned, full infectious virus expression in BALB/Mo mice takes place only 7 to 14 days after birth. Therefore, lack of antibody production in *Mov-13* V^+ mice might be related to the high sensitivity of B cells to tolerigenic signals during embryogenesis.

Moreover, *Mov-13* V^+ mice failed to generate virus-specific CTL in secondary mixed-leukocyte tumor cell cultures (MLTC), whereas V^- mice showed a high cytotoxic response. This lack of reactivity in V^+ mice was due to a strong reduction in virus-specific CTL precursors in the spleen, as determined by limiting dilution analysis (Ronchese *et al.*, 1984). In addition, natural suppressor cells have been demonstrated within the thymus of *Mov-13* V^+ mice. These cells, which are absent in mice of other lines carrying endogenous M-MuLV (including BALB/Mo), appeared to inhibit the cytotoxic response of M-MuLV-specific CTL (Tilkin *et al.*, 1985).

The high incidence of thymic lymphomas observed in V^+ but not in V^- mice (Ronchese *et al.*, 1984) is also worthy of note, as this finding suggests once more that the host's immunological inability to restrict high virus production greatly increases the risk of neoplastic transformation of target cells; conversely, it follows that an efficient immune response is essential to prevent leukemogenesis.

IV. Immune Reactivity to Viral Antigens in Mice Infected with Exogenous M-MuLV

A. Expression of Virus-Coded Antigens on Lymphoreticular Cells

In vivo and *in vitro* observations indicate that the rapidly replicating cells of the immune system represent one of the sites that better support retrovirus growth (Burns and Allison, 1975; Meruelo and Bach, 1983; Bendinelli *et al.*, 1985). That lymphoid cells are very susceptible to MuLV infection is demonstrated by the observation that mice of some conventional strains (C57BL/6, BALB/c, and CBA) infected at birth with M-MuLV express viral antigens on the surface of cells from different lymphoid organs after a few days. In fact, approximately 50% of the thymus cells and 30% of the spleen cells from C57BL/6 mice are stained by anti-M-MuLV fluorescent sera as early as 10 days after virus infection, and the percentage of positive cells increases with increasing postinfection time (Collavo *et al.*, 1981b). More interesting, the presence of these antigens on lymphocytes is not only detectable by serological methods but also by CTL generated in MLTC against M-MuLV-induced antigens, as shown by the lytic activity of virus-specific CTL on lipopolysaccharide (LPS)-induced B blasts or concanavalin A (Con A)-induced T blasts from virus "carrier" (i.e., neonatally virus-infected, viremic) mice (Collavo *et al.*, 1981b; Chieco-Bianchi *et al.*, 1983). Thus, M-MuLV replication and expression occur in both lymphocyte populations even though most lymphomas arising in these mice are of T cell origin.

In addition, thymus and peripheral lymphoid organs from M-MuLV carrier mice induce the generation of virus-specific CTL when used in mixed culture as stimulators of syngeneic spleen cells obtained from M-MSV-immune mice (Collavo *et al.*, 1981b; Chieco-Bianchi *et al.*, 1983). It should be noted that thymus or spleen cells from C57BL/6 mice injected with M-MuLV as adults do not express virus-induced antigens and are devoid of stimulatory capacity, a finding suggesting that immunocompetent hosts are able to prevent the establishment of a persistent M-MuLV infection.

As mentioned earlier, a few days are required after neonatal infection before the M-MuLV antigens can be recognized by CTL on the infected cell surface. On day 4, thymus and spleen cells do not show stimulatory capacity and are not lysed by virus-specific CTL; both these properties are not acquired until day 10. Moreover, as described in Section VI, M-MuLV antigens are expressed in the lymphoid organs by macrophages and other cells with accessory cell function.

Cold target inhibition assays, using Con A blasts from M-MuLV carrier mice and M-MuLV-induced leukemia cells (MBL-2) as unlabeled competitive inhibitors, revealed that common antigens are recognized by virus-specific CTL on infected nontransformed as well as transformed cells (Collavo *et al.*, 1981b). M-MuLV antigens, however, are expressed in a lower concentration on nontransformed cells, because these showed a weaker capacity to inhibit effector cell cytotoxicity than did leukemic cells.

That a relationship exists between persistence of M-MuLV infection and leukemia onset is evident. In fact, only mice that showed continuous virus production and expressed virus-induced antigens on lymphoid cells developed lymphomas; the few mice that were injected at birth but whose hematopoietic and lymphoid cells did not release infectious virus or express M-MuLV antigen remained disease free (Collavo *et al.*, 1981b). This finding is in line with those reported by Gisselbrecht *et al.* (1978) on a good correlation between the level of viremia and the appearance of lymphomas in young-adult, M-MuLV-infected mice of different strains, and it indicates that viremia and viral cell surface antigen expression represent suitable parameters to evaluate the risk for developing leukemia.

B. Effect of Neonatal M-MuLV Infection on Nonspecific Immune Reactivity

That retroviruses infect and replicate preferentially in lymphoreticular cells and adversely affect the host's immune reactivity against a variety of antigens was demonstrated a quarter of a century ago in animals, but only recently in man. For a detailed account of the vast array of immune functions that are affected in naturally or experimentally virus-infected animals, the reader is referred to Dent (1972), Friedman *et al.* (1979), and Bendinelli *et al.* (1985).

Regarding mice injected with exogenous MuLV, evidence has been provided that Friend (F-) and Rauscher (R-) MuLV exert a strong inhibition of both T and B lymphocyte activity and of accessory cell function (Ceglowski and Friedman, 1968; Bendinelli *et al.*, 1975). However, the precise mechanisms that initiate and sustain this immunodepression are not yet understood and are still subject to speculation (Bendinelli *et al.*, 1985).

Contradictory results have been reported for other chronic transforming retroviruses, because immunological deficiencies, if present, apparently are quite subtle before the clinical onset of leukemia (Metcalf and Moulds, 1967; Biasi *et al.*, 1973; Collavo *et al.*, 1975a,b; Hatten and Dunton, 1978). For example, injection of G- or Gi-MuLV in newborn mice did not reduce the percentage of Thy-1 positive cells in peripheral blood and in lymphoid organs, nor did it affect T and B lymphocyte *in vitro* reactivity to selective mitogens (Collavo *et al.*, 1975c). Moreover, even though the response to T-independent antigens was similar to that of uninfected control mice, a slight but significant reduction in antibody-producing cells to thymus-dependent antigens was observed only in mice infected with Gi-MuLV. In neonatally M-MuLV-infected mice, CTL generation following stimulation with cells differing for H-2 or for minor (H-Y) histocompatibility antigens was similar to that of uninfected control mice (Collavo *et al.*, 1981b, and unpublished observations).

The possibility that the residual uninfected lymphocyte population in these mice accounts for the normal reactivity was discarded in view of the observation that antibody production and viral replication may coexist in individual cells of M-MuLV-infected mice (Celada and Asjo, 1973). Moreover, in M-MuLV carrier mice, T lymphocytes responding to mitogen or alloantigen stimulations are lysed by virus-specific CTL (Collavo *et al.*, 1981b), a finding indicating that lymphocytes may still perform normal functions even though they carry and express an MuLV genome.

C. M-MSV Tumor Progression in Neonatally M-MuLV Infected Mice

It has been clearly shown that T lymphocytes represent the cell population mainly involved in the regression of M-MSV tumors (Herberman *et al.*, 1973; Collavo *et al.*, 1974; Plata *et al.*, 1976; Levy and Leclerc, 1977). In fact, T cell-deficient mice (i.e., mice subjected to thymectomy, lethal X irradiation, and syngeneic bone marrow intravenous infusion), which are highly susceptible to M-MSV oncogenesis, can have their immunocompetence restored by syngeneic thymus graft or by injection of normal syngeneic T lymphocytes (Collavo *et al.*, 1974). Moreover, adoptive immunity experiments involving transfer of different M-MuLV-specific T lymphocyte subpopulations or CTL clones indicate that CTL play a major role in M-MSV tumor prevention and regression (Collavo *et al.*, 1980a,b; Engers *et al.*, 1984; Cerundolo *et al.*, 1987). Instead, when thymus or peripheral T lymphocytes obtained from M-MuLV carrier mice were transferred into syngeneic immunodepressed recipient mice, no protection against M-MSV-induced tumors was observed (Chieco-Bianchi *et al.*, 1980; Collavo *et al.*, 1982). Interestingly enough, the time required for M-MuLV antigen expression on infected thymocytes parallels that required for tolerance induction at the thymus level. In fact, 4 days after M-MuLV subcutaneous injection in newborns, when viral antigens were not yet detected on thymic cells, the grafted thymus conferred protection; conversely, M-MuLV antigen-positive thymus obtained a few days later induced tolerance (Chieco-Bianchi *et al.*, 1980; Collavo *et al.*, 1981b). In agreement with our *in vitro* data (Section V), adoptive immunity experiments did not show the presence of suppressive effects in tolerant mice: transfer of cell mixtures consisting of lymphocytes from M-MSV-immune mice and lymphocytes from M-MuLV-carrier or M-MSV-tumor progressor mice, fully protected M-MSV-infected T cell-deficient mice (Collavo *et al.*, 1982).

V. Lack of Virus-Specific T Lymphocyte Generation in Neonatally M-MuLV-Infected Mice

As described in the previous sections, a split tolerance is induced in mice infected at birth with exogenous MuLV; although these mice are capable of antibody production, their T lymphocytes and especially their CTL apparently become unresponsive to viral antigens. This inability to generate virus-specific CTL persists even when these mice are challenged in adult life with M-MSV or when their spleen cells are restimulated *in vitro* with leukemic cells bearing the relevant antigens. These data indicate that neonatal infection with M-MuLV renders CTL tolerant to the viral antigens; the early appearance of M-MuLV antigens on the surface of infected cells and the persistent viremia substantiate this hypothesis.

The mechanism underlying immunological tolerance is by no means unique, and it may vary depending on the lymphoid cell population involved, the nature of the antigen considered, the time and site of antigen introduction. Regarding the injection of self-replicating agents, such as viruses, the presence of humoral "blocking factors," the induction of suppressor T cells, or the deletion or abortion of virus-specific precursors have been commonly evoked to explain T cell tolerance.

The possibility that immunological unresponsiveness to MuLVs might be linked to the inefficacy of T cells physically present but unable to react owing to an antigen excess or antigen–antibody complexes was investigated. Myburgh and Mitchinson (1976) found that spleen cells from rats neonatally infected with G-MuLV failed to mount a cellular immune response to viral antigens. Following *in vivo* adoptive transfer experiments and *in vitro* assessment of cell-mediated cytotoxicity after trypsinization of effector cells, these workers concluded that the failure to react was likely due to humoral blocking factors. Repeated attempts to rescue the cytotoxic activity of spleen cells from M-MuLV carrier mice by using appropriate procedures to eliminate the antigen excess or the immune complexes from the lymphoid cell surface were unsuccessful in our hands. Spleen cell trypsinization to remove or overnight incubation to shed virus–antibody complexes that might possibly be blocking effector cell antigen receptors did not reverse the unresponsive state of these cells (Collavo *et al.*, 1981b). On the other hand, in view of recent reports that T lymphocytes recognize virus-processed antigens on the surface of infected cells (Towensend *et al.*, 1985; Morrison *et al.*, 1986), it is unlikely that virus particles per se or virus–antibody complexes block the interaction of T lymphocytes with the appropriate target cells.

A state of tolerance due to inactivation of virus-specific CTL by suppressor T lymphocytes has been described in M-MuLV-carrier mice infected with M-MSV in adult life (Plater *et al.*, 1981). These mice bear progressively growing sarcomas, and lack of tumor regression was attributed to the presence of suppressor T cells able to inhibit *in vitro* the generation of M-MuLV-specific CTL. The suppressor cells apparently enhanced tumor growth when transferred into syngeneic mice infected with M-MSV. We have observed, however, that lymphoid cells from M-MuLV-carrier mice do not inhibit virus-specific CTL generation when added as a "third party" in MLTC (Collavo *et al.*, 1981b). Inhibitory effects were also not observed following addition of spleen cells from M-MSV-tumor progressor mice to cultures consisting of M-MSV-immune spleen cells stimulated with syngeneic M-MuLV-induced leukemic cells (Collavo *et al.*, 1982; Chieco-Bianchi *et al.*, 1983). Moreover, as reported in Section IV,C, M-MSV immune spleen cells mixed with spleen cells from M-MuLV-carrier or M-MSV-tumor progressor mice were still protective when transferred into T cell-deficient virus-infected mice (Collavo *et al.*, 1982).

The preceding results suggested that the unresponsiveness in M-MuLV-carrier mice to virus-coded antigens was not maintained through the activity of specific suppressor T cells (Plata *et al.*, 1979; Collavo *et al.*, 1981a).

As a further possibility, deletion of virus-specific lymphocyte precursors had to be considered. Direct evidence of CTL precursor deletion in M-MuLV-carrier mice was obtained in experiments that employed a limiting dilution assay, in the presence of interleukin 2 (IL-2), to enumerate CTL precursors (CTLp) (Brunner *et al.*, 1980; Weiss *et al.*, 1980). The results of repeated experiments indicated a 70- to 150-fold reduction in virus-specific CTLp frequency in M-MuLV-carrier mice relative to virus-specific CTLp frequency in syngeneic uninfected controls (Fig. 4). Following challenge with M-MSV, this difference was even more striking (up to 450-fold reduction), because CTLp frequency remained low in the M-MuLV-carrier mice but increased considerably in mice receiving M-MSV only (Fig. 4). Whereas a low CTLp frequency (1/10,000) was also detected when the spleen cells from double virus-infected mice were restimulated in MLTC, in control cultures obtained from virus-immune mice, CTLp frequency ranged from 1/4 to 1/15 (Collavo *et al.*, 1982).

In an attempt to evaluate virus-specific helper T cell reactivity, spleen cells from M-MuLV-infected mice were pretreated with anti-Lyt-2 serum and complement (to enrich the Lyt-2⁻ helper T cell fraction) and then analyzed by limiting dilution in the presence of stimulator cells and IL-2

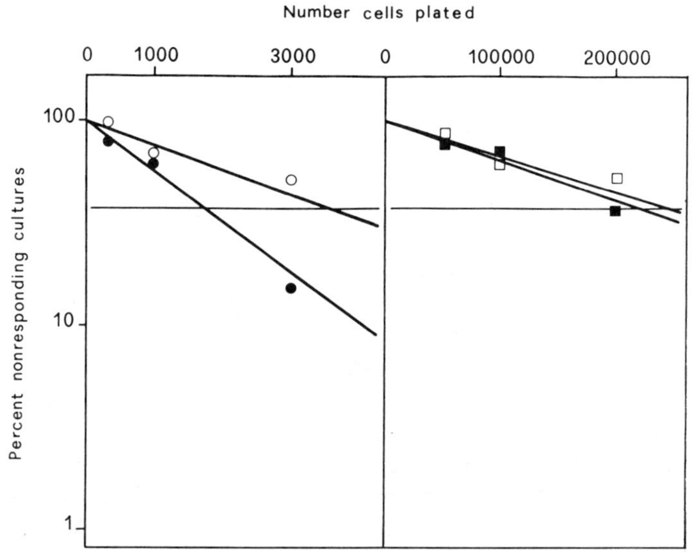

FIG. 4. Minimal estimate of M-MuLV-specific CTLp frequency (*f*) in uninjected control (○; *f* = 1/3500); M-MuLV-carrier (□; *f* = 1/240,000); and M-MSV-tumor regressor (●; *f* = 1/1600) or progressor (■; *f* = 1/220,000) mice, calculated by linear regression analysis of the data.

(D. Collavo and F. Ronchese, unpublished). The frequency of proliferating precursors in M-MuLV-carrier mice was almost similar (1/10,700) to that observed in M-MuLV-immune mice (1/9100); but in carrier mice, proliferating cells were for the most part non-T cells, because they were unaffected following anti-Thy-1 serum and complement treatment (D. Collavo and F. Ronchese, unpublished).

The limiting dilution analysis also provided a highly sensitive assay for detecting the presence of suppressor T cells under clonal growth conditions. When different doses of spleen cells from M-MuLV-carrier or M-MSV-tumor progressor mice were added to microcultures containing limiting numbers (10^3) of immune cells, no reduction in CTLp frequency was detected in comparison with CTLp frequency in control cultures in which normal cells or cells from progressor mice, pretreated with anti-Lyt-2 monoclonal antibodies and complement were added (Collavo *et al.*, 1982).

These findings demonstrate that the major factor responsible for the immune tolerance to MuLV-coded antigens is the deletion or abortion of CTLp, which specifically recognize MuLV-cell surface determinants. On the other hand, less conclusive data are available on deletion of virus-specific helper T lymphocyte precursors, and further work is required to clarify this point.

VI. Role of Antigen-Presenting Cells in Immune Reactivity to M-MuLV

The role of antigen-presenting cells (APC) in immune responses has been investigated in many systems, including experimental tumors. Ia-positive APC from different sources may process and/or present antigens to T cells *in vivo* as well as *in vitro*, but how APC participate in antigen presentation for the generation of effector T lymphocytes is not yet fully understood. Nonetheless, their role in the induction of tumor immunity may be deduced from investigations on the cytotoxic response in the M-MSV tumor system.

Taniyama and Holden (1979) observed that spleen cells from M-MSV-immune macrophage-depleted mice fail to mount an *in vitro* secondary cytotoxic response to syngeneic tumors, and they suggested that macrophages have an accessory function in CTL generation when intact tumor cells are used as stimulators. Subsequently, Gomard *et al.* (1981) reported that macrophages are necessary for *in vitro* primary CTL-mediated responses to exogenous M-MuLV, but not for secondary responses. In further studies using a more stringent APC depletion, spleen cells from M-MSV-immune A.TL ($K^sI^kD^d$) mice, stimulated in MLTC with Ia-negative syngeneic M-MuLV leukemic cells, failed to generate virus-specific CTL (Biasi *et al.*, 1983a). However, CTL generation could be restored by addition in culture of syngeneic T cell-depleted immune spleen cells, as well as by addition of untreated spleen cells or peritoneal macrophages from nonimmune adult mice. These results, in line with findings previously reported for immune response to SV40 (Glaser, 1980), confirmed that an interaction between T lymphocytes and APC is required for *in vitro* anti-M-MSV CTL induction.

That Ia antigens are crucial for the presentation of virally induced antigens was further demonstrated in A.TL mice, where addition of anti-Ia^k serum in culture brought about specific inhibition of CTL generation (Biasi *et al.*, 1983a). Moreover, because APC from nonpresensitized donors also restored M-MSV-specific CTL generation *in vitro*, it is likely that these cells could have acquired the viral antigens from the stimulator leukemic cells in culture and then presented them in an immunogenic form.

In investigating the ability of spleen cells from mice of various age groups to reconstitute M-MSV-specific CTL generation in Ia-depleted immune cells, a lack of activity was detected in spleen cells from mice less than 2 weeks old (Biasi *et al.*, 1983b). Thus, an ontogenetic delay in accessory cell function, similar to that observed in other antigen responses (Lu *et al.*, 1979), appeared evident for viral antigens as well. As will be discussed later, it is highly possible that this peripheral APC function delay contributes to tolerigenesis when exogenous MuLVs infect neonatal or very young animals.

It has been shown that soluble factors secreted by immunocompetent cells may bypass the APC requirement for CTL differentiation (Farrar *et al.*, 1982). Employing the M-MSV tumor system, it was also confirmed that in primary and secondary *in vitro* responses IL-2-containing culture supernatants are able to induce virus-specific CTL generation in MLTC set up with APC-depleted responder cell populations (Gomard *et al.*, 1981; Biasi *et al.*, 1983a). IL-2-induced restoration of the CTL response in Ia-depleted immune spleen cells was also observed in the presence of anti-Ia^k serum, provided that relevant Ia-negative stimulator leukemic cells were in culture (G. Biasi, unpublished results). Furthermore, by investigating the genetic restriction between APC and T lymphocytes for CTL generation, it was observed that soluble factors with CTL differentiating activity could also be produced in I region-incompatible cell culture combinations (Biasi *et al.*, 1983a). These findings indicate that class I-restricted CTL are set up to express their functional programs in the presence of Ia-negative leukemic cells, whether the soluble factors are exogenously provided or produced in culture, as a result of class II-restricted antigen recognitions.

With the aim of better elucidating APC functional activity in neonatally M-MuLV-infected mice, the ability of spleen cells from these mice to participate as APC in virus-specific CTL generation was also investigated (Biasi *et al.*, 1983b,c). It was observed that Ia-positive APC from M-MuLV carrier mice of different ages fail to reconstitute CTL generation of syngeneic M-MSV-immune Ia-depleted spleen cells. On the other hand, the same cell population stimulates the generation of virus-specific CTL and provides an adequate target for class I-restricted effectors. Using adult M-MuLV-carrier mice, the existence of suppressor cell activity was again ruled out, because their spleen cells did not affect the activity of APC from normal mice when mixed together in MLTC. Furthermore, the demonstration that spleen cells from M-MuLV-carrier mice were a good source of APC for CTL generation to M-MuLV unrelated antigens (Biasi *et al.*, 1983c) indicates that the defect is specific for the virus-induced antigens.

Therefore, a clear difference between normal and neonatally virus-injected mice emerged regarding APC function. Following M-MuLV infection early in life, it is likely that APC progenitors become productively infected like other target cells and thus may propagate the provirus-encoded information to the cell progeny as part of their genetic makeup. Indeed, M-MuLV antigens are detected by class I-restricted CTL and by anti-M-MuLV fluorescent serum on the macrophage surface and can be transferred to normal APC to induce specific CTL (Biasi *et al.*, 1983a). To explain the specific failure observed, the hypothesis was advanced that fully differentiated APC from M-MuLV carrier mice do not present viral polypeptides adequately as immunogenic moieties because of their "self" nature. This failure contrasts with the efficient presentation of other "self" molecules, such as H-Y antigen (Biasi *et al.*, 1985), and indicates that M-MuLV-induced antigens require processing steps before presentation in an immunogenic form. Numerous studies indicating that T lymphocyte recognition of soluble proteins and viral antigens occurs after antigen processing events support this possibility (Shimonkevitz, 1983; Matis *et al.*, 1985; Townsend *et al.*, 1985, 1986; Morrison *et al.*, 1986).

In agreement with our hypothesis, it has been reported that class II-restricted influenza virus-specific CTL do not recognize the influenza hemagglutinin introduced and displayed on the cell surface via a recombinant vaccinia expression vector, even if the same targets are recognized by class I-restricted CTL clones as in the M-MuLV system (Morrison *et al.*, 1986). These results indicate that different cellular pathways are used for processing exogenously or endogenously synthetized viral antigens; thus, as a consequence of the integration of viral sequences in cellular DNA, some yet unknown cellular mechanisms interfere with the production of immunogenic viral protein fragments recognizable in association with class II MHC molecules. Therefore, it is likely that APC from M-MuLV-carrier mice do not induce virus-specific CTL in M-MSV-immune Ia-depleted spleen cells, because they are incapable of triggering class II-restricted recognition. Indeed, class I-restricted CTL can be expanded in the presence of exogenous IL-2 provided M-MuLV-infected stimulator cells are in culture, a finding reinforcing the thesis that differences exist in viral antigen presentation and recognition by MHC class I- and class II-restricted T lymphocytes (Morrison *et al.*, 1986).

VII. Role of Immune Reactivity on Lymphoma Development in Mice with Persistent M-MuLV Infection

In mice neonatally infected with M-MuLV, chronic virus infection and lack of specific CTL reactivity are always connected events; consequently, whether or not lymphoma may be induced by persistence of virus-infected cells in the presence of an efficient immunological response remains an open question. This important point has been in part clarified by a set of experiments carried out in mice receiving an intrathymus (i.t.) injection of M-MuLV in adult life (Collavo *et al.*, 1983; Zanovello *et al.*, 1984a,b). Thymic and peripheral T lymphocytes from these mice expressed virus-induced antigens, because they were lysed by virus-specific CTL and stained by anti-M-MuLV fluorescent serum; no viral antigens, however, were detected on B lymphocytes and macrophages. The percentage of antigen-positive T cells increased progressively with increasing postinoculation times. Instead, i.t.-injected mice could mount a strong cellular immune response against M-MuLV-infected cells, as detected by secondary MLTC and evaluation of virus-specific CTLp frequency; furthermore, these mice did not become viremic and, more interesting, did not develop lymphomas. These findings are at variance with those usually observed in mice infected at birth or, on the other hand, in mice receiving M-MuLV intraperitoneally at adult age (see Table I), and indicate that the CTL response is sufficient for prevention of lymphoma outgrowth despite a persistent viral infection of the thymus and the peripheral T lymphocytes.

This conclusion has been further substantiated by other studies on M-MuLV i.t.-injected adult mice treated with an immunodepressive agent, such as cyclophosphamide (P. Zanovello, unpublished observation). Repeated injections of the drug, at a dose that greatly reduced virus-specific CTLp (Collavo *et al.*, 1985), allowed virus spreading, as shown by infection of either T and B cells and macrophages. In these mice, the lymphoma incidence was similar to that of neonatally M-MuLV-infected mice (Table 1).

These results suggest that lymphomas induced by exogenous MuLV infection are triggered by the lack of virus-specific CTL surveillance, a deficiency that favors continuous infection of new target cells and increases the risk for neoplastic transformation.

VIII. Discussion

Since the pioneer studies by Gross (1951), the age of host mice at the time of MuLV infection has been recognized as a critical factor in leukemia induction. In fact, only newborn or very young mice become viremic following infection and subsequently show a high incidence of lymphoid neoplasms. It was soon realized that the influence of age on susceptibility to leukemogenesis reflected the inefficiency of newborn mice to mount immune

TABLE I

RELATIONSHIP BETWEEN VIRUS EXPRESSION, VIREMIA, VIRUS-SPECIFIC CTLP FREQUENCY AND LYMPHOMA DEVELOPMENT IN M-MULV-INFECTED MICE[a]

Strains	Treatment	Age at treatment	M-MuLV antigen expression[b]			Viremia[c]	Reciprocal virus-specific CTLp frequency[d]	Lymphoma development
			T	B	M			
C57BL/6	None		−	−	−	−	3750	−
C57BL/6 Mov 13	None		+	+	+	+	900,000	+
C57BL/6	M-MuLV i.p.	Newborn	+	+	+	+	225,000	+
C57BL/6	M-MuLV i.p.	Adult	−	−	−	−	2200	−
C57BL/6	M-MuLV i.t.	Adult	+	−	−	−	35,000	−
C57BL/6	M-MuLV i.t. + CY[e]	Adult	+	+	+	+	230,000	+

[a] Antigen expression, viremia, and CTLp frequency have been evaluated at 2–3 months of age.
[b] Evaluated by anti M-MuLV fluorescent serum. T, T lymphocyte; B, B lymphocyte; M, macrophage.
[c] Typing for M-MuLV performed in tail biopsies using UV-XC plaque assay.
[d] Minimal estimate of M-MuLV-specific CTLp frequency evaluated in limiting dilution assay and calculated by linear regression analysis of data.
[e] CY, cyclophosphamide.

responses against foreign antigens, and, accordingly, a persistent MuLV infection could be easily established.

In the experimental systems described in the preceding sections, MuLV expression on lymphoreticular cells during the perinatal period must be considered the initial step of multiple events eventually leading to lymphoma development. Endogenous M-MuLV activation during embryogenesis in *Mov-13* mice or in the few days following birth in BALB/Mo mice, as well as exogenous M-MuLV infection and expression in newborn mice, render the still immature immune system tolerant to viral antigens, thus enabling the establishment of a lifelong virus carrier state. The different susceptibility of T and B lymphocytes to tolerigenic signals would explain the observation that both humoral and cellular M-MuLV-specific immune responses appear impaired in *Mov-13* mice, whereas only the T cell branch is affected in the other experimental systems. That T lymphocytes become tolerant more rapidly and with a lower antigen dose than B lymphocytes is an old notion (Weigle *et al.*, 1972). A split tolerance involving only T cell-mediated immunity is commonly observed in mice perinatally infected with MuLV (Ihle *et al.*, 1982), and a similar observation was previously reported in mice bearing LCMV infection (Oldstone and Dixon, 1967). In the latter system, the production of specific IgG antibodies in the absence of both CTL generation and a delayed hypersensivity reaction to viral antigens suggests the existence of a selective T cell tolerance that spares virus-specific helper T cells as well (Nash, 1985). In effect, the role of virus-specific helper T cell reactivity on pathogenesis of T cell lymphomas in MuLV-infected mice is quite controversial. While Boyer *et al.* (1982) reported that mice with a high virus-specific helper T cell response are less sensitive to leukemia development, extensive studies by Lee *et al.* (1979, 1981) demonstrated that enhanced M-MuLV-specific helper T cell reactivity represents the initial event that, through production of blastogenic factors, induces chronic T lymphocyte stimulation and eventual transformation. Although the higher *in vitro* responsiveness of lymphocytes from M-MuLV-infected mice to blastogenic factors is unquestionable, the evidence that these factors are produced primarily by a virus-specific helper T cell population is less convincing. Indeed, it has been shown that both T and non-T lymphocyte populations are strongly stimulated by MuLV gp70 (Bubbers *et al.*, 1980). Moreover, it seems unusual that helper T cell activation reportedly did not require APC presence (Enjuanes *et al.*, 1981), even though it is widely accepted that helper T cells recognize antigens only if presented by APC in association with class II MHC molecules (Unanue, 1981).

An additional argument in favor of the "chronic immune stimulation hypothesis" derived from the finding that CBA/N mice inoculated at birth with M-MuLV became viremic but, unlike mice of the closely related CBA/J strain, did not mount a virus-specific T cell response and did not develop lymphomas (Lee and Ihle, 1981). However, it was subsequently reported that these mice do develop T cell lymphomas following virus infection, albeit after a much longer latent period (Storch and Chused, 1984). Interestingly, unlike CBA/J mice, CBA/N mice lack an endogenous ecotropic virus and possess a chromosome 5-linked locus that, at least *in vitro*, restricts cell susceptibility to infection with recombinant MuLV (Hartley *et al.*, 1983).

Discovery of the technique for enumerating antigen-specific CTLp by limiting dilution analysis has fostered renewed interest in the concept that tolerance to *self* antigens is due to functional clonal delection of T lymphocytes. In fact, clonal deletion has been formally demonstrated for anti-hapten and anti-allo-MHC CTLp (Nossal and Pike, 1981; Good and Nossal, 1983; Feng *et al.*, 1983). In the MuLV system, proviral integration in the cell genome and its expression on the surface of the infected cells early in life renders the virus-induced antigens comparable to *self* antigens. Therefore, tolerance in MuLV-infected mice may be due to the same mechanisms that may explain *self* tolerance induction (Nossal, 1983). Accordingly, in these mice deletion of virus-specifc CTLp has been observed in the absence of any active suppression exerted by T lymphocytes (Section V).

Recent evidence indicates that T cell tolerance is MHC-restricted (Matzinger *et al.*, 1984; Rammensee and Bevan, 1984), thus requiring antigen presentation in the context of *self* MHC molecules during ontogeny of the T cell repertoire (Schwartz, 1986). In peripheral lymphoid organs from normal young or neonatally M-MuLV-infected mice, APC are unable to present viral antigens to virus-specific T lymphocytes (Section VI). This inadequacy in antigen presentation is due to an ontogenic delay in APC function and, in M-MuLV infected mice, to a specific APC defect in properly processing viral antigens. It is likely that the accessory cell function deficiency may contribute to M-MuLV spreading by precluding peripheral activation of the few virus-specific CTLp that escape tolerization.

Whether tolerance to self-antigens is achieved during T cell differentiation before or after thymus entry is still under debate (Cowing, 1985). That the thymus plays a leading role in M-MuLV tolerance emerges from the experiments in which the thymus from neonatally virus-infected mice was grafted to T cell-depleted uninfected recipient mice (Sections II,B and IV,C). In these mice, tolerance could be transferred by grafting thymus obtained from 7-day-old M-MuLV-infected mice. At this time, while thymus cells of the donors already express virus-induced antigens, peripheral APC are still unable to present viral antigens to T lymphocytes and therefore cannot account for T cell tolerance induction.

Lack of CTL able to lyse M-MuLV-infected cells facilitates virus spread and establishment of lifelong viremia. It is noteworthy that persistent M-MuLV infection per se is not sufficient for lymphoma development, because in i.t. M-MuLV-injected adult mice, the generation of virus-specific

CTL, albeit reduced, is competent to restrict virus spreading and prevent lymphoma onset (Section VII).

Another important issue in leukemogenesis by chronic transforming retroviruses is the significance of the prolonged latent period between establishment of viremia and tumor appearance. As already discussed, stimulation of cell proliferation by viral antigens or blastogenic factors during this interval could increase the target cell population at risk for additional neoplastic changes. Time would also be required for the emergence of novel recombinant viruses that may act as ultimate leukemogenic agents. Following the initial report by Hartley *et al.* (1977) of recombinant dualtropic virus detection in preleukemic and leukemic AKR thymuses, several studies have shown that MuLV genomic properties per se may play a crucial role in leukemogenesis. Intragenic recombination between ecotropic and endogenous xenotropic viruses may generate dualtropic oncogenic viruses, and sequences in the *env* and *gag–pol* genes as well as in noncoding LTR regions appear to be responsible for the tumorigenic activity (Holland *et al.*, 1985a,b; Celander and Haseltine, 1984; Des Groseillers and Jolicoeur, 1984; Lenz *et al.*, 1984). Not all dualtropic viruses, however, seem capable of inducing tumors, and in some instances they may even protect against lymphoma development (Stockert *et al.*, 1980; De Rossi *et al.*, 1983). Furthermore, even when highly oncogenic recombinant viruses are injected, a considerable latency is observed before tumor onset (Fischinger *et al.*, 1975; Cloyd *et al.*, 1980).

Mutagenesis by proviral sequence insertion appears to be an additional time-requiring leukemogenic process, but deregulation of cellular protooncogenes has been demonstrated only in a portion of induced or spontaneous lymphomas, with the c-*myc* and *pim-1* genes principally involved (Selten *et al.*, 1984, 1985). Thus, insertional mutagenesis also does not seem to be a general mechanism of neoplastic transformation, although the possibility that yet unknown cellular protooncogenes become activated or structurally altered following retrovirus integration cannot be ruled out.

Clearly multiple events may occur, and additive cell changes may be required before the outgrowth of the leukemic T cell clone (Fig. 5). Central to this issue are the nonrandom chromosome abnormalities usually observed in a number of virus-induced mouse lymphomas. For instance chromosome 15, which contains the c-*myc* and c-*sis* genes as well as the MuLV common integration sites (Zijlstra and Melief, 1986), is frequently trisomic in spontaneous T cell lymphomas, and in lymphomas induced by M-MuLV, X rays, or chemical carcinogens (Klein and Klein, 1985). How MuLV can induce chromosome aberration is not clear, but it should be recognized that MuLV infection can exert a direct mutagenic effect on host cells (Brown and Crossen, 1976; Majone *et al.*, 1983; Chieco-Bianchi *et al.*, 1984). In any case, the outgrowth of cell clones bearing given chromosomal defects is often a necessary step in tumor progression (Klein, 1981).

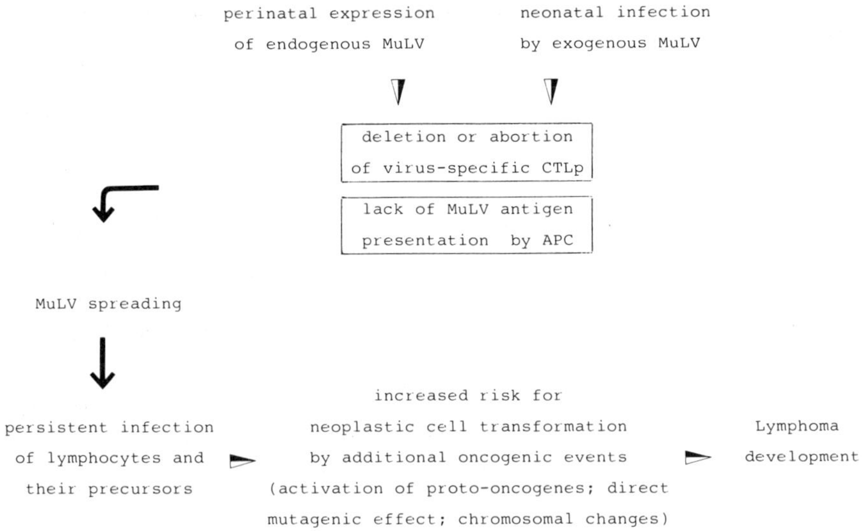

FIG. 5. Events related to leukemic clone outgrowth.

It is commonly held that the MuLV system is a misleading model for studies of retrovirus-induced human diseases and that better human analogs are the feline and bovine leukemia virus systems (Gallo, 1985). Clearly, human retroviruses are very different from MuLV as far as genomic structure and virus–cell interactions are concerned. However, even if extensively studied, the immune responses to human retroviruses are far from being clarified. For instance, the virus-specific CTL generation in the infected host is still to be explored, and there are as yet no data for the existence of a split tolerance following perinatal virus transmission. No doubt these questions will be answered shortly.

ACKNOWLEDGMENTS

We thank Drs. E. D'Andrea, A. De Rossi, F. Ronchese, and P. Zanovello for their contributions; Mrs. G. Miazzo and Mr. S. Mezzalira for technical assistance; Mrs. W. Tognon and P. Segato for manuscript preparation. The authors' studies were supported by Consiglio Nazionale delle Ricerche, P. F. Oncologia, Ministero Pubblica Istruzione; and Associazione Italiana per la Ricerca sul Cancro.

REFERENCES

Axelrad, A. (1965). *Prog. Exp. Tumor Res.* **6**, 30–81.

Bendinelli, M., Kaplan, G. S., and Friedman, H. (1975). *J. Natl. Cancer Inst.* **55**, 1425–1432.

Bendinelli, M., Matteucci, D., and Friedman, H. (1985). *Adv. Cancer Res.* **45**, 125–181.

Biasi, G., Collavo, D., Biasi, A., and Chieco-Bianchi, L. (1973). *In* "Characterization of Human Tumors" (W. Davis and C. Maltoni, eds.), pp. 261–265. Excerpta Medica, Amsterdam.

Biasi, G., Collavo, D., Zanovello, P., Colombatti, A., and Chieco-Bianchi, L. (1979). *J. Immunogenet.* **6**, 341–351.

Biasi, G., Saggin, L., Dazzi, F., De Rossi, A., and Collavo, D. (1983a). *J. Immunol.* **130**, 1447–1450.

Biasi, G., Saggin, L., Dazzi, F., and Collavo, D. (1983b). *Transplant. Proc.* **15**, 2125–2127.

Biasi, G., Collavo, D., and Chieco-Bianchi, L. (1983c). *J. Immunol.* **131**, 16–18.

Biasi, G., Dazzi, F., Loveland , B., Rivarollo, R., and Asherson, G. (1985). *Immunogenetics* **22**, 177–181.

Bosselman, R. A., van Griensven, L. J. L. D., Vogt, M., and Verma, I. (1979). *J. Virol.* **32**, 968–978.

Boyer, B., Debré, P., Seman, M., Zilberfarb, V., and Lévy, I. P. (1982). *Eur. J. Immunol.* **12**, 692–697.

Breindl, M., Doehmer, J., Willecke, K., Dansman, J., and Jaenisch, R. (1979). *Proc. Natl. Acad. Sci. U.S.A.* **76**, 1938–1942.

Brown, R. L., and Crossen, P. E. (1976). *Exp. Cell Res.* **103**, 418–420.

Brunner, K. T., MacDonald, H. R., and Cerottini, J. C. (1980). *J. Immunol.* **124**, 1627–1633.

Bubbers, J. E., Elder, J. H., and Dixon, F. (1980). *J. Immunol.* **124**, 388–394.

Bubenik, J., Turano, A., and Fadda, G. (1969). *Int. J. Cancer* **4**, 648–654.

Burns, W. H., and Allison, A. (1975). *In* "The Antigens" (M. Sela, ed.), pp 479–574. Academic Press, New York.

Ceglowski, W. S., and Friedman, H. (1968). *J. Natl. Cancer Inst.* **40**, 983–986.

Celada, G., and Asjö, B. (1973). *In* "Virus Tumorigenesis and Immunogenesis" (W. S. Ceglowski and H. Friedman, eds.), pp. 263–270. Academic Press, New York.

Celander, D., and Haseltine, W. A. (1984). *Nature (London)* **312**, 159–162.

Cerundolo, V., Lahaye, T., Horvath, C., Zanovello, P., Collavo, D., and Engers, H. (1987). *Eur. J. Immunol.* **17**, 173–178.

Chieco-Bianchi, L. (1972). *In* "Immunopathologie und Therapie der akuten Leukose im Kindesalter" (W. Plenert, G. Aurich, and F. Zinti, eds.), pp. 28–39. Friederich-Schiller-Universität Jena.

Chieco-Bianchi, L., and Collavo, D. (1977). *In* "Scientific Foundation of Oncology" (T. Symington and R. L. Carter, eds.), pp. 388–393. Heinemann, London.

Chieco-Bianchi, L., Fiore-Donati, L., Tridente, G., and Pennelli, N. (1967). *Nature (London)* **214**, 1227–1228.

Chieco-Bianchi, L., Fiore-Donati, L., Collavo, D., and Tridente, G. (1970). *In* "Immunity and Tolerance in Oncogenesis (L. Severi, ed.), pp. 599–612. Division of Cancer Research, Perugia.

Chieco-Bianchi, L., Pennelli, N., Collavo, D., and Tridente, G. (1971). *In* "Morphological and Functional Aspects of Immunity" (K. Lindahl-Kiessling, G. Alm, and M. G. Hanna, eds.) pp. 555 – 565. Plenum, New York.

Chieco-Bianchi, L., Collavo, D., Biasi, G., and Colombatti, A. (1973). *Br. J. Cancer* **28**, 238–244.

Chieco-Bianchi, L., Colombatti, A., Collavo, D., Sendo, F., Aoki, T., and Fischinger, P. J. (1974a). *J. Exp. Med.* **140**, 1162–1179.

Chieco-Bianchi, L., Sendo, F., Aoki, T., and Barrera, O. L. (1974b). *J. Natl. Cancer Inst.* **52**, 1345–1350.

Chieco-Bianchi, L., Collavo, D., Colombatti, A., and Biasi, G. (1975). *In* "Comparative Leukemia Research 1973, Leukemogenesis" (Y. Ito and R. M. Dutcher, eds.), pp. 613–620. Univ. of Tokyo Press/Karger, Basel.

Chieco-Bianchi, L., Colombatti, A., De Rossi, A., and D'Andrea, E. (1979). *In* "Advances in Medical Oncology, Research and Education, Vol. I, Carcinogenesis" (G. P. Margison, ed.), pp. 61–69. Pergamon, Oxford.

Chieco-Bianchi, L., Collavo, D., Zanovello, P., De Rossi, A., and Davies, A. J. S. (1980). *Nature (London)* **285**, 667–668.

Chieco-Bianchi, L., D'Andrea, E., De Rossi, A., Zanovello, P., Ronchese, F., and Collavo, D. (1983). *In* "Modern Trends in Human Leukemia" (R. Neth, R. C. Gallo, M. Greaves, M. A. S. Moore, and K. Winkler, eds.), Vol. 1, pp. 275–279. Springer-Verlag, Berlin.

Chieco-Bianchi, L., Aldovini, A., Ronchese, F., De Rossi, A., Majone, F., Montaldi, A., and Levis, A. G. (1984). *Toxicol. Pathol.* **12**, 361–368.

Cloyd, M. W., Hartley, J. W., and Rowe, W. P. (1980). *J. Exp. Med.* **151**, 542–552.

Collavo, D., Colombatti, A., Chieco-Bianchi, L., and Davies, A. J. S. (1974). *Nature (London)* **249**, 169–170.

Collavo, D., Biasi, G., Colombatti, A., and Chieco-Bianchi, L. (1975a). *Br. J. Cancer* **32**, 331–338.

Collavo, D., Biasi, G., Colombatti, A., and Fabbris, R. (1975b). *Tumori* **61**, 339–349.

Collavo, D., Colombatti, A., Biasi, G., and Chieco-Bianchi, L. (1975c). *Eur. J. Cancer* **11**, 443–449.

Collavo, D., Colombatti, A., Biasi, G., Chieco-Bianchi, L., and Davies, A. J. S. (1976). *J. Natl. Cancer Inst.* **56**, 603–608.

Collavo, D., Parenti, A., Biasi, G., Chieco-Bianchi, L., and Colombatti, A. (1978). *J. Natl. Cancer Inst.* **61**, 885–890.

Collavo, D., Biasi, G., Colombatti A., Parenti, A., Zanovello, P., and Chieco-Bianchi, L. (1979a). *In* "Tumor-Associated Antigens and their Specific Immune Response" (R. Arnon and F. Spreafico, eds.), pp. 109–127. Academic Press, New York.

Collavo, D., Biasi, G., Zanovello, P., Chieco-Bianchi, L., and Colombatti, A. (1979b). *In* "Current Trends in Tumor Immunology" (S. Ferrone, R. Herberman, R. A. Reisfield, and L. Gorini, eds.), pp. 301–322. Garland, New York.

Collavo, D., Zanovello, P., Leuchars, E., Davies, A., Chieco-Bianchi, L. and Biasi, G. (1980a). *J. Natl. Cancer Inst.* **64**, 97–104.

Collavo, D., Zanovello, P., Biasi, G., and Chieco-Bianchi, L. (1980b). *Cell. Mol. Biol.* **26**, 155–158.

Collavo, D., Ronchese, F., Zanovello, P., and Biasi, G. (1981a). *In* "Hemolymphopoiesis: Normal and Pathological Cell Differentiation" (F. Gavosto, G. P. Bagnara, M. A. Brunelli, and C. Castaldini, eds.), pp. 85–88. Esculapio, Bologna.

Collavo, D., Zanovello, P., Biasi, G., and Chieco-Bianchi, L. (1981b). *J. Immunol.* **126**, 187–193.

Collavo, D., Ronchese, F., Zanovello, P., Biasi, G., and Chieco-Bianchi, L. (1982). *J. Immunol.* **128**, 774–779.

Collavo, D., Ronchese, F., Zanovello, P., De Rossi, A., and Cerundolo, V. (1983). *In* "Frontiers of Experimental Hematology" (U. Torelli, G. P. Bagnara, M. A. Brunelli, C. Castaldini, and A. U. Di Prisco, eds.), pp. 169–199. Serono Symposia, Milano.

Collavo, D., Ronchese, F., Zanovello, P., Cerundolo, V., and Biasi, G. (1985). *Int. J. Immunopharmacol.* **6**, 529–535.

Colombatti, A., Collavo, D., Biasi, G., and Chieco-Bianchi, L. (1976). *In* "Comparative Leukemia Research 1975" (J. Clemmesen and D. S. Yohn, eds.), pp. 448–450. Karger, Basel.

Colombatti, A., Chieco-Bianchi, L., De Rossi, A., D'Andrea, E., and Collavo, D. (1977). *Int. J. Cancer* **19**, 565–575.

Colombatti, A., D'Andrea, E., De Rossi, A., Collavo, D., and Chieco-Bianchi, L. (1978a). *In* "Advances in Comparative Leukemia Research 1977" (P. Bentvelzen, J. Hilgers, and D. Yohn, eds.), pp. 94–97. Elsevier, Amsterdam.

Colombatti, A., De Rossi, A., Taylor, B. A., Chieco-Bianchi, L., and Meir, H. (1978b). *Int. J. Cancer* **21**, 179–185.

Cowing, C. (1985). *Immunol. Today* **6**, 72–74.

D'Andrea, E., De Rossi, A., and Chieco-Biancho, L. (1981). *Tumori* **67**, 511–520.

De Clerq, E. (1975). *J. Natl. Cancer Inst.* **54**, 474–477.

Dent, P. (1972). *Prog. Med. Virol.* **14**, 1–35.

De Rossi, A., D'Andrea, E., Biasi, G., Collavo, D., and Chieco-Bianchi, L. (1983). *Proc. Natl. Acad. Sci. U.S.A.* **80**, 2775–2779.

Des Groseillers, L., and Jolicoeur, P. (1984). *J. Virol.* **52**, 945–952.
Engers, H., Lahaye, T., Sorenson, G. D., Glasebrook, A. L., Horvat, C., and Brunner, K. T. (1984). *J. Immunol.* **133**, 1664–1670.
Enjuanes, L., Lee, J., and Ihle, J. N. (1981). *J. Immunol.* **126**, 1478–1484.
Farrar, J. J., Benjamin, W. R., Hilfiker, M. L., Howard, M., Farrar, W. L., and Fuller-Farrar, J. (1982). *Immunol. Rev.* **63**, 129–166.
Feng, H. M., Glasebrook, A. L., Engers, H. D., and Lovis, J. A. (1983). *J. Immunol.* **131**, 2165–2169.
Fischinger, P. J., Nomura, S., and Bolognesi, D. P. (1975). *Proc. Natl. Acad. Sci. U.S.A.* **72**, 5150–5155.
Friedman, H., Specter, S., Farber, P., and Ceglowski, W. S. (1979). *Proc. Leukocyte Cult. Conf.* **12**, 783–802.
Gallo, R. C. (1985). *Cancer Res.* **45**, 4524s–4533s.
Gisselbrect, S., Pozo, F., Debré, P., Hurot, M. A., Lacombe, M. J., and Levy, J. P. (1978). *Int. J. Cancer* **21**, 626–634.
Glaser, M. (1980). *Eur. J. Immunol.* **10**, 342–346.
Good, M. F., and Nossal, G. J. (1983). *J. Immunol.* **180**, 78–85.
Gomard, E., Duprez, V., Henin, Y., and Lévy, J. P. (1976). *Nature (London)* **260**, 707–708.
Gomard, E., Wybier-Franqui, J., and Lévy, J. P. (1981). *J. Immunol.* **126**, 891–896.
Gross, L. (1951). *Proc. Soc. Exp. Biol. Med.* **76**, 27–32.
Hartley, J. W., Wolford, N. K., Old, L. J., and Rowe, W. P. (1977). *Proc. Natl. Acad. Sci. U.S.A.* **74**, 789–792.
Hartley, J. W., Yetter, R. A., and Morse, H. C. (1983). *J. Exp. Med.* **185**, 16–24.
Hatten, B. A., and Dunton, H. (1978). *Immunology* **35**, 707–713.
Hayward, W. S., Neel, B. G., and Astrin, S. M. (1981). *Nature (London)* **290**, 475–480.
Herberman, R. B., Nunn, M. E., Lavrin, H., and Asofski, R. (1973). *J. Natl. Cancer Inst.* **51**, 1509–1512.
Hirsch, M. D., Allison, A. C., and Harvey, J. J. (1969). *Nature (London)* **223**, 739–740.
Holland, C. A., Wozney, J., Chatis, P. A., Hopkins, N., and Hartley, J. W. (1985a). *J. Virol.* **53**, 152–157.
Holland, C. A., Hartley, J. W., Rowe, W. P., and Hopkins, N. (1985b). *J. Virol.* **53**, 158–165.
Hollis, V. W., Jr., Aoki, T., Barrera, O., Oldstone, M., and Dixon, F. J. (1974). *J. Virol.* **13**, 448–454.
Ihle, J. N., and Hanna, M. G. (1977). *Contemp. Top. Immunobiol.* **6**, 169–194.
Ihle, J. N., and Lee, J. C. (1982). *Curr. Top. Microbiol. Immunol.* **98**, 85–101.
Jaenisch, R. (1979). *Virology* **93**, 80–90.
Jaenisch, R., Fan, H., and Croker, B. (1975). *Proc. Natl. Acad. Sci. U.S.A.* **72**, 4008–4012.
Jaenisch, R. (1976). *Proc. Natl. Acad. Sci. U.S.A.* **73**, 1260–1264.
Jaenisch, R., Jähner, D., Nobis, P., Simon, I., Löhler, J., Harbers, K., and Grotkopp, D. (1981). *Cell* **24**, 519–529.
Klein, E., and Klein, G. (1966). *Nature (London)* **209**, 163–165.
Klein, G. (1981). *Nature (London)* **294**, 313–318.
Klein, G., and Klein, E. (1985). *Nature (London)* **315**, 190–195.
Lee, J. C., and Ihle, J. N. (1977). *J. Immunol.* **118**, 928–934.
Lee, J. C., and Ihle, J. N. (1979). *J. Immunol.* **123**, 2351–2358.
Lee, J. C., and Ihle, J. N. (1981). *Nature (London)* **289**, 407–409.
Lee, J. C., Horak, I., and Ihle, J. N. (1981). *J. Immunol.* **126**, 715–722.
Lenz, J., Celander, D., Crowther, R. L., Patarca, R., Perkins, D. W., and Haseltine, W. A. (1984). *Nature (London)* **308**, 467–470.
Levy, J. P., and Leclerc, J. C. (1977). *Adv. Cancer Res.* **24**, 1–66.
Lu, C. Y., Calamai, E. G., and Unanue, E. R. (1979). *Nature (London)* **282**, 327–329.

McGrath, M. S., and Weissman, I. L. (1979). *Cell* **17**, 65–75.
Majone, F., Montaldi, A., Ronchese, F., De Rossi, A., Chieco-Bianchi, L., and Levis, A. G. (1983). *Carcinogenesis* **4**, 33–37.
Massey, R. J., and Schochetman, G. (1981). *Science* **213**, 447–449.
Matis, L. A., Ruscetti, S. K., Longo, D. L., Jacobson, S., Brown, E. J., Zinn, S., and Kruisbeek, A. M. (1985). *J. Immunol.* **135**, 703–713.
Matzinger, P., Zamoyska, R., and Waldmann, H. (1984). *Nature (London)* **308**, 738–741.
Meruelo, D., and Bach, R. (1983). *Adv. Cancer Res.* **40**, 107–188.
Metcalf, D., and Moulds, R. (1967). *Int. J. Cancer* **2**, 53–58.
Mirand, E. A., Grace, J. T., Jr., and Buffet, R. F. (1966). *Nature (London)* **209**, 696–698.
Morrison, L. A., Lukacher, A. E., Braciale, U. L., Fan, D. P., and Braciale, T. J. (1986). *J. Exp. Med.* **163**, 903–921.
Myburgh, J. A., and Mitchinson, N. A. (1976). *Transplantation* **22**, 236–244.
Nash, A. (1985). *Br. Med. Bull.* **41**, 41–45.
Nossal, G. J. (1983). *Annu. Rev. Immunol.* **1**, 33–62.
Nossal, G. J., and Pike, B. L. (1981). *Proc. Natl. Acad. Sci. U.S.A.* **78**, 3844–3847.
Oldstone, M. B. A., and Dixon, F. J. (1967). *Science* **158**, 1193–1195.
Oldstone, M. B. A., Aoki, T., and Dixon, F. J. (1972). *Proc. Natl. Acad. Sci. U.S.A.* **69**, 134–138.
Plata, F., Cerottini, J. C., and Brunner, K. T. (1975). *Eur. J. Immunol.* **5**, 227–233.
Plata, F., Jongeneel, V., Cerottini, J. C., and Brunner, K. T. (1976). *Eur. J. Immunol.* **6**, 823–828.
Plata, F., MacDonald, H. R., and Shain, B. (1979). *J. Immunol.* **123**, 852–858.
Plater, C. P., Debré, P., and Leclerc, J. C. (1981). *Eur. J. Immunol.* **11**, 39–46.
Rammensee, H., and Bevan, J. M. (1984). *Nature (London)* **308**, 741–744.
Ronchese, F., D'Andrea, E., Collavo, D., De Rossi, A., Zanovello, P., and Chieco-Bianchi, L. (1984). *Cell. Immunol.* **83**, 379–388.
Rubin, H., Fanshier, L., Cornelins, A., and Hughes, W. F. (1962). *Virology* **17**, 143–156.
Schwartz, R. H. (1986). *Adv. Immunol.* **38**, 31–201.
Selten, G., Cuypers, H. T., Zijlstra, M., Melief, C., and Berns, A. (1984). *Embo J.* **3**, 3215–3222.
Selten, G., Cuypers, H. T., and Berns, A. (1985). *Embo J.* **4**, 1793–1798.
Shimonkevitz, R., Kappler, J., Marrack, P., and Grey, H. (1983). *J. Exp. Med.* **158**, 303–316.
Simon, I., Löhler, J., and Jaenisch, R. (1982). *Virology* **120**, 106–121.
Sodroski, J., Rosen, C., Wong-Staal, F., Salahuddin, S. Z., Popovic, M., Arya, S., Gallo, R. C., and Haseltine, W. A. (1985). *Science* **227**, 171–173.
Spärck, J. V., and Volkert, M. (1965). *Nature (London)* **206**, 578–583.
Stockert, E., O'Donnell, P. V., Ohata, Y., and Old, L. J. (1980). *Proc. Natl. Acad. Sci. U.S.A.* **77**, 3720–3724.
Storch, G. T., and Chused, T. M. (1984). *J. Immunol.* **135**, 2797–2800.
Stutman, O. (1975). *Adv. Cancer Res.* **22**, 261–422.
Taniyama, T., and Holden, H. T. (1979). *J. Immunol.* **123**, 43–49.
Teich, N., Wyke, J., Mak, T., Bernstein, A., and Hardy, W. (1984). *In* "RNA Tumor Viruses" (R. Weiss, N. Teich, H. Varmus, and J. Coffin, eds.), 2nd Ed., Vol. I, pp. 785–998. Cold Spring Harbor Laboratory, Cold Spring Harbor, New York.
Tilkin, A. F., Bègue, B., Gomard, E., and Levy, J. P. (1985). *J. Immunol.* **134**, 2779–2782.
Townsend, A. R. M., Gotch, F. M., and Davet, J. (1985). *Cell* **42**, 457–467.
Townsend, A. R. M., Rothrard, J., Gotch, F. M., Bahadur, G., Wraith, D., and McMichael, A. J. (1986). *Cell* **44**, 959–968.
Unanue, E. R. (1981). *Adv. Immunol.* **31**, 1–136.
Van der Putten, H., Quint, W., van Raaij, J., Robanus Maandag, E., Verma, I. M., and Berns, A. (1981). *Cell* **24**, 729–739.
Vogt, M. (1979). *Virology* **93**, 226–236.
Volkert, M., and Hannover Larsen, J. (1965). *Prog. Med. Virol.* **7**, 160–207.

Wahren, B. (1968). *J. Natl. Cancer Inst.* **41**, 923–929.
Weigle, W. O., Chiller, J. M., and Habicth, C. S. (1972). *Transplant. Rev.* **8**, 3–25.
Weiss, A., Brunner, K. T., MacDonald, R., and Cerottini, J. C. (1980). *J. Exp. Med.* **152**, 1210–1225.
Zanovello, P., Collavo, D., Ronchese, F., De Rossi, A., Biasi, G., and Chieco-Bianchi, L. (1984a). *Cell. Immunol.* **83**, 379–388.
Zanovello, P., D'Andrea, E., Ronchese, F., De Rossi, A., Collavo, D., and Chieco-Bianchi, L. (1984b). *Tumori* **70**, 1–8.
Zijlstra, M., and Melief, C. J. M. (1986). *Biochim. Biophys. Acta* **865**, 197–231.

ADVANCES IN HUMAN RETROVIRUSES

Angus Dalgleish and Miroslav Malkovský

MRC Clinical Research Centre, Divison of Immunology,
Watford Road, Harrow, Middlesex HA1 3UJ, England

I. Introduction 307
II. The Search for Human Retroviral Isolates 309
III. Specific Isolates 311
IV. The Significance of the SSAV/BaEV Human Isolates 312
V. HTLV-I 313
A. Epidemiology 315
B. Causative Agent of ATLL 315
VI. HTLV-II 315
VII. AIDS and HIV 316
VIII. Simian AIDS (SAIDS) and the New African Isolates 317
IX. Cell Biology and Immunology of Human Retroviral Infections 320
X. HIV 321
XI. Molecular Biology of HTLV-I and HTLV-II 327
XII. Molecular Biology of HIV 329
XIII. Epidemiology of Human Retroviruses 335
A. Epidemiology of HIV 336
B. Evidence of Heterosexual Transmission 336
C. AIDS and Africa 337
D. Earliest Evidence of HIVs 339
XIV. Origin of the AIDS Virus 339
XV. AIDS and Children 340
XVI. From Infection to Disease 341
XVII. AIDS and Cancer 342
XVIII. Approaches to Treatment 344
A. Therapy for HIV-Asssociated Disease 345
B. Immunotherapy 348
C. Vaccines 349
D. Genetic Approaches to Treatment 350
E. Conclusions 350
XIX. Conclusions and Prospects 351
References 352

I. Introduction

The term *retroviruses* encompasses all viruses containing an RNA-dependent DNA polymerase (reverse transcriptase) enzyme activity (Fenner, 1975). The family is divided into three subfamilies: (1) Oncoviridinae, which

ADVANCES IN CANCER RESEARCH, VOLUME 51

includes all oncogenic members and many closely related nononcogenic viruses; endogenous viruses are also included in this group, (2) Lentiviridinae, or the "slow" viruses, such as the visna virus and (3) Spumaviridinae, or the "foamy" viruses, which induce persistent infections without any clinical disease but cause vacuolization of cultured cells. Recently, some other viruses including DNA viruses such as hepatitis B virus have also been shown to possess a reverse transcriptase activity (Tiollais *et al.*, 1985). Nevertheless, the only retroviruses associated with human disease were foamy viruses isolated from patients with nasopharyngeal carcinoma (Achong *et al.*, 1971; Epstein *et al.*, 1974). The "human" isolate is closely related to the Simian foamy virus (SFV) serotype 6 (Nemo *et al.*, 1978), however, the relationship to disease is unclear. The suspicion that the Achong isolate represents a nonhuman laboratory contaminant or a rare zoonosis (Brown *et al.*, 1978, 1982) has been challenged by Achong and Epstein (1978, 1983) and by Loh *et al.* (1977, 1980), on the grounds that human sera from East and West Africa and from the Pacific islands (where there are no nonhuman primates) react in immunofluorescence tests with infected cells. It is possible that a virus closely related to SFV-6 could represent a natural infection of humans, just as monkeys are natural hosts to viruses closely related to the human T cell-tropic retroviruses. Several isolates have been obtained from patients with de Quervain's subacute granulomatous thyroiditis (Stancek *et al.*, 1975), and again the relationship between virus and disease is unclear. However, examples of retrovirus-induced diseases in animals abound. They are caused by exogenous viruses presenting as endemic or epidemic infections. The viruses may be transmitted horizontally or congenitally, and infection is usually more widespread in the affected population than is the incidence of disease. Animal models include avian, murine, feline, bovine, and simian examples, although retroviruses have been found in such diverse species as vipers and pike. Oncoviridinae- and Lentiviridinae-induced diseases are well documented and will not be described in detail, except to mention that many of these diseases have obvious human counterparts, which include lymphomas, sarcomas, carcinomas (including breast cancer), leukemias and a wide variety of other hematological conditions, acquired immunological deficiencies, arthritis, and a spectrum of neurological conditions reminiscent of multiple sclerosis (see Table I; for a further review, see Weiss *et al.*, 1985a).

With so many good animal models for so many human diseases of unknown etiology, it is not surprising to learn that the complete failure to associate human retroviruses with specific diseases until 1980, when the first human tumor retrovirus was reported, was not due to lack of effort. Indeed, so many retroviruses were isolated from a variety of human malignant tissues that they became known as "human rumor viruses." In order to appreciate the advances in our knowledge of human retroviruses brought about by the

TABLE I
DISEASES CAUSED BY RETROVIRUSES IN ANIMALS

Disease	Species
Leukemia	Avian, mouse, cat, primates
Lymphoma	Avian, mouse, cat, primates, fish
Carcinoma	Mouse (mammary), chicken (renal)
Sarcoma	Mouse, cow, hampster, rat, avian, reptiles
Wasting and autoimmune disease	Cat, primates, mouse
Arthritis	Goat
Nervous system	Sheep, goat, mouse, rat
Osteopetrosis	Chicken
Anemia	Horse

discovery of the human T cell leukemia/lymphoma viruses (HTLV) and the human immunodeficiency virus (HIV) isolates, the history of putative human retroviral isolates prior to HTLV and HIV will be briefly reviewed.

II. The Search for Human Retroviral Isolates

Retroviruses may be detected by a variety of methods that include electron microscopy (EM), reverse transcriptase (RT) assays, the detection of known viral antigens, the nucleic acid hybridization techniques, and the rescue and activation of retroviral particles (thus allowing serological studies). Often evidence of retroviruses has been detected by one method only, and hence further characterization has not been possible. EM studies have suggested the presence of C-type particles in tissues and cultures from patients with leukemia, sarcoma, and melanoma. However, they have also been seen in normal embryonic tissue and normal placentas. B-type particles resembling the mouse mammary tumor virus have been observed in milk and normal mammary cells (Fellet and Chopra, 1969; Furmanski *et al.*, 1974).

RT activity similar to those of primate viral RTs have been reported in acute and chronic leukemias (Gallagher *et al.*, 1974; Van Muyen *et al.*, 1979), in myelofibrosis (Steel *et al.*, 1977), in breast cancer (Axel *et al.*, 1972), in melanoma and other skin tumors, and in normal human placentas, which occasionally produce retroviral-like particles visible by EM (Nelson *et al.*, 1978). Because RT activity cannot usually be detected in an enzymatically active form until it has been proteolytically cleaved from an inactive precursor during packaging into virions, one may not be able to detect it in the absence of virions. An assay to detect both the enzyme and high-molecular-weight RNA unique to retroviruses was therefore devised to increase the certainty with which a positive outcome can be interpreted (Schlom and Spiegelman, 1971). The assay led to positive results from numerous researchers in a great variety of malignant conditions, results that unfortunately have not been confirmed or further characterized since the mid-1970s.

Viral antigens (p30 and p70) are often expressed in animal retrovirus systems that do not produce complete virions, and antibodies to these proteins have been used as "probes" to detect latent retroviral infection in human cells. Positive results have been reported in a variety of malignant tissues and in normal human placenta, using antibodies prepared against a variety of animal retroviruses, especially the gibbon ape leukemia virus—Simian sarcoma-associated virus (GALV-SSAV) groups, baboon endogenous virus (BaEV), and the Mason-Pfizer monkey virus (MPMV). Molecular studies using animal probes showed that although normal human DNA, like other mammalian DNAs, has conserved cellular genes homologous to viral oncogenes (Wong-Staal *et al.*, 1981), no significant homology to animal B-type, C-type, or D-type viruses was found (Bishop *et al.*, 1974; Gallo and Wong-Staal, 1980), with the exception of sequences distantly related to the sequence of BaEV (Benveniste and Todaro, 1974; Wong-Staal *et al.*, 1976). More recently, however, genetic elements bearing the structure of retroviruses have been isolated from DNA libraries by their homology to murine leukemia virus (MuLV) (Martin *et al.*, 1981), BaEV (Bonner *et al.*, 1982), or mouse mammary tumor virus (MMTV) (Callahan *et al.*, 1982). Several copies of these endogenous sequences exist in the human genome and are polymorphic. Some sequences represent full-length genomes, whereas other lack long terminal repeat sequences (LTRs) and other components of the genome (*gag–pol–env*); these sequences contain the viral elements in a variety of combinations, i.e., as incomplete viral genomes. Some human tumors express endogenous retroviral-like genes, although whether or not they are causally related or just amplified is still not clear. Testicular teratocarcinoma cell lines have been shown to release C-type retroviral particles that are immunologically unrelated to animal retrovirus strains, synthesized only in a fraction of cells, and possess high molecular weight (GOS) RNA (Boller *et al.*, 1983; Bronson *et al.*, 1984; Lower *et al.*, 1984, 1987). Interestingly, choriocarcinoma cells are also reported to react with a monoclonal antibody specific for the p19 protein of HTLV-I (12/1-2) and a similar reactivity has been observed in syncytiotrophoblasts, which, in addition, express the retrovirus RD114 p30-related antigen (Suni *et al.*, 1981, 1984).

In view of the difficulty of detecting retroviruses in human tissues, a variety of agents that activate retrovirus production in animal systems, such as the halogenated pyrimidines—iododeoxyuridine (IdU) and bromodeoxyuridine (BrdU), have been tried, with disappointing results. Similarly, cocultivation with "indicator" cell lines has been used to rescue from animal cells endogenous viruses that are otherwise very difficult to isolate (Weiss *et al.*, 1971). Again, various viruses have been rescued from human tissues, but they remain poorly characterized; they may even be endogenous viruses of the indicator cell line. Serological studies of human populations have implicated Simian virus antigens that may be heterophile carbohydrate moieties to which antibodies are ubiquitous in humans. High titers of these antibodies are seen in Hodgkin's disease (Ebbesen *et al.*, 1979), myeloid leukemia, testicular teratocarcinoma, pregnancy, and in laboratory workers handling of primate retroviruses (Kurth and Mikschy, 1978). Specific antiodies capable of neutralizing RT activity have been reported from patients with myeloid leukemias; these antibodies have specificity for SSAV (acute) and feline leukemia viruses (chronic) (Jacquemin *et al.*, 1978).

III. Specific Isolates

Certain isolates suspected of being of human origin have been clearly shown to be of animal origin. RD114 is a virus "isolated" from a human rhabdomyosarcoma passaged through the brain of a fetal kitten; it is now known that human cells rescued a feline endogenous xenotropic C-type virus. ESP-1 was isolated from a cell line derived from a lymphoma patient but appears to be a xenotropic mouse leukemia virus variant selected for growth in the human cell it contaminated. A virus islolated from HeLa cells by Zhdanov and his colleagues (1972) in Moscow turned out to be MPMV that must have contaminated the HeLa cells at some stage of their passage history.

Other retroviral detections in human tissue remain elusive, however. A plethora of EM, RT, and hybridization reports suggest the presence of a virus similar to MMTV and MPMV in human breast cancer tissue. It is interesting that, even though there is little homology genetically between these two diverse viruses, they do share common antigenic determinants on their virion proteins. A paucity of both human breast cell lines and confirmation of alleged retroviruses in their culture make further comment speculative. If there is a hitherto undiscovered group of retroviruses associated with human disease, the strongest contender for animal relatedness could be the GALV-SSAV and BaEV groups. Investigators in several laboratories have detected the presence of retroviral particles in leukemia cells that, where they have been adequately characterized, appear to be closely related to GALV-SSAV, with some components related to BaEV. Similar viruses have not been obtained from normal bone marrow cultures. Such viruses include the HL23 virus, which was isolated from a patient with acute myeloid leukemia (Gallagher and Gallo, 1975) and was shown to be very close to a mixture of SSAV and BaEV. Suspected laboratory contamination would appear unlikely, because further independent isolates were made; and DNA prepared from the spleen of the patient at autopsy hybridized to BaEV but not that of SSAV probe. Hybridization to BaEV RNA (but not to SSAV RNA) has been reported for five out of eight myeloid leukemic patients but not for normal subjects (Wong-Staal *et al.*, 1976). Viruses isolated from a patient with a lymphosarcoma that progressed to a leukemic phase and from two children with acute lymphoblastic leukemia (Nooter *et al.*, 1975, 1977) are also very similar to SSAV and BaEV, although further detailed characterization has not permitted definitive interpretation. Kaplan *et al.* (1977, 1979) describes the production of C-type particles from 8 of 14 lymphoma cell lines. They are said to be able to transform human hematopoietic cell lines in culture. Characterization of these isolates again shows a close relationship to SSAV, GALV, and BaEV. Not all SSAV/BaEV-like isolates are from malignant cells; HEL-12 was obtained by Panem *et al.* (1975) from human embryonic fibroblasts, and antigens reacting with anti-HEL-12 sera have been found in tissues from patients with systemic lupus erythematosus (SLE) (Panem *et al.*, 1976, 1978) and in villous stromal cells from normal placentas.

IV. The Significance of the SSAV/BaEV Human Isolates

There has been an enthusiasm by some authors to regard these isolates as monkey contaminants. However, there are considerable grounds for doubt, which need airing. Not only had Nooter, Panem, and Kaplan never knowingly handled primary retroviral isolates before their discoveries, but also the "primate" origin of the monkey viruses is not certain (Weiss *et al.*, 1985a). GALV was isolated from colonies of baboons that had been inoculated with human tissues, and, moreover, little is known about GALV infection in feral gibbons. Simian sarcoma virus (SSV) and SSAV were first isolated from a New World woolly monkey that was a Californian pet in close contact with humans and a gibbon (Thielen *et al.*, 1971). The serological data on human infection with BaEV has been challenged on the grounds of heterophile carbohydrate moiety interactions. BaEV, which is clearly endogenous in the baboon, has already spread to other host species, such as the adaptation by ancestral cats of the BaEV-related RD114 virus, and may have done so in humans. The detection of retroviral-like particles in normal placentas suggests the possibility of prenatal exogenous viral infection in humans, an infection engendering immunological tolerance similar to that seen in chickens infected with leukemia viruses. Furthermore, characterization of some isolates makes it hard to interpret whether both SSAV and BaEV or one virus related to both groups are present. Studies by Schnitzer *et al.* (1977, 1979) suggest that two viruses exist and that productive infection is possible only when mixed infection occurs, although reports of one or the other isolate only being associated with leukemia continue (Derks *et al.*, 1982). It is possible therefore that if a cofactor or helper virus is essential, then it does not have to be SSAV or GALV.

In the light of the foregoing information, coupled with the close similarity of not only the HTLVs and HIVs (see later) but also the more distant homology of human endogenous sequences (Martin *et al.*, 1981; Rabson *et al.*, 1983) to their monkey counterparts, the idea either that SSAV and GALV are human viruses or that human counterparts of these viruses (including BaEV) exist demands further investigation. There are still some investigators who feel that a virus similar to SSAV is involved in human leukemias, and these investigators are continuing their research in this fascinating area (Maeda *et al.*, 1986). Pseudotypes, or hybrid viruses, have frequently been used to examine the host range and neutralization properties of retroviruses in animals (Zavada, 1982). Recently this method has been used to rescue presumptive viral information from human melanoma cell lines by a helper oncovirus (the Harvey murine leukemia and sarcoma virus complex) (Zavada *et al.*, 1986). Further developments using this exciting technique are eagerly awaited. Reasons to be optimistic about further advances in "new" human retroviruses lie in the discovery of the human T cell lymphotropic viruses, HTLVs and HIVs, which were first isolated seven decades after retroviruses were described (Vallée and Carré, 1904; Ellermann and Bang, 1908; Rous, 1911). More recently, human teratocarcinoma-derived retroviruses have been genomically and enzymatically characterized and shown to be different from MTLV and HIV (Löwer *et al.*, 1987). Retroviral particles have also been described in patients with psoriasis and continue to be characterized (Iverson *et al.*, 1983).

V. HTLV-I

Two lines of inquiry led to the discovery of the first human T cell lymphotropic virus. One was the belief that such viruses existed and therefore new methods of isolation and detection would need to be employed to detect them, and the second was the recognition of a new disease entity termed adult T cell leukemia/lymphoma (ATLL) in southern Japan (Uchiyama *et al.*, 1977; Tajima *et al.*, 1979). The marked clustering of ATLL and its distinct clinical features strongly suggested a viral etiology. Because C-type particles had already been reported in patients with T cell lymphomas (van der Loo, 1979) the viral hypothesis was tested by looking for antibodies in the serum of ATLL patients against an established cell line from one such patient (Miyoshi *et al.*, 1980). All patients with ATLL had antibodies against cytoplasmic antigens in Miyoshi's T cell line (MT-1); in addition, 26% of healthy adults living in the endemic area had ATLL antibodies, whereas only 2% of healthy adults living in nonendemic areas possessed these antibodies. However, only after the isolation of HTLV-I by Gallo and colleagues were C-type particles reported in MT-1 cells examined by EM. The virus was therefore presumed to be etiologically linked to ATLL and was called the adult T cell leukemia virus (ATLV) by Hinuma *et al.* (1981). The infectivity of this virus was established in co-cultivation experiments with fresh cord cells, which could be immortalized by ATLV (Miyoshi *et al.*, 1981). Prior to this time, Gallo and his co-workers had been working on the theory that human retroviral particles were too few to be detected by EM. Therefore, they attempted to refine the reverse transcriptase (RT) assay to detect purified DNA polymerases that seemed to have all the properties of RT (Sarngadharan *et al.*, 1972; Gallo *et al.*, 1973).

It was difficult to grow T lymphocytes in the laboratory, and it therefore seemed logical to look for a growth factor that would enhance the proliferation of particular lymphocytes in which retroviruses could replicate. In 1976 Gallo and his colleagues discovered a T cell growth factor (TCGF) or interleukin 2 (IL-2) (Morgan *et al.*, 1976); this growth factor permitted the selective growth of T lymphocyte populations *in vitro*. The stage was then set for the first isolation of a human T cell retrovirus (achieved in 1978) from cultured T lymphocytes from a patient with a skin T cell lymphoma called mycosis fungoides (Poiesz *et al.*, 1980). A second isolate was obtained from a patient with Sézary syndrome (Poiesz *et al.*, 1981). The detailed characterization of virus that followed showed that the RT was magnesium- and not manganese-dependent as in most retroviruses (Rho *et al.*, 1981). Subsequently, specific monoclonal antibodies (Robert-Guroff *et al.*, 1981) and nucleic acid probes (Reitz *et al.*, 1981) were prepared. The cells from which HTLV-I was isolated were $OKT4^{+}$ lymphocytes, the same subtype as the tumor cells of ATLL. Because no definitive serological data had been obtained in the United States to link HTLV-I with a specific disease (Posner *et al.*, 1981), coded sera, provided by Y. Ito, N. Nakao, T. Aoki, and their colleagues, were examined in Gallo's laboratory. These studies showed that almost 100% of the sera of ATLL patients were positive (Robert-Guroff *et al.*, 1982; Kalyanaraman *et al.*, 1982). These data were published at the same time as the immunofluorescence studies of Hinuma and the EM pictures of a C-type retrovirus by Miyoshi. Subsequent studies showed that both isolates were the same virus (Wong-Staal *et al.*, 1983) and, in addition, that all subsequent isolates from the United States, Japan, and the United Kingdom represented the same serotype (Clapham *et al.*, 1984). The clinical features of ATLL were first recognized as a distinct clinical entity in the West by Catovsky and his colleagues at the Hammersmith Hospital in London, who described the occurrence of ATLL in Carribbean immigrants to the United Kingdom (Catovsky *et al.*, 1982). This report directed attention to the Carribbean as the second endemic HTLV-I area after Japan (Gallo *et al.*, 1984). In the light of later findings, it now seems likely that the American patients from whom the first isolates were obtained suffered from ATLL with predominant skin involvement. The clinical features of ATLL include hypercalcemia with or without bone lesions, hepatosplenomegaly, and lymphadenopathy, features that are characteristic of sarcoidosis, which is also prominent in the natives of the Caribbean area and in Blacks in the southeastern part of the United States. This raises the possibility that sarcoidosis is due to a similar agent (Dalgleish, 1985), although an extensive investigation by both biological and molecular techniques has been negative so far.

A. Epidemiology

HTLV-I has now been shown to be endemic in the southeastern portion of the United States (Blayney *et al.*, 1983), parts of South America, parts of southern Italy, and the Arctic, as well as in many parts of Africa. The virus has also been detected in American Indians and Canadian immigrants to Cayenne, in the Surinam population of Holland, and in populations at risk from AIDS. HTLV-I has also been found in association with T cell malignancies in Caucasian people living in the United Kingdom (Dalgleish and Weiss, 1987).

B. Causative Agent of ATLL

The etiological association of HTLV-I with ATLL is based on the following observations: (1) Geographically the areas of high incidence of ATLL correspond closely with those of high prevalence of HTLV-I infection as adduced from seroepidemiological surveys; (2) all individuals with ATLL have evidence of HTLV-I infection; (3) the ATLL tumor cells carry HTLV-I proviruses, whereas nontumorous cells from the same patient are not necessarily infected; (4) HTLV-I transforms human and animal T cells *in vitro*; (5) HTLV-I is closely related to Simian retroviruses, which are oncogenic in experimental animals (Weiss *et al.*, 1985a). In addition, seroepidemiological studies suggest that only about 1 in 80 infected people develop ATLL and that it may take several decades to do so. These data suggest that a cofactor, or a "second hit," is necessary for malignancy to develop. The mechanisms whereby HTLV-I infection leads to malignancy will be discussed in further detail in Sections IX and XI.

VI. HTLV-II

The first isolate of HTLV-II was from a patient with a T cell variant of hairy cell leukemia (Kalyanaraman *et al.*, 1982). Although subsequent studies have failed to link HTLV-II to hairy cell leukemia (Dalgleish, 1985), a second isolate of HTLV-II has recently been reported from a patient with atypical hairy cell leukemia (Rosenblatt *et al.*, 1986), and antibodies to HTLV-II have been reported in a patient with a "new" T cell lymphoproliferative disease (Sohn *et al.*, 1986), a report that suggests a possible causal role in some T cell malignancies. Two other isolates of HTLV-II were obtained from a New York drug addict with acquired immune deficiency syndrome (AIDS) and a hemophiliac who did not show evidence of malignancy. The epidemiology of HTLV-II has not been thoroughly studied, although it has been reported in London drug addicts (Tedder *et al.*, 1984). The increasing association with malignancy is in keeping with the ability of HTLV-II, like HTLV-I, to transform human lymphocytes *in vitro* (Chen *et al.*, 1983a). In spite of the paucity of isolates and seroepidemiology, HTLV-II is very similar to HTLV-I in genomic structure and function and therefore future associations with T cell malignancies should not be surprising.

VII. AIDS and HIV

In spite of HTLV-I and -II, human retroviruses would probably have remained in comparative obscurity if it had not been for the sudden emergence of AIDS. Although it was first recognized as a distinct disease entity in early 1981, it probably did not exist (outside Africa) until 1978, when the first cases appeared in the United States and Haiti. AIDS was first recognized as a result of the occurrence of *Pneumocystis carinii* infections and Kaposi sarcoma (KS) in previously healthy young homosexual men (Center for Disease Control [CDC], 1981). Both conditions were extremely rare outside immunosuppressed populations (such as patients with renal transplants), although a relatively benign form of KS manifesting on the lower limbs is not uncommon in older men of Mediterranean extraction. It rapidly became clear that AIDS was endemic in American homosexuals, drug addicts, and people from Haiti, all of whom manifested many and varied opportunistic infections and immunoblastic lymphomas, in addition to the early presentations described. Furthermore, it became apparent that many people in the AIDS at-risk categories were developing ominous signs of ill health: persistent generalized lymphadenopathy and serious systemic symptoms, such as severe weight loss, night sweats, fevers, diarrhea, and malaise. These symptoms did not qualify for a diagnosis of AIDS, which was defined by the CDC as a disease with symptoms indicative of cellular immune deficiency and with no known underlying cause (CDC, 1982) and was referred to as AIDS-related complex (ARC). Any doubt that the sudden emergence of these conditions in three well-defined groups was not due to an infectious agent was quickly dispelled with the recognition that AIDS was spreading through blood and blood products, such as Factors VIII and IX used to treat hemophiliacs (CDC, 1982).

As the exponential rise in the number of AIDS cases continued (Allen, 1984), a search for a likely candidate ensued. A new retrovirus was an attractive idea, because many animal retroviruses cause immunodeficiency and allied disease. For instance, Friend virus and avian leukosis viruses cause wasting syndromes in rats and birds, respectively (Takeichi *et al.*, 1974; Weiss and Frisby, 1982), equine infectious anemia virus induces multiple immunopathies (Henson and McGuire, 1974), and Mason-Pfizer monkey virus has been associated with immunodeficiency (Fine *et al.*, 1975). However, it was the feline leukemia viruses, which cause leukemia–lymphoma in some cats (reminiscent of HTLV-I-induced disease in humans) and T cell depletions and opportunistic infections in others (Hardy, 1985), that suggested that a virus similar to HTLV-I (and therefore a retrovirus) might be the cause of AIDS.

Although some AIDS patients are HTLV-I carriers, HTLV-I is not the cause of AIDS. Indeed, the first isolation of a new human virus subsequently shown to be the causal agent of AIDS was reported in 1983 by Montagnier and his colleagues at the Pasteur Institute (Barré-Sinoussi *et al.*, 1983). They detected reverse transcriptase, cytopathic activity, and viral particles in phytohemagglutinin- (PHA) and IL-2-stimulated lymphocytes from a patient with lymphadenopathy. Although the report by Barre-Sinoussi *et al.* commented on the similarities of the new isolate to HTLV and suggested the name T lymphotropic retrovirus, this isolate was called LAV-1 (lymphadenopathy-associated virus). Other similar cultures followed (Montagnier *et al.*, 1984), and the causal association of LAV and AIDS remained obscure until Popovic and Gallo reported isolations from AIDS and at-risk patients of a new retrovirus, which they called human T cell lymphotropic virus type 3 (HTLV-III). This retrovirus was "replicated" in a virus-producing cell line, thus enabling characterization and confirmation of the causative link with AIDS and related conditions (Popovic *et al.*, 1984; Gallo *et al.*, 1984) (Fig. 1). Subsequent studies have shown HTLV-III and LAV to be virtually identical (Cheingsong-Popov *et al.*, 1984; Wain-Hobson *et al.*, 1985; Muesing *et al.*, 1985; Ratner *et al.*, 1985). Levy *et al.* (1984) have reported the isolation of similar viruses, which they called AIDS-related viruses (ARV) and which, although similar to the LAV and HTLV-III isolates, are clearly more distant (Sanchez-Pescador *et al.*, 1985) and markedly different with respect to neutralization properties (Weiss *et al.*, 1986). In view of the confusing terminology, an international committee has decided that all the different isolates should be called human immunodeficiency viruses (HIV).

VIII. Simian AIDS (SAIDS) and the New African Isolates

SAIDS was first recognized in 1983 at both the New England and California primate centers (Henrickson *et al.*, 1983; Letvin *et al.*, 1983). D-type and C-type retroviruses were isolated from the afflicted primate colonies. The similarity of some of the C-type viruses to HTLV-III has resulted in the term STLV-III (Kanki *et al.*, 1985; Daniel *et al.*, 1985). Serological studies have shown that STLV-III (SIV) is present in approximately 50% of African green monkeys (AGM), but not in chimpanzees, baboons, or colobus monkeys

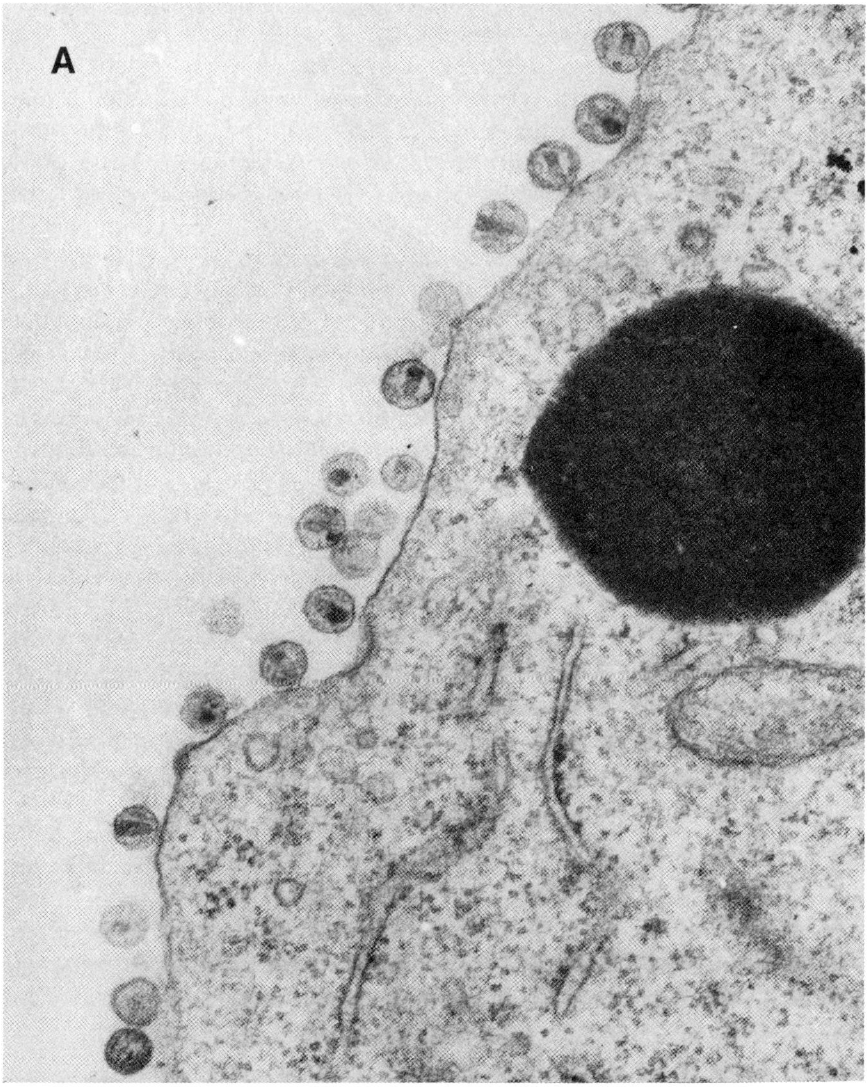

FIG. 1. A. Electron micrograph of HIV (from a British patient, MA). B. The typical budding crescents (arrows) usually associated with C-type retroviruses (the Ma isolate of HIV).

(Kanki *et al.*, 1985). African green vervets infected with SIV do not become ill, however, unlike macaques (MAC), which manifest overt SAIDS following infection. These observations suggested Africa as a possible origin of the AIDS virus. Serological screening studies in West Africa (where AIDS is not endemic) showed that antibodies to SIV were detected in healthy Senegalese prostitutes (Barin *et al.*, 1985). This finding led to the isolation of a new

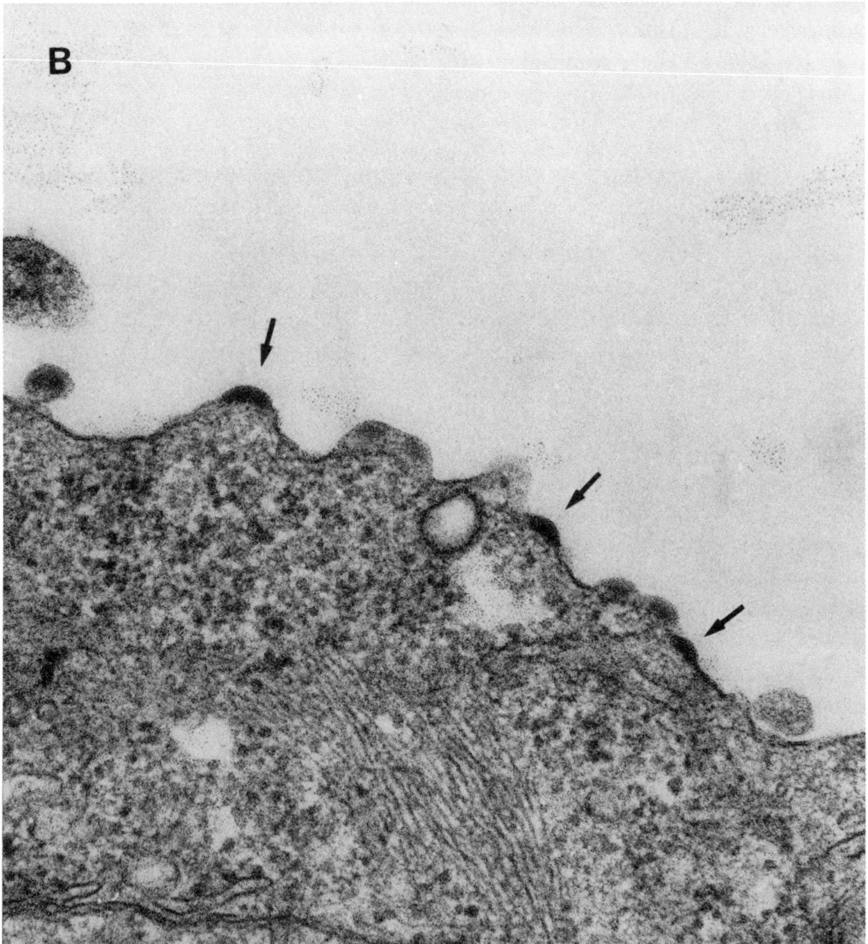

FIG. 1. *(continued)*

virus from these Senegalese. The isolate was named HTLV-IV and is similar, yet distinct antigenically from other HIV isolates, although it is nearly identical to SIV (Kanki *et al.*, 1986).

Another new isolate, called LAV-II, has been made by the Pasteur team (Clavel *et al.*, 1986). They noticed that some African AIDS patients were repeatedly negative for serum antibodies to HIV. Like HTLV-IV, LAV-II was isolated from patients from West Africa. However, whereas HTLV-IV is said to be noncytopathic, both *in vivo* and *in vitro*, LAV-II is clearly associated with disease. Nevertheless, the close relationship of both viruses to STLV-III and their serological similarities (reviewed later) suggest that LAV-II and HTLV-IV may be closely related.

IX. Cell Biology and Immunology of Human Retroviral Infections

One of the most distinctive properties of the HTLVs is the ability to reproduce some of their *in vivo* biological properties, *in vitro*. HTLV-I and -II can both immortalize and transform T lymphocytes, whereas HIV induces cytopathic effects with substantial cell killing. Normal lymphocytes, whether cord-, peripheral blood-, or marrow-derived, grow actively following PHA and IL-2 activation for about 30 days; then growth slows or terminates. However, in the presence of HTLV-I, some cells grow indefinitely. A notable feature of HTLV-I-infected T cells is the constitutive expression of IL-2 receptors, which are often abundant (Poiesz *et al.*, 1980; Leonard *et al.*, 1982; Greene and Robb, 1985; Tsudo *et al.*, 1983). The growth of HTLV-I-infected cells also becomes independent of exogenous IL-2. Furthermore, infected cells often display lobulated nuclei and multinucleated giant cells, and they express transferrin receptors and human leukocyte antigens class II (HLA-Dr) in addition to IL-2 receptors (Popovic *et al.*, 1983). Interestingly, binding of HTLV-I particles to T lymphocytes induces IL-2 production and IL-2 receptor expression and triggers T cell proliferation (Gazzola and Dodon, 1987).

In vitro transmission from cell to cell has been well documented by irradiating virus-infected cells and co-cultivating with cord feeder cells. The transformed lines can be shown to be of recipient-cell origin by genotype characterization (Popovic *et al.*, 1983). HTLV-I-transformed cell lines *in vivo* do not usually have the cross-chromosomal abnormalities seen in ATL leukemia cell lines, and their malignant potential is unclear, although tumor formation has been seen with HTLV-I immortalized cells in immunosuppressed hamsters (Miyoshi *et al.*, 1983). Whereas the immortalized cell lines *in vivo* are nearly always $CD4^+$, a variety of other cells can be infected *in vitro*, including human $CD8^+$ cells and B cells as well as rabbit, rat, and monkey lymphocytes. Nonlymphoid cells that can be productively infected with HTLV-I include human osteosarcoma cells (HOS) (Clapham *et al.*, 1983), feline kidney epithelial cells, fibrosarcoma cells (HT1080), feline CCC cells (Weiss *et al.*, 1985a), human fibroblasts, and human endothelial cells. Induction of syncytia (multinucleated cells) by HTLV-I allows not only for a test for virus production but also for screening of patients' sera for antibodies that will effectively inhibit syncytial formation induced by HTLV-I positive cells (Nagy *et al.*, 1984). Some sera from HTLV-II-infected people and most positive African green monkey and chimpanzee sera also cross-inhibit syncytial formation induced by HTLV-I (Clapham *et al.*, 1984).

Vesicular stomatitis virus (VSV)–HTLV-I pseudotypes can be used as probes for neutralizing antibodies and for cell surface receptors specific to HTLV. ATLL patients have high neutralizing titers ranging from 1:50 to 1:30,000 dilutions, and pseudotypes have been prepared from HTLV-I isolates from Japan, the United States, and the United Kingdom to show that all of these isolates represent the same serotype (Clapham *et al.*, 1984).

X. HIV

The tropism from $CD4^+$ lymphocytes reported *in vivo* is also seen *in vitro* (Klatzmann *et al.*, 1984a). Short-term cultures show marked cytopathogenic effects and early, within 2–3 weeks, selective cell death of the $CD4^+$ but not the $CD8^+$ subsets in marked contrast to those infected with HTLV-I. Using the induction of syncytia and VSV (HIV) pseudotypes as assays, only cells bearing the CD4 antigen can be infected. A wide range of T cell lines, a B cell line LCO (EBV) and a monocyte cell line (U937) are also infectable with HIV (Dalgleish *et al.*, 1984). Furthermore, the surface CD4 antigen is seen to down regulate, following infection (Dalgleish *et al.*, 1984; Klatzmann *et al.*, 1984b; Hoxie *et al.*, 1985; Lifson *et al.*, 1986a). The nature of cell fusion in infected $CD4^+$ cultures is known to involve the CD4 antigen itself, as this process is blocked by anti-CD4 antibodies (Dalgleish *et al.*, 1984) (Fig. 2). It also involves the

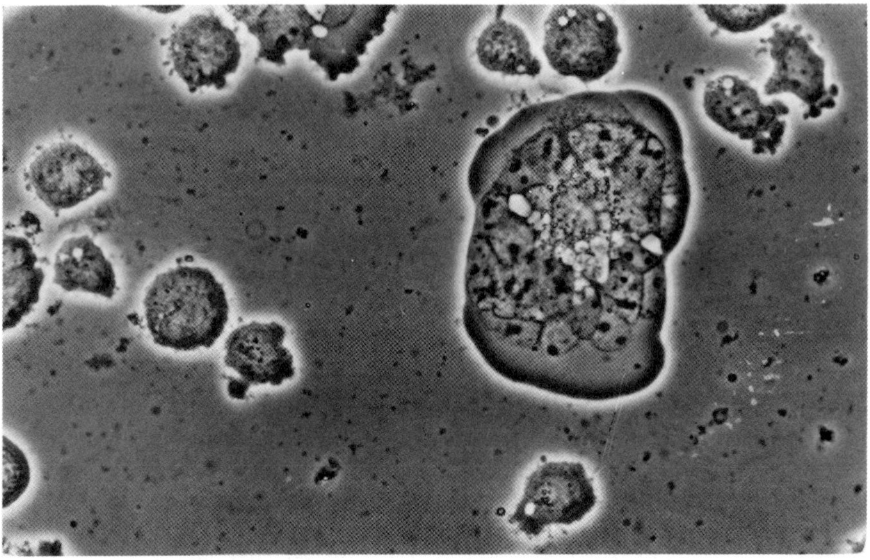

FIG. 2. A typical syncytia formed by $CD4^+$ cells (JM) after virus infection.

envelope glycoprotein of HIV as shown by experiments using cells expressing subclones of HIV (Lifson *et al.*, 1986b,c; Sodroski *et al.*, 1986a). The importance of this CD4/HIV mediated cell fusion is that fused cells are unstable in culture, do not proliferate, and produce numerous virions at the cell surface. If this were to happen *in vivo*, then CD4 cells could be depleted in this way, a result that could have unfortunate consequences for an HIV envelope-based vaccine.

Using a panel of monoclonal antibodies to a wide range of T cell antigens, investigators found that in the syncytial and pseudotype assay all the anti-CD4 monoclonal antibodies blocked HIV infection, whereas the other monoclonal antibodies did not—with the exception of Leu 8 and an anti-class II (HLA-DR) antibody in which weak blocking only was seen (Dalgleish *et al.*, 1984). This work implied that the HIV receptor involved the CD4 antigen. In order to confirm this, the recently cloned CD4 molecule (Maddon *et al.*, 1986) was transfected into a variety of mouse and human cell lines. All human cell lines, whether or not they were of lymphoid origin—but none of the mouse cell lines (Maddon *et al.*, 1986)—were rendered infectable by the expression of the CD4 antigen. Clearly, then, in humans the CD4 molecule (CD4 antigen) is the receptor for HIV. But what do the mouse results mean? Either there is a second component present on human but not mouse cells or the human CD4 molecule is not endocytosable in the mouse. The CD4 molecule binds to the glycoprotein gp120 (110–130) of HIV, which has been shown to co-precipitate with CD4 but not with any other molecule (McDougal *et al.*, 1986). Binding to *all* the CD4-transfected cells (both murine and human) was shown to be as effective as on naturally ocurring CD4-bearing cell lines. The reader is also referred to a more recent review of what happens between binding to the receptor and productive infection (Marsh and Dalgleish, 1987).

Not all of the CD4 molecule is required in binding, however, because some anti-CD4s fail to block HIV infection (Dalgleish, 1986a). Moreover, a panel of radiolabeled anti-CD4 antibodies were used to map the putative HIV binding site; the results suggest that the binding site is relatively large (Sattentau *et al.*, 1986). Further studies on the binding of HIV and CD4 indicate that glycosylation is not important, but combined alkylation and reduction of HIV will destroy binding (McDougal *et al.*, 1986). Mannose-containing carbohydrate moieties on the viral envelope glycoproteins may be important, either directly or indirectly (Lifson *et al.*, 1986b). These studies demonstrate that the binding site on the gp120 molecule requires a proper protein conformation and not simply the primary amino acid sequence, a finding that implies it is unlikely that synthetic polypeptides or cloned gene products of the gp120 will inhibit virus binding to CD4, unless they assume the appropriate tertiary structure. It is becoming increasingly unlikely that an alternative receptor exists. Many B cells that are surface $CD4^-$ and HIV infectable express CD4 mRNA on Northern blots. Recently a B cell in our laboratory that is eminently infectable with HIV but negative for CD4 mRNA on Northern blots was positive for CD4 mRNA using Sl nuclease analysis (which is a more sensitive method for detecting mRNA). Uninfectable cells remained negative for CD4 by the Sl nuclease test (M. Malkovsky and A. Dalgleish, unpublished observations). Even brain cells that are infectable *in vitro* express CD4 mRNA.

Unlike the HIV receptor, the receptors for HTLV-I and HTLV-II remain elusive. Using techniques similar to those described for defining the HIV receptor (Dalgleish *et al.*, 1984), no known T cell surface antigen [including IL-2 receptor, transferrin, or class II (HLA-DR) molecules] has been implicated. Nevertheless, whereas sera from HTLV-I-infected patients readily neutralize in syncytial and pseudotype assays, no significant inhibition is seen with HIV-positive sera in syncytial assays; and only low-level neutralizing activity is detected in pseudotype assays and infectivity assays, even when antibodies to viral membrane antigens are present in high titer (Weiss *et al.*, 1985b). The protective effect of sera was found to be higher in healthy HIV-seropositive individuals than in symptomatic and AIDS patients, a finding suggesting that these low titers may be effective *in vivo* (Robert-Guroff *et al.*, 1985). More recently, pseudotypes were prepared from HIV isolates with distinct envelope genomes. The serum neutralized the isolate derived from the same subject, at a slightly higher titer than unrelated isolates, although in a selection of sera from British and Ugandan HIV-infected patients, significantly higher neutralization titers were seen against the ARV-II isolate from San Francisco. Furthermore, sera that were raised in rabbits and guinea pigs to a recombinant envelope glycoprotein gpl20 only weakly neutralized the pseudotype from which the isolate was cloned (H9IIIB) and virtually none of the other isolates (Weiss *et al.*, 1986). This does not auger well for a recombinant vaccine, although it would be interesting to raise sera against the ARV-II envelope. Similar assays using LAV-II and HTLV-IV are in progress.

Once inside the cell, HIV may either integrate into the host cell DNA (and lie dormant waiting to be activated—see Fig. 3) or undergo replication and cause cell death. How it does so is the subject of much controversy. Some workers propose that activation of a cytotoxic protein could be responsible (Dayton *et al.*, 1986); others blame HIV-induced acceleration of cell senescence (Zagury *et al.*, 1986) or interactions between viral proteins and the CD4 molecule (Sodroski *et al.*, 1986a). Another possibility is that the major cause of cell death is the accumulation of enormous amounts of viral DNA and RNA in cells. This accumulation causes chaos in cell metabolism, which is further complemented by cell membrane damage (soon after the beginning of viral replication, cells looking seemingly normal "leak" fluorescein-labeled antibodies). The membrane damage is of unknown

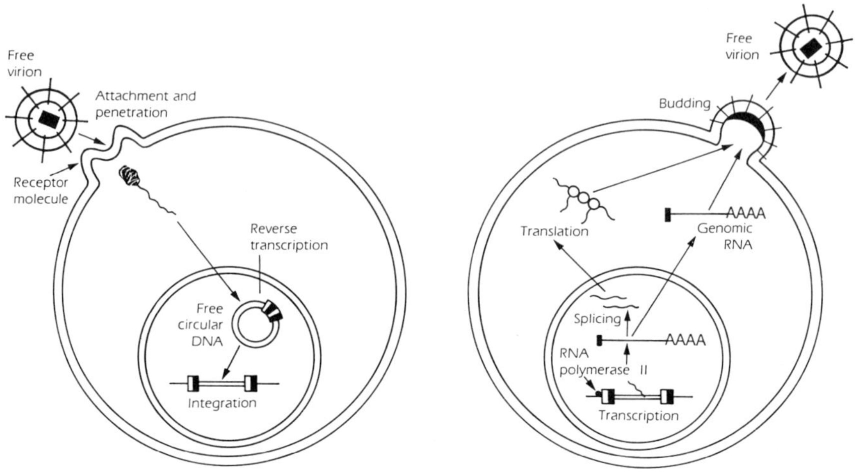

FIG. 3. Life cycle of a retrovirus showing attachment, penetration, integration, transcription, translation, and budding stages.

origin, but it could either be due to the metabolic chaos or, as suggested by Haseltine, be caused by a direct HIV–membrane interaction. Although all these suggestions are acceptable and not mutually exclusive, the question of cell death remains unresolved. This mystery is even more puzzling in the light of the results of Hoxie *et al.* (1985), results clearly demonstrating that T cells cultured in medium supplemented with interleukin 2 can remain productively infected with HIV without showing any cytopathic effect.

The interaction of HIV with the immune system of an individual, resulting in a marked decrease in the numbers of helper–inducer $CD4^+$ lymphocytes and elevated, normal, or decreased numbers of suppressor/cytotoxic $CD8^+$ lymphocytes was one of the first recognized HIV-associated disorders on the level of organism. A possible explanation of this phenomenon is that the $CD4^+$ cells are attacked and destroyed by HIV, whereas the elevation in $CD8^+$ lymphocyte numbers, an increase that often follows infection with Epstein-Barr virus or cytomegalovirus, could reflect the usual response to these herpes viruses, which are present in more than 90% of AIDS patients. In this context, it is noteworthy that the AIDS patients' T cells often react by elevated spontaneous proliferation when cultured *in vitro*. These T cell alterations are accompanied by an increased host susceptibility to both bacterial and viral infections (in particular, to opportunistic ones such as *Pneumocystis carinii* pneumonia or cytomegalovirus retinitis) and/or neoplasms (e.g., Kaposi sarcoma or lymphomas). Interestingly, Walker *et al.* (1986) reported that autologous but not allogeneic $CD8^+$ lymphocytes could control HIV infection *in vitro* by suppressing virus replication. The same authors also suggested that autologous $CD8^+$ lymphocytes could be expanded *in vitro* and administered to AIDS sufferers to inhibit HIV replication and progression of disease. Recently, HIV-specific cytotoxic T lymphocytes that are class I HLA restricted and directed against *env* and *gag* gene products have been described (Walker *et al.*, 1987; Plata *et al.*, 1987). Similarly, antibody-directed cell-mediated responses (against *env*) are also seen in HIV-infected persons, although the clinical significance of these responses with regard to controlling HIV-associated disease is still far from clear (A. G. Dalgleish *et al.*, unpublished observations).

HIV-infected persons tend to display decreased delayed-type hypersensitivity responses *in vivo*. For instance, in tests using seven skin-test antigens, the positive responses of a group of AIDS patients were approximately 25% those of the control group (Lane and Fauci, 1985). Because various functions of both nonspecific mononuclear cells (for antigen processing) and antigen-specific T lymphocytes (for antigen recognition), which are required to be effective for mounting such responses, have not been studied in the particular patients, the precise nature of this disorder remains to be elucidated.

T cells isolated from peripheral blood of HIV-infected persons usually show a decrease in (1) proliferative responses to mitogens and antigens, (2) cytotoxic functions, (3) helper activities for B lymphocytes, (4) the expression of the receptor for IL-2, and (5) the production of IL-2. These defects could be due to nonspecific suppressive molecules, which are released by T cells from AIDS patients (Laurence and Mayer, 1984). Interestingly, similar inhibitory molecules, whose production is associated with immunization, have been postulated to provide a mechanism limiting the entry of new cells into an immune response (Malkovsky *et al.*, 1982). This mechanism could be inappropriately activated in AIDS patients, i.e., it is possible that HIV-associated trans-activating proteins (for details see Section XI) augment the expression of these nonspecific inhibitory molecules, just as some HTLV-I proteins activate (in trans) the expression of IL-2 and its receptor. Large amounts of these inhibitory proteins could be toxic for immunocompetent cells, thus contributing to the functional or somatic death of immunocompetent cells and to the profound AIDS patients' immunological defects, whose severity may not always correlate directly with the deficit in immunocompetent cell numbers. Also, HIV proteins may have direct suppressive influences on T cells. This effect could result in substantial quantitative and qualitative abnormalities of the IL-2 system, which have been recognized in HIV-seropositive persons (Borzy, 1987) and are probably important contributing factors to the impaired immune functions in HIV-associated diseases.

An interesting feature of humoral immunity in AIDS patients is a polyclonal B cell activation similar to that in systemic lupus erythematosus. It is manifested by (1) elevated levels of serum immunoglobulin and circulating immune complexes, (2) increased numbers of spontaneous plaque-forming cells in the peripheral blood, (3) an augmented spontaneous proliferation of B lymphocytes and hyperresponsiveness to B cell growth factors *in vitro*, (4) meager or absent antigen-specific antibody responses following immunization, and (5) refractoriness to some B cell activation signals *in vitro*. A direct polyclonal activation of human B lymphocytes by HIV (Schnittman *et al.*, 1986) in the absence of the normal regulatory T cell environment could partly explain these abnormalities. More recently, Pahwa *et al.* (1986) demonstrated both stimulatory and inhibitory influences of an HIV protein preparation on normal B lymphocyte differentiation. Their results are compatible with the possibility that both direct effects (on B cells) and indirect effects (through T cells) of HIV are responsible for the AIDS-associated B lymphocyte dysfunction.

The number of monocytes in the peripheral blood of AIDS patients is normal, although monocytes expressing the CD4 antigen are depleted in a manner similar to helper T lymphocytes (Rieber and Riethmuller, 1986). AIDS patients' monocytes are also normal with respect to phagocytosis, intracellular killing of microorganisms, and enhancement of hydrogen peroxide release, and to cytotoxicity in response to γ interferon. However, their chemotactic activity is markedly decreased, especially in patients in the later stages of disease. Also, patients with AIDS display a substantially decreased rate of removal of autologous erythrocytes coated with anti-Rh antibodies. This defect in Fc receptor-mediated clearance, which is again most striking in patients with the most advanced illness, may be related to the blockage of Fc receptors by circulating immune complexes. Langerhans cells from AIDS patients are deficient in the expression of HLA class II molecules, but their immunological competence has not been studied. Viruses isolated from different sources, e.g., brain or lymphocytes from the same individual, will show different tropisms *in vitro* for lymphocytes or monocytes, i.e., one isolate will grow well in both lymphocytes and monocytes whereas another will only grow well in lymphocytes (Koyanagi *et al.*, 1987).

The sera of approximately 90% of HIV-infected people contain antibodies that react with an 18-kDa antigen restricted to lectin-stimulated or HIV-infected CD4 T cells *in vitro* and that are cytotoxic in the presence of complement (Stricker *et al.*, 1987). It is possible that these antibodies may contribute to the development of immunodeficiency.

In AIDS patients and in many healthy risk-group members, serum levels of acid-labile interferon, α_1-thymosin and β_2-microglobulin are elevated, whereas levels of thymulin are decreased. Acid-labile interferon was originally described in the sera of patients with systematic lupus erythematosus. It may be synthetized by B lymphocytes infected with retroviruses (Boumpas *et al.*, 1984).

In contrast to children with immunodeficiencies, increased α_1-thymosin levels have been detected in patients with AIDS and healthy homosexual men. This observation does not seem to correlate with a severe thymic involution (characterized by thymocyte depletion, absence of a definitive cortex or medulla, and lack of Hassall's corpuscles) found at autopsy in thymus glands from AIDS patients. There is also a lack of correlation between serum levels of α_1-thymosin, which induces T cell maturation, and total mature T cell numbers. The mechanism underlying these thymic abnormalities remains to be determined.

β_2-Microglobulin is the light chain of all HLA class I molecules, which are present on the surface of practically all cells in the body. The increase in serum levels could reflect a higher rate of cell-membrane turnover and signal the development of acquired immune deficiency syndrome. The meaning of the decreased serum level of thymulin in AIDS patients is unclear, however. For a further review of the immunopathogenesis of HIV, see Spickett and Dalgleish (1988) and Fauci (1988).

XI. Molecular Biology of HTLV-I and HTLV-II

Structurally and functionally, most exogenous oncogenic animal retroviruses belong to two categories (Fig. 4). HTLV-I and HTLV-II form a third category. They are replication-competent, their latency period (HTLV-I) is long (up to several decades), and they possess *in vitro* transforming ability.

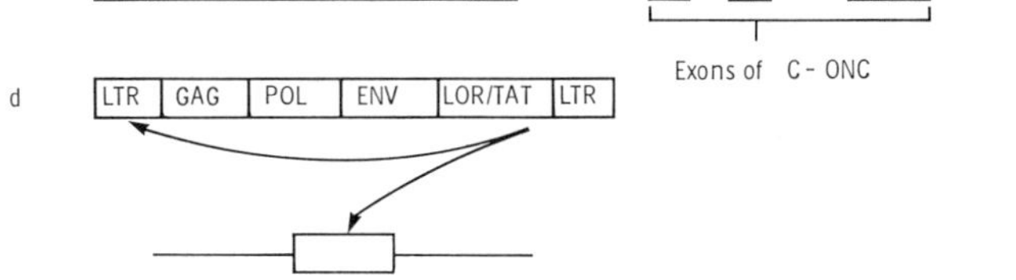

FIG. 4. Genomic structure of retroviruses and mechanisms of oncogenesis. (a) Transduction of an oncogene (*v-onc*) into a nondefective viral genome. (b) The transduced oncogene (within a viral genome that may be defective) can be transcribed *via* LTR-initiated transcription. (c) A cellular protooncogene may be activated (through the viral *cis*-acting transcriptional elements) when a provirus is integrated in its vicinity. (d) The product of the *tat* gene of HTLVs has a positive *trans*-acting role for viral transcriptional activation, probably by increasing the efficiency of mRNA utilization (post-transcriptional activation) or the level of steady-state mRNA either by direct transcriptional activation or mRNA stabilization. It can also cause transcriptional *trans*-activation of nonviral transcription units.

The wild-type proviral DNA genomes of HTLV-I (9032 kb) and HTLV-II (8952 kb) contain the *gag*, *pol*, and *env* structural genes (Seiki *et al.*, 1983; Chen *et al.*, 1983b; Shimotohno *et al.*, 1985). The *gag*, *pol*, and *env* open reading frames of HTLV-I and HTLV-II encode precursor core proteins of 429 and 433 amino acids, reverse transcriptase precursors of 896 and 982 amino acids, and precursors of envelope proteins of 488 and 487 amino acids, respectively (Seiki *et al.*, 1983; Shimotohno *et al.*, 1985). A protease gene is situated in a region between *gag* and *pol* genes in HTLV-II and can encode a sequence of 178 amino acids (Shimotohno *et al.*, 1985). This region is noncoding in HTLV-I (Wong-Staal and Gallo, 1985). The function of these major structural genes is analogous to that of HIV, as described below. Both proviruses have two LTRs, one at each end, which are 755 bp (HTLV-I) and 763 bp (HTLV-II) in length and, like the LTRs of HIV and other retroviruses (see below) contain regulatory elements critical with respect to viral integration, transcription, and replication as well as to target cell specificity (Chen *et al.*, 1984).

The overall nucleic acid sequence homology between the two types of HTLVs is approximately 60% (Shimotohno *et al.*, 1985), and under high stringency conditions there is no hybridization of HTLV-I with HTLV-II (Chen *et al.*, 1983b). Also, there is little overall homology between the HTLV-I and HTLV-II LTRs. However, comparative sequence analysis has revealed similarities in several LTR regions including the TATAA box, the cap site, the polyadenylation signal, and a unique 21-bp triple repeat sequence in U3 upstream of the TATAA box, which may function as an enhancer (Shimotohno *et al.*, 1984a). The most interesting genomic feature is a region of about 1.6 kb between the carboxyl terminus of the *env* gene and 3′ LTR, which according to its original description contains four open reading frames in HTLV-I and three in HTLV-II (Shimotohno *et al.*, 1984b). However, Haseltine and colleagues (1985) have noted that there are at least ten long open reading frames in this region and that numerous polypeptides could be made from this sequence provided that splicing events occur. This region—originally called the pX region (Seiki *et al.*, 1983) or long open reading frame (*lor*)—does not appear to be a typical oncogene, because it is not homologous to known human cellular sequences. It contains a gene, variably termed *x*, *x-lor*, or *tat-I/tat-II*. Its product acts on upstream promoter elements to increase the rate of transcription, and the mechanism of its product's function appears to be different from that of the product of *tat-III* (Sodroski *et al.*, 1984, 1985a,b; Slamon *et al.*, 1984; Chen *et al.*, 1985; Felber *et al.*, 1985; Fujisawa *et al.*, 1986). Greene and colleagues (1986) have shown that the transfection of T cells with the *tat-II* gene upregulates the expression of the interleukin 2 gene and the IL-2 receptor gene. These data are consistent with one of the hallmarks of HTLV-I, HTLV-II transformed cells as well as ATLL cells: the constitutive expression of high levels of the receptor for IL-2. The enhanced co-expression of these growth-promoting genes on both the mRNA and protein level could induce intensive DNA synthesis in T lymphocytes. This, in turn, may favor a gene rearrangement which is probably a pivotal event in leukemogenesis.

XII. Molecular Biology of HIV

The HIV family of viruses displays the general properties of retroviruses:

1. 5′LTR-*gag-pol-env*-3′LTR genomic organization
2. Presence of a unique nonstructural protein necessary for replication—the enzyme reverse transcriptase (RNA-dependent DNA synthetase), which is similar to reverse transcriptases of other retroviruses
3. High-molecular-weight RNA
4. Glycoprotein envelope
5. 1.16–1.17 g/ml buoyant density in sucrose gradient
6. Budding at the cell surface

Mature HIV virions are 100–130 nm in diameter and have a small, electron-dense core, which is round or bar-shaped, depending on the section. HIV virions contain several antigenic proteins. The precursor protein p55 and its cleavage products, p7, p9, p17, and p24, are associated with the core. The p24 is the major antigenic protein of HIV. The two structural envelope proteins, gp120 and gp41, are glycosylated and are derived from a single precursor, gp160. Antibodies against this glycoprotein also recognize its cleavage products: gp120, gp70, gp41, and gp34. Interestingly, certain regions of the HIV *env* gene product have been predicted to be highly antigenic (Robson *et al.*, 1987). The sera of most persons infected with HIV contain antibodies against the core and envelope proteins, whereas antibodies against other antigenic proteins of HIV have been detected less frequently.

The HIV particle contains two identical molecules of genomic RNA. The complete HIV genome has been cloned as DNA and sequenced. Unlike many animal proviruses, HIV does not contain any DNA that is homologous to DNA found in the human genome. Integration of HIV proviruses does not occur at a specific site in the host cell genome. The lengths of proviral DNAs sequenced independently by five groups (Ratner *et al.*, 1985; Sanchez-Pescador *et al.*, 1985; Wain-Hobson *et al.*, 1985; Muesing *et al.*, 1985; Desai *et al.*, 1986) are in the range of 9193 to 9749 bp. The complete provirus is flanked by a 7-bp direct repeat: TAGTAGT (Starcich *et al.*, 1985).

The sequences that encode viral proteins (Fig. 5) are flanked by LTRs. The LTRs contain signals that participate in the integration of transcription of viral genes (viral RNA synthesis). The LTRs also specify the cap site and a portion of the 5′ untranslated sequence of viral messenger RNA. The

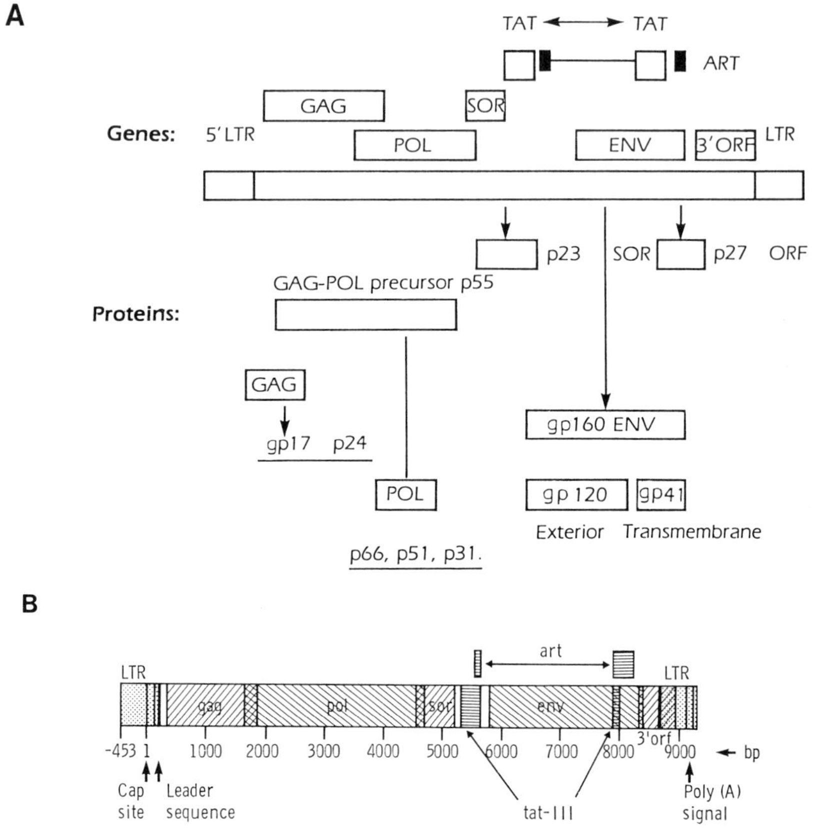

FIG. 5. A. Genetic structure of HIV, showing major proteins. B. The number of base pairs in each coding region.

HIV LTR itself is 634 bp in length and consists of the usual U3, R, and U5 regions of 453, 98, and 83 bp, respectively (for HTLV-III B). The alignment of LTR sequences of various HIV isolates indicates that the R and U5 sequences are very well conserved, whereas the U3 sequences show 8% variation among HIV isolates (Desai *et al.*, 1986). No open reading frame is found in U3. The LTR is bound by conserved pairs of nucleotides (Temin, 1981), beginning with the TG dinucleotide and terminating with the inverted sequence CA at position 634. The CA dinucleotide ending the U5 region of the leftward (5′) LTR is followed by a sequence that has 18 bp complementary to the 3′ terminus of transfer RNA-lysine ($tRNA_{lys}$). Initiation of minus (viral)-strand DNA synthesis in retroviruses requires a host cell tRNA molecule as a primer, and this sequence functions as such a primer site. The same primer is used by the mouse mammary tumor virus, whereas other known mammalian retroviruses, including HTLV-I and HTLV-II, have a tRNA-proline primer. Preceding the 3′ LTR is a 15-bp polypurine tract (similarly positioned in other retroviruses), which plays an important role in the initiation of plus-strand DNA synthesis.

A TATAA sequence typical of eucaryotic transcriptional promoters (the TATA box) is situated 27 bp upstream (5′) from the transcriptional initiation site (cap site, U3–R boundary). The sequence CCAAT, which usually occurs in U3 about 70–80 bp before R, is located upstream (5′) at position 178. A consensus sequence that signals addition of polyadenylated tails, AATAAA, is positioned 24 bp upstream (5′) from the polyadenylation site at nucleotide 551. It is noteworthy that the polyadenylation signal is positioned much further upstream in HTLV-I and HTLV-II. The polyadenylation site is also flanked by sequences related to the transcriptional termination consensus signals TTTGCN(G/C)TTGCA and TTGT. The latter is 20 bp downstream (3′) from this site at position 571. Large repeats, characteristic of some retroviral-enhanced elements, which are generally located upstream (5′) from the TATA box and are an important feature of transcriptional regulation of some eucaryotic and viral genes are not present. Sequences related to the consensus sequence for enhancer elements, GTGG(A/T)(A/T)-(A/T)G, include TGGATGG at position 128 and TGGTTAG at position 463. Within the HIV LTR, there is also a sequence element responsive to the trans-activation gene product (Rosen *et al.*, 1985a). It is termed TAR and located in the R region, which encodes the 5′ leader sequence of viral mRNA. Okamoto and Wong-Staal (1986) have predicted a stable hairpin RNA structure within the TAR element of the viral mRNA that may be essential for trans-activation. Other cis-acting sequences involved in the regulation of HIV expression are three sites that bind the cellular transcription factor Spl and act to increase transcription initiation *in vitro* (Jones *et al.*, 1986).

The genome of HIV, like that of other retroviruses, contains three structural genes—*gag*, *pol*, and *env*—that encode the capsid (core) proteins, Mg^{2+}-dependent reverse transcriptase, protease, integrase, and the envelope proteins. In addition, the HIV genome harbors *at least* five other genes—*sor*, *R*, *tat-III*, *3′orf*, and *art/trs*—that are not common to most retroviruses and whose functions are now under investigation.

The *gag* open reading frame contains the *gag* gene (512 codons), which encodes the internal structural proteins of the virion. The *gag* gene codes for a capsid structure that is somewhat different from that of other retroviruses. For example, there is no protein interposed between the amino terminus and the major capsid proteins for HIV as there is for most of the other retroviruses. Also, two (rather than one) small proteins are derived from the carboxyl-terminal end of the *gag* precursor. In contrast to most other retroviruses, the HIV *gag* gene precursor appears to be associated with the nucleus or the perinuclear space. The precursor polypeptide, p55, is synthetized and then cleaved to yield the mature *gag* proteins described earlier. The calculated relative molecular mass of 55,841 is consistent with detection of the 55,000 *gag* precursor polypeptide in immunoprecipitates of HIV-infected cells using sera from HIV-infected persons. The protein coded 5′ (upstream) of the p24 coding sequence is hydrophilic. Its calculated M_r of 14,866 corresponds to the *gag* protein p17. The 3′ part of the *gag* region codes for the basic (because of a high content of lysine and arginine residues) retroviral acid-binding protein. The alignment of the *gag* gene sequence of various HIV isolates shows that the majority of changes in amino acids are localized in the carboxyl-terminal sequence. The amino-terminal sequences display intermediate changes, whereas the regions encoding p24 are conserved. These data are similar to those obtained from other known retroviruses in which the major internal protein with group-specific antigenic determinants is well conserved, whereas the amino and carboxy termini, which carry type-specific antigenic determinants, are more heterogenous. The amino terminus of p24 is generated by a cleavage between tyrosine and proline. Interestingly, proline is also present at the amino terminus of p25 *gag* of HTLV-I, p27 *gag* of Rous sarcoma virus (RSV) and p30 *gag* of murine leukemia virus.

The *pol* open reading frame (1003 codons) overlaps the *gag* open reading frame by 80 amino acids. This long overlap is in contrast to the shorter overlap in this region for most of the other retroviruses. In the *pol* open reading frame, the region coding for the enzyme reverse transcriptase is shorter than that of most retroviruses and appears to comprise two subunits: 66 kDa and 51 kDa. It has numerous regions where the predicted amino acid sequence shows considerable homology to *pol* gene products of HTLV-I, RSV, and MuLV ($\sim$20–30%). The amino terminus is to a certain extent homologous to portions of the putative viral polymerases of hepatitis B virus and cauliflower mosaic virus. The carboxyl termini of HIV, HTLV-I, RSV, and MuLV are also appreciably homologous in protein structure. The second open reading frame codes not only for reverse transcriptase but also for a protease and an endonuclease (Ratner *et al.*, 1985). Interestingly, 3′-azido-3′-deoxythymidine phosphorylated to its 5′-triphosphate derivative is a potent inhibitor of HIV reverse transcriptase, a finding indicating that the product of this open reading frame can be a specific target for antiviral therapy (Furman *et al.*, 1986). Several important functional regions of HIV RT have been identified, including components of the triphosphate binding site and pyrophosphate exchange sites (Larder *et al.*, 1987). It is also noteworthy that the reverse transcriptase of HIV exhibits a preference for the divalent magnesium rather than manganese.

The *env* open reading frame can code a protein 863 amino acids long. The *env* gene encodes the major glycoprotein found in the envelope of the virus and in the cytoplasmic membrane of infected cells. The *env* protein is synthesized from a subgenomic 4.3 kb mRNA,in contrast to the *gag* and *pol* proteins which are probably synthesized from full-length mRNA (Muesing *et al.*, 1985; Rabson *et al.*, 1985; Arya *et al.*, 1985). The external portion of the HIV envelope glycoprotein is so extensively glycosylated that almost 50% of its weight is accounted for by sugar residues. Generally, retroviral *env* proteins arise from a precursor polypeptide, which is processed at two or more sites. There are 32 potential *N*-glycosylation sites (Asp-X-Ser/Thr) and three hydrophobic regions characteristic of the retroviral envelope proteins. The size of the predicted products is in accordance with the detection of a 120-kDa glycoprotein (from 517 to 523 amino acids) and a virion-associated gp41 (346 amino acids), which is the transmembrane protein. This transmembrane protein is unusually long, almost twice that of other retroviruses. The comparison of nucleotide sequences of various HIV isolates indicates approximately a 13% heterogeneity in the gp120 coding sequence and 7% in the gp41 coding sequence, resulting in an amino acid sequence divergence of up to 25% and 16%, respectively. These defined regions of amino acid sequence homology and heterogeneity could have important implications for infectivity and pathogenicity and play a role in escaping the host's immune surveillance, as described for the visna virus (Clements *et al.*, 1980).

The protein products of *sor*, *tat*, and *3'orf* have been identified serologically in infected cells (Lee *et al.*, 1986; Sodroski *et al.*, 1986a; Kan *et al.*, 1986; Allan *et al.*, 1985; Arya and Gallo, 1986; Franchini *et al.*, 1986). Recent evidence strongly suggests that there is a protein encoded by the open reading frame termed *art* or *trs* (Sodroski *et al.*, 1986c; Feinberg *et al.*, 1986). The *sor* (short open reading frame) gene encodes a protein of M_r 23,000, which is thought to be translated from 5.0-kb and 5.5-kb mRNAs. The *3'orf* (open reading frame) extends into the 3′ LTR, consists of three exons, and codes for a 27,000 M_r protein and similar to the *tat-III* and *art/trs* products appears to be synthesized from a subgenomic mRNA (2 kb). Mutations in these two open reading frames neither interfere with the initiation of viral infection *in vitro* (Sodroski *et al.*, 1986b; Fisher *et al.*, 1986), nor impair the ability of the virus to induce cytopathic effects, although *sor* mutants replicate with somewhat delayed kinetics. In contrast, deletions in the *3'orf* region result in mutant viruses that are more virulent than the original wild-type isolates, a finding indicating that the *3'orf* gene could be involved in downregulating virus replication (Luciw *et al.*, 1987). The function of the *R* gene is unknown (Wong-Staal *et al.*, 1987).

The *tat-III* (trans-activating transcriptional regulation) gene also consists of three exons, the first of which does not code for protein structure. Its transcription into a functional messenger RNA involves double splicing, which brings together sequences from the 5′ part (287 bp), middle part

(268 bp), and 3′ part (1258 bp) of the HIV genome (Arya *et al.*, 1985; Sodroski *et al.*, 1985a). The second and third exon code for the *tat-III* protein (86 amino acids in the HTLV-III and LAV isolates and 101 in the ARV-2 and CDC-451 isolates). The second exon, which codes for 72 amino acids and represents the major functional domain of the trans-activator gene is located between the *sor* and *env* genes, in a region originally thought to be noncoding. The remaining amino acids are coded by a small exon within the *env* gene, where the open reading frame terminates at 86 or 101 amino acids, depending upon the isolate. The *tat-III* gene product stimulates LTR-directed gene expression through the interaction with specific sequences (TAR) in the leader of viral messages. Mutations in the 5′ portion of the first coding exon result in inefficient synthesis of structural proteins and hinder virus replication. It has been shown that, in cell lines constitutively expressing the *tat-III* protein, these mutations are fully complemented in trans (Dayton *et al.*, 1986). Because the first 58 amino acids of the *tat* product are sufficient to carry its trans-activation and replication functions (Seigel *et al.*, 1986), the role of the *tat-III* carboxyl-terminal region remains to be elucidated. Some authors (Rosen *et al.*, 1986; Feinberg *et al.*, 1986) suggest that *tat* is required for the translation of viral mRNA even though it does not substantially affect mRNA levels. In these studies, cells transfected with mutant HIV genomes defective for *tat* expression contained normal levels of viral mRNA but no viral proteins. In contrast to these findings, others have reported that *tat* expression does increase mRNA levels. Using recombinant constructs—the HIV LTR linked to the interleukin 2 gene (Culen, 1986) or to the chloramphenicol acetyltransferase gene (Peterlin *et al.*, 1986)—these authors showed that the levels of the heterologous mRNA transcripts became elevated in the presence of *tat*. The fact that the TAR element is downstream of the cap site and does not behave as a transcriptional enhancer would suggest that augmented mRNA stability rather than an increased rate of transcription initiation is responsible for the observed phenomenon. A possible explanation for the described *tat-III* effects at both the mRNA and protein level could be a concomitant increase in mRNA stability and derepression of translation (Chen, 1986). However, recently Okamoto and Wong-Staal (1986) demonstrated that nuclear extracts from HIV-infected cells contained a factor (probably a protein) that stimulated the initiation of transcription (approximately 12-fold) from the HIV promoter, possibly by binding to the DNA. It is conceivable that this factor is the *tat* gene product. Therefore, it remains possible that *tat-III* primarily influences the rate of transcription initiation. However, results of Kao *et al.* (1987) indicate that *tat* does not affect the rate of HIV transcription initiation, but it *trans*-activates HIV transcription by relieving a specific block to transcriptional elongation within the TAR sequence. Interestingly, a transcription factor called NF-κB acts in synergy with the viral *tat-III* gene product to enhance HIV expression (Nabel and Baltimore, 1987). Trans-acting factors in HTLV-I, HTLV-II, and bovine leukemia virus (BLV) similar

to *tat-III* are products of a viral gene termed *tat* or *x-lor* (Sodroski *et al.*, 1984; Slamon *et al.*, 1984; Rosen *et al.*, 1985b).

The observation that diminished expression of *gag* and *env* proteins associated with mutations near the two coding exons of the *tat-III* gene cannot be complemented by the *tat-III* gene product alone suggested the existence of another trans-activator gene. It has been postulated that the coding exons of this gene use alternative reading frames of both coding exons of the *tat-III* gene. The splicing events needed to generate this alternative reading-frame product are essentially the same as those required for the *tat-III* gene expression. The product of the alternative reading frame is 116 amino acids long and contains a number of basic hydrophilic residues similar to those found in the *tat-III* gene product as well as in other nucleic acid-binding proteins. The gene known as *art* (anti-repression trans-activator), or *trs*, appears to neutralize the effects of cis-acting negative-regulatory sequences present on viral mRNA coding for the HIV structural proteins (Sodroski *et al.*, 1986b) or to control the extent of mRNA processing, such that larger mRNA species are maintained (Feinberg *et al.*, 1986). In addition, both *art/trs* and *tat* are absolutely required for the synthesis of gp120 from its cognate mRNA, and they influence the level of gp120 mRNA (Knight *et al.*, 1987). Finally, although the *art/trs* gene product is essential for expression of HIV structural proteins, it may have a negative *trans*-regulatory role in transcription (Sadaie *et al.*, 1988).

Despite the genomic diversity of HIV that is well documented (Wong-Staal and Gallo, 1985), proviral DNAs from different HIV isolates hybridize with each other even under high stringency conditions. The most divergent part of the HIV genome is the part of the *env* gene coding for the exterior glycoprotein, where HIV isolates differ from each other in up to 20% of amino acids. Therefore, it appears that the HIV family consists of a spectrum of genetically similar but divergent retroviruses. The genetic variability of HIV could reflect a selective advantage of mutations, for instance on the basis of "sneaking through the immune response" mechanism similar to that of the equine infectious anemia virus (EIAV) (Montelaro *et al.*, 1984).

However, the one consistent feature between all known HIV-I isolates as well as HIV-II and SIV isolates, is that they bind to CD4, thus suggesting a conserved binding site that is present on a diverse range of HIVs.

XIII. Epidemiology of Human Retroviruses

The worldwide distribution of HTLV-I and HTLV-II infections has already been discussed. What remains to be seen, however, is whether these viruses spread into other communities by sexual or other modes of infection. One route of transmission that has received a lot of speculative attention is that of insect vector transmission. A recent study in Trinidad (Miller *et al.*, 1986) suggests that the most at-risk population in the case of HTLV-I are the poor living near open water courses. This evidence strongly suggests that mosquitos may be responsible for HTLV-I transmission in Trinidad. There is as yet no direct evidence of mosquito transmission in man, although transmission studies using the bovine leukemia virus (which is very similar to HTLV-I) in cows show that a minimum number of 900 lymphocytes are required before transmission is possible (A. Burny, personal communication). Hence, "large" mosquito or multiple bites may be required in order to transmit humam retroviruses by this route. Nevertheless, there is no evidence that HIV can be transmitted by mosquitos. Replication in mosquitos is required for most pathogens to be transmitted, and it is unlikely that HIV can replicate in mosquitos as it is heavily CD4-dependent.

A. Epidemiology of HIV

Initially HIV infection appeared to be confined to homosexuals, hemophiliacs (or receivers of blood and its products), intravenous drug abusers, and Haitians. The involvement of the last group was taken by some to suggest that the virus came to the West from Africa. However, it is more likely that Haitians contracted the virus from American homosexuals for whom Haiti was a popular vacation resort, particularly in view of the fact that the earliest evidence of the virus in the Americas suggests it appeared in New York, San Francisco, and Haiti simultaneously. Nevertheless, the transmission of HIV in Haiti as well as in Haitian immigrants to Florida appears to be mainly heterosexual, as it is in Africa. Indeed, it is the ability to spread through heterosexual contact that puts AIDS into a league different from that of the initial stages of recognition of AIDS, when only the aforementioned groups appeared to be at risk. Although AIDS has always been a heterosexual disease in Africa, there was very little evidence for that in the United States and Europe until recently.

B. Evidence for Heterosexual Transmission

Wives of hemophiliacs have become seropositive for HIV antibodies (approximately 10%), whereas other family members remain seronegative (Melbye *et al.*, 1985; Kreiss *et al.*, 1986). Virus has been isolated from semen and cervical secretions, and the documentation of HIV transmission via artificial insemination contributes additional proof to this mode of transmission (Stewart *et al.*, 1985). Antibodies to HIV have been reported in female prostitutes (CDC, 1985); and, whereas they may have had other risk factors (i.e., intravenous drug abuse), at least 200 women whose only admitted risk factor was exposure to a risk group member developed AIDS (CDC, 1985). Indeed, several such cases are known to one of us (A.G.D.). The risk of female to male transmission appears to be low, although at least 40 AIDS cases among men whose only at-risk behavior was to have sex with a female risk group member (CDC, 1986; Redfield *et al.*, 1985) have been reported.

Although the detailed history of the epidemiology of AIDS will not be reviewed in detail here (for fuller reviews, see Weiss *et al.*, 1985a; Dalgleish and Weiss, 1987; Biggar, 1986), it should be remembered that only a handful of cases of AIDS initially appeared in the homosexual community, following which the incidence was seen to rise exponentially.

C. AIDS AND AFRICA

AIDS is now widespread throughout Central Africa. It was first recognized there as a potential source of the disease when clinicians in Paris and Brussels reported AIDS-like illnesses among African patients without any known risk factors for AIDS. Those observations directed attention to Rwanda and Zaire, where AIDS was found to be prevalent in heterosexually promiscuous members of the urban communities of the new modern cities. The clinical features are generally similar to those seen in Western AIDS patients except that a different pattern of opportunistic infections is seen. It is now clear that the spectrum of opportunistic infections seen in AIDS reflects those organisms found in the environment. Although *Pneumocystis* pneumonia is commonly seen in the West, it is rare in Africa where oroesophageal candidiasis and tuberculosis are more common (see Tables II and III).

Starting in 1984, physicians recognized in Uganda a new disease entity (known locally as "slim" disease) characterized by extensive oral candidiasis, diarrhea, extreme wasting and weight loss, fever, an itchy maculopapular

TABLE II

DISEASES MODERATELY INDICATIVE OF UNDERLYING IMMUNODEFICIENCY AND SEEN IN AIDS

Protozoan infection	*Viruses*
Pneumocystis carinii pneumonitis	Cytomegalovirus of an organ other than a lymph node
Toxoplasma gondii encephalitis or disseminated infection	Progressive multifocal leukoencephalopathy
Chronic *Crytosporidium* enteritis (>1 month)	Herpesvirus (chronic infection—simplex or zoster)
	Polyomavirus
Fungal Diseases	
Candida oral/esophagitis/bronchitis	*Bacterial infection*
Cryptococcal meningitis or disseminated infection	*Mycobacterium avium* complex or *M. Kansasii* (and disseminated tuberculosis)
Histoplasmosis (disseminated)	*Legionella* sp.
Chronic enteric isosporosis	*Nocardia* sp.
Helminthic infections	*Salmonella* sp.
Strongyloidiasis (disseminated beyond the gastroinetestinal tract)	*Shigella* sp.
	Listeria monocytogenes

TABLE III

DERMATOLOGICAL MANIFESTATIONS

Infections	*Bacteria*
Herpes simplex and zoster	*Staphylococcus*
Pox viruses (molluscum contagiosum)	*M. intracellulare* and *tuberculosis*
Papilloma viruses (verruca vulgaris, condyloma acuminatum)	
	Cancers
	Kaposi's sarcoma
Fungi	Hodgkin's and non-Hodgkin's lymphomas including Burkitt's lymphoma
Candida albicans (thrush)	Squamous and small cell carcinomas
Cryptococcus neoformans	
Histoplasma capsulatum	
Trichophyton rubrum	*Other*
	Primary HIV infection
Protozoa	Seborrheic dermatitis
Acathamoeba castellani (amoebiasis)	Oral "hairy" leukoplasia
	Granuloma anulare-like eruption
	Drug eruptions
	Sulfonamides

rash, and occasional respiratory symptoms (Serwadda *et al.*, 1985). The clinical features were similar to those reported in some HIV subjects in the United States (Mathur-Wagh and Mildvan, 1984). Indeed, the majority of Ugandan slim patients were positive to a highly specific competitive ELISA assay that uses an early isolate (CBL-I), which is similar to HTLV-III and LAV isolates. This study showed the following important points: (1) the disease was new to Uganda; (2) the populations affected were heterosexually promiscuous; (3) children and old people were largely free of virus infection, a finding providing strong indirect evidence against mosquito or insect vector transmission; (4) contact with traders from Tanzania, many of whom were HIV seropositive, implicated spread from or to other regions in eastern Africa. However, an isolate from a Tanzanian resident is considerably different in the envelope region (Dalgleish and Popovic, unpublished observations), yet this serum reacts in standard ELISA assays using earlier isolates. Subsequent studies have shown that at least 10% of healthy mothers in Kampala tested positive for HIV antibodies in 1986, and the numbers have since risen (W. Carswell, A. Dalgleish, and R. Weiss, unpublished observations). Recently, slim disease has appeared in epidemic proportions in western Tanzania (Biggar, 1986), and it now appears to be spreading rapidly across the whole of central Africa. The important message from these and other studies is that AIDS is a heterosexual disease in Africa, affecting men and women in roughly equal proportions. Longitudinal studies involving prostitutes and their male customers add further evidence that not only is AIDS spread from men to women but also that it may spread from women to men, although the latter is evidently less efficient, as is probably the case with gonorrhea (Van de Perre *et al.*, 1985). At present, heterosexual transmission in the West appears to be much less common, a situation suggesting that a cofactor is involved. Although no clear agent has been identified, the increased incidence of venereal disease in Africa coupled with the apparent association between recently contracted sexual diseases and the progression from healthy to seropositive for HIV in homosexuals in the West (Weber *et al.*, 1987) demands further attention.

D. Earliest Evidence of HIVs

The earliest recorded cases that are consistent with AIDS occurred in Zairian citizens in 1976 and 1977 (Bygbjerg, 1983; Vandepitte *et al.*, 1983). Further evidence that a virus similar to HIV was present in Central Africa in 1959 has been obtained by thorough investigation of stored sera samples (Nahmias *et al.*, 1986). Interestingly, a number of sera from Africa (collected in the 1960s and early 1970s) also contain antibodies specific for HTLV-I (Saxinger *et al.*, 1984). A high degree of false reactivity by ELISA to both HTLV-I and HIV has been reported in sera samples from Africa, a report necessitating confirmation by Western blots or competitive ELISA assays to determine definite positivity. Because most of these sera were collected from the "malarial belt," the question was raised as to whether or not the reactivity was due to antibodies to *Plasmodium falciparum*. However, this has been shown not to be the case. The real reason remains unresolved. Early reports that false-positive reactions could be due to antibodies against DR4 or other HLA types should no longer be a problem, because of the use of cloned virus products or the use of non-DR-containing cell lines like CEM to produce the virus antigen.

XIV. Origin of the AIDS Virus

With mounting evidence that AIDS originated in Africa, the question must be asked as to why it has only recently emerged as a pathogenic disease. A clue may be provided by monkeys. A similar virus (STLV-III, or SIV) has been isolated from monkeys (Kanki *et al.*, 1985). Although green vervet monkeys from Africa are seropositive for SIV, they appear to remain healthy, whereas the virus causes immunodeficiency among macaques (which are seronegative in the wild). The case that African green vervet monkeys represent a reservoir of SIV is strengthened by the fact that sera collected over 20 years ago are positive for STLV-III antibodies (Daniel *et al.*, 1985; Kanki *et al.*, 1985). Possible routes of transmission of SIV-like viruses from monkey to man aside, these data provide a possible model that suggests that a small isolated population of humans could have carried HIV for many years without any obvious pathogenic effects. The fact that the spread of AIDS through Africa appears to have started at the time of widespread civil unrest and subsequent troop movements offers a scenario for the sudden mixing of infected carrier and susceptible populations.

Indeed, further studies with SIV indicated that a group of healthy prostitutes were infected with a virus more similar to SIV than to HIV. This finding led to the isolation of a virus called HTLV-IV, which now appears to be pathogenic *in vitro* and *in vivo* (Kanki, 1986), in marked contrast to another recent isolate made from West Africa by workers at the Pasteur Institute, an isolate that has been called LAV-II (HIV-2) (Clavel *et al.*, 1986). This virus was isolated from West African AIDS patients (Guinea-Bissau and the Cape Verde Islands), and is obviously pathogenic *in vivo* as well as *in vitro*. The low pathogenicity of HTLV-IV has recently been challenged, and a complete, direct-comparison analysis between HTLV-IV and LAV-II is not available at this time. Nevertheless, analysis of HTLV-IV shows that it bears many proteins of SIV_{AGM}—notably, a 32-kDa protein thought to be a transmembrane envelope protein. Sequence data suggests that they are nearly identical (B. Hahn, personal communication). Furthermore, the envelope proteins of SIV_{AGM} are recognized by the human sera which, in contrast, do not recognize the proteins of HIV-I. Sera from LAV-II (HIV-2)-infected patients only precipitate the envelope proteins from SIV_{MAC} and not those of LAV (HIV-1); however, the precipitation of the p32 of SIV as described for HTLV-IV is not obvious.

It seems likely that these new isolates are just further evidence of a wide variation of human retroviruses of the HIV family present in Africa. Further studies on these and other primate isolates (as well as on those yet to be discovered) should increase our understanding of what makes HIV pathogenic in humans.

XV. AIDS and Children

Whereas a detailed account of pediatric AIDS is outside the scope of this review, the increasing occurrence of AIDS in children has resulted in important epidemiological data with regard to transmission and the response of the immature immune system to HIV. Although only approximately 2% of AIDS cases diagnosed in the West occur in children under the age of 13 years, 76% of these cases occur in infants born to HIV-infected mothers. It is likely that infected mothers transmit the virus at some point near parturition. A case of transmission via breast milk has been reported. The other cases are due to transmission via blood and its products. The risk of perinatal infection is controversial, although studies are underway to detail the exact incidence. Earlier studies suggest that 65% of subsequent births to HIV-infected mothers who had already produced one offspring with AIDS were infected. The natural history of pediatric AIDS depends on presentation, and this, in turn, depends on what constitutes pediatric AIDS. It is clear that there is a widespread clinical picture of HIV infection in children. The common presentations are failure to thrive, persistent *Candida* infections and generalized lymphadenopathy. An increasing variety of other conditions are associated with HIV infection in addition to the recognized opportunistic infections and Kaposi sarcoma. These include lymphoid interstitial pneumonitis, encephalopathy, protein malnutrition, hepatitis, and recurrent bacterial infections. A high index of suspicion is needed to diagnose an HIV-infected infant, a situation that might, in part, explain why the majority of pediatric HIV-infected cases in the United States have been reported from Miami and New York. The number of infected children who will develop disease and die is not known. Several children are known to have remained asymptomatic several years after infection. Definite studies are awaited with interest. Nevertheless, it would appear that the reaction of children to infection may be different from that of adults, because hypogammaglobulinemia (in contrast to hypergammaglobulinemia in adults) is increasingly recognized in HIV-infected children. For detailed reviews, see Parks and Scott (1987), and Thomson and Dalgleish (1987).

XVI. From Infection to Disease

Initial studies on HIV infection and disease predicted that up to 10% of those infected will develop AIDS. Numerous cohort studies have since described various degrees of progression, from 6 to 20%, of HIV-infected people to AIDS over a 2-year period. Whatever confusion may be apparent in the different figures, one thing is clear and that is that the risk that infected persons will develop AIDS increases with the length of time they have been infected. The second point is that the definition of AIDS is a very limiting diagnosis, and a more appropriate description is HIV-related disease. With this in mind, Redfield and his colleagues at the Walter Reed Medical Center have proposed the Walter Reed staging classification for HIV infection (Redfield *et al.*, 1986). Basically, this defines six major categories of HIV infection ranging from well through lymphadenopathy, decreased helper lymphocyte number (less than 400) and decreased or absent resistance to opportunistic infections. On the basis of this classification, it appears that the majority of patients with decreased helper cell numbers will relentlessly progress to the next stage over an 18-month period. The trigger to move from totally asymptomatic to symptomatic is still unknown, although cofactors such as other sexually transmitted diseases or certain viral infections (Nabel *et al.*, 1988) have been implicated, as mentioned previously (Weber *et al.*, 1986). Longitudinal studies on homosexual cohorts with blood samples collected since 1978 show that the subsequent annual seroconversion rates vary from 5 to 10% per year and that the rate for developing AIDS varies from 3% per year to 34% for a 3-year period for subjects in New York. It is noteworthy that differences between New York and San Francisco suggest a much higher incidence of disease in HIV seropositive homosexuals in New York.

It is possible that this is a consequence of the more effective neutralization characteristics of the San Francisco isolate (ARV-II) (Weiss *et al.*, 1986). Nevertheless, on the basis of these studies and similar ones conducted in Germany, the predicted rates for HIV-infected persons developing AIDS are now in the region of 75 to greater than 90% over a 7- to 12-year period. The need for preventive measures, effective treatment, and above all a vaccine is surely obvious.

Moreover, the increasing recognition of devastating neurological complications in HIV-infected people (reviewed by Berger and Resnick, 1987) serve only to underlie the importance of the documentation of HIV-related disease and reduced reliance on the terminal AIDS categorization (Table IV).

XVII. AIDS and Cancer

HIV infection is associated with Kaposi sarcoma, malignant B cell lymphomas, and an increasing number of other cancers such as oropharyngeal or perirectal carcinomas, and small cell cancers. Most of these cancers may be due to oncogenic virus induction in an overall immunosuppressed state, e.g., EBV and HTLV-I in lymphomas and papilloma virus in squamous cell carcinomas. Nevertheless, Kaposi sarcoma (KS) remains an enigma. KS has been recognized for a long time as a benign endemic condition of African and Meditteranean elderly men, and only recently its aggressive form (which often kills by strangulation or obstruction of the gastrointestinal tract) has been diagnosed in previously healthy HIV-infected young men. It has also been reported as a new epidemic phenomenon in Africa, where it is associated with HIV infection (Bayley *et al.*, 1985). However, it appears associated but not necessarily caused by HIV infection. No known virus, including earlier suspicions pertaining to cytomegalovirus, can be implicated. In particular, HIV is not associated with KS in that it is not integrated into KS DNA (R. C. Gallo, personal communication). Furthermore, KS is seen in HIV-infected homosexuals more than it is seen in other HIV-infected groups and other immunosuppressed populations, e.g., transplant patients. It is attractive to speculate that another as yet undiscovered virus is the causative agent. Another possibility is that HIV infects a subset of T cells that controls proliferation of endothelial tissues or, on infection, secretes angiogenic endothelial growth factors. Perhaps certain isolates are more prone to do so than others, for some explanation as to why HIV-infected promiscuous homosexuals are more likely to develop KS than other at-risk groups is required.

TABLE IV

NEUROLOGICAL MANIFESTATIONS

Encephalitis
Viral
HIV
Cytomegalovirus (CMV)
Herpes simplex I, II, and zoster
Other
Bacterial
Treponema pallidum
Parasitic
Toxoplasma gondii
Taenia solium (cysticercosis)
Meningitis
Viral
HIV or other
Bacterial
Mycobacterium intracellulare or *tuberculosis*
Escherichia coli
Treponema pallidum
Other
Fungal
Cryptococcus neoformans
Aspergillus fumigatus
Histoplasma capsulatum
Coccidioides immitis
Brain abscess
Bacterial
Mycobacterium or other
Fungal
Candida and others
Parasitic
Toxoplasma gondii
Taenia solium
Myelopathy
Viral
HIV vascular myelopathy
CMV
Herpes simplex and zoster
Epstein-Barr virus
Others
Bacteria
Syphilitic meningomyelitis
Neuropathy
Viral
HIV
CMV
Herpes simplex or zoster

(*continued*)

TABLE IV (*continued*)

Myositis
Of unknown origin
Progressive multifocal leukoencephalopathy
Neoplastic
Brain lymphoma
Metastatic disease including carcinomatous meningitis and compressive myelopathy
Lymphomas, Kaposi's sarcoma, and plasmacytoma
Vascular complications
Hemorrhage secondary to immune thrombocytopenia
Embolic stroke and cerebral arteritis
Vascular compromise secondary to *Aspergillus fumigatus* infection
Metabolic disorders
Drug effects
Electrolytic imbalance
Vitamin deficiency

Although it is attractive to postulate that HIV-associated lymphomas may be due to EBV or HTLV-I activation, many patients are negative for these viruses, a finding suggesting the possibility that other agents, such as the human B lymphotropic virus (HBLV) reported by Salahuddin *et al.* (1986), may play a role. It is harder to ascribe a viral etiology to the occurrence of small cell carcinomas or primitive neuroendocrine tumors that have been described in the lung, gastointestinal tract, and the pancreas (Reed *et al.*, 1985; Nusbaum *et al.*, 1985; Moser *et al.*, 1985). Yet why should these tumors not have some hitherto unrecognized viral component in their oncogenic pathway?

Hodgkin disease (HD) has been a long-standing contender for a viral etiology, and its extraordinary association epidemiologically to multiple sclerosis and paralytic poliomyelitis suggests that it may be the rare outcome of a common viral infection. The occurrence of HD in the anorectal region in homosexuals provides further tantalizing evidence for a possible viral etiology (Dalgleish and McElwain, 1986).

XVIII. Approaches to Treatment

ATLL is a particularly aggressive neoplasm, with few people surviving more than 6 months after diagnosis in spite of intensive chemotherapeutic regimens. Studies with the anti-Tac monoclonal antibody, specific for p55 of the IL-2 receptor, have shown that all HTLV-I- associated ATLL express the Tac antigen. Furthermore, the expression differs from that of normal cells in that the ATLL cells do not have to be activated before they express IL-2 receptors. Moreover, HTLV-I-infected cell lines express 5–10 times more receptors per cell than do maximally PHA-stimulated lymphocytes, and ATLL cells in culture do not show a decline in IL-2 receptors, unlike normal lymphocytes. Also the IL-2 receptors are not downregulated by anti-Tac. It is known that the long open reading frame of HTLV-I and HTLV-II, the *x-lor*, or *tat* gene as it is commonly described, whose normal function is to regulate transcription of the virus, also activates in *trans* the genes for IL-2 and its receptor.

Waldmann and his colleagues have attempted to treat ATLL using intravenous anti-Tac monoclonal antibody either alone or conjugated to toxins (e.g., ricin A chains). Of three patients with progressive ATLL, two had a partial response whereas the third had a 6-month remission prior to disease recurrence, which again responded to renewed therapy for a further 3 months (Waldmann, 1986).

A. Therapy for HIV-Associated Disease

A logical therapeutic strategy against HIV requires an understanding of its life cycle (Fig. 1). Possible strategies may be developed by inducing or giving neutralizing antibodies or boosting cell-mediated immunity. The specificity for the CD4 antigen suggests that anti-CD4 monoclonal antibodies may have a role in the blocking of binding between the gp120 of HIV and CD4. Clinical studies to investigate the effect of anti-CD4 therapy *in vivo* are currently underway. As all known isolates of HIV, including LAV-II, bind to CD4 irrespective of their neutralization characteristics, this route is particularly attractive. A further extrapolation of this approach is the use of anti-idiotypes to a specific epitope of the CD4 antigen. This epitope appears to be recognized by anti-Leu 3a and OKT4a monoclonal antibodies, because anti-idiotypes to these epitopes appear to have some neutralizing activity to a range of HIV isolates tested (Dalgleish *et al.*, 1987). Obviously, a highly specific antibody with a high affinity and specificity to the viral envelope (binding region) could have considerable therapeutic and vaccine implications.

Following binding to the CD4, the virus–receptor complex probably undergoes endocytosis. Whether this route is pH-dependent and therefore susceptible to ammonium chloride and amantidine is still not clear, because preliminary studies showing inhibition by these agents do not exclude an effect on the virus assembly and budding (Maddon *et al.*, 1986).

Once inside the cell, virus replication depends upon the cellular replicative machinery for transcription as well as on the activity of reverse transcriptase. An attractive therapeutic strategy therefore is to use reverse transcriptase (RT) inhibitors (which are known to be effective in animal retroviral systems), since RT is an enzyme unique to retroviral systems and not expressed in normal eukaryotic cells. Drugs that appear to inhibit RT are listed in Table V.

Other compounds that are known to inhibit replication but are still being evaluated include AL-721 which alters viral binding to cells, and α-interferon, which may inhibit viral budding. α-Interferon also appears to have some activity against KS, although it is not clear whether this activity is due to its antiviral properties.

Because early studies have shown that any RT inhibitor is only virustatic while being administered, any effective compound would need to satisfy the following requirements: (1) effective inhibition of HIV at levels readily achieved over long periods *in vivo*; (2) minimum toxicity, especially after long-term use; (3) penetration into the CNS (particularly important in view of the increasing incidence of HIV neurological morbidity and mortality). Other features rendered necessary by these dictates would include the possibility to be administered orally, a long half-life, a low cost, and the possibility to be produced on a large scale. Of the drugs mentioned in Table V, the following are worthy of further mention.

Suramin. This drug has been available for a number of years and has been used in the treatment of trypanosomiasis and onchocerciasis. It can bind and inhibit a large variety of enzymes and is known to be effective against animal RT. The demonstration that it was active against HIV (Mitsuya *et al.*, 1984) *in vitro* led to a limited clinical trial, which showed that it was virustatic during the period of administration. However, the treatment was also associated with considerable toxicity, which included fevers, macular rashes, nephrotoxicity, and hepatic dysfunction. These features led to its discontinuation as a potential agent (Broder *et al.*, 1985).

TABLE V
DRUGS THAT INHIBIT RT

Drug	*In vitro* inhibition	*In vivo* effects
Suramin	25–50 μM	Virustatic
HPA.23	Observed	Virustatic
Phosphonoformate	132–680 μM	Virustatic
Ribavirine[a]	100 μg/ml (partial)	?
AZT[b]	1–10 μM	Virustatic
Dideoxycytidine[b]	0.5–5 μM	Under trial
Rifabutine[a]	10–100 μg/ml (partial)	Under trial

[a]Action not clear.
[b]Probably inhibit by chain termination (see text).

HPA-23. Ammonium 21-tungsto-9-antimoniate (HPA-23) is known to inhibit the RT of a number of animal retroviruses. Unfortunately, it has a short half-life and induces thrombocytopenia. No large-scale trials have been reported, although it is known to be virustatic in man (Rozenbaum *et al.*, 1984).

Phophonoformate. This is another agent that is known to be effective against animal RT and has been used to treat CMV *in vivo.* A clinical trial in London has shown that it has virustatic properties similar to those of suramin and AZT. But, unfortunately, no marked clinical improvement has been reported, and it can only be given intravenously. Toxicity is not a major problem, however, although nephrotoxicity and bone retention after prolonged administration have been reported (Farthing *et al.*, 1987).

*AZT (3′-*Azido-3′-deoxythymidine). Some chain terminators for DNA synthesis can also act as potent inhibitors of retroviral replication. AZT is one such drug and is a thymidine analog in which the 3-hydroxy (OH) group is replaced by an azido (N_3) group. AZT is converted by cellular enzymes to a triphosphate form that is utilized by RT. Because of the 3′ modification, subsequent 5′ → *3′* phosphodiester linkages cannot be formed. Cellular DNA polymerase alpha is approximately 100-fold less susceptible to inhibition by AZT-triphosphate than is the RT of HIV. *In vitro* inhibition of HIV at concentrations of 1–3 μM was demonstrated by Mitsuya *et al.* (1985). Clinical trials have shown that AZT can be given by oral administration, is virustatic, and enters the cerebrospinal fluid. A large-scale study has shown a significant improvement in AZT-treated patients with respect to mortality and even neurological complications have been reported to improve during administration (Yarchoan *et al.*, 1987). However, although the drug was well tolerated, side effects included significant hematocrit reductions, headaches, tremors, and confusions. Unlike in previous drugs mentioned, significantly improved immunological parameters have been reported in that increases in the number of helper T cells have been observed and positive skin tests were seen in previously anergic patients. Complete regression of KS lesions have also been reported. Unfortunately, the decrease in hematocrit seen in some patients may turn out to be a major problem with regard to long-term administration.

What is important, however, is that AZT is one member of a family of nucleoside analogs that can act as chain terminators. Other analogs with 3′ modifications are also potent inhibitors of HIV. One of these, 2′,3′-dideoxycytidine, is presently being tested in animals prior to clinical trials in patients.

A full review of other drugs will not be given here except to mention that antiviral activity as well as immunomodulation activity has been claimed for isoprinosine, which is undergoing clinical trials alone and in combination with ribavirin. Conflicting claims have been reported with regard to the *in vivo* efficacy of ribavirin for HIV, and further studies are awaited.

B. Immunotherapy

The CD4-positive helper lymphocyte is effectively the conductor of the immunological "orchestra" exerting control functions or interacting with many of the other cells of the immune system (Dalgleish, 1986b). It is not surprising therefore that infection of this cell with a cytopathic virus should inevitably lead to gross immunological dysfunction. It would be of considerable practical advantage to restore the immune system of infected patients in whom it has been severely disrupted if not destroyed. Therapeutic strategies have focused on the following potential therapies: interferons, thymic replacement hormones, other cytokines, bone marrow transplantation, lymphocyte replacement, intravenous γ-globulin therapy, plasmapheresis, and on those drugs claimed to have immunomodulation properties, such as isoprinosine and cimetidine.

The role of interferons has been mentioned in that an anti-HIV activity of interferon-α (produced by leukocytes and fibroblasts) can be demonstrated *in vitro*. Unfortunately, clinical trials have been disappointing, with the possible exception of some patients with KS (Krown *et al.*, 1983). Trials with interferon-γ (produced by lymphocytes and monocytes) are now in progress and should theoretically be more likely to have beneficial activity in AIDS. However, preliminary studies suggest that patients with KS actually do worse than with interferon-α. It should be noted that serum interferon levels are already raised in AIDS patients (Abbott *et al.*, 1984).

Thymic replacement therapies in patients with AIDS are unfortunately anecdotal and uninspiring. However, numerous different thymic peptides are now available and have yet to be fully assessed. Thymopentin (TP-5) appears particularly interesting, as it has been shown to restore proliferative responses and reverse the inhibition of T cell function in AIDS patients. There may be a role for this compound in pre-AIDS patients (Mascort-Lemone *et al.*, 1983). A more interesting observation is that an antiserum prepared against α-thymosin, a thymic hormone, effectively neutralized the HTLV-III isolate. The antiviral activity of the antiserum was found to be due to a region of homology between α-thymosin and p17, a product of the *gag* gene of HIV (Sarin *et al.*, 1980). Further studies on this fascinating observation are needed, particularly in view of the preparation's obvious potential as a vaccine.

IL-2 is a lymphokine that is known to reconstitute deficient *in vitro* immune responses (Malkovsky and Sodel, 1987). Although IL-2 may improve some immune parameters *in vivo*, no dramatic responses have been reported from numerous clinical studies. This may not be surprising because although IL-2 helps restore the immune system, it also activates and expands the CD4 helper lymphocyte pool. This action may in fact have the effect of "adding fuel to the fire," because it is known from *in vitro* studies that one of the best ways to "heat up" virus production is to add fresh uninfected cells to the culture. Similarly, the poor response to marrow transplants and lymphocyte transfusions may be due to a similar "fuel for the fire" phenomenon.

Although there may be cautious grounds for optimism in some cases, it should be noted that in the majority of trials reviewed, the improvements in *in vivo* immune function and clinical condition remainn curiously uncoordinated. Indeed, the only sensible approach in the light of the studies reviewed in this article would be to use an RT inhibitor as well as an immune regulatory agent. A small study using suramin with interfon-α gives supportive evidence to this approach (Zagury *et al.*, 1985).

C. Vaccines

Because of the ability of HIV to infect and lie dormant in cells without undergoing replication and producing cytopathogenicity itself (Folks *et al.*, 1986), any treatment of infected persons may need to be continued for life. The only long-term solution is the development of an efficient and cheap vaccine. Many viruses have been contained by a vaccine (Dalgleish, 1986a) and hopes were therefore high when the causal agent of AIDS was discovered. Unfortunately, HIV is a term encompassing a range of isolates that express considerable genetic diversity, mainly in the envelope coding sequence (Wong-Staal and Gallo, 1985; Desai *et al.*, 1986). Although HIV elicits a strong antibody response to envelope (as well as *gag*) proteins, the antibody response to neutralizing epitopes is extremely poor. Neutralizing antibodies can be detected in most infected patients, but their titers are extremely low and they do not cross-neutralize a range of isolates better than do antibodies raised to a specific envelope region (Weiss *et al.*, 1986). An exception to these generalizations is the San Francisco isolate ARV-II, which appears to be more readily neutralizable by the autologous serum and sera from patients infected with other isolates.

HIV has been cloned and subcloned and many isolates extensively characterized. The HIV envelope gene has been inserted into a vaccinia virus vector, which readily induces envelope antibodies that do not have effective neutralizing function (Chakrabarti *et al.*, 1986; Hu *et al.*, 1986). Further subclones and peptides from these regions are undergoing extensive testing worldwide, and a plethora of reports should appear in the near future. The main objective is to obtain a vaccine that will neutralize all known isolates. Numerous delivery systems such as vaccinia and adenovirus are currently being evaluated. Any virus vaccine will need to undergo extensive evaluation in a primate model, the best of which is still very unsatisfactory. Also, chimpanzees (test animals) are very expensive.

The vaccine approach will not be easy and may well require that more than one epitopic determinant be used. The *gag* protein may be important particularly in view of the studies of the influenza nucleoprotein, which can be recognized by cytotoxic lymphocytes (Townsend *et al.*, 1986). Neutralization may not be associated directly with the antibody binding site, as, for instance, in polio virus type I (Diamond *et al.*, 1985) or enveloped viruses (Gollins and Porterfield, 1986). Moreover, to be protective, a monoclonal antibody does not need to be neutralizing in some systems (Gould *et al.*, 1986). On the brighter side, protection with synthetic peptides has now been reported for several viral systems, and their selection has become easier (Geysen *et al.*, 1984, 1985).

D. Genetic Approaches to Treatment

The great advances in cloning and sequencing different isolates has enabled specific analysis of the role of the different genes, as previously reviewed. Whereas the role of *tat* and *art/trs*, in viral replication has been studied in some detail, the cytopathic effects are less clear. Available information allows for armchair speculation on the possibilities of constructing viruses with the *tat* gene reversed, so that the viruses would encode antisense RNA. Bone marrow cells would be infected with the "antivirus," re-injected into the same AIDS patient and this is expected to result in production of "protected" lymphocytes (Mariman, 1985; Tellier and Weber, 1985).

E. Conclusions

In spite of the great variety of possible treatment strategies outlined here, we want to stress that many specific observations or small studies as well as detailed discussion of potential immunosuppressive therapies, e.g., cyclosporin A (Klatzmann and Montagnier, 1986) have been ommitted. We believe that the most promising therapeutic strategy is to exploit the ability of all the different viral isolates to bind to the CD4 antigen. Obviously, any specific antibody or peptide that could inhibit this binding may have considerable therapeutic potential. Furthermore, this site may be preserved and coded for by a fixed component of the CD4 antigen. This observation implies that the obvious route is to make anti-idiotypes to antibodies recognizing this specific component of the CD4 antigen, which in turn should neutralize the virus (Dalgleish *et al.*, 1988). Many practical problems, such as differential affinity to the virus or receptor, not to mention class II HLA antigens with which CD4 interacts, will need to be thoroughly researched. The CD4 gene, which has now been cloned, can be used to make soluble CD4 that may have the same effect *in vivo* as a CD4 anti-idiotype (Smith *et al.*, 1987).

XIX. Conclusions and Prospects

Advances in knowledge about human retroviruses over the last few years have been made at an unparalleled rate. Whereas the sociopolitical implications of AIDS will keep the pressure on therapeutic and vaccine strategies, the "spin off" from these programs into other areas of medicine, such as oncology and neurological disease, should be considerable. The review of human retrovirus research prior to the discovery of the T lymphotropic viruses suggests that in view of the major advances in technology over the last few years, some other diseases, such as some lymphomas and leukemias, may well be shown to have a viral component in their pathogenesis. Other diseases, such as Kawasaki disease, have already been proposed as having a retroviral etiology (with some supportive evidence), as has non-A, non-B hepatitis, where the evidence is not convincing. Sarcoidosis may also have a viral etiology. The impact of human retroviruses on neurological diseases has already revealed some interesting surprises. HTLV-I appears to be the causal agent of tropical spastic paraparesis (Gessain *et al.*, 1985; Newton *et al.*, 1987), although it is probably not the cause of multiple sclerosis as tentatively suggested (Koprowski *et al.*, 1985).

Nevertheless, the recognition that HTLV-II can transactivate the IL-2 gene and its receptor suggests that such a scenario (gene *trans*-activation) with similar, yet different, viruses could be involved in many disorders of unknown etiology—e.g. the autoimmunity seen in multiple sclerosis (Dalgleish *et al.*, 1987).

One thing is certain: advances in our knowledge of human retroviruses is growing so fast that many topics here described as "under investigation" or "not yet known" may be well-characterized by the time this review is read.

REFERENCES

Abbott, S. R., Buimovici-Klein, E., Cooper, L. Z., Lange, M., Briggs, M., and Weller, I. V. (1984). *Lancet* **1**, 564.

Achong, B. G., and Epstein, M. A. (1978). *J. Gen. Virol.* **40**, 175–181.

Achong, B. G., and Epstein, M. A. (1983). *Med. Virol.* **11**, 53–57.

Achong, B. G., Mansell, P. G. A., Epstein, M. A., and Clifford, P. (1971). *J. Natl. Cancer Inst.* **46**, 299–307.

Allan *et al.* (1985). *Science* **230**, 810–813.

Allen, J. R. (1984). *Semin. Oncol.* **11**, 4–11.

Arya, S. K., and Gallo, R. C. (1986). *Proc. Natl. Acad. Sci. U.S.A.* **83**, 2209–2213.

Arya, S. K., Guo, C., Josephs, S. F., and Wong-Staal, F. (1985). *Science* **229**, 69–73.

Azel, R., Gulati, S. C., and Spiegelman, S. (1972). *Proc. Natl. Acad. Sci. U.S.A.* **69**, 3133–3137.

Barin, F., M'Boup, S., Denis, F., Kanki, P., Allan, J. S., Lee, T. H., and Essex, M. (1985). *Lancet* **2**, 1387–1389.

Barré-Sinoussi, F., Chermann, J. C., Rey, M. T., Nugeyre, M. T., Chamaret, S., Gurest, J., Danguet, C., Axler-Blin, C., Vézinet-Brun, F., Rouzioux, C., Rozenbaum, W., and Montagnier, L. (1983). *Science* **220**, 868–870.

Bayley, A. C., Downing, R. G., Cheingsong-Popov, R. Tedder, R. S., Dalgleish, A. G., and Weiss, R. A. (1985). *Lancet* **1**, 359–361.
Benveniste, R. E., and Todaro, G. J. (1974). *Nature (London)* **252**, 456–459.
Berger and Resnick. (1987). *In* AIDS (S. Broder, ed.), pp. 263–283. Dekker, New York.
Biggar, R. J. (1986). *Lancet* **1**, 79–82.
Bishop, J. M., Quinwell, N., Medeiros, E., and Varmus, H. E. (1974). *Cancer* **34**, 1421–1426.
Blayney, D. W., Blattner, W. A., Robert-Guroff, M., Jaffe, E. S., Fisher, R. I., Bunn, P. A., Patton, M. G., Rosick, H. R., and Gallo, R. C. (1983). *J. Am. Med. Assoc.* **250**, 1048–1052.
Boller, K., Frank, H., Lower, J., Lower, R., and Kurth, R. (1983). *J. Gen. Virol.* **64**, 2549–2559.
Bonner, T. A., O'Connell, C. O., and Cohen, M. (1982). *Proc. Natl. Acad. Sci. U.S.A.* **80**, 4709–4713.
Borzy, M. S. (1987). *Cell. Immunol.* **104**, 142–153.
Boumpas, D., Harris, C., Hooks, J., Popovic, M., and Mann, D. (1984). *Clin. Res.* **32**, 343A.
Broder, S., Yarchoan, R., Collins, J. M., Lane, H. C., Markham, P. D., Klecker, R. W., Redfield, R. R., Mitsuya, H., Hoth, D. F., Gelman, E., *et al.* (1985). *Lancet* **2**, 627–630.
Bronson, D. L., Saxinger, W. C., Ritzi, D. M., and Fraley, E. E. (1984). *J. Gen. Virol.* **65**, 1043–1051.
Brown, P., Nemo, G., and Gajdusek, C. (1978). *J. Infect. Dis.* **137**, 421–427.
Brown, P., Moreau-Dubois, M. C., and Gajdusek, C. (1982). *Arch. Virol.* **71**, 229–234.
Bygbjerg, I. C. (1983). *Lancet* **1**, 925.
Callahan, R., Drohan, W., Tronick, S., and Schlom, J. (1982). *Proc. Natl. Acad. Sci. U.S.A.* **79**, 5503–5507.
Catovsky, D., Greaves, M., Rose, M., Galton, D. A. G., Goolden, A., McClusky, J., Blattner, W., and Gallo, R. E. (1982). *Lancet* **1**, 639–645.
Centers for Disease Control (1981). *Morbid. Mortal. Weekly Rep.* **30**, 305–308.
Centers for Disease Control (1982). *Morbid. Mortal. Weekly Rep.* **31**, 652–654.
Centers for Disease Control (1985a). *Morbid. Mortal. Weekly Rep.* **34**, 1–5.
Centers for Disease Control (1985b). *Morbid. Mortal. Weekly Rep.* **34**, 561–563.
Centers for Disease Control (1986a). *Morbid. Mortal. Weekly Rep.* **35**, 17–21.
Centers for Disease Control (1986b). *Morbid. Mortal. Weekly Rep.* **35**, 35–46.
Chakrabarti, S., Robert-Guroff, M., Wong-Staal, F., Gallo, R. C., and Moss, B. (1986). *Nature (London)* **320**, 535–537.
Cheingsong-Popov, R., Weiss, R. A., Dalgleish, A., Tedder, R. S., Shanson, D. C., Jeffries, D. J., Ferns, R. B., Briggs, E. M., Weller, I. V. D., Mitton, S., Adler, M. W., Farthing, C., Lawrence, A. G., Gazzard, B., Weber, J., Harris, J. W. R., Pinching, A. J., Craske, J., and Barbara, J. A. J. (1984). *Lancet* **2**, 477–480.
Chen, I. S. Y. (1980). *Cell* **47**, 1–2.
Chen, I. S. Y., Quan, S. G., and Golde, D. W. (1983a). *Proc. Natl. Acad. Sci. U.S.A.* **80**, 7006–7009.
Chen, I. S. Y., McLaughlin, J., Gasson, J. C., Clark, S. C., and Golde, D. W. (1983b). *Nature (London)* **305**, 502–505.
Chen, I. S. Y., McLaughlin, J., and Golde, D. W. (1984). *Nature (London)* **309**, 276–279.
Clapham, P., Nagy, K., Cheingsong-Popov, R., Exley, M., and Weiss, R. A. (1983). *Science* **222**, 1125–1127.
Clapham, P., Nagy, K., and Weiss, R. A. (1984). *Proc. Natl. Acad. Sci. U.S.A.* **81**, 2886–2889.
Clavel, F., Guetard, D., Brun-Vezinet, F., Chamaret, S., Rey, M.-A., Santos-Ferreira, M. O., Laurent, A. G., Dauguet, C., Katlama, C., Rouzious, C., Klatzman, D., Champalimaud, J. L., and Montaigner, L. (1986). *Science* **233**, 343–346.
Clements, J. E., Pederson, F. S., Narayan, O., and Haseltine, W. A. (1980). *Proc. Natl. Acad. Sci. U.S.A.* **77**, 4454–4458.
Culen, (1986). *Cell* **46**, 973–982.

Dalgleish, A. G. (1985). *Aust. N.Z. J. Med.* **15**, 375–385.
Dalgleish, A. G. (1986a). *J. R. Coll. Phys. (London)* **20;4**, 258–267.
Dalgleish, A. G. (1986b). *Immunol. Today* **7**, 142–144.
Dalgleish, A. G., and McElwain, T. (1986). *Aust. N.Z.J. Med.* **16**, 823–827.
Dalgleish, A. G., and Weiss, R. A. (1987). *In* "Clinical Virology" (A. Zuckerman, J. E. Banatvala, and J. R. Pattison, eds.), pp. 517–544. Wiley, Chichester.
Dalgleish, A. G., Beverley, P. C. L., Clapham, P. R., Crawford, D. H., Greaves, M. R., and Weiss, R. A. (1984). *Nature (London)* **312**, 763–767.
Dalgleish, A. G., Fazakerley, J., and Webb, H. (1987). *J. Neuropathol. Neurobiol.* **13**, 241–250.
Dalgleish, A. G., Thomson, B. J., Chanh, T. C., Malkovský, M., and Kennedy, R. C. (1987). *Lancet* **2**, 1047–1050.
Dalgleish, A. G., Kennedy, R. C., Sattentau, Q., Chanh, T., Beverley, P., Maddon, P., Axel, R., and Malkovský, M. (1988). *In* "Human Retroviruses, Cancer and AIDS: Approaches to Prevention and Therapy" (D. Bolognesi, ed.), pp. 283–288. Alan R. Liss, Inc., New York.
Daniel, M. D., King, N. W., Letvin, N. L., Hunt, R. D., Sehgal, P. L., and Desrosiers, R. C. (1984). *Science* **223**, 602–605.
Daniel, M. D., Letvin, N. L., King, N. W., Kannagi, M., Sehgal, P. K., Hunt, R. D., Kanki, P. J., Essex, M., and Desrosiers, R. C. (1985). *Science* **228**, 1201–1204.
Dayton, A., Sodroski, J. G., Rosen, C. A., Goh, W. C., and Haseltine, W. A. (1986). *Cell* **44**, 941–947.
Derks, J. P. A., Hofmans, L., Bruning, H., and Rood, J. (1982). *Cancer Res.* **42**, 681–686.
Desai, S. M., Kalyanaraman, V. S., Casey, J. M., Srinivasan, A., Anderson, P. R., and Devare, S. G. (1986). *Proc. Natl. Acad. Sci. U.S.A.* **83**, 8380–8384.
Diamond, D. C., Jameson, B. A., Bonin, J., Kohara, M., Abe, S., Hoh, H., Komatsu, T., Arita, M., Kuge, S., Nomoto, A., Osterhaus, A. D. M. E., Crainic, R. and Wimmer, E. (1985). *Science* **229**, 1090–1093.
Ebbesen, P. C., Due, J., Hesse, J., Kurth, G. R., Noble, R., and Jensen, G. (1979). *Int. J. Cancer* **24**, 1–5.
Ellermann, V., and Bang, O. (1908). *Centralbl. Bacteriol. Parasit. Infektionskrank.* **46**, 595–609.
Epstein, M. A., Achong, B. G., and Ball, G. (1974). *J. Natl. Cancer Inst.* **53**, 681–688.
Farthing, C. F., Dalgleish, A. G., Clark, A., McClure, M., Chanas, A., and Gazzard, B. G. (1987). *AIDS* **1**, 21–25.
Fauci, A. S. (1988). *Science* **239**, 617–622.
Feinberg, M. B., Jarret, R. F., Aldovini, A., Gallo, R. C., and Wong-Staal, F. (1986). *Cell* **46**, 807–811.
Felber, B., Paskalis, H., Kleinman-Ewing, C., Wong-Staal, F., and Pavlakis, G. (1985). *Science* **229**, 675–679.
Feller, W. F., and Chopra, H. C. (1969). *Cancer* **24**, 1250–1254.
Fenner, F. (1975). *Intervirology* **6**, 1–12.
Fine, D. L., Landon, J. C., Pienta, R. J., Kubicek, M. T., Valerio, M. G., Loeb, W. F., and Chopra, H. C. (1975). *J. Natl. Cancer Inst.* **54**, 651–658.
Fisher, A., Ratner, L., Mitsuya, H., Marselle, L., Harper, M., Broder, S., and Wong-Staal, F. (1986). *Science* **233**, 655–659.
Folks, T., Powell, D. M., Lightfoote, M., Benns, S., Martin, M., and Fauci, A. (1986). *Science* **231**, 600–604.
Franchini, G., Robert-Guroff, M., Wong-Staal, F., Ghrayeb, J., Kato, I., Chang, T. W., and Chang, N. T. (1986). *Proc. Natl. Acad. Sci. U.S.A.* **83**, 5282–5285.
Fujisawa, J.-L., Seiki, M., Sato, M., and Yoshida, M. (1986). *EMBO J.* **5**, 713–718.
Furman, P. A., Fyfe, J. A., St. Clair, M. H., Weinhold, K., Rideout, J. L., Freeman, G. A., Nusinoff Lehrman, S., Bolognersi, D. P., Broder, S., Mitsuya, H., and Barry, D. W. (1986). *Proc. Natl. Acad. Sci. U.S.A.* **83**, 8333–8337.

Furmanski, P., Longley, C., Fouchey, D., Rich, R., and Rich, M. A. (1974). *J. Natl. Cancer Inst.* **52**, 975–977.

Gallagher, R. E., and Gallo, R. C. (1975). *Science* **187**, 350–353.

Gallagher, R. E., Todaro, G. J., Smith, R. G., Livingston, D. M., and Gallo, R. C. (1974). *Proc. Natl. Acad. Sci. U.S.A.* **72**, 4137–4141.

Gallo, R. C. (1984). *Cancer Surv.* **3**, 113–159.

Gallo, R. C. (1985). *Cancer Res. Suppl.* **45**, 4524–4533.

Gallo, R. C., and Wong-Staal, F. (1980). *In* "Viral Oncology" (G. Klein, ed.), pp. 399–431. Raven, New York.

Gallo, R. C., Miller, N. R., Saxinger, W. C., and Gillespie, D. (1973). *Proc. Natl. Acad. Sci. U.S.A.* **70**, 3219–3224.

Gallo, R. C., Salahuddin, S. Z., Popovic, M., Shearer, G. M., Kaplan, M., Haynes, B. F., Palker, T. J., Redfield, R., Oleskie, J., Safai, B., White, G., Foster, P., and Markham, P. D. (1984). *Science* **224**, 500–503.

Gazzola, L., and Dodon, M. D. (1987). *Nature (London)* **326**, 714–717.

Gessain, A., Vernaut, J. C., and Maiurs, L. (1985). *Lancet* **2**, 407–410.

Geysen, M. H., Meloen, R. H., and Barteling, S. J. (1984). *Proc. Natl. Acad. Sci. U.S.A.* **81**, 3998–4002.

Geysen, H. M., Barteling, S. J., and Meloen, R. H. (1985). *Proc. Natl. Acad. Sci. U.S.A.* **82**, 178–182.

Gollins, S. W., and Porterfield, J. S. (1986). *Nature (London)* **321**, 244–246.

Gould, E. A., Buckley, A., Barrett, A. D. T., and Cammack, N. (1986). *J. Gen. Virol.* **67**, 591–595.

Greene, W. C., and Robb, R. J. (1985). *Contemp. Top. Mol. Immunol.* **10**, 1–34.

Greene, W. C., Leonard, W. J., Wano, Y., Svetlik, P. B., Peffer, N. J., Sodroski, J. G., Rosen, C. A., Goh, W. C., and Haseltine, W. A. (1986). *Science* **232**, 877–880.

Guyacler, M., Emerman, M., Sonigo, P., Clavel, F., Montagnier, M., and Alizon, M. (1987). *Nature (London)* **326**, 662–668.

Hardy, W. D. (1985). *Adv. Viral Oncol.* **5**, 1–37.

Haseltine, W. A., Sodroski, J., and Rosen, C. (1985). *Cancer Res. (Suppl.)* **45**, 4545s–4549s.

Henrickson, R. V., Maul, D. H., Osborn, R. G., Sever, J. L., Madden, L. R., Ellingsworth, L. R., Anderson, J. H., Lowenstine, L. J., and Gardner, M. B. (1983). *Lancet* **7**, 388–390.

Henson, J. B., and McGuire, T. C. (1974). *Prog. Med. Virol.* **18**, 143–159.

Hess, J. L., Clements, J. C., and Narayan, O. (1985). *Science* **229**, 482–485.

Hinuma, Y., Nagata, K., and Hanaoka, M. (1981). *Proc. Natl. Acad. Sci. U.S.A.* **78**, 6476–6480.

Hoshino, H., Esumi, H., Miwa, M., Shimoyama, M., Minato, K., Tobinai, K., Hirose, M., Watanabe, S., Inada, H., Kinoshita, K., Kamihira, S., Ichimaru, M., and Sugimura, T. (1983). *Proc. Natl. Acad. Sci. U.S.A.* **80**, 6061–6065.

Hoxie, J. A., Haggarty, B. S., Rackowski, J. L., Pillsbury, N., and Levy, J. A. (1985). *Science* **229**, 1400–1402.

Hu, S.-L., Kosowski, S. G., and Dalrymple, J. M. (1986). *Nature (London)* **320**, 537–540.

Iverson, O. J. (1983). *Acta. Pathol. Microbiol. Immunol. Scand.* **1391**, 407–412.

Jacquemin, P. C., and Strijckmans, R. (1985). *Int. J. Cancer* **36**, 535–539.

Jacquemin, P. C., Saxinger, C., and Gallo, R. C. (1978). *Nature (London)* **276**, 230–236.

Jones, K. A., Kadonaga, J. T., Luciw, P. A., and Tjian, R. (1986). *Science* **232**, 755–759.

Kalyanaraman, V., Sarngadharan, M., Nakao, Y., Ito, Y., and Gallo, R. C. (1982). *Proc. Natl. Acad. Sci. U.S.A.* **79**, 1207–1210.

Kan, N. C., Franchini, G., Wong-Staal, F., DuBois, G. C., Rogey, W. G., Lantenberger, J. A., and Papas, T. S. (1986). *Science* **231**, 1553–1555.

Kanki, P. J., McLane, M. F., King, N. W., Jr., Letvin, N. L., Hunt, R. D., Sehgal, P., Daniel, M. D., Desrosiers, R. C., and Essex, M. (1985). *Science* **228**, 1199–1201.

Kanki, P., Barin, F., M'Boup, A. J., Romet-Lemonne, J., Marlink, McLane, M., Lee, T. H., Arbeille, B., Dennis, F., and Essex, M. (1986). *Science* **232**, 238–243.
Kao, S.-Y., Calman, A. F., Luciw, P. A., and Peterlin, B. M. (1987). *Nature (London)* **330**, 489–493.
Kaplan, H. S., Goodenhow, R. S., Epstein, A. L., and Rosenthal, P. N. (1977). *Proc. Natl. Acad. Sci. U.S.A.* **74**, 2564–2568.
Kaplan, H. S., Goodenhow, R. S., Gartner, S., and Bieber, M. (1979). *Cancer* **43**, 1–24.
Klatzmann, D., and Gluckman, J.-C. (1986). *Immunol. Today* **7**, 291–296.
Klatzmann, D., Barré-Sinoussi, F., Nugeyre, M. T., Dauguet, C., Vilmer, E., Griscelli, C., Brun-Vézinet, F., Rouzioux, C., Gluckman, J.-C., and Montagnier, L. (1984a). *Science* **225**, 59–63.
Klatzmann, D., Champagne, E., Chamaret, S., Gruest, J., Guetard, D., Hercend, T., Gluckman, J.-C., and Montagnier, L. (1984b). *Nature (London)* **312**, 767–768.
Knight, D. M., Flomerfelt, F. A., and Shrayeb, J. (1987). *Science* **236**, 837–840.
Koprowski, H., DeFreitas, E. C., and Harper, M. (1985). *Nature (London)* **318**, 154–160.
Koyanagi, Y., Miles, S., Mitsuyasu, R. T., Merrill, J. E., Vinters, H. V., and Chen, I. S. Y. (1987). *Science* **236**, 819–822.
Kreiss, J. K., Koech, D., Plummer, F. A., Holmes, K. K., Lightfoote, M., Piot, P., Ronald, A. R., Ndinya-Achola, J. O., D'Costa, L. J., Roberts, P., Ngugi, E. N., and Quinn, T. C. (1986). *N. Engl. J. Med.* **314**, 414–418.
Krown, S. E., Real, F. X., Cunningham-Rundles, S., Myskowski, P. L., Koziner, B., Fein, S., Mittelman, A., Oettgen, H. F., and Safai, B. (1983). *N. Engl. J. Med.* **308**, 1071–1076.
Kurth, R., and Mikschy, U. (1978). *Proc. Natl. Acad. Sci. U.S.A.* **70**, 737–741.
Lane, H. C., and Fauci, A. S. (1985). *Annu. Rev. Immunol.* **3**, 477.
Larder, B. A., Purifoy, D. J. M., Powell, K. L., and Darby, G. (1987). *Nature (London)* **327**, 716–717.
Laurence, J., and Mayer, L. (1984). *Science* **225**, 66.
Lee, T.-H., Coligan, J. E., Allan, J. S., McLane, M. F., Groopman, J. E., and Essex, M. (1986). *Science* **231**, 1546–1549.
Leonard, W. J., Depper, J. M., Uchiyama, T., Smith, K. A., Waldmann, T. A., and Greene, W. C. (1982). *Nature (London)* **300**, 267–269.
Letvin, N. L., Eaton, K. A., Aldrich, W. R., Sehgal, P. K., Blake, B. J., Schlossman, S. F., King, N. W., and Hunt, R. D. (1983). *Proc. Natl. Acad. Sci. U.S.A.* **80**, 2718–2722.
Levy, J. A., Hoffman, A. D., Kramer, S. M., Landis, J. A., Shimabukuro, J. M., and Oshino, L. S. (1984). *Science* **225**, 840–842.
Levy, J. A., Cheng-Mayer, D. D., and Luciw, P. A. (1986). *Science* **232**, 998.
Lifson, J. D., Reyes, G. R., McGrath, M. S., Stein, B. S., and Engleman, E. G. (1986a). *Science* **232**, 1123–1127.
Lifson, J., Coutre, S., Huang, E., and Engleman, E. (1986b). *J. Exp. Med.* **164**, 2101–2106.
Lifson, J. D., Feinberg, M. B., Reyes, G. R., Rabin, L., Banapour, B., Chakrabarti, S., Moss, B., Wong-Staal, F., Steimer, K. S., and Engleman, E. G. (1986c). *Nature (London)* **323**, 725–728.
Loh, P. C., Achong, B. C., and Epstein, M. A. (1977). *Intervirology* **8**, 204–217.
Loh, P. C., Matsumura, F., and Mizumoto, C. (1980). *Intervirology* **13**, 87–90.
Loo, E. M., van der, van Muijen, W. A., and Meijer, C. J. (1979). *Virchows Arch. B. Cell Pathol.* **31**, 193–203.
Löwer, R., Löwer, J., Frank, H., Harzmann, R., and Kurth, R. (1984). *J. Gen. Virol.* **65**, 887–898.
Löwer, J., Wondrak, E. M., and Kurth, R. (1987). *J. Gen. Virol.* **68**, 2807–2815.
Luciw, P., Cheng-Mayer, C., and Levy, J. A. (1987). *Proc. Natl. Acad. Sci. U.S.A.* **84**, 1434–1438.
McDougal, J. S., Kennedy, M. S., Sligh, J., Cort, S., Marle, A., and Nicholson, J. K. A. (1986). *Science* **231**, 382–385.

Maddon, P. J., Dalgleish, A. G., McDougal, J. S., Clapham, P., Weiss, R. A., and Axel, R. (1986). *Cell* **47**, 333–348.

Maeda, S., Yonezawa, K., Yoshizaki, H., Mori, M., Kobayashi, T., Akahonai, Y., Yachi, A., and Mellors, R. C. (1986). *Int. J. Cancer* **38**, 309–316.

Malkovský, M., Asherson, G. L., Stockinger, B. V., and Watkins, M. C. (1982). *Nature (London)* **300**, 652–655.

Malkovský, M., and Sondel, P. M. (1987). *Blood Rev.* **1**, 254–266.

Mariman, E. C. M. (1985). *Nature (London)* **318**, 414.

Marsh, M., and Dalgleish, A. G. (1987). *Immunol. Today* **8**, 369–371.

Martin, M. A., Bryan, T., Rasheed, S., and Khan, A. S. (1981). *Proc. Natl. Acad. Sci. U.S.A.* **78**, 4892–4896.

Mascart-Lemone, F., Huygen, K., Clumeck, N., Brenez, D., Bolla, K., and Duchateau, J. (1983). *Lancet* **2**, 735–736.

Mathur-Wagh, U., and Mildvan, D. (1984). *Ann N.Y. Acad. Sci.* **437**, 184–191.

Melbye, M., Ingersleri, J., Biggar, R., Sarin, P., Goedest, J., Zachariae, E., Ebbesen, P., and Steinbjerg, S. (1985). *N. Engl. J. Med.* **312**, 857.

Miller, G., Pegram, S., Kirkwood, B., Beckles, G., Byam, N., Clyadew, S., Kinlen, L., Chan, L. C., Cawson, D., and Greaves, M. F. (1986). *Int. J. Cancer* **38**, 801–808.

Mitsuya, H., Popovic, M., Yarchoan, R., Matsushita, S., Gallo, R. C., and Broder, S. (1984). *Science* **226**, 172–174.

Mitsuya, H., Weinhold, K. J., Furman, P. A., St. Clair, M. H., Lehrman, S. N., Gallo, R. C., Bolognesi, D., Barry, D. W., and Broder, S. (1985). *Proc. Natl. Acad. Sci. U.S.A.* **82**, 7096–7100.

Miyoshi, I., Kubonishi, I., Sumida, M., Hiraki, S., Tsubota, T., Kimura, I., Miyamoto, K., and Sato, J. (1980). *Gan* **71**, 155–156.

Miyoshi, I., Kubonishi, I., Yoshimoto, S., Aai, T., Ohtsuki, Y., Shiraishi, Y., Nagata, K., and Hinuma, Y. (1981). *Nature (London)* **294**, 770–771.

Miyoshi, I., Fujishita, M., Taguchi, M., Matsubayashi, K., Miwa, N., and Tanioka, Y. (1983). *Int. J. Cancer* **32**, 333–336.

Montagnier, L., Dauguet, C., Axler, C., Chamanet, S., Gruest, J., Nugere, N., Rey, F., Barré-Sinoussi, F., and Chermann, J.-C. (1984). *Ann. Virol.* **135E**, 119–134.

Montalero, R. C., Parekh, B., Orrego, A., and Issel, C. J. (1984). *J. Biol. Chem.* **259**, 10539–10544.

Morgan, D. A., Ruscetti, F., and Gallo, R. C. (1976). *Science* **193**, 1007–1008.

Moser, R. J., Tenholder, M. F., and Ridenour, R. (1985). *Ann. Intern. Med.* **103**, 478.

Muesing, M. A., Smith, D. H., Cabridilla, C. D., Benton, C. V., Lasky, L. A., and Capon, D. J. (1984). *Nature (London)* **313**, 450–458.

Muijen, G. N. P., van, te Velde, and den Ottolander, G. J. (1979). *Cancer* **43**, 1682–1688.

Nabel, G., and Baltimore, D. (1987). *Nature (London)* **326**, 711–713.

Nabel, G. J., Rice, S. A., Knipe, D. M., and Baltimore, D. (1988). *Science* **239**, 1299–1302.

Nagy, K., Weiss, R. A., Clapham, P., and Cheingsong-Popov, R. (1984). *In* "Human T-Cell Leukemia/Lymphoma Virus" (R. C. Gallo *et al.*, eds.), pp. 121–131. Cold Spring Harbor Laboratory, Cold Spring Harbor, New York.

Nahmias, A. J., Weiss, J., Yao, X., Lee, F., Kodsi, R., Schanfield, M., Matthews, T., Bolognesi, D., Durack, D., Motulsky, A., Kanki, P., and Essex, M. (1986). *Lancet* **1**, 1279–1280.

Nelson, J., Leong, J. A., and Levy, J. A. (1978). *Proc. Natl. Acad. Sci. U.S.A.* **75**, 6263–6267.

Nemo, G. I., Brown, P. W., Gibbs, C. J., and Gajdusek, D. C. (1978). *Infect. Immun.* **20**, 69–72.

Newton, M., Cruickshank, K., Miller, D., Dalgleish, A. G., Rudge, P., Clayden, S., and Moseley, I. (1987). *Lancet* **1**, 415–416.

Nooter, K., Aarssen, A. M., Bentvelzen, P., de Groot, F. G., and van Pelt, P. (1975). *Nature (London)* **256**, 595–597.

Nooter, K., Bentvelzen, P., Zurcher, C., and Rhim, J. (1977). *Int. J. Cancer* **19**, 59–65.

Nusbaum, N. J. (1985). *N. Engl. J. Med.* **312**, 1706.

Okamoto, T., and Wong-Staal, F. (1986). *Cell* **47**, 29–35.

Pahwa, S., Pahwa, R., Good, R., Gallo, R., and Saxiger, C. (1986). *Proc. Natl. Acad. Sci. U.S.A.* **83**, 9124–9128.

Panem, S. (1976). *ICN-UCLA Symp. Mol. Cell Biol.* 409–417.

Panem, S., Prochouinik, E. V., Real, R., and Kirsten, W. H. (1975). *Science* **189**, 297–299.

Panem, S., Ordonez, N. G., Dalton, H., and Soltani, K. (1978). *J. Invest. Dermatol.* **71**, 260–262.

Parks, W., and Scott, G. (1987). *In* "AIDS" (S. Broder, ed.), pp. 245–261. Dekker, New York.

Peterlin, B. M., Luciw, P. A., Barr, P. J., and Walker, M. D. (1986). *Proc. Natl. Acad. Sci. U.S.A.* **83**, 9734–9738.

Plata, F., Autran, B., Martins, L. P., Wain-Hobson, S., Raphael, M., Mayand, C., Denis, M., Guillon, J. M., and Debre, P. (1987). *Nature (London)* **328**, 348–351.

Poiesz, B. J., Ruscetti, F. W., Gazdar, A. F., Bunn, P. A., Minna, J. D., and Gallo, R. C. (1980). *Proc. Natl. Acad. Sci. U.S.A.* **77**, 7415–7419.

Poiesz, B. J., Ruscetti, F. W., Reitz, M. S., Kalyanaraman, V. S., and Gallo, R. C. (1981). *Nature (London)* **294**, 268–271.

Popovic, M., Lange-Wantzin, G., Sarin, P. S., Mann, D., and Gallo, R. C. (1983). *Proc. Natl. Acad. Sci. U.S.A.* **80**, 5402–5406.

Popovic, M., Sarngadharan, M. G., Read, E., and Gallo, R. C. (1984). *Science* **224**, 497–500.

Posner, L. E., Robert-Guroff, M., Kalyanaraman, V. S., Poiesz, B. J., Ruscetti, F. W., Fossieck, B., Bunn, Jr., P. A., Minna, J. D., and Gallo, R. C. (1981). *J. Exp. Med.* **154**, 333–346.

Rabson, A. B., Sheele, P. E., Garon, C. F., and Martin, M. (1983). *Nature (London)* **306**, 604–607.

Ratner, L., Haseltine, W., Patarca, R., Livak, K. J., Starcich, B., Josephs, S. F., Doran, E. R., Rafalski, J. A., Whitwhoen, E. A., Baumeister, K., Ivanoff, L., Petteway, S. R., Pearson, M. L., Lautenberger, J. A., Papas, T. S., Ghrayeb, J., Chang, N. T., Gallo, R. C., and Wong-Staal, F. (1985). *Nature (London)* **313**, 277–284.

Redfield, R. R., Markham, P., Salahuddin, S. Z., Wright, D. C., Sarngadharan, M. G., and Gallo, R. C. (1985). *J. Am. Med. Assoc.* **254**, 2094–2096.

Redfield, R. R., Wright, D. C., and Tramont, E. C. (1986). *N. Engl. J. Med.* **314**, 131–132.

Reed, E. J., Orenstein, J. M., and Chorba, T. L. (1985). *Am. J. Clin. Pathol.* **83**, 385–384.

Reitz, M. S., Poiesz, B. J., Ruscetti, F. W., and Gallo, R. C. (1981). *Proc. Natl. Acad. Sci. U.S.A.* **78**, 1887–1891.

Rho, H. M., Poiesz, B., Ruscetti, F. W., and Gallo, R. C. (1981). *Virology* **112**, 355–360.

Rieber, P., and Riethmuller, G. (1986). *Lancet* **1**, 270.

Robert-Guroff, M., Ruscetti, F. W., Posner, L. E., Poiesz, B. J., and Gallo, R. C. (1981). *J. Exp. Med.* **154**, 1957–1964.

Robert-Guroff, M., Fahey, A., Maeda, M., Nakao, Y., Ito, Y., and Gallo, R. C. (1982). *Virology* **122**, 297–305.

Robert-Guroff, M., Brown, M., and Gallo, R. C. (1985). *Nature (London)* **316**, 72–75.

Robson, B., Fishleigh, R. V., and Morrison, C. A. (1987). *Nature (London)* **325**, 395.

Rosen, C. A., Sodroski, J. G., and Haseltine, W. A. (1985a). *Cell* **41**, 813–823.

Rosen, C. A., Sodroski, J. G., Kettman, R., Burny, A., and Haseltine, W. (1985b). *Science* **227**, 320–322.

Rosen, C. A., Sodroski, J. G., Goh, W. C., Dayton, A. I., Lippke, J., and Haseltine, W. A. (1986). *Nature (London)* **319**, 555–559.

Rosenblatt, J. D., Golde, D. W., Wachsman, W., Giorgi, J. V., Jacobs, A., Schmidt, G. M., Quan, S., Gasson, J. C., and Chen, I. S. Y. (1986). *N. Engl. J. Med.* **315**, 372–377.

Rous, P. (1911). *J. Exp. Med.* **13**, 397–411.

Rozenbaum, W., Dormont, D., Spire, B., Vilmer, E., Gentilini, M., Griscelli, C., Montagnier, L., Barré-Sinoussi, F., and Chermann, J. C. (1985). *Lancet* **1**, 450–451.

Sadaie, M. R., Benter, T., and Wong-Staal, F. (1988). *Science* **239**, 910–913.

Salahuddin, S. Z., Ablashi, D., Markham, P. D., Josephs, S., Sturzenegger, S., Kaplan, M., Halligan, G., Biberfield, P., Wong-Staal, F., Kramansky, B., and Gallo, R. C. (1986). *Science* **234**, 596–603.

Sanchez-Pescador, R., Power, M. D., Barr, P. J., Steimer, K. S., Stempien, M. M., Brown-Shimer, S. L., Gee, W. W., Renard, A., Randolph, A., Levy, J. A., Dina, D., and Luciw, P. A. (1985). *Science* **227**, 485–492.

Sarin, P., Sun, D., Thornton, A., Naylor, P., and Goldstein, A. (1986). *Science* **232**, 1135–1137.

Sarngadharan, M. G., Sarin, P. S., Reitz, M. S., and Gallo, R. C. (1972). *Nature (London) New Biol.* **240**, 67–72.

Sattentau, Q., Dalgleish, A. G., Beverley, P. C. L., and Weiss, R. A. (1986). *Science* **234**, 1120–1123.

Saxinger, W., Blattner, W. A., Levine, P. H., Clark, J., Biggar, R., Hoh, M., Moghissi, J., Jacobs, P., Wilson, L., Jacobson, R., Crookes, R., Strong, M., Ansari, A. A., Dean, A. G., Nkrumah, F. K., Mourali, N., and Gallo, R. C. (1984). *Science* **225**, 1473–1476.

Schlom, J., and Spiegelman, S. (1971). *Science* **174**, 840–843.

Schnittman, S. M., Lane, M. E., Higgins, S. E., Folks, T., and Fauci, A. S. (1986). *Science* **233**, 1084–1086.

Schnitzer, T. Z. (1979). *J. Gen. Virol.* **42**, 199–206.

Schnitzer, T. Z., Weiss, R. A., and Zavada, J. (1977). *J. Virol.* **23**, 449–454.

Seigel, L. J., Ratner, L., Josephs, S. F., Derse, D., Feinberg, M. B., Reyes, G. R., O'Brien, S. J., and Wong-Staal, F. (1986). *Virology* **148**, 226–231.

Seiki, M., Hattori, S., Hirayama, Y., and Yoshida, M. (1983). *Proc. Natl. Acad. Sci. U.S.A.* **80**, 3618–3622.

Serwadda, D., Mugerwa, R., Sewankambo, N., Lwegaba, A., Carswell, J., Kirya, G., Bayley, A. C., Downing, R. G., Tedder, R. S., Clayden, S. A., Weiss, R. A., and Dalgleish, A. G. (1985). *Lancet* **2**, 849–853.

Shaw, G. M., Hahn, B. H., Arya, S. K., Froopman, J. E., Gallo, R. C., and Wong-Staal, F. (1984). *Science* **226**, 1165–1171.

Shimotohno, K., Golde, D. W., Miwa, N., Sugimura, T., and Chen, I. S. Y. (1984a). *Proc. Natl. Acad. Sci. U.S.A.* **81**, 1079–1083.

Shimotohno, K., Wachsman, W., Takahashi, Y., Golde, D. W., Miwa, M., Sugimura, T., and Chen, I. S. Y. (1984b). *Proc. Natl. Acad. Sci. U.S.A.* **81**, 6657–6661.

Shimotohno, K., Takahashi, Y., Shimizu, N., Gojobori, T., Golde, D. W., Chen, I. S. Y., Miwa, M., and Sugimura, T. (1985). *Proc. Natl. Acad. Sci. U.S.A.* **82**, 3101–3105.

Slamon, D. J., Shimotohno, K., Cline, M., Golde, D. W., and Chen, I. S. Y. (1984). *Science* **226**, 61–64.

Smith, D. H., Byrn, R. A., Marsters, S. A., Gregory, T., Groopman, J. E., and Capon, D. J. (1987). *Science* **238**, 1704–1707.

Sodroski, J. G., Rosen, C. A., and Haseltine, W. A. (1984). *Science* **225**, 381–385.

Sodroski, J., Patarca, R., Rosen, C., Wong-Staal, F., and Haseltine, W. (1985a). *Science* **229**, 74–78.

Sodroski, J., Rosen, Wong-Staal, F., Salahuddin, S. Z., Popovic, M., Arya, S., Gallo, R. C., and Haseltine, W. A. (1985b). *Science* **227**, 171–173.

Sodroski, J., Goh, W. C., Rosen, C., Campbell, K., and Haseltine, W. (1986a). *Nature (London)* **322**, 470–474.

Sodroski, J., Goh, W. C., Rosen, C., Tartar, A., Portetelle, D., Burny, A., and Haseltine, W. (1986b). *Science* **231**, 1549–1553.

Sodroski, J., Goh, W. C., Rosen, C., Dayton, A., Terwilliger, E., and Haseltine, W. (1986c). *Nature (London)* **321**, 412–417.

Sohn, C. C., Blayney, D., Miset, J. L., Mathé, G., Flandrin, G., Moran, E., Jensen, F., Winberg,

C., and Rappaport, R. (1986). *Blood* **67**, 949–956.
Sonigo, P., Alizen, M., Staskus, K., Klatzman, D., Cole, S., Danos, O., Retzel, E., Tiollais, P., Haase, A., and Wain-Hobson, S. (1985). *Cell* **42**, 369.
Spickett, G., and Dalgleish, A. G. (1988). *Clin Exp. Immunol.* **71**, 1–7.
Stancek, D., Stancekova-Gressnerova, M., Janotka, M., Hnilica, P., and Orovec, D. (1975). *Med. Microbiol. Immunol.* **161**, 133–144.
Starcich, B., Ratner, L., Josephs, S. F., Okamoto, T., Gallo, R. C., and Wong-Staal, F. (1985). *Science* **227**, 538–540.
Steel, L. K., Laube, H., and Chandra, C. (1977). *Cancer Lett.* **2**, 291–298.
Stewart, G. J., Tyler, J. P., Cunningham, A. L., Barr, J. A., Driscoll, G. L., Gold, J., and Lamont, B. J. (1985). *Lancet* **2**, 581–585.
Stricker, P. B., McHugh, T. M., Moody, D. J., Morrow, W. J. N., Stibes, D. P., Shuman, M. A., and Levy, J. A. (1987). *Nature (London)* **327**, 710–713.
Suni, J., Wahlström, T., and Vaheri, A. (1981). *Int. J. Cancer* **28**, 559–566.
Suni, J., Narvanen, A., Wahlström, T., Lehtovirta, P., and Vaheri, A. (1984). *Int. J. Cancer* **33**, 293–298.
Tajima, K., Tominaga, S., Kuroishi, T., Shimizu, H., and Suchi, T. (1979). *Jpn. J. Clin. Oncol.* **9**, 495–504.
Takeichi, N., Kaji, N., and Kodama, K. (1974). *Cancer Res.* **34**, 543–550.
Tedder, R. S., Shanson, D., Jeffries, D., Cheingsong-Popov, R., Clapham, P., Dalgleish, A. G., Nagy, K., and Weiss, R. A. (1984). *Lancet* **2**, 125–128.
Tellier, R., and Weber, J. M. (1985). *Nature (London)* **318**, 414.
Temin, H. (1981). *Cell* **27**, 1–3.
Thielen, G. H., Gould, D., Fowler, M., and Dungworth, D. (1971). *J. Natl. Cancer Inst.* **47**, 881–889.
Thomson, B. J., and Dalgleish, A. G. (1987). *Arch. Dis. Child.* **62**, 631–634.
Tiollais, P., Pourcel, C., and Dejean, A. (1985). *Nature (London)* **317**, 489–495.
Townsend, A. R. M., Rothbard, J., Gotch, F. M., Bahadur, G., Wraith, D., and McMichael, A. J. (1986). *Cell* **44**, 959–968.
Tsudo, M., Uchiyama, T., Uchino, H., and Yodoi, J. (1983). *Blood* **61**, 1014–1016.
Uchiyama, Y., Yodoi, J., Sagawa, K., Takatsuki, K., and Uchino, H. (1977). *Blood* **50**, 481–492.
Vallée and Carré. (1904). *Compt. Rend. Acad. Sci. (Paris)* **139**, 331–333.
Van de Perre, P., Clumeck, N., Carael, M., Nzabihimana, E., Robert-Guroff, M., De Mol, P., Freyens, P., Butzler, J. P., Gallo, R. C., and Kanyamupira, J. B. (1985). *Lancet* **2**, 524–527.
Van Muijen, G. N. P., te Velde, G. T., den Ottolander, G. J., Brand, A., Kroopman-Broekhuyzen, N., Schaberg, A., and Warnaar, N. (1979). *Cancer* **43**, 1682–1688.
Vandepitte, J., Verwilghen, R., and Zachee, P. (1983). *Lancet* **1**, 925–926.
Wain-Hobson, S., Sonigo, P., Danos, O., Cole, S., and Alizon, M. (1985). *Cell* **40**, 9–17.
Waldmann, T. A. (1986). *Science* **232**, 727–732.
Walker, B. D., Chakrabarti, S., Moss, B., Paradis, T. J., Flynn, T., Durno, A. G., Blumberg, R. S., Kaplan, J. S., Hirsh, M. S., and Schooley, R. T. (1987). *Nature (London)* **328**, 345–348.
Walker, C., Devey, M., Stites, D., and Levy, J. A. (1986). *Science* **234**, 1563–1566.
Weber, J. N., Wadsworth, J., Rogers, L. A., Moshtael, O., Scott, K., McManus, T., Berrie, E., Jefferies, D. J., Harris, J. R. W., and Pinching, A. J. (1986). *Lancet* **1**, 1179–1182.
Weber, J. N., Clapham, P., Weiss, R. A., Parker, D., Roberts, C., Duncan, J., Weller, I. V. D., Carne, C., Tedder, R. S., Pinching, A., and Cheingsong-Popov, R. (1987). *Lancet* **1**, 119–121.
Weiss, R. A., and Frisby, D. P. (1982). *In* "Advances in Leukaemia Research 1981," pp. 303–311. Elsevier, Amsterdam.
Weiss, R. A., Friis, R. R., Katz, E., and Vogt, P. K. (1971). *Virology* **46**, 920–938.
Weiss, R. A., Teich, N., Varmus, H., and Coffin, J. (1985a). "RNA Tumour Viruses." Cold

Spring Harbor Laboratory, Cold Spring Harbor, New York.
Weiss, R. A., Clapham, P. R., Cheingsong-Popov, R., Dalgleish, A. G., Carne, C. A., Weller, V. D., and Tedder, R. S. (1985b). *Nature (London)* **316**, 69–72.
Weiss, R. A., Clapham, P. R., Weber, J. N., Dalgleish, A. G., Laskey, L. A., and Berman, P. W. (1986). *Nature (London)* **324**, 572–575.
Wong-Staal, F., Gillespie, D., and Gallo, R. C. (1976). *Nature (London)* **262**, 190–195.
Wong-Staal, F., Dalla-Favera, R., Franchini, G., Gellmann, E. P., and Gallo, R. C. (1981). *Science* **213**, 226–228.
Wong-Staal, F., Hahn, B., Manzari, V., Colombini, S., Franchini, G., Gelmann, E. P., and Gallo, R. C. (1983). *Nature (London)* **302**, 626–628.
Wong-Staal, F., and Gallo, R. C. (1985). *Nature (London)* **317**, 395–400.
Wong-Staal, F., Chandra, P.-K., and Shrayeb, J. (1987). *AIDS Res. Hum. Retroviruses* **3**, 33–39.
Yarchoan, R., Berg, G., Brouwers, P., Fischl, M., Spitzer, A. R., Wichman, A., Grafman, J., Thomas, R. V., Safai, B., Brunetti, A., Perno, C. F., Schmidt, P. J., Larson, S. M., Myers, C. E., and Broder, S. (1987). *Lancet* **1**, 132–135.
Zagury, D., Gagne, I., Réveil, B., Bernard, J., Zagury, J.-F., Saimot, A. G., Sarin, P. S., and Gallo, R. C. (1985). *Lancet* **2**, 449.
Zagury, D., Bernard, J., Leonard, R., Cheynnier, R., Feldman, M., Sarin, P. S., and Gallo, R. C. (1986). *Science* **231**, 850–853.
Zavada, J. (1982). *J. Gen. Virol.* **63**, 15–24.
Zavada, J., Zavadova, Z., and Russ, G. (1986). *J. Gen. Virol.* **67**, 1561–1569.
Zhdanov, V. M., Solovieu, V. D., Filatov, F., and Bykovsky, R. (1972). *Arch. Gesamte Virusforsch.* **39**, 309–316.

NOTE ADDED IN PROOF: Recent results (Kestler III, H. W. *et al.*, *Nature* **331**, 619–621, 1988) indicate that retroviral isolates previously referred to as STLV-III_{AGM} and HTLV-IV are not authentic, but were derived from cell cultures infected with $SIV_{MAC\text{-}251}$.

HOMING RECEPTORS AND METASTASIS

Beverly Taylor Sher, Robert Bargatze, Bernard Holzmann, W. Michael Gallatin, Dana Matthews, Nora Wu, Louis Picker, Eugene C. Butcher, and Irving L. Weissman

Department of Pathology, Stanford University School of Medicine, Stanford, California, 94305

I. Introduction 361
II. Metastasis, Adhesion, and the Cell Surface 362
A. Metastatic Potential and Heterotypic Aggregation 362
B. Antibody Blocking *in Vivo* and/or *in Vitro* 363
C. Adhesion to Cryostat Sections 364
D. Adhesion to Endothelial Monolayers 365
E. Known Adhesion Systems Involved in Metastasis 365
III. Lymphocyte Homing Receptors 367
A. Lymphocyte Recirculation 367
B. Evidence for Specific Homing Receptors *in Vivo* and *in Vitro* 368
C. Mouse Lymphocyte Homing Receptors 370
D. Human Lymphocyte Homing Receptors 372
E. Rat Lymphocyte Homing Receptors 372
F. Other Potential Lymphocyte Homing Receptors 373
IV. Lymphocyte Homing Receptors and Metastasis 376
A. Somatic Fusions of Nonmetastatic Tumors with Normal Lymphocytes 376
B. HEV Binding and Metastasis 377
C. MEL-14 and Metastasis 380
D. Hermes-1 and Metastasis 385
V. Summary and Conclusions 386
References 387

I. Introduction

Metastasis is a complex process involving many separate steps. These steps include the establishment and maintenance of the primary tumor, its vascularization, the escape of metastatic cells into the circulatory system, the arrest of these cells in the vasculature of a distant organ and their subsequent extravasation, and, finally, the establishment and growth of the secondary tumor (Nicolson and Poste, 1983; Schirrmacher, 1985). Metastasis is not necessarily a random process as many types of tumors have characteristic metastatic patterns, forming metastases in particular target organs (Nicolson, 1982b, 1984b; Nicolson and Custead, 1982; Schirrmacher, 1985). The final two steps of the metastatic cascade are particularly relevant to the process of organ-specific metastasis. It is clear that the microenvironment created by the organ that tumor cells enter can affect their subsequent growth

ADVANCES IN CANCER RESEARCH, VOLUME 51

(Nicolson and Dulski, 1986; Nicolson and Custead, 1982). It is also clear that blood-borne tumor cells do not necessarily become arrested and extravasate in the first capillary bed they encounter (Tarin *et al.*, 1984). In this review, we will concentrate on the entry of blood-borne cells into tissues through the microvasculature.

A normal equivalent of the entry of blood-borne metastatic cells into organs by way of the microvasculature is the entry of lymphocytes into tissues from the blood. Lymphocyte entry into lymphoid organs such as the peripheral nodes and Peyer's patches—a process known as homing—depends upon specific adhesive cell–cell interactions between entering lymphocytes and endothelial cells lining specialized postcapillary venules (Gowans and Knight, 1964). These interactions are mediated by lymphocyte cell-surface receptors, known as lymphocyte homing receptors, that bind to specific molecules on the endothelial cell surface (Gallatin *et al.*, 1983, 1986).

Neoplastic processes often involve the subversion of normal cellular functions for the benefit of the tumor, so it seems quite possible that the lymphocyte homing receptor system could be involved in organ-specific metastasis. In this review, we will first discuss the evidence for the involvement of specific adhesive interactions between tumor cells and cells of their target organs; we will then review the biology of lymphocyte homing; and finally we will discuss evidence for the involvement of the lymphocyte homing receptor system in metastasis.

II. Metastasis, Adhesion, and the Cell Surface

A. Metastatic Potential and Heterotypic Aggregation

In 1975, Nicolson and Winkelhake suggested that the organ specificity of blood-borne tumor metastasis could be related to the ability of tumor cells to adhere to cells of the target organ. B16 melanoma cell lines with increasing ability to form lung metastases were mixed with single-cell suspensions of several different organs, including lung, liver, kidney, brain, and spleen; and the formation of hererotypic cellular aggregates was measured. The degree of aggregation observed was related to the organ specificity of the tumor lines *in vivo*: lung > liver, kidney, spleen, and erythrocytes. The degree of specific aggregation of the tumor cells with the lung cells also reflected the number of *in vivo* selection steps that the different B16 lines had undergone, with those lines that were more highly selected for lung metastic capacity forming more aggregates with lung cells and fewer aggregates with cells from the other organs tested. The ability of tumor cells to form specific heterotypic aggregates with cells from their target organs has been observed in other systems as well (Phondke *et al.*, 1981; DeBaetselier *et al.*, 1984; Nicolson, 1982a, 1984b; Kamenov and Longenecker, 1985; Collard *et al.*, 1986; Kamenov *et al.*, 1984).

B. Antibody Blocking *in Vitro* and/or *in Vivo*

In a number of experiments, treatment of tumor cells with antibodies against cell-surface components that have been correlated with the organ-specific metastatic capacity of the tumor appear to block the ability of the tumor cells to adhere to normal cells *in vitro*. In one such experiment, the invasive mouse sarcoma line FS9 was used to immunize rabbits, and the resulting antiserum was absorbed with the noninvasive, H-2-identical cell line L929 (Steinemann *et al.*, 1984). Fab fragments from the absorbed antiserum blocked the ability of FS9 cells to invade monolayers of the chicken heart fibroblasts *in vitro*. The absorbed antiserum was found to react predominantly with a 37-kDa cell-surface glycoprotein expressed at high levels on FS9 cells, but at low levels by L929 cells. Fab fragments of a monoclonal antibody directed against the 37-kDa glycoprotein also blocked FS9 invasion. The expression of the 37-kDa glycoprotein by FS9 cells is thus probably responsible for their invasive capacity.

A similar experiment showed that monoclonal antibodies against cell-surface proteins expressed by normal cells can block the adhesion of metastatic cells. Two monoclonal antibodies, OPAR-1 and OPAR-2, were found to bind to two rat liver cell-surface proteins with molecular weights of 125,000 and 100,000 (Middlekoop *et al.*, 1985). These proteins were found predominantly on the sinusoidal surface of hepatocytes and on Kupffer cells but were not present on sinusoidal endothelial cells. The OPAR antibodies inhibited the adhesion of mouse metastatic TA3 mammary carcinoma cells to rat liver cells *in vitro* but failed to block the adhesion of MB6A lymphosarcoma cells. *In vivo* testing of the effect of these antibodies on hepatic metastasis was not reported. It thus appears that different tumors can use different adhesive molecules to interact with cells from their target organs.

A number of groups have generated monoclonal antibodies that are capable of blocking experimental metastasis *in vivo*. Shearman *et al.* (1980) described a monoclonal antibody that blocked organ-specific metastasis of AL2, a Marek's disease chicken lymphoma cell line. This cell line, which had been selected for its ability to metastasize to liver, was used to immunize mice. Monoclonal antibodies from the subsequent fusion were tested for their ability to react with the AL2 line but not with nonmetastatic Marek's disease lines, and one antibody with these characteristics, 1.20, was found. Preincubation of AL2 cells with the 1.20 antibody specifically blocked their ability to metastasize to embryonic liver but not to the chorioallantoic membrane in chicken embryos. Preincubation of AL2 cells with isotype-matched control antibodies that reacted with the cells had no effect on AL2 metastasis to either site. Furthermore, expression of the 1.20 antigen by other Marek's disease sublines was found to be positively correlated with their ability to form liver metastases. Thus, treatment of the AL2 line with a monoclonal antibody against a cell-surface determinant found only on cells capable of experimental metastasis to liver blocked metastasis *in vivo*. Similar results in another system have been obtained by Gunji and Taniguchi (1986), who generated a monoclonal antibody, M2590, which recognizes a melanoma cell-surface protein. This antibody specifically inhibited experimental metastasis of melanoma cells to lung, whereas isotype-matched controls had no effect.

McGuire *et al.* (1984) have correlated the blocking of experimental metastasis by antibodies *in vivo* with the inhibition of adhesive interactions *in vitro*. Sublines of the mouse RAW117 lymphosarcoma were selected for enhanced ability to metastasize to liver *in vivo*. RAW117-H10 was obtained after ten selection steps, while RAW117-H5 was obtained after five selection steps. *In vitro*, the selected sublines adhered better to liver cells than to brain cells, whereas the parental line was nonselective in its adhesion properties. The sublines were then tested with a polyclonal xenoantiserum raised against fetal liver cells and known to block organ-specific homotypic aggregation between fetal liver cells *in vitro*. RAW117-H10 expressed higher levels of the fetal liver determinants than did RAW117-H5, which in turn expressed more of these determinants than did RAW117. Treatment of RAW117-H10 cells with Fab′ or $F(ab')_2$ fragments of the xenoantiserum inhibited liver metastasis *in vivo*, whereas treatment of these cells with the appropriate fragments of a polyclonal anti-H-2 antiserum did not affect their metastic capacity. Thus, tumor cell adhesive behavior *in vitro* was correlated with metastatic potential *in vivo*, and a xenoantiserum known to block adhesion *in vitro* also blocked experimental metastasis *in vivo*. It may be that further work on the other experimental systems described in this section will also result in such direct adhesion–metastasis correlations.

C. Adhesion to Cryostat Sections

A modified version of the procedure used to assay lymphocyte homing capacity *in vitro* (discussed in Section III,B) has been used to select metastatic tumor variants with enhanced organ specificity. Netland and Zetter (1985) allowed B16 melanoma cells to adhere to cryostat sections of mouse lung and brain. The adherent cells were cultured and the selection procedure was then repeated a number of times. The selection subpopulations were then tested for their ability to adhere specifically to cryostat sections of the appropriate organ and for their metastatic potential *in vivo*. A subpopulation selected on cryostat sections of lung showed enhanced adhesion to cryostat sections of lung tissue and a sixfold increase in the frequency of lung metastases *in vivo* over that of the parental B16 population. Selection of B16 cells on brain sections, however, failed to produce a brain-specific subpopulation. Still, these experiments demonstrate a direct correlation between the ability of tumor cells to adhere to the tissue of a target organ and their ability to metastasize to that organ *in vivo*. The cryostat section adherence technique has also been used to demonstrate positive correlations between organ-specific metastasis *in vivo* and the ability of the metastatic cells to adhere to sections of the target organ (Barnett and Eccles, 1984; Netland and Zetter, 1984).

D. Adhesion to Endothelial Monolayers

In the metastatic process, the cells in the target organ that are actually involved in adhesion of blood-borne tumor cells are only a small subpopulation of the cells in the organ- the endothelial cells and other cells lining the blood vessels through which the tumor cells enter the organ. In some organs, such as the liver, parenchymal cells may come into direct contact with cells in the blood. Most tissues, however, have the more usual structure in which the capillary endothelium, its basement membrane, an interstitial connective tissue matrix, and the basement membrane of the epithelial cell (if the tissue is epithelial) separate the tissue parenchyma from the blood. This fact of tissue architecture has led to experiments in which the ability of tumor cells to adhere to and invade cultured endothelial monolayers has been correlated with their metastatic capacity (Kramer and Nicolson, 1979; Nicolson, 1982b; Stanford *et al.*, 1986; Korach *et al.*, 1986). In these experiments, endothelia from blood vessels other than those of the tumor target organ, indeed from species other than that of the tumor cells, are frequently used to assay the adhesive behavior of tumor cells (Stanford *et al.*, 1986; Nicolson, 1982b; Korach *et al.*, 1986). Still, in these experiments, positive correlations between the capacity to bind endothelial cells and high metastatic capacity *in vivo* have been observed.

There is evidence, however, that endothelia from different tissues are not necessarily alike. Monoclonal antibodies and antisera have been used to detect organ-specific patterns of surface antigen expression by endothelial cells (Auerbach *et al.*, 1985). If endothelia of different organs express different adhesive determinants, this uniqueness could contribute to the organ specificity of metastasis of blood-borne tumor cells. The binding capacities of several tumor lines to cell lines derived from different types of vascular endothelia have been examined (Alby and Auerbach, 1984). Adhesion experiments with endothelia cells derived from mouse brain capillaries (MBE cells) and mouse ovary capillaries (MOE cells) revealed that mouse ovary-derived teratoma cells adhered preferentially to MOE cells, whereas glioma cells adhered preferentially to MBE cells. In addition, a testicular teratoma that metastasizes preferentially to ovary adhered preferentially to MOE cells. These experiments suggest that endothelial cells from different locations do indeed differ in their adhesive properties in ways that correlate with organ-specific metastasis.

E. Known Adhesion Systems Involved in Metastasis

In the experiments discussed in the preceding sections, adhesive interactions between metastatic cells and normal cells have been shown to be involved in organ-specific metastasis. The adhesive molecules involved, however, were not identified, although in some cases they were partially described. In this section, we will discuss the involvement of two different well-characterized molecular adhesion systems in metastasis.

Investigation of the mechanism of metastasis to liver has implicated a number of hepatic asialoglycoprotein-binding proteins involved in the adhesion of metastatic cells to normal liver cells (Schirrmacher *et al.*, 1980; Cheinsong-Popov *et al.*, 1983; Schirrmacher, 1985). The experimental system involves two related cells lines: Eb, a line of low metastatic potential; and Esb, a spontaneous variant of Eb with high metastatic capacity for liver. *In vitro*, Esb binds to isolated hepatocytes, whereas Eb cells do not. When iodinated hepatocyte cell-surface proteins are allowed to bind to Esb cells, eluted, and separated on sodium dodecyl suflfate (SDS) gels, three different hepatocyte Esb-binding proteins are found, with molecular weights of 52,000, 56,000, and 110,000 under reducing conditions (Cheinsong-Popov *et al.*, 1983). The binding of these proteins to Esb cells can be specifically inhibited by prior incubation of the hepatocyte lysate with *N*-acetyl-*O*-galactosamine or D-galactose, a result indicating that these proteins are lectins. These lectins bind to more than ten different Esb cell-surface proteins but bind no proteins on the surfaces of Eb cells. Treatment of Eb cells with neuraminidase, however, allows Eb cells to bind isolated hepatocytes, a result suggesting that the lectin-binding structures on these cells are masked by sialic acid. The specific adhesive interactions between the hepatocyte lectins and cell-surface proteins on Esb cells may thus explain, at least in part, the preferential liver metastasis of Esb cells.

The involvement of a cell-surface receptor for the matrix protein laminin has been postulated to be important in experimental metastasis to lung (Terranova *et al.*, 1982; Vollmers *et al.*, 1984). Laminin forms a bridge between cell surface laminin receptors and type IV collagen, a constituent of the extracellular matrix (McCarthy *et al.*, 1985). After exposure to laminin, metastatic mouse BL6 and PM2 cells have an increased ability to bind to isolated type IV collagen, whereas a nonmetastatic mouse fibrosarcoma cell line does not (Terranova *et al.*, 1982). Incubation of the metastatic cell lines with antibody to laminin prior to their intravenous injection into mice substantially reduced the number of subsequent lung metastases. Although the authors propose that this results from blockade of an adhesive event, other effects of the antibodies on the cells are possible.

The involvement of laminin in experimental lung metastasis has also been demonstrated in an independent series of experiments. Vollmers and Birchmeier generated monoclonal antibodies that could block the ability of metastic B16 melanoma cells to adhere to extracellular matrices in culture (Vollmers and Birchmeier, 1983a,b). The antibodies specifically blocked the experimental metastasis of B16 melanoma sublines selected for high metastatic capacity to lung. Subsequent experiments have demonstrated that these antibodies specifically block the binding of B16 cells to laminin, although the B16 cell-surface protein that they immunoprecipitate does not appear to be the same as the previously identified laminin receptor (Vollmers *et al.*, 1984).

The ability to bind laminin, however, is not always correlated with high metastatic capacity. Low-metastatic MDW4 cells bind to laminin better than do cells of their high metastatic variant, MDAY-D2 (Dennis, 1985). When injected subcutaneously, MDW4 cells almost exclusively form localized tumors at the site of injection. The author suggested that the ability of these cells to bind laminin, and thus to adhere to the extracellular matrix at the site of injection, resulted in their failure to leave that site and form widely disseminated metastases.

Other well-characterized molecular adhesion systems have been proposed to be involved in metastasis. These include fibronectin and other adhesive extracellular matrix glycoproteins (for review, see McCarthy *et al.*, 1985) and the cell–cell adhesion CAM system (for review, see Brackenbury, 1985). In the remainder of this review, we will concentrate on another such cell–cell adhesion system, the lymphocyte homing receptor system.

III. Lymphocyte Homing Receptors

A. Lymphocyte Recirculation

The immune system acts to defend the body against foreign antigens. It comprises a series of lymphoid organs and cellular elements, including the lymphocytes. Each lymphocyte, whether a B cell or a T cell, bears surface receptors for a foreign antigen. The number of foreign antigens that the body can encounter over a lifetime is potentially very large. The number of different T and B cell antigen receptors is correspondingly large, so only a rare subpopulation of the lymphocytes in the body can recognize any given antigen. Therefore, the development of an effective immune response depends not only upon the entry of an antigen into a site where it can be processed and presented to lymphocytes but also upon the presence of lymphocytes bearing receptors for that particular antigen.

Small lymphocytes, the population that includes the mature T and B cells as well as memory cells, are mobile and are capable of recirculating through the blood, the peripheral lymphoid organs, and the lymph (Ford, 1975). This capacity facilitates the development of immune responses by ensuring that lymphocytes with many different antigenic specificities can encounter antigen that has been trapped and processed in a particular place (reviewed in Rouse *et al.*, 1984). In order to enter lymphoid organs such as the Peyer's patches and the peripheral lymph nodes, blood-borne lymphocytes must cross specialized endothelia. This process of lymphocyte extravasation occurs in specialized postcapillary venules that are lined with high endothelium

(Gowans and Knight, 1964) and are known as high endothelial venules, or HEV. The process is mediated by specific interactions between the endothelial cells and the entering lymphocytes; both T and B lymphocytes enter lymphoid organs by common HEVs (Gutman and Weissman, 1973; Howard *et al.*, 1972). It is unclear whether the migrating lymphocytes pass through the endothelial cells or whether they pass through areas where two endothelial cells border each other, but close membrane apposition between the two cell types is a key feature of the process. By electron microscopy, it has been shown that some of these close membrane contacts resemble gap junctions (Campbell, 1983). The migration of recirculating lymphocytes from the blood to particular lymphoid sites has been referred to as homing, and the specific lymphocyte cell-surface molecules that mediate the process are known as "homing receptors" (Gallatin *et al.*, 1983).

B. Evidence for Specific Homing Receptors *in Vivo* and *in Vitro*

Early experiments dealing with lymphocyte recirculation revealed that lymphocytes from different sources have different migratory preferences. For example, small lymphocytes derived from peripheral nodes or from the efferent lymphatics draining peripheral nodes, when labeled and reintroduced into the bloodstream of a syngeneic animal, migrate preferentially to peripheral nodes, whereas lymphocytes leaving gut lymphatics migrate preferentially to Peyer's patches (Griscelli *et al.*, 1969; Guy-Grand *et al.*, 1974; Scollay *et al.*, 1976; Smith *et al.*, 1980). These preferential homing patterns can be correlated with the ability of lymphocyte populations to bind to cryostat sections of high endothelial venules in peripheral lymphoid organs. This assay, known as the HEV assay, was first described by Stamper and Woodruff (1976) and was modified by Butcher *et al.* (1979) to include the ability to compare the binding of two different lymphocyte populations to the same cryostat sections.

The HEV assay is performed as follows (Butcher *et al.*, 1979). The lymphocytes whose binding properties are to be tested are mixed at a 1:1 ratio in tube A with a fluoresceinated control population of lymphocytes. The mixture is then incubated at 4°C on cryostat sections of the appropriate lymphoid organ. Nonadherent lymphocytes are washed off the section at the end of the incubation period and the sections are fixed in glutaraldehyde. Fluoresceinated and unfluoresceinated lymphocytes adhering to HEV are observed by fluorescence and dark-field microscopy. The same procedure is performed for a mixture of fluoresceinated and unfluoresceinated control lymphocytes in tube B to control for the effect of fluoresceination on HEV binding. The HEV binding ability of the test population relative to that of the control population is expressed as a relative adherence ratio, or RAR, calculated as follows:

$$\text{RAR} = \frac{\dfrac{\text{number of test lymphocytes on HEV, tube A}}{\text{number of fluoresceinated control lymphocytes on HEV, tube A}}}{\dfrac{\text{number of unfluoresceinated control lymphocytes on HEV, tube B}}{\text{number of fluoresceinated control lymphocytes on HEV, tube B}}}$$

The HEV assay has been used to study the HEV binding properties of various populations of lymphocytes, and correlations between their *in vitro* HEV binding behavior and their *in vivo* homing behavior have been observed. For example, about 1.4 times as many Peyer's patch lymphocytes as lymph node lymphocytes bind to Peyer's patch HEV, whereas approximately twice as many lymph node lymphocytes as Peyer's patch lymphocytes bind lymph node HEV (Butcher *et al.*, 1980), results reflecting the *in vivo* homing behavior of these populations (Griscelli *et al.*, 1969). In addition, B cells bind better to Peyer's patch HEV than to lymph node HEV, whereas T cells bind peripheral node HEV better than Peyer's patch HEV, these results again reflecting their *in vivo* homing properties and tissue distribution (Stevens *et al.*, 1982). The distributions of T cell subsets in different peripheral lymphoid organs is also reflected by their HEV adherence properties. In short-term *in vivo* homing experiments, Lyt-2 T cells from peripheral blood localized approximately 1.5 times as well as Lyt-2^+ T cells in Peyer's patches, whereas both populations localized equally well in peripheral nodes (Kraal *et al.*, 1982). In the HEV binding assay, the Lyt-2^- cells bound Peyer's patch HEV considerably better than did Lyt-2^+ T cells. These homing and HEV recognition properties reflect the distribution of these T cell subsets *in vivo*: mucosal lymphoid organs such as the Peyer's patches are enriched, relative to the nonmucosal peripheral nodes, in Lyt-2^- T cells relative to Lyt-2^+ T cells. The specific lymphocyte–HEV interactions measured in the HEV assay are therefore likely to be important in the establishment of the patterns of recirculatory behavior observed *in vivo*.

The HEV assay has also been used to examine the specificity of lymphoma–endothelial cell interactions. A series of spontaneous AKR/Cum thymic lymphomas was characterized by the HEV assay, and four different binding patterns emerged (Butcher *et al.*, 1980; Butcher and Weissman, 1980). Some tumors were incapable of binding to HEV at all; some bound only Peyer's patch HEV but not peripheral node HEV; some bound peripheral node HEV but not Peyer's patch HEV; and some bound to both HEV types. There must therefore be at least two different lymphocyte homing receptors, one specific for peripheral node HEV and the other specific for Peyer's patch HEV. Both Peyer's patch and peripheral node-specific tumors bound to mesenteric node HEV: mesenteric node HEV must therefore bear the biding determinants found on Peyer's patch HEV as well as those found on peripheral node HEV (Butcher *et al.*, 1980).

C. Mouse Lymphocyte Homing Receptors

The existence of cell lines with known HEV-binding properties was exploited to study lymphocyte homing at the molecular level. A peripheral node-specific B cell lymphoma, 38C-13, was used to immunize a Fischer rat, and the rat's spleen was fused with the SP20 mouse myeloma to generate hybridomas (Gallatin *et al.*, 1983). The supernatants of these hybridomas were tested by immunofluorescence for reactivity with the surfaces of 38C-13 and of normal lymphocytes and for the absence of reactivity with two non-binding cell lines, RAW112 and EL4. Antibodies from one hybridoma, MEL-14, upon further testing, showed a pattern of reactivity with cell lines capable of binding peripheral node HEV and an absence of reactivity with cells incapable of binding peripheral node HEV.

When 38C-13 cells were incubated with saturating amounts of MEL-14, washed, and then tested in the HEV assay, their ability to bind to peripheral node HEV was almost completely blocked. The same was true for normal mesenteric node lymphocytes; however, their ability to bind to Peyer's patch HEV was essentially unaffected by this treatment. When mesenteric node lymphocytes were pretreated with MEL-14 and then injected intravenously into a syngeneic mouse, their entry into peripheral nodes was sharply reduced, but their homing to Peyer's patches was only modestly affected, perhaps by Fc-mediated effects. Thus, the molecule recognized by the MEL-14 antibody is necessary both for peripheral node HEV binding *in vitro* and for lymphocyte homing to peripheral nodes *in vivo*.

The expression of the MEL-14 determinant by lymphocytes changes during development. In the thymus, only 3–6% of the thymocytes are MEL-14^{hi} (Reichert *et al.*, 1984, 1986). These cortically located cells are predominantly of mature phenotype and represent a major source of thymic emigrants. A high proportion of mature T and B cells in peripheral blood and lymphoid organs express high levels of the MEL-14 antigen. Antigen-activated lymphocytes, both *in vitro* and *in vivo*, lose the ability to home and to bind HEV and also lose high levels of MEL-14 expression (Reichert *et al.*, 1983; Dailey *et al.*, 1985). High levels of MEL-14 expression are thus characteristic of mature, recirculation-competent, unstimulated lymphocytes.

The lymphocyte cell-surface molecule recognized by the MEL-14 antibody has a number of interesting features. MEL-14 immunoprecipitates a cell-surface glycoprotein of approximately 90,000 molecular weight under nonreducing conditions (Gallatin *et al.*, 1983). Under reducing conditions, the electrophoretic mobility of this molecule decreases, a finding suggesting that it contains multiple intrachain disulfide bonds, although this anomalous behavior may depend on other posttranslational modifications of this molecule (see later). Endo F digestion reduces the size of the isolated glycoprotein to approximately 55 kDa in at least three separate digestion steps (Siegelman *et al.*, 1986). Thus, the molecule is heavily glycosylated.

The MEL-14 antibody was used to screen a λgt11 expression vector cDNA library constructed using mRNA from the 38C-13 cell line (St. John *et al.*, 1986). Surprisingly, only clones encoding the highly conserved ubiquitin molecule were obtained from this screen. Amino-terminal protein sequencing of the 90-kDa glycoprotein immunoprecipitated by MEL-14 revealed the presence of not one but two different amino termini on the molecule (Siegelman *et al.*, 1986). One of these amino-terminal sequences exactly matched the ubiquitin protein sequence; the other represents a previously unsequenced protein. There is a precedent for such an arrangement: ubiquitin has been found to be covalently linked to histone 2A(H2A) through an isopeptide bond between its carboxyl terminus and an ε-amino group of a lysine residue of H2A (Goldknopf and Busch, 1977). The glycoprotein immunoprecipitated by MEL-14 therefore consists of a core polypeptide modified by glycosylation and ubiquitination.

The MEL-14 antibody probably recognizes an epitope formed by ubiquitination of the core polypeptide, as it does not react with native ubiquitin (St. John *et al.*, 1986). In addition, MEL-14 did not detect every ubiquitin-encoding cDNA clone in the gt11 library, a result suggesting that only certain ubiquitin–galactosidase fusion proteins can present the MEL-14 epitope in a library screen. MEL-14 does, however, react with a peptide containing the carboxyl terminus of ubiquitin (amino acids 64–76), albeit less avidly. This peptide corresponds not only to the conjugation site of ubiquitin with H2A but also to a portion of the otherwise compactly organized ubiquitin molecule that is relatively free to move (Vijay-Kumar *et al.*, 1985).

The mouse peripheral node lymphocyte homing receptor, presumably the 90-kDa molecule recognized by MEL-14, is a lectin (Stoolman *et al.*, 1984). Mannose 6-phosphate, and to a lesser extent, L-fucose and D-mannose, specifically inhibit the binding of lymphocytes to peripheral node HEV. MEL-14 specifically blocks the ability of lymphocytes to bind to microspheres derivatized with mannans including mannose 6-phosphate (Yednock *et al.*, 1985). Treatment of cryostat sections with sialidase prior to the HEV assay prevents the binding of normal lymphocytes to peripheral node but not to Peyer's patch HEV (Rosen *et al.*, 1985).

An immunization protocol similar to that used to generate the MEL-14 monoclonal antibody has been used to generate hybridomas against a Peyer's patch binding T lymphoma, TK-1; several hybridomas (Bill 1–4) produce supernatant antibodies that are specific for Peyer's patch binding cells and specifically, although so far only partially, block the adherence of lymphocytes to Peyer's patch HEV (B. T. Sher, unpublished observations). Characterization of these antibodies is in progress.

D. Human Lymphocyte Homing Receptors

The HEV assay system has also been used with human lymphocytes (Jalkanen *et al.*, 1986a; Jalkanen and Butcher, 1985). A series of *in vitro* B lymphoblastoid lines and neoplastic human cell lines has been used to demonstrate the existence of separate lymphocyte homing receptors for peripheral node and mucosal HEV (Jalkanen *et al.*, 1986a). In addition, a monoclonal antibody, Hermes-1, has been demonstrated to stain all of the neoplastic cell lines that bind to either type of HEV as well as to stain normal lymphocytes (Jalkanen *et al.*, 1986c). Although this monoclonal antibody fails to block adhesion to either peripheral node HEV or to mucosal HEV in the HEV assay, an antiserum directed agaist the material immunoprecipitated by Hermes-1 blocks binding to both HEV types, an observation suggesting that in humans the peripheral node and mucosallymphocyte homing receptors share common antigenic determinants. In immunohistological studies, Hermes-1 stains lymphocytes in T cell and B cell areas of tonsils, adenoids, and lymph nodes. It fails to stain germinal center cells strongly but stains the majority of peripheral blood lymphocytes. It stains roughly 15% of thymocytes, mostly medullary cells but also some scattered cortical cells.

Hermes-1 immunoprecipitates a 90-kDa molecule from human cells that has precisely the same mass as that of the MEL-14-reactive glycoprotein on normal mouse lymphocytes (Jalkanen *et al.*, 1986c; W. M. Gallatin, unpublished observations). In addition, MEL-14 weakly cross-reacts with Hermes-1 on human material (Jalkanen *et al.*, 1986a); and when included in the HEV assay, it blocks the adhesion of human lymphocytes to peripheral node but not to appendix HEV (Jalkanen *et al.*, 1987). It appears, therefore, that the molecules recognized by the MEL-14 antibody in mice are related to those recognized by the Hermes-1 antibody in humans.

E. Rat Lymphocyte Homing Receptors

There is also evidence for distinct lymphocyte homing receptors for peripheral nodes and Peyer's patches in the rat. A soluble factor from thoracic duct lymph, HEBF, when applied to cryostat sections, blocks the binding of lymphocytes to peripheral node HEV but not to Peyer's patch HEV (Chin *et al.*, 1980a,b). HEBF was used to immunize a BALB/c/J mouse for the generation of monoclonal antibodies (Rasmussen *et al.*, 1985). One of these monoclonal antibodies, A.11, was found to block the adherence of lymphocytes to peripheral node HEV but not to Peyer's patch HEV *in vitro*. The A.11 antibody stained the surfaces of 50–60% of thoracic duct lymphocytes, 35–45% of lymph node cells, 52–55% of Peyer's patch lymphoid cells, 35—45% of splenocytes, 2–10% of thymocytes, and 1–10% of bone marrow cells. The A.11 antibody immunoprecipitates under nonreducing conditions four different protein species with molecular weights of approximately 200,000, 135,000, 63,000, and 40,000. Under reducing conditions, these bands reduce to bands of 135,000, 63,000, and 40,000.

Similarly, a second soluble factor from thoracic duct lymph, $HEBF_{pp}$, which blocks the adherence of lymphocytes to Peyer's patch but not to peripheral node HEV (Chin *et al.*, 1984), was used to immunize mice to generate monoclonal antibodies (Chin *et al.*, 1986). The monoclonal antibody 1B2 was isolated and shown to block specifically the adherence of lymphocytes to Peyer's patch but not to peripheral node HEV *in vitro*. This antibody stains 55–56% of thoracid duct lymphocytes, 45–50% of lymph node lymphocytes, 50–60% of Peyer's patch lymphocytes, 48–53% of splenic lymphocytes, 5–10% of thymocytes, and 2–8% of bone marrow cells. The 1B.2 antibody precipitates an 80-kDa protein from the surface of rat thoracic duct lymphocytes whose size does not change upon reduction.

The rat system differs from the mouse and human systems in several respects. First, multiple, non-90-kDa proteins are immunoprecipitated by the A.11 antibody, and an 80-kDa protein is precipitated by the 1B.2 antibody. Thus, the molecular similarity between a human glycoprotein and the mouse glycoprotein recognized by MEL-14 is not obviously shared by the rat proteins so far demonstrated to be involved in lymphocyte binding to either peripheral node or Peyer's patch HEV. Second, in the human system, the putative lymphocyte homing receptor molecules appear to be very cloely related to each other, as they appear to be the same size and to share serological determinants, whereas this is not obviously true for the rat system. At the molecular level, therefore, comparisons between the moieties identifed as being important in the binding of lymphocytes to HEV in mice, humans, and rats make it clear that the lymphocyte homing receptor system may be molecularly complex. It is possible that each homing receptor is a multimolecular complex and that the different classes of molecules immunoprecipitated reflect the particular specificity of the monoclonal antibody used rather than any fundamental difference in the components of the complex between species.

F. Other Potential Lymphocyte Homing Receptors

In addition to the peripheral node and Peyer's patch lymphocyte homing receptors, other homing receptors are almost certainly expressed by lymphocytes. Migration phenomena involved in normal lymphocyte development suggest the existence of at least two additional lymphocyte homing receptors. Blood-borne lymphocyte precursors enter the bone marrow and the thymus at particluar stages in development (Lepault and Weissman, 1981; LeDouarin, 1984; Ford *et al.*, 1966; Metcalf and Moore, 1971; Weissman *et al.*, 1978). This seeding process, at least in thymus, has been proposed to involve the interaction of the precursor cells with the vascular endothelium of the fetal thymus (Champion *et al.*, 1986), a process that could easily involve a thymus-specific lymphocyte homing receptor. A similar bone marrow-specific lymphocyte homing receptor could also exist.

Another process that could be mediated by a specific homing receptor is the migrration of $sIgA^+$ lymphoblasts into the lamina propria of the gut. These lymphoblasts arise in the Peyer's patches and mesenteric node and travel by way of the thoracic duct lymph into the bloodstream, from which they enter the gut lamina propria (Gowans and Knight, 1964; Griscelli *et al.*, 1969; Craig and Cebra, 1971; Guy-Grand *et al.*, 1974; Pierce and Gowans, 1975; Cebra *et al.*, 1977; McWilliams *et al.*, 1977). This process could conceivably require a lamina propria endothelium-specific lymphocyte homing receptor.

Another potentially unique homing receptor could be involved in the traffic of lymphocytes to skin. Several clinical syndromes, including the Sezary syndrome and mycosis fungoides, which have been classified as subtypes of cutaneous T cell lymphoma, involve the presence of large numbers of neoplastic T cells in skin (Bunn, *et al.*, 1981; Wood *et al.*, 1982; Chu *et al.*, 1984). In the Sezary syndrome there is evidence from cell labeling studies that Sezary cells proliferate extensively in the skin and in lymph nodes but do not proliferate actively in the blood (Bunn *et al.*, 1981). Short-term homing studies with malignant cutaneous T lymphoma cells reveal their propensity to relocalize to the skin following intravenous injection (Miller *et al.*, 1980). These studies further suggest that circulating Sezary cells originate in extracutaneous sites and that they then enter the skin.

In addition to the evidence from these clinical conditions, a series of experiments in mice suggests the existence of homing receptors for skin (Daynes *et al.*, 1985; Spangrude *et al.*, 1985). Pertussis toxin has been shown to inhibit homing receptor-mediated lymphocyte entry into peripheral lymph nodes (Spangrude *et al.*, 1984). When lymphocytes previously primed with the contact hypersensitivity-inducing agent DNFB are treated with pertussis toxin, transferred into the bloodstream of a syngeneic animal, and then challenged with the same antigen, they fail to enter the skin upon which the antigen was applied (Spangrude *et al.*, 1985). The inhibition of contact hypersensitivity in this system is specific for lymphocyte extravasation, as the treated cells can produce an immune response against DNFB when injected directly into the skin upon which the antigen was applied. The similarity between the inhibition of lymphocyte entry into lymph nodes and into skin suggests that lymphocyte entry into skin may be a homing receptor-mediated event.

A final process that may involve additional lymphocyte homing receptors is inflammation. A subset of blood-borne lymphocytes enters sites of inflammation by first adhering to the endothelia of capillaries adjoining the inflammatory site in a process known as margination and then by passing through those blood vessel walls into the inflamed tissue (reviewed in Coldits, 1985). Lymphokines released by activated lymphoid and myelomonocytic cells during inflammatory responses, including γ-interferon and interleukin 1, have been shown to increase the ability of cultured endothelial cells to be bound by normal, untreated B and T cells (Cavender *et al.*, 1986). This change in the endothelial cell that permits higher levels of lymphocyte binding is reminiscent of the effect of an ongoing immune response upon lymph node HEV endothelial cells; the HEV bind lymphocytes better than do HEV in nonstimulated lymph nodes, but the types of lymphocytes bound are not different from the lymphocytes bound by unstimulated HEV (Kraal and Twisk, 1984). Lymphokines have also been shown to enhance expression of Class II molecules by endothelial cells and, therefore, perhaps to increase their ability to present specific antigen to circulating T and B cells (Pober *et al.*, 1984). Perhaps these lymphokines also increase the levels of an endothelial ligand for a lymphocyte homing receptor specific for that type of endothelium and thus facilitate entry of "activated" B and T cells irrespective of antigen reactivity from the blood. In fact, in the mouse most antigen- or mitogen-activated T and B cell lymphoblasts rapidly lose receptors enabling them to bind to either lymph node or Peyer's patch HEV; and they also become MEL-14-negative (Reichert *et al.*, 1983; Kraal *et al.*, 1982; Butcher *et al.*, 1982). These cells can be immunohistochemically localized mainly to (antigen-dependent) germinal centers in lymphoid tissues, and most isolated germinal center cells neither bind or home to lymphoid organ HEV (Reichert *et al.*, 1983). All murine T cell clones isolated to date also lack MEL-14 determinants and homing receptors for lymphoid organ HEV; and when released into the bloodstream, they fail to home to lymphoid organs but collect in large numbers in lung and liver (Dailey *et al.*, 1982a, 1985). This population of cells are therefore unlikely and in one case has been shown to be unable (Dailey *et al.*, 1982a)—to localize to sites of lymphoid organ metastasis for *in vivo* adoptive immunotherapy; but they might well respond locally to hematogenous metastasis in lung and liver, as described in some human adoptive immunotherapy trials (Rosenberg *et al.*, 1986). We have elsewhere proposed (Gallatin *et al.*, 1986; Weissman, 1987) that loss of lymphoid organ HEV specific homing receptors might allow antigen-activated lymphoblasts released into the bloodstream to home specifically to sites of local inflammatory endothelia without (unwanted) removal by high avidity interactions (Bjerknes *et al.*, 1986) with each lymphoid organ HEV they pass.

An interesting candidate for an inflammation-specific homing receptor is the lymphocyte cell adhesion molecule LFA-1, a member of the fibronectin family of cell surface adhesive proteins (for review, see Springer *et al.*, 1987; Hynes, 1987). Antigen- or mitogen-activated lymphocytes markedly increase levels of surface LFA-1, whereas endothelia (and several other cells) markedly increase surface expression of the LFA-1 cognate ligand, ICAM-1 (Rothlein *et al.*, 1986), following induction with the inflammatory lymphokines IL-1 and TNF.

Site-specific entry of immune T cells has been observed even in the central nervous system, normally thought to be an immunologically privileged compartment. It is possible to transfer cloned T cells that are specific for myelin basic protein ito syngeneic normal animals and induce experimental autoimmune encephalitis (Zamvil *et al.*, 1985). This process might involve the recognition of antigen by the T cells on the surfaces of brain endothelial cells, but more likely it represents homing by lymphocyte subsets that express homing receptors for specific CNS endothelia. Brain endothelial cells would therefore express a ligand for a lymphocyte homing receptor.

In rheumatoid arthritis, endothelial structures resembling HEV are present in inflamed synovia (Jalkanen *et al.*, 1986b). MEL-14, which inhibits mouse and human lymphocyte binding to lymph node HEV, fails to inhibit binding to synovial HEV. Furthermore, synovial HEV fail to bind either a lymph node HEV-specific or a mucosal HEV-specific human cell line. Thus, HEV in inflamed joints are distinct from those in organized lymphoid tissues, a finding implying that a unique homing receptor system is involved in lymphocyte traffic to joints. Whether this system is joint-specific or is shared by other inflamed tissues remains to be determined.

There could be one (e.g., LFA-1) or more than one lymphocyte homing receptor involved in these inflammatory processes. If endothelia in different parts of the body each have distinct ligands for lymphocyte homing receptors, the potential number of lymphocyte homing receptors could be quite large.

IV. Lymphocyte Homing Receptors and Metastasis

A. Somatic Fusions of Nonmetastatic Tumors with Normal Lymphocytes

The ability of lymphocytes bearing homing receptors to leave the blood and enter surrounding tissues is strongly reminiscent of the ability of metastatic cells to do likewise. Metastatic cells that expressed lymphocyte homing receptors could, in theory, use this normal mechanism to enter any tissue that lymphocytes could enter. It is thus interesting to look at the metastatic behavior of tumors that express lymphocyte homing receptors. The products of fusion events between tumor cells and normal lymphocytes could be expected to bear homing receptors in some cases, and indeed, normal lymphocytes, when fused with nonmetastatic tumor cells, can confer metastatic capacity upon the resulting hybrids (DeBaetselier *et al.*, 1982, 1984; Larizza *et al.*, 1984a; Kamenov and Longenecker, 1984; Collard *et al.*,

1986). As an example, highly metastatic hybridomas were derived from an *in vitro* fusion between normal C57Bl/6 spleen cells and the nonmetastatic NSl plasmocytoma (DeBaetselier *et al.*, 1982). Various of these hybridomas demonstrated different metastatic capacities for spleen, liver, and lung, an observation suggesting that the normal fusion partners in each case had different migratory abilities. Such fusion events might occur spontaneously *in vivo* as well as artificially *in vitro*. For example, the BW-Li tumor line was derived from a rare metastatic liver nodule from a CBA mouse that had received an intravenous injection of cells of the AKR-derived BW tumor (DeBaetselier *et al.*, 1984). The BW tumor is not inherently invasive, whereas the BW-Li tumor infiltrates hepatocyte monolayers *in vitro*. BW-Li cells, unlike cells of the BW parental line, were found to bear CBA-derived T cell markers and to be capable of forming large liver metastases. This experiment was repeated with a semiallogeneic (CBA x AKR)-F_1 mouse, and again a metastatic cell line bearing CBA-derived markers—the BW-O-Li line—was derived from a rare tumor nodule in the liver.

In each of these cases it is clear that the metastatic variant acquired something that altered the previously nonmetastatic phenotype of the tumor cell parent line from the normmal lymphocyte partner. In each case, a good candidate for this normal factor could be a lymphocyte homing receptor (or receptors).

It has been suggested that the highly metastatic Esb variant of the Eb T cell lymphoma line (see Section II,E) was derived from a spontaneous fusion with a host macrophage (Larizza *et al.*, 1984a). The Esb line expresses the antigen Mac-1, which is not found on the Eb line. In addition, when Eb cells were fused with normal macrophages *in vitro*, highly metastatic hybridomas resulted. In this case, the normal cell partner was not a lymphocyte but a macrophage. Normal cells other than lymphocytes can express lymphocyte homing receptors, however; a subset of neutrophils, for example, can express the MEL-14 antigen (Lewinsohn *et al.*, 1986).

From these experiments it is clear that fusion of tumor cells with normal cells might occur spontaneously *in vivo* and result in enhanced metastatic capacity for the tumor. This process, which under some circumstances must involve the acquisition of lymphocyte homing receptors by the tumor, could be a major feature of tumor progression *in vivo*.

B. HEV Binding and Metastasis

Bargatze *et al.* (1987) have analyzed the metastatic behavior of a number of different lymphomas upon passage into syngeneic recipients. Lymphomas were selected on the basis of their HEV-binding phenotypes as defined in the HEV assay. Four different groups of tumors were studied: peripheral node binders, Peyer's patch binders, double binders, and nonbinders. Cells of each tumor type were injected intramuscularly into mice that had received

400 roentgens of whole-body irradiation 18–24 hr before passage. Recipients were sacrificed when they had developed obvious signs of lymphoma—either large palpable lymph nodes or a large mass at the site of injection. Tumor involvement of peripheral and mucosal lymphoid organs were assessed by weight and/or histology. A summary of the HEV binding of these tumors is shown in Table I. The HEV binding groups gave rise to gross enlargement of all of the lymph nodes assayed. Surprisingly, this included tumors initially assayed to be Peyer's patch HEV binders; these were later shown to contain MEL-14^{hi} revertants (Holzmann and Weissman, 1987, and see later). Nonbinding lymphomas alternatively grew as large tumors at the site of injection and were present in the lymph nodes draining this site but were not found in distant lymph nodes. All of the lymphomas tested had access to the bloodstream; both binders and nonbinders exhibited significant blood levels of tumor cells and gave rise to significant splenic enlargement and bone marrow involvement.

The apparent nonspecificity of metastasis by Peyer's patch-specific HEV binding lymphomas (TK1, TKJ43) to all of the lymph nodes tested could be explained in several ways. One possibility is that the binding capacities of the tumors in the HEV assay might not reflect true binding potential; tumors that appeared Peyer's patch-specific in the HEV assay might also have a very low level of the peripheral node lymphocyte homing receptor on their surfaces that would still be sufficient for a few cells to enter lymph nodes. It is also possible that binding is never absolutely specific or that homing receptor expression is merely one important component of a constellation of coregulated phenotypic features that determines the localization and growth of lymphomas. It should be pointed out, however, that (1) the Peyer's patch-specific lymphomas produced a preferential enlargement of the mesenteric lymph nodes compared with the lymph node-specific lymphomas (i.e., the ratio of weights of the mesenteric node, which contains HEV capable of binding mucosa-specific cells, to peripheral nodes was greater in the case of the mucosal HEV-specific lines); (2) the involvement of Peyer's patches by the peripheral node HEV-binding lymphoma BK37 was usually focal; and (3) only the Peyer's patch-preferring lymphomas TK1 and TKJ43 replaced the mucosal lamina propria. These observations suggest that HEV receptor specificity may play a quantitative role in determining organ metastases even in this experimental setting of rapid spread and growth of tumors following adoptive transfer.

Alternatively, as tumors passaged *in vivo* are highly heterogeneous and their heterogeneity increases with time (Nicolson, 1982a, 1984a,b; Nicolson and Custead, 1982; Nicolson and Poste, 1983), perhaps a few cells in the tumor population expressed relatively high levels of the opposite lymphocyte homing receptor specificity. As the metastatic behavior of the tumors was assayed in animals with advanced lymphomas, even if only a relatively small

TABLE I

MURINE LYMPHOMAS: HEV BINDING PHENOTYPE AND EXPRESSION OF MEL-14 ANTIGEN[a]

Cell line[a]	Strain of source	Cell type	Binding to HEV[b]: Peripheral lymph node	Binding to HEV[b]: Peyer's patches	Expression of MEL-14 antigen
Nonbinding lymphomas					
L1-2	C57L	Pre-B	–	–	–
RAW112	BALB/c	Pre-B	–	–	–
ABE 8.1/2	BALB/c	Pre-B	±	–	–
EL-4	C57BL	T cell	–	–	–
BW5147	AKR	T cell	–	–	–
TK2	AKR	T cell	–	–	–
TK5	AKR	T cell	–	–	–
TK52	AKR	T cell	–	–	–
HEV-binding lymphomas					
TK1	AKR	T cell	±	+++++	–
TK23	AKR	T cell	+	++	+++
TK40	AKR	T cell	±	+	±
TKJ43	AKR	T cell	+	++++	±
BK37	AKR	B cell	++	–	++++
38C13	C3H	B cell	++	–	+++
Control cells					
Normal	BALB/c	Lymph node cells	+	+	++

[a]Tumor cells lines used in these studies: L1-2, an Abelson virus-induced C57L lymphoma; RAW112, an Abelson virus-induced BALB/c lymphoma; ABE 8.1/2 (American Type Culture Collection), an Abelson virus-induced BALB/c lymphoma; EL-4, a chemical carcinogen-induced C57BL lymphoma; BW5147 (American Type Culture Collection), an AKR T cell lymphoma; 38C13, a C3H Ig surface-positive nonsecreting B cell lymphoma. TK2, TK5, TK52, TK1, TK23, TK40, spontaneous AKR/Cum T cell lymphomas; TKJ43, an AKR/J lymphoma; BK37, an AKR/Cum B cell lymphoma.

[b]Based on the value of the relative adherence ratio (RAR; see Section III,B) ± standard error.

number of metastatic lymphoma cells from a Peyer's patch HEV binding lymphoma initially entered a lymph node from the blood, their resulting growth in the (presumably) favorable environment of the lymph node could result in a considerable enlargement of the node. Furthermore, the levels of MEL-14 can be modulated by antibody selection *in vitro* (W. M. Gallatin, unpublished observations) and by developmental events *in vivo*, so the cells that seeded the peripheral nodes might very well have different MEL-14 antigen levels than their descendants in the fully developed metastases. In fact, as shown later, that appears to be the case for at least some lymphomas. The dramatic difference between the behavior of binders and nonbinders, however, makes it clear that the expression of lymphocyte homing receptors is important to the metastatic spread of these lymphomas.

The metastic behavior of one of the AKR/Cum spontaneous lymphomas, TK1.PP, has been examined kinetically (B. T. Sher, unpublished data). TK1.PP is an uncloned variant of TK1 (Butcher *et al.*, 1980) that was derived by multiple passages of TK1 through mice and selection of those cells found in Peyer's patches. TK1.PP retains TK1's ability to bind to Peyer's patch HEV but in addition has acquired heterogeneous expression of the MEL-14 antigen, as shown in Fig. 1. The time course of TK1.PP metastasis is shown in Fig. 2. At day 0, 8-week-old AKR/Cum mice were given 2.5×10^6 TK1.PP cells subcutaneously. The metastatic course of the tumor was followed by weight of the organs involved. Each time point represents data from a single mouse, whose sex is given below the time point. At the first time point, day 8, there is already obvious involvement of some of the organs observed, although the mouse appeared healthy externally. Mice did not appear ill, as evidenced by ruffled fur and grossly enlarged palpable lymph nodes, until day 14, at which time there was gross involvement of all lymphoid organs examined. By day 18, mice were moribund and the weights of Peyer's patches and peripheral nodes had not increased in several days. Two points emerge from this analysis. First it is dangerous to compare the weights of organs from mice that may be at different stages of tumor growth, as one would be simply relying on externally evident illness. Second, it is clear that TK1.PP metastasizes to every organ for which it bears lymphocyte homing receptors, and again, it is likely that the possession of these homing receptors influences this phenomenon.

C. MEL-14 AND METASTASIS

To circumvent these problems, the following experiments were performed. A MEL-14-negative population of TK1.PP lymphoma cells was isolated with a fluorescence-activated cell sorter and then reinjected into nonirradiated syngeneic recipients. Despite this selection, large lymph node metastases again developed (B. Holzmann and I. L. Weissman, unpublished data). However, it was found that metastatic lymphoma cells had reverted

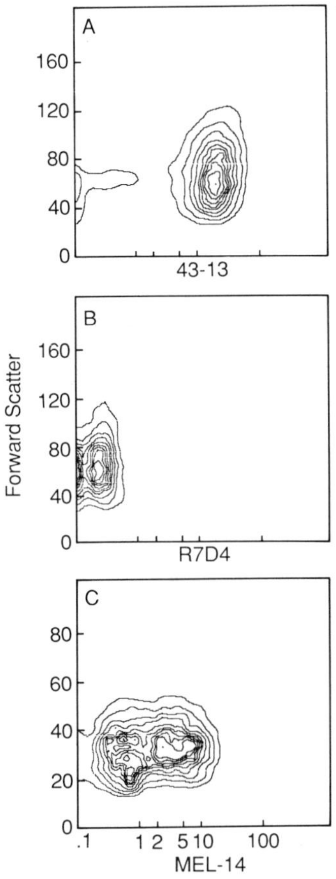

FIG. 1. Staining with MEL-14, R7D4, and 43-13. TK1.PP cells were isolated from peripheral lymph nodes of an AKR/Cum mouse with externally evident lymphoma. A. 43-13 staining reveals that <99% of the cells in this preparation are tumor cells, as the 43-13 antibody is specific for the glycosylated *gag* membrane protein of the AKR/Cum lymphoma virus (Pillemer *et al.*, 1986). B. R7D4 is an isotype-matched negative control for MEL-14, and its staining of the same cells is shown here. C. MEL-14 clearly stains a subpopulation of TK1.PP cells, although the levels of staining are heterogeneous.

to a MEL-14-positive phenotype. Interestingly, a higher proportion of lymph node metastatic cells were MEL-14^{hi} than were Peyer's patch metastatic cells (Fig. 3). A different spontaneous AKR/Cum lymphoma (TK40) gave rise to both locally growing and metastatic tumors when injected subcutaneously. Whereas MEL-14 staining was close to background levels in locally growing tumors, the lymph node metastases were strongly enriched for MEL-14-positive cells (Fig. 4). Moreover, a subline of TK40 selected for

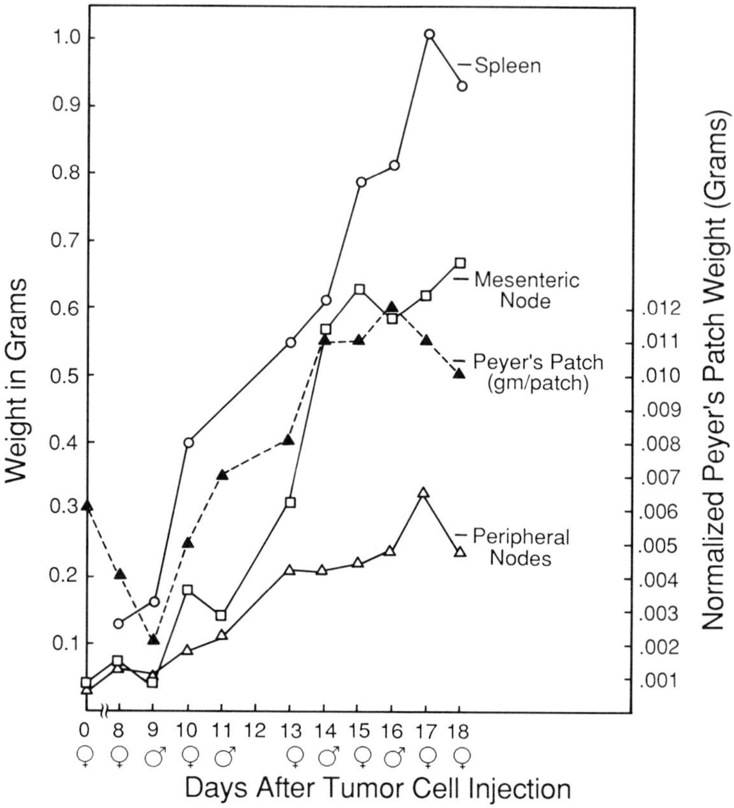

FIG. 2. Time course of TK1.PP metastasis. At day 0, 8-week-old AKR/Cum mice were given a 2.5×10^6 TK1.PP cells. Weights of organs from one mouse per time point were subsequently determined. The sex of the mouse is given next to the time scale.

its high metastatic capacity showed a high expression of the MEL-14 surface antigen. These data are consistent with the hypothesis that the MEL-14-defined homing receptor can also function as a mediator of lymphoma metastasis. It should be apparent from these experiments that the tested MEL-14-negative PP-binding T lymphomas undergo a high rate of variation to the MEL-14^{hi} phenotype and to lymph node metastases. Whether this represents a heritable genetic event (mutation) with a high frequency or some microenvironmentally defined event(s) of differential gene expression has not been determined. It is of interest that a similar high rate of variation in the ability of a murine sarcoma (KHT) to form pulmonary metastases has been reported and has led to a model of "dynamic heterogeneity" of unstable mutations relating to metastasis among clonal tumor lines (Harris *et al.*, 1982).

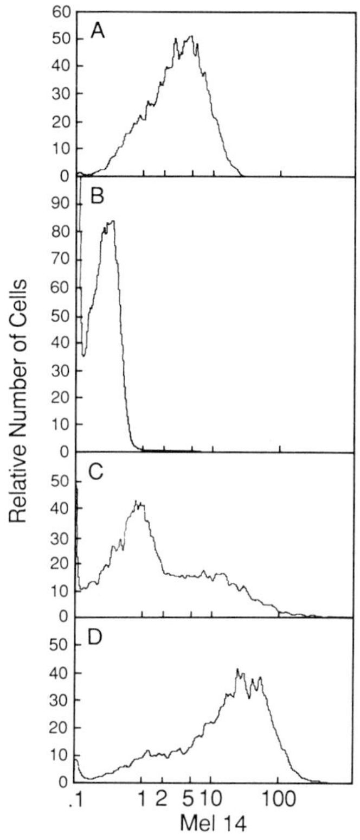

FIG. 3. MEL-14 levels reflect the propensity for lymph node metastases by the dual HEV binding AKR lymphoma, TK1. TK1 tumor cells were isolated from a mesenteric node metastasis and stained with MEL-14. A. FACS profile of this population; values on the x-axis ≥ 10 units usually correlate with lymph node HEV binding. B. MEL-14-negative population used for passage (5×10^4 to each recipient). C, D. MEL-14 staining profiles of a Peyer's patch metastasis (C) and a peripheral lymph node metastasis (D) from one of those recipients, and was typical of all recipients. The lymph node metastases regularly contained a higher proportion of MEL-14^{hi} metastic cells than did the Peyer's patches. R7D4 controls were uniformly below 2 FACS units.

In an attempt to establish further the significance of the peripheral lymph node homing receptor in both *in vitro* binding of murine lymphoma cells to HEV and in short- and long-term *in vivo* tumor behavior, tumor variants of the spontaneous AKR/thymic lymphomas were selected for "high" or "low" expression of the MEL-14 antigen by clonal selection with the fluorescence activated cell sorter (FACS). Although many of the "low" and 'high" cloned variant lines were quite unstable with respect to their MEL-14 phenotype, a few more stable lines continued to differ by greater than one

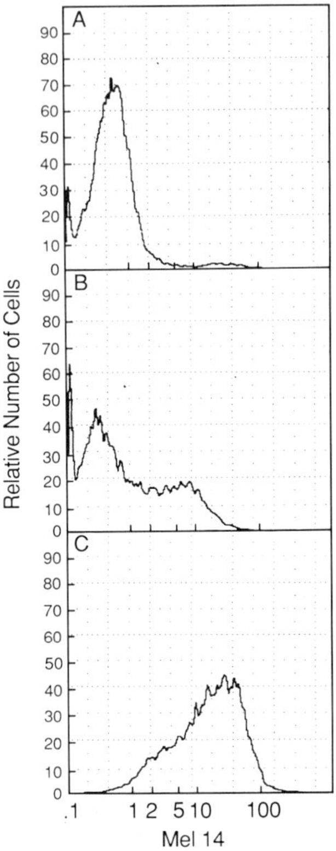

FIG. 4. MEL-14 expression by local tumors and lymph node metastases of the AKR lymphoma TK40. A. The MEL-14 staining of the subcutaneous tumor shows very few cells with significant staining. B. The MEL-14 staining of another passage of TK40 selected for high metastatic potential to lymph nodes. C. The MEL-14 staining of a lymph node metastasis from a mouse injected with the tumor shown in B. The isotype matched control, RA3-6B2, gave tumor cell fluorescence of ≤ 2 FACS units in all 3 cases.

log in degree of modal fluorescence when stained with the MEL-14 antibody. As would be predicted from their lower MEL-14 phenotype, the "low" lines bound almost ten times less well to HEV on frozen sections of lymph nodes than their "high" counterparts. These "low" variants showed a quantitatively similar decrease in the amount of radiolabeled antigen precipitated by the MEL-14 antibody. The antigen was not absent, however, in keeping with the low but definite MEL-14 reactivity and HEV binding. No gross modification of the glycoprotein was evident in these one-dimensional polyacrylamide gel electrophoretic (PAGE) analyses, although minor alterations yielding a nonfunctional form lacking the MEL-14 epitope would not be resolved by these methods. No striking differences in expression of $gp90^{MEL\text{-}14}$ within the phases of the cell cycle were seen between the "high" and "low" variants.

They did not differ with respect to other T cell differentiation antigens (T200, L3T4, and Lyt-2). As these tumor variants were selected (from a clonal tumor line) to differ *only* in MEL-14 phenotype and do not differ in any other demonstrable way, this direct correlation between MEL-14 phenotype and peripheral node HEV binding is perhaps the strongest evidence yet that the glycoprotein recognized by the MEL-14 antibody mediates the binding of malignant derivatives of lymphocyte precursors to lymph node HEV.

Preliminary studies of short-term dissemination of murine lymphoma cells suggest that the presence of $gp90^{MEL\text{-}14}$ is important in at least the early localization of lymphoma cells to peripheral lymph nodes. In these experiments, fluorescein labeled tumor variants were injected intravenously into syngeneic mice, and 24 hr later cell suspensions of peripheral lymph nodes and spleen underwent two-color FACS analysis to determine tumor localization and MEL-14 phenotype. In this study, a variant line that actually had a bimodal distribution of MEL-14 phenotype (i.e., 50% "low," 50% "high" secondary to phenotypic drift) was used. Whereas the tumor cells present in the spleen had the same bimodal distribution of MEL-14 phenotype as the injected population, every tumor cell analyzed in the peripheral nodes was $MEL\text{-}14^{hi}$ (Matthews *et al.*, 1987). This finding strongly suggests that the peripheral node lymphocyte homing receptor on these lymphoma cells at least facilitates, and may even be required for, entry of such tumor cells into the parenchyma of peripheral lymph nodes. Attempts thus far to correlate this short-term homing with long-term patterns of metastatic growth of lymphoma have not confirmed a difference in peripheral node tumor between "high" and "low" variants; this negative outcome may be due to the presence of enough "high" cells in the "low" variant line to prevent detection of a significant difference from the "high" line, and/or to other factors influencing the growth of tumor cells once they have located in the node. Although the presence or absence of the peripheral node lymphocyte homing receptor is very likely one determinant of lymphoma dissemination to lymph nodes, other elements in the multistep process of metastasis must also contribute to the ultimate successful localization and growth of such cells at these sites.

D. Hermes-1 and Metastasis

Preliminary studies of a random selection of non-Hodgkin's lymphoma patients revealed a general correlation between the extent of involvement of multiple lymph node groups and immunohistological staining with Hermes-1 (Jalkanen *et al.*, 1987). These preliminary analyses, however, included multiple morphological classifications of lymphomas. To determine whether Hermes-1 antigen expression provided an independent predictor of lymphoma/leukemia spread to lymph nodes via the blood, additional studies were carried out comparing the clinical presentation of Hermes-1$^+$ *versus* Hermes-1$^-$ lymphomas within morphologically uniform cases. For this purpose, we selected diffuse histiocytic lymphomas and common acute lymphoblastic leukemias, two relatively common and fairly homogeneous types of lymphoid neoplasms that displayed a reasonable frequency of Hermes-1$^-$ and Hermes-1$^+$ cases. Within each of these classifications, studies to date allow the followig generalizations: (1) All neoplasms producing generalized adenophathy, with involvement of all lymph node groups in a more or less symmetric pattern, have been Hermes-1^{hi}. (2) Lymph node involvement of Hermes-1$^-$ lymphomas and leukemias is often absent, localized, or explainable by local contiguous spread and is always asymmetric and never generalized. (3) A significant population of both diffuse histiocytic lymphomas and common acute leukemias are Hermes-1$^+$, yet fail to produce generalized adenopathy and behave as if lacking functional homing properties. This latter population is particularly prominent in diffuse histiocytic lymphomas, in which only 5/57 cases displayed truly generalized adenopathy, but 41/57 cases were Hermes$-$1$^+$ (Picker *et al.*, 1987). The results indicate that Hermes-1 antigen expression is probably necessary but certainly not sufficient for efficient, population-based blood-borne homing to lymph nodes.

The lack of direct correspondence between Hermes-1 positivity and lymph node dissemination in many neoplasms may reflect a quantitative discordance between antigen positivity and functional HEV binding ability: In studies of mouse and human cell lines, there is an excellent qualitative correspondence between the ability to bind detectably to HEV and expression of homing receptor antigens, but many cell lines bearing substantial levels of antigen bind poorly. In quantitative analyses, Hermes-1$^+$ lymphomas displaying poor functional binding ability would not be expected to produce generalized adenopathy. It is also possible that some cases immunohistologically assessed as positive express cytoplasmic but not surface antigen. Finally, because Hermes-1 appears to define a common determinant present on gp85–95 involved in multiple tissue-specific endothelial recognition events, some or many positive lymphomas may express members of this putative homing receptor family that are specific for endothelial cell determinants not present in organized lymph nodes and mucosal lymphoid tissues. Additional studies at the functional level will be required to determine precisely the relationship between HEV-binding ability and lymphoma/leukemia metastasis in humans.

V. Summary and Conclusions

As discussed in the preceding sections, there are several indications that the lymphocyte homing receptors involved in the normal process of lymphocyte recirculation are also relevant to the behavior of metastatic cells.

Cell fusion experiments indicate that previously nonmetastatic cells can acquire metastatic capacity from fusion with normal lymphocytes. Murine T lymphomas that bear high levels of functional homing receptors can metastasize to peripheral lymphoid organs, whereas those lymphomas lacking homing receptors cannot. Virtually all lymph node metastases of lymphomas contain a high proportion of MEL-14^{hi} cells, even if the primary tumor has been selected to be relatively deficient in these cells. Further investigations of the biology of lymphocyte homing receptors will reveal whether or not there are additional lymphocyte homing receptors and will clarify the role of lymphocyte homing receptors in metastasis. Antibodies against these lymphocyte homing receptors could therefore be useful for diagnosis and treatment of metastatic disease.

References

Alby, L., and Auerbach, R. (1984). *Proc. Natl. Acad. Sci. U.S.A.* **84**, 5739–5743.

Auerbach, R., Alby, L., Morrisey, L. W., Tu, M., and Joseph, J. (1985). *Microvasc. Res.* **29**, 401–411.

Bargatze, R. F., Wu, N. W., Weissman, I. L., and Butcher, E. C. (1987). *J. Exp. Med.* **166**, 1125–1131.

Barnett, S. C., and Eccles, S. A. (1984). *Clin. Exp. Metastasis* **2**, 297–310.

Bjerknes, M., Cheng, M., and Ottaway, C. A. (1986). *Science* **231**, 402–404.

Brackenbury, R. (1985). *Cancer Metastasis Rev.* **4**, 41–58.

Bunn, P. A., Edelson, R., Ford, S. S., and Shackney, S. E. (1981). *Blood* **57**, 452–563.

Butcher, E. C., and Weissman, I. L. (1980). *Ciba Found. Symp.* **71**, 265–586.

Butcher, E. C., Scollay, R. G., and Weissman, I. L. (1979). *J. Immunol.* **123**, 1996–2003.

Butcher, E. C., Scollay, R. G., and Weissman, I. L. (1980). *Eur. J. Immunol.* **10**, 556–561.

Butcher, E. C., Rouse, R. V., Coffman, R. L., Nottenburg, C. N., Hardy, R. R., and Weissman, I. L. (1982). *J. Immunol.* **129**, 2698.

Butcher, E. C., Lewinsohn, D., Duijvestijn, A., Bargatze, R., Wu, N., and Jalkanen, S. (1986). *J. Cell Biochem.* **30**, 121–131.

Campbell, F. R. (1983). *Anat. Record* **297**, 643–652.

Cavender, D. E., Haskard, D. O., Joseph, B., and Ziff, M. (1986). *J. Immunol.* **136**, 203–207.

Cebra, J. J., Gearhart, P. F., Kamat, R., Robertson, S. M., and Tseng, J. (1977). *Cold Spring Harbor Symp. Quant. Biol.* **41**, 201–215.

Champion, S., Imhof, B. A., Savagner, P., and Thiery, J. P. (1986). *Cell* **44**, 781–790.

Cheinsong-Popov, R., Robinson, P., Altevogt, P., and Schirrmacher, V. (1983). *Int. J. Cancer* **32**, 359–360.

Chin, Y.-H., Carey, G. D., and Woodruff, J. J. (1980a). *J. Immunol.* **125**, 1764–1769.

Chin, Y.-H., Carey, G. D., and Woodruff, J. J. (1980b). *J. Immunol.* **125**, 1770–1774.

Chin, Y.-H., Rasmussen, R., Cakiroglu, A. G., and Woodruff, J. J. (1984). *J. Immunol.* **133**, 2961–2965.

Chin, Y.-H., Rasmussen, R. A., Woodruff, J. J., and Easton, T. G. (1986). *J. Immunol.* **136**, 2556–2561.

Chu, A., Patterson, J., Berger, C., Vonderheid, E., and Edelson, R. (1984). *Cancer* **54**, 2414–2422.

Colditz, I. G. (1985). *Surv. Synth. Pathol. Res.* **4**, 44–68.

Collard, J. G., Schijven, J. F., Bikker, A., LaRiviere, G., Bolscher, J. G. M., and Roos, E. (1986). *Cancer Res.* **46**, 3521–3527.

Craig, S. W., and Cebra, J. J. (1971). *J. Exp. Med.* **134**, 188–200.

Dailey, M. O., Fathman, C. G., Butcher, E., Pillemer, E., and Weissman, I. (1982a). *J. Immunol.* **128**, 2134.

Dailey, M. O., Pillemer, E., and Weissman, I. L. (1982b). *Proc. Natl. Acad. Sci. U.S.A.* **79**, 5384.

Dailey, M. O., Gallatin, W. M., and Weissman, I. L. (1985). *J. Mol. Cell Immunol.* **2**, 27–36.

Daynes, R. A., Spangrude, G. J., Roberts, L. K., and Krueger, G. G. (1985). *J. Invest. Dermatol.* **85**, 14s–20s.

DeBaetselier, P., Gorelik, E., Eshhar, A., Ron, Y., Katsav, S., Feldman, M., and Segal, S. (1982). *Adv. Exp. Med. Biol.* **149**, 179–185.

DeBaetselier, P., Roos, E., Brys, L., Remels, L., and Feldman, M. (1984). *Int. J. Cancer* **34**, 731–738.

Dennis, J. W. (1985). *J. Natl. Cancer Inst.* **74**, 1111–119.

Ford, C. E., Micklem, H. S., Evans, H. P., Gray, J. G., and Ogden, D. A. (1966). *Ann. N.Y. Acad. Sci.* **129**, 283–295.

Ford, W. L. (1975). *Prog. Allergy* **19**, 1–59.

Gallatin, W. M., Weissman, I. L., and Butcher, E. C. (1983). *Nature (London)* **304**, 30–34.

Gallatin, W. M., St. John, T. P., Siegelman, M., Reichert, R., Butcher, E. C., and Weissman, I. L. (1986). *Cell* 44, 673.

Goldknopf, I. L., and Busch, H. (1977). *Proc. Natl. Acad. Sci. U.S.A.* **74**, 864–868.

Gowans, J. L., and Knight, E. J. (1964). *Philos. Trans R. Soc. London Ser. B*159 257–282.

Griscelli, C., Vassali, P., and McCluskey, R. T. (1969). *J. Exp. Med.* **130**, 1427–1451.

Gunji, Y., and Taniguchi, M. (1986). *Japn. J. Cancer Res.* **77**, 595–601.

Gutman, C., and Weissman, I. (1973). *Transplantation* **16**, 621.

Guy-Grand, D., Griscelli, C., and Vassali, P. (1974). *Eur. J. Immunol.* **4**, 435–443.

Guy-Grand, D., Griscelli, C., and Vassali, P. (1978). *J. Exp. Med.* **148**, 1661–1677.

Harris, J. F., Chambers, A. F., Hall, R. P., and Lang, V. (1982). *Proc. Natl. Acad. Sci. U.S.A.* **79**, 5547–5551.

Holzmann, B., and Weissman, I. L. (1987). In preparation.

Howard, J. C., Hunt, S. V., and Gowans, J. L. (1972). *J. Exp. Med.* **135**, 206–219.

Hynes, R. (1987). *Cell* **48**, 549–554.

Jalkanen, S. T., and Butcher, E. C. (1985). *Blood* **66**, 557–582.

Jalkanen, S., Reichert, R. A., Gallatin, W. M., Bargatze, R. F., Weissman, I. L., and Butcher, E. C. (1986a). *Immunol. Rev.* **91**, 39–60.

Jalkanen, S., Steere, A. C., Fox, R. I., and Butcher, E. C. (1986b). *Science* **233**, 556–558.

Jalkanen, S. T., Bargatze, R., Herron, L., and Butcher, E. C. (1986c). *Eur. J. Immunol.* **16**, 1195–1202.

Jalkanen, S. T., Wu, N., Bargatze, R. F., and Butcher, E. C. (1987). *Annu. Rev. Med.* **38**, 467–476.

Kamenov, B., and Longenecker, B. M. (1985). *Leuk. Res.* **9**, 1529–1537.

Kamenov, B., Kieran, M. W., Barrington-Leigh, J., and Longenecker, B. M. (1984). *Proc. Soc. Exp. Biol. Med.* **177**, 211–219.

Korach, S., Poupon, M.-F., DuVillard, J.-A., and Becker, M. (1986). *Cancer Res.* **46**, 3624–3629.

Kraal, G., and Twisk, A. (1984). *Eur. J. Immunol.* **14**, 586–588.

Kraal, G., Weissman, I. L., and Butcher, E. C. (1982). *Nature (London)* **298**, 377.

Kraal, G., Weissman, I. L., and Butcher, E. C. (1983). *J. Immunol.* **130**, 1097–1102.

Kramer, R. H., and Nicolson, G. L. (1979). *Proc. Natl. Acad. Sci. U.S.A.* **76**, 504–55704–5708.

Larizza, L., Schirrmacher, V., Graf, L. Pfluger, E., Peres-Martinex, M., and Stohr, M. (1984a). *Int. J. Cancer* **34**, 699–707.

Larizza, L., Schirrmacher, V., Stohr, M., Pfluger, E., and Dzarlieva, R. (1984b). *J. Natl. Cancer Inst.* **72**, 1371–1378.

LeDouarin, N. M. (1984). *Cell* **38**, 353–360.

LePault, F., and Weissman, I. L. (1981). *Nature (London)* **293**, 151–154.

Lewinsohn, D. M., Bargatze, R. F., and Butcher, E. C. (1987). *J. Immunol.* **138**, 4313–4321.

McCarthy, J. B., Basara, M. L., Palm, S. L., Sas, D. F., and Furcht, L. T. (1985). *Cancer Met. Rev.* **4**, 125–152.

McGuire, E. J., Mascali, J. J., Grady, S. R., and Nicolson, G. L. (1984). *Clin. Exp. Metastasis* **2**, 214–222.

McWilliams, M., Phillips-Quagliata, J. M., and Lamm, M. E. (1977). *J. Exp. Med.* **145**, 866–875.
Matthews, D. C., Weissman, I. L., and Gallatin, W. M. (1988). In preparation.
Metcalf, D., and Moore, M. (1971). "Frontiers of Biology," Vol. 24. North Holland Publ., Amsterdam.
Middlekoop, O. P., van Bavel, P., Calafat, J., and Roos, E. (1985). *Cancer Res.* **45**, 3825–3835.
Miller, R. A., Coleman, C. N., Fawcett, H. D., Hoppe, R. T., and McDougell, I. R. (1980). *N. Engl. J. Med.* **303**, 89–92.
Netland, P. A., and Zetter, B. R. (1984). *Science* **224**, 1113–1115.
Netland, P. A., and Zetter, B. R. (1985). *J. Cell Biol.* **101**, 720–724.
Nicolson, G. L. (1982a). *Biochim. Biophys. Acta* **695**, 113–176.
Nicolson, G. L. (1982b). *J. Histochem. Cytochem.* **30**, 214–220.
Nicolson, G. L. (1984a). *Cancer Metastasis Rev.* **3**, 25–42.
Nicolson, G. L. (1984b). *Exp. Cell Res.* **150**, 3–22.
Nicolson, G. L., and Custead, S. (1982). *Science* **215**, 176–178.
Nicolson, G. L., and Dulski, K. M. (1986). *Int. J. Cancer* **38**, 289–294.
Nicolson, G. L., and Poste, G. (1983). *Int. Rev. Exp. Pathol.* **25**, 77–181.
Nicolson, G. L., and Winkelhake, J. L. (1975). *Nature (London)* **255**, 230–232.
Phondke, G. P., Madyastha, K. R., Madyastha, P. R., and Barth, R. F. (1981a). *J. Natl. Cancer Inst.* **66**, 643–647.
Picker, L. J., Medeiros, L. J., Weiss, L. M., Warnke, R. A., and Butcher, E. C. (1988). *Amer. J. Path.* **130**, 496–504.
Pierce, N. F., and Gowans, J. L. (1975). *J. Exp. Med.* **142**, 1550–1563.
Pillemer, E. A., Kooistra, D. A., Witte, O. N., and Weissman, I. L. (1986). *J. Virol.* **57**, 413.
Pober, J. S., Gimbrone, M. A., Jr., Collins, T., Cotran, R. S., Ault, K. A., Fiers, W., Krensky, A. M., Clayberger, C., Reiss, C. S., and Burakoff, S. J. (1984). *Immunobiology* **168**, 483–494.
Rasmussen, R., Chin, Y.-H., Woodruff, J. J., and Easton, T. G., (1985). *J. Immunol.* **135**, 19–24.
Reichert, R. A., Gallatin, W. M., Weissman, I. L., and Butcher, E. C. (1983). *J. Exp. Med.* **157**, 813–827.
Reichert, R. A., Gallatin, W. M., Butcher, E. C., and Weissman, I. L. (1984). *Cell* **38**, 89–99.
Reichert, R. A., Weissman, I. L., and Butcher, E. C. (1986). *J. Immunol.* **136**, 3521–3528.
Rosen, S. D., Singer, M. D., Yednock, T. A., and Stoolman, L. M. (1985). *Science* **228**, 1005–1007.
Rosenberg, S. A., Lotze, M. T., Muul, L. M., Leitman, S., Cheng, A. E., Ettinghausen, S. E., Matory, U. L., Skibber, J. M., Shiloni, E., Vetto, J. T., Seipps, C. A., Simpson, C., and Reichert, C. M. (1986). *N. Engl. J. Med.* **313**, 1485–1492.
Rothlein, R., Dustin, M. L., Martin, S. D., and Springer, T. A. (1986). *J. Immunol.* **137**, 1270–1274.
Rouse, R. V., Reichert, R. A., Gallatin, W. M., Weissman, I. L., and Butcher, E. C. (1984). *Am. J. Anat.* **130**, 391–405.
Schirrmacher, V. (1985). *Adv. Cancer Res.* **43**, 1–73.
Schirrmacher, V., Cheinsong-Popov, R., and Arnheiter, H. (1980). *J. Exp. Med.* **151**, 984–989.
Scollay, R., Hopkins, J., and Hall, J. (1976). *Nature (London)* **260**, 528–529.
Shearman, P. J., Gallatin, W. M., and Longenecker, B. M. (1980). *Nature (London)* **286**, 267–269.
Siegelman, M., Bond, M. W., Gallatin, W. M., St. John, T., Smith, H. T., Fried, V. A., and Weissman, I. L. (1986). *Science* **231**, 823–829.
Smith, M. E., Martin, A. F., and Ford, W. L. (1980). *Monogr. Allergy* **16**, 203–232.
Spangrude, G. J., Braaten, B. A., and Daynes, R. A. (1984). *J. Immunol.* **132**, 354–362.
Spangrude, G. J., Araneo, B. A., and Daynes, R. A. (1985). *J. Immunol.* **134**, 2900–2907.
Springer, T. A., Dustin, M. L., Kishimoto, T. K., and Marlin, S.D. (1987). *Annu. Rev. Immunol.* **5**, 223–252.
Stamper, H. B., and Woodruff, J. J. (1976). *J. Exp. Med.* **144**, 828–833.
Stanford, D. R., Starkey, J. R., and Magnuson, J. A. (1986). *Int. J. Cancer* **37**, 435–444.

Steinemann, C., Fenner, M., Binz, H., and Parish, R. (1984). *Proc. Natl. Acad. Sci. U.S.A.* **81**, 3747–3750.

Stevens, S. K., Weissman, I. L., and Butcher, E. C. (1982). *J. Immunol.* **128**, 844–851.

St. John, T., Gallatin, W. M., Siegelman, M., Smith, H. T., Fried, V. A., and Weissman, I. L. *Science* **231**, 845–850.

Stoolman, L. M., Tenforde, T. S., and Rosen, S. D. (1984). *J. Cell Biol.* **99**, 1535–1540.

Tarin, D., Price, J. E., Kettlewell, M. G. W., Souter, R. G., Vass, A. C. R., and Crossley, B. (1984). *Cancer Res.* **44**, 3584–3592.

Terranova, V. P., Liotta, L. A., Russo, R. G., and Martin, G. R. (1982). *Cancer Res.* **42**, 2265–2269.

Vijav-Kumar, S., Bugg, C. E., Wilkinson, R. D., and Cook, W. J. (1985). *Proc. Natl. Acad. Sci. U.S.A.* **82**, 3582–3586.

Vollmers, H. P., and Birchmeier, W. (1983a). *Proc. Natl. Acad. Sci. U.S.A.* **80**, 6863–6867.

Vollmers, H. P., and Birchmeier, W. (1983b). *Proc. Natl. Acad. Sci. U.S.A.* **80**, 3729–3733.

Vollmers, H. P., Imhog, B. A., Braun, S., Waller, C. A., Schirrmacher, V., and Birchmeier, W. (1984). *FEBS Lett.* **172**, 17–20.

Weissman, I. L. (1986). *Bioessays* **5**, 112.

Weissman, I. L., Papaioannou, V., and Gardner, R. (1978). *In* "Differentiation of Normal and Neoplastic Cells" (B. Clarkson, P. A. Marks, and J. E. Tills, eds.), pp. 33–47, Cold Spring Harbor Laboratory, Cold Spring Harbor, New York.

Wood, G. S., Deneau, D. G., Miller, R. A., Levy, R., Hoppe, R. T., and Warnke, R. A. (1982). *Blood* **59**, 876–882.

Yednock, T. A., Butcher, E. C., Stoolman, L. M., and Rosen, S. D. (1985). *J. Cell Biol.* **101**, 233a.

Zamvil, S., Nelson, P., Trotter, J., Mitchell, D., Knobler, R., Fritz, R., and Steinman, L. (1985). *Nature (London)* **317**, 355–358.

DEHYDROEPIANDROSTERONE AND STRUCTURAL ANALOGS: A NEW CLASS OF CANCER CHEMOPREVENTIVE AGENTS

Arthur G. Schwartz,* Jeannette M. Whitcomb,* Jonathan W. Nyce,†
Marvin L. Lewbart,‡ and Laura L. Pashko*

I. Introduction 391
II. DHEA and Breast Cancer 392
III. Glucose-6-Phosphate Dehydrogenase Inhibition 394
IV. Antiobesity Action of DHEA 396
V. Cancer Prevention 400
VI. Mechanism of Cancer Preventive Effect 404
A. Inhibition of DNA Synthesis 407
B. Inhibition of Superoxide Formation 412
VII. Glucose-6-Phosphate Dehydrogenase Deficiency and Human Cancer 415
VIII. Other Therapeutic Effects of DHEA 417
A. Antidiabetic Activity 417
B. Antiautoimmune and Possible Antiaging Effects 418
C. Possible Antiatherogenic Effect 419
D. Synthetic DHEA Analogs: Their Use as Potential Drugs and as Tools for Understanding the Mechanisms of Therapeutic Action of DHEA 420
References 421

I. Introduction

The biological significance of dehydroepiandrosterone (DHEA) and its sulfate ester, dehydroepiandrosterone sulfate (DHEAS), major secretory products of the human adrenal gland, is unclear (Vande Wiele *et al.*, 1963). DHEA was first isolated in 1934 by Butenandt and Tscherning from human urine, and 10 years later DHEAS was also extracted from urine (Munson *et al.*, 1944). Callow (1936) originally suggested that DHEA was secreted by the adrenal gland, because the level of the steroid increased in urine samples after adrenocorticotropic hormone (ACTH) administration and in hyperadrenocorticism and decreased after suppression of ACTH secretion. Baulieu *et al.* (1965) first demonstrated that DHEA is secreted by the human adrenal gland

*Fels Research Institute, Temple University School of Medicine, 3420 North Broad Street, Philadelphia, Pennsylvania, 19140, †Department of Pharmacology, East Carolina University, Greenville, North Carolina, 27834–4354, ‡Steroid Laboratory, Crozer-Chester Hospital, Chester, Pennsylvania, 19013.

ADVANCES IN CANCER RESEARCH, VOLUME 51

primarily as the sulfate ester, an unusual steroid secretory product because steroid sulfates are normally formed in the liver as metabolic degradation products prior to excretion. Over 99% of the circulating DHEA in humans is sulfated, with less than 1% representing the free steroid (Zumoff *et al.*, 1980)

Over the past several years this laboratory and others have demonstrated several therapeutic effects of DHEA in laboratory mice and rats that, in their diversity, appear rather remarkable. These include cancer preventive, possible antiautoimmune, and antiatherogenic effects as well as antiobesity and antidiabetic activities. However, a certain simplicity in the mechanism of action of the DHEA class of steroids is now beginning to emerge. The well-documented capacity of DHEA to inhibit mammalian glucose-6-phosphate dehydrogenase (G6PDH)—the rate-limiting enzyme in the pentose phosphate pathway, a major source of cytosolic NADPH—now appears central to the mechanism of the cancer preventive action of this steroid. It would not be surprising if inhibition of this enzyme contributes to some of the other beneficial effects of DHEA as well.

II. DHEA and Breast Cancer

DHEA and DHEAS plasma levels undergo a marked and progressive age-related decline beginning in the second decade and eventually fall to 10–20% of their maximal values in the seventh decade (Migeon *et al.*, 1957; Orentreich *et al.*, 1984; Zumoff *et al.*, 1980) (Fig. 1). In contrast, during the normal aging process basal plasma levels of cortisol and aldosterone show little change (Gherondache *et al.*, 1967; Weidman *et al.*, 1975). The stimulaton of cortisol and aldosterone levels following ACTH administration also shows no apparent change with age, whereas the ability of DHEA and DHEAS to be stimulated declines markedly (Parker *et al.*, 1981).

In 1962 Bulbrook *et al.* reported that women with primary operable breast cancer excrete subnormal amounts of 11-deoxy-17-ketosteroids (derived primarily from DHEA and DHEAS) prior to mastectomy and suggested that this hormone abnormality might precede the onset of the disease. In order to test this hypothesis, Bulbrook *et al.* undertook a prospective study in which 24-hr urine specimens were collected from approximately 5000 women on the island of Guernsey who had no apparent breast cancer and were followed for 9 years. At the end of that time, 27 women had developed malignant breast tumors. The excretion of various urinary steroids in the women who had developed breast cancer was compared with that of 187 carefully matched controls from the same population that had not developed a tumor, and it was found that the excretion of androsterone and etiocholanolone (two principal metabolites of DHEA) was lower in the women who had developed breast cancer (Bulbrook *et al.*, 1971).

With the development of suitable analytical techniques, several laboratories have undertaken determinations of DHEAS plasma levels in

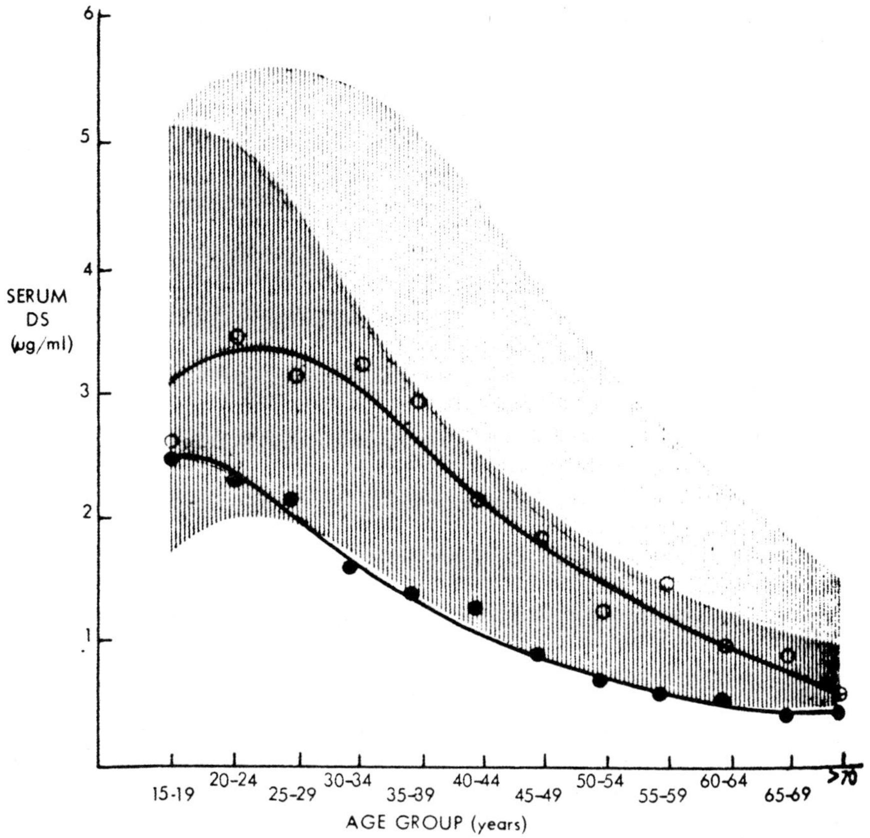

FIG. 1. Serum (DS) concentrations versus age in men (○) and women (●). Data points are antilogs of mean log DS values. Shaded areas delineate normal ranges for men (lighter shaded area) and women (darker shaded area). Normal limits for each age and sex group were computed by the equation: minimum or maximum = antilog [mean of log DS values ± (1 + log 2) SD] corresponding to the log equivalent of the mean ± SD and including about 90% of measured values. To obtain smooth curves for means and limits, curves were computer fitted to the general equation: $y = K \text{ Exp } [ax^3 + bx^2 + cx + d]$, where y is the DS value in micrograms per milliliter and x is the mean age of the group. (From Orentreich *et al.*, 1984.)

women with breast cancer and in matched controls. Several retrospective studies have shown subnormal plasma levels of DHEA and DHEAS in advanced breast cancer patients (Brownsey *et al.*, 1972; Rose *et al.*, 1977; Wang *et al.*, 1974). The findings of Zumoff *et al.* (1981) are of particular interest, because these investigators addressed the problem of the marked fluctuations in DHEA levels over a 24-hr cycle. DHEA and cortisol are secreted episodically and synchronously, and their levels may vary by as much as 100% on individual spot determinations; DHEAS levels, however, show much less variability (Rosenfeld *et al.*, 1981). Zumoff *et al.* (1981) measured 24-hr mean plasma concentrations of DHEA and DHEAS by sampling blood every 20 min, pooling aliquots of the 72 samples, and determining the concentration of steroid in the pooled samples. When these determinations were made on plasma from 11 women with primary operable breast cancer and from 37 normal women, ages 21 to 75, they found that in contrast to the marked and progressive decline of DHEA and DHEAS concentrations with age in the normal women, the concentrations of both steroids were age-invariant in the cancer patients. The premenopausal patients had subnormal plasma DHEA and DHEAS levels, whereas the postmenopausal patients had supranormal levels.

The preponderance of evidence in these case-control studies suggests that women with breast cancer have subnormal DHEAS plasma concentrations. However, as in all case-control studies, it is uncertain whether the presence of the measured abnormality precedes or is a consequence of the disease. The prospective study of Bulbrook *et al.* provides the strongest evidence suggesting that women with subnormal DHEAS levels experience an increased risk of breast cancer.

III. Glucose-6-Phosphate Dehydrogenase Inhibition

DHEA is a potent noncompetitive inhibitor (with respect to glucose 6-phosphate and NADP) of mammalian G6PDH but not of algal or yeast enzyme (Marks and Banks, 1960; Oertel and Benes, 1972; Raineri and Levy, 1970). Not only do DHEA and specific steroids in the androstane series inhibit G6PDH but so do pregnenolone and related pregnane steroids. In the androstane series, a keto group at C-17 is required for inhibition; steroids possessing either no functional group at C-17 or a hydroxy or carboxy group at this position are inactive as inhibitors. The introduction of a double bond between C-5 and C-6 reduces inhibitory activity; DHEA (3β-hydroxy-5-androsten-17-one) is a less effective inhibitor than epiandrosterone (3β-hydroxy-5α-androstan-17-one). The presence of a 16α bromide (Br) group in the androstan series markedly enhances inhibitory action. 16α-Br-epiandrosterone (Epi-Br) has an inhibitory constant (K_i) of 0.571 μM against purified rat mammary gland G6PDH; K_i is 3.56 μM for epiandrosterone and 18.4 μM for DHEA (Raineri and Levy, 1970). Similarly, greater potency is seen with bovine adrenal G6PDH; a K_i of 0.3 μM and 17.6 μM is obtained with Epi-Br and DHEA, respectively (Pashko *et al.*, 1981).

Changing the ring structure at the A–B ring juncture from the 5α configuration to the 5β markedly reduces inhibitory activity. In the pregnane series, a 20-keto group is necessary for inhibition and appears to serve the same function as the 17-keto group does in the androstane series (Raineri and Levy, 1970).

That the DHEA inhibition of G6PDH is of physiological significance has been questioned by Nielson and Warren (1965). The K_i for DHEA against several purified mammalian G6PDH preparations is approximately 18 μM, whereas the concentration of DHEA in human plasma is 0.01 to 0.02 μM, a level that would produce neglibible inhibition of G6PDH (Zumoff *et al.*, 1980). The concentration of DHEAS in human plasma, approximately 5 to 7 μM in the second decade (Orentreich *et al.*, 1984), is well within the range that produces G6PDH inhibition by the free steroid, but not for DHEAS, which is inactive as an inhibitor (Oertel and Benes, 1972). Oertel, however, has isolated from human plasma an unstable lipoidal conjugate between DHEA and sulfatidic acid (fatty diesters of glycerosulfuric acid) known as DHEA-sulfatide (Oertel, 1964, 1966) (Fig. 2), which is a more potent inhibitor of G6PDH than is DHEA (K_i of sulfatide, 3 μM; K_i of DHEA, 8 μM; against human placental G6PDH) (Oertel and Benes, 1972). The sulfatide, according to Oertel and Benes (1972), may represent up to 90% of the DHEAS in human plasma and could therefore be a physiological regulator of G6PDH.

Hochberg *et al.* have reported the isolation of lipoidal derivatives of pregnenolone, 17α-hydroxypregnenolone, and DHEA from extracts of bovine adrenals (Hochberg *et al.*, 1979). These lipoidal compounds, which were present in adrenal extracts in quantities that are of the same order of magnitude as those of the free steroids, appear to be esters of the steroids with various long-chain fatty acids. Incubation of pregnenolone or DHEA with bovine or rat adrenal homogenates resulted in the formation of non-polar metabolites of these steroids that had properties similar to the endogenous lipoidal derivatives. The related steroids, 17α-hydroxypregnenolone, 17α-hydroxyprogesterone, progesterone, and testosterone were not converted into lipoidal derivatives when incubated with bovine adrenal

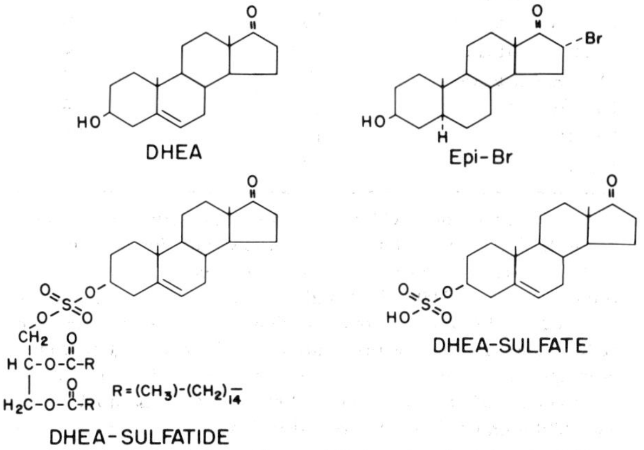

FIG. 2. Structures of steroids. (From Pashko *et al.*, 1981.)

homogenates, a result indicating specificity of this enzymatic conversion for certain steroids (Mellon-Nussenbaum and Hochberg, 1980).

Our laboratory has found that synthetically prepared DHEA-sulfatide was a more effective inhibitor of mouse epidermal G6PDH than DHEA was (Table I) (Pashko *et al.*, 1981). We have also observed that the sulfatide is a labile substance, which may explain the failure to isolate this conjugate from human plasma with routine extraction procedures. The sulfatide, when injected intraperitoneally into mice, was highly effective in blocking the stimulaton in epidermal DNA synthesis rate produced by topical application of the tumor promoter tetradecanoylphorbol-13-acetate (TPA), a biological effect that is very likely mediated through inhibition of G6PDH (Fig. 3) (see Section VI,A).

IV. Antiobesity Action of DHEA

In 1977 Yen *et al.* reported that DHEA treatment of VY mice bearing the A^{vy} mutation, which produces a metabolic obesity—i.e., an obesity that results from an enhanced efficiency of food utilization rather than from

TABLE I

INHIBITION OF MOUSE EPIDERMAL G6PDH ACTIVITY BY DHEA AND RELATED STEROIDS

Steroid	Concentratoin (*M*)	Percentage of control activity[a]
DHEA	10^{-5}	54
DHEA	10^{-6}	90
DHEA	10^{-7}	90
DHEA-sulfate	10^{-5}	96
DHEA-sulfatide	10^{-5}	46
DHEA-sulfatide	10^{-6}	64
DHEA-sulfatide	10^{-7}	67
Epi-Br	10^{-5}	9
Epi-Br	10^{-6}	51
Epi-Br	10^{-7}	71

[a]Steroid inhibition of G6PDH activity was determined as described in Pashko *et al.* (1981). Steroids were dissolved in dioxane immediately before testing. The reaction medium consisted of 3.0 ml of 0.05 *M* triethanolamine—0.005 EDTA buffer (pH 7.6), 0.01 *M* NADP solution, and 0.02 ml of dioxane or steroid in dioxane. The reaction was run at 25°C and was initiated by the addition of 0.005 ml of a 0.031 *M* glucose 6-phosphate solution. Activity was measured in munits from changes in absorbance at 340 nm on a Gilford 2400-S recording spectrophotometer. The inhibition produced by the added steroid was expressed as a percentage of the control value. (From Pashko *et al.*, 1981.)

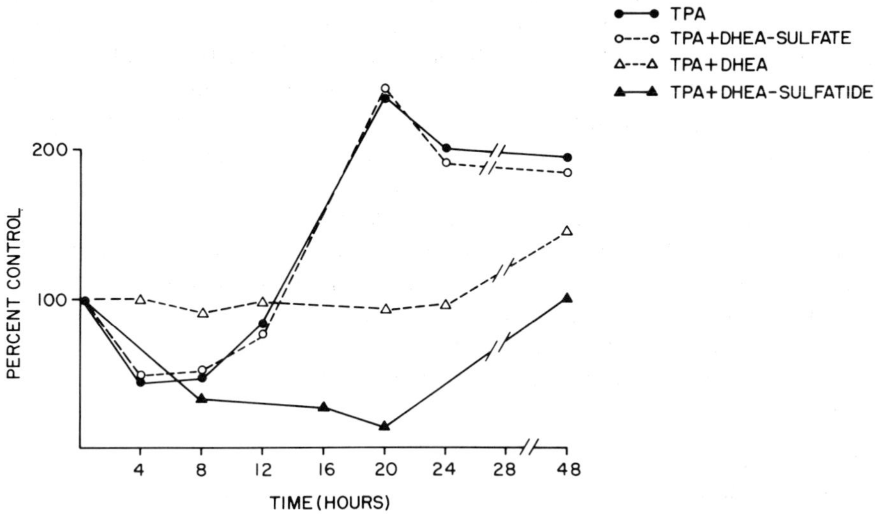

FIG. 3. Inhibition of TPA stimulation of [^{3}H]thymidine incorporation in mouse epidermis by DHEA and DHEA-sulfatide. Mice were injected with either DHEA (15 mg/kg), DHEA-sulfate (20 mg/kg), or DHEA-sulfatide (48 mg/kg) 1 hr before TPA application. The doses used are equivalent to 50 μmol of steroid per kilogram of body weight. [^{3}H]Thymidine was administered at various time intervals, and the amount incorporated per microgram of DNA in the epidermis was determined as described in Pashko *et al.* (1981). Each point is the mean of the percentage of control specific incorporation for three separately treated mice with a standard error of <15%. (From Pashko *et al.*, 1981.)

hyperphagia (Richerson and Gowen, 1947)—markedly inhibited weight gain. DHEA was administered orally as a suspension in sesame oil at a dose of 500 mg/kg thrice weekly. Measurements of food consumption indicated that treated and untreated mice consumed equivalent amounts of food and that consequently DHEA produced its antiweight effect through a metabolic alteration in the efficiency of food utilization rather than as a result of appetite suppression. Hepatic lipogenesis rates, as measured by the incorporation of $^3H_20$ into lipid, were depressed. Yen *et al.* hypothesized that DHEA treatment reduced weight gain by inhibiting lipogenesis as a result of G6PDH depression. NADPH is an essential cofactor for fatty acid biosynthesis, and this synthetic pathway might be depressed under conditions of reduced NADPH availability.

Yen *et al.* subsequently reported that 5α-androstan-17-one, an even more potent G6PDH inhibitor than DHEA (Raineri and Levy, 1970), also reduced weight gain in VY-A^{vy}/a mice when injected subcutaneously at 200 mg/kg thrice weekly (Yen *et al.*, 1978). This finding would appear to support the hypothesis that G6PDH inhibition by DHEA is responsible for its antiobesity action.

That DHEA treatment produces an antiweight effect in both mice and rats of many different strains has been confirmed in this and other laboratories (Cleary *et al.*, 1984a,b; Schwartz *et al.*, 1981; Tagliaferro and Davis, 1983; Weindruch *et al.*, 1984). DHEA is effective when administered orally at 450 mg/kg thrice weekly (Fig. 4) or when given in the diet from 0.2 to 0.6%. In many strains of mice and rats, DHEA given in the diet at >0.2% leads to suppression in food consumption. Frequently this is a transient effect, with an eventual rise in food intake equal to that of untreated animals. Pair-feeding experiments have demonstrated that DHEA-treated animals weigh significantly less than those with an equal food intake, a result indicating that the antiweight effect of steroid treatment results, at least in part, from an alteration in the efficiency of food utilization rather than simply from appetite suppression (Pashko *et al.*, 1986) (Fig. 5).

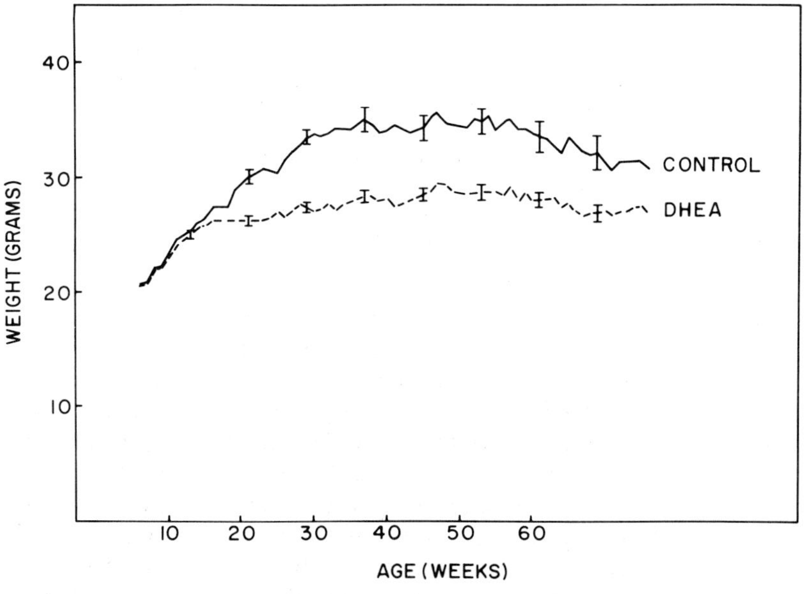

FIG. 4. Growth curves for control and DHEA-treated C3H-*A/A* mice. One hundred and sixty weanling C3H-*A/A* female mice were obtained from the Leonell C. Strong Research Foundation, Del Mar, CA. At 5 to 6 weeks of age, the animals were divided into two groups and housed in plastic cages with four animals per cage. One group received 450 mg/kg of DHEA (prepared as a suspension in sesame oil) by peroral intubation three times weekly, and the other group received the sesame oil vehicle. Purina® laboratory chow (11% fat) and water were provided *ad libitum*. The animal quarters were maintained at 24 ± 1°C and at 40 to 45% relative humidity with 12 hr of light and 12 hr of darkness each day. All mice were identified by earmark and were weighed weekly. Points are weekly determinations of mean weights, with the standard error indicated at 8-week intervals. The differences in the mean weights of the two groups are statistically significant ($P < 0.001$, Student's *t*-test) at all points after the nineteenth week. (From Schwartz *et al.*, 1981.)

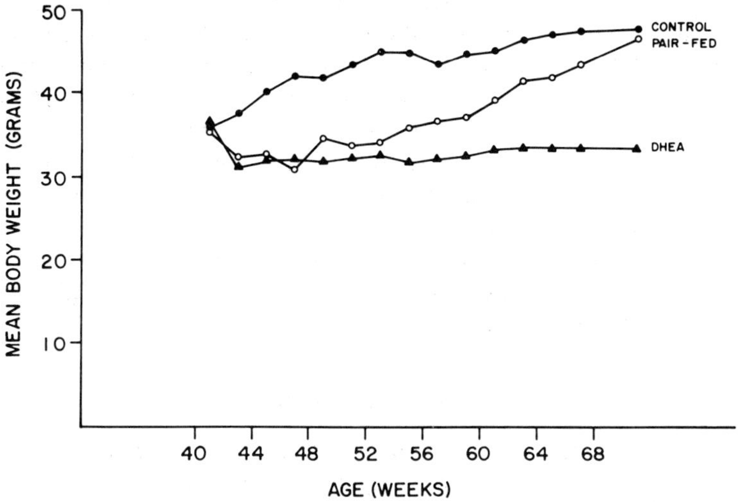

FIG. 5. Mean weights for experimental groups of mice. Male C57BL/6 (C57BL/6 N Nial) mice were obtained at 9 months of age from the National Institute on Aging Colony maintained by the Charles River Laboratories, Kingston, NY. The animals were housed four per cage in 11.5 × 7 × 5 in. filter-topped plastic cages with hardwood bedding in an animal facility with a 12:12 hr light/dark cycle at 70 ± 2°F and 50 ± 5% relative humidity. The control group was given *ad libitum* access to a control diet that consisted of powdered Breeder's chow containing a minimum of 23% protein and 12% fat with 3% acacia added as a binder, which was pelleted by Bioserve, Inc. The pair-fed group was also fed the control diet but was limited to the amount of food eaten weekly by the DHEA group. The DHEA diet was identical to control diet but contained 0.3% (w/w) DHEA. Each point is the mean value for 34 to 40 mice. The standard deviation was equal to or less than 15% of the mean for each experimental group. (From Pashko and Schwartz, 1985.)

That the antiobesity action of DHEA is competely the result of G6PDH inhibition appears unlikely. Coleman *et al.*, (1984) reported that Epi-Br, a much more potent G6PDH inhibitor than DHEA, failed to produce an antiweight effect or lower blood sugar in genetically diabetic (*db/db*) C57BL/KsJ mice when fed in the diet at 0.4%. In contrast, feeding of DHEA at 0.4% had a dramatic effect on control of diabetes in the aforementioned mutant and in regulating weight gain in similar mutant strains. Although inhibition of G6PDH by DHEA and structural analogs may contribute to the antiobesity effect of these steroids, it appears unlikely that this biochemical action alone is responsible for the regulation of weight gain.

DHEA treatment of Zucker rats (Shepherd and Cleary, 1984) or BHE rats (Cleary *et al.*, 1984a) enhanced long-chain fatty acyl-CoA hydrolase activity in the liver, and it has been postulated that this may represent the stimulation of an energy-wasting cycle, or futile cycle, that may contribute to the reduced caloric efficiency of the DHEA-treated rat. However, various agents that stimulate liver peroxisome formation, such as clofibric acid and diethylhexylphthalate, also stimulate fatty acyl-CoA hydrolase activity (Katoh *et al.*, 1984). Peroxisome proliferators also produce hepatomegaly and stimulate liver catalase activity (Reddy *et al.*, 1982) but do not inhibit weight gain. DHEA shares with these compounds the property of producing hepatomegaly and stimulating liver catalase activity (Schwartz *et al.*, 1987). Fatty acyl-CoA hydrolase stimulation may therefore be a consequence of peroxisome proliferation rather than a specific property of an antiobesity steroid. However, it is reasonable to assume that energy-wasting processes may play an important role in the mechanism of the antiweight activity of DHEA and specific congeners.

V. Cancer Prevention

This laboratory demonstrated in 1975 that DHEA protected rat liver epithelial-like cells and hamster embryonic fibroblasts against aflatoxin B_1 and 7,12-dimethylbenz[*a*]anthracene (DMBA)-induced cytotoxicity and transformation (Schwartz and Perantoni, 1975) (Tables II and III). Treatment with the steroid also inhibited the rate of metabolism of [^{3}H]DMBA to water-soluble products by the cultured fibroblasts. Related steroids, such as testosterone or etiocholanolone, produced significantly less protection.

Epiandrosterone, a more effective inhibitor of G6PDH than DHEA, was also more active in inhibiting the rate of metabolism of [^{3}H]DMBA to

TABLE II

EFFECT OF ANDROGENIC STEROIDS ON AFLATOXIN B_1-INDUCED TRANSFORMATION

Steroid	Total no. of clones	Cloning efficiency[a] (%)	Transformed[a] Total no.	Transformed[a] %
No steroid (control)	776	3.9	35	4.5
DHEA	1126	3.8	25	2.2
Testosterone	980	3.0	42	4.3
Etiocholanolone	1289	4.3	40	3.1
Aflatoxin	876	1.9	237	30.5
Aflatoxin-DHEA	1060	2.8	103	9.7
Aflatoxin-testosterone	804	2.3	235	29.3
Aflatoxin-etiocholanolone	950	2.1	159	16.7

[a]Hamster embryo cells were plated in 60-mm culture dishes containing rat feeder-layer cells, as described by Schwartz and Perantoni (1975). The following day the test media were added to the cultures for 24 hr, after which the cells were incubated in normal medium (with changes every 2 to 3 days) for 6 days. Cultures were fixed and stained, and the number of normal and transformed clones in each group was determined. Cloning efficiency is the percentage of the total clones counted per number of cells plated. The transformation frequency is expressed as the percentage of transformed clones per total number of clones. The aflatoxin B_1 concentration was 10^{-6} *M*, and the steroid concentration was 10^{-4} *M*. (From Schwartz and Perantoni, 1975.)

TABLE III

EFFECT OF ANDROGENIC STEROIDS ON DMBA-INDUCED TRANSFORMATION

Steroid[a]	Total no. of clones	Cloning efficiency (%)	Transformed	
			Total no.	%
No steroid (control)	419	2.6	7	1.7
DHEA	374	2.3	7	1.9
Testosterone	478	3.0	7	1.5
DMBA	403	1.7	70	17.3
DMBA-DHEA	438	2.1	38	8.7
DMBA-testosterone	329	1.5	46	14

[a]The experimental conditions are the same as those given in Table II. The DMBA concentration was 7.5×10^{-7} *M*, and the steroid concentration was 10^{-4} *M*. (From Schwartz and Perantoni, 1975.)

water-soluble products (Fig. 6). Based on these observations, we hypothesized that DHEA protected cultured cells against aflatoxin B_1- and DMBA-induced cytotoxicity and transformation through inhibition of the rate of carcinogen activation by mixed-function oxidases as a result of depression of the NADPH pool size, since NADPH is a necessary cofactor for mixed-function oxidase activity (Schwartz and Perantoni, 1975).

DHEA produced two biological effects that suggested that it might demonstrate cancer preventive activity *in vivo*: the steroid protected cultured cells against chemical carcinogen-induced cytotoxicity and transformation, and DHEA treatment of mice produced a striking antiweight effect, primarily through a reduction in caloric efficiency rather than through appetite suppression. Reducing weight gain of laboratory mice and rats through food restriction produces what may be the most marked cancer preventive action of any known regimen (Tannenbaum and Silverstone, 1953). Spontaneous, chemically induced, and radiation-induced tumors in many different organs are all reduced in frequency in food-restricted rodents. Not only does underfeeding inhibit tumor development, it retards the rate of appearance of autoimmune disease processes as well as many age-related pathological changes and is believed to slow the rate of aging (Fernandes *et al.*, 1978; McCay *et al.*, 1935; Weindruch and Walford, 1983; Yu *et al.*, 1982). The fundamental mechanism by which underfeeding protects aginst such a broad spectrum of pathological changes is obscure, and its elucidation is obviously of the greatest importance.

The data from several human epidemiological studies also suggest a positive correlation with high relative body weight and incidence of cancer of the breast, colon, rectum, prostate, endometrium, kidney, cervix, ovary, thyroid, and gallbladder (Albanes, 1987). In contrast, lung, bladder, and stomach cancer appear to be inversely associated with body weight. However, the effect of cigarette smoking, which is positively associated with these

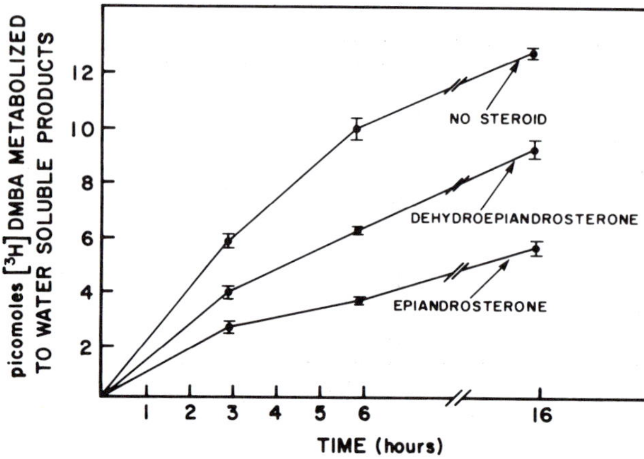

FIG. 6. Comparative effects of DHEA and epiandrosterone on the rate of metabolism of [^{3}H]DMBA to water-soluble products by E-3 cells. A rat liver epithelial-like cell line (E-3) was established from an adult male Sprague-Dawley rat and propagated in monolayer culture in minimal essential medium (Schwartz and Perantoni, 1975). A constant number (100,000) of E-3 cells was inoculated into T-15 flasks and fed on alternate days. Five days after inoculation, cultures received medium containing a specific steroid (10^{-4} *M*) or control medium with ethanol (0.07%). Following a 30-min incubation at 37°C, cultures received [^{3}H]DMBA (13 Ci/mmol) at a final concentration of 10^{-8} *M*. The [^{3}H]DMBA was dissolved in dimethylsulfoxide and added to the cells to give a final dimethylsulfoxide concentration of 0.01%. The concentration of [^{3}H]DMBA used (10^{-8} *M*) had no apparent cytotoxic effect. At various intervals, the medium was collected, the cultures were washed with 2 ml of cold Earle's balanced salt solution (without phenol red), and the washes were pooled with the medium. Five milliliters of acetone and 5 ml of hexane were added to the pooled medium–wash mixture, which was shaken and centrifuged at 900 *g* for 5 min. The aqueous phase was reextracted with 5 ml of hexane and centrifuged. Aliquots of the aqueous phase (0.2 ml) and of the combined organic phases (0.5 ml) were each dissolved in 20 ml of toluene–Triton X solution and counted in an Intertechnique scintillation counter. The radioactivity in the aqueous phase following incubation of medium in T-15 flasks without cells was subtracted as background for each of the aqueous points. The background radioactivity was approximately 10% of the combined radioactivity recovered in the aqueous and organic phases, and it did not increase with time of incubation over a 16-hr period. In the presence of E-3 cells, there was a progressive increase in the amount of radioactivity recovered in the aqueous phase with incubation time, with approximately 80% of the radioactivity appearing in the aqueous phase after 16 hr of incubation in the nonsteroid cultures. (From Schwartz and Perantoni, 1975.)

three latter cancers, was not considered in many of these studies. Lew and Garfinkel (1979) carried out a large-scale prospective study on 750,000 American men and women for 13 years to determine the effect of weight on mortality from cancer, coronary artery disease, and all causes. The authors compared overall cancer mortality in both men and women who smoked 20+ cigarettes a day as well as in those who never smoked (Table IV). The cancer mortality in smokers showed a biphasic response with respect to

TABLE IV

MORTALITY RATIOS FOR ALL AGES COMBINED ACCORDING TO SMOKING HABITS IN RELATION TO THOSE 90–109% OF AVERAGE AGE[a]

Cause of death	Sex		Weight index <80	080–089	090–109	110–119	120–129	130–139	140+
All causes of death	M	Never smoked	0.88	0.75	0.75	0.91	0.98	1.16	1.69
		20+ cigarettes	1.68	1.40	1.34	1.53	1.76	2.00	2.21
		Other	1.22	1.01	0.93	1.04	1.15	1.29	1.66
	F	Never smoked	1.10	0.88	0.93	1.08	1.20	1.37	1.74
		20+ cigarettes	1.98	1.59	1.64	1.82	2.22	2.30	2.73
		Other	1.53	1.13	1.12	1.40	1.42	1.62	2.04
Coronary artery disease	M	Never smoked	0.72	0.66	0.76	0.96	1.04	1.24	1.73
		20+ cigarettes	1.06	1.13	1.33	1.66	1.81	2.11	2.11
		Other	0.91	0.90	0.93	1.12	1.19	1.37	1.84
	F	Never smoked	0.93	0.82	0.92	1.10	1.29	1.39	1.86
		20+ cigarettes	1.51	1.70	2.12	2.20	3.48	3.79	4.74
		Other	1.54	1.14	1.18	1.88	1.44	2.01	2.33
Cancer, all sites	M	Never smoked	0.60	0.60	0.66	0.69	0.79	0.90	0.76
		20+ cigarettes	2.07	1.71	1.43	1.46	1.55	1.71	2.00
		Other	1.20	1.03	1.90	0.89	1.05	0.87	1.22
	F	Never smoked	0.85	0.85	0.96	1.06	1.16	1.19	1.50
		20+ cigarettes	1.49	1.36	1.34	1.50	1.34	1.70	1.49
		Other	1.11	0.98	1.03	1.06	1.16	1.11	1.60

[a]These data were obtained from a long-term prospective study conducted by the American Cancer Society over the period 1959–1972 on 750,000 men and women drawn from the general population. (From Lew and Garfinkel, 1979.)

weight, with thin and heavy invidivuals demonstrating the highest mortality. In contrast, the nonsmokers showed a progressive increase in cancer mortality with increasing weight. While relations between caloric intake and body weight are complex, a complete review of the literature data suggests that reducing caloric intake and relative body weight may lead to a decrease in cancer risk in humans (Albanes, 1987).

We undertook experiments to determine whether DHEA treatment would reduce cancer susceptibility in laboratory mice. It should be emphasized that DHEA-treated mice, unlike their food-restricted counterparts, are fed *ad libitum*; and pair-feeding experiments have shown that for most strains of mice a large part of the antiweight effect results from a diminished efficiency of the rate of conversion of ingested calories into body mass. DHEA treatment would therefore represent a much more efficacious regimen than food restriction.

We did indeed find that long-term DHEA treatment inhibited the development of spontaneous breast cancer in C3H-A^{vy}/*A* (obese) and C3H-*A*/*A* mice (Schwartz, 1979; Schwartz *et al.*, 1981) (Table V), of DMBA- and urethane-induced lung adenomas in A/J mice (Schwartz and Tannen, 1981) (Table VI), and of 1,2-dimethylhydrazine (DMH)-induced colon tumors in BALB/c mice (Nyce *et al.*, 1984) (Table VII). Garcea *et al.* (1985, 1987) reported that DHEA administration to Wistar rats inhibited the development of liver preneoplastic foci induced by diethylnitrosamine initiation followed by partial hepatectomy and treatment with *N*-acetylaminofluorene and phenobarbital. Similarly Moore *et al.* (1986) found the DHEA administration to F344 rats previously treated with dihydroxy-di-*n*-propylnitrosamine inhibited the development of thyroid tumors and preneoplastic liver foci.

VI. Mechanism of Cancer Preventive Effect

In all of the preceding studies demonstrating tumor prophylaxis by DHEA in mice and rats, DHEA treatment produced a concomitant antiobesity effect. Thus, the tumor preventive action of DHEA may have resulted from a mechanism similar to that of weight loss through food restriction rather than from a direct action of DHEA on target cells. In order to determine whether DHEA has any direct-acting anticarcinogenic activity, we employed the two-stage procedure for induction of skin papillomas (DMBA initiation and TPA promotion) (Boutwell, 1964) and the complete model (weekly applications of DMBA to skin) for induction of skin papillomas and carcinomas (Terracini *et al.*, 1960). In these experiments DHEA was applied topically to mouse skin 1 hr before DMBA or TPA treatment. Under these conditions of topical treatment, DHEA has no effect on body weight and it is likely that any inhibition of tumor development by DHEA results from a direct action of the steroid on cells in the skin. We found that topical DHEA

TABLE V

EFFECT OF LONG-TERM DHEA TREATMENT ON BREAST CANCER INCIDENCE IN C3H-A/A AND C3H-A^{vy}/A MICE[a]

	Length of treatment (months)														
	4	5	6	7	8	9	10	11	12	13	14	15	16	17	18
C3H-A/A															
No. controls living	78	78	75	72	67	60	54	49	42	35	35	33	30	29	20
No. controls with cancer (cumulative)	0	0	1	3	4	6	6	7	8	13	13	13	13	14	21
No. DHEA living	77	76	75	75	75	73	63	54	52	48	44	42	38	32	29
No. DHEA with cancer (cumulative)	0	1	1	1	1	1	1	3	4	5	6	6	7	7	9
C3H-A^{vy}/A															
No. controls living	27	26	26	24	21	17	15	12	11	9	7	7			
No. controls with cancer (cumulative)	0	0	0	2	5	9	11	14	15	17	19	19			
No. DHEA living	23	22	22	22	21	19	19	16	16	15	12	9			
No. DHEA with cancer (cumulative)	0	0	0	0	0	0	0	0	0	1	4	5			

[a]DHEA-treated mice received 450 mg/kg of DHEA (prepared as a suspension in sesame oil) by peroral intubation 3 times weekly. Spontaneous breast tumors were detected by weekly palpation. (From Schwartz *et al.*, 1981.)

TABLE VI

EFFECT OF DHEA ON DMBA- AND URETHANE-INDUCED LUNG TUMORIGENESIS[a]

Tumors per mouse	Number of mice having the indicated number of tumors			
	DMBA alone	DMBA + DHEA	Urethane alone	Urethane + DHEA
0		3		
1		5		
2		5		
3	2	5		
4	1	1		1
5	1	1		
6	2	2		
8	3		1	2
9	3			1
10	2		1	
11	2	1		1
12			1	3
13				1
14	2			1
15	2		4	1
16	1		2	2
17	1		2	2
18			1	
19	2		3	
20			1	1
21			1	
22	1		1	1
23			1	2
24	1		2	
25			2	
26	1		1	
28				1
35	1			
Number of mice per group	28	23	23	20

[a]Groups of A/J mice were treated with either DMBA (0.5 mg in 0.2 ml sesame oil administered perorally) or urethane (1 mg/kg intraperitoneally of a sterile saline solution of urethane). Nine days after carcinogen treatment, mice received a diet containing 0.6% DHEA or a control diet. Fourteen weeks later, the mice were sacrificed and the number of lung adenomas was determined. DHEA produced a marked reduction in the incidence of lung tumors in DMBA-treated mice ($P < 0.001$, $\chi^2 = 25.2$) and a smaller effect in the urethane-treated animals ($P < 0.05$, $\chi^2 = 5.7$). (From Schwartz and Tannen, 1981.)

TABLE VII

REDUCTIONS IN COLON TUMOR YIELD INDUCED BY DHEA[a]

Protocol	Average number of tumors per animal	
	20 weeks	26 weeks
DMH plus DHEA	0.5 ± 0.71	2.5 ± 1.3
DMH only	8.3 ± 6.2	13.2 ± 6.4
Control diet	0.0	0.0
DHEA only	0.0	0.0

[a]BALB/c female mice were placed on either a control diet or a diet supplemented with 0.6% DHEA. Two weeks later all mice were injected subcutaneously and weekly thereafter with 21 mg/kg of DMH. Autopsy of ten animals from each group following 20 weeks of carcinogen treatment revealed a 16-fold reduction in colonic tumor yield per animal in DHM + DHEA-treated animals relative to the tumor yield in those treated with DMH alone. Autopsies at 26 weeks showed over a fivefold reduction in colonic tumor yield in the DHEA-treated animals. [From Nyce, J. W., Magee, P. N., and Schwartz, A. G. (1982). *Ann. N.Y. Acad. Sci.* **397**, 317–319.]

application to the skin of CD-1 mice inhibited DMBA-initiated and TPA-promoted papilloma formation at both the initiation and promotion stages and inhibited DMBA-induced papilloma and carcinoma development in the complete carcinogenesis model (Pashko *et al.*, 1984, 1985).

In the mouse, either topical application of DHEA to the skin at 100 or 400 μg (Pashko *et al.*, 1984) or oral administration in the diet at 0.6% for 2 weeks (Pashko and Schwartz, 1985) inhibits the rate of binding of [^{3}H]DMBA to skin DNA. This inhibition of [^{3}H]DMBA-binding to skin DNA may result from depression of G6PDH activity and inhibition of carcinogen activation as was suggested for the mechanism by which DHEA protects cultured cells against DMBA- and aflatoxin B_1-induced toxicity and transformation. Very probably the reduction in [^{3}H]DMBA-binding to skin DNA by DHEA accounts for the antiinitiating activity of the steroid against DMBA-initiated papillomas as well as for the inhibition in development of DMBA-induced papillomas and carcinomas in the complete carcinogenesis model.

A. INHIBITION OF DNA SYNTHESIS

Topical DHEA treatment also inhibits papilloma formation when applied 1 hr before TPA treatment, a result indicating that the steroid also blocks tumor promotion. The following experimental evidence suggests that DHEA inhibition of tumor promotion may also result from G6PDH inhibition by the steroid. Tumor promoters such as TPA produce diverse effects on mammalian cells (Slaga, 1983), and the mechanism by which they enhance skin papilloma formation is not fully understood. TPA application to mouse skin stimulates epidermal DNA synthesis and hyperplasia (Argyris, 1980b; Baird *et al.*, 1971). It was suggested by Frei and Stephens (1968), Setala *et al.* (1959), and Argyris (1983) that chronic regenerative hyperplasia induced by topical application of tumor promoters was critical to their tumor-enhancing action. Argyris (1980a,b) and Argyris and Slaga (1981) demonstrated that the production of chronic regenerative hyperplasia by abrasion of the skin promotes epidermal tumorigenesis in the skin of mice initiated with DMBA. Kinzel *et al.* (1984) have provided strong experimental support for the notion that the induction of DNA synthesis by TPA is a necessary condition for its tumor-promoting action. The tumor-promotion phase can be subdivided into two stages (Furstenburger *et al.*, 1981; Slaga *et al.*, 1980). Stage I is brought about by a single application of TPA; it must be followed in stage II by repeated treatment with incomplete promoters such as 12-*O*-retinoylphorbol-13-acetate or mezerein. Kinzel *et al.* (1984) produced tumors in mice by an initiating dose of DMBA followed by a single treatment with TPA (stage I) and then twice weekly applications of 12-*O*-retinoylphorbol-13-acetate (stage II). They found that a single intraperitoneal injection of mice with hydroxyurea, a reversible nontoxic inhibitor of DNA synthesis in mouse epidermis, given at different times before or after treatment with TPA interfered with tumor formation. Hydroxyurea treatment produced an almost complete inhibition of tumor formation if administered 18 hr after TPA application—i.e., at the time of maximal DNA synthesis.

A single intraperitoneal injection of DHEA (10 mg/kg) into ICR mice immediately before TPA application also abolishes the TPA stimulation in epidermal [^{3}H]thymidine incorporation (Pashko *et al.*, 1981). The synthetic steroid, Epi-Br, a compound that is 30 to 50 times more potent as an inhibitor of mammalian G6PDH (Raineri and Levy, 1970), is also much more active as an inhibitor of the TPA stimulation of [^3H]thymidine incorporation—an injected dose of 0.4 mg/kg of Epi-Br was more effective than 10 mg/kg of DHEA (Pashko *et al.*, 1981) (Table VIII). Of various sex steroids and a glucocorticoid that were tested, all of which are inactive G6PDH inhibitors, only corticosterone inhibited the rate of [^{3}H]thymidine incorporation. Glucocorticoids are known to inhibit epidermal DNA synthesis (Castor and Baker, 1950).

Specific 3T3 fibroblast clones can, under carefully defined conditions, be stimulated to undergo highly efficient differentiation into adipocytes (Bernohr *et al.*, 1985; Green and Kehinde, 1975). Adipocyte differentiation is a multistep process, the mechanism of which is unclear. Increases in thymidine incorporation, in cell number, and in translatable mRNAs precede the elevation of marker enzymes of lipid synthesis, and of increased incorporation of acetate into lipid (Bernohr *et al.*, 1985; Green and Kehinde,

TABLE VIII

EFFECT OF DIFFERENT STEROIDS ON THE RATE OF [^{3}H]THYMIDINE INCORPORATION IN NORMAL AND TPA-STIMULATED MOUSE EPIDERMIS[a]

Steroid	Dose (mg/kg, i.p.)	Specific activity (cpm/μg DNA)	
		Acetone	TPA
Saline–Emulphor	—	42.0 ± 0.9	113 ± 4.0
Epi-Br	10.0	6.3 ± 1.2	26 ± 4.4
Epi-Br	2.0	8.1 ± 0.3	27 ± 7.0
Epi-Br	0.4	6.5 ± 0.4	29 ± 4.0
Epi-Br	0.1	41.0 ± 7.0	100 ± 0.2
DHEA	15.0	23.0 ± 1.0	39 ± 5.9
DHEA	10.0	—	51 ± 1.3
DHEA	2.0	—	64 ± 2.3
DHEA	0.4	—	122 ± 11.0
Estradiol-17β	15.0	—	119 ± 19.0
Progesterone	15.0	—	120 ± 17.0
Corticosterone	15.0	—	80 ± 5.0
Testosterone	15.0	—	118 ± 13.0

[a]Mice were treated with steroid and TPA, and the rate of [^{3}H]thymidine incorporation was determined 20 hr later as described by Pashko *et al.* (1981). ICR male mice (7–9 weeks old) were shaved on the back 1–2 days before use. Mice were housed in polycarbonate cages (5 mice/cage) in animal quarters maintained at 24 ± 1°C and 40–45% relative humidity with 12 hr of light and 12 hr of darkness each day. Only mice showing no hair regrowth following shaving were used. Animals were injected intraperitoneally (i.p.) with a particular steroid suspended by homogenization in 95% saline–5% Emulphor (GAF Corp., New York) or were injected with vehicle alone. One hour later TPA (10 μg in 0.2 ml of acetone) or acetone vehicle was applied topically to the shaved skin. After 20 hr, mice were injected i.p. with 60 μCi of [^{3}H]thymidine (2 Ci/mmol) 20 min before sacrifice. The animals were killed by cervical dislocation and the residual hair was removed with a depilatory agent. Epidermal scrapings were prepared, homogenized in distilled water at 4°C, and the macromolecules precipitated with 0.4 *N* trichloracetic acid (TCA). Following 6 washes with 0.2 *N* TCA at 4°C and 2 washes with absolute ethanol at room temperature, the nucleic acids wre hydrolyzed with 0.5 *N* TCA at 90°C for 5 min. The hydrolysates (0.2-ml aliquots) were counted in an Intertechnique scintillation counter and assayed for DNA. Each value is the mean ± range for two or three separately treated mice. Each counted aliquot (0.2 ml) contained approximately 10 μg of DNA. (From Pashko *et al.*, 1981.)

1976). Using the above assay of conversion of 3T3 preadipocytes to adipocytes, Gordon *et al.* (1986a) found that DHEA and Epi-Br blocked the conversion to adipocytes of the 3T3-L1 and 3T3-F442A mouse embryo fibroblast clones. They also observed that Epi-Br was much more potent than DHEA in blocking conversion and suggested that G6PDH inhibition by these steroids very likely accounted for this effect (Fig. 7).

Two major functions usually ascribed to the oxidative branch of the pentose phosphate cycle are the generation of NADPH for reductive biosyntheses and other specific metabolic reactions as well as the formation of ribose

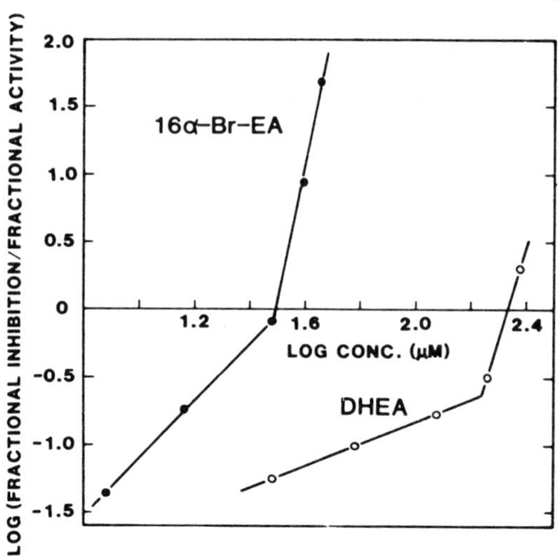

FIG. 7. Effect of concentration of DHEA and 16α-bromoepiandrosterone (16α-Br-EA) on the glycerol-3-phosphate dehydrogenase-specific activities of differentiating 3T3-L1 preadipocytes. The cells were differentiated as described in Gordon *et al.* (1986a). Various concentrations of DHEA (30–240 μM) and 16α-bromoepiandrosterone (7.5–45 μM) were added simultaneously with the differentiation stimuli (days 7–9), and the cells were harvested on day 12. The results are expressed as percentages of fully differentiated controls and are plotted here according to the median effect plot (50) in which the logarithm of the ratio of the fractional inhibition to the fractional activity is plotted as a function of the logarithm of the concentration of the blocking steroid. (From Gordon *et al.*, 1986a.)

5-phosphate, which is utilized in nucleotide biosynthesis via the intermediate 5-phosphoribosyl 1-pyrophosphate. Purine ribonucleotide and thymidylic acid biosynthesis are dependent upon tetrahydrofolic acid, which requires NADPH for its reductive synthesis from folic acid. Also the enzymatic formation of deoxyribonucleotide diphosphates from their corresponding ribonucleotide diphosphates by ribonucleotide reductase in NADPH dependent.

If DHEA and related steroids repress DNA synthesis in cells by reducing ribonucleotide and deoxyribonucleotide synthesis as a result of G6PDH inhibition, then provision of these nucleosides would be expected to reverse the DHEA-induced inhibition. This was indeed shown to be the case with cultured HeLa TCRC-2 cells. DHEA at a concentration of 10^{-5} *M* inhibited the growth rate of these cells in culture, and this growth inhibition was almost completely overcome by adding to the culture medium a mixture of the deoxynucleosides of adenine, guanine, thymine, and cytosine (Dworkin *et al.*, 1986) (Fig. 8). Gordon *et al.* (1987) have also found that the addition of the four ribonucleosides (uridine, cytidine, adenosine, and guanosine) to

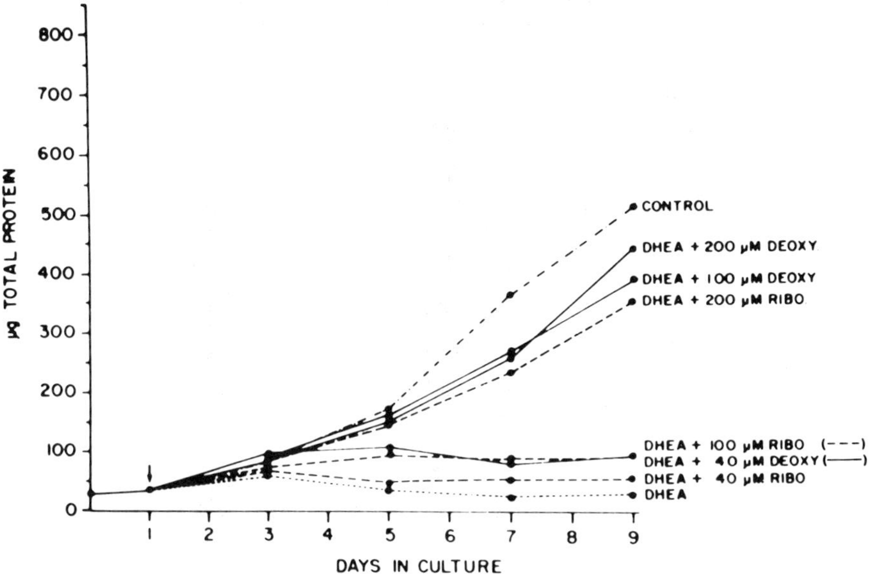

FIG. 8. Reversal of DHEA-induced growth inhibition of HeLa TCRC-2 cells by deoxy- or ribonucleosides. Cells were seeded at 0.3×10^6 cells per T-15 flask with 3 ml of Eagle's minimal essential medium supplemented with 10% dialyzed fetal calf serum. Twenty-four hours after seeding, triplicate flasks received DHEA (10 *µM*) or DHEA supplemented with deoxyribonucleosides (deoxyadenosine, deoxyguanosine, deoxycytidine, and thymidine) and ribonucleosides (adenosine, guanosine, cytidine, and uridine). The individual nucleosides are indicated in micromolar concentrations. Cells were fed daily with fresh media containing the various additives. Points are mean cellular protein contents for four T-15 flasks with an average standard error of <10%. (From Dworkin *et al.*, 1986.)

cultured 3T3-L1 cells almost completely prevented the blocking action of Epi-Br on the differentiation of these cells to adipocytes (Fig. 9).

Other investigators have found that G6PDH is stimulated in cells undergoing increased rates of cell proliferation. Ledda-Columbano *et al.* (1985) have found in the rat higher rates of cholesterol synthesis and enhanced G6PDH levels in chemical carcinogen-induced hepatocyte nodules than in surrounding normal tissue. Similar biochemical changes were found when liver cell proliferation was induced by either partial hepatectomy, lead administration, or insulin treatment of diabetic and fasted rats (Columbano *et al.*, 1985). Rao *et al.* (1984) have also reported a positive correlation between cell proliferation and G6PDH activity in both the pancreas and liver of rats. Yoshimoto *et al.* (1983) reported that epidermal growth factor (EGF) and insulin, both of which stimulate growth of primary cultured hepatocytes from adult rats, induced G6PDH activity in these cells. Induction of G6PDH

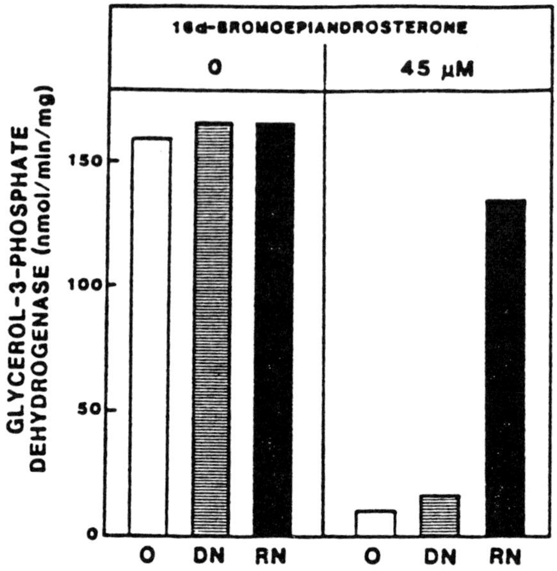

FIG. 9. Reversal by ribonucleosides of the blocking action of 16α-bromoepiandrosterone on the differentiation of 3T3-L1 cells to adipocytes, as measured by the specific activity of cytosolic glycerol-3-phosphate dehydrogenase. The cells were grown and differentiated as described in Gordon *et al.* (1986a). Exposure to 45 μM 16α-bromoepiandrosterone occurred from day 7 to day 9 simultaneously with the differentiation mixture (insulin, fetal calf serum, dexamethasone, and 1-methyl-3-isobutylxanthine). The cells were also exposed on days 6–9 either to a mixture of thymidine, deoxycytidine, deoxyadenosine, and deoxyguanosine (DN) or to a mixture of uridine, cytidine, adenosine and guanosine (RN). The final concentrations of all nucleosides were 200 μM. The addition of the nucleosides was made on day 6 to the same medium that was already present on the plates, in order to avoid the perturbing effects of fresh medium. Note that the nucleosides had little effect on glycerol-3-phosphate dehydrogenase activity of the control cells, and that the ribonucleosides, but not the deoxyribonucleosides, nearly completely reversed the blocking effect of the steroid. (From Gordon *et al.*, 1987.)

by these two hormones was greater at low cell density, when the hepatocytes were actively growing, than it was at high cell density, when growth was inhibited. Moreover, they found that the induction of malic enzyme, another NADPH-supplying enzyme, was inhibited by EGF and that cell density had opposite effects on malic enzyme activity and G6PDH activity. The authors concluded that malic enzyme acts mostly in lipogenesis, whereas G6PDH functions in both cell growth and lipogenesis.

B. INHIBITION OF SUPEROXIDE FORMATION

In addition to an NADPH requirement for mixed function oxidase activity and for specific enzymatic reactions in the biosynthesis of ribonucleotides and deoxyribonucleotides, NADPH is a coenzyme for a membrane-bound oxidase that is found in granulocytes and macrophages and generates superoxide anion (O_2^-) (Babior, 1982). O_2^- and other forms of reactive oxygen can induce deletion mutations and chromosomal aberrations (Emerit and Cerutti, 1983; Hsie *et al.*, 1986) and may exert critical effects in the tumor promotion process. X irradiation of cultured hamster embryonic fibroblasts followed by TPA treatment induces malignant transformation, and this process can be blocked by treatment with superoxide dismutase (SOD) and TPA (Borek and Troll, 1983). Kensler *et al.* (1983) found that topical application of a low-molecular-weight copper complex, bis[(3,5-diisopropyl)salicylato](*O*,*O*)copper(II), which has SOD-mimetic action, together with TPA in the two-stage skin tumor system markedly inhibited papilloma formation. TPA rapidly stimulates O_2^- formation by granulocytes *in vitro* (Goldstein *et al.*, 1981). DHEA inhibits this stimulation and the synthetic steroid, Epi-Br, is a more potent inhibitor, again a result suggesting that G6PDH inhibition and a reduction in NADPH pool size is the probable mechanism of inhibition (Whitcomb and Schwartz, 1985) (Table IX).

Thus three processes which contribute to tumor development: (1) metabolic activation of a carcinogen through the action of mixed-function oxidases, (2) tumor promoter stimulation of cell proliferation, and (3) tumor promoter stimulation of O_2^- formation are all inhibited by DHEA, probably as a result of G6PDH inhibition and a lowering of the NADPH cellular pool. We have recently obtained evidence indicating that these first two processes may also be inhibited in mouse epidermis following a regimen of 40% food restriction for 2 weeks, a result suggesting a similarity in the mechanism by which underfeeding and DHEA inhibit tumorigenesis. Specifically, reducing the food intake of A/J mice (60% of *ad libitum* fed) for 2 weeks inhibits the rate of binding of [^{3}H]DMBA to mouse skin DNA by 50% (Schwartz and Pashko, 1986) (Table X). A similar reduction in [^{3}H]DMBA binding to skin DNA is produced by topical application of DHEA immediately before DMBA treatment (Schwartz and Pashko, 1986) (Table X). The TPA stimulation in the rate of [^{3}H]thymidine incorporation in mouse epidermis is also abolished in food-restricted animals, an effect that is also seen with topical DHEA treatment (Table XI). We found that mouse epidermal G6PDH activity was depressed by 60% following 2 weeks of food restriction (Schwartz and Pashko, 1986) (Table XII), and when considered with the evidence that the inhibition of [^{3}H]DMBA binding to DNA and TPA stimulation in [^{3}H]thymidine incorporation by DHEA very possibly results from G6PDH inhibition, it is reasonable to assume that the depression in epidermal G6PDH activity following underfeeding may exert a similar effect. Although further experimental evidence in other organs on G6PDH activity levels following food restriction is clearly needed, it is an intriguing possibility

TABLE IX
EFFECT OF STEROIDS ON TPA STIMULATION OF SUPEROXIDE (O_2^-) PRODUCTION BY HUMAN POLYMORPHONUCLEAR LEUKOCYTES[a]

Steroid	Percentage of inhibition, O_2^-	Percentage of inhibition, G6PDH
DHEA		
1×10^{-4} *M*	59 ± 13 (6)	73 ± 6 (2)
5×10^{-5} *M*	43 ± 10 (4)	63 ± 6 (3)
1×10^{-5} *M*	24 ± 9 (5)	31 ± 8 (3)
Epi-Br		
1×10^{-4} *M*	99 ± 2 (3)	100 ± 0 (2)
5×10^{-5} *M*	74 ± 14 (4)	83 ± 1 (3)
1×10^{-5} *M*	44 ± 11 (4)	61 ± 0.7 (2)
Testosterone		
1×10^{-4} *M*	22 ± 11 (3)	10 ± 0 (3)
5×10^{-5} *M*	None	None
1×10^{-5} *M*	—	—
DHEA-sulfate or hydrocortisone		
1×10^{-4} *M*	None	None
5×10^{-5} *M*	None	None

[a]Polymorphonuclear leukocytes (PMNs) were isolated from whole human blood. The rate of O_2^- production was measured by the rate of cytochrome *c* reduction as described by Goldstein *et al.* (1981). 100 μl of horse heart cytochrome *c* (4 mg/ml in H_2O) and 50 μl of PMN cell suspension were added to 400 μl of Earle's balanced salt solution (BSS) and brought to 37°C in a heated cuvette holder. Steroids to be tested were added in 3 μl of ethanol. This concentration of ethanol did not demonstrably affect the rate of O_2^- production. The PMNs were activated by the addition of 50 μl of TPA (1 μg/ml in BSS), and the reduction of cytochrome *c* was monitored by the change in absorbance at 550 nm. The reference cuvette contained 500 μl of BSS and 100 μl of cytochrome *c*. The addition of superoxide dismutate completely inhibited the reduction of cytochrome *c*.

Each value is the mean percentage of inhibition ± S.D. with the number of experiments indicated in parentheses. In the absence of steroid, 10^7 PMNs produced ~3.4 nmol O_2^- per minute. Addition of 20 μg/ml of SOD completely inhibited the production of O_2^-. Steroids were dissolved in ethanol and added to the reaction cuvette at a final ethanol concentration of 0.5%. TPA was prepared as a stock solution of 1 mg/ml in acetone and diluted to 1 μg/ml in BSS on the day of use. 50 μl of this prepartion was added to 550 μl of reaction mixture at a final acetone concentration of 0.01%.

G6PDH activity was measured as described in Whitcomb and Schwartz (1985).

TABLE X

EFFECT OF STEROID TREATMENT OR TWO WEEKS OF FOOD RESTRICTION ON [^{3}H]DMBA BINDING TO SKIN DNA[a]

Treatment	[^{3}H]DMBA bound to DNA (cpm/μg DNA)
Ad libitum fed	116 ± 5.2
Ad libitum fed plus DHEA	66 ± 13
Ad libitum fed plus testosterone	164 ± 8.4
Food restricted	57 ± 14

[a]Male A/J mice (6 weeks old) were housed four per cage in 11½ × 7 × 5 in. plastic cages with hardwood bedding in an animal facility with 12 hr of alternating light and dark at 70 ± 2°F and 50 ± 5% relative humidity.

Ad libitum fed mice were given free access to pelleted Purina mouse chow #5015. Food consumption was determined as described in Schwartz and Pashko (1986). Food-restricted mice were given daily rations of approximately 60% of the amount of food eaten per day by the *ad libitum*-fed mice.

[^{3}H] DMBA Binding to mouse skin DNA. Mice were shaved 2 to 3 days before use. Only those showing no hair regrowth were used. In experiments in which mice were food-restricted, a regimen of food restriction was initiated in and continued for 2 weeks prior to [^{3}H]DMBA application. Topical DHEA or testosterone was applied at a does of 400 μg in 0.2 ml of acetone 1 hr before [^{3}H] DMBA (100 μCi, nmol total, in 0.2 ml acetone) was applied; 0.2 ml of acetone was applied to mice not receiving steroid.

The DMBA was applied in a darkened room, and the mice were kept in the dark until sacrifice 12 hr later in order to minimize the loss of DMBA-DNA adducts due to light exposure. The skin was excised and placed in cold 0.25 *M* sucrose–0.05 *M* Tris buffer (pH 7.5), and the epidermis and dermis were scraped off with a surgical scalpel. DNA was isolated as described in Schwartz and Pashko (1986).

Values are mean ± S.D. for three individual determinations, with pooled tissue from two mice used for each determination. From Schwartz and Pashko, 1986.

that underfeeding depresses G6PDH activity, with a consequent inhibition of initiation and promotion, and that this may contribute to the tumor preventive activity of this regimen.

VII. Glucose-6-Phosphate Dehydrogenase Deficiency and Human Cancer

We are postulating that depression of G6PDH activity by DHEA and specific structural analogs is central to the mechanism by which these steroids inhibit tumorigenesis. We would therefore anticipate that individuals who are carriers of hereditary G6PDH deficiency would experience a lowered cancer incidence and also that isolated cells from such individuals would show responses to tumor initiators and promoters similar to DHEA-treated cells. Evidence discussed later does indeed suggest this.

TABLE XI

EFFECT OF TWO WEEKS OF FOOD RESTRICTION ON TPA STIMULATION OF EPIDERMAL [^{3}H]THYMIDINE INCORPORATION[a]

Treatment	[^{3}H]Thymidine incorporation (cpm/μg DNA)
Ad libitum fed	58 ± 5.0
Ad libitum fed plus TPA	119 ± 13
Food restricted	41 ± 8.9
Food restricted plus TPA	41 ± 5.7

[a]A/J mice were shaved on the back 2 to 3 days before use. Only mice showing no hair regrowth following shaving were used. Food-restricted mice received approximately 60% of *ad libitum* levels of food for 2 weeks prior to TPA (10 μg in 0.2 ml acetone) application. Twenty hours after TPA application, mice were injected intraperitoneally with 60 μCi of [^{3}H]thymidine (2 Ci/nmol) 20 min before sacrifice. The animals were killed by cervical dislocation, residual hair was removed with a depilatory agent, and DNA was prepared from epidermal scrapings as described in Schwartz and Pashko (1986). Values are mean ± S.D. for three separately treated mice in each group. (From Schwartz and Pashko, 1986).

G6PDH deficiency is a sex-linked hereditary defect occurring with high frequency in certain populations. Among the most prevalent deficiency mutants are the Mediterranean variant, found primarily among Sephardic Jews, Greeks, and Sardinians, and G6PDH A$^-$, common in Black populations. The Mediterranean deficiency is more severe than the A$^-$ deficiency and occurs in many cells and tissues other than erythrocytes, including fibroblasts, lymphocytes, neutrophils, liver, adrenals, kidneys, and the lens of the eye (Beutler, 1971).

TABLE XII

EFFECT OF TWO WEEKS OF FOOD RESTRICTION ON EPIDERMAL G6PDH ACTIVITY[a]

Treatment	Specific activity (nmol NADPH/mg protein–min)
Ad libitum fed	43.4 ± 6.0
Food restricted	18.1 ± 5.1

[a]Male A/J mice were shaved on the back 2 to 3 days before use. Only those mice showing no hair regrowth were used. Food-restricted mice received approximately 60% of the food consumed by *ad libitum* fed mice for 2 weeks prior to sacrifice and G6PDH measurement. G6PDH activity was determined as described in Schwartz and Pashko (1986). Values are mean ± S.D. for three separate determinations, with pooled epidermal tissue from four mice used for each determination. (From Schwartz and Pashko, 1986).

Feo *et al.* (1984a,b) recently reported that cultured fibroblasts and lymphocytes from individuals with the Mediterranean variant of G6PDH deficiency are less sensitive to the cytotoxic and transforming effects of benzo[*a*]pyrene (BP) and are less efficient in metabolizing [^{3}H]BP to water-soluble products than are fibroblasts from normal individuals. Treatment of normal fibroblasts or lymphocytes with DHEA mimicked the effect of the G6PDH deficiency. The authors also reported a marked reduction in pentose phosphate shunt activity and a lowering of the NADPH:NADP pool ratio in the G6PDH-deficient cells. Pascale *et al.* (1987) have also found that TPA stimulation of O_2^- formation by neutrophils, a process that is inhibited by DHEA and even more strongly by Epi-Br, is reduced in neutrophils from G6PDH-deficient individuals. Thus, both the rate of metabolic activation of a polycyclic hydrocarbon carcinogen and tumor promoter stimulation of O_2^-, processes that are both inhibited by DHEA and specific structural analogs, are also impaired in cells from G6PDH-deficient people.

Beaconsfield *et al.* (1965) first proposed that the lowered cancer rates in Israelis of North African or Asian origin relative to the rates in those of Western European or American origin might be due to the higher frequency of G6PDH deficiency in the former population. Sulis (1972) noted that among 320 male Sardinians with cancer who came from the area near Cagliari (where G6PDH deficiency affects 25–35% of the male population) the prevalence of the enzyme deficiency was only 13% ($p < 0.01$). In a case-control study among 70 Bantu hepatoma patients in Zaire, Mbensa *et al.* (1978) found that only 9 (12.9%) had G6PDH deficiency, whereas in a male control group 23% (11 out of 49) were G6PDH deficient. The discrepancy was most pronounced in the young adult group: under 40 years only 3 out of 47 patients (6.4%) were G6PDH deficient. Naik and Anderson (1971) determined the frequencies of G6PDH deficiency in 241 consecutive Black cancer patients (66 male and 175 female) admitted to M. D. Anderson Hospital in 1969 and in a control group of 266 healthy Black males and 142 Black females. A lower frequency of G6PDH deficiency was observed in both male (4.5%) and female (0.57%) cancer patients relative to that in male (9.4%) and female (3.8%) controls. While additional work is clearly needed to establish a causal relationship between the incidence of G6PDH deficiency and tumor development, these studies suggest an inverse correlation and are consistent with the hypothesis that G6PDH deficiency may protect against cancer.

VIII. Other Therapeutic Effects of DHEA

A. Antidiabetic Activity

The mutation diabetes (*db*) produces obesity and a hyperinsulinemic insulin-resistant state that progresses to a severe diabetes syndrome only when the mutation is placed on a susceptible inbred strain of mouse (Coleman, 1978). On the C57BL/KsJ (*BL/Ks*) background the *db* trait is characterized by obesity and transient hyperinsulinemia, followed by beta cell necrosis and atrophy. In *BL/Ks db/db* mice, DHEA treatment (0.4% of diet) initiated between 1 and 4 months of age produced a rapid remission of hyperglycemia, a preservation of beta cell structure and function, and an increased insulin sensitivity as measured by glucose tolerance tests (Coleman *et al.*, 1982). DHEA feeding was also therapeutic to normal *BL/Ks* mice made diabetic by multiple low doses of streptozotocin. DHEA treatment of *BL/Ks db/db* mice only slightly reduced the rate of weight gain, although the final body weights attained in treated and control mice were the same. However, daily food intake as measured over a period of 2 weeks was increased by 48% in the DHEA-treated animals.

Introduction of the *db* gene into C57BL/6J (*BL/6*) mice produces obesity with a transient well-compensated diabetes that is less severe than that observed in KsJ mice. The mild hyperglycemia observed in the *BL/6 db/db* mouse was prevented by feeding 0.1% DHEA diet, and both body weight and food consumption were also decreased (Coleman *et al.*, 1984).

The mechanism of the antidiabetic effect of DHEA in the mouse is not clear. Epi-Br, the potent G6PDH inhibitor that is more active than DHEA in several biological assays, when fed at 0.4% in the diet of *BL/Ks db/db* mice, had no effect on blood sugar levels or on the rate of weight gain, a result suggesting that G6PDH inhibition is not the primary mechanism of action of the antidiabetic and antiobesity effects (Coleman *et al.*, 1984).

B. Antiautoimmune and Possible Antiaging Effects

Administration of DHEA (0.4% of the diet) to NZB mice, an autoimmune susceptible strain that develops a Coomb's-positive hemolytic anemia, inhibited anemia development (Tannen and Schwartz, 1982). DHEA treatment also produced a significant reduction in weight gain in this mouse strain. The NZB/NZW mouse, which is considered an excellent model for the development of systemic lupus erythematosus, develops an autoimmune disorder that is characterized by the formation of anti-DNA and antinuclear antibodies (Dubois *et al.*, 1966; Holmes and Burnet, 1963). These mice develop a severe immune complex glomerulonephritis that produces death in the majority of animals before 12 months of age. Lucas *et al.* (1985) found that DHEA (0.45% in the diet) prevented the formation of antibodies to double-stranded DNA and prolonged survival. But unlike the NZB mouse, the NZB/NZW strain responded to DHEA treatment with reduced autoimmune disease development without reduced weight gain.

Treatment of Sprague-Dawley rats with a diet containing 0.4% DHEA from 2 to 19 months of age inhibited the appearance of proteinuria at 19 months (Pashko and Schwartz, 1985). Chronic progressive nephrosis with concomitant proteinuria appears at an early age in the Sprague-Dawley rat and is a principal cause of death (Gray *et al.*, 1974). Much less severe proteinuria develops with age in the C57BL/6 mouse, and this was also inhibited by DHEA treatment (Pashko and Schwartz, 1985). Not only was proteinuria development retarded, but when DHEA treatment was continued throughout the life span of the mice and rats, their longevity was greater than that of nontreated controls (unpublished observation). Thus, DHEA treatment may share with caloric restriction the ability to retard aging.

C. Possible Antiatherogenic Effect

Gordon *et al.* recently tested the effect of DHEA against experimentally induced atherosclerosis in rabbits (Gordon *et al.*, 1986b). The authors used a model in which severe aortic atherosclerosis occurs. A 2% cholesterol diet was given to ten New Zealand white male rabbits for 11 weeks: five received 0.5% DHEA in the diet, five did not. After 1 week on the diet, a balloon catheter-induced aortic intimal injury was performed in all animals. On day 77 the rabbits were sacrificed, the aortas were removed, and atherosclerosis was assessed by Sudan stain. Plaque thickness in five regions was quantified, and the authors noted a 39% decrease in plaque thickness in the DHEA-treated group. The effect was not due to differences in food intake, body weight, total serum cholesterol, or triglycerides.

A recently reported epidemiological study by Barrett-Connor *et al.* (1986) may be related to these findings of Gordon *et al.* These investigators reported the results of a prospective study that examined the relationship of plasma DHEAS levels to subsequent 12-year mortality in a population-based cohort of 242 men aged 50–79 years. After adjusting for age, systolic blood pressure, serum cholesterol level, obesity, fasting plasma glucose level, cigarette smoking status, and personal history of heart disease, they found that the DHEAS level was independently and inversely related to death from any cause and death from cardiovascular disease in particular in men over age 50.

A recent finding in this laboratory may be relevant to the observations of Gordon *et al.* and Barrett-Connor *et al.* Stimulated production of various eicosanoid compounds, such as leukotrienes and prostaglandins, is believed to play an important role in the development of atherosclerosis (Glomset, 1985) and also in the enhancement of tumorigenesis by tumor promoters, such as TPA in the skin (Aizu *et al.*, 1986) and bile salts in the colon (Craven *et al.*, 1986). The beneficial effects of diets high in fish oil fatty acids, which contain ω-3-fatty acids instead of arachidonic acid, in populations such as Eskimos, who experience a low incidence of atherosclerotic heart disease, is well documented (Bang and Dyerberg, 1980; Kromhout *et al.*, 1985).

We have found that topical application of TPA to mouse skin stimulates prostaglandin E_2 (PGE_2) levels from a baseline of 8.4 ± 1.0 (pg $PGE_2/\mu g$ DNA)

($n = 2$) to 77.1 ± 3.3 ($n = 2$). Pretreatment of mice for 10 days with a diet containing 0.2% of either DHEA, 16α-fluoro-androsten-17-one (8354), or 16α-fluoro-5α-androstan-17-one (8356) reduced the stimulated values from 77.1 ± 3.3 ($n = 2$) to 22.7 ± 8.2 ($n = 3$), 4.2 ± 0.4 ($n = 3$), and 5.6 ± 0.4 ($n = 3$), respectively. Compounds 8354 and 8356 are more potent inhibitors of G6PDH than DHEA, again a finding suggesting a role for inhibition of this enzyme in an important biological effect. One possible explanation is that these steroids reduce the rate of conversion of linoleic acid to arachidonic acid, a process requiring NADPH (Mohrhauer *et al.*, 1967; Chapkin *et al.*, 1986). However, further work is clearly needed to establish the mechanism of this biological action.

D. Synthetic DHEA Analogs: Their Use as Potential Drugs and as Tools for Understanding the Mechanism of Therapeutic Action of DHEA

The studies reported in this review have demonstrated that oral treatment of mice and rats with DHEA protects against the development of a broad spectrum of tumors, delays the development of an autoimmune hemolytic anemia and lupus erythematosus-like disease, and may retard aging. In all of these studies, with the exception of that of Lucas *et al.* (1985), oral DHEA administration simultaneously reduced weight, and because inhibiting weight gain through food restriction has similar protective effects, it is not clear to what extent these actions of DHEA are mediated by direct effects on target cells or are an indirect consequence of weight reduction. However, one series of experimental observations does indicate that DHEA treatment inhibits tumorigenesis through a direct action on target cells. Topical application of DHEA or 3β-methyl-5-androsten-17-one to mouse skin at a dose of 100 or 400 μg per application, which has no effect on weight gain, blocks the action of both locally applied DMBA and TPA in producing skin papillomas and carcinomas (Pashko *et al*, 1984, 1985). As previously discussed, these effects of DHEA very likely result from G6PDH inhibition and a lowering of the NADPH cellular pool.

Although long-term DHEA treatment of mice and rats is without apparent side effect, DHEA is convertible into estrone and testosterone. DHEA is uterotrophic at therapeutic doses in the sexually immature rat (Knudsen and Mahesh, 1975), and conversion into sex steroids could limit the usefulness of DHEA as a cancer chemopreventive drug. The synthetic steroid 3β-methylandrost-5-en-17-one, in which the *3β-hydroxy* group of DHEA is replaced with a *3β-methyl* group, was specifically designed to prevent conversion into androstenedione, an intermediate on the pathway to testosterone and estrone. 3β-Methylandrost-5-en-17-one was indeed without activity in the rat uterotrophic test at doses at which DHEA was highly active (Pashko *et al.*, 1984). On oral administration the synthetic steroid was about 3 times as active as DHEA as an antiobesity and antidiabetic agent in the mouse (unpublished observation).

Two other synthetic steroids, 16α-fluoro-5-androsten-17-one (8354) and 16α-fluoro-5α-androstan-17-one (8356), which also lack the uterotrophic and seminal vesicle enlarging effects of DHEA, have shown 15 times greater potency than DHEA when given orally in blocking both [^{3}H]DMBA binding to skin DNA and TPA stimulation in epidermal [^{3}H]thymidine incorporation; a dose of 25 mg/kg of either analog is as effective as 400 mg/kg of DHEA. At the 25 mg/kg dose, the analogs do not inhibit weight gain, and it should now be possible to determine whether the cancer preventive activity, and possibly other therapeutic effects of these steroids as well, is mediated through G6PDH inhibition and can be dissociated from the weight reducing effect (unpublished observation). The lack of estrogenic and androgenic activity of compounds 8354 and 8356 along with their greater potency suggest that such analogs may find application as cancer chemopreventive drugs in the human.

References

Aizu, E., Nakadate, T., Yamamoto, S., and Kato, R. (1986). *Carcinogenesis* **7**, 1809–1812.

Albanes, D. (1987). *Nutr. Cancer* **9**, 199–217.

Argyris, T. S. (1980a). *Am. J. Pathol.* **98**, 639–648.

Argyris, T. S. (1980b). *J. Invest. Dermatol.* **75**, 360–362.

Argyris, T. S. (1983). *Cancer Res.* **43**, 1768–1773.

Argyris, T. S., and Slaga, T. J. (1981). *Cancer Res.* **41**, 5193–5195.

Babior, B. M. (1982). *Can. J. Physiol. Pharmacol.* **60**, 1353–1358.

Baird, W. M., Sedgwick, J. A., and Boutwell, R. K. (1971). *Cancer Res.* **31**, 1434–1439.

Bang, H. O., and Dyerberg, J. (1980). *Adv. Nutr. Res.* **3**, 1–22.

Barrett-Connor, E., Khow, K.-T., and Yen, S. S. C. (1986). *N. Engl. J. Med.* **315**, 1519–1524.

Baulieu, E.-E., Corpéchot, C., Dray, F., Emiliozzi, R., Lebeau, M.-C., Mauvais-Jarvis, P., and Robel, P. (1965). *Recent Prog. Horm. Res.* **21**, 411–500.

Beaconsfield, P., Rainsbury, R., and Kalton, G. (1965). *Oncologia* **19**, 11–19.

Bernohr, D. A., Bolanowski, M. A., Kelly, J. J., Jr., and Lane, M. D. (1985). *J. Biol. Chem.* **260**, 5563–5567.

Beutler, E. (1971). *Semin. Hematol.* **8**, 311–340.

Borek, C., and Troll, W. (1983). *Proc. Natl. Acad. Sci. U.S.A.* **80**, 1304–1307.

Boutwell, R. K. (1964). *CRC Crit. Rev. Toxicol.* **2**, 419–443.

Brownsey, B., Cameron, E. H. D., Griffiths, K., Gleave, E. N., Forrest, A. P. M., and Campbell, H. (1972). *Eur. J. Cancer* **8**, 131–137.

Bulbrook, R. D., Hayward, J. L., Spicer, C. C., and Thomas, B. S. (1962) *Lancet* **2**, 1235–1240.

Bulbrook, R. D., Hayward, J. L., and Spicer, C. C. (1971). *Lancet* **1**, 519–522.

Butenandt, A., and Tscherning, K. (1934). *Hoppe-Seyler's Z. Physiol. Chem.* **229**, 167–184.

Callow, R. K. (1936). *J. Soc. Chem. Ind. London* **55**, 1030–1040.

Castor, E. W., and Baker, B. L. (1950). *Endocrinology* **47**, 234–241.

Chapkin, R. S., Ziboh, V. A., Marcelo, C. L., and Voorhees, J. J. (1986). *J. Lipid Res.* **27**, 945–954.

Cleary, M. P., Hood, S. S., Chando, C., Han, C. T., and Billheimer, J. T. (1984a). *Nutr. Rev.* 4, 485–494.

Cleary, M. P., Shepherd, A., and Jenks, B. (1984b). *J. Nutr.* **114**, 1242–1251.
Cleary, M. P., Fox, N., Lazin, G., and Billheimer, J. T. (1985). *Nutr. Res.* **5**, 1247–1257.
Coleman, D. L. (1978). *Diabetologia* **14**, 141–144.
Coleman, D. L., Leiter, E. H., and Schwizer, R. W. (1982). *Diabetes* **31**, 830–833.
Coleman, D. L., Schwizer, R. W., and Leiter, E. H. (1984). *Diabetes* **33**, 26–32.
Columbano, A., Dessi, S., Ledda-Columbano, G. M., Chiodino, C., Corie, P., and Pani, P. (1985). *Abstr. Agents Process. Chem. Carcinogenesis; Sardinian Int. Meet., 3rd*, p. 35.
Craven, P. A., Pfanstiel, J., and DeRubertis, F. R. (1986). *J. Clin. Invest.* **77**, 850–859.
Dubois, E. L., Horowitz, R. E., Demopoulos, H. B., and Teplitz, R. (1966). *J. Am. Med. Assoc.* **195**, 285–289.
Dworkin, C. R., Gorman, S. D., Pashko, L. L., Cristofallo, V. J., and Schwartz, A. G. (1986). *Life Sci.* **38**, 1451–1457.
Emerit, I., and Cerutti, P. (1983). *Carcinogenesis* **4**, 1313–1316.
Feo, F., Pirisi, L., Pascale, R., Daino, L., Frassetto, S., Garcea, R., and Gaspa, L. (1984a). *Cancer Res.* **44**, 3419–3425.
Feo, F., Pirisi, L., Pascale, R., Daino, L., Frassetto, S., Zanetti, S., and Garcea, R. (1984b). *Toxicol. Pathol.* **11**, 261–268.
Fernandes, G., Friend, P., Yunis, E. J., and Good, R. A. (1978). *Proc. Natl. Acad. Sci. U.S.A.* **75**, 1500–1504.
Frei, J. V., and Stephens, P. (1968). *Br. J. Cancer* **22**, 83–92.
Furstenberger, G., Berry, D. L., Sorg, B., and Marks, F. (1981). *Proc. Natl. Acad. Sci. U.S.A.* **78**, 7722–7726.
Garcea, R., Daino, L., Pascale, R., Frassetto, S., Cozzolino, P., Ruggiu, M. E., and Feo, F. (1985). *Abstr. Agents Process. Chem. Carcinogenesis, Sardinian Int. Meet., 3rd.*
Garcea, R., Daino, L., Pascale, R., Frassetto, S., Cozzolino, P., Ruggiu, M. E., and Feo, F. (1987). *Toxicol. Pathol.*, in press.
Gherondache, C., Romanoff, L., and Pincus, G. (1967). *In* "Endocrines and Aging" (L. Gitman, ed.), pp. 76–101. Thomas, Springfield, Illinois.
Glomset, J. A. (1985). *N. Engl. J. Med.* **312**, 1253.
Goldstein, B. D., Witz, G., Amoruso, M., Stove, D. S., and Troll, W. (1981). *Cancer Lett.* **11**, 257–262.
Gordon, G., Newitt, J. A., Shantz, L. M., Weng, D. E., and Talalay, P. (1986a). *Cancer Res.* **46**, 3389–3395.
Gordon, G. B., Bush, D. E., and Weisman, H. F. (1986b). *Arteriosclerosis* **6**, 558a (Abstr.).
Gordon, G. B., Shantz, L. M., and Talalay, P. (1987). *Adv. Enzyme Regul.* **26**, 355–382.
Gray, J. E., Weaver, R. N., and Purmalis, A. (1974). *Vet. Pathol.* **11**, 153–164.
Green, H., and Kehinde, O. (1975). *Cell* **5**, 19–27.
Green, H., and Kehinde, O. (1976). *Cell* **7**, 105–113.
Hochberg, R., Bandy, L., Ponticorvo, L., Welch, M., and Lieberman, S. (1979). *J. Steroid Biochem.* **11**, 1333–1340.
Holmes, M. C. and Burnet, F. M. (1963). *Ann. Intern. Med.* **59**, 265–276.
Hsie, A. W., Recio, L., Katz, D. S., Lee, C. Q., Wagner, M., and Schenley, R. L. (1986). *Proc. Natl. Acad. Sci. U.S.A.* **83**, 9616–9620.
Katoh, H., Nakajima, S., Kawashima, T., Kozuka, H., and Uchiyama, M. (1984). *Biochem. Pharmacol.* **33**, 1081–1085.
Kensler, T. W., Bush, D. M., and Kozumbo, W. J. (1983). *Science* **221**, 75–77.
Kinzel, V., Loehrke, H., Goerttler, K., Furstenberger, G., and Marks, F. (1984). *Proc. Natl. Acad. Sci. U.S.A.* **81**, 5858–5862.
Knudsen, T. T. and Mahesh, V. B. (1975). *Endocrinology* **97**, 458–468.
Kromhout, D., Bosschieter, E. B., deLezenne Coulander, C. (1985). *N. Engl. J. Med.* **312**, 1205–1209.

Ledda-Columbano, G. M., Columbano, A., Dessi, S., Coni, P., Chiodino, C., and Pani, P. (1985). *Carcinogenesis* **6**, 1371–1373.
Lew, E. A. and Garfinkel, L. (1979). *J. Chron. Dis.* **32**, 563–576.
Lucas, J. A., Ahmed, S. A., Casey, M. L., and MacDonald, P. C. (1985). *J. Clin. Invest.* **75**, 2091–2093.
McCay, C. M., Crowell, M. F., and Maynard, L. M. (1935). *J. Nutr.* **10**, 63–74.
Marks, P. A., and Banks, J. (1960). *Proc. Natl. Acad. Sci. U.S.A.* **46**, 447–452.
Mbensa, M., Rwakunda, C., and Vergilghen, R. L. (1978). *East Afr. Med. J.* **55**, 17–19.
Mellon-Nussbaum, S., and Hochberg, R. B. (1980). *J. Biol. Chem.* **225**, 5566–5572.
Migeon, C. J., Keller, A. R., Lawrence, B., and Shepart, T. H. (1957). *J. Clin. Endocrinol. Metab.* **17**, 1051–1062.
Mohrhauer, H., Christiansen, K., Gan, M. V., Deubig, M., and Holman, R. T. (1967). *J. Biol. Chem.* **242**, 4507–4514.
Moore, M. A., Thamavit, W., Truda, H., Sato, K., Ichihara, S., and Ito, N. (1986). *Carcinogenesis* **7**, 311–316.
Munson, P. L., Gallagher, T. F., and Koch, F. C. (1944). *J. Biol. Chem.* **152**, 67–77.
Naik, S. N., and Anderson, D. E. (1971). *Oncologia* **25**, 356–364.
Nielson, M. H., and Warren, J. C. (1965). *Biochim. Biophys. Acta* **97**, 532–541.
Nyce, J. W., Magee, P. N., Hard, G. C., and Schwartz, A. G. (1984). *Carcinogenesis* **5**, 57–62.
Oertel, G. W. (1964). *Hoppe-Seylers Z. Physiol. Chem.* **336**, 236–247.
Oertel, G. W. (1966). *Hoppe-Seylers Z. Physiol. Chem.* **343**, 276–281.
Oertel, G. W., and Benes, P. (1972). *J. Steroid Biochem.* **3**, 493–496.
Orentreich, N., Brind, J. L., Rizer, R. L., and Vogelman, J. H. (1984). *J. Clin. Endocrinol. Metab.* **59**, 551–555.
Parker, L., Gral, T., Perrigo, V., and Skowsky, R. (1981). *Metabolism* **6**, 601–604.
Pascale, R., Garcea, R., Ruggiu, M. E., Daino, L., Frassetto, S., Vannini, G., Cozzolino, P., Lenzerini, L., Feo, F., and Schwartz, A. G. (1987). *Carcinogenesis* **8**, 1567–1570.
Pashko, L. L., and Schwartz, A. G. (1985). *J. Gerontol*, **38**, 8–12.
Pashko, L. L., Schwartz, A. G., Abou-Gharbia, M., and Swern, D. (1981). *Carcinogenesis* **2**, 717–721.
Pashko, L. L., Rovito, R. J., Williams, J. R., Sobel, E. L., and Schwartz, A. G. (1984). *Carcinogenesis* **5**, 463–466.
Pashko, L. L., Hard, G. C., Rovito, R. J., Williams, J. R., Sobel, E. L., and Schwartz, A. G. (1985). *Cancer Res.* **45**, 164–166.
Pashko, L. L., Fairman, D. K., and Schwartz, A. G. (1986). *J. Gerontol.* **41**, 433–438.
Raineri, R. and Levy, H. R. (1970). *Biochemistry* **9**, 2233–2243.
Rao, K. V., Kottapally, S., and Shinozuka, H. (1984). *Toxicol. Pathol.* **12**, 62–68.
Reddy, J. K., Warren, J. R., Reddy, M. K., and Lalwani, N. D. (1982). *Ann. N.Y. Acad. Sci.* **386**, 81–110.
Richerson, G. E., and Gowen, J. W. (1947). *Science* **105**, 496–498.
Rose, D. P., Stauber, P., Thiel, A., Crowley, J. J., and Milbrath, J. R. (1977). *Eur. J. Cancer* **13**, 43–47.
Rosenfeld, R. S., Hellman, L., Roffwarg, H., Weitzman, E. D., Fukushima, P. K., and Gallagher, T. F. (1971). *J. Clin. Endocrinol. Metab.* **33**, 87–92.
Schwartz, A. G. (1979). *Cancer Res.* **39**, 1129–1132.
Schwartz, A. G., and Pashko, L. L. (1986). *Anticancer Res.* **6**, 1279–1282.
Schwartz, A. G., and Perantoni, A. (1975). *Cancer Res.* **35**, 2482–2487.
Schwartz, A. G., and Tannen, R. H. (1981). *Carcinogenesis* **2**, 1335–1337.
Schwartz, A. G., Hard, G. C., Pashko, L. L., Abou-Gharbia, M., and Swern, D. (1981). *Nutr. Cancer* **3**, 46–53.
Schwartz, A. G., Lewbart, M. L., and Pashko, L. L. (1987). In preparation.

Setala, K., Merenmies, L., Stjernvall, L., Aho, Y., and Kajanne, P. (1959). *J. Natl. Cancer Inst.* **23**, 925–951.

Shepherd, A., and Cleary, M. P. (1984). *Am. J. Physiol.* **246**, E123–128.

Slaga, T. J. (1983). *Environ. Health Perspect.* **50**, 3–14.

Slaga, T. J., Fischer, S. M., Nelson, K., and Gleason, G. L. (1980). *Proc. Natl. Acad. Sci. U.S.A.* **77**, 3659–3663.

Sulis, E. (1972). *Lancet* **1**, 1185.

Tagliaferro, A. R., and Davis, J. R. (1983). *Abstr. Fed. Proc., Fed Am. Soc. Exp. Biol.* **43**, 326.

Tannen, R. H., and Schwartz, A. G. (1982). *Abstr. Fed. Proc., Fed. Am. Soc. Exp. Biol.* **41**, 463.

Tannenbaum, A., and Silverstone, H. (1953). *Adv. in Cancer Res.* **1**, 451–501.

Terracini, B., Shubik, P., and Della Porta, A. (1960). *Cancer Res.* **20**, 1538–1542.

Vande Wiele, R. L., MacDonald, P. C., Gurpide, E., and Lieberman, S. (1963). *Recent Prog. Horm. Res.* **19**, 275–310.

Wang, D. Y., Bulbrook, R. D., Herian, M., and Hayward, J. L. (1974). *Eur. J. Cancer* **10**, 477–482.

Weidman, P., de Myttenaere-Bursztein, S., Maxwell, M., and de Lima, J. (1975). *Kidney Int.* **8**, 325–333.

Weindruch, R., and Walford, R. L. (1983). *Science* **215**, 1415–1418.

Weindruch, R., McFeeters, G., and Walford, R. (1984). *Exp. Gerontol.* **41**, 433–438.

Whitcomb, J. M., and Schwartz, A. G. (1985). *Carcinogenesis* **6**, 333–335.

Yen, T. T., Allan, J. A., Pearson, D. V., and Acton, J. M. (1977). *Lipids* **12**, 409–413.

Yen, T. T., Allan, J. A., Pearson, D. V., and Acton, J. M. (1978). *Experientia* **34**, 1542–1543.

Yoshimoto, K., Nakamura, T., and Ichihora, A. (1983). *J. Biol. Chem.* **258**, 12355–12360.

Yu, B. P., Masoro, E. J., Murata, I., Bertrand, H. A., and Lynd, F. T. (1982). *J. Gerontol.* **37**, 130–141.

Zumoff, B., Rosenfeld, R. S., Strain, G. W., Levin, J. and Fukushima, P. K. (1980). *J. Clin. Endocrinol. Metab.* **51**, 330–333.

Zumoff, B., Levin, J., Rosenfeld, R. S., Markham, M., Strain, G. W., and Fukushima, D. K. (1981). *Cancer Res.* **41**, 3360–3363.

INDEX

A

Acquired immune deficiency syndrome (AIDS), *see also* Human immunodeficiency viruses; Human T cell lymphotropic virus; Retroviruses, human
in Africa, 317–320, 337–339
cancer and, 338(*t*), 342, 344
children and, 338, 340–341
dermatological manifestations of, 337–338
diseases indicative of, 337–339
earliest evidence of, 339
fungal diseases and, 337, 338(*t*)
Haitians and, 335–336
herpes viruses and, 324
heterosexual transmission of, 336–339
female to male transmission, 336, 338–339
from infection to disease in, 341–342
insect vector transmission and, 335–336, 338
neurological manifestations of, 342, 343(*t*)
opportunistic infections and, 337–338
origins of, 339–340
therapy for, *see* HIV-associated disease, therapy for
ACTH, DHEA and, 391
Activins, TGF and, 121–123
Acute lymphoblastic leukemia, retroviruses and, 312
Acute transforming viruses, 278, 280–282, *see also* Murine leukemia virus antigens
Adhesion, metastasis and, 364–367, *see also* Metastasis, organ-specific
Adoptive immunization, MuLV and, 279–280
Adrenal gland, DHEA and, 391–392
Adrenocorticotropic hormone (ACTH), DHEA and, 391
Adriamycin, TGF and, 138
Adult T cell leukemia (ATL), treatment of, 344–345
Adult T cell leukemia/lymphoma (ATLL)
HTLV-I and, 313–315
retroviruses and, 321
Adult T cell leukemia virus (ATLV), 313
Aflatoxin B_1-induced transformation, androgenic steroids and, 400(*t*)
Africa, AIDS and, 337–339
Age factor, prostatic cancer and, 2, 17–18
AIDS, *see* Acquired immune deficiency syndrome
AIDS-related complex (ARC), 316
AIDS-related viruses (ARV), 317
Air pollution, prostatic cancer and, 76–79
AL-721, AIDS and, 346
Alcohol, prostatic cancer and, 41–42
Ammonium 21 tungsto-9-antimoniate (HPA-23), AIDS and, 347, 356(*t*)
Androgen
diet and, 63–64
prostatic cancer and, 31–32
Anemia, DHEA and, 418
Animal models
oncogene activation and, *see* Oncogene activation in chemical carcinogenesis, *in vivo*
prostatic cancer and, 2, 28–31, 72–73
retroviruses and, 308, 309(*t*), 310
Antiandrogens, prostatic cancer and, 2
Antibody, *see also* Monoclonal antibody
A.11, 372–373
CD4, 321–322
MEL-14, 370–371
metastasis and, 363–364
M-MuLV and, 284–287
MuLV and, 280

Antiestrogens, TGF and, 133
Antigen, *see also* Murine leukemia virus antigens
CD4, 322–323, 345, 350–351
Hermes-1, metastasis and, 385–386
lymphocyte recirculation and, 367–368
Antigen presenting cells (APC), M-MuLV and, 293–295
Anti-Tac monoclonal antibody, 345
ARC, 316
Artificial insemination, HIV and, 336
ARV, 317
Atherosclerosis, DHEA and, 419–420
ATL, treatment of, 344–345
ATLL, retroviruses and, 321
ATLV, 313
Atomic bomb explosions, prostatic cancer and, 76–79
Avian leukemia virus, 278, 279
3'-Azido-3'-deoxythymidine (AZT), AIDS and, 346(*t*), 347
AZT, 346(*t*), 347

B

Baboon endogenous virus (BaEV), 310, 311–313
Bacterial infection, AIDS and, 337, 338(t)
BaEV, 310, 311–313
Benign prostatic hyperplasia, prostatic cancer and
latent carcinoma and, 9–14
prostatitis and, 19–21
Benzo[a]pyrene (BP), oncogene activation and, 154, 157, 159, 170(*t*)
Birth cohorts, prostatic cancer and, 18, 25, 32–38
Black populations, prostatic cancer and, 3–4, 7–9, 17, 25–28, 89–90
diet and, 33
hormonal system and, 83–85
latent carcinoma and, 10
Bladder cancer, prostatic cancer and, 19
Blast cells, IAPs in, 265
B lymphocyte dysfunction, AIDS and, 325–326
Body weight
cancer and, 401–404
DHEA and, 396–400
Bombesin, *ras* genes and, 149
Bone, TGF and, 114–117, 132
Bone marrow-specific lymphocyte homing receptor, 374
BP, oncogene activation and, 154, 157, 159, 170(*t*)
Brain abscess, AIDS and, 343(*t*)
Brain IAP gene expression in mouse somatic cells, 228–230, *see also* Intracisternal A-particle gene family
Breast cancer
correlation with prostatic cancer, 18–19
DHEA and, 392–394, 405(*f*)
dietary factors and, 27–28
geographic variations in, 18–19
life-style and, 27
retroviruses and, 309, 311
tamoxifen and, 129–130
TGF and, 133
Breast milk, AIDS and, 340

C

Cadmium, prostatic cancer and, 51–55, 73–75
Caffeine, prostatic cancer and, 35–37, 42–43
Carbohydrate intake, prostatic cancer and, 40, 44–45, 60–62
Castration, prostatic cancer and, 2, 83
Cathepsin D, TGF and, 129
Cat tumors, IAP gene family and, 259
CD4
antibody, 321–322
antigen, 322–323, 345, 350–351
Cell selection, tumor promoters and, 162
Cellular differentiation, TGF and, 135
Cellular metabolism, TGF and, 135–136
Cerebellum IAP gene expression in mouse somatic cells, 228–230, *see also* Intracisternal A-particle gene family
Cervical cancer, prostatic cancer and, 67
Cervical secretions, HIV and, 336
Chemical carcinogens, prostatic cancer and, 80–82, *see also* specific chemical carcinogens
Chemotherapy, prostatic cancer and, 2
Children, AIDS and, 338, 340–341, *see also* Acquired immune deficiency syndrome
Chronic immune stimulation hypothesis, 298–299
Chronic transforming viruses, 278, *see also* Murine leukemia virus antigens

Circumcision, prostatic cancer and, 67
Cirrhosis, prostatic cancer and, 83
C-*mos* gene, IAP element transposition in, 244–249
C-*myb* protooncogenes, IAPs and, 229
C-*myc* gene
  IAPs and, 229, 265, 266
  mineral oil and, 151(*t*), 160
Coffee, prostatic cancer and, 28, 36–37, 42–43
Cold target inhibition assay, MuLV and, 288–289
Collagen, TGF and, 137–138
Colon cancer
  correlation with prostatic cancer, 18–19
  dietary factors and, 27–28
  geographic variations in, 18–19
  life-style and, 27
Colon tumor, DHEA and, 407(*t*)
ConA protooncogenes, IAPs and, 229
Connective tissue, TGF and, 134
Cortisol, TGF and, 135
Cryostat section adherence technique, metastasis and, 364–365
Cycloheximide, IAPs and, 229–230
Cyclophosphamide, lymphoma and, 296
Cyproterone acetate, prostatic cancer and, 2
Cysteine residues, TGF and, 121–123
Cytomegalovirus, 324
Cytotoxic T lymphocytes (CTL), MuLV and, 280, 282, *see also* Murine leukemia virus antigens

D

Decapentaplegic gene complex (DPP-C), TGF and, 121–123
Dehydroepiandrosterone (DHEA)
  antiaging effects of, 418–419
  antiatherogenic effects of, 419–420
  antiautoimmune effects of, 418–419
  antidiabetic activity of, 417–418
  antiobesity action of, 396–400
  breast cancer and, 392–394
  cancer preventive effects of
    general considerations, 400–404, 406
    inhibition of DNA synthesis, 407–412
    inhibition of superoxide formation, 412–415
  general considerations for, 391–392
  G6PDH and, 394–396, 397(*f*), 399, 415–417
  NADPH and, 397, 409–413, 417, 420
  synthetic analogs and, 420–421
  topical, 404, 407–408
  TPA and, 396, 397(*f*), 408, 409(*t*), 413, 414(*t*), 416(*t*), 419–421
Dehydroepiandrosterone sulfate (DHEAS), *see* Dehydroepiandrosterone
DEN, oncogene activation and, 170(t)
De Quervian subacute granulomatous thyroiditis, 308
Dermatological manifestations, AIDS and, 337–338
DHEA, *see* Dehydroepiandrosterone
Diabetes
  DHEA and, 417–418
  IAP gene expression and, 252–253
Diet
  Pritikin, 65
  prostatic cancer and, *see* Prostatic cancer, environmental factors and
Diethylnitrosamine (DEN), oncogene activation and, 170(*t*)
Dimethylbenzanthracene (DMBA)
  androgenic steroids and, 400, 401(*t*)
  oncogene activation and, 150(*t*), 153(*t*), 154, 156–158, 169, 170(*t*), 171
    in vivo, 173–176
  tumor promoters and, 161
DMBA, *see* Dimethylbenzanthracene
DNA
  DHEA inhibition of, 407–412
  IAP gene expression and, 195–202, 221–224
  TGF and, 136
Dog tumors, IAP gene family and, 259
Drosophila,
  BP and, 154
  TGF and, 121–123
Drug-metabolizing enzymes, prostatic cancer and, 80–81

E

EGF, *see* Epidermal growth factor
Eggs, prostatic cancer and, 39
Ejaculation, prostatic cancer and, 56, 66–67
Electron microscopy (EM), retroviruses and, 309
EM, retroviruses and, 309

Embryo, mouse, IAPs in, 230–236
EMS, oncogene activation and, 170(*t*)
Encephalitis
AIDS and, 343(*t*)
experimental immune, 376
Endocrine system
diet and, 63–66
prostatic cancer and, 83
Endothelia
adhesive properties of, 365
lymphocyte homing receptors and, 376
ENU, *see* Ethylnitrosourea
Env-gene recombinants of M-MuLV, 283
Environmental factors, prostatic cancer and, *see* Prostatic cancer, environmental factors and
Enzymes, chemical carcinogens and, 80–81
Epiandrosterone, 400
Epidermal growth factor (EGF)
G6PDH and, 411–412
TGF and, 108, 110–114
Epidermis IAP gene expression in mouse somatic cells, 228–230, *see also* Intracisternal A-particle gene family
Epithelia, TGF and, 132–133
Epstein-Barr virus, 324
Escherichia coli, oncogene activation and, 157
Estradiol, diet and, 65
Estrogen
diet and, 63–64
prostatic cancer and, 2
TGF and, 135
Ethylmethanesulfonate (EMS), oncogene activation and, 170(*t*)
Ethylnitrosourea (ENU), oncogene activation and, 154, 159, 160

F

FACS, 383–385
Familial aggregation, prostatic cancer and, 21–22, 25–26
Farmworkers, prostatic cancer and, 68–69, 79–80
Fat intake, prostatic cancer and, 32–34, 37–39, 43–44, 60–66
Fc receptor-mediated clearance, HIV and, 326
Feline leukemia viruses, AIDS and, 317
Fertility, prostatic cancer and, 22–23, 28
Fertilizers, prostatic cancer and, 69
Fiber intake, prostatic cancer and, 41, 45
Fibroblasts
embryonic, TGF and, 131–132
IAP gene expression and, 228–230, *see also* Intracisternal A-particle gene family
oncogene activation and, 171, 173
TGF and, 131–132, 134
Fibrosarcoma, oncogene activation in, 151–153(*t*), *see also* Oncogene activation in chemical carcinogenesis
Fluorescence activated cell sorter (FACS), 383–385
Foods and foodstuffs, prostatic cancer and, 38–41
FSH secretion, TGF and, 135
Fungal diseases, AIDS and, 337, 338(*t*)

G

Gag proteins, IAPs and, 187, 204–208
GALV, *see* Gibbon ape leukemia virus
Gene amplification, oncogenes and, 167
Genetic approaches to AIDS treatment, 350
Genetic mechanisms
prostatic cancer and, 21–22
TPA and, 166–167
Genomic organization
of IAPs, 185–191
of retroviruses, 327–329
Geographic variation, prostatic cancer and, 3–6, 23–24, 32–33
Gerbil cells, IAP gene family and, 258
Gibbon ape leukemia virus (GALV), 310, 312–313
Glandular cells, TGF and, 135
Glioblastoma, oncogene activation and, 153(*t*), *see also* Oncogene activation in chemical carcinogenesis
Gliomas, oncogene activation and, 155, 159
Glucose-6-phosphate dehydrogenase (G6PDH) inhibition, DHEA and, 394–396, 397(*f*), 399, 415–417
GnH-RH, prostatic cancer and, 2
Gonadotropin releasing hormone (GnH-RH), prostatic cancer and, 2
Gonorrhea, prostatic cancer and, 57–58, 67, 91

G6PDH, *see* Glucose-6-phosphate dehydrogenase
Guinea pig leukemia, IAP gene family and, 258–259

H

Hairy cell leukemia, HTLV-II and, 315
Haitian population, AIDS and, 335–336
Hallogenated pyrimidines, IAPs and, 226
Hawaiian population, prostatic cancer and
 diet and, 33–34
 vitamin A, 46–49
Heart IAP gene expression in mouse somatic cells, 228–230, *see also* Intracisternal A-particle gene family
HEBF, 372–373
Hemophiliac patient, HIV and, 336
Hepatocellular adenoma, oncogene activation in, 151–153(*t*), *see also* Oncogene activation in chemical carcinogenesis
Hepatocellular carcinoma, oncogene activation in, 151–153(*t*), *see also* Oncogene activation in chemical carcinogenesis
Hepatoma, oncogene activation and, 151–153(*t*), 157, *see also* Oncogene activation in chemical carcinogenesis
Hermes-1 antigen expression, metastasis and, 385–386
Herpes viruses, AIDS and, 324
Heterosexual transmission, AIDS and, 336
HEV, 368–373, 375, 377–380
High endothelial venules (HEV), 368–373, 375, 377–380
HIV, *see* Human immunodeficiency viruses
Hodgkin's disease
 retroviruses and, 311
 viral etiology of, 344
Homing receptors, metastasis and, *see* Metastasis, organ-specific, lymphocyte homing receptors and
Hormone abnormality, breast cancer and, 392–394
Hormone therapy, prostatic cancer and, 2
HPA-23, AIDS and, 347, 356(*t*)
HTLV, *see* Human T cell lymphotropic virus
Human B lymphotropic virus (HBLV), 344
Human immunodeficiency viruses (HIV), *see also* Acquired immune deficiency syndrome; Human T cell lymphotropic virus; Retroviruses, human
 B lymphocyte dysfunction and, 326
 cancer and, 342, 344
 cell death and, 323–324
 earliest evidence of, 339
 EM of, 318–319(*f*)
 epidemiology of, 336
 Fc receptor-mediated clearance and, 326
 heterosexual transmission of, 336–339
 human T-4 molecule and, 322–324
 humoral immunity and, 325–326
 KS and, 342
 LAV and, 319–320, 321–327
 molecular biology of, 329–335
 monoclonal antibodies and, 322
 pathogenesis of, 339–340
 pediatric AIDS and, 340–341
 proteins, 325
 serum levels and, 326–327
 skin test antigens and, 325
 T cell isolates from, 325
 terminology and, 317
 thymic abnormalities and, 327
Human immunodeficiency virus (HIV)-associated disease, 341–342
 therapy for
  drugs, 346–348
  general considerations, 345–346, 350–351
  genetic approaches, 349–350
  immunotherapy, 348–349
  vaccines, 349–350
Human T cell lymphotropic virus (HTLV), *see also* Acquired immune deficiency syndrome; Human immunodeficiency viruses; Retroviruses, human
 cell biology of, 320–321
 receptors, 323
 type 1, 313–315, 320–321
  molecular biology, 327–329
 type 2, 315–316, 320–321
  molecular biology, 327–329
 type 3, 317
 type 4, 319–320, 340
Humoral immunity, AIDS and, 325–326
Hydroxytamoxifen, TGF and, 133
Hypogammaglobulinemia, pediatric AIDS and, 341

I

IAP gene family, *see* Intracisternal A-particle gene family
IL-2, *see* Interleukin 2
Immune system, TGF and, 135
Immunoglobulins
  IAP gene family and, 249–252
  TGF and, 135
Immunological tolerance, MuLV and, *see* Murine leukemia virus antigens
Immunotherapy, AIDS and, 348–349
Infections, AIDS and, 338(*t*)
Inflammation, lymphocyte homing receptors and, 374–376
Inhibins, TGF and, 121–123
Insect vector transmission, AIDS and, 335–336, 338
Insertional mutagenesis hypothesis, 278
Insulin, G6PDH and, 411–412
Insulin-like growth factor, 114
Interferon
  HIV and, 326, 348
  IAP gene family and, 227
Interleukin 2 (IL-2)
  AIDS and, 349
  retroviruses and, 314, 317, 320
Interleukins, TGF and, 135, 136
Intracisternal A-particle (IAP) gene family
  cat tumors and, 259
  chromosomal distribution of, 201–203
  component proteins
    envelope, 211
    gag, 187, 204–208
    general considerations, 203–204
    integrase, 211
    reverse transcriptase, 208–211, 213
  diabetes and, 252–253
  dog tumors and, 259
  element transposition and, 243–249
  embryonic development and, 230–236
  general considerations for, 184–185
  genomic organization of, 185–191
  gerbil cells and, 258
  guinea pig leukemia and, 258–259
  immunoglobulin regulatory factors and, 249–252
  mus muculus and, 184–193, 194(*t*)
  neoplastic transformation and, 259–269
  normal somatic cells and, 227–230
  other retroviruses and, 193–201
  rat DNA and, 195–196, 257–258
  regulation
    cell proliferation, 225–226
    DNA methylation, 221–224
    general considerations, 219–221
    halogenated pyrimidines, 226
    interferon effects, 227
    oncogene effects, 224–225
  Syrian hamster DNA and, 195–202
  teratocarcinoma cells and, 236–243
  transcription of, 217–219
  transmission, 212–214
  type I elements, 187–189
  type II elements, 189–190
  type R particles, 253–257
Ionizing radiation, prostatic cancer and, 76–79
Iron and steel foundry workers, prostatic cancer and, 75–76
Italian population, diet and, 34–35

J

Japanese population
  breast cancer and, 18
  prostatic cancer and, 3–7, 18, 23
    diet, 35, 36–37, 63–64
    latent, 9–14

K

Kaposi sarcoma (KS), 316, 342
Karyotypic changes, tumor progression and, 169
Kidney IAP gene expression in mouse somatic cells, 228–230, *see also* Intracisternal A-particle gene family
Kirsten sarcoma virus, TGF and, 108
KS, 316, 342

L

Laminin, lung metastasis and, 366–367
Latent carcinoma, prostatic, 9–14
LAV, *see* Lymphadenopathy-associated virus
Lentiviridinae, 308, *see also* Retroviruses, human
Leukemia, *see also* Murine leukemia virus antigens
  myeloid, retroviruses and, 311

prostatic cancer and, 19
retroviruses and, 310, 311-312
Leydig cell IAP gene expression in mouse somatic cells, 228-230, *see also* Intracisternal A-particle gene family
Life-style
breast cancer and, 27
colon cancer and, 27
prostatic cancer and, *see* Prostatic cancer, environmental factors and
LIT tumors, prostatic cancer and, 9-11, 14, 25, 88-89
Liver cirrhosis, prostatic cancer and, 83
Liver IAP gene expression in mouse somatic cells, 228-230, *see also* Intracisternal A-particle gene family
Liver metastasis, 364, *see also* Metastasis, organ-specific
adhesion and, 366
Lung cancer
oncogene activation and, 150-151(*t*), *see also* Oncogene activation in chemical carcinogenesis
TGF and, 133
Lung IAP gene expression in mouse somatic cells, 228-230, *see also* Intracisternal A-particle gene family
Lung metastasis, adhesion and, 366-367
Lung tumorigenesis, DHEA and, 406(*t*)
Lymphadenopathy-associated virus (LAV), 317, 319-320, *see also* Human immunodeficiency viruses
HTLV-IV and, 340
Lymphocyte homing receptors, *see* Metastasis, organ-specific, lyphocyte homing receptors and
Lymphocytes, *see also* B lymphocyte dysfunction, AIDS and; T lymphocytes
TGF and, 133, 136, 138
Lymphokines, lymphocyte homing receptors and, 375, 376
Lymphoma, *see also* Thymic lymphoma
HIV-associated, 344
metastasis and
Hermes-1, 385-386
HEV binding, 377-380
metastasis and, HEV assay, 369-370
M-MuLV and, 296, 297(t), *see also* Murine leukemia virus antigens
Lymphoreticular cells, M-MuLV and, 287-289
Lymphosarcoma
metastasis and, 364
retroviruses and, 311-312

M

Macroglobulin
HIV and, 326-327
TGF and, 130
Macrophage IAP gene expression in mouse somatic cells, 228-230, *see also* Intracisternal A-particle gene family
Macrophage tumor, oncogene activation and, 150-151(*t*), *see also* Oncogene activation in chemical carcinogenesis
Malic enzyme, 412
Malignancy, *see also* Metastasis, organ-specific; specific malignancy
AIDS and, 338(*t*), 342, 344
HTLV-II and, 316
IAP expression and, 259-267
Mammary carcinoma, oncogene activation and, 150-151(*t*), 153(*t*), 155-156, *see also* Oncogene activation in chemical carcinogenesis
Marek's disease, metastasis and, 363-364
Marital status, prostatic cancer and, 22-23, 28
Mason-Pfizer monkey virus (MPMV), 310-311, 317, *see also* Monkey viruses
MAV, IA gene family elements and, 191-192
MCA, oncogene activation and, 150-151, 154, 157, 159, 170(*t*), 171
Meat consumption, prostatic cancer and, 34-36, 38-39
MEL-14, metastasis and, 380-385
Meningitis, AIDS and, 343(*t*)
Metalloproteinases (TIMP), TGF and, 134
Metastasis, organ-specific
adhesion systems involved in, 365-367
cryostat sections, 364-365
endothelial monolayers, 365
antibody blocking and, 363-364
general considerations for, 361-362
heterotropic aggregation and, 362
lymphocyte homing receptors and
Hermes-1, 385-386
HEV binding, 377-380
human, 372
lung recirculation, 367-368

MEL-14, 380–385
mouse, 370–371
other, 373–376
peripheral mode, 370–371
rat, 372–373
somatic fusions, 376–377
Methylcholanthrene (MCA), oncogene activation and, 150–151, 154, 157, 159, 170(*t*), 171
N-Methyl-*N*'-nitro-*N*-nitrosoguanidine (MNNG), oncogene activation and, 169, 170(*t*), 171
N-Methyl-*N*-nitrosourea (MNU), prostatic cancer and, 30–31
Migration studies, prostatic cancer and, 6, 25
Milk consumption, prostatic cancer and, 34–36, 39–40
Mineral oil, c-*myc* gene and, 151(*t*), 160
MIS, TGF and, 121–123
M-MSV, *see* Moloney murine sarcoma virus
MNNG, *see* *N*-Methyl-*N*'-nitro-*N*-nitrosoguanidine
MNU, *see* *N*-Methyl-*N*-nitrosourea
Moloney murine sarcoma virus (M-MSV), 280–282, *see also* Murine leukemia virus antigens
Monkey viruses, 310–313, 317–320
Monoclonal antibodies
anti-TAC, 345
HIV and, 322
metastasis and, 363–364, 371–373
Mormon population, prostatic cancer and, 14–15
Mosquitos, AIDS and, 335–336, 338
Mouse IAP genetic elements, 184–191, 228–230, *see also* Intracisternal A-particle gene family
MPMV, *see* Mason-Pfizer monkey virus
Mullerian inhibitory substance (MIS), TGF and, 121–123
MuLV, *see* Murine leukemia virus; Murine leukemia virus antigens
Murine leukemia virus (MuLV), IAP elements and, 191–192
Murine leukemia virus (MuLV) antigens, 296, 297(*t*)
APC and, 293–295
early work on immunological tolerance to, 279–282
endogenous, 282–287
exogenous, 287–290
general considerations for, 277–279, 296–301
lymphoma development and, 296, 297(t)
M-MSV and, 280–282
Mycobacteria, AIDS and, 338(*t*)
Mycosis fungoides, retroviruses and, 314, 317
Myeloid leukemias, retroviruses and, 311
Myeloma, IAP element transposition in, 244–246
Myeloma-associated virus (MAV), IAP elements and, 191–192
Myelopathy, AIDS and, 343(*t*)
Myositis, AIDS and, 344(*t*)

N

NADPH, DHEA and, 397, 409–413, 417, 420
Nasopharyngeal carcinoma, oncogene activation and, 153(*t*), *see also* Oncogene activation in chemical carcinogenesis
Neoplastic transformation, IAP gene family and, 259–269
Neuroblastoma, oncogene activation and, 153(*t*), *see also* Oncogene activation in chemical carcinogenesis
gene amplification and, 167
Neurological manifestations, AIDS and, 342, 343(*t*)
Niacin, prostatic cancer and, 50–51
Nitrogen cavitation, IAPs and, 203
Nitrosomethylurea (NMU), oncogene activation and, 154, 159
NMU, prostatic cancer and, 30–31
NOB mice, retroviruses and, 253
Non-Hodgkin's lymphoma, metastasis and, 385–386
Nonobese diabetic (NOB) mice, retroviruses and, 253
Northern blotting
IAPs and, 220(*f*), 227, 229
T-4 mRNA and, 322–323
Northern hybridization, TGF and, 119–120

Nutrition, prostatic cancer and, *see* Prostatic cancer, environmental factors and

O

Obesity
DHEA and, 396–400
endocrine effects of, 65
prostatic cancer and, 60
Obesity, DHEA and, 396–400
Occupational factors, prostatic cancer and, 68–76
Oncogene activation in chemical carcinogenesis
direct *v* indirect
alternative routes, 160–161
carcinogen-specific mutations, 156–158
general considerations, 155–156
neu gene, 159
ras genes, 159
general consideration for, 147–148
tumor progression and
gene amplification, 167
karyotypic changes, 169
loss of *ras* alleles, 168
tumor promotion and
cell communication, 162–164
cell selection, 162
general considerations, 161–162
genetic mechanisms, 166–167
signal transduction and gene activation, 164–166
TGFs, 164
in vitro
carcinogens, 169–171
comparison of *in vivo*, 173–176
stage specificity, 171–173
in vivo, 150–153
comparison of *in vitro*, 173–176
ras genes, 148–154
tissue-specificity, 150–155
Oncogene products, IAPs and, 224–225
Oncogenesis, retroviruses and, 278, 327, *see also* Murine leukemia virus antigens
Oncoviridinae, 307–308, *see also* Retroviruses, human
Opportunistic infections, AIDS and, 337–338
Osteoblasts, TGF and, 132, 138
Osteosarcoma, IAPs and, 214
Ovary IAP gene expression in mouse somatic cells, 228–230, *see also* Intracisternal A-particle gene family
Overweight, endocrine effects of, 65

P

PAI, TGF and, 134
Pancreas B cells IAP gene expression in mouse somatic cells, 228–230, *see also* Intracisternal A-particle gene family
Papillomas
oncogene activation and, 174–176
TPA and, 165
tumor promoters and, 162
PBNA, prostatic cancer and, 72–73
Pediatric AIDS, 340–341
Peptide growth factors, *see also* Transforming growth factor-α; Transforming growth factor-β
Pertussis toxin, lymphocyte homing receptors and, 374–375
Pesticides, prostatic cancer and, 69
Peyer's patch
HEV and, 369–370, 371
HEV binding lymphomas, 378–380
N-Phenyl-2-napthylamine (PBNA), prostatic cancer and, 72–73
Phophonoformate, AIDS and, 347, 356(*t*)
Pituitary, TGF and, 135
Plasma cell IAP gene expression in mouse somatic cells, 228–230, *see also* Intracisternal A-particle gene family
Plasmacytoma, oncogene activation and, 150–151(*t*), *see also* Oncogene activation in chemical carcinogenesis
Plasma prolactin levels, diet and, 64–65
Plasmin, TGF and, 129
Plasminogen activator inhibitors (PAIs), TGF and, 134
Plutonium exposure, prostatic cancer and, 78–79
Pneumocystis carinii infection, 316
Postmenopausal patient, DHEA and, 394
Premenopausal patient, DHEA and, 394
Pritikin diet, endocrine effects of, 65
Progressive multifocal leukoencephalopathy, AIDS and, 344(*t*)
Prostatic cancer
androgen administration and, 31–32

animal models for, 28–31, 72–73
birth cohorts and, 18, 25, 32–38
endocrine system and, 63–64
environmental factors and
  air pollution, 76–77
  diet and nutrition, 28, 31–55, 59–66
    alcohol, 41–42
    animal models, 28
    cadmium, 51–55
    caffeine, 35–37, 42–43
    carbohydrate intake, 40, 44–45, 60–62
    dietary fiber, 41, 45
    fat intake, 32–34, 37–39, 43–44, 60–66
    foods and foodstuffs, 38–41
    protein intake, 44, 60–66
    studies, 31–38
    trace elements, 50–51, 62–63
    vitamins, 40–41, 45–50
  general considerations, 25, 27–28, 31–32
  ionizing radiation, 77–79
  occupational factors, 26–27, 51–55, 68–76, 79–82
  sexual factors, 55–58, 66–68
  smoking, 58
  water hardness, 79
epidemiology and
  age factor, 2, 17–18
  benign prostatic hyperplasia and, 19–21
  correlation with other sites and tumors, 18–19
  familial aggregation, 21–22, 25–26
  fertility, 22–23, 28
  geographic variation, 3–6, 23–24, 32–33
    latent carcinoma, 9–14
  marital status, 22–23, 28
  migration studies, 6, 25
  prostatitis, 21, 68
  racial differences, 6–9, 24, 26, 33–34, 89–91
    latent carcinoma, 9–14
  socioeconomic status, 4–5, 15–16, 27, 89–90
  special populations, 14–15, 28
  summary, 22–28
  urban-rural differences, 16–17, 26–27
general considerations for, 1–3, 87–94
genetic factors and, 21–22, 25–26
hormonal system and, 30–31, 82–86
latent, 9–14, 24–25
LIT tumors and, 9–11, 14, 25, 88–89
MNU and, 30–31
obesity and, 60
risk factors for, 87–88
testosterone and, 31, 37–38, 39
viral etiology of, 67–68
vitamin A and, 34–35, 40–41, 45–49, 61–63
vitamin C and, 33, 45–49
Prostatic schistosomiasis, prostatic cancer and, 68
Prostatitis, prostatic cancer and, 21, 68
Prostitutes, HIV and, 336
Protein intake, prostatic cancer and, 44, 60–66
Protein kinase C, tumor promoters and, 164–165
Proteins
  HIV and, 325
  ras, 149
Protozoan infection, AIDS and, 337, 338(*t*)
Purkinje cells IAP gene expression in mouse somatic cells, 228–230, *see also* Intracisternal A-particle gene family
Pyrimidines
  IAP and, 226
  retroviruses and, 310

R

Racial differences, prostatic cancer and, 6–9, 24, 26, 33–34, 83–84, 89–91
RAR, HEV assay and, 368–369
Rat
  DNA, IAP gene family and, 195–196, 257–258
  lymphocyte homing receptors, 372–373
Receptor
  EGF, TGF-α and, 112–113
  HTLV-I, 323
  lymphocyte, 367, *see also* Metastasis, organ-specific, lymphocyte homing receptors and
  TGF and, 123–127, 136
Relative adherence ratio (RAR), HEV assay and, 368–369
Renal carcinoma, oncogene activation and, 153(*t*), *see also* Oncogene activation in chemical carcinogenesis
Retroviruses, human
  animal models and, 308, 309(*t*), 310
    NOB mice, 253

ATLL and, 313–315
ATLV and, 313
BaEV and, 310, 311–313
CD4 and, 322–323, 345, 350–351
cell biology and immunology of, 320–321
epidemiology of
AIDS and Africa, 337–339
general considerations, 335–336
heterosexual transmission, 336–337
HIV, 336, 339
GALV and, 310, 312–313
general considerations for, 351
general properties of, 329
HIV and, *see* Human immunodeficiency viruses
HTLV and, *see* Human T cell lymphotropic virus
IL-2 and, 314, 320
LAV and, 317, 319–320
LAV-II and, 319–320
life cycle of, 323–324
lymphomas and, 344
oncogenesis and, 278, *see also* Murine leukemia virus antigens
SAIDS and, 317–320
search for, 309–311
specific isolates of, 311–312
SSAV and, 310, 311–313
Reverse transcriptase (RT)
IAP and, 208–211, 213
retroviruses and, 309
AIDS, 345–346
Rheumatoid arthritis, lymphocyte homing receptors and, 376
Riboflavin, prostatic cancer and, 50–51
RNA in IAPs, 214–217
RT, *see* Reverse transcriptase
Rubber industry, prostatic cancer and, 69–73, 79, 90–91
Rural-urban differences, prostatic cancer and, 16–17, 26–27

S

SAIDS, 317–320
Salivary gland IAP gene expression in mouse somatic cells, 228–230, *see also* Intracisternal A-particle gene family
San Francisco isolate ARV-II, 342, 349
Sarcoidosis, ATLL and, 315
Sarcoma, *see* Moloney murine sarcoma virus; specific sarcoma
Sarcoma growth factors (SGFs), TGF and, 107–108
Schwann cells, TGF and, 132
Schwannoma, oncogene activation and, 153(*t*), 155, 159, *see also* Oncogene activation in chemical carcinogenesis
SDS gel, TGF and, 118–119
Selenium, prostatic cancer and, 50–51, 63
Semen, HIV and, 336
Seminal vesicle IAP gene expression in mouse somatic cells, 228–230, *see also* Intracisternal A-particle gene family
Seventh Day Adventist population
diet and, 35–36
prostatic cancer and, 14–15
Sezary syndrome, 374
retroviruses and, 314, 317
SGF, TGF and, 107–108
Simian AIDS (SAIDS), 317–320
Simian sarcoma-associated virus (SSAV), 310, 311–313
Simian sarcoma virus (SSV), retroviruses and, 312
Simian virus glycoproteins, retroviruses and, 311
Simultaneous detect test, retroviruses and, 309–310
SIV, 317–318, 339
Skeletal muscle IAP gene expression in mouse somatic cells, 228–230, *see also* Intracisternal A-particle gene family
Skin abnormalities, AIDS and, 337–338
Skin carcinoma, oncogene activation and, 150–151(*t*), *see also* Oncogene activation in chemical carcinogenesis
TPA, 165
Skin papilloma
DHEA and, 404, 406–408
oncogene activation and, 150–151(*t*), *see also* Oncogene activation in chemical carcinogenesis
TPA and, 165
SLE, *see* Systemic lupus erythematosus
'Slim' disease, 337–338
Small lymphocyte IAP gene expression in mouse somatic cells, 228–230, *see also* Intracisternal A-particle gene family
Smoking
DHEA and, 402–404

prostatic cancer and, 58
Socioeconomic status, prostatic cancer and, 4-5, 15-16, 27, 89-90
Southern blotting, *ras* genes and, 159
Special populations, prostatic cancer and, 14-15, 28
Spleen IAP gene expression in mouse somatic cells, 228-230, *see also* Intracisternal A-particle gene family
Spumaviridinae, 308, *see also* Retroviruses, human
SSAV, 310, 311-313
SSV, 312
Steel foundry workers, prostatic cancer and, 75-76
Stellate cells IAP gene expression in mouse somatic cells, 228-230, *see also* Intracisternal A-particle gene family
STLV-III, 317-318
AIDS and, 339
Superoxide formation, DHEA inhibition of, 412-415
Suramin, AIDS and, 346
Syrian hamster, IAP and, 184, 193, 195-201, *see also* Intracisternal A-particle gene family
Systemic lupus erythematosus (SLE), retroviruses and, 312
HIV and, 326

T

Tamoxifen
breast cancer and, 129-130
TGF and, 133
Tat viral gene, 278
T cell
HEV adherence properties of, 369
HIV-infected persons and, 325
lymphocyte homing receptors and, 376
T cell growth factor (TCGF), 314, *see also* Interleukin 2
TCGF, *see* T cell growth factor
Tea, prostatic cancer and, 28, 36-37, 43
Teratocarcinoma cells, IAP and, 236-243
Testosterone, prostatic cancer and, 31, 37-39
diet and, 63-64, 65
x-ray exposure and, 78
12-O-Tetradecanoylphorbol-13-acetate (TPA), oncogene activation and, 154, 163-167
Tetradecanoylphorbos-13-acetate (TPA), DHEA and, 396, 397(*f*), 408, 409(*t*), 413, 414(*t*), 416(*t*), 419-421
TGF, *see* Transforming growth factor-*alpha*; Transforming growth factor-*beta*
Thiamin, prostatic cancer and, 50-51
Thymic lymphoma, M-MuLV and, 282, 287
T lymphocytes and, 290-293
Thymic replacement therapies, AIDS and, 348
Thymosin, HIV and, 326-327
Thymulin, HIV and, 326, 327
Thymus
IAP gene expression in mouse somatic cells and, 228-230, *see also* Intracisternal A-particle gene family
lymphocyte homing receptors and, 373-374
TIMP, TGF and, 134
T lymphocytes, *see also* Lymphocytes
HIV and, 324-325
neonatally M-MuLV infected mice and, 290-293
T lymphoma, oncogene activation and, 150-151(*t*), *see also* Oncogene activation in chemical carcinogenesis
T-4 molecule, HIV and, 322-323
TPA, 396, 397(*f*), 408, 409(*t*), 413, 414(*t*), 416(*t*), 419-421
Trace elements, prostatic cancer and, 50-51, 62-63
Transforming growth factor-α (TGF-α)
amino acid sequences of, 110-112
biological activity of, 112-113
EGF and, 108, 110-113
general considerations for, 107-110
oncogene activation and, 164
SGF and, 107-108
structure of, 110-112
TGF-β and, 107-110, *see also* Transforming growth factor-β
Transforming growth factor-β (TGF-β)
amino acid sequences of, 116-117, 119(*f*), 122-123
anchorage-independent growth of cells and, 113-114, 131
binding proteins, 125-127
biological actions of, 130-136
antiproliferative effects, 132-133
cellular metabolism, 135-136
other effects, 133-135
proliferative effects, 131-132
cartilage-inducing factors and, 114-115

gene encoding, 120
high-pressure liquid chromatography and, 108
homologies among, 119(*f*), 122
inhibition of growth and, 114
isolation of, 113–115
latent, 128–130
membrane receptors for, 123–127
Northern hybridization and, 119–120
oncogene activation and, 164
peptides related to, 119(*f*), 121–123
physical properties of, 116–119
purification of, 115–116
SDS gels and, 118–119
SGF and, 107–108
structure of precursor of, 118(*f*), 119–120
TGF-α and, 107–110, *see also* Transforming growth factor-α
therapeutic uses of, 136–138
tyrosin kinase activity of, 127
in vivo, 136–138
Western blots and, 117–118
Trigeminal ganglion IAP gene expression in mouse somatic cells, 228–230, *see also* Intracisternal A-particle gene family
Triton X-100, IAP and, 203
Tumor promoters, oncogenes and, 154, 161–167
Type R particles, IAP gene family and, 253–257
Tyrosin kinase activity, TGF-β and, 127

U

Ulcers, TGF and, 138
Urban-rural differences, prostatic cancer and, 16–17, 26–27

V

Vaccine, AIDS and, 349–350
Vascular endothelium, TGF and, 133
Vegetables, prostatic cancer and, 32–35, 40–41
Venereal disease, prostatic cancer and, 57–58, 67
Vesicular stomatitis virus (VSV), HTLV and, 321
Viruses, *see also* Retroviruses, human
AIDS and, 337
prostatic cancer and, 67–68
Vitamin A, prostatic cancer and, 34–35, 40–41, 45–49, 61–62, 63
Vitamin C, prostatic cancer and, 33, 40–41, 45–49
VSV, 321

W

Walter Reed staging classification for HIV infection, 341
Water hardness, prostatic cancer and, 79
Weight
cancer and, 401–404
DHEA and, 396–400
Western blotting, TGF and, 117–118
Wound-healing, TGF and, 129, 137–138

X

X-ray exposure, prostatic cancer and, 77–79

Z

Zinc intake, prostatic cancer and, 50–51, 63–64